THE MAP

Also by Nick Page

The Church Invisible
street life (with Rob Lacey)
Blue

Making the Bible
Meaningful • Accessible • Practical

NICK PAGE

GRAND RAPIDS, MICHIGAN 49530 USA

To Lily, Madeleine and Martha,

in the hope that, one day, we will all

go exploring together.

ZONDERVAN™

The MAP: Making the Bible Meaningful, Accessible, Practical
Copyright © 2002 by Nick Page
Originally titled *The Bible Book*
First published in Great Britain in 2002 by HarperCollins*Publishers*

Nick Page asserts the moral right to be identified as the author of this work.

Unless otherwise indicated, all Scripture quotations are from the *Contemporary English Version Bible* published by HarperCollins*Publishers* © American Bible Society 1991, 1992, 1995. Scripture quotations marked (NIV) are from the *Holy Bible, New International Version* © International Bible Society 1973, 1978, 1984. Used by permission of Zondervan. All rights reserved

ISBN 0-310-25239-3

Written and designed by Nick Page

Printed in the United States of America

07 08 09 10 /❖ DC/ 10 09 08 07 06 05

Contents

Part One: Mapping Out the Territory

Part Two: The Old Testament

Part Three: The New Testament

Part Four: Who, Where, What

Special Features

Landmarks

Maps and Charts

Postcards

Brief Lives

Part One
Mapping Out the Territory

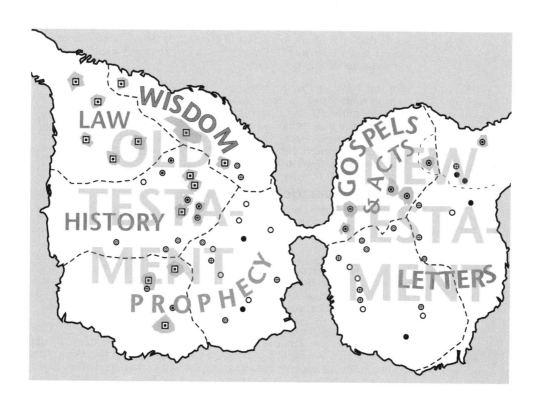

Introduction

Let's start with a story

It's 1966 and I am in Sunday school. (For those of you who have never heard of such a thing, it was what used to go on while the grown-ups did "proper church.")

Anyway, on the wall of the Sunday school was a picture, painted sometime in the 1930s. It was called "What Happened To Your Hands?" and it featured someone who, I was reliably informed, was Jesus. He was a weird figure. He was sitting in a garden, wearing a long, white dress. His skin was ivory white, and his hair fell in glossy waves to his shoulders. He looked like an actor in a shampoo advertisement. At his feet, two cherubic children gazed at him with adoration. I couldn't share their devotion. But for years this was my image of Jesus—a pale, unreal, unexciting hippy who had absolutely nothing to do with real life.

Fast-forward to 1979. In a lonely, quiet hour, I picked up a copy of the Bible and started reading the book of Luke—a book that is a kind of biography of Jesus. The effect was remarkable. Nothing in life had prepared me for the real figure. Here was a real man; passionate, angry, full of life. A man who, far from sitting politely in an English garden, went to parties, enjoyed a good argument and spent his time with entirely the wrong people. As I read the stories about him and listened to his words, I began to realize that I'd wasted a lot of time. If I'd read the Bible properly in the first place, I might have met this man a lot earlier. Here was a real hero. Here was someone I could believe in.

Why am I telling you this? Because I believe it shows the truth—if we want to understand the Bible, make up our minds about it, we have to read it for ourselves. As I learned in subsequent years—indeed, as I am still learning—the Bible is like no other book. There are passages in the Bible that lift and inspire—and there are parts that disgust and shock. The Bible is challenging, unsettling, comforting and encouraging. **What we have to do is encounter it for ourselves.**

Not your average Bible scholar

A quick note about me. I am not a Bible scholar. I am not a trained theologian. I am not an archaeologist or ancient historian. My Hebrew is nonexistent and my Greek is limited to two words: "doner" and "kebab."

You might think that this is not exactly the best recommendation for someone who is writing a guide to the Bible. You might be right. But I thought it best to be honest right at the beginning, because then, if you want an in-depth, academically rigorous commentary written entirely in ancient Phoenician, you can go and buy one.

What I have tried to do is to share my enthusiasm for the Bible and for what it has to say. I'm not an expert: I'm a fan. I don't know all the answers, which is why, I hope, I can be honest about the questions. This is not a reference book written by an expert, but an honest attempt to get across my enthusiasm and excitement about the Bible. I have relied heavily on the work of experts, but ultimately the views expressed in this book are my ideas and responses. You may agree with my opinions, you may find them stupid. The important thing is that you read the Bible and make up your own mind.

How This Book Is Organized

For each book of the Bible we start with the same basic features:

Who, When, What

Who: who wrote it? who is it aimed at?

When: when was it written? when did the events it describes take place?

What: what happens in the book? What is its purpose?

Genesis
In the beginning...

Genesis is the book of beginnings. It is not only the start of the Bible – it is the start of all creation.

Who: The traditional view is that Moses wrote the Pentateuch. Nowadays most people believe that the books are the work of several hands and come from different traditions.

When: Genesis was written over a long period of time. It was probably begun in the time of Moses, but later generations added other material and edited the book together. The book probably reached its final form around the time of Solomon (970-930BC).

What: Genesis is about origins. It tells the readers where we came from and why we are here. In the opening chapters of Genesis we have all the themes that will fill the rest of the Bible – creation, sin and rebellion; love, grace and mercy. For, following the fall of Adam and Eve, God was not concerned solely with punishment, he was also planning for salvation.

The book is structured around the lives of several figures; people like Adam, Noah, Abraham, Jacob and Joseph. There are, of course, interludes which cover other topics, but these are the key characters. They are known as the Patriarchs, the 'fathers' and they remind us that the Bible is not a book about God – it is a book about God and man.

God is personal. He speaks, he thinks, he relates to humans. This is not some impersonal 'life-force', still less some distant, alien being. This is a 'someone', a being who wants to communicate with the world he has created. Indeed, the whole of the Bible is about God's attempts to make himself known to his creations, to inspire, cajole, correct and above all, to love, these people he made.

Quick Guide
Author Various, including Moses
Type Pentateuch
Purpose To explain where we all came from and why we are all here.
Key verses 1.1 In the beginning. God created the heavens and the earth.
If you remember one thing about this book... God created this world to be good, but things went badly wrong.
Your 15 minutes start now Read chaps 1–3, 28, 38

The Route Through Genesis

Quick Guide

The Quick Guide is a kind of snapshot of the book. It will tell you the title, theme and purpose and give you something to remember.

Your 15 minutes/10 minutes/5 minutes start now

Just a few chapters, to give you a representative sample of the book. Of course, there is much more in each book, but this will give you a start.

The Route Through

A graphical overview of the book with numbers indicating specific events or topics.

Extra Features

There are loads of other features along the way, including

Landmarks—explain key themes or topics of the Bible

Puzzling Points—look at those difficult passages

Brief Lives—introduce the major characters

Details, Details . . . the little facts that you might otherwise miss

Timelines—show you how and when the action took place

Postcards—introduce you to the key locations of the Bible

Maps—show you the layout of countries and nations

Cross-References—the arrows ▷ point you to other relevant pages

Verse References

Bible verses are given in the following format: Book Chapter:Verse. Bible books are indicated by the first letters of their name (e.g., Ne = Nehemiah, He = Hebrews), except where there are duplications (see p. 14 for the full list). So, Ge 1:1 means Genesis, chapter 1, verse 1.

Six Myths about the Bible

1. It's written in weird language

You said to yourself, "I really should read the Bible." You knew there was one in the house somewhere. Eventually you found it—hidden at the back of the bookcase, behind some photographs of your great-aunt and some old Agatha Christie novels. You blew the dust off it, opened the black covers with a creak and read, *"Yea, verily, I say unto thee . . ."*

It's nice language, but completely incomprehensible to anyone without a degree in English. What's happened is that you are using an old translation. Unless you are fluent in ancient Hebrew or first-century Greek, then you will read the Bible in translation. First, then, you need to buy a modern version. Find one that you can read easily—which means not just one where the language is modern, but one that is well designed and laid out.

> **Details, Details . . .**
> **New users start here—**
> **Bible translations**
> There are many versions of the Bible available, each with their own strengths and weaknesses. In my opinion, however, the accessible versions are:
>
> • **New International Version**
> • **Contemporary English Version**
> • **New Living Translation**
> • **Good News Translation**
>
> In this book, I've used the Contemporary English Version, unless indicated otherwise.

2. Only the experts can understand it

There are, of course, puzzling parts. There are parts of the Bible that no one understands, where even the experts are baffled. Similarly, there are many passages on which people hold different views. But despite these "problem areas," the vast majority of the Bible is really very straightforward.

Jesus, for example, boiled the Old Testament Law down to two commandments: "Love the Lord your God with all your heart and mind and soul" and "love your neighbor as yourself." That's not exactly complicated. It's not brain surgery. (It might be hard to do, but that's another issue.)

So there will be parts that you don't understand. There will be far more numerous parts where the meaning is plain and clear and where you can put it into action.

3. It takes too much time

The Bible has been arranged to allow you to read it in bits, so you can read as little, or as much, as you like. I wouldn't necessarily recommend that you read only one verse a day, but neither do you have to tackle all of Genesis at one sitting. What is important is that you make some time to read it and think about it. Time is always a problem, but if an activity is worthwhile, you can make the space for it.

4. It's boring

The Bible undoubtedly has its dull parts—such as dimensions of buildings, complicated family trees, lists of numbers and detailed descriptions of ancient religious ritual. (By the way, some cultures find these exciting—they're just not our kind of thing.) But it also has fascinating history, stirring stories, moving poetry, thought-provoking wisdom and life-changing insights. So if you find a passage that you consider dull, simply move on. There is something exciting just around the corner.

5. It's too big

The Bible contains a lot of writing, it is true—around 750,000 words—but the people who put it together broke it down into bite-sized chunks. So we can read as little, or as much, as we like. And there are good reasons why it's so big. For a start, it's a lot of books joined together. The Bible contains 66 books, split into 1,189 chapters and written by at least 40 authors. It took 1,000 years to compile.

Most importantly, it's about life, death and everything between. You'd expect more than 32 pages and a few cartoons.

6. It's irrelevant

It's about you and me

The people in the Bible are much like us. They may dress differently, they may act in unusual ways, but the issues they wrestle with are the same issues that face us all. The Bible talks about love, peace, war, happiness, freedom, greed, forgiveness, sex, possessions, truth . . . and a whole lot more. All these issues are just as relevant today.

It's historically important

Historically speaking, the Bible is the most important book ever published. It has influenced the actions of more people around the world than any other book; in the Western world it has inspired most of the great art, poetry and literature of the past centuries. Its influence on politicians, writers, artists, revolutionaries, visionaries and religious leaders is unmistakable. Its laws—the famous Ten Commandments—are at the basis of most judicial systems. Many of the everyday proverbs and phrases we use are found in the Bible.

It addresses the big questions

Many believe the Bible gives us the answers to the big questions. It tells us why we are here, what we are supposed to do on earth and where we are going to end up in the future. It tells us about God. If the Bible is true, then it changes everything: how we look at the world, how we treat each other, the way we should live our lives. You might disagree with that, but shouldn't you find out first?

It's the Word of God

For Christians, the Bible is more than just another book. Christians talk about the Bible as "the Word of God." It is a book through which God speaks to his people. Just as Christians believe that God speaks to us through prayer, we also believe that God speaks to us through the Bible. That is why the Bible is often referred to as the "living" Word of God. The Bible is a truly interactive book. It challenges, inspires, thrills, excites and changes all those who read it.

Why should you read the Bible? Because it's more than another book. It's a marvelous country to explore . . .

Exploring the Bible

The thing that really annoys me about the way many people talk about the Bible is that they make it seem so boring.

I believe the problem is often to do with how we approach the Bible. We approach it almost in fear, as if it's going to be an unpleasant experience. It's not meant to be an exciting experience—it's just something you have to do. Like going to the dentist: it's good for you, but you don't actually enjoy it.

Well, I don't think the Bible is like that. I prefer to think of Bible study as exploration. Reading the Bible should be less like visiting the dentist and more like exploring another land. We should approach the Bible with the spirit of pioneers, "boldly going" into brave new chapters, seeking to understand the natives and to learn from their wisdom.

The map

So, how do we map the Bible? How is it laid out? What does the country look like?

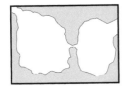

The continent

At first glance the Bible appears to be a huge, forbidding land mass. Open the covers and you will see that it is split into two "land masses," the Old Testament and the New Testament. The Old Testament is the larger—and older—of the two and both masses are linked by what looks like a small, thin strip.

Look a bit closer and you can see that the huge continent is really two land masses joined by a small bridge.

The regions

The Bible is split into "regions" or types of writing. There are the rocky, ancient areas, a large flat plain, dense forest lands, even some difficult and dangerous swamps—different regions, all distinct.

The Old Testament is split into four different regions: History, Prophecy, Wisdom and what some people call "the Pentateuch" or "the Books of the Law."

The New Testament is divided into three regions: the Gospels (sort of mini-biographies of Jesus), the book of Acts (a history of the early Church) and the Letters. The Letters are subdivided into letters from Paul and letters from other people, such as John and Peter.

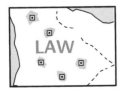

The cities

Each region is full of cities—which correspond to the books of the Bible. The Law, for example, consists of five "cities": Genesis, Exodus, Leviticus, Numbers, Deuteronomy. The Gospels "region" in the New Testament contains Matthew, Mark, Luke and John. Within all the regions there are cities and towns. Some of these are huge and ancient. Some are smaller. Some are tiny. They are all linked by a crisscrossing of roads and tracks.

The longest book in the Bible is over one hundred times the size of the smallest book. And just as cities and towns look different, the books are written in different styles. Some books—the Psalms, for instance—are collections of poems. Some are long histories. Some of these "cities" are very similar in architecture. There are parts of Chronicles and Kings that echo each other very closely, but from a different standpoint.

The streets

Just as there are streets within every city, each book of the Bible is broken down into chapters. Some of these are long streets—more like highways. Others are very short. Some of them look like other streets; in some of them the architecture is completely different. Some of the streets are identical to streets in other towns on that continent.

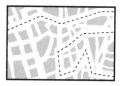

The houses

And just as streets are made up of houses with numbers, each chapter of the Bible is made up of different amounts of numbered verses. Again, some houses are replicas of houses in other cities, other towns. Most of the houses are different, although they might be built in a particular style.

Finding your way around

When someone says, "Look up John 3:16," what they are actually doing is giving you an address. All you have to do is go to the city of John, find street number 3 and go to the house numbered 16. Ring the bell, open the door, read it and see what's inside.

Broken down in this way, we can see that the Bible isn't meant to be taken in all at once. You can no more grasp the "whole of the Bible" at once than you can spend a day in a continent and think that you have seen it. Reading the Bible should be an adventure, an exploration, a visit to a different land. If you really want to understand it, you have to spend some time there. There are, of course, the famous "sights." There are the places that every traveler visits—the chapters that we all should read, the passages that should be on everyone's itinerary. But the smaller, less visited places have their delights and their importance too. There is always something to discover. Each city has its own charms, its own sights. Hidden streets and half-forgotten alleys can help you to understand a place in a way that the tourist traps never can.

Whatever the case, the point is this: reading the Bible should not be seen as either a test or a chore. It's not a painful duty to be performed. It's a place to explore.

Sometimes that journey will be slow and tough, sometimes it will require slogging through foothills or climbing mountains. Sometimes it will be easy and smooth. Some sights we will see will make us stop in awe. Some will make us simply stop and think. All of it is important. All of it requires that we set out and make the journey.

The land we're going to explore

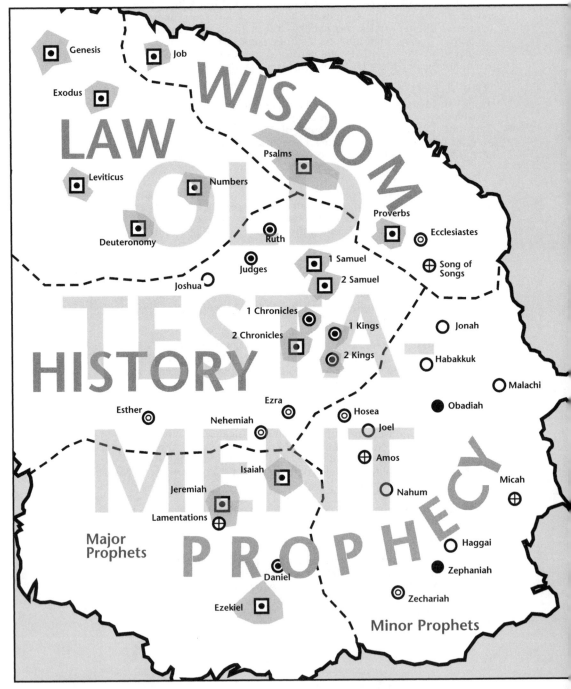

Bible books and their abbreviations

Genesis	Ge	1 Samuel	1 Sa	Esther	Es	Lamentations	La	Micah	Mic
Exodus	Ex	2 Samuel	2 Sa	Job	Jb	Ezekiel	Ek	Nahum	Na
Leviticus	Le	1 Kings	1 Ki	Psalms	Ps	Daniel	Da	Habakkuk	Ha
Numbers	Nu	2 Kings	2 Ki	Proverbs	Pr	Hosea	Hos	Zephaniah	Ze
Deuteronomy	De	1 Chronicles	1 Ch	Ecclesiastes	Ec	Joel	Jo	Haggai	Hag
Joshua	Jos	2 Chronicles	2 Ch	Song of Solomon	So	Amos	Am	Zechariah	Zec
Judges	Jg	Ezra	Ez	Isaiah	Is	Obadiah	Ob	Malachi	Mal
Ruth	Ru	Nehemiah	Ne	Jeremiah	Je	Jonah	Jon		

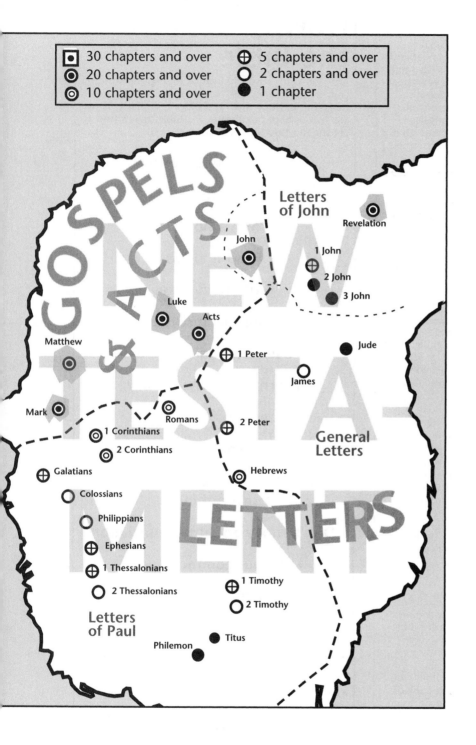

		30 chapters and over		⊕	5 chapters and over
	⊙	20 chapters and over		○	2 chapters and over
	⊚	10 chapters and over		●	1 chapter

GOSPELS
ACTS
NEW
& TESTA-
MENT
LETTERS

Letters of John

John

Revelation

1 John

2 John

3 John

Luke

Acts

Matthew

1 Peter

James

Jude

Mark

Romans

1 Corinthians

2 Peter

2 Corinthians

General Letters

Galatians

Hebrews

Colossians

Philippians

Ephesians

1 Thessalonians

2 Thessalonians

1 Timothy

2 Timothy

Letters of Paul

Philemon   Titus

Matthew	Mt	Galatians	Ga	Titus	Ti	3 John	3 Jn
Mark	Mk	Ephesians	Ep	Philemon	Phm	Jude	Ju
Luke	Lk	Philippians	Ph	Hebrews	He	Revelation	Re
John	Jn	Colossians	Col	James	Ja		
Acts	Ac	1 Thessalonians	1 Th	1 Peter	1 Pe		
Romans	Ro	2 Thessalonians	2 Th	2 Peter	2 Pe		
1 Corinthians	1 Co	1 Timothy	1 Ti	1 John	1 Jn		
2 Corinthians	2 Co	2 Timothy	2 Ti	2 John	2 Jn		

How to Explore the Bible

Anyone who seriously wants to explore another country has to follow certain rules if they are to make the most of their expedition. Similarly, if you are serious about exploring the Bible, here's how to get the most out of your journey.

Approach with respect

Work with a plan

Move slowly

Read it aloud

Write field notes

Look around you

Use some guidebooks

Learn about the history

Understand the culture

Get to know the locals

Don't expect to understand everything

Don't worry about pronunciation

Use your common sense

Always ask questions

If I visit an Indian temple, I act with respect. I take my shoes off. I speak quietly. I don't go in there in size twelve Timberlands playing my kazoo. It's the same with the Bible. We have to treat it with respect. This doesn't mean being boring and stone-faced about it; it means listening, trying to understand what it says, not just blindly rejecting or accepting it.

It helps to have a plan of action —an itinerary—to help you explore. You might want to work through a particular book, or really get to know one chapter in detail. You might want to follow a particular person and study his or her life. Or you could study a topic such as "prayer," "the temple," or "forgiveness."

When I travel I take along reference materials—like guidebooks, maps and phrase books. The deeper you begin to explore, the more help you will need. Some key reference books are:

Concordance
Basically a list of key words used in the Bible and where to find them. For example, to read everything the Bible has to say about camels, you look up the word "camel" and it lists all the verses where that word occurs. (There are twelve verses, actually. To be honest, camels are not one of the hot topics of the Bible. It's the principle that counts.)

Dictionary
A Bible dictionary will tell you much more about the meanings and history of significant Bible words.

Commentary
This book, I hope, will tell you quite a lot about each book of the Bible, but if you want to go deeper, get a single-volume commentary. That will cover each book of the Bible in much more depth.

God has given us wisdom. Some of us could do with a little more, admittedly, but we all have it. So, when you read the Bible, try to use the wisdom God has given you. Don't fly off into fanciful theories and ideas based on one verse. Try to identify when people are speaking metaphorically or literally. Use your common sense.

Take your time with the reading. Read slowly. Stop and think. Don't try to rush around. We are not in a race. If we really want to get to know the region of the Bible that we are visiting, we have to spend time there and move at an easy, relaxed pace.

The Bible was originally more of an audio book. It was read to people. That's why so much of it uses repetition: to help it stick in the memory. So, sometimes, it helps to read the Bible out loud. It will slow down your reading, it will bring out the rhythm of the passage, it will help you to identify the parts that really stand out.

Keep a traveler's journal as you visit each street and city. That way the thoughts that you have, the images that spring to mind, will stick in your memory. Make your own maps. Draw your own pictures. Write down your thoughts and observations. You might like to keep a separate book for the purpose or, as I do, you might like to scribble in the margins or place Post-It notes on the pages.

Make sure that you don't just take one verse out of context. Try to look around you at the passages that surround that verse. Find out about the time it was written and the situation of the writer.

If there is one thing that has really helped my journeys through the Bible, it has been a broad understanding of the history. Each book of the Bible was written at a particular point in history, and understanding this can help our understanding of the entire book.

The Bible often seems baffling and mysterious to us—but some of this at least is because we simply don't understand the culture. As we visit the Bible we have to accept that it is the product of a vastly different culture. That culture had very different attitudes toward women, marriage, food, work, etc. True explorers don't try to impose their culture on the land they visit; instead they try to understand—and learn from—the culture around them.

The Bible is full of fascinating individuals and characters. You will find tricksters and frauds, psychos and prophets, doom merchants and happy-go-lucky figures. Try to understand their character, to find out what makes them tick.

I was speaking to a French friend who has lived in England for many years. "There are things I still don't understand," he said, before launching into a full-scale rant about cricket. However long we stay in a country, there will always be some things that baffle us. There are some areas where we will always be visitors. In the Bible there are things that we will never understand. But that doesn't mean we should stop exploring.

For some reason, people can get very hung up on the right way to say Bible places and names. I've never understood this—I mean, how do we know how the ancient Israelites pronounced "Zerubbabel"? They might have called him "Zubble" for all we know. Just don't worry about it.

Ask questions. Ask *lots* of questions. And if you can't think of what questions to ask, turn the page . . .

Ask questions

The most important thing to bring to the Bible is the ability to ask questions. We have to be willing to engage with the text, to ask questions and look for the answers. When I was growing up, I felt that if I had questions or doubts or worries about a Bible passage, then I was somehow being sinful or unbelieving. In fact, the Bible is full of people who asked God challenging questions. If they weren't afraid, then neither should we be.

Bible study has three key parts:

Understanding the origin of the passage

Understanding the contents of the passage

Understanding the meaning of the passage

Without wanting to sound too much like someone from a kung-fu film, the way to understanding, my child, is to ask questions. Here are just a few questions that will help you start to come to grips with any Bible passage. Of course, not all of them are relevant to all parts of the Bible—just choose the most appropriate ones.

	Understanding the **origin** of the passage	Understanding the **contents** of the passage	Understanding the **meaning** of the passage
Who?	Who wrote the passage?	Who appears in the passage?	Who is the writer talking to?
What?	What happens in the passage?	What style is it in?	What's the big idea behind this passage?
Why?	Why was this written?	Why did the events take place?	Why does the writer use certain words or phrases?
When?	When was it written?	When is the action set?	When did it take place in the overall scheme of things?
Where?	Where was it written?	Where does the action take place?	Where is God leading me through this?
How?	How is the passage put together?	How would the original audience have responded?	How can I apply this to my life?

The aim of exploration

Explorers have one goal: to explore. They want to visit new places, to climb new heights, to discover things that no one has ever discovered before. All exploration is about the gathering of knowledge—and exploring the Bible is no different. Reading the Bible will give us knowledge in many ways, but particularly in three key areas:

Knowledge of the Bible

Sounds obvious, but there we go. The more you read the Bible, the more you understand about it, the more you pick up on the references, spot the links, see the big picture. You understand more about how the thing works and more about how to use it.

Knowledge of life

The Bible is not merely a book of nice ideas, it's a book that claims to offer a practical foundation for living. Throughout the Bible you will find advice on how to live; things we should do, attitudes we should adopt, actions we should avoid. As we explore the Bible we will find rules and principles that we can apply to our own lives.

Knowledge of God

Christians believe that the real purpose and aim of Bible exploration is to deepen our relationship with God. They believe that, through reading the Bible, they will come into contact with the creator of humankind, with the being who made us all in the first place. That, ultimately, is what makes the Bible unlike any other book—for by exploring the Bible, I believe, you can actually get to meet the main character of the book.

Divine Inspiration

Christians talk about the Bible as being "divinely inspired." They take this idea from verses such as 2 Timothy 3:16, which says, *Everything in the Scriptures is God's Word. All of it is useful for teaching and helping people and for correcting them and showing them how to live.* In fact, the phrase Paul uses of the Scriptures is "God-breathed," which Christians interpret as meaning that the Scriptures are not merely the production of men, but of men working under the command and inspiration of God.

Some people believe in what is called verbal inspiration—the idea that every word in the Bible came directly from God. "After all," the argument goes, "God is perfect and cannot make mistakes—so divinely inspired Scriptures must also be perfect and without error." At its extreme, followers of this view believe that everything in the Bible is free from error, not only in terms of religion, but also in terms of history and science. "Fundamentalists" reject scientific theories such as evolution, or archaeological theories that conflict with Bible history.

Some talk about "moral inspiration," by which they mean that the Bible is inspired in its moral and ethical teaching, but not in its religious and mystical teachings. Subscribers to this view would, for example, agree with Jesus' moral teaching but reject his miracles or resurrection. Or they might explain those events in a metaphorical or symbolic way.

Others prefer what is called "plenary inspiration," which means that the subjects and themes that the Bible deals with are inspired by God, but the grammar, the sentences, the details were left to the original writers. This view takes the position that the writers were prompted and inspired by the Holy Spirit, but the words they used were their own. They might make mistakes and errors as they wrote, but the meaning and significance of their words would be inspired by God.

Perhaps the key factor here is what we mean by "inspire." The word comes from two Latin words: *spirare* meaning "breathe," and *in* meaning ... um ... "in." Inspire literally means to breathe in. If the Bible is "God-breathed," therefore, to read it is to inhale something—to feel what he feels, hear his words, feel his life within us. So, whatever your view of the Bible, perhaps the most important question is, "How has it changed your life?" To breathe in something of God is to be more loving, kind, forgiving, faithful, patient, understanding, compassionate in ourselves and to recognize and respond to those qualities in God. If we do that, then we will truly be inspired and the Bible will truly be inspirational.

How Did We Get the Bible?

The Hebrew Scriptures

At first there were just the Hebrew Scriptures. The Hebrew Scriptures are the same as the Christian Old Testament, but arranged under three headings—Law, Prophets and Writings. This is more of a chronological arrangement, reflecting the three stages in which the Scriptures were gathered together. First came the Law of Moses, then the work of the prophets and finally the miscellaneous writings. They group some of the books together that the Christian Bible splits up. Samuel, Chronicles and Kings are each one book, rather than two; and all the minor prophets are brought together in one book. Thus the Hebrew version has twenty-four books, where the Christian Old Testament has thirty-nine.

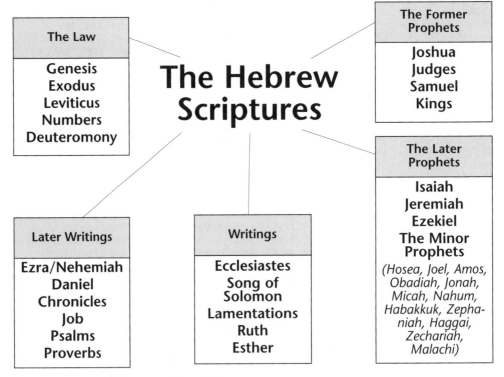

The Law

Genesis
Exodus
Leviticus
Numbers
Deuteromony

The Hebrew Scriptures

The Former Prophets

Joshua
Judges
Samuel
Kings

The Later Prophets

Isaiah
Jeremiah
Ezekiel
The Minor Prophets

(Hosea, Joel, Amos, Obadiah, Jonah, Micah, Nahum, Habakkuk, Zephaniah, Haggai, Zechariah, Malachi)

Later Writings

Ezra/Nehemiah
Daniel
Chronicles
Job
Psalms
Proverbs

Writings

Ecclesiastes
Song of Solomon
Lamentations
Ruth
Esther

The oral tradition

The early Church used the Jewish Scriptures, probably singing from the Psalms and reading the passages to see how they pointed to Jesus. But in addition they told stories of Jesus' life on earth and shared memories and favorite quotes. These were spoken memories—an oral tradition—that were passed on from group to group, from one eyewitness to another. In the early days the Church was restricted to a fairly limited geographical location, many of the eyewitnesses were still alive and the followers believed strongly that the return of Jesus was imminent. For these reasons, they probably did not feel the need to write the accounts down.

The first accounts

After a while, however, the Church began to spread throughout Asia Minor. Similarly, it became apparent that the Lord's return was not going to be quite as quick as had been anticipated and the original eyewitnesses began to die off (or were killed). Thus it became urgent that these stories and recollections be gathered together so that new converts would have something to tell them about the story of Jesus. So various people began to write down their own accounts, drawing on a range of material and their own observations.

In the mail

At the same time, well-known figures such as Paul, Peter and John began to write to different churches helping them to solve problems and offering spiritual advice. There were other documents by respected figures in the Church—leaders such as Irenaeus and Polycarp. These letters, which contained a lot of valuable teaching and insight, were collected and copied and passed around the early Church.

True or false

So far, so good. But then other documents began to be circulated, fake "gospels" full of fantastic details and strange stories. Some of these were written by opponents of Christianity in order to discredit it, or by people who wanted others to follow their own brand of false Christian teaching. Others were written by well-meaning supporters who had, perhaps, let their imagination get the better of them. Much of the material in these "gospels" focused on the early years of Jesus, particularly his childhood and upbringing about which so little was really known. One of these invented gospels gave him a wife and a family, others showed him performing miracles in his childhood, including turning his school friends into birds and murdering his teacher.

So the scriptures available to the Christian Church looked like this:

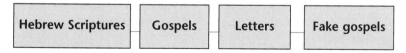

The Church was faced with a difficult and urgent question: what was the official teaching? What were the "approved" documents?

The reading list

In response, various Church leaders began to draw up their lists of approved and recommended reading. Again there were problems, because Christianity was still an evolving faith with no centralized leadership, so many of these lists reflected the personal preferences of local Christian leaders. The earliest surviving list is a vivid example of this. It was issued by Marcion in AD 144. Marcion was very anti-Jewish, so his list omitted the entire Old Testament and every Gospel except for Luke (and even then he edited out parts he didn't like). He did include some letters of Paul (but then again, Paul was Greek, so that made him OK).

Other lists followed, each including its own selection. Gradually a consensus emerged and most lists included the four Gospels, the book of Acts and the letters of Paul. However, there was a lot of debate about some of the other letters, especially about James, Jude, Hebrews, 2 Peter, 2 and 3 John and Revelation.

The main criterion on which books were admitted into the collection of Christian writings lay in their authorship. Books that were agreed to have been written by an apostle, or by a close associate of an apostle, were generally admitted. Books that had question marks against their authorship were often included in the "disputed" sections. Books that were definitely not written by apostles were rejected.

All this came to a head in AD 376. That was the year that Bishop Athanasius wrote an Easter letter to the churches in his region in which he listed his idea of what constituted "Holy Scripture." His list of books—the same as we have in our Bibles today—was eventually confirmed by two councils, one in Rome in 382 and one in Carthage in 397. It eventually became the list; the official, approved, recognized documents. Even then there was some debate, and Revelation only just made it into the finished collection.

Thus the Bible that we have today "grew." No single person decided on its contents; instead it is the result of agreement and consensus and debate. But it is worth remembering that the early Church did not have a Bible as such; the collection of books that we know as the Bible was not agreed on until around 400.

So, the Bible as we know it is made up of the following sections:

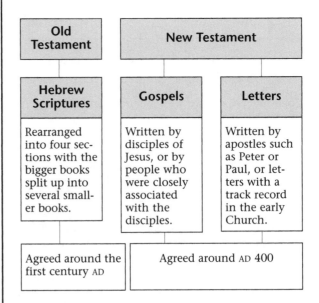

Old Testament	New Testament	
Hebrew Scriptures	**Gospels**	**Letters**
Rearranged into four sections with the bigger books split up into several smaller books.	Written by disciples of Jesus, or by people who were closely associated with the disciples.	Written by apostles such as Peter or Paul, or letters with a track record in the early Church.
Agreed around the first century AD	Agreed around AD 400	

22

The Big Picture
The events and times of the Bible

Creation and the early times

God creates the heavens and the earth. He creates a world that is good. He creates men and women. They are given a garden to inhabit and only one rule to obey. However, they give in to temptation and choose to turn away from God. They are exiled from the garden. Sin and evil pollute God's creation.

Humanity starts to spread throughout the earth, and with its spread comes the spread of evil. Adam and Eve's eldest son kills his brother. Eventually God decides to wipe out all of humanity and start again. Well . . . not quite all. Noah is a good man and he and his family are saved from the flood. Noah is given the task of repopulating the earth. God vows never to destroy humanity again.

The patriarchs

The problem of evil is not eradicated, however, and now God begins a new scheme. He decides to work through a nation, a chosen people. As the father of these people, he chooses Abraham. God promises Abraham that his descendants will be a great nation—the Jews—and they will have a land to inhabit—the land of Canaan. He also promises that all of humanity will be blessed by one of Abraham's descendants.

Abraham, in his old age, fathers a son, Isaac. Isaac fathers twins, Esau and Jacob, and the line progresses through the younger son. Jacob has twelve children—one of whom, Joseph, ends up in Egypt. In the end, this son is joined by the rest of the clan, who flee to Egypt to escape famine. Jacob changes his name to Israel, and it is by this name that the people will henceforth be known.

In Egypt, the descendants of Abraham start to multiply and, a few hundred years further on, there is some good news and some bad news. The good news is that part, at least, of the promise has come true—Abraham's descendants have become a nation. The bad news is that the entire nation is in slavery.

The exodus

God raises up a leader—Moses—who commands the Egyptian leader to let the Israelites go. After a series of plagues on the Egyptians, the Israelites are freed. The Israelites make their way back to the land that God had promised their ancestor Abraham. On the way God gives them commandments and detailed instructions on how the Jews should behave as a nation and how they should worship their God.

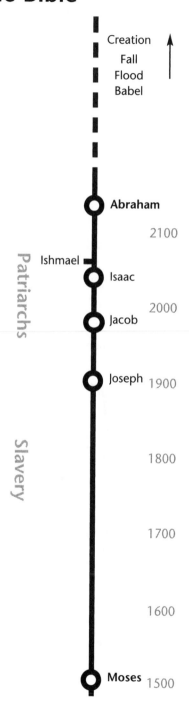

Creation
Fall
Flood
Babel

Abraham
2100

Patriarchs

Ishmael
Isaac
2000
Jacob

Joseph 1900

Slavery

1800

1700

1600

Moses 1500

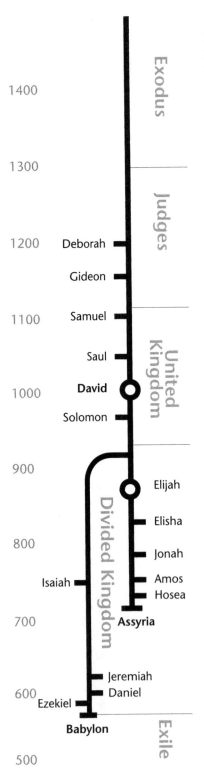

At the very borders of the Promised Land, however, their faith fails—they are too scared to cross into the land. This lack of faith means they spend the next forty years wandering in the desert.

Moses never makes it into the Promised Land. He dies on a mountain overlooking Canaan and hands over leadership to Joshua, under whose command the Israelites cross the River Jordan and take possession of the land. However, even after the first successful battles the old pattern repeats itself. God gave his people explicit instructions to conquer *all* the land, but the people settle for a compromise. Some of the old inhabitants—the Canaanites—remain and, with them, their own ways of worship. For the next 800 years Israel's history is a battle between the worship of God and the worship of false gods.

The judges

First there is the period of the judges—a period when the country was filled with lawlessness and violence and when "each man did what he thought was right." The judges—leaders like Deborah and Gideon and Samson—bring only occasional light into the darkness.

The united kingdom

Then the Israelites ask for a king. God doesn't want them to have a king—they do not need one with him as their leader—but in the end he gives in and Saul becomes the first king of Israel. It is a false start. Saul is a headstrong but foolish leader and he is succeeded by David, Israel's greatest king. Under the leadership of David and his son Solomon, Israel achieves the height of its power and influence. David defeats the enemies of Israel and Solomon builds a magnificent temple in Jerusalem.

The divided kingdom

It was not to last. On Solomon's death, the country falls into civil war, and the "Promised Land" splits into two countries: Israel in the north and Judah in the south. The next 300 years are a long, slow descent. The two nations are constantly attacked by powerful enemies, while they are weakened by a succession of evil kings who follow false gods. In an attempt to turn them around, God sends a series of messengers—the prophets —who bring challenges and rebukes and predictions of the fate that is awaiting the two nations. It doesn't do much good. In 722 BC the northern kingdom of Israel is captured and the inhabitants taken into captivity in Assyria. They are never heard of again. A hundred years later, the southern kingdom of Judah falls to another mighty empire, the Babylonians, and the people are taken captive in Babylon. Yet not all hope is lost. In the years before and during the exile, the prophets talked of a Messiah—a "chosen one"—a mighty leader whom God would send to save his people.

The exile and return

Their exile lasts seventy years, before the Babylonian empire falls and the exiles start to return to Israel. Despite opposition, they rebuild Jerusalem and the temple. But the glory days—such as they were—have gone. God sends no more prophets and Israel remains at the mercy of invading nations, first the Greeks and then the mighty Roman Empire. Increasingly, the people of Israel place their hopes in the long-awaited Messiah.

Jesus

The promise given so long ago to Abraham was to be worked out in a remarkable way. A poor young woman called Mary becomes pregnant with a son, a son whose father is God himself. This son, Jesus, is born in poverty and raised in obscurity in an unremarkable town in northern Israel.

Jesus' real work begins when he is around 30 years old. After a short spell in the desert, he travels through Israel preaching, teaching and performing miracles. He starts to make claims for himself, claims that go beyond those of a teacher or even a prophet. He forgives people their sins and raises the dead; he challenges the establishment. With his small band of followers he enters Jerusalem in triumph. Then it all seems to go wrong. Betrayed by one of his followers, Jesus is tried by the authorities, taken outside the city and executed.

Three days later, his followers start to make remarkable claims. They claim that Jesus has risen from the dead, that he has appeared to many of his followers. More, they claim that Jesus is the Messiah, that his death has changed the world, and that he has sent them a new helper, the Holy Spirit, to empower and inspire them. These followers spread the message far and wide.

The early Church

As the message catches hold, the followers face persecution from the Jewish and Roman authorities. New leaders emerge: Peter, the fisherman who was one of Jesus' first followers; Paul, who began his career persecuting Jesus' followers and who, after a dramatic vision of Jesus, becomes one of the gospel's most outspoken exponents. Gradually the stories about Jesus are written down and sent around the world. The followers set up local groups—called churches. People of all nationalities start to believe in this Messiah.

The future

Some look even further. In exile on a small island, John, one of Jesus' earliest followers, has a vision of the end of time. Jesus will return and gain the final victory over darkness. The world will end as it began—with creation, with God creating a new heaven and a new earth, where all his followers will live in peace.

Well, that's the story anyway. Now read on . . .

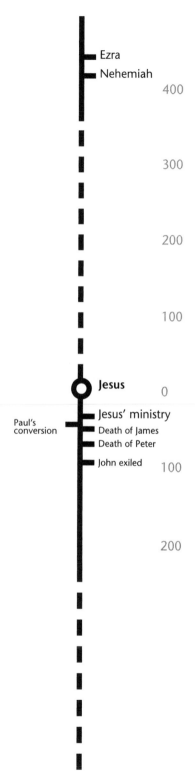

Ezra
Nehemiah
400

300

200

100

Jesus   0

Paul's conversion   Jesus' ministry
Death of James
Death of Peter

John exiled   100

200

Part Two
The Old Testament

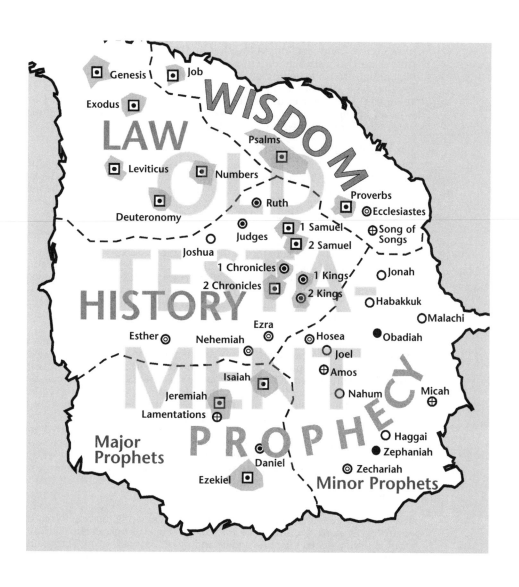

The Old Testament

The books that we group together under the name "Old Testament" are some of the most remarkable works ever written. But to really appreciate the Old Testament we have to understand a few highly important facts.

• It wasn't written by Christians

The Old Testament is only given that title when it is put together with the New Testament—that is, when it is part of the Christian Bible. It is "old" because, in Christian eyes, it describes a relationship with God that was preparatory to, and superseded by, the new relationship revealed through Jesus Christ. Thus you cannot expect the people in the Old Testament to behave like Christians—they lived thousands of years before Jesus arrived.

• It was written over a huge period of time

The Old Testament comes from a wide range of cultures and backgrounds and took around 1,500 years to put together. So the culture described in the early parts of the Old Testament differs, not merely from the culture of the New Testament, but from the culture of other parts of the Old Testament itself. During that time attitudes and behavior changed vastly. By the end of the Old Testament period, for example, it was assumed that one man married one woman. Much earlier it was not uncommon for one man to have several wives (or several hundred if you're King Solomon).

• It was specifically organized and edited

The Old Testament is a collection of documents that were deliberately edited and gathered together by a series of editors and compilers. That means it is very hard to give a specific author and date for many of the books, because many were put together many years after the original material was written by an editor who sometimes added his own comments and insertions.

• It is not a system

For all these reasons, it is hard, if not impossible, to talk about one comprehensive system of Old Testament faith. Ideas and attitudes changed over time. God reveals himself in different ways to different people. Abraham is cited in the New Testament as a "man of faith," but his understanding of God was very different from ours. He lived before God saved the Israelites from Egypt, before the giving of the Law, before, most crucially, the arrival of Jesus.

Over the years this has led to huge problems for Christians in particular as the God of the Old Testament seems so different from the God of the New Testament. Some people could reconcile the differences only by dismissing the Old Testament completely. Others argue that there is no difference—that God is the same yesterday, today and forever. Most readers, however, will find things that are puzzling and that simply don't "fit." That is not to say that there are not themes that run through the Old Testament. Ideas of love, justice, mercy, compassion are found woven into the pattern of many books of the Bible. And the people in the Old Testament show many characteristics that we can see in our own lives and in the lives of people around us—hope, fear, joy, greed, treachery, selfishness and many more universal human emotions. But we will find much that we don't understand, and behavior that we find difficult even to condone.

The key thing to remember is that they too were exploring, finding things out as they went along. We should be wary of looking at people in the Old Testament as if they shared the same understanding of God that we do. They didn't. But they were humans for all that, and there is still an awful lot that we can learn from their faith and their lives.

The Books of the Law

The Pentateuch

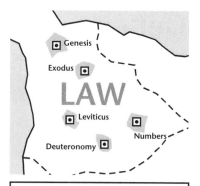

The first five books of the Bible are called the Pentateuch, from the Greek word *pentateuchos*, meaning "five-volumed book." They are traditionally associated with Moses. Some claim that he wrote them himself, others that his words and his encounter with God were the inspiration for their composition. For this reason they are often referred to as the Law of Moses. When other parts of the Bible talk about "the Law," they generally mean the Pentateuch.

Genesis

Begins with the creation of man, and then traces the origins of the people of Israel through ancestors like Abraham, Jacob and Isaac. Although it begins with a global perspective (you can't get much more global than the creation of the world), it soon begins to narrow down into the story of Israel. By the end of Genesis, the people of Israel are in slavery in Egypt.

Exodus

With Exodus we enter Moses' own time. Exodus tells the story of the escape from Egypt—the exodus itself. The book ends with Moses receiving the Ten Commandments from God and the instructions for the building of the tabernacle.

Leviticus

Leviticus is almost completely a book of rules and regulations. It consists of a huge amount of what might be called religious red tape. Most people find it a difficult and even dull book, but there are gems inside.

Numbers

Gets its name because it is full of ... er ... numbers, actually. It contains a census of the people of Israel, taken while they were on their journey. It also records the failure of Israel to enter the Promised Land and their forty years in the wilderness.

Deuteronomy

This is mainly Moses' farewell speech. It is a summary, in a way, of the other books, given just before his death and before the Israelites' entry to the Promised Land.

Details, Details . . .
Other names for the Pentateuch

The Law (Ez 10:3; Mt 12:5, Lk 16:16)

The book of the Law (Ne 8:3, Ga 3:10)

The book of the Law of Moses (are you spotting a theme yet?) (Ne 8:1, Lk 2:22)

The book of Moses (2 Ch 25:4, Mk 12:26)

The law of the Lord (Ez 7:10, Lk 2:23–24)

The law of God (Ne 10:28, 29)

The book of the Law of God (2 Ch 17:9)

That part at the beginning of the Bible (everyone else)

Details, Details . . .
Five or six?

Some experts argue that the Pentateuch should really be the Hexateuch, with the book of Joshua added in. (Hex = six, as if you didn't know.) Other experts advocate a "tetrateuch" of four books—removing Deuteronomy from the list.

None of this really matters, but I thought you might like to know the kinds of things that scholars do to fill their time.

Genesis
In the beginning . . .

Genesis is the book of beginnings. It is not only the start of the Bible—it is the start of all creation.

Who: The traditional view is that Moses wrote the Pentateuch. Nowadays most experts believe that the books are the work of several hands and come from different traditions.

When: Genesis was written over a long period of time. It was probably begun in the time of Moses, but later generations added other material and edited the book together. The book probably reached its final form around the time of Solomon (970–930 BC).

What: Genesis is about origins. It tells the readers where we came from and why we are here. In the opening chapters of Genesis, we have all the themes that will fill the rest of the Bible—creation, sin and rebellion; love, grace and mercy. For, following the fall of Adam and Eve, God was not concerned solely with punishment, he was also planning for salvation.

The book is structured around the lives of several key figures, people like Adam, Noah, Abraham, Jacob and Joseph. There are, of course, interludes that cover other topics, but these are the key characters. They are known as the patriarchs, the "fathers," and they remind us that the Bible is not a book about God—it is a book about God and man.

God is personal. He speaks, he thinks, he relates to humans. This is not some impersonal "life force," still less some distant, alien being. This is a "someone," a being who wants to communicate with the world he has created. Indeed, the whole of the Bible is about God's attempts to make himself known to his creations, to inspire, cajole, correct and above all to love these people he made.

Quick Guide

Author
Various, including Moses

Type
Books of the Law

Purpose
To explain where we all came from and why we are all here.

Key verse
1:1 "In the beginning God created the heavens and the earth."

If you remember one thing about this book . . .
God created this world to be good, but things went badly wrong.

Your 15 minutes start now
Read chapters 1–3, 28, 38, 41–42

The Route Through Genesis

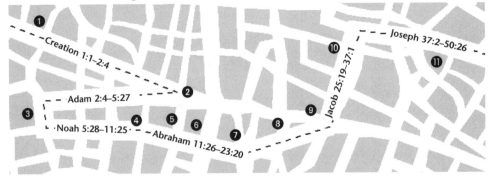

Creation 1:1–2:4
Adam 2:4–5:27
Noah 5:28–11:25
Abraham 11:26–23:20
Jacob 25:19–37:1
Joseph 37:2–50:26

Creation 1:1–2:4

Genesis 1:1–2:4 describes the creation of the universe. It is created in a set pattern and order, and arranged in a timescale. With the exception of the "lights," creation fits a reasonably consistent pattern. The first four days *prepare* the place—the universe, the land, the seas, the energy source. The last two days *populate* the place, with animals, birds, fish and, of course, humans.

Scientifically, there is a problem with the "lights"—the stars—which are not created until the fourth day. Surely the lights should be the first thing created? But the chronology is not necessarily the important thing. Genesis is talking about who put the stars in place, more than when it happened.

TIMETABLE—CREATION

	Day	Verse
LIGHT	1	1:3–5
SKY	2	1:6–8
WATER AND LAND	3	1:9–13
LIGHTS Stars, etc.	4	1:14–19
FISH AND BIRDS	5	1:20–23
ANIMALS AND HUMANS	6	1:24–31
REST	7	2:2–3

View Points

Just six days? (2:1–2)

On one hand:
God did all this, exactly as Genesis states, in six, twent-four-hour days.
For: Does exactly what it says in the Bible.
Against: Does not agree with geological and scientific findings. Does not allow for poetic symbolism.

On the other hand:
Not literal, but a poetic and symbolic description of God's actions.
For: Avoids scientific difficulties and problems within the text.
Against: Relies on interpretation of text rather than literal acceptance.

Moving on: The word used for day has several meanings in the Old Testament. In its simple form it means "twenty-four hours," but it can also be used to describe a certain moment (as in the "day of the Lord") or an indefinite period of time (e.g., "day of temptation" [Ps 95:8]). Psalm 90:4 also indicates that God's time is different from ours—a thousand years to him is like a day.

Puzzling Points

Is it scientifically accurate?

OK. Let's start with what we know. Genesis is not a scientific book. It does not deal with the detail of how God formed the world, what atoms he brought together, what swirling clouds of particles he parted in order to make the thing happen.

Those who look to Genesis for a detailed, scientific account of the origins of the universe will find themselves in difficulties, because it's simply not that kind of book. Genesis looks at causes rather than processes; it asserts that God made the universe and God made humans. It claims that creation did not happen by accident. Whatever scientific process brought about humans and the universe, God was the prime mover. It was God's hand that first made the lights, and God's hand that created living, breathing beings.

It is worth remembering, when we come to Genesis, that it is opposed not by scientific facts but by a number of other theories. Evolution is a theory. The big bang is a theory. Both have been developed by scientists and astronomers to explain the evidence, but they are still theories, nevertheless. Archaeology, anthropology, astronomy—and any other "ology" you care to name—all, when it comes to the origins of the planet and its inhabitants, deal in theories. The origins of humankind are still very obscure.

Genesis offers one such theory: God made everything. It does not explain how he did it. Indeed, it does not know how he did it. It just says that he did.

Details, Details . . .
What does "in his image" mean?

It doesn't mean physical image. God, despite the way that paintings over the years have depicted him, is not white, and old, with a beard. The Bible is vague about what God looks like. He appears sometimes in human form, sometimes as a burning bush. Physically mankind looks like . . . er . . . mankind actually.

The image of God in us is something different. It is the spirit, the inborn dignity and sacredness of each individual. We are like God in that we can respond to God.

Things you don't find in the Bible: The garden of Eden

There is no such thing as the garden of Eden. There is a garden *in* Eden, which is not the same thing. Elsewhere there are references to "the garden of God" (Ek 28:13 NIV or "the garden of the Lord" (Is 51:3 NIV). Eden is described as a region with a river with four tributaries: the Pishon, Gihon, Tigris and Euphrates. The latter two are identified, but we don't know where the others were, nor do we know where the garden itself was. The most common theory is that the garden lay somewhere in southern Mesopotamia.

What the garden was is much more important than *where* it was. It was a place where man and God worked and lived in harmony; a place of innocence, peace and happiness. Later, when people used the word "paradise" to describe heaven, they were looking back to that place in Eden, for "paradise" is the Persian word for "garden."

Adam and Eve 2:4–5:27

❶ The first humans

On the sixth "day," God created his first human—Adam. The name derives from the ancient name for mankind. This is the first of the species, the representative man, the original.

There are two accounts in Genesis. The first, Genesis 1:26–30, is a general account. The second, in Genesis 2:7–25, is a more detailed account of the creation of men and women. Some have seen a conflict between these two accounts, but it is not clear why. The first account occurs within the passage that is describing the broad sweep of creation, so the writer does not pause to describe the detail of what happened. The second account is much more detailed, describing Adam's creation and his need for a partner.

The key word here is partnership. God creates, not a servant, but a partner. Many people have seen Eve as subservient to Adam because she came second. One might equally argue that she was an improved version —human version 2.0! But the truth is, she was meant to be a partner. And the end of the chapter indicates that this partnership was part of the natural order: a man and a woman, joining together to become like one being.

Adam was different from the rest of the animals for one reason: he was made in God's image. He was also given control over the animals. In these environmentally conscious days, that is a bone of contention—why should man be in charge? Apart from the fact that this ignores the obvious (i.e., humans are obviously in control—I know of no countries that are being ruled by dolphins), the fact is that this dominion is balanced by another command from God: responsibility. Adam was put into the garden to take care of it (2:15). I try to avoid gardening, on the whole, but I do know that taking care of a garden means not polluting it, not destroying the environment and not ripping the whole thing up to dig for minerals.

❷ The fall

Chapters 2 and 3 of Genesis are the Bible's answer to the question of how sin came into the world. The answer is plain: it came through the choice of humankind. Adam and Eve are given only one rule: there is one tree, the fruit of which they must not touch—the tree of the knowledge of good and evil.

Knowledge of good and evil here cannot mean knowing right or wrong: Adam must already have known that when God spoke to him. If he did not know right from wrong, then he would not have known enough to take any notice of God's commands. It is more a matter of who was to be in charge.

The question here is: who makes the rules? God was asserting his position as the one authority—his right as creator and carer to make the rules. By choosing to disobey him, Adam and Eve challenged that right. They chose their own path—a path that led them out of paradise and into a harsher world.

Doubt 3:1

The serpent tempts Eve to question the truth of God's words. This is the fundamental truth of sin: it is a rebellion against the goodness of God, a belief that we know best, that we are the only ones who matter.

Action 3:6

Doubt turns to action as each one eats the fruit. Although they later blame others, they are each responsible for their own sin.

Guilt 3:7

The minute they do this thing, they know that something has happened. Things are not the same.

Separation 3:8

They have broken the rules. They have chosen their own path. They cannot stay in the garden. From now on there is a separation between man and God, and between man and nature. Things will get a lot tougher now—for all parties involved.

Love 3:22

Yet there is still something there. Man cannot get rid of his relationship with God. It is part of our very being—we are created in his image. And God himself is determined not to leave the situation as it is. As they leave, he gives them a gift. God does not let Adam and Eve go out of the garden without giving them warm clothes to wear. He is a father and he still cares.

The rest of the Bible tells of how God strove to repair the relationship and how human beings can satisfy the desire that still gnaws at every human heart: the desire to return to Eden, to live with and be loved by our true Father.

❸ Cain and Abel 4:1–16

Far from sin stopping with Adam and Eve, things soon get worse. Their firstborn child, Cain, is also the first murderer. By the time we get to Lamech, a few generations further on, murder has become a habit. Once again the root of sin is selfishness and pride; the belief that only I matter. Cain's offerings were not acceptable because of the spirit in which they were given. From the start, the point about sacrifices is not their content but their intent; not so much what is given but the heart of the giver. It was a lesson that Jesus was to illustrate in Mark 12:41–44.

Things you don't find in the Bible: The apple

The Bible doesn't mention an apple in Genesis. All it talks about is a fruit. It could have been a banana for all we know. It could have been any fruit. All right, probably not a gooseberry.

Puzzling Points
The serpent (3:1)

The serpent is not like the other creatures. What is he? Some argue that the serpent is a metaphor for man's own desire and pride. In that sense, Eve is listening to her own doubt. The traditional view, however, is that the serpent is Satan— the "accuser" who tempts humanity to disobedience. ▷276

Why were they evicted?

Even if the earth has somehow been affected by their choice, it is not easy to grasp why Adam and Eve have to leave the garden. The Bible says that God exiles them because he does not want them to live forever. He is putting a limit on their powers. It is also a symbol of how sin means that we cannot live with God. Only through Jesus will we be able to live forever. Only through him will we be able to get back to the garden.

Why did God "mark" Cain? (4:15)

The mark indicated to everyone that it was up to God to punish, not man. Abel's blood cries out to God for vengeance. Cain's punishment is banishment. He has to live in the Land of Nod—i.e., the Land of Wandering.

Who was Cain's wife? (4:17)

His sister. Look, incest is later banned in the Bible. But when there are only five human beings in the world, you've got to start somewhere. Verse 5:4 tells us that Adam had more children, although only Seth, Abel and Cain are mentioned.

Questions, Questions

Were they really that old?

OK. Let's get serious here—it says in Genesis 5:26 that Methuselah died at the age of 969!
Yes.

Oh come on. No one lives that long. I mean, I think my grandad's been hanging around for ages, and he's only 86.
Well, other ancient accounts also have traditions of long life: the Babylonian tradition identifies nine or ten kings before the flood who totaled between 18,000 and 65,000 years!

So? They probably made it up as well.
Not necessarily. The most popular explanation is that the effects of the fall were slow to wear off physically. Adam and Eve had been promised long life—their descendants appear to share this physical attribute in differing degrees. Long life—very long life—was hereditary in the family of Adam.

So you're saying it was genetic?
Maybe. Another explanation is that the numbers don't mean literal years but are merely to give us an account of long periods of time.

All right, when was the retirement age, then?
Men retired at 612 and women at 586.

Really?
No. Don't be stupid.

Puzzling Points

Did angels really have sex with women (6:1–2)?

Difficult to say. The exact phrase is "sons of God," which normally means angels in the Old Testament. Some experts interpret these as angels, as part of the fallen angels who rebelled against God. Others believe the phrase refers to the descendants of Seth—the ancient, original lineage.

Whatever the case, the offspring of this relationship were not exactly normal. They are called Nephilim, which means "fallen ones." Although described as "heroes" and warriors, they were also evil—the verse describing them is followed immediately by God's observation on the terrible state of the world. The tradition of huge, powerful, completely amoral men lived on for many years—it is mentioned in Numbers 13:33, where the shocked and hysterical Israelites claim to have seen the Nephilim in the Promised Land.

▷278

Noah
5:28–11:25

At the beginning of Genesis, God looks on his creation with optimism and hope and satisfaction. It was good. Now he looks and the opposite is true. Humanity is irretrievably evil. So he decides to wipe it out and start again. Almost all of it. There is one good man: Noah and his family. He out of all creation would be spared.

❹ The flood
6:5–8:18

The word used to describe the flood is *mabbûl*—a word that occurs only one other time in the Bible—in Psalm 39:10. So this is not the common, ordinary, run-of-the-(water)mill flood. This is the big one. This is an awesome, cataclysmic, all-devouring deluge. Water comes from all directions—from the windows of heaven and from the depths of the earth.

Along with Noah, the ark contained his wife, their three sons and their wives. The Bible tells us that Noah took into the ark two of each "kind" of animal. This doesn't necessarily mean species—it might be more general than that. it also tells us that he took seven pairs of each "clean" animal. This is confusing because the distinction between clean and unclean animals didn't occur until much later—in the time of Moses. Some see this as evidence of later authorship of this story.

The covenant

After the flood, God makes a covenant or a promise to Noah. God promises never again to send a flood, and he gives Noah and his descendants the earth to look after. So the story of Noah ends with a great promise, with a reconciliation between God and his creation, and with a sign of God's love written in the sky. From now on, the great sign from God is not the rain, but the rainbow.

Brief Lives: Noah

Background: Son of Lamech. Wife and three boys.

Occupation: Boatbuilder. Winemaker.

Achievements: A righteous person (6:9), Noah is noted for his trust in God and his faithfulness, despite the prevailing culture. He trusted God enough to build the ark and to get into it and to believe that he would be saved. He also invented wine (9:20–27). Anyone who is ultimately responsible for the invention of Shiraz is OK in my book.

Character: Faithful. Patient. Soggy.

Pros: Believes and obeys God.

Cons: Perhaps a little *too* fond of a glass of wine.

Details, Details . . . Different accounts of the flood

There are accounts of a large flood in a number of ancient cultures. A Sumerian tablet from around 2000 BC describes how the king was warned by the gods of an approaching deluge and built a boat in which to escape. Similarly, epics from Babylonia and Assyria contain accounts. The Epic of Gilgamesh tells how Gilgamesh was warned by the god Ea that a flood was coming. He builds a boat in which he shelters his family, some animals, treasure and some craftsmen. It also contains a parallel of Noah sending out the birds to seek land. These are not, of course, biblical renditions, but the parallels suggest a common memory of a huge, cataclysmic event.

Anyone got any air freshener?

Things you don't find in the Bible: **Noah's boat**

The word used for Noah's vessel is "ark," which means box. This was not a yacht, but a great, big, waterproof crate. It had different decks for different purposes, but its main aim was simply to float. It didn't need steering, because God was directing it. It didn't need power, because all it needed to do was float. All it needed was space, some very good waterproofing and very, very, very good ventilation.

View Points

Was it really the whole earth?

On one hand:
The whole world was covered, and the only life preserved was in the ark. All species were in there. Everything was blotted out. The mountains were covered in floodwaters.

On the other hand:
Only a limited region was covered—the "known world" as it were. The flood, therefore, was restricted to the Middle East. A vast environmental zone was to be washed away. The mountains were covered with mist and cloud that accompanied the deluge.

Moving on A cataclysmic event, the wiping out of sinful mankind and the saving of one family to carry on God's purpose. This is the message of the flood epic. Whether you think the flood covered the whole earth or just a large part of it, the point is that God saved the people who were faithful to him. And humankind continued on the earth.

Puzzling Points

Why does Noah curse Ham? (9:20–27)

After the flood Noah plants a vineyard and gets drunk. Ham enters the tent and sees him naked. Why this should result in a curse is unclear. The others were very careful not to look at their father when they covered him—perhaps it was Ham's lack of concern for his father's dignity that reflected a lack of respect and earned him a curse. On the other hand, I can't help thinking that Noah shouldn't have got quite so drunk in the first place.

❺ The tower of Babel

Babel means "Gate of God" and that is what they thought this project was—an entry to greatness, a way for man to become as powerful as God. He is trying to get hold of that fruit he missed out on. The flood had taught them nothing—indeed, the story of the tower of Babel is one that has been worked out century after century, time after time.

"Babel" is the usual Old Testament form of Babylon, so it is probable that the writer has in mind a Babylonian ziggurat, or stepped tower. Either way, God intervenes and the unity of humankind is shattered.

Abraham   11:27–23:20

Chapter 11 of Genesis is a turning point. This is the point where God decides to work through one man. God makes a promise to Abram, a promise that will bring all of creation back to him. Abram is promised that he will be the father of a great and mighty nation and, more than that, through this nation the whole world will be blessed.

This promise now becomes the main theme of the rest of the Bible. Abram will become Abraham and the history of his family will form the theme of much of the Old Testament. There is a new direction to the narrative—we start to look forward, to the fulfillment of God's promises, to the new plan that God has put into action. There is also a deeper, more spiritual feel to the book as God reveals more of himself and his nature to Abraham.

In many of these encounters, God is decidedly mysterious. There is much that the patriarchs did not know about him, or that he did not reveal to them. Indeed, when he later speaks to Moses, he tells Moses that he kept some things hidden (Ex 6:3).

❻ The covenant with Abram   12:1–3

"I will bless you and make you a great nation," says God.

The promise comes as Abram is called to leave Haran and go to a new land. The great nation that is promised is a long way off—indeed, Abram was already seventy-five and childless. Since the average life span of the biblical figures of this time is roughly double ours, we can, perhaps, get an idea of Abram's physical state by imagining a man of forty. The land is granted quickly. Abram arrives in Canaan and is given the land (12:7). The nation, not unnaturally, was to take slightly longer to achieve. Give the man a break. He was seventy-five, after all.

In chapter 15, God repeats his promise to Abram, this time sealing it with a covenant. Along with the covenant ceremony, God introduces a historical perspective: he lays out the future for Abram. His people will be enslaved but will be released and will eventually reach the Promised Land.

The ceremony is sealed with a smoking cooking pot and a flaming fire. This seems like an odd kind of barbecue ritual, but it is a clear reference to the future release of Israel from captivity, when God will go before his people as a pillar of fire and a pillar of smoke. Indeed, God appears as smoke or fire several times in the Old Testament.

The promise to Abram is repeated several times, in chapters 12, 15 and 17. In chapter 17, there is a further injunction on Abram to "obey me and always do right" (v. 1). Abram has a responsibility as his part of the covenant. There is also the injunction to mark the covenant by circumcision, symbolizing an allegiance to God. He also has a name change, from Abram to Abraham, which is really just a change of dialect. The name means the same thing, but the longer form sounds a bit like "father of many nations." God was making a pun. Sarai changes her name to Sarah —both names mean "princess"—to signify this new start. It is clear that chapter 17 is something of a turning point.

Landmark: Covenant

A covenant is a biblical term for a legally binding agreement. It is used primarily in the Bible for the agreement that God has made with humankind. So important is this term that it was used to describe the two sections of the Bible. *Testamentum* is the Latin word for covenant, so the two parts of the Bible are really the stories of the Old and New covenants.

Old Testament covenants

Noah. After the flood, God makes a promise to Noah never to destroy humankind in that way again (Ge 6:18)

Abraham. God tells Abraham that he will make a great nation out of his descendants. The agreement between the two is sealed by circumcision (Ge 15:9–21; 17:1–27).

Moses. After God saves the Israelites from Egypt he declares that they are now his people and he is their God. This covenant calls for the Israelites to be "holy as I am holy." To enable them to do this, God gives them the Law, written on two tablets of stone. These stones are kept in a special box called "the ark of the covenant" (Ex 19–24).

These covenants usually take the form of legal agreements and treaties of the time, consisting of a preamble naming the author, a historical setting showing the relationship between the two parties, a declaration of the mutual responsibilities of the parties, details of when the covenant should be read out and finally a list of the consequences should the covenant be broken.

New covenant

Humankind never kept their part of the bargain. They worshiped false gods and failed to keep the Law. Through the later prophets, God began to show that he would therefore make a new agreement, one that would not be expressed through external aspects like sacrifices and circumcision, but that would be an attitude of heart and mind (Je 31:31–34).

This agreement was fulfilled by Jesus, who established it at the last supper (Mk 14:24) and whose death sealed the agreement (He 8:8–13). The new covenant means that anyone from any nation who has faith in Jesus will be saved.

Abram and Lot 13:1–14:16

Lot is a curious character. He is, in some ways, a bit of a buffoon. Here he makes his choice—the apparently fertile part of Canaan will be his. It is the right choice materially, but the wrong choice spiritually, for he ends up living near Sodom, which, in real estate terms, is not a good move.

Sodom is attacked by several kings and Lot is captured, only to be rescued by Abram, and later he only just escapes with his life after his dwelling is attacked by the men of Sodom and God destroys the place. Lot is not criticized for his part in the events, but neither is he praised. He just seems to carry on getting it wrong . . .

Brief Lives: Abram, aka Abraham

Background: Son of Terah. Resident of Ur.

Occupation: Nomadic shepherd, although given the scale of his enterprise, "sheep management executive" might be a more appropriate title.

Achievements: Abraham is *the* man of faith of the Old Testament. He had no prior experience on which to base his faith. He had no Scriptures, no history to examine. He had only a God who spoke to him and made promises.

Yet Abraham believed the promises and acted on them. He left his home and traveled south. He believed that he would be a father, even though he was in his old age. He was even prepared to give up his precious son if God asked. He had faith that God would do what he said he would do. Of course, there were times when he was not so sure—such as the times when he passed his wife off as his sister. But generally, "Abram believed the LORD, and the LORD was pleased with him" (15:6). And for that he is one of the great heroes of the Old Testament.

Character: Trusting, but not afraid to question.

Pros: Trusts in the Lord.

Cons: Occasionally does *not* trust in the Lord.

Landmark: What's in a Name?

The Bible places a great emphasis on the importance of names. Names are not just what you are called; they are who you are, or who the Lord intends you to be. Nobody in the Bible was named because the name sounded nice. Names had a significance, a meaning, a depth.

A name change is often a sign of changed ownership or changed allegiance. When the Babylonian and Egyptian empires took control of Jerusalem, they changed the kings' names to show them that they owned them, lock, stock and double-barreled surname (2 Ki 23:34; 24:17).

Equally it can indicate a change of purpose. God changes Abram's name to Abraham and Sarai to Sarah (Ge 17:5). Jesus changed Simon's name to Cephas (Jn 1:42).

Names can indicate character. Jacob's name means "trickster" and Esau's name means "hairy."

Names are prophetic. Several prophets called their children by names that gave a message from God. The most extreme example of this is Hosea, whose children included "Not Wanted," "Not My People" and "Please Call My Lawyer." (Actually I made the last one up.)

▷**52, 263**

Abram's journey

Abram left Ur and settled in Haran (Ge 11:31). He then traveled to Shechem (12:6), on to Bethel (12:8), and then into Egypt (12:10). He returned via Bethel, where he separated from Lot (13:3), and finally settled at Hebron (13:18).

Haran · Nineveh

Shechem · Damascus

Hebron · Bethel · Babylon

Memphis · Sodom · Ur

Let's hear it for Hagar   16:1–16; 21:9–21

Time goes by and no child appears, so Abram tries to take matters into his own hands by fathering a child through his wife's slave, Hagar. It was customary for men whose wives could not have children to sleep with a slave. The slave's child would then be adopted by the wife.

When the child is born, Sarai, Abram's wife, drives Hagar away. God rescues her and promises her too that her son—who is eventually called Ishmael—will be the father of many descendants. He too has a covenant of sorts. He too will be the father of a "great nation" (21:17–18) although, unlike the promise he gave to Abram, he does not promise that blessing will come through them. Ishmaelites—a nomadic tribe—appear in the story of Joseph, and it is part of Islamic theology that all Arabs are descended from Ishmael.

Nevertheless, it is important to note that Hagar is extremely unusual in that God appears before her. The status and position of women in the Bible has always been a cause of much discussion, debate and, it has to be admitted, distress. But here we have a simple servant girl, and an Egyptian servant girl at that, receiving rescue and comfort from the Lord.

God's decision to work through the descendants of Isaac does not mean that he does not care for his other children. Nor, indeed, that he would not be at work among them. Throughout the history of the Old Testament there are many examples where the prophets point to the other nations as a rebuke to Israel, where individuals and communities from other nations are blessed by God.

❼ Sodom and Gomorrah   18:16–19:38

Archaeological evidence shows that something happened in the plain surrounding the Dead Sea around 2000 BC, some catastrophe that rendered the area unfit for human life. The most likely explanation is an earthquake of some kind. The biblical explanation is more direct: God did it.

Sodom was a byword for sin of all kinds. It would be wrong to assume that the main evil in Sodom was the sin that has come to bear its name. Although the men of the town wanted to have sex with the strangers and the town was clearly in the grip of sexual perversion, the main sins are attempted rape and abuse of hospitality. In ancient times the rules of hospitality were sacred, hence Lot's appeal to the men not to harm his guests (19:8). Lot shows how much he too has been infected by the atmosphere of the place—offering his daughters as a replacement. Later his daughters were to treat him in a similar way.

In the end the angels assert themselves. Lot and his family are given every opportunity to leave. Once again, Lot comes across as a foolish figure. He has to be cajoled into hurrying, he fails to persuade his potential sons-in-law of the danger, he has to be virtually dragged out of the city. His wife pauses as they flee and is turned

---

Details, Details . . .
Melchizedek (14:17–20)

An intriguing figure. This incident would probably have been one of those "fascinating-but-not-terribly-important" parts of the Bible, had it not been for the use of Melchizedek by the writer of Hebrews as a kind of prefigurement of Christ.

The name Melchizedek can be translated as "the king of righteousness." It is obvious from the passage that the god he worships is the same as the God of Abram. He lives in Jerusalem (here called Salem). Contrast this to the king of Sodom whose name, Bera, means "in evil." The whole incident is about the perennial choice facing Abram and his descendants—a choice between righteousness and evil.

"to salt," perhaps covered by debris. The mechanics, as with so much of Genesis, are less important than the lack of faith. She yearned still for Sodom, and in the end she shared its fate.

Then there occurs one of the strangest events in Genesis. Lot, in a cave in the hills, is raped by his daughters. Specifically they get him drunk and sleep with him. What is the point of this story? Certainly their excuse—that there are no men around—is ridiculous: they had just come from the town of Zoar, which, although small, must have had *some* eligible bachelors. Perhaps it merely illustrates—like Lot's attempt to offer his daughters to the mob—how far the atmosphere of Sodom had polluted their judgment and their morals.

❽ The birth of Isaac
21:1–21

The Lord's promises come to fruition and Sarah bears a son, Isaac. Sarah—perhaps remembering her own scornful laughter—says, "God has made me laugh" (20:6). Joyous laughter has replaced bitter cynicism.

Isaac was a great joy and blessing to Abraham and Sarah, but their faith was about to be tested. Chapter 22 opens with the statement that "God decided to test Abraham" (22:1). He tells the old man to take his son to Moriah and sacrifice him there on an altar. Abraham takes the boy, ties him to the altar and even gets as far as raising the knife before God calls out and stops him.

What is going on here? Isn't this the cruelest test? Why would God be so mean as to put a father and son through that ordeal?

It is an unsettling story. Even as a test of faith it seems harsh and cruel and unnecessary. However, there are some features we need to take into account.

Puzzling Points

Why are there three versions of the same story?

Genesis 20:1–18 seems to be a repeat of Genesis 12:10–20. Then there's Genesis 26:6–16, which is essentially the same story, but involving Isaac.

In the first two cases, Abraham is in a foreign land and pretends that his wife is his sister in order to protect his own life. The logic seems to go something like this:

• the king will want to sleep with my attractive wife.

• If he *knows* she is my wife, he will kill me first.

• So I shall pretend she is my sister.

• Admittedly, he will still sleep with her, but at least we'll be alive.

It is, like so many stories in Genesis, a curious tale—and all the more curious because it occurs in three places, with the cast changed slightly each time. In Genesis 12 the protagonists are Abraham and Sarah and the king of Egypt. In Genesis 20 the protagonists are Abraham, Sarah and Abimelech, King of Gerar. And in Genesis 26 the protagonists are Isaac, Rebekah and, wait for it, Abimelech again.

As for its triple occurrence, there are only two real explanations:

1. That it did occur three times. That Isaac made the same mistake his father made, that Abraham did the same thing twice.

2. It is simply three versions of the same story, with different traditions ascribing it to slightly different people.

There are some differences between the accounts—in Genesis 20, for example, Abraham tries to excuse the sin with a half-truth about how Sarah is actually his sister because she is kind of a half-sister. In 26, Isaac remains in the land and grows rich—so much so that the king begs him to move away. Perhaps it is better to focus on the main point of the story: each time the point of the story is that the husbands do not have faith in God to protect them. Each time they completely misjudge the honor of the foreign leaders, whose generosity and compassion offer an implicit condemnation of Abraham's dishonesty and lack of faith.

• The Bible does indeed call us to put God first, to love God above everything else. Even our closest relations can become to us like selfish possessions. We forget that they do not belong to us. We forget that everything is God's, for him to do with as he pleases.

• The nations around Israel had a history of human sacrifice. God consistently condemned this as abhorrent. This command to Abraham is a graphic demonstration of how God does not want children to be sacrificed.

Details, Details . . .
You want me to put my hand where? (24:2)

When Abraham commissions the servant to find a wife for Isaac, he makes him swear by placing his hand under Abraham's thigh. This was an ancient custom. Since the promise involved the succession of Abraham's family, this oath seemed to involve the servant placing his hand near to Abraham's . . . er . . . equipment. It's symbolic. Not to mention unhygienic.

Questions, Questions

Rewards for trickery

All this seems terribly unfair.
Yes. It is.
Then why did God allow it? Why did he reward Jacob?
There is nothing in the text to indicate that God approved of Jacob's conduct. But throughout the Bible God works with human beings and takes their faults and actions into account.
But he's such a liar.
Um . . . yes. But it's important to view this event in the context of Jacob's life. He is a man who not only tricks, but who is tricked.
Like how?
His Uncle Laban tricks him. Although he was given the birthright by Esau, he doesn't really gain because he has to flee from the family and live in exile. His estrangement from his brother causes him a lot of grief. And, in the end, it's pretty apparent that Esau doesn't really suffer from it.

• The region of Moriah mentioned here (22:2) is later identified with the Temple Mount in Jerusalem (2 Ch 3:1). Perhaps this was an "echo" of a future event. There would come a time when God would see his own son sacrificed in the same place. Perhaps God is simply sharing how he will one day feel, how he will have to see his own son face death and how, unlike Abraham, he will not stay his hand.

Jacob   25:19–37:1

Isaac's wife is found from relatives in Mesopotamia—northern Syria. The task is undertaken with prayers to God—prayers that were answered before the servant had even finished praying (24:15), with the appearance of Rebekah. She agrees to return with the servant and marry Isaac. Perhaps her brother, Laban, thought the whole thing happened far too easily. Later he was to make the marriage agreement with Isaac's son a lot trickier to negotiate . . .

The story of Isaac and Rebekah has distinct parallels with Abraham and Sarah. There is the incident with Abimelech (26:1–11). His wife is barren, like Sarah, and her pregnancy is the result of divine intervention (25:21). He is a wealthy man with large herds. And, like Isaac and Ishmael, there is conflict between his two sons: Esau and Jacob.

❾ Jacob and Esau   25:19–34; 27:1–46

They fought, according to the Bible, even before they were born (25:22). Esau is a hairy redhead, a pun on his names, for Esau means "hairy" and Edom, his other name, means "red." His brother emerges grasping Esau's heel. His name—Jacob—means "he grasps the heel." This is a figurative expression meaning "he tricks." Our equivalent is surely "he pulls your leg."

Their names sum up their characters and the enmity that was to arise between them: Esau the hairy hunter, the red-headed, hot-tempered man of action; Jacob the scheming trickster, the cunning plotter, the man of strategy and schemes.

God works through the second-born. Isaac was not the firstborn son of Abraham, Jacob was not the firstborn son of Isaac. Isaac loved Esau, but God's planning involved Jacob. So Jacob tricks Esau out of his birthright (25:29–34). This might seem unfair, but the Bible is clear that the blame is to be shared. Jacob might be a schemer, but Esau thinks so little of his birthright that he is willing to sell it for a pot of stew.

The next trick, however, is worse. While Esau is out hunting, Rebekah and Jacob trick a blind Isaac into thinking that Jacob is his elder son. Isaac therefore pronounces his blessing on Jacob—and a blessing once given could not be taken back. The whole event is curious. Rebekah and Jacob act disgracefully—Jacob even lies that God has provided him with the meat for his father's meal (27:20) and he betrays his father with a kiss (27:27).

Isaac shakes with shock when he finds out the truth, but then, it was a serious situation in that age and culture. The "blessing" was a powerful statement—a legally binding announcement that Isaac could not withdraw. In it, he gives Jacob the power over Esau, making him "lord" over his brother (27:27–29). When Esau begs for another blessing, he gets little comfort from his father.

Stairway to heaven
28:10–22

So Jacob leaves home and travels to his Uncle Laban at Haran—the same journey made by his grandfather's servant.

Here he has a significant dream: he sees a stairway reaching up to heaven and angels ascending and descending, like travelers on some vast celestial escalator. Once again, the covenant is reiterated by God. It is something of a turning point for Jacob—an encounter with God that turns him away from his life of trickery and toward a trust in the Lord. From now on he vows to trust God and asks the Lord to watch over him and to bring him safely home.

I have hidden depths.

Puzzling Points
Why doesn't Jacob recognize his bride? (29:15–35)

After seven years of waiting, Jacob marries … the wrong woman. Why didn't he notice? Mainly because in ancient wedding ceremonies the bride was entirely covered. It was an offense for a man to see the woman's face (think Afghanistan under the Taliban rule). So Jacob couldn't actually see Leah during the ceremony, and at night, presumably, it was too dark. Jacob does not realize he has actually married Leah, Rachel's elder sister. It is a delicious irony: the second son who tricked his way into first place is tricked into marrying the first-born daughter.

Poor Leah with her weak eyesight is looked on with compassion by God, just as he looked after Hagar all those years ago. She is given children—half of all the sons of Jacob—while Rachel struggles to conceive. Both wives compete with each other by giving their respective servants to Jacob as well (29:31–30:24).

▷75

Questions, Questions
The sheep and the goats
Oh come on.
What now?
This part about Jacob managing a kind of early genetic engineering program. You're not seriously telling me that sticking a load of twigs in front of mating goats and sheep is going to produce speckled offspring? You might as well argue that if two people have sex in a room with red wallpaper their child will be a redhead.
Well, it does seem a little odd. But the real point is that actually it is all God's doing. Jacob later ascribes the technique to a dream he was given by God (31:4–13).
But Jacob believed it made a difference.
Well, the whole thing is also laced with humor. You see, the author of these parts of Genesis was a real pun-lover and all of Jacob's tricks have an element of the joke about them. Esau's name means "red," and he is tricked out of his blessing by a red stew. Laban's name means "white," and he is tricked out of his sheep by white sticks. Jacob isn't just adding to his own wealth by this technique—he's actually making fun of Laban.

Landmark: Birthright

Birthright is a common theme in the Bible. It refers to the inheritance rights of the sons in Hebrew families—especially to the rights of the firstborn, or eldest son. At the father's death, the property was divided among the surviving sons. However, the firstborn always got a larger share—usually a double portion (De 21:17). He also had other responsibilities, such as looking after his mother or any unmarried sisters. Daughters did not inherit from their father unless there were no surviving sons.

Birthright, however, was not automatic. It could be forfeited if the behavior of the son was particularly bad. Reuben lost his birthright because he committed incest with his father's concubine (Ge 35:22; 49:3–4), Esau swapped his birthright for a meat stew (Ge 25:29–34). Nonetheless, removing the birthright was a significant act and there are warnings against giving it away (De 21:17).

In the absence of the father, the firstborn son was also assumed to have authority over his brothers and sisters. In royal families, the firstborn son succeeded to the title, and the family "line" was assumed to pass through the eldest son. Firstborn sons were considered to be holy to the Lord, and were supposed to be consecrated by the priests when only a month old. Jesus was the firstborn child of Mary and Joseph, and his parents took him and consecrated him at the temple (Lk 2:27).

By the time of the New Testament, the obligations and practices had changed. The Greeks and Romans used written wills to pass on their property, and if no will existed the property was divided equally among the sons, or, in the case of Roman law, among the wife and children. It is against this background that Paul uses the theme of birthright to show how all Christians are "heirs" to God. We will all share equally in his glory (Ro 8:16–17).

Details, Details . . .
The household gods (31:22–35)

Once again, Jacob's tricks force him to move on and sensing a growing resentment from Laban and his sons, he answers God's call to return home. It goes all right, but Rachel steals her father's household gods. These were idols, which Rachel probably took thinking they would bring her luck or blessing. Rachel was obviously still partly pagan at heart and, like her Aunt Rebekah, was prone to more than a little deceitfulness. She lies about stealing them, hides them in a box and sits on it, claiming to be unable to move because of her period. Since any women menstruating were considered ritually impure, no man would go near her. Or they may have recognized that she was just in one of those moods . . .

⑩ Jacob's struggle   32:1–32

By Genesis 32, Jacob is in a difficult position. Behind him is the land of Laban, and ahead of him is the land of Esau. Both are his "enemies." It is in this crisis that Jacob meets with God in an incredible and powerful way.

His first encounter is with the angels of God (32:1), presumably the same angels he had seen in his dream at Bethel. His second encounter comes when he is alone. No wives, no children, no possessions: they have all gone ahead of him. It is night, and he is utterly alone.

"A man came," says the Bible, "and fought with Jacob until just before daybreak" (32:34). Jacob wrestles with the figure who, seeing that Jacob will never surrender, simply reaches out and dislocates Jacob's hip. Still Jacob grabs hold of the man and demands a blessing.

It is an immensely profound moment. All his life Jacob had fought—first against Esau and then against Laban. But it was never really them he was fighting: it was God himself. He never truly trusted God until this moment; he never truly believed that his destiny was in God's hand. This fight—and God's victory—showed Jacob that he could not succeed on his own.

God gives him a new name: no longer is he "Jacob" but "Israel." The name Israel means "he struggles with God." Jacob, in return, demands to know the name of his opponent, but God does not give him an answer. This too is a profound moment—for it differentiates God from the cheap, easy, useless symbols that Rachel hid in that box. God, unlike the idols, is not a statue on the mantelpiece, but a powerful, mysterious, creative being. Jacob struggled and survived—but for the rest of his life he would walk with a limp.

This encounter seems to change Jacob. He calls Esau "master" or "my lord." In a curious phrase he describes seeing Esau as "like seeing the face of God" (33:10). It was not that Esau resembled physically the appearance of the wrestler from the previous night; it was that Esau's welcome for Jacob was an answer to his prayers. Whenever our prayers are answered, whoever answers them, it is like seeing the face of God.

Brief Lives: Jacob

Background: Son of Isaac. Brother of Esau. Married Leah and Rachel.

Sons by Leah: Reuben, Simeon, Levi, Judah, Issachar, Zebulun (Daughter: Dinah)

Sons by Bilhah: Dan, Naphtali

Sons by Zilpah: Gad, Asher

Sons by Rachel: Joseph, Benjamin

Occupation: Confidence trickster. Herdsman. Genetic engineer.

Achievements: Jacob relied on his wits, but he was to learn that trust is better than trickery. He was to encounter God in several powerful and moving ways. The central encounter of his life took place in his struggle with the stranger by the river. After this, he was given a new name—Israel—a name that means "he struggles with God." The twelve tribes who were to descend from his children became the nation of Israel. They took from Israel not only his name, but his character —a people who struggle with God and man and overcome.

Character: Cunning, manipulative; then faithful and determined.

Pros: Encountered God. Good with sheep.

Cons: Make sure he signs the contract.

Puzzling Points

Judah and Tamar (38:1–30)

Simeon and Levi were not the only problem children. In chapter 35 we learn that Reuben slept with his father's concubine Bilhah (35:21), and the story of Joseph is interrupted by the strange tale of Judah and his daughter-in-law Tamar. Judah leaves his brothers and goes to live among the Canaanites. His eldest son, Er, marries a woman called Tamar. When Er dies, by custom, his brother Onan takes Tamar as his wife. Onan, however, refuses to do his duty and makes sure she won't get pregnant by never fully consummating the marriage. His refusal to do his duty is seen as a great sin, and his death comes as a consequence. Judah now fears for the life of his third son, Shelah, so refuses to marry him to Tamar.

Tamar then takes her future in her own hands. Disguised as a prostitute, she waylays her father-in-law and sleeps with him. As a pledge of payment she takes his seal—which was the way that Judah would sign and seal legal documents. It was his ID card, his PIN number—his unique identifier. Three months go by and Tamar is discovered to be pregnant. As she is dragged out to be punished, she reveals who the true father of her baby is. Judah realizes that it is he who has been in the wrong.

It is a difficult passage. How could God approve of someone behaving in this way? To understand Tamar's behavior, however, we have to understand marital customs of the time. It was the custom for widows to be married to their husband's nearest living relative—usually the brother. The practice is described in Deuteronomy 25:5–6. The idea is that it would not leave the woman unprotected and would provide her with offspring to continue the line. In ancient times, not having male offspring was seen as a great shame—indeed, it still is in some countries. Which is why Tamar goes to such great lengths to secure her child. It is not just some woman's desperate desire to have a baby; it is to establish her status, her importance, her entire future. It is important to note that Judah "never slept with her again." This is not about lust, but about Tamar asserting her rights as a woman and securing a future for her and her family. And one of the interesting things about Tamar is that she is one of the few women mentioned in the family tree of Christ (Mt 1:3). Her actions were to secure the line of King David and, ultimately, Jesus.

The rape of Dinah   34:1–31

Dinah, Jacob's daughter by Leah, is courted and then raped by the prince of Shechem. However, the lad truly loves Dinah and decides to marry her. Jacob's sons declare that, in return, all the men of Shechem must be circumcised. When the citizens are lying in their beds incapacitated, Simeon and Levi systematically butcher every man in the town. It seems remarkable that two men could take on a whole town, but a recently circumcised male is in a great deal of pain: their opponents could hardly move, let alone wield a sword. It is a brutal reprisal and Jacob reacts with disgust. They are forced to move on. Because of this crime, Simeon and Levi would face their father's curse in the future (49:7).

Joseph   37:2–50:26

Rachel was always Jacob's favorite wife, and the sons she gave him—Joseph and Benjamin—were his favorite sons. The other sons actively hated their brother Joseph (37:4). Such favoritism was to have dire consequences, for when Joseph started to have rather self-aggrandizing dreams, the other children reacted angrily. Joseph's crime was not the dreams—which were prophecies after all—but his complete lack of tact. His brothers faked his death and the lad was taken into slavery in Egypt.

⑪ Joseph in Egypt
       39:1–47:12

It is a biblical principle that in order to become somebody, you have to be a nobody first. Jacob, Joseph, Moses, Elijah—all of them had to lose their identities in order to find them. Sometimes this meant going into the wilderness, sometimes it meant fleeing from the family home. Joseph becomes a slave and then a prisoner, but through it he finds a deep and powerful relationship with God.

Ironically, the very ability that got him into trouble—the ability to interpret dreams—proves his salvation. He interprets the dream of Pharaoh and becomes the prime minister of Egypt. His interpretation includes not only the meaning, but also a suggestion of action. It also leads to the salvation of his family—who can call on the brother they thought lost when they need to escape the famine.

The twelve tribes
48:1–22

On Jacob's deathbed, he blesses Joseph. Because of his sinful act at Shechem, Reuben, Jacob's firstborn, loses his birthright to Joseph (49:3–4). What is more, Jacob blesses Joseph's second son, Ephraim, above his first, Manasseh. Why he does this is not made clear, but it is not really surprising. Jacob was the younger son, who fell in love with the younger sister. It is hardly surprising that he always preferred the younger of the two.

Chapter 49—often called the blessing of Jacob—is the longest poem in Genesis and contains blessings, not just for his sons, but for the tribes that were to proceed from them. Simeon and Levi are punished. Simeon will see his descendants scattered (Jos 19:1, 9). His place in the twelve tribes will be taken by the two "half-tribes" of Ephraim and Manasseh. Levi's tribe was, eventually, not to be given any land for their own, becoming the priestly tribe. The poem describes the characteristics of the people who would descend from the brothers and the kinds of territories they would inhabit. So Zebulun will be the closest to the sea and Asher will dwell in rich and fertile farmland. Benjamin is likened to a savage wolf—a reference to the savagery of the tribe in later years (Jg 19–21).

Joseph's story, more than any other in Genesis, echoes the story of Israel the nation. He was to be taken into exile; he was to struggle with God and with man; he was, finally, to be used as a source of blessing for many other nations and peoples. Joseph's story moves us from the stories of individuals—the patriarchs—to the story of the nation, for after Joseph, the tribes of Israel move to Egypt and become a slave nation.

> **Details, Details . . .**
> **The coat of many colors (37:3)**
>
> Actually a robe, richly and lavishly embroidered and ornamented. Nobody gets excited about a coat with a lot of colors on it, but a robe with gold and silver and all the trimmings . . .

Jacob's sons

Twelve Tribes

The twelve tribes of Israel were descended from the twelve sons of Jacob. Well, not all of the sons. Simeon was dispossessed and his inheritance given to Joseph, and then further split between the two "half-tribes" of Manasseh and Ephraim.

Reuben Levi Issachar

Simeon Judah Gad Zebulun

Asher

Jacob

Naphtali

Benjamin

Dan

Joseph

Manasseh

Ephraim

Mothers of Jacob's sons
- Leah
- Zilpah
- Bilhah
- Rachel

Landmark: Weights, Measures and Currency

Weight

Old Testament

The standard unit of weight was the shekel, which weighed 11.4g. Fifty shekels made one mina and 60 minas made one talent. So, a talent was 3,000 shekels.

New Testament

By the time of Jesus, Roman measures had taken over and the standard measure was the Roman "pound," which weighed 325g or 11.5 oz.

Currency

Old Testament

The standard unit of currency was the shekel . . . Hang on, I'm getting a strange sense of déjà vu. Yes, it is the same as the unit of weight. And here's how it happened.

In the early days nobody used coins. Most business was carried out by bartering goods such as livestock, timber, wine or honey. This was eventually replaced by metal, mainly in the form of silver, which was the most common metal, and people measured out the price of goods in certain weights of silver.

So, for example, Solomon purchased chariots at 600 shekels of silver— that is, 6.84kg of silver. Thus, the shekel also became the unit of currency. People would value their property and products in so much weight of precious metal. And just as in the weights, the talent and the mina were used to indicate bigger value items. For example, Jeremiah's field cost him 17 shekels of silver (Je 32:9), but Omri bought the hill and city of Samaria for two *talents* of silver—around 68kg.

As time went by, people started to make their shekels more portable. The metal was often carried around in convenient weights. Abraham gave Rebekah bracelets weighing 10 shekels (Ge 24:22) and gold was often carried around in thin bars weighing, for example, 50 shekels.

New Testament

Coins came in around the seventh and eighth centuries BC, but they spread slowly to Israel and Judah—perhaps because the coins had images on them. By New Testament times, however, there were three major currencies available: Jewish, Greek and Roman. These were basically still units of measurement. All that had happened was that the thin bars and the bracelets had turned into coins.

The shekel was now an 11.4g coin. And, once again, 50 shekels made a mina and 60 minas made a talent. The Greek currency, meanwhile, was the drachma, and the Roman currency, the denarius.

The exchange rate was:

Jewish		Greek		Roman
1 shekel	=	1 tetradrachma (also known as 10 stater)	=	4 denarii

 =  =

The denarius was roughly one day's pay for a working man. The Jews also had smaller currency, notably the *lepton*—a bronze coin that represented the smallest coin imaginable. It is this coin that Jesus talks about when he sees the poor widow giving it in Luke 21:2.

Linear measures

The standard unit of length in the Bible was the cubit—roughly the length of an arm, from elbow to fingertips. (Of course, if you have exceptionally long or short arms, then you're in trouble.) Accordingly, the value of the cubit varied between 44 and 53 cm.

The Old Testament cubit was around 450mm, the New Testament cubit around 550mm. In the New Testament, the Roman system of measurements is more apparent; ships measured depths in fathoms (1.8m), and longer distances included the stadion (furlong) at 185m and the milion (mile) at 1,478m.

Span

1 Cubit

Exodus

This way out . . .

Exodus means, literally, "exit." Which more or less sums up the theme of the book—as it deals with the departure of the Israelites from slavery in Egypt.

Who: Tradition ascribes the book to Moses—and there are indications that he might have had a hand in some sections (17:14; 24:4; 34:27). Joshua mentions "the Book of the Law of Moses" (Jos 8:31) and the New Testament claims that Moses was responsible for certain passages. However, later hands were almost certainly involved in shaping and editing the original materials.

When: If we take Moses as the prime mover, it would mean that the book dates from the fifteenth century BC. However, later hands may well have played a role.

As to when the action took place, there is considerable debate. According to 1 Kings 6:1, the event took place 480 years before the fourth year of Solomon's reign—which would make it 1446 BC. This would make the pharaohs Thutmose III and his son Amunhotep II. However, you will not be surprised to find that there are difficulties. The mention of the city of Rameses in 1:11 has led some to argue for a later date, to fit in with the Pharaoh Rameses II who ruled around 1290 BC. It may well be that this name is the result of a later editor.

What: The book deals with the escape of the Israelites from slavery in Egypt. It also includes a great deal of religious rite and ceremony and legal issues. In addition it contains some of the deepest and most mysterious insights into the nature of God, and the relationship between God and his people.

Quick Guide

Author
Various, including Moses

Type
Books of the Law

Purpose
To show how God rescued his people from slavery in Egypt.

Key verses

3:14–15 "I am the eternal God. So tell them that the LORD, whose name is 'I Am,' has sent you. This is my name forever, and it is the name that people must use from now on."

20:2–3 "I am the LORD your God, the one who brought you out of Egypt where you were slaves. Do not worship any god except me."

If you remember one thing about this book . . .

God keeps his promises.

Your 15 minutes start now

Read chapters 1–3, 11–12, 19–20

The Route Through Exodus

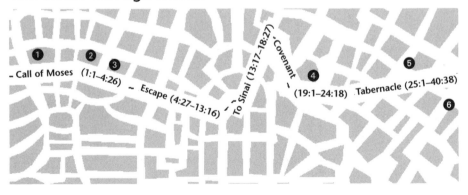

Call of Moses (1:1–4:26) — Escape (4:27–13:16) — To Sinai (13:17–18:27) — Covenant (19:1–24:18) — Tabernacle (25:1–40:38)

POSTCARD

The ancient land of Egypt stretches down in a narrow strip alongside the River Nile. Indeed, we rely on the river for our prosperity, trusting in the annual flooding to make the land fertile and the crops grow. It is the abundance of our crops that has made us such a popular destination for starving people from other countries.

We are famous for our building projects, including the cities of Rameses and Pithom, and the visitor will note the happy, cheerful singing of slaves as they merrily erect another enormous pointy building. Chief architect of all this is, of course, our Pharaoh Rameses II, latest in a long line of slightly psychotic gods-in-human-form.

Visitors can enjoy the splendor of our temples while taking an early morning dip in the wonderful, pure, frog-, gnat- and blood-free Nile.

Welcome to Egypt!

Lower Egypt
Rameses
Memphis
R. Nile
Upper Egypt
Thebes
Aswan

The call of Moses 1:1–4:26

Exodus opens with the Israelites in slavery. In the centuries after the death of Joseph the Israelites who settled in Egypt have multiplied so much that the ruling Pharaoh views them as a kind of plague. In the end the Pharaoh announces that a cull will take place: he decrees that every male child born to the Israelites will be drowned. In these desperate straits, a mother tries to hide her baby boy. When he becomes too big, she makes a miniature version of the boats that plied their trade along the Nile—boats that were made out of reeds and waterproofed with tar—and lets him float away.

❶ The burning bush 3:–4:17

Chapter 3 contains one of the most vivid and important scenes of the entire Bible. Moses has fled to Horeb after murdering a guard and is tending sheep in the desert. It is not certain where Horeb was, but it could be another name for Mount Sinai. (Since we don't know where Mount Sinai was either, we're not much wiser.)

God—here described as "the angel of the Lord"—appears to Moses in the guise of a burning bush. God identifies himself and assures Moses that he has heard the cry of his people (3:7–10). More, he tells Moses that he is to be the one who will lead the Israelites out of Egypt. After being assured that the Lord will be with him, Moses asks God his name. And God answers that his name is "I Am" (3:14).

The name is important. God is in the present tense. He has no beginning and no end; he simply is. He is such an all-encompassing God that his name cannot fully describe all that he represents. (Jesus was later to apply the phrase to himself—unmistakably identifying himself with God.)

Landmark: Names of God

Many names and images are used to describe God. Some of the main ones are:

Yahweh

Always written in Scriptures as YHWH, and never uttered by the Jews out of reverence for God. Some modern Jewish writers maintain this tradition and write G-d instead of God. Jews would substitute the phrase Adonai ("my great Lord") when reading out aloud. The term Jehovah, is a confused mix of these two words and arises out of combining the vowels from Adonai with YHWH. It does not occur before the twelfth century AD.

There is a lot of dispute about what the name means, and some experts believe that it doesn't, in fact, mean anything. Others believe that it means "he causes to be what exists" and refers to God as Creator. Instead of printing Yahweh or YHWH, most modern Bibles use "the LORD" (with small caps).

Elohim

Usually rendered "God." Although the word is actually plural (i.e., "Gods"), it is commonly used of God as the one, supreme deity.

El

The singular form of "Elohim." It is sometimes used of God himself, but can also be used of any god, true or false. It is usually used as a predicate—that is, something that comes before another term, for example "El Elyon," which means "God Most High" (Ge 14:18), or in Genesis 31:13, where God says, "I am the God (El) of Bethel." The most well-known derivation is El Shaddai, which is translated "God Almighty." Shaddai probably means "mountain," giving the sense of permanence and majesty. Used in lots of places, including Genesis 17:1; 28:3; 49:25; and throughout Job.

Here's an example of all three being used together: ". . . for I, the Lord [YHWH], your God [Elohim], am a jealous God [El]" (De 5:9 NIV).

Some other terms for God

Lord God of Israel

In Hebrew, *Yahweh elohe Yisrael*. Frequently used by the prophets (e.g., Is 18:6; Ze 2:9).

Lord of Hosts

In Hebrew, *Yahweh sebaot*. A divine title used in the histories and prophets. The "hosts" are the heavenly powers, under the command of God (e.g., 1 Sa 1:3; Ps 24:10).

Holy One of Israel

Lots in Isaiah, and also in Jeremiah and Psalms (e.g., Is 1:24 and 1 Sa 15:29).

Images used to describe God

The Bible abounds with a host of images that are used to describe what God is like. Examples include a rock (Ex 7:1–7), a shepherd (Ps 23:1), a stronghold (Ps 18:2), a refuge (Ps 37:39) and a redeemer (Is 41:14). Jesus uses perhaps the most potent image, which is that of a father.

▷263

Brief Lives: Moses

Background: Adopted son of an Egyptian princess.

Occupation: Prince. Murderer. Shepherd. Leader. Lawgiver.

Achievements: Despite personal limitations and a difficult upbringing, Moses led his recalcitrant and frequently disobedient people with courage and vision.

He had a unique relationship with God—only Moses was allowed to see the true appearance of the Lord (although only the back view). He was honest before God and willing to sacrifice his own desires for his people.

Moses was 40 when he fled Egypt, and he stayed in Midian for another 40 years. His life could be said to be in three parts: Egyptian prince (1–40), Midian shepherd (41–80), Israelite leader (81–120).

Character: Faithful, obedient, sometimes frustrated and angry or fearful.

Pros: Led his people to the Promised Land.

Cons: Like his people, failed to enter the Promised Land.

A Little Local Difficulty
Zipporah's son   4:24–26

Chapter 4 includes one of the most unfathomable parts of the Bible—which is saying something. On the way back to Egypt, we are told that the Lord was about to kill Moses. His wife Zipporah "touches his legs"—probably a euphemism for his genitals—with a flint knife in a kind of circumcision and Moses is saved. It's a very strange passage. Some interpret this as God being about to punish Moses for not being circumcised. Some see the story as a throwback to some incredibly bloodthirsty primal legend. The truth is, no one really knows what it means. We're not sure even if it's referring to Moses or his son. Nor do we know what Zipporah means when she refers to Moses as a "bridegroom of blood." It does link in with one of the central images of Exodus—people being saved through blood. But it is, at heart, a mystery. Sorry I can't be more helpful.

Puzzling Points

Does God harden Pharaoh's heart?

Nine times in Exodus we are told that God hardened the heart of Pharaoh—as if it were God who was causing Pharaoh to remain stubborn against the Israelites. So does this mean that God is manipulating Pharaoh? That Pharaoh really wants to let the children of Israel go, but God willfully and maliciously changes his mind in order to make the Egyptians suffer?

Some argue that this doesn't mean that God is directly involved as such, that it is merely a kind of shorthand for saying that "it happened," or "it will happen." God, after all, knows the future, and nothing happens unless he permits it, so in that sense he doesn't need to be directly involved. He knows precisely how Pharaoh is going to act. Pharaoh has the freedom to let the Israelites go or make them stay. His heart is hardened because God allows it to be hardened.

Even if you take it absolutely literally, you must first remember that all this started with Pharaoh. If we are told nine times that God hardened Pharaoh's heart, we are also told nine times that Pharaoh hardened his own heart. For the first five plagues it was Pharaoh alone who hardened his heart. It was his decision. God merely confirmed what he had already decided. So there is an element that suggests God is merely saying that he knew what was going to happen—that he knew what Pharaoh's answer was going to be.

We also have to remember that all pharaohs considered themselves to be gods. They wielded enormous power, power they used to oppress people and make them suffer. There is also a sense here in which God is saying: he thinks he's pulling the strings, but I will show him who is in charge. The plagues are not mere punishments, but defeats for Egypt's gods. Many of their gods had the heads of cattle—and they were killed. The darkness is an insult to the sun god, Ra. Pharaoh usually wore a headdress in the shape of a cobra—but his snakes were eaten by the one made by Moses. This is God demonstrating that he is the one, true, powerful God.

It is quite clear that at every point, Pharaoh had a genuine chance to let the Israelites go. But at every point he decided against it. He challenged God. He lost.

Details, Details . . .
Bricks without straw (5:6)

Straw was used to bind the clay together so that the bricks kept their shape while drying. Without it, producing usable bricks was virtually impossible.

The escape from Egypt
4:27–13:16

Moses returns to Egypt and the people accept him when he shows them the signs of God's power (4:29–31). Things have grown tougher than ever. Pharaoh, however, responds by making the Israelites work harder and harder, making bricks, while vital supplies are denied them. The Israelites, in a way that was to happen throughout the exodus, blamed Moses for making things worse.

Moses and Aaron go to Pharaoh and demonstrate God's power to him. Just as in the desert during his first encounter with God, Moses' staff turns into a snake. What is interesting here is that Pharaoh's magicians can do the same thing. Only all their snakes get eaten by Moses' snake. When Pharaoh takes no notice of this, God responds by visiting a series of plagues on Egypt —the famous ten plagues. Each time, Moses and Aaron challenge Pharaoh to let the Israelites go, and each time he refuses. Only after the last and most terrible plague does Pharaoh finally come to his senses.

❷ The ten plagues
7:14–11:10

Some interpret these plagues as a series of natural disasters, intensified by God and occurring with a supernatural frequency. In this interpretation Moses scattering the soot (9:8) and turning the dust into gnats (8:16) are symbolic, indicative of the huge extent of the disasters. Equally it might be that the dust really did turn into swarms of gnats—just as the staff turned into a snake. Either way, the point is that these occurrences were brought on by God as a demonstration of power and a punishment on the Egyptians.

They occur, roughly, in three groups of three and one final, terrible disaster. Each group is introduced when Moses confronts Pharaoh early in the morning (7:14; 8:20; 9:13). They can also be traced within a calendar year—beginning with the floods in late summer and early autumn and the resulting plagues of infestation and diseases.

❸ Passover
11:1–13:16

Pharaoh tries a succession of negotiations, but always falls short of freeing the Israelites. In the end, he dismisses Moses with a final rebuke. "If you ever come back," he says, "you're dead" (10:29). Given all Egypt has been through, it is something of a weak threat. But it has a terrible consequence, for if the first nine plagues were extensions of natural disasters, the tenth plague is supernaturally terrifying.

God tells Moses that he will pass through the country, killing the firstborn of Egyptian men and animals. God will be accompanied by another being, called simply "the destroyer" (12:23 NIV)—apparently an angel or a group of angels.

The instructions are detailed and precise: every Israelite household is to take a lamb, slaughter it and then paint their doorposts with blood and eat the meat together. Houses thus marked will be "passed over" by the devastation.

May indicate a huge flooding, with red sediment being washed down from Ethiopia (see also 2 Ki 3:22).	**River of blood** (7:14–24)
With the fish dead there was nothing to eat the frogs, so they began to swarm.	**Frogs** (7:25–8:15)
The flooded fields of Egypt then proved a potent breeding ground for gnats.	**Gnats** (8:16–19)
As the waters receded, flies infested the land.	**Flies** (8:20–32)
The flies carried anthrax that killed Egyptian livestock.	**Dead animals** (9:1–7)
The anthrax poisoned the skins of the humans.	**Sores** (9:1–7)
The winter brought a massive hailstorm that destroyed the crops.	**Hailstorm** (9:13–35)
In March/April the east winds brought in the locusts to destroy what little food the Egyptians had left.	**Locusts** (10:1–20)
The darkness could well have been a remarkably severe sandstorm—the *khamsin*—which blows in each year in the early spring.	**Darkness** (10:21–29)
The end of the line.	**Passover** (11:1–12:30)

Summer Autumn

Winter

Spring

A Little Local Difficulty
What's with the yeast?
12:14

God instructs the Israelites to remove all yeast from their houses. Quite why is a mystery. The bread they eat in celebration of the event is meant to symbolize the haste with which they had to leave—they were so rushed that they did not have time for the bread to rise. But yeast here seems to be a symbol for sin—perhaps because the yeast meant fermentation, and fermentation meant corruption, and that meant uncleanliness. Or perhaps they were just allergic.

The Israelites obey God's instructions, and that night the firstborn of the Egyptians die. It is a shattering blow for Pharaoh; he summons Moses and tells him and his people to get out quick. (Chapter 12 includes detailed instructions on how they were to celebrate this event in the future—possibly these were given later, but inserted here by an editor.)

There are two key things to remember about the Passover. First, the Egyptians were not innocent; they had previously done exactly the same thing to the sons of the Israelites. Second, God said he would "punish the gods of Egypt" (12:12). Pharaoh believed that he was a god; the Lord would show him what a *real* God can do.

This event was a defining moment for the Israelites. It was to be celebrated every year for thousands of years—and is still celebrated today in the Feast of Passover and the Festival of Unleavened Bread. Chapters 12 and 13, along with the account of the escape, include detailed regulations for the celebration of the Passover. And just as God had taken away the Egyptian firstborn, he gave instructions for the consecration of the Israelite firstborn—for the way that the Israelites are supposed to give their firstborn sheep, goats, whatever, to the Lord in sacrifice. They are, basically, supposed to remember this event forever: it was the moment when God punished a proud nation and brought his people out of slavery.

The route of the exodus

The Way of the Sea (13:17–18)

The precise route is uncertain, but we know the Israelites avoided the main trading routes, which ran through Philistine country, along the north coast, and took the "Way of the Sea," which led to the mining district around Mount Sinai.

The Wilderness

Many of the places named in the account have disappeared. However, we do know that, after reaching Hebron, they rebelled against God and then spent forty years wandering in the eastern wilderness of the Sinai, before eventually moving up to the east of the Dead Sea, and crossing the Jordan to Jericho.

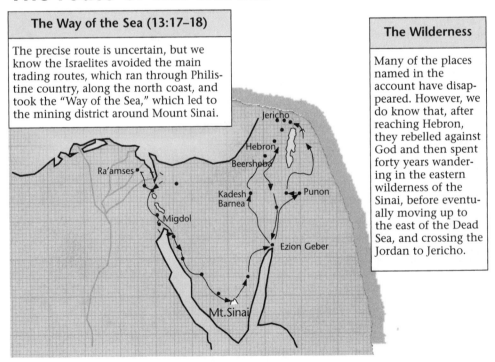

To Sinai 13:17–18:27

The Israelites are led by God himself, in the form of a pillar of cloud during the day and a pillar of fire at night. The Israelites have been miraculously delivered. They have been freed from slavery, rescued from death, brought out of Egypt. And three days later they start to moan.

This is the start of a pattern. During their wanderings whenever the people face a difficulty they moan about Moses and Aaron. Here they moan first about the lack of water—so Moses provides water (15:22–27, 17:1–7). They moan about the lack of food—and Moses provides them with food (16:1–34). God provides for his people and protects them in a war with the Amalekites (17:8–15). This passage introduces a warrior who was to become a major figure in the future: Joshua was to be Moses' assistant and then leader of the Israelites in his own right. He was to be the only one out of all his generation to enter the Promised Land.

Things you don't find in the Bible: The crossing of the Red Sea

Despite what Charlton Heston wants you to think, Moses never parted the Red Sea and the Israelites never crossed it. This sea is actually *Yam Suph* in Hebrew, i.e., "sea of reeds." Since reeds don't grow in salt water, it must have been a shallower inland lake. Nevertheless, the troops are closing in, Moses raises his hand, the sea parts and the people pass through on dry land. The Egyptians try to follow and they are drowned. Not one survives.

Covenant 19:1–24:18

Three months after their escape from Egypt, the people come to the foot of Mount Sinai. And here, following on from the appointment of the judges, God provides for them in perhaps the most lasting way. Here he gives Moses the complete instructions for the nation. The blueprint of how they should live, how they should worship, what are the fundamental ethical and moral codes for them to follow. Here, at Mount Sinai, God is to turn these ragtag nomads into a nation.

It begins with a recognition of God's power. The people prepare by ritually cleansing themselves (19:10–15). On the third day a massive storm descends onto the mountain—a storm that contains God. The holiness of God is something here that is actually dangerous. God orders that the people are to be kept back for their own good. We see examples of this later in the Bible, where people who come into contact with the ark of the covenant are consumed. God is, at times, dangerous. Only Moses is allowed at this time to enter the cloud.

❹ The Ten Commandments 20:1–17

Sometimes called the *Decalogue*—but only if you're trying to show off—the Commandments form the basis for all the Law. They begin with a bit of context—"I am the Lord your God, the one who brought you out of Egypt where you were slaves" (20:2). In other words, this is not a case of God saying, "Obey these commandments and you will get a reward." The history of Israel does show that obedience is linked with blessing—and it is linked here (20:5–6). But God has already given his people the reward. He has shown his love and power and concern—it is now up to them to respond.

Details, Details . . . Forty days and nights

It rains on Noah for forty days and nights (Ge 7:4). Moses spends forty days and nights on Mount Sinai with God (Ex 34:28). Elijah travels for forty days and nights through the desert to encounter God at Mount Horeb. Finally Jesus goes into the desert for forty days and forty nights (Lk 4:2). Forty seems to have been a significant figure for the Israelites, signifying "a long time."

Forty years was also held to represent a generation—hence the forty years that the Israelites spent in the desert.

In some ways the number serves as a kind of theme, a "sign" of true service and dedication to God. The fact that Moses, Noah, Elijah and Jesus all spent forty days in seclusion serves to link them all together as true servants of the Lord.

The Ten Commandments

1. Only worship God (20:3)

No god, either real or imagined, is to take the place of the one true God. Not Zeus or Baal or Dagon from the ancient world, not money, success or sex from our modern world. Nothing should replace God in our worship.

2. Don't make or worship idols (20:4)

An idol is not merely an image—it is something that is worshiped in and of itself. The ancient world did not just make statues of their gods, they worshiped the statues. Some people use this verse to argue that any representation of God is therefore wrong, but the key issue here is not representation but worship. Images can point us to God, can tell us things about God, can help us understand God better. But they have no power in themselves. The representation is not the reality.

3. Don't misuse God's name (20:7)

God's name is holy and we should use it carefully. Nowadays we tend to take this as meaning we should not use it as any kind of swearword—to do so cheapens the name. But it also means we should not swear falsely on it in court or use it like some kind of cheap magic formula. God demands to be taken seriously.

4. Keep the Sabbath holy (20:8)

The Sabbath was given for two reasons: rest and reflection. It is not right that people should work all the hours there are. In today's 24/7 culture, overworking is seen as a badge of honor. It's not. It's against God's rules. But the Sabbath is not just about rest, but also about worship. It's about spending time with God, making sure that there is time in the week for him, keeping your priorities set on God and not on work and the world around you.

5. Respect your parents (20:12)

The word translated "respect" actually means "honor," "prize highly," "care about." We may not like it, but we owe our parents. So does this mean that we should "honor" those who abuse their children? Should the children of all the evil men in the Bible "honor" their fathers? Quite obviously not: this code is about preserving a stable social structure and family life.

6. Do not murder (20:13)

Pretty obvious really. The word here usually refers to a deliberate and premeditated act.

7. Do not commit adultery (20:14)

Again, a commandment that is centered on preserving the sanctity of the social structure. Adultery is a sin against God as well as the marriage partner.

8. Do not steal (20:15)

Again. Pretty obvious.

9. Do not lie about others (20:16)

The text actually has "Don't lie about your neighbor," but since Christ pointed out that everyone is our neighbor, it doesn't make much difference.

10. Do not covet what others have (20:17)

To covet means to desire in a bad way. It's not necessarily bad to look at what people own and wish to have it: there are plenty of homeless people in the world who would love a house. It is more the evil desire of possession, the lust to own. Often covetousness leads to breaking the other commandments—the desire to possess can lead a person to lie or steal or murder. But even if it doesn't, God makes clear that the inward desire is as bad as the outward act—a fact Jesus reinforces (Mt 5:21–30).

Landmark: The Law

Why the Law? Why all these regulations? What on earth is the point?

The Hebrew word *Torah* actually means "instruction"; the Law is intended more as a framework for living than a restrictive set of practices.

Justice

At the basic level it was intended to protect the poor and the innocent, to preserve health and to ensure that society operated justly. There is much in the Law that is about the rights of the poor, the oppressed and the refugee. The Ten Commandments are, at a very basic level, a way for society to operate with fairness and safety.

It is wrong, therefore, to see the Law as entirely harsh. It contained many commands based on compassion and mercy. It ordered fair treatment for all, regardless of wealth or status. The Israelites were told not to oppress foreigners living among them, they were told to make provision for the poor. One of the most astonishing of its decrees was the Jubilee provision, which declared a Sabbath for the land and, once every fifty years, a complete reversion of society to what was fair and right.

Hygiene

The laws on cleanliness have, at their root, a hygiene function and include things like dealing with skin diseases and avoiding eating foods such as pork and seafood.

Culture and society

There is also a cultural level, which reflects the prevailing culture of the time. Thus rules on marriage and, for example, menstruating women, reflect the views of the culture. No one now can seriously argue that a woman with a period is "unclean," but the culture of the time did not understand what was happening. The Bible has to be understood in the context of its times. We might wish that God had put these people right, had explained everything and ushered in a new era of political correctness, but God always works through the culture of the people he is dealing with. So, a large chunk of the Law reflects the culture and expectations of the period.

Religious observance

The laws about religious observance and worship deal with sacrifices and worship, with the activities of temple and tabernacle. These seem, to a modern mind, to be ridiculously legalistic, but in their time they served an important purpose: they kept Israel holy. Israel was not supposed to act in the same way as the nations around it. At least part of the laws about the priestly functions were about keeping Israel focused on God.

Identity

Part of the role of the Law was to establish a kingdom (23:20–33). The Law was what made Israel special, what made the people unique. It was through obeying God's commands that Israel found unity and purpose. The Law was what distinguished Israel from the "lawless" nations surrounding them.

The tabernacle 25:1–40:38

In his time spent on the mountain, Moses is given detailed instructions from God on the construction of a special place of worship.

There are also detailed instructions as to the kind of garments to be worn by the priest (28:1–43). The priests were to be Aaron and his family, and they were appointed in a special ceremony (29:1–44; 30:22–33; Le 8:1–36).

Courtyard (27:9–21)	Altar (27:1–8)	Basin (30:17–21)	Tabernacle (26:1–37)
The tabernacle, altar and basin were enclosed in a large, fenced area.	Made of hard, dark acacia wood, the altar was a square structure housing a bronze grid on which the sacred offerings were burned. It is curious that something built for burning things was built of wood (wooden barbecues are not recommended), but probably it was filled with earth when it was used.	Made of bronze, this huge basin was filled with water so that the priests could wash their hands and feet before entering the tabernacle.	Literally "dwelling place"—a kind of portable temple. A large tent made from an inner tent of embroidered linen (26:1–6), covered with layers of goat hair (26:7–13), rams' leather and the hides of "sea cows" (26:14 NIV). (Presumably these were seals.) A large curtain divided the tabernacle into two rooms: "the holy place" and "the most holy place" (26:31–35). Only the high priest could enter the most holy place.

50 cubits

100 cubits

The holy place contained . . .			The most holy place contained . . .
Table (25:23–30)	**Lampstand (25:31–40)**	**Incense altar (30:1–10)**	**Ark of the covenant (25:10–22)**
On this was put the sacred bread—twelve loaves, one loaf from each tribe—which represented a perpetual offering to the Lord.	The light represented the glory of the Lord.	The incense— which was burned by the high priest— represented the prayers of the people ascending to God.	The only thing in the most holy place was a special box that contained the stone tablets given to Moses by God, on which were carved the Ten Commandments. Although we call this the ark, the word used is not the same as that used of Noah's boat. It actually means "chest." The chest was specially decorated and carried on long poles.

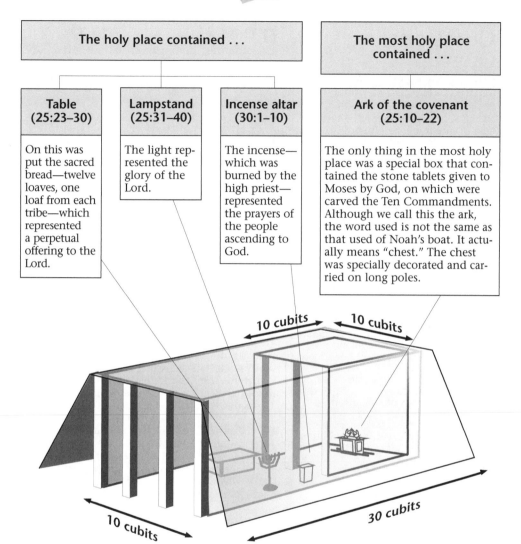

10 cubits
10 cubits
10 cubits
30 cubits

Puzzling Points

Why did God need all this?

All this ritual, all this detail, all these special clothes and implements. Surely God didn't need all this for the people to worship him? He didn't. But the people did. Later prophets make it clear that God isn't interested in rite and ritual if they are not accompanied by the right attitude. And God, who is everywhere, doesn't need a house or a tent to live in. In this culture and at this time, however, it was necessary to remind the people that God was present among them. They required a presence and a place. We're not so different today. We know that God doesn't need a church to live in, but all religions need focal points.

The Israelites didn't just believe that God was in the Holy of Holies, they believed that he spoke to them from between the two angels on the cover of the ark—the so-called atonement cover. It was not because God needed it, but because the Israelites needed it. Without something visible, they were apt to get off track. Which is exactly what happened.

▷63, 137, 366

Questions, Questions

Blind and toothless (21:23)

What about this verse?

What about it?

"If she is seriously injured," it says, "the payment will be life for life, eye for eye, tooth for tooth, hand for hand, foot for foot," etc., etc.

Ah. You noticed. Well it's talking about a specific instance—when a man hits a pregnant woman.

But it occurs elsewhere. Deuteronomy 19:21, where it's talking about a punishment for people who give false witness.

Yes, but . . .

And Leviticus 24:17 where it's perfectly clear. "Death is also the penalty for murder."

Yes, but . . .

Eye for eye. Tooth for tooth. Pancreas for pancreas.

Eh?

All right, not the last one. But how do we square this with what Jesus said in Matthew 5:38–42? He explicitly says we are not to do that. And here, God says we are to do it.

Well, some people don't think that they are contradictory. They argue that this law—the "law of retaliation"—was intended to make the punishment fit the crime. Indeed, it acted as a corrective against excessive retribution.

But it's still based on retribution rather than mercy.

Well, it's very black and white, certainly. Then again, these were tough times. There had to be clear ways of working in any given situation, ways that could easily and fairly be applied.

BUT IT WAS WRONG!

There's no need to shout.

Sorry.

Look, you have to understand that the Law was given at a specific time for a specific purpose. From a Christian point of view, the Law was only ever intended as a stepping-stone. The whole point of the New Testament is that the Law, by itself, was not enough. Nobody was good enough to live up to it. When Jesus came he fulfilled the Law because he looked to the spirit.

So Jesus did change it?

He went *beyond* it. He said that to think about the act was as bad as doing it. He emphasized the spirit of the Law rather than the letter of the Law. He changed the rules. But then he was allowed to: he was God.

❺ The Law   20:22–24:18

After the Ten Commandments are given, God gives Moses detailed commands dealing with worship (20:22–26), social justice (21:1–36, 23:1–9), property (22:1–15) and a host of other questions (22:16–31).

The golden calf 32:1–35; De 9:6–29

The Israelites' ability to forget is remarkable. With regard to God and his commands, they had the attention span of goldfish. At the very time that Moses was up the mountain speaking with God, the Israelites were preparing to make an idol to worship. They think that their leader has disappeared and decide that it is time for a new god.

This is astonishing. Only a few short weeks before, they had been amazingly rescued. Forty days before, they had agreed to abide by the Ten Commandments—one of which specifically forbade making idols. Now they were willing to turn their backs on all that. Even more amazingly, Aaron agrees to their demands.

Their idol was made of gold—or of wood plated with gold—and shaped like a calf, possibly drawing on their knowledge of the Egyptian bull-god *Apis*. They celebrate in a drunken orgy—a noise that sounds to the descending Joshua and Moses like the sound of battle.

God is, understandably, furious. He determines to wipe them out and start again. He says to Moses, in words that take us right back to Abraham, "I will make your descendants into a great nation" (32:10). Moses begs the Lord to hold back, and God changes his mind.

Moses hurries down the mountain to confront the people. He smashes the stone tablets—symbolizing the way in which the people have broken the agreement. He crushes the calf, scatters the powder on water, and forces the people to drink it. He calls those who are faithful to him, and part of the tribe of Levi respond (not all of them—Deuteronomy indicates that there were Levite offenders as well). They go through the camp killing the worst offenders—an act that leads Moses to set them apart to serve as priests for Israel (Nu 25:7–13). Moses offers to take the sin of the people upon himself, but this time his arguments do not convince God: each individual must bear the responsibility for their own sin, and as punishment, a plague sweeps through the camp (32:31–35).

❻ The back of God   33:1–23; De 10:1–5

The peoples' sin leads to a temporary separation; God withdraws from these stubborn people. Moses goes to the Tent of Meeting—a tent outside the camp where he would meet with God—and he asks the Lord how he is to lead the people without God. In response, God allows Moses an unparalleled privilege: he will be allowed to see God, to "hear my holy name," to glimpse the very nature of God. When God appears earlier in the Old Testament it is usually in a human form, like the man with whom Jacob wrestled. Now Moses sees God in his raw power. But not his face. Even Moses cannot see God "full on," as it were. When Moses returns from the mountain, his face is shining, such is the power of the reflected glory of God. Even the back of God.

The remainder of Exodus describes the building of the tabernacle and repeats much of the previous chapters. Bezalel and Oholiab, the craftsmen chosen by God for the work, lead their team of craftsmen in creating the fittings, and the people—perhaps out of shame—bring so many offerings for the work that Moses has to beg them to stop (35:30–36:7). Only Moses is entrusted with setting up the tabernacle. Only he can place the tablets in the ark. And when the tabernacle is finished, the glory of the Lord fills it with such power that even Moses cannot enter (40:1–38). From then on, wherever the Israelites went, the Lord would be with them, dwelling among them, leading them to the land he had promised them.

Landmark: Ark of the Covenant

The ark was a rectangular wooden box in which the two tablets containing the Ten Commandments were stored. It was made at Sinai by Bezalel and served as a symbol of God's presence, guiding his people. During the exodus it was stored in the most holy place in the tabernacle. After the Israelites had conquered the Promised Land, it was stored first at Bethel (Jg 20:27) and then Shiloh (1 Sa 1:3). David brought it to Jerusalem, where his son, Solomon, installed it in the Holy of Holies in his temple. Its eventual fate is unknown. It was probably lost during the Babylonian siege of Jerusalem in 587 BC. Stories of its recovery by Indiana Jones are unsubstantiated.

The ark was a dangerous object. It could not be touched directly, and it was associated with various strange, powerful happenings. It was as if it contained some kind of raw power and it had to be handled with care.

Cover
The lid—or "mercy seat"—was made of gold and surmounted by two cherubs with their wings outstretched. This was regarded as a kind of "throne" where God appeared.

Box
Made of acacia wood and covered with gold leaf.

Poles
Long poles were inserted in metal rings to allow the ark to be carried.

1.5 cubits

1.5 cubits

2.5 cubits

Leviticus
How to be holy

Who: Modern criticism tends to assign the composition of Leviticus to a much later priestly tradition. However, the book is full of references to Moses being given the Law—it is quite explicit in this.

When: It depends on your view. If you view it as the work of a priestly editor or writer, then it would have been written around 600 BC. If you view it as primarily Moses' work, then it dates from c. 1400 BC.

What: Leviticus takes its name from the priestly tribe of Israel: the Levites. It is basically a book of laws—laws governing worship, ritual, social behavior, criminal justice, health and safety, food production and even clothing manufacture.

Primarily Leviticus is about holiness. In the culture of the time, this holiness is characterized by physical perfection. No one with any blemish on them can serve at the tabernacle. Sores, burns, skin diseases, even a woman's monthly period—all these were supposed to make a person unclean. This is not an equal opportunities book. Disabled people and women don't get a look in when it comes to Leviticus. They were, in the culture of the time, seen as imperfect, and only the perfect were good enough for God.

Quick Guide

Author
Various, including Moses

Type
Books of the Law

Purpose
Provides the rules for the Israelites that were intended to keep them holy.

Key verses
20:7–8 "Dedicate yourselves to me and be holy because I am the LORD your God. I have chosen you as my people, and I expect you to obey my laws."

If you remember one thing about this book . . .
God wants people to be like him; that is why we have to obey his rules.

Your 10 minutes start now
Read chapters 9–11, 23, 25

Why should this be? Why should God look down on women and those suffering from illnesses and disabilities? It is not an easy question to answer. After all, Moses may have had a speech impediment (he complains about his slowness of speech) and he was acceptable to God. But when it comes to the tabernacle, Leviticus is about perfection. And that meant perfect sacrifices, perfect animals, perfect priests.

We would be wrong, however, in thinking that Leviticus is concerned only with the rite and ritual of the tabernacle. Along with the offerings and sacrifices, the clean and unclean, there is also profound social legislation—especially the Jubilee, a revolutionary economic and political concept unlike anything else of its time—or any other time, come to that.

The Route Through Leviticus

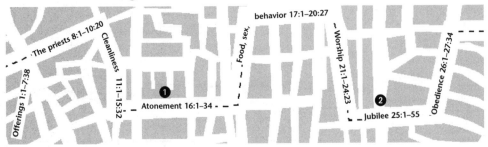

behavior 17:1–20:27

The priests 8:1–10:20

Cleanliness 11:1–15:32

Food, sex,

Worship 21:1–24:23

Obedience 26:1–27:34

Offerings 1:1–7:38

❶ Atonement 16:1–34

❷ Jubilee 25:1–55

Offerings   1:1–7:38

Offerings brought to the Lord were expected to be perfect and without defect. They were gifts to God and were therefore supposed to be of the highest value and quality—not something that the giver didn't want in the first place. The offerings were governed by strict regulations.

OFFERINGS			
Type	**When**	**What**	**Why**
Burnt offering 1:1–17; 6:8–13	Offered every morning and evening in the tabernacle, but individuals could make special offerings.	Bulls, rams, doves, pigeons. Males only.	An act of devotion. Atonement for unintentional sin. Expression of commitment to God.
Grain offering 2:1–16; 6:14–23	Same time as the burnt offering and the peace offering.	Grain, flour, olive oil, unleavened bread, salt. No yeast or honey.	An act of devotion. Thankfulness for God's provision.
Peace offering 3:1–17; 7:11–36	Same time as the burnt offering and the grain offering.	Any animal from the herd, as long as it was without defect.	Symbolizing peace between humans and God. A sign of friendship and wholeness. It was often accompanied by a communal meal and, at certain festivals, it could include huge numbers of animals (1 Ki 8:63–5; Nu 29:39).
Sin offering 4:1–5:13; 6:24–30	When an unintentional sin had been committed by the priest (4:3–12), the whole community (4:13–21), a leader (4:22–26) or an individual (4:27–35).	Priests would bring a young bull, leaders a goat, individuals a she-goat or a lamb, while the poor would bring a dove and the very poor some flour.	An atonement for unintentional sin, an act of confession and request for forgiveness.
Guilt offering 5:14–6:7; 7:1–10	When a sin had been committed that required some form of restitution, or where someone else had been hurt.	A ram or lamb, plus 120 percent of the full value of whatever had been done, which was to be given to the person who was wronged.	Atonement for sins that required restitution. Thus, a guilt offering was used to atone for sins like theft and cheating.

Details, Details . . .

Urim and thummim (8:8; Ex 28:30; Nu 27:21 NIV)
Nobody really knows what these were. (The CEV translates them as "two small objects" and generally avoids the issue.) The Hebrew actually means "curses and perfections" which is not very helpful. They appear to have been a kind of lottery device—objects of wood, metal or stone that were drawn or cast to decide the will of God in times of crisis. A bit like rolling a dice or drawing straws.

▷366

The priests 8:1–10:20

The people who were to receive these offerings and oversee the worship in the tabernacle were Aaron and his sons. They were brought before the Lord and anointed. A ram was cleaned and made perfect and then slaughtered. Its blood was put on their right ears, thumbs and big toe. What this was supposed to symbolize is unknown.

Cleanliness 11:1–15:32

Leviticus contains a large number of laws to do with food and health issues. These are known as cleanliness laws; food was declared clean or unclean, as, indeed, were people who were suffering from various diseases or conditions.

Most of this can be explained in terms of primitive health and hygiene: pork, for example, is notoriously prone to viral infection, as is seafood—as many unwary tourists can attest. But other food laws are more difficult to understand, such as the command that a kid cannot be cooked in its mother's milk. It should be noted, as well, that this is not a manual of zoology—the hare, for example, is classed with other ruminants such as the cow simply because of the movement of its jaws.

CLEAN AND UNCLEAN FOOD

Type	OK	Not OK
Ruminants 11:1–8	Anything with clean fur and cloven hooves, e.g., cattle, sheep, etc.	Camels, hyrax (rock badgers), rabbits, pigs.
Fish 11:9–12	Anything with scales and fins.	Anything without scales or fins, e.g., oysters, lobsters, submarines.
Birds 11:13–19	Not defined.	Eagles, vultures, buzzard, kites, crows, ostriches, hawks, seagulls, owls, pelicans, storks, herons, hoopoes, bats (I know it's not a bird, but *they* didn't know that).
Insects 11:20–23	Anything with jointed legs that hops, e.g., locusts, grasshoppers, crickets.	Any other kind of insect.
Others 11:29–30	Not defined.	Moles, rats, mice, lizards, geckos, skinks, chameleons, snakes (v. 42).

When it comes to people, women after childbirth are to be purified (12:1–8). People with skin diseases are to be examined by the priests (13:1–46). Thankfully for this author at least, bald people are clean (13:40). Mildew—understandably in a city composed of tents—is to be kept outside the camp (13:47–59), but the controls are also extended to houses (14:33–57).

Chapter 15 deals with sexual impurities, including infections of male sexual organs and women with periods. Culturally, a woman with a period was considered unclean. Whatever we make of these cleanliness laws, the prophets were to go further: a person's skin is irrelevant; what matters is that his or her heart is clean (Ps 5:10; Is 1:16).

The Day of Atonement
16:1–34

Chapter 16 gives regulations for the Day of Atonement. Many experts argue that this chapter is a later insertion on the grounds that there is no evidence that the Jews celebrated the Day of Atonement before the exile.

❶ The scapegoat   16:20–22

However, the detail about the Day of Atonement is interesting, for it includes a ritual whereby the sin of Israel is "transferred" to a goat. Two goats were brought forward, one of which would be sacrificed and the other driven out into the desert, taking away the sin of the people with it. From this we get the expression "scapegoat." Later in the New Testament this ritual—which had to happen annually—was to be contrasted with Christ's "once for all" sacrifice.

Food, sex, general behavior   17:1–20:27

Chapters 17–20 contain a mixed bag of regulations, some continuing the food laws, others going into more detail about sexual behavior. Chapter 18 is mostly a list of taboo incestual relationships. Verses 24–30 indicate that part of the reason for these prohibitions is that they are customary practices of the nations around Israel. Israel was to keep itself pure.

Worship   21:1–24:23

The priests have special laws and directives controlling their conduct. They are to stay clear of dead bodies and to avoid cutting their hair (21:1–12). They are also to be perfect physical specimens—or, at least, should not suffer from any physical deformities (21:16–21).

A Little Local Difficulty
A dangerous occupation
10:1–3

The first service overseen by the new priesthood is a tragic one. Or a just one, depending on your point of view. Nadab and Abihu, two sons of Aaron, burn incense when they are not supposed to and are immediately consumed by fire. Their death seems incredibly harsh: there is no indication of any motive other than mistake. But the Lord's power, in the Pentateuch at least, is a dangerous substance; it is to be handled with care and the instructions are to be strictly followed.

The root of this is a mystery: the same kind of thing happened to people who touched the ark, and even Ananias and Sapphira in the New Testament. At the end of the day, we don't know why this happened, or whether the people to whom it happened deserved it. Sometimes the raw power of God seems to operate according to its own laws. The rules and regulations outlined in Leviticus were more than just symbolic: they were a kind of spiritual safety regulation.

Details, Details . . .
Manna

The food that God gives to the Israelites is called manna, or bread from heaven. We don't know what it was. It can't have been a naturally appearing food, because it appeared double on the sixth day and not at all on the Sabbath in order to save the people from collecting it. That they kept samples of it for future generations (16:31) indicates that it was, indeed, a miraculous provision from God. The manna was given to them all the time they were in the desert, but stopped when they eventually entered Canaan. Jesus was later to use the image of himself, calling himself the true bread from heaven (Jn 6:32, 51).

Puzzling Points

Does Leviticus condemn homosexuality?

Yes. At least it did at the time. You see, this is the difficulty with taking moral universals from the laws in Leviticus.

Experts agree that Leviticus contains different kinds of laws—some of which are cultural, some of which belong to the old covenant and have been rendered redundant by Jesus, and others that are universals and persevere for all time. The difficulty is deciding which is which.

For example, if you take 18:22 as a universal, a statement that is as applicable now as then, then why don't you also take 19:19, which forbids us to wear clothing made of two kinds of materials? Or 19:27, which forbids cutting the hair at the side of the head? We have to read these laws with an understanding of their cultural significance, but unless they are reinforced elsewhere in Scripture, they cannot be taken as universals.

There *are* arguments against homosexuality that can be based on Scripture, but they cannot be based on Leviticus alone.

Festivals and Jubilee
25:1–55

Chapters 23 and 24 contain instructions for the observation of various festivals and holy days. It includes a number of lesser-known festivals, including the offering of firstfruits, which instructs the Israelites to bring their first grain and "wave" it in front of the Lord.

However, the list of festivals culminates in the provisions for the Year of Jubilee and the Sabbath year. This astonishing piece of social legislation was probably the most demanding of all the levitical laws. It was one thing to make sure that your sacrifice was free of physical defects; it was another thing entirely to hand back the property you owned and free your slaves.

The Sabbath year was a Sabbath for the land. Every seventh year the land was allowed to rest and recover. This is a primitive form of agricultural improvement, allowing the land to lie fallow and recover and avoiding over-farming. This concept was also applied to social structures. Slaves were only enslaved for a maximum of six years, and in the seventh year they were to be freed (Ex 21:2). Debts were to be cancelled in the Sabbath year (De 15:1–11).

❷ Jubilee 25:8–17

Every fiftieth year—that is, after seven lots of seven years—the entire social structure of Israel was to be reset. It was a kind of "Sabbath of Sabbaths," in which much of the property (although not houses inside walled cities) was to revert to its original owners (25:18–34). Slaves were to be released and could return to their property. The idea seems to be that it would give everyone the chance to start again. No matter how life had treated them or what misfortune had happened to them, in the Jubilee year they could wipe the slate clean and start again. Unsurprisingly, this legislation was rarely, if ever, enacted. The only time it is definitely said to have happened, the slaves were freed—and then promptly taken back into slavery (Jer 34:8–22).

Obedience 26:1–27:34

Leviticus ends with promises and warnings; promises of blessings if the laws are obeyed (26:1–12), and warnings of punishments if they are not (26:14–46). If the laws were kept, then God would be with his people—"I will walk with you—I will be your God, and you will be my people" (26:12). The holy God would have a holy people.

The final chapter is about objects, people or property that have been dedicated or promised to the Lord. Some vows or promises could be commuted into cash payments, and this chapter gives guidance as to fair prices. Some people were dedicated for service as a special thanksgiving (e.g., 1 Sa 1:11). They could be bought back either at a set price (27:3–7) or at a fair price set by the priest.

Numbers
The long and winding road

Numbers is largely just that: a book of statistics and accounts. A list of the tribes of Israel and the number of people in each tribe.

Yet, despite the administrative details that fill the book, there are some fascinating passages and perhaps the Hebrew title *Bemidbar* is more appropriate—it means "in the desert."

Who: Again, the traditional authorship is ascribed to Moses, but there are passages that indicate that perhaps a later writer was involved. And anyway, parts of Numbers are more like a telephone directory than anything else. If Moses was responsible it was only because he ordered the information to be gathered together.

When: See introduction to Leviticus.

What: Numbers tells of Israel's journey to the edge of the Promised Land. But more than that, it tells of their failure to enter their land, their continual bickering and grumbling against God, and the final judgment on their faithlessness and disobedience. Their God had enabled them to escape from Egypt, but their own sin meant that they were never to escape the desert.

Exodus tells how Israel became a worshiping community; Numbers tells how they became an army. After the giving of the Law and the creation of the tabernacle at Sinai, the Israelites marched out to conquer the lands around them. Leviticus only covers a timescale of about a month; Numbers covers forty years. Leviticus takes place in one location; Numbers zooms around the desert like a camel on steroids.

Quick Guide
Author
Moses and a later editor
Type
Books of the Law
Purpose
The tale of how Israel came to the Promised Land . . . eventually.
Key verses
14:22–23 "I swear that not one of these Israelites will enter the land I promised to give their ancestors. These people have seen my power in Egypt and in the desert, but they will never see Canaan. They have disobeyed and tested me too many times."
If you remember one thing about this book . . .
Rebellion against God will always leave you in the wilderness.
Your 15 minutes start now
Read chapters 6, 13–14, 20, 22, 31–33

The Route Through Numbers

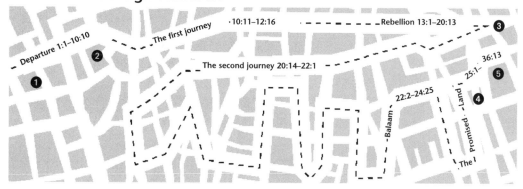

Departure 1:1–10:10
The first journey
10:11–12:16
Rebellion 13:1–20:13
The second journey 20:14–22:1
22:2–24:25
Balaam
25:1–
36:13
The Promised Land
The

Questions, Questions

Why isn't Aaron punished?

How does he get away with it?
What do you mean?
Well, Aaron goes along with the creation of the golden calf and he isn't punished. He criticizes Moses and he isn't punished— even though Miriam contracts a skin disease. Why doesn't he ever get what he deserves?
Perhaps he does. Some experts believe that Aaron was punished, but that, because this book was written by a priest, he didn't want to record anything bad against Aaron.
You mean this is biased history?
Well, that might be the case, but the problem with this theory is that Aaron is shown clearly to be at fault.
So he doesn't come across in a good light.
No. Just the opposite. Possibly Aaron's punishment was less obvious. His two sons died, after all, and he, like Moses, never got to the Promised Land. But he also seems to recognize his sins and repent. Maybe his failing was that he was too easily led. What do you think?
Oh, I don't know. I'll go along with you . . .

Puzzling Points

The numbers don't work

For a book so concerned with numbers, it comes as a surprise to the reader to realize that the numbers don't really work. The problem is that they are simply too vast. If we take the figures as given then the number of men in the Israelite army would require a total population of over 2,000,000 people. This is an impossible figure, both in comparison to the neighboring nations of the time, and especially when we think that they are wandering in the desert.

Various possibilities are suggested, most of which revolve around reinterpreting the word used for "thousand." None of these possibilities really solve the problem and in the end, all we can say is that the numbers, while probably not exact, certainly indicate that this was a nation on the move, rather than a small group of tribes.

Preparing for departure
1:1–10:10

After the laws have been given on Mount Sinai and the tabernacle established, the Israelites prepare to leave Sinai and journey to their destination.

In preparation for this a census is taken of all the tribes (1:1–54) and a map drawn up of their arrangement in the camp (2:1–34). Detailed accounts of the responsibilities of various clans are given. The Levites are to carry the ark, the Gershonites and Merarites are to carry the tabernacle and the Kohathites are to carry the furnishings.

❶ Unfaithfulness   5:11–31

Chapter 5 consists of extra material that includes one of the strangest pieces of the Law: the test of unfaithfulness.

This deals with the suspicions of a husband about the conduct of his wife and involves what seems to be a trial by ordeal. The accused woman has to drink what is described as "bitter water" (5:18). If she is innocent, nothing happens, but if she is guilty, then she will be unable to bear children. Throughout this the name of the Lord is invoked, indicating that it is he who will reveal the truth rather than a magic potion or ritual. But even so, the rite seems harsh and sexist, certainly by our standards. Yet this was evidently an ancient custom and reflects the social values of the time.

❷ Nazirites   6:1–21

Chapter 6 introduces the Nazirites—a special group who took strict vows. Nazirite means "vowed." Their vows meant total devotion to the Lord. They did not cut their hair, drank no alcohol and had no contact with dead bodies—not even their parents.

This vow could be perpetual or for a set period. Famous Nazirites include Samson, Samuel and John the Baptist.

Chapters 7–10 lead on from Exodus 40 with a description of the inauguration and dedication of the tabernacle. Chapter 7 is the longest chapter in the Pentateuch and contains a lot of repetition, describing in detail the gifts brought from each tribe. The section also describes the purification of the Levites (8:5–26; see also Le 8) and the celebration of the Passover (9:1–14).

Then it is time for departure. Trumpets are sounded, a triumphant battle cry is yelled and the people start to march. Their departure is governed by the cloud that indicates the presence of God (9:15–23).

The first journey 10:11–12:16

Only three days into the march, and the people start complaining. "The fire of the Lord" breaks out among them (11:1)—perhaps similar to that which consumed Aaron's sons. However, this display of God's anger does nothing to dampen their disobedience and moaning, and soon they are back on one of their favorite topics: food. Exasperated, Moses complains to God of the strain he feels in leading these people. God, despite his anger with the Israelites, is also a God of compassion. He answers Moses' cry and provides meat for the people.

Tensions within the camp are not restricted to the people, however, but also extend to the leadership. Aaron and Miriam also criticize Moses. Miriam is punished by God for her criticism.

❸ Rebellion 13:1–20:13

By chapter 13 the Israelites are near enough to Canaan to send out spies. Two men from each tribe are sent to bring back their reports.

Their reports are a mix of excitement and sheer fear. The land is amazingly fertile, but the inhabitants are strong and powerful. As the spies' reports are spread about, the Canaanites develop into mythical giants—the legendary Nephilim (13:33; Ge 6:4). In the face of these rumors the people rebel and refuse to enter the land. The Canaanites were strong, it is true, but the Israelites had a God who was stronger. However, at that moment they cannot believe that and their faithlessness is finally too much for God, who declares that the people will never enter the land. Only Joshua and Caleb—two of the spies who declared that they should invade—are to make it into Canaan.

As an abortive attempt to make up for their faithlessness, the Israelites try to invade by themselves, but it is too late. They are defeated and forced to retreat (14:39–45). It is the first of several rebellions against Moses in this section.

A Little Local Difficulty
Moses and the rock 20:1–13

The Israelites demand water, so Moses and Aaron plead with the Lord, and the Lord tells them to go to a rock, speak to it, and water will come. So Moses does that. Well, *almost*. He strikes it with a branch, and water flows. But because Moses and Aaron struck the rock, instead of speaking to it, they are told that they will not lead Israel into the Promised Land.

Why? Did Moses really suffer this punishment just because, out of rage and frustration, he hit the rock with a twig instead of shouting at it? What is going on here? The Bible is slightly opaque as to the real nature of Moses' offense. There are certainly indications that he did not trust a word alone to open the rock, and that he did not obey the Lord precisely. The punishment seems to imply that his offense was a lack of faith in the Lord—the same lack of faith that saw the Israelites doubt their ability to conquer Canaan. We have seen, elsewhere in Numbers, the result of disobeying the Lord. But given Moses' service, this seems a remarkable overreaction. Perhaps there was more to Moses' actions than mere mistake. The only thing we can take from this is that, whatever the reason behind the story, it shows that no one is immune from God's commands. Moses, despite his service, gets no special treatment. He would see the Promised Land, but never enter it.

And so the old guard will pass away. Miriam is already dead. Aaron dies on Mount Horeb and his garments are passed on to his son Eleazar.

Details, Details . . .
The bronze snake (21:4–9)
Another day, another grumble. The people—perhaps complacent after their defeat of the Canaanites at Hormah (21:1–3)—moan about the lack of water and the awful food. There is more to this than simply moaning about the food. The manna God provided was a sign of his grace and mercy—he didn't have to provide anything. So when the Israelites moaned about the food, they were actually questioning the grace of God. This time God sends a plague of snakes among the people. Moses' intercession leads to the erection of a bronze snake. Anyone who looked at the snake would survive. This image was to be picked up and used later in John 3:14–15.

Personal rebellion   15:32–6

People bear a personal responsibility for their decisions. This seems tough sometimes—such as in the case of the man who was executed for collecting wood on the Sabbath—but the penalty for Sabbath-breaking was clear and had always been clear from the beginning. He was guilty of what is called in 15:30 "deliberate rebellion," and he had to bear the consequences.

Rebellion against Moses   16:1–35

Chapter 16 sees yet more rebellion, this time from Korah and his followers. This is a rebellion born of arrogance and ambition. Korah has already been selected from the Levites for a special role, but that is not enough for him; he wants to be priest. In the end he fails the test and he and his followers are destroyed by earthquake and fire.

Ingratitude to God   16:41–50

This divine punishment only leads to more rebellion against Moses—which results in a plague breaking out among the people. Thousands of people die through the plague, but more specifically through their own ingratitude and rebellion.

Aaron and the priesthood   17:1–18:32

In both of these events Aaron has a key part. It is he who is chosen by God in the contest with Korah. It is he who stands between the living and the dead during the plague outbreak, who makes atonement for the people. The flowering of his staff, described in 17:1–13, is one of a series of stories that emphasize the importance of the Aaronic priesthood—the priesthood descended from his line. In this final story the staffs of the heads of each tribe are planted in front of the tabernacle. The next morning, Aaron's staff has burst into bloom—a sign that God has chosen the house of Levi as his special servants and priesthood.

This is not a life of luxury, and the onerous duties of the Levites are detailed in the next chapter. They bore responsibility for the correct worship of the Lord and for any infringements against the tabernacle. They would receive a proportion of the sacrifices made by the Israelites and a tithe—that is, a proportion of the earnings of the people. But the tribe of Levi would never have any land to call their own.

The second journey   20:14–22:1

Forty years have passed since Israel first entered the desert. (Although the year is not mentioned, we can work it out from the list of places given in Numbers 33:38. At least, you can if you're into that sort of thing.)

Balaam   22:2–24:25

By now the Israelites have developed into a formidable enemy. After years in the desert, they are now preparing to attack Canaan and take possession of the land.

Balak, King of Moab, calls on Balaam, a well-known holy man, to come and curse the Israelites and bring down misfortune on them. Balaam is an unusual figure: a soothsayer from the banks of the Euphrates who acknowledges God as his Lord. However, he seems to have viewed God as one among many—for later he is condemned for bringing Israel into idolatry (31:7–8; De 23:3–6; Jos 13:22; Ne 13:1–3; among others). This time he listens to God and then sets out.

There is a problem here, for in 22:20 God gives Balaam permission to go, and then two verses later we learn that God is angry at Balaam for going. Possibly the explanation is similar to that concerning God's anger against Moses—that Balaam did not fully obey the Lord, that the Lord had told Balaam to go and say one thing, but he intended to go and say another. Nonetheless it is difficult to resolve the contradiction. In the end, however, God sends an angel to block his way. Balaam cannot see the angel until his donkey speaks to him. There is a richly comic picture here —the internationally renowned soothsayer cannot see the angel, but the proverbially dumb and stubborn beast sees only too well. Balaam is told to say only what the Lord gives him to say.

Balaam is later killed in the war against Moab. He is marked as responsible for a plan to defeat the Israelites, not by cursing them, but by luring them into the ways of the Midianites, to make them "go native." He was obviously unable to learn from his experience. He should have spent more time talking to his donkey.

The Promised Land   25:1–36:13

❹ Moabite women   25:1–17

When the Israelites stay at Shittim, they become exposed to foreign gods again. In particular they indulge in sexual relationships with Moabite women. This is not just going to bed with them, but sex as part of their religious rituals. The worship of foreign gods was often tied in with sexual immorality and abhorrent practices such as child sacrifice. For most of their history as recorded in the Bible, the lure of foreign gods was to be Israel's downfall. Time and again they were to indulge in the worship of Baal and the other gods of the neighboring countries. That is why the reaction is so swift and strong. To our eyes it is ridiculously brutal—the high priest takes a spear and personally impales an errant Israelite and his Midianite woman (25:6–9). But then, perhaps we don't take false worship seriously enough. At the time, God's commands were clear: stay pure. If that took extreme measures, then so be it.

After forty years, the Israelites are back at the river, preparing to cross into the Promised Land. Chapter 26 contains the second census—the first was taken thirty-eight years earlier. The first generation of those who had left Egypt had now all died. A new task needed new preparation—and this time Moses and Eleazar re-count the numbers in the tribes. The numbers of warriors have declined overall in the intervening years—from 603,550 to 601,730. Some tribes have declined considerably, a result, perhaps, of the plague and the divine judgment on Korah and his supporters.

The preparation for the final attack includes the handover of leadership. Joshua is appointed by God to succeed Moses (27:12–23). For many years he has been the leader's assistant. He was with him on the mountain and has been faithful ever since. Joshua will be the one to lead Israel into the Promised Land.

Details, Details . . .
Wrists and foreheads (6:8–9)

Some Jews still take this verse literally. They tie what are called phylacteries to their arms or foreheads—small boxes that contain passages from the Law (Ex 13:1–16; De 6:4–9; 11:13–21). They also attach small boxes called mezuzot to the door frames of their houses. Jesus was to criticize those who wore these phylacteries ostentatiously, who wore the Law on their arms and heads, but without love in their hearts.

In this war the women and men of the enemy are killed, but the children and unmarried women are taken as plunder. It is an example of the kind of war that God commanded Israel to engage in at the time of the conquest: a total war where entire nations were expelled or killed.

❺ Cities of refuge

The remainder of Numbers is about the various occupations and allocations of land. The Reubenites and Gadites decide to settle where they are and not cross the Jordan. This is agreed, providing they promise to join their fellow Israelites in the battle. The Levites, who would not receive land as such, are allotted towns to live in. These are also to be cities of refuge—places people can flee to in the case of unintentional killing —what we might call manslaughter. The perpetrator would have to stay in the city of refuge. The idea was to prevent the rise of blood feuds between families, so that an innocent man would not be killed before a trial could take place.

Numbers ends with the Israelites on the verge of conquering the Promised Land. Their journey has been long and unnecessary, for if they had trusted the Lord they could have taken the land forty years earlier. But now the faithless generation has passed away. The new nation is about to enter the land and claim what has been promised them for so long.

Landmark: Circumcision

Circumcision is a ritual operation that removes all, or part, of the foreskin from the male penis. The practice dates back to very early times—there are depictions of the act on Egyptian tombs. Personally, I'd have preferred a picture of a nice kitten, but some people have funny tastes. Anyway, it has been practiced by many cultures, including African, South American, Australian and Native American tribes, generally as a kind of initiation, a rite of passage from being a boy to being a man.

The Jews, however, used it in a very different way. They circumcised their babies on the eighth day after their birth—so it was nothing to do with manhood. Instead it was a physical sign of belonging to God, a sign of the covenant between God and his people. God says that any male not circumcised "hasn't kept his promise to me and cannot be one of my people" (Ge 17:14).

Circumcision, therefore, was not a sign of belonging to a tribe, or even a nation, but a sign of belonging to God. As the years went by, though, this meaning was increasingly ignored, and Jews began to forget that circumcision was a symbol—and not a guarantee— of purity and holiness. Thus they believed that as long as they were circumcised they were OK. This attitude was criticized by prophets such as Jeremiah, who said to the people, "Your bodies are circumcised, but your hearts are unchanged" (Je 9:26).

In New Testament times, the issue became a crucial bone of contention between Jewish and Greek Christians. Some argued that the Greeks should be circumcised, like the Jewish believers. Peter, and later Paul, fought this, arguing that Christians were justified by faith in Christ and did not need the physical act of circumcision (Ro 4:9–13).

Deuteronomy
A few words in closing . . .

Deuteronomy is Moses' farewell speech. It is a reminder of all that has happened to Israel, of the way that God has brought them out of slavery and—despite their own lack of faith—had brought them to the verge of the Promised Land. Indeed, the name Deuteronomy means "repetition of the law."

Who: The traditional view is that Moses wrote it—although obviously the introduction and the account of Moses' death were by a different hand. Jesus himself talks about Moses' authorship, and the New Testament regards Deuteronomy highly: there are nearly one hundred quotations from Deuteronomy in the New Testament.

When: Around 1400 BC.

What: At the time of writing, Moses and the Israelites are in Moab, just where the Jordan flows into the Dead Sea. The leadership has been handed over to Joshua, and Moses is saying farewell. In his address he reminds the people of the things that have happened to them and the laws they are to obey. This is a renewal of the covenant between the Lord and his people.

The God who comes across in Deuteronomy is more caring and personal than he often seems in the other books of the Pentateuch. He teaches his people through their trials. In all their wanderings they never go hungry, their clothes don't wear out and they don't even get swollen feet! Now this loving God has led them to a land of plenty (8:1–9).

The Route Through Deuteronomy

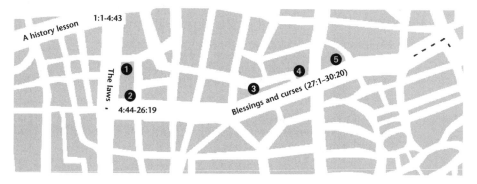

A history lesson 1:1-4:43

The laws

1
2
4:44-26:19

3
4
5
Blessings and curses (27:1–30:20)

PARALLEL LINES
Now where have I seen that before?

	Deuteronomy	Numbers	Exodus	Leviticus	▷ Page
LEADERS APPOINTED	1:9–18		18:13–27		...
Men sent to explore	1:19–25	13:1–33	...	...	71
Israel refuses to enter	1:26–45	14:1–45	...	...	71
Defeat of King Sihon	2:26–37	21:21–30	...	...	...
Defeat of King Og	3:1–11	21:31–5	...	...	...
Land divided	3:12–22	32:1–42	...	...	...
TEN COMMANDMENTS	5:1–22	...	20:1–17	...	58
Fear and trembling	5:23–33	...	20:18–21	...	...
Force other nations out	7:1–5	...	34:11–16	...	...
Blessings	7:12–26	...	...	26:3–13	...
GOLDEN CALF	9:7–29	...	32:1–35	...	62
More commandments	10:1–5	...	34:1–10	...	...
AARON'S DEATH	10:6–7	20:22–9	...	...	...
Prayers answered	10:10–11	...	34:9–10, 27–29	...	...
Dietary laws	14:3–29	...	...	11:1–47	66
Loan laws	15:1–11	...	...	25:1–7	68
Freeing slaves	15:12–18		21:1–11	...	...
Firstborn animals	15:19–23	18:15–18	...	27:26–27	68
PASSOVER	16:1–8	...	12:1–20	23:4–8	55
Harvest festival	16:9–12	...		23:15–21	68
Festival of Shelters	16:13–15	29:12–38	...	23:33–43	...
Three festivals	16:16–17	...	23:14–17	...	...
Rights of priests	18:1–8	18:8–32	...	...	...
Safe towns	19:1–13	35:9–28	...	...	74
Curses for disobedience	28:1–14	35:9–28	...	26:3–13	...

A history lesson   1:1–4:43

In his first speech, Moses looks back on the past. Most of these events are recounted elsewhere, but Moses' speech gives them a more personal flavor. He recounts Israel's history of disobedience and focuses on their relations with the neighboring countries such as Moab, Ammon and Bashan. Here, in his own words, we get a glimpse of the man behind the leader. We also see the personal pain of Moses. He prays and begs God to let him cross the Jordan, but it is not to be. He is allowed to stand on the top of Mount Pisgah and look. He can look, but he can't touch (3:23–29).

His first speech ends with a reminder of the dangers of idol worship. This will be a major issue in the lives of the Israelites in the years to come, living, as they will, in the midst of pagan nations.

"You must be very careful not to forget the things you have seen God do for you. Keep reminding yourselves, and tell your children and grandchildren as well" (4:9).

The laws   4:44–26:19

Moses' second speech picks up on the theme of the laws and repeats a great many of the commands that God has given his people. It begins with the Ten Commandments and concentrates on the theme of worship and holiness. The great battle for the Israelites will not be against the forces of Canaan; it will be a battle against impurity and sin. The primary purpose of the Law was to keep Israel holy, to set them apart and give them a different set of values.

Between the repetitions, Moses reminds the Israelites time and again of how great their God is. The most important commandment, he tells them, is to love their God with all their heart, soul and strength (6:4). He tells the people to memorize the laws, to talk about them all the time, to hold them in their memory (6:6). They are the weakest of nations (7:6), but they have the strongest God. He cares for each of them.

Most of all, their eyes have seen the glory. They have seen what God has done for them. They are involved in glory. The Lord defeated the Egyptian army and he will defeat the Canaanites (11:1–32). So it doesn't matter who is talking—their brother or sister or even a prophet (13:1–2, 6–10): if that person is trying to take them away from God then he or she must be dealt with strongly. It is, literally, a matter of life and death.

❶ The king   17:14–20

In the midst of his reiteration of the laws and his injunctions to the Israelites about how they should act in the new land, Moses looks ahead and warns them of the dangers of a king. In words that are repeated through Samuel the prophet (1 Sa 8:4–9), he talks of these dangers. Israel should not need a king, because God is their ruler—but here, perhaps, Moses is recognizing that there will come a time when they will demand a monarch.

In particular he warns of an overreliance on Egypt (symbolic of any foreign power) and gives a warning against taking too many wives. (Evidently Solomon never read this part.) God did not want the Israelites to be overreliant on any one country, or to form alliances that would lead to trouble. The bottom line is that any future king will rule only through God's permission. He will be obliged to read and obey the laws. Previous to this passage, Moses has been talking about justice (16:18–17:13) and the king will be subject to the same laws.

❷ Crime and punishment

Chapters 16–26 contain a lot of material dealing with social and criminal justice. Much of this is repeated from other places, but some of it involves developments and explanations of the code already given. It is often in the form of case studies, such as the man whose ax-head flies off, killing his coworker (19:5–7), or the woman who is raped out in the countryside (22:25–7). It even includes laws for digging the latrines (23:12–14).

Some of these laws seem archaic and stern—as with a lot of the laws in the Old Testament. But others surprise us with their contemporary relevance. Runaway slaves are to be given a haven (23:15–16). Newlyweds are to be given time to settle in (24:5). Loans are to be fair and just (24:10–13). Children are not to be punished for the crimes of their parents (24:16). The poor are to be cared for (24:17–22).

Blessings and curses 27:1–30:20

This section includes a long list of curses and blessings given to those who disobey or obey the laws. It paints a picture of two kinds of society: one that is fruitful and strong, and one that is disease-ridden, weak, powerless and enslaved (27:9–28:68). It ends with Moses calling the people to renew their agreement with the Lord. It really is very simple, in the end. Choose life, Moses says. Choose the way of the Lord (30:15).

"The LORD our God hasn't explained the present or the future, but he has commanded us to obey the laws he gave to us and our descendants" (29:29). The future scares us, the past confuses us. In the meantime, we are to obey God, to follow his laws, to live in his presence.

❸ Change of leadership 31:1–34:12

After these speeches, Moses announces a change of leadership. The old man hands power over to his young commander. Well, relatively young. He was probably around 75. Retirement was evidently not an option in those days.

❹ The song of Moses 32:1–43

In the sacred tent the future is revealed to Moses. The people of Israel, despite his warnings, despite all the blessings and the curses, will turn their backs on the Lord. God will give them the land, but he knows exactly what they're going to do with it. It must have been a sad and dispiriting moment for the great man. He gave his life to his people, he gave all he had to make them pure and holy, and it was all going to come to nothing (31:14–29). Yet the song he sings is not one of total defeat. Although it tells of Israel's rejection, it ends with forgiveness and purification. Moses knows that it will come out good in the end, that God will achieve his purpose despite Israel as much as because of Israel.

❺ Death of Moses 34:1–12

And so, after blessing the tribes (33:2–29), the old man dies. He stands on the mountaintop and sees the Promised Land, but he dies in Moab. And yet, this is not the end of the story. The truth is that Moses did get to see the Promised Land and he did get to meet the one true king of Israel. It happened centuries later, in Jerusalem, when he met Jesus (Mt 17:1–9). But that, as they say, is another story.

The Histories

The twelve books of history take the story on from the conquest of the Promised Land, through the decline of the monarchy, into exile under foreign powers and finally to the return from exile of the Jewish nation.

Joshua

Joshua was the successor to Moses, and, unlike his mentor, he actually got to enter the Promised Land. The book tells of the invasion and conquest of the land and the division of the territory between the twelve tribes of Israel.

Judges

Judges is one of the bleakest books of the Bible. It tells of the dark, anarchic era that followed the conquest, when every man acted as he thought fit and violence and barbarism ruled. The only exceptions were the "judges," leaders raised by God who brought occasional order to the chaos.

Ruth

A small book telling of Ruth the Moabitess and her faithfulness and love.

1 & 2 Samuel

The story of the first kings of Israel: Saul and David The name comes from the prophet Samuel, who anointed both kings.

1 & 2 Kings

Could equally be called 3 & 4 Samuel, because it continues the story from the previous books. It starts with the reign of Solomon and then goes downhill as the kingdom splits in two, and a succession of bad kings get their hands on the throne. The book tells of the downfall of Israel and the fate of its inhabitants—taken into slavery by foreign powers.

1 & 2 Chronicles

The books of Chronicles are a condensed version of the Samuel-Kings story. The books concentrate mainly on the kings of Judah—the southern kingdom—and have a particular focus on the building of the temple and the religious ceremonies.

Esther

The story of Queen Esther, a Jewess who became Queen of Persia and saved her people from extermination at the hands of their enemies.

Ezra & Nehemiah

Two books telling of the return of the Jews from exile in Babylon, their struggles to rebuild the shattered city of Jerusalem, the reestablishment of the temple and the rediscovery of the books of the Law.

Joshua
Into the Promised Land

When: The date and authorship of Joshua are open to debate. Some scholars argue that the book was written a lot later than the events it describes—possibly as late as 800 years after the events. But there are arguments that place the book earlier and closer to the time of the action. A lot of the descriptions of the cities use antiquated names that would have been prevalent at the time, such as "the Jebusite city" for Jerusalem (15:8). The probable truth is that the book dates from the early years of the monarchy, but also includes material that was inserted at a later date.

Who: Although Joshua orders his men to make a survey of the land (18:8) and he draws up commands and laws (24:25), we don't know who the author was.

What: The subject of the book is the conquest of Canaan. After their years of wandering in the desert, the Israelites finally make it across the Jordan and into the land God had given them.

Following these first victories, Israel goes on to take much of Canaan, conquering city-state after city-state. The less important cities are burned, while those on hills—that is, the cities that can be defended and used —are kept. The only exception is Hazor, the most powerful city in the land, which is burned. Finally, there is peace in the land (11:23). And yet the land is never fully conquered, and the previous inhabitants are never fully driven out. Israel is sowing the seeds of its future faithlessness and destruction.

The Route Through Joshua

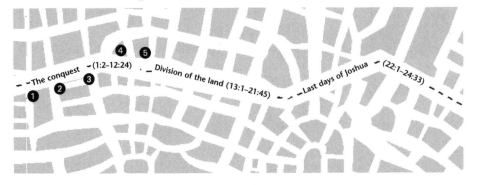

The conquest (1:2–12:24) — Division of the land (13:1–21:45) — Last days of Joshua (22:1–24:33)

Landmark: The Bible and Ethnic Cleansing

Joshua is, in some ways, a troubling book. It describes a triumphant conquest for Israel, but that, by definition, means that another nation is defeated. At times that conquest seems more like ethnic cleansing than anything else, with entire city populations deliberately and systematically wiped out.

The first thing to bear in mind about Joshua is that it is not an account of military success for one country, but of God's purpose for his world. The role of Israel was to demonstrate the power, holiness and mercy of God—to show to the kingdoms around what God was like. The Bible is the story of the kingdom of God being established among the earthly kingdoms. That could not be achieved without a battle.

Practical realities

There was a practical reality to overcome. This was the only way to establish a kingdom. There was no United Nations at the time, no international law, no media to mobilize "world opinion." There was, generally speaking, only a load of large hairy dudes with sharp swords. It was a tough and brutal time. If Israel was not prepared to fight then they would die. The establishment of the kingdom was supposed to be for the benefit of other nations. First, therefore, it had to become a kingdom.

Defeat of false gods

The Bible tells how God gave a portion of his world to one people on condition that they followed his ways. It also tells how God's judgment fell on the Canaanites—a nation that worshiped false gods and engaged in terrible practices. Nations were viewed, not as political or even military identities, but as expressions of their gods. The success or otherwise of a nation was viewed as proof of its power, in much the same way as success at the Olympic Games used to be viewed as proof of the value of communism or capitalism. We must also note that when Israel followed the same false gods, they were treated as harshly.

Leased not given

The land did not belong to Joshua and his people, but to the Lord. The riches they obtained through victory were to be distributed as God saw fit. The conquest was a particular mission at a particular time.

Even so . . .

All of this is true, but still we have to face the fact that innocent men, women and children, who had no say in their country's government or in their state religion, were killed. At that point all we can do is trust in the mercy and justice of God. The Bible teaches us that death is not the end.

God's methods change according to culture and time. With the coming of Jesus, God's redemptive purpose was fulfilled on earth. If the conquest of Canaan was part of that redemption, its purpose has been achieved. Therefore, the kind of warfare described in Joshua is not necessary anymore.

There is still judgment waiting for nations and individuals, but it is not for us to achieve it with the bullet and the bomb. Instead we are to go out into the world and make disciples of every nation. We are still called to establish a kingdom, but this time it has to be in people's hearts.

Brief Lives: Joshua

Background: Son of a nun. Sorry, son of Nun.

Occupation: Slave. Personal assistant to Moses. Then leader of Israel.

Achievements: Joshua was originally called Hoshea (Nu 13:8, 16) which means "salvation." Moses changed his name to Joshua, meaning "the Lord saves." The Greek version of this name was "Jesus."

Joshua's life combines the two aspects of a man of faith and a military commander. He left Egypt as a young man, took over the leadership of Israel when he was around 75 and died at 110. As a man of faith, he was the only other person allowed up the mountain with Moses (Ex 24:13–14), as well as being appointed to stand guard outside the tent when Moses was meeting God (Ex 33:11). As a military commander, he led the Israelites to victory over the Amalekites in the early days of the exodus (Ex 17:8–13) and it was Joshua who commanded the Israelites in their battles to take the Promised Land.

These two sides to his character are seen, perhaps, at their strongest when he was one of the twelve spies who entered Canaan secretly the first time around (Nu 14:26–34). Only Joshua and his partner Caleb argued that God would bring the victory, his military knowledge backed up by his deep faith.

Character: Hardworking. Faithful. Tough.

Pros: Tough fighter. Man of faith.

Cons: Don't mention his age.

The conquest   1:1–12:24

Joshua begins with a promise. God sets out the boundaries of the land that he will give Israel. The dimensions described here in fact only happened during the time of David and Solomon, if then. The first half of the book deals with the possession of the land.

❶ Rahab   2:1–21

The position of prostitutes in the Old Testament is ambiguous, to say the least. There were two kinds:

• Temple prostitutes who performed sex in the context of false and idolatrous worship, and whose earnings were used to support the temples of false gods. These are always condemned.

• "Ordinary" prostitutes who stood on street corners or worked in brothels. Generally these prostitutes were seen as bad—Proverbs, for example, is full of injunctions to stop young men falling into their "trap." However, there is also some kind of acceptance that these things happen, just as the early kings had multiple wives and harems.

Rahab was the latter kind of prostitute, a working girl who probably combined her trade with that of an innkeeper. All part of the service, as it were. However, when the two spies stay the night at her establishment, she becomes a convert to the God of Israel and she protects the spies. The spies agree to return her protection. She will not be killed, as long as she hangs a red cord outside her house—a subtle echo of the Passover blood in Exodus.

Rahab's actions made her a heroine for the Israelites. The New Testament honors her faith (He 11:31) and her good works (Ja 2:25). The issue of her occupation is, apparently, less important than her role in the establishment of God's kingdom.

> ### Details, Details . . .
> ### The ban (6:18–19)
>
> God commanded that no one in the invading Israelite army should keep any of the "spoils of war." Valuable items were to be put into the treasury of the Lord. This is important because it indicates that this was not a battle for wealth. Most wars in history have their origin in human greed—normally in greed for land and wealth. This was not such a war. No one was to make themselves rich through this war —only rich in faith.
>
> Not everyone observed the ban on possession. Achan (7:1–26) kept a rich robe, some silver and gold. His sin had both personal and communal consequences: personal because it led to his death (7:25–26), and communal because it led to the death of thirty-six soldiers in battle (7:2–5).

❷ The crossing of the Jordan   3:1–4:24

After the spies report back, the Israelites cross the Jordan and enter the country. They are led by the ark of the covenant and the waters divide to let them pass over. Just as the waters of the reed sea parted to lead them out of Egypt, the waters of the Jordan part to lead them into the Promised Land. Their entry is followed by a service of rededication, at which the men are circumcised.

❸ The fall of Jericho   5:13–6:27

One of the most famous events of the Bible, the fall of Jericho, has been subject to an enormous amount of archaeological examination. Jericho is certainly one of the oldest cities in the world—if not the oldest. There are traces of more than twenty cities built on top of each other and stretching back more than 8,000 years. Argument still rages over whether the fallen walls really existed, and whether their remains can actually be identified. Indeed, there is some debate as to whether the cities described in Joshua existed at all, and if so, where they were. In the end, however, we must admit that archaeology can only take us so far.

The fall of Jericho, like the conquest of the land, was the work of God. It was preceded by Joshua meeting with an angel (5:13–15) and, although the Israelites practiced a form of psychological warfare, marching round the city in silence and then finally shouting, the collapse of the walls was an act of God.

POSTCARD

Not far from the Jordan, and just to the north of the Dead Sea, Jericho is one of the most ancient cities in the world. There were people living here in 7000 BC!

And we're not just one of the oldest, we're one of the lowest as well—800 feet below sea level to be precise—a position that gives us a hot tropical climate. This climate is one of the reasons that so many palm trees grow in Jericho, giving us the nickname the "city of palms."

Throughout the millennia, the city of Jericho has risen and fallen. Several times the city has been abandoned, or moved, or has fallen down due to earthquakes or excessive trumpet playing.

Visitors are advised to check out our many Canaanite temples, purchase from our world-famous potteries or have a look at our strong, sturdy, and, we like to think, impregnable walls.

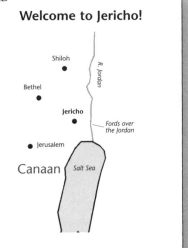

Welcome to Jericho!

❹ Ai and Gibeon: two deceptions — 8:1–9:27

The battle at Ai is interesting because it is the first recorded instance of the strategic retreat. The king of Ai believes that the Israelites are in retreat and foolishly chases them, only to be ambushed.

But those who trick can also be tricked, and the rulers of Gibeon engineer a peace treaty with the Israelites by claiming that they live a long way away. The key verse here is 9:14, "The Israelites tried some of the food, but they did not ask the LORD if he wanted them to make a treaty." They relied on their own judgment and the Gibeonites were spared destruction.

❺ The standing sun — 10:1–27

The treaty is soon invoked when the Amorites attack Gibeon. The Israelites go to their defense. More than that, the Lord goes to their defense: first the Amorite army is pelted by enormous hailstones (10:11) and then the day is supernaturally extended. Many of us have prayed for more hours in the day. Joshua is one of the few people who have received an answer. The sun, according to this passage, doesn't go down "for a whole day." Various theories have been put forward to explain this apparently impossible phenomenon. Some theorize that God extended the hours of daylight, others that the sun remained overcast, allowing the Israelites to fight through the afternoon, when normally the sun would be too hot. We really don't know what happened—except that, as at Jericho, the defeat was the result of the Lord's power and not just the Israelites' military strength.

Division of the land   13:1–21:45

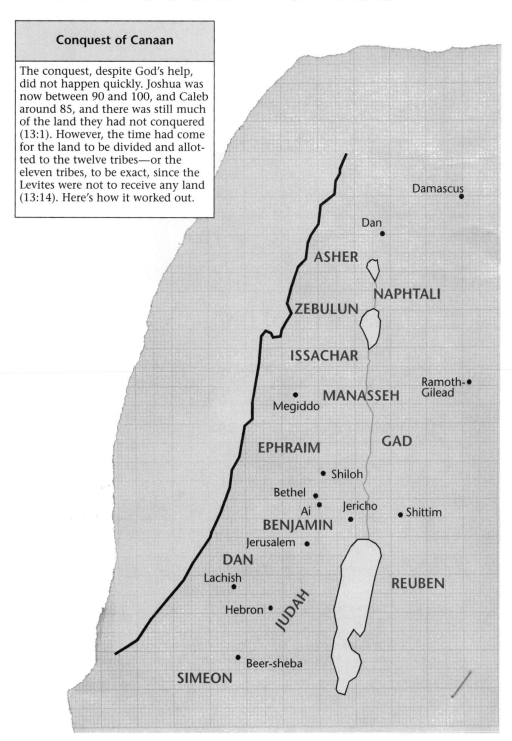

Conquest of Canaan

The conquest, despite God's help, did not happen quickly. Joshua was now between 90 and 100, and Caleb around 85, and there was still much of the land they had not conquered (13:1). However, the time had come for the land to be divided and allotted to the twelve tribes—or the eleven tribes, to be exact, since the Levites were not to receive any land (13:14). Here's how it worked out.

Damascus

Dan

ASHER

NAPHTALI

ZEBULUN

ISSACHAR

Ramoth-Gilead

MANASSEH

Megiddo

EPHRAIM

GAD

Shiloh

Bethel

Ai   Jericho   Shittim

BENJAMIN

Jerusalem

DAN

Lachish

REUBEN

JUDAH

Hebron

Beer-sheba

SIMEON

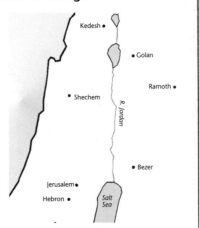

POSTCARD

Welcome to the Cities of Refuge!

Have you accidentally killed someone? Maybe you've run someone over in your chariot, or had an unfortunate accident during sword fighting practice. Whatever the case, if you're on the run, then run in our direction!

The cities of refuge are places where all those who have accidentally slain someone can find a haven. Here, you can escape vengeful relatives of the victim—sorry, accidentally dead person. With three cities on either side of the Jordan, we offer easy access for accidental killers wherever they are.

Admittedly you will have to have your application approved by a committee and, if approved, you'll have to stay in the city until the death of the high priest, but that seems a small price to pay compared with having your head kicked in by an angry relative.

Last days of Joshua   22:1–24:33

The division of the land brings immediate conflict. The tribes on the west of the Jordan build an altar on their return, and the rest of the Israelites see this as disobedience. According to Deuteronomy 12:5–14, Israel was only to have one altar. However, their actions are not because they want to become independent of the rest of the tribes, but because they want to prove their commitment to the entire nation. Even though they live outside the Promised Land, their altar is testimony to their allegiance and conflict is avoided.

The story of Joshua is the story of a job almost done. Joshua leaves his people with work still remaining. There are still lands to be taken—but he promises that they will take them if they only have faith in the Lord. His final speech is a condensed history of Israel, from Abraham's calling onward, a reminder to the Israelites that they are part of a grand scheme (24:1–13). The Lord has blessed them. They live in towns they didn't build and eat from trees they didn't plant (24:13).

The people respond with a renewed commitment to serve the Lord and to remain faithful. Yet the seeds of doubt remain. There are still those in Israel who have idols (24:23), although they promise to throw them away. After all the Lord has done for them, there are still people who turn to other gods.

For all its victories, for all the final promises from the people, the book ends on a knife edge: will the Israelites complete the task begun by Joshua? Or will they fall at the final hurdle?

Judges
A mad, bad world

The book of Judges takes us from the time of Joshua to the establishment of the monarchy. Its title comes from 2:16, "From time to time, the Lord would choose special leaders known as judges . . ." These judges were not only leaders in battle, they decided legal cases and in some cases performed religious rituals.

Who: Traditionally the authorship has been assigned to Samuel, but there is no evidence of this. It is certainly possible that he assembled some of the accounts, but Judges is probably the work of several hands.

When: The book probably dates from the tenth century BC, around the time of the monarchy (hence the constant refrain about Israel having no king). The events described take place following the death of Joshua around 1390 BC.

What: Judges paints a picture of a dark and often violent society. It starts with a captured king having his thumbs and big toes cut off (1:6–7) and goes downhill from there. Faced with one of the grimmest books of the Bible, many readers wonder what moral purpose it has. But Judges is a book about a real society—a society that abandons God. One recurring phrase sums up the book: "Israel wasn't ruled by a king, and everyone did what they thought was right."

Quick Guide

Author
Unknown

Type
History

Purpose
The history of the violent early years in the Promised Land: a depiction of a society without God.

Key verse
17:6: "This was before kings ruled Israel, so all the Israelites did whatever they thought was right."

If you remember one thing about this book . . .
A society without rules is not freedom, but anarchy.

Your 15 minutes start now
Read chapters 2, 4–5, 7–8, 13–16

Israel had the choice of following the God who had led them out of Egypt, the God who had made covenants with Moses and Abraham, or choosing the gods of Canaan. Time and time again they chose Canaan, and so the book is a slow, painful, brutal descent into anarchy and lawlessness. It's like a vicious circle: the people turn away from God; God sends a foreign nation to punish them; the people cry out to God for deliverance; God sends them a "judge" to deliver them. Then the people turn away again . . . Judges is about the faithlessness of the people, but it is also about the faithfulness of God. He, unlike his people, took promises seriously.

The Route Through Judges

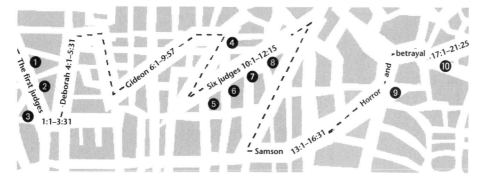

87

The judges

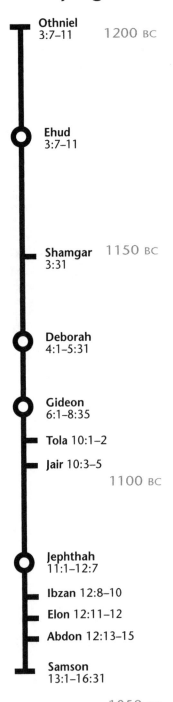

Othniel
3:7–11   1200 BC

Ehud
3:7–11

Shamgar   1150 BC
3:31

Deborah
4:1–5:31

Gideon
6:1–8:35

Tola 10:1–2

Jair 10:3–5

1100 BC

Jephthah
11:1–12:7

Ibzan 12:8–10

Elon 12:11–12

Abdon 12:13–15

Samson
13:1–16:31

1050 BC

The first judges   1:1–3:31

The Israelites are encamped at Gilgal, near Jericho. The Canaanites, although beaten, are still living in the cities—mainly located in the central hill country. God wanted the Israelites to take over a clean, pure land. That meant completely expelling the people who lived there before, but soon the Israelites are starting to compromise and to forget their task. One after another, the tribes fail to complete the task (1:21, 27–36).

And so the Canaanites remained in the land, like an infection in the body. The cure was not complete, the infection flared up again, the Israelites forgot their God and turned to the gods of the Canaanites. Instead of turning Canaan into the Lord's land, they managed to adopt the ways, customs, morals and religion of the Canaanites. God outlines the consequences. They will not be secure and safe. Other nations will defeat them. They wanted to be like the Canaanites; now they will know what it is to be a defeated and weak nation. Just like the Canaanites.

The section begins with a flashback to the death of Joshua. Following his death, Israel remains faithful for a while, but after only one generation, they start to worship Baal and Astarte and other gods from nearby nations (2:10–13).

Then we are introduced to the judges—leaders who would come to Israel's rescue. But even the judges could not change Israel's stubbornness and refusal to obey God (2:18–19). God therefore uses the enemies of Israel as instruments of his justice: the Canaanites, the Sidonians, Hivites, Amorites, Perizzites, Hivites, Jebusites. And, of course, the Philistines (3:1–6).

❶ Othniel   3:7–11

Defeats King Cushan Rishathaim.

❷ Ehud   3:12–30

Assassinates Eglon, the fat Moabite king. He attacks the king in his private apartments, leaving his sword in the body of the dead man, because the fat closes over the hilt and he can't get it out again. The servants are reluctant to go and investigate because they think the king is on the toilet!

Ehud is described as a left-handed man. This meant that he could conceal his dagger on the other side of his body. A right-handed man would have his dagger on the left-hand side so that he could reach across and draw it easily. The guards checked the wrong side. Ironically, Ehud was from the tribe of Benjamin, and "Benjamin" means "son of my right hand." Ehud leads the Israelites and routs the Moab army.

❸ Shamgar 3:31

Shamgar kills six hundred with a cattle prod—a pole sharpened with a metal tip. He is not given the title of judge—and some experts believe he may actually have been a Canaanite rather than an Israelite—but he fits the profile. And he was very handy with a sharp stick.

Deborah 4:1–5:31

Deborah is the only female judge and also a prophetess. She calls Barak to attack the Canaanites, but he puts a condition on obeying her—insisting that she should accompany him. Because of this, he does not get the honor of completing the victory.

Barak defeats Sisera's army, as his iron chariots are bogged down in the flooded Kidron valley. Sisera escapes and hides in the tent of Jael. The custom of the time forbade any man other than her husband to enter a woman's tent. Sisera must have thought it the ideal hiding place, but while he is sleeping, Jael drives a tent peg through his head.

This, to put it mildly, is against the laws of hospitality, which put an obligation on the host to protect guests from harm. But it appears that Jael's husband, Heber, had already decided to join with Israel, so although she was breaking the laws of hospitality, she was keeping faith with her husband.

The song of Deborah that follows is one of the oldest poems in the Bible. It celebrates the victory, praises Jael and ends with a prayer to God to keep them strong.

Gideon 6:1–8:35

For seven years the country is oppressed by the Midianites—a particularly harsh oppression that led to many Israelites hiding in the mountains. Enter Gideon—who is also called Jerub-Baal—who initially is not sure of his calling and asks God for signs, which the Lord gives him (6:20–23, 36–40). He leads his men against the Midianites but not before God reduces the force from 32,000 to 300. God wants to demonstrate that it is he who will deliver Israel, not Israel's own strength. He attacks in the night and such confusion is caused in the Midianite camp that they start to kill each other (7:15–25).

Gideon is offered the kingship of Israel, but refuses. Then, a shocking event happens. He asks the people to give him gold earrings from the plunder. He melts them down and makes an idol, which is worshiped in his hometown. This from the man who had started his career tearing down the altars to Canaanite gods. Gideon is like the book of Judges in one man. He is blessed by God, he is hugely successful, and then he turns to foreign gods. He embodies the moral confusion and decay of the times.

❹ Abimelech 9:1–57

Gideon's son, Abimelech, becomes the ruler of Israel through the simple, if brutal, act of murdering all his brothers. Well, not *quite* all. Jotham, the youngest son, escapes after telling a fable against his brother. After three

---

Questions, Questions
Superheroes

What about these numbers?
What about them?
Well, six hundred with nothing more than an oversized toothpick.
It was like a spear, actually.
And then there's Samson killing a thousand men with a jawbone.
Um. Yes.
Well?
There are two views: one is that the numbers aren't literal, but signify large amounts. So it may not have been an exact thousand but he did an awful lot of damage. It's like saying your favorite football player has scored tons of goals. It just means "a lot."
And the other view?
Well, it does say that the Spirit of the Lord came on Samson, so we're not talking about an ordinary soldier here. This is a man who is fighting with the power of God.
I see. So a sort of nuclear-powered jawbone then.
A God-powered jawbone.
Even better.

years, Abimelech faces a revolt at Shechem where, after initial success, he is killed when, during the siege, a woman drops a millstone on his head. To avoid the shame of being slain by a woman, his servant stabs him.

Six judges   10:1–12:15

❺ Tola   10:1–2
Nothing is known of Tola beyond the fact that he led Israel for 23 years.

❻ Jair   10:3–5
Another judge with a lot of donkey-riding sons. The donkeys indicate considerable wealth, or so I am told.

❼ Jephthah   11:1–12:7
Israel is once again oppressed, this time by the Philistines and Ammonites. Their rescuer is Jephthah, who had been driven from his home because he was an illegitimate child, and who became an outlaw. When his tribe members come to him and ask him to help, he agrees, providing that he will be their ruler if successful.

Before fighting the enemy he makes a vow: if God grants him victory, then he will sacrifice the first creature that comes out of his house to greet him on his return. It is a stupid vow and it has a terrible consequence. He returns home after the victory and the first creature to greet him is not a dog or domestic animal, but his daughter and only child. She is sacrificed.

Throughout the Old Testament, God condemns human sacrifice. It was a custom of some of the cultures around Israel, but God viewed it with disgust. Jephthah made a bad vow and it led to an even worse sacrifice. It is a sign of how far the society of the judges had fallen that even the "good men" acted with such folly and evil.

Details, Details . . .
You say shibboleth, I say sibboleth (12:5–6)

Jephthah's final battle is against the Ephraimites. When the Ephraimites try to escape across the river held by the Gilead forces, they were asked to say the word "shibboleth" which, ironically, means "flood." Apparently their accent gave them away; they pronounced the word with a hard "s," and they were killed.

---

❽ Ibzan, Elon and Abdon   12:8–15
Three minor judges who judged Israel for seven, ten and eight years respectively. It appears to have been a time of relative peace, since none of these judges is a military leader.

Samson   13:1–16:31

Samson, like Ehud earlier, was a lone hero, a man who single-handedly triumphed over his enemies. An angel appears to his parents and tells them that he is to be special. He is to be a Nazirite, which is from the Hebrew word meaning "dedicated." Samson is never to drink alcohol, never to cut his hair, never to eat or touch anything unclean and, indeed, his parents have to obey the same rules before their son is born.

Samson is a strange judge. He is motivated by an intense hatred for Philistines, but at the same time chases one of their women to be his wife. He is clever, witty and prodigiously strong; a man of God who sleeps with prostitutes and falls for totally unsuitable women.

There are times when he almost treats his high calling as a bit of a joke. He never really grasps that his power comes from, and can be taken away by, God. He is a man of passions and self-indulgence, a man who "does what he thinks right." Motivated by faith, he is also motivated by lust. His is a story of continual compromise and spiraling violence. His marriage to a Philistine woman ends in disaster, with his wife and father-in-law burned to death and thousands of Philistines killed. He has superhuman strength and all-too-human weaknesses. Samson is, in some ways, a picture of Israel —a set-apart and special hero, who constantly compromises and blurs the rules. However, Samson is always careful to give the glory to God and God supernaturally provides for him (15:11–20). For 20 years, Samson brings relative peace to Israel.

> **Details, Details . . .**
> **The city gates (16:1–3)**
>
> The city gates were more than just a large piece of joinery: they were a symbol of the national strength. By taking them, Samson is humiliating his enemies. Again.

Unsurprisingly, it was a woman who was his downfall. Samson's relationship with Delilah has become the stuff of Hollywood legend, a kind of romantic coupling like Romeo and Juliet. This is a complete misconception. It was not a romantic love, but a single-minded obsession. Samson was obsessed with Delilah from the moment he saw her, but Delilah was only in it for the money. Three times she asks him for the secret of his strength and tries to betray him; three times he resists telling her the truth and escapes. (You'd have thought that he was beginning to suspect something, but apparently not.) Finally she nags him into telling the truth.

He has compromised with the rules once too often. "He did not realize that the Lord had stopped helping him," runs the chilling verse (16:20). Finally, blind and chained, he is paraded before the Philistines for their entertainment. His eyes are darkened, but, perhaps for the first time, Samson can see clearly. His strength always came from God and now he calls on God for the last time. The Lord hears him and Samson pushes apart the columns that hold up the roof. The Philistines brought out Samson to provide entertainment, and he brought the house down.

POSTCARD

Our coastal nation has always had an affinity for the sea. We started life as inhabitants of the island of Crete—or Caphtor as it was known then—and settled along the Mediterranean coast during the time of the Egyptians.

We are a seagoing people, and four of our five major cities are along the coast.

Despite the rumors spread by some of our near neighbors, we are a cultured and sophisticated civilization with advanced techniques in pottery, weaponry and assorted metalwork (especially shackles). The temples to gods such as Dagon and Ashtoreth are full of fine arts and crafts.

We like to think that our gates are always open to visitors, but this is mainly because someone has ripped them off.

Welcome to Philistia!

Philistia

Ekron

Ashdod

Gath

Ashkelon

Gaza

Jerusalem

Israel

Horror and betrayal   17:1–21:25

The final section of Judges contains shocking scenes of almost meaning-less violence. It is not clear whether they follow on from Samson, or whether they occurred at an earlier date. They appear to form a kind of appendix to the main narrative.

❾ Micah and the priest   17:1–31

The story of Micah and the Levite priest begins with a curious tale that illustrates the terrible way in which the Israelite religion had become cor-rupted. Micah steals money from his mother, then returns it when she places a curse on whoever has taken it. They turn the silver into an idol to worship. Then a young Levite arrives and Micah takes him into his employment, apparently under the belief that all he has to do is employ a priest and he will be all right (17:13).

The tribe of Dan, however, takes Micah's priest and his idol and sets up a new place of worship in Laish. The story seems to imply that the people, far from having faith in God, had faith in priests and statues. They believed in possessions, either possessing the idol, or possessing the "holy man." The priest, for his part, is only interested in gaining power and influence, and tells whoever employs him whatever they wish to hear.

❿ The Levite's wife   19:1–30

The second story shows that Israel at this time was every bit as bad as Sodom. The story parallels almost exactly the story of Lot in Sodom, but this time there is no divine vengeance to destroy the town. A Levite is given shelter by an old man in Gibeah. With him is his wife, who has been unfaithful to him, but whom he has persuaded to return with him. The men of Gibeah demand that the Levite is given to them to have sex with. The old man refuses, even offering his daughters instead. In the end, the panicking Levite throws his wife out and she is brutally raped and mur-dered. The Levite then cuts her body into twelve pieces, and sends the pieces to the rest of the tribes of Israel. Shocked and outraged, the other tribes descend on the Benjaminites and almost completely annihilate them.

The other tribes take a vow never to marry anyone from Benjamin, but even this vow is "evaded." The Benjaminites are tacitly allowed to go and abduct women. After all, if the women are taken by force, then no one is guilty of giving their daughter and no oaths have been broken.

The whole episode is a grubby and brutal end to a frequently brutal book. No one comes out of it with any credit, not even the poor, abused woman, who, after all, was only there because she had been unfaithful to her hus-band and had run away. It is as if all the moral degradation and ethical confusion has been distilled into one chain of events. Thus we have adul-terous women, sex-crazed men, husbands who will callously sacrifice their wives to save their skins, tribes who take an oath and then find a way round it. It is a violent, filthy and morally corrupt episode.

But then, that's what happens when "everyone does as he sees fit."

Aram

Hadad
Hadad might mean "maker of loud noise," indicating perhaps a thunder-god, or the god of hi-fi.

Rimmon
Rimmon was worshiped in Damascus. He has been linked with Rammanu, the Assyrian god of wind, rain and storm.

Philistia

Dagon
Dagon may have been some kind of vegetation or harvest deity. Or his name may have been derived from *dagh*, meaning "fish." So perhaps he was a fish and vegetable deity. Maybe he was the god of fish and chips.

Baal-zebul
The name means "Baal the prince," but it is deliberately changed by the Jews to Baal-zebub, which means "lord of the flies." This Philistine deity was worshiped at Ekron (2 Ki 1:2, 3, 6, 16). His name has been appropriated as the name of the devil, but in fact, he wasn't that important. And anyway, they were only making fun of the Philistines.

Moab

Chemosh
A tricky one. While one part in the Bible says Chemosh is the god of the Ammonites (Jg 11:24), he was actually a historical figure. However, it might simply be that the king took the name of his god. The Bible also implies that Chemosh demanded human sacrifice (2 Ki 3:27).

PHOENICIA

ARAM (Syria)

ISRAEL

AMMON

PHILISTIA

MOAB

JUDAH

EDOM

Ammon

Molech aka Milcom.
The name probably meant simply "king." He was worshiped at places such as the Valley of Hinnom, —for this was a god who demanded the burning of the sacrificial victims. His worship becomes increasingly frequent in the later history of Israel and Judah. King Ahaz of Judah was a keen follower, who sacrificed his son (2 Ki 16:3).

Gods of other nations

The Israelites were surrounded by other nations, each with their own gods, and, throughout their history, God's chosen people chose someone else to worship. Many of these gods were primitive fertility gods, worshiped because they were thought to produce crops and livestock. The Israelites, however, worshiped a God who had power over the whole of creation, not just the agricultural part.

Ruth

Love and duty

Ruth is a book about family duty and, more importantly, affection and friendship. The events of the book are set in the time of the judges, during a period of peace between Israel and Moab. As the book records an incident in the history of the family of David, it is likely that it was written during the time of the monarchy.

Who: Author unknown.

When: Date unknown, but probably written later than the time of the judges.

What: The striking element here is that the person who most embodies selfless love is not an Israelite, but a Moabite. Several times in the book the author reminds his reader that she is "Ruth the Moabitess"—a woman from a despised and hated enemy of Israel. Her goodness and love shine through. She is a prime example of how participation in the kingdom of God is nothing to do with nationality, but a matter of loving God and following his commands.

Quick Guide

Author

Unknown

Type

History

Purpose

A story showing dutiful love and friendship.

Key verse

1:16 "Please don't tell me to leave you and return home! I will go where you go, I will live where you live; your people will be my people, your God will be my God."

If you remember one thing about this book . . .

God is a God for all nations and all people.

Your 10 minutes start now

Read the whole thing. It's only four chapters.

Landmark: Redemption

The word "redemption" occurs twenty-three times in Ruth. The concept is a key one in the history of Israel. Redemption means paying a price to save someone from evil. Through the selfless love of Ruth and Boaz, Naomi is redeemed. She is given a grandson, and through that, a future. She is brought back from hunger and homelessness to security and contentment.

The author may intend a parallel with the way David—a descendant of Ruth—saved his people. But, more than that, Ruth points to the way in which God's selfless love redeems his people. The way in which Boaz recognizes his obligations is an echo of the way in which God keeps his promises. And it is through another descendant of David—Jesus—that God was truly to bring his people back to him.

The Route Through Ruth

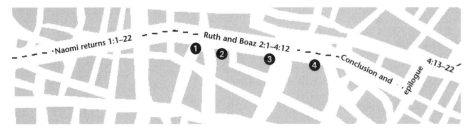

Naomi returns 1:1–22   Ruth and Boaz 2:1–4:12   ❶ ❷ ❸ ❹   Conclusion and epilogue 4:13–22

Naomi returns   1:1–22

The book opens in the time of the judges (1:1). Due to a famine in Israel, Elimelech, a citizen of Bethlehem, took refuge in Moab. There both he and his two sons died, leaving his wife Naomi and Orpah and Ruth, her two widowed daughter-in-laws (1:5). Naomi decides to return to Israel and, initially, Orpah and Ruth accompany her. Orpah decides to return to her home (1:14) but Ruth, in a moving display of fidelity and affection, commits herself to Naomi (1:16–17). Even though Naomi pleads with her three times to return to Moab, Ruth is determined to stay with her mother-in-law. They arrive in Bethlehem empty, penniless and destitute. Ironically, it is the beginning of harvest.

Ruth and Boaz   2:1–4:12

❶ Ruth gleans

Ruth gleans in the fields of Boaz—a rich relative of her father-in-law Elimelech. Old Testament laws insisted that grain that had been dropped on the ground should be left there for the poor to glean (Le 19:10; 23:22). Boaz notices Ruth and offers protection, allowing her to glean as long as she wants in his field, protecting her from harassment of any kind and providing refreshment for her (2:8–9). Indeed, he goes way beyond his duties, instructing his men to deliberately drop grain in her path so that she has plenty to collect. It is a remarkably sensitive response to her position—but he has heard of her support and affection for Naomi and it is clear that he admires her commitment.

❷ Ruth loves Boaz

As a single woman Ruth was vulnerable. There are clear times in Ruth when Boaz acts to protect her from violence or sexual harassment, so it is vital for her future that she finds a family to be a part of. Naomi helps Ruth with her dress and appearance and sends her to Boaz. When Boaz goes to sleep, Ruth goes and lies at his feet, symbolically requesting his protection. Moved by her loyalty, he agrees to marry her (3:6–13).

❸ Boaz redeems Ruth

Duty is not done for profit. A relative is interested because he wants to get Elimelech's land, but when Boaz points out that buying the land also commits the man to marrying Ruth and giving her children, he backs out. That would mean that the property he already owned would have to be shared between his present children and any that Ruth might have (4:1–6).

❹ The agreement

So Boaz and he make a legal agreement, sealed by handing each other one of their sandals. Exchanging footwear might seem odd—all right it *is* odd—but this was the customary way to show that the agreement was sealed. (I don't suggest you try handing over one of your trainers next time you sign a contract.) Everything has been done with thoroughness and propriety, and the elders pronounce their blessing.

Puzzling Points

Does Ruth seduce Boaz?

There are some experts who believe that Ruth manipulates Boaz; that by going and lying with him she implicates him. They argue that "lying at his feet" is a euphemism for "having sex with." In this hypothesis, Ruth and Naomi appear to work together to "catch" Boaz. However, this interpretation doesn't really take into account the context of the action and Boaz's reaction.

First, we're in the time of the judges. The country was in a state of general moral degradation. Considering that Tamar posed as a prostitute in order to secure her marriage to Judah, Ruth's actions are the height of propriety.

Second, there is no indication that Boaz acts like a trapped man. He gives Ruth more than she asks for, and he persuades her closer kinsman not to redeem her.

Finally, the Bible is not coy about sex. If it had wanted to say that Ruth and Boaz slept together, it would have said it. Ruth's actions are symbolic and moving. Boaz is inspired by her, not ensnared.

Boaz and Ruth are likened to Jacob and Leah and Rachel, and also to Perez —one of Boaz's ancestors. Perez was an appropriate model, since his parents—Judah and Tamar—were married in accordance with custom and obligation (although, admittedly, Judah had to be somewhat maneuvered into following the marriage customs).

Conclusion and epilogue   4:13–22

This book is not just about devotion and duty. It is also about the preservation of the "house of David." The book was probably written as an episode in the history of David's family. Ruth and Boaz marry and they have a son, Obed. The book ends showing that the line of David was preserved. Obed was David's grandfather. Through Boaz and Ruth recognizing their obligations and acting with love, generosity and courage, the family line was preserved—the line that would lead to King David, and beyond to Jesus.

Landmark: Harvest

Harvest in Old Testament times usually took place around April and May. Barley was the first crop to be harvested, followed by wheat a few weeks later.

The men would move through the field cutting the wheat or barley with sickles, followed by the women who would gather up the cuttings into sheaves. Gleaning was the act of going through the field and collecting the stalks that had been missed.

The wheat was then taken to the threshing floor, where the grains were removed from the stalks. The wheat would then be winnowed—tossed or thrown in the air, either by hand or with winnowing forks, to separate the straw from the wheat grains. Threshing floors were wide open spaces that allowed the wind to get in and blow away the straw, while the grains would simply fall to the ground. The wheat would then be sifted to remove any other impurities, put into bags and then either stored or taken to be milled into flour.

It's about time someone invented the tractor.

For ancient peoples a successful harvest was cause for great celebration, providing the staple foodstuff for a country or area. There were laws and traditions about harvest that had to be obeyed. Gleaning had to be left to the poor, whose right it was to go through the fields and gather up what was left. The owners were not to take absolutely everything.

The best of the harvest was supposed to be presented to God—a symbolic reminder of who it was who gave them the harvest in the first place.

1 Samuel
Shepherds and kings

First and Second Samuel are actually one book that is divided into two parts for the simple reason you couldn't fit the whole thing on one scroll. The history continues in the book of Kings which, again, originally formed one book. They are named after the prophet Samuel—the man used by God to establish a kingship in Israel. Samuel was a kingmaker, a prophet who not only anointed both Saul and David, but was also responsible for defining the new structure of the kingdom.

Who: It is not known who the author was; it may have been edited from a variety of original sources.

Samuel mentions one such source—*The Book of Jashar* (2 Sa 1:18), but there are others mentioned in Chronicles, including *The Book of the Annals of King David* (1 Ch 27:24), *The Records of Samuel the Seer*, *The Records of Nathan the Prophet* and *The Records of Gad the Seer* (1 Ch 29:29).

When: Whoever the author was, he probably lived after the death of Solomon, since he makes reference to the two kingdoms that only came into existence after Solomon's death.

Quick Guide

Author
Variety of sources

Type
History

Purpose
A history of Israel's first king, Saul, and the rise of its second, David.

Key verse
15:22 "Does the LORD really want sacrifices and offerings? No! He doesn't want your sacrifices. He wants you to obey him."

If you remember one thing about this book . . .
God wants our obedience, not just our good intentions.

Your 15 minutes start now
Read chapters 1–3, 8, 10, 16–17, 20, 31

What: 1 and 2 Samuel cover about one hundred years, from the close of the time of the judges to the establishment of the kingdom under David. It also records the terms and conditions, as it were, of that kingship, the fact that all kings were under the rule of God.

The tale is traced through the lives of three men: Samuel, Saul and David; the kingmaker and the first two kings. The first part deals with Samuel and Saul and is a contrast between the faithful prophet and the tragically disobedient king. Saul should have had it all, but he was constantly relying on his own judgment, rather than obeying God's commands. As the book continues, we see Saul as an increasingly unstable figure, prone to mood swings and ever more desperate to hold on to his kingdom—a kingdom that God has already promised to someone else.

The Route Through 1 Samuel

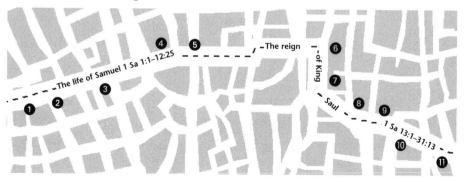

The life of Samuel 1 Sa 1:1–12:25

The reign of King Saul

1 Sa 13:1–31:13

The life of Samuel   1:1–12:25

❶ Birth and childhood   1:1–4:1

Like many of the great men of the Bible, Samuel's birth is special. His mother is unable to have children—for which she is mocked by her husband's other wife. In tears at the temple in Shiloh, she is assured by Eli the priest that she will have a son and, sure enough, she gives birth to a boy. She names him Samuel, which sounds like "heard from God," and when he is just a few years old, she presents him to Eli to help him in the temple. In her prayers, Hannah remembers God's care for the poor and the helpless. Life and death, riches and poverty are determined by God (2:1–10).

Eli's sons are dishonest priests, cheating the people and taking sacrificial meat for themselves. Although Eli rebukes them (2:22–25), it is clear that he is too indulgent to their vices (2:29). God sends a prophet to tell Eli that his sons will die, that his family will bear the consequences of their sins and that another will be chosen (2:26–36).

"In those days, the LORD hardly ever spoke directly to people . . ." (3:1). In the night the boy Samuel hears the voice of the Lord. The Lord repeats his message to Eli and from then on the people realize that God speaks to Samuel (3:1–4:1).

Puzzling Points

Why don't some of the details match?

The writer of the Old Testament histories took his material from a variety of sources and documents.

However, he doesn't write history as we would write it today. There are no footnotes, no references. Sometimes the chronology is out. Duplicate and parallel accounts are given of the same event, sometimes with differences in the details. There are, for example, two accounts of Saul's crowning, and two of David's introduction to Saul. There are different accounts of Saul's death.

While most of these discrepancies can be explained, it is curious to most readers they are there at all. Why didn't the historian do his work better? Why didn't he sort the mess out? But the writer wasn't thinking that way. He was simply setting down the events as honestly and comprehensively as he could, using whatever materials came to hand.

❷ The ark is captured   4:1–7:2

This episode demonstrates how far understanding of God and his Law has fallen in the days since the conquest. The ark has been residing at Hebron. Hophni and Phinehas, the two sons of Eli, treat the ark as if it were a kind of pagan idol, as if God could be controlled by it. The Philistines overcome their fear, defeat Israel, capture the ark and kill the two evil priests. Eli literally falls over with the shock, and dies (4:12–18).

Ironically, it is the Philistines who understand the power with whom they are dealing. After their god is smashed and their towns are hit with the plague, they send the ark back, not leading it, but letting God guide the transport (6:1–18). And what do the Israelites do when it returns? Of course. They peer inside it and treat it like a curiosity (6:19–21). The consequences are severe. The presence of God in your life is not always a very comfortable thing.

❸ National renewal   7:3–17

In the light of danger from the Philistines, Samuel calls for a national renewal of faith. The people destroy their pagan idols and meet together at Mizpah for prayer and sacrifice. Before the sacrifice can be completed, however, the Philistines attack. Their forces are caught in a huge thunderstorm and they panic. Samuel is appointed the last—and greatest—judge of Israel.

❹ We want a king   8:1–11:15

Even the holiest of men have trouble with their families. Samuel's sons are a copy of Eli's—dishonest and corrupt priests and leaders—and the people clamor for a king.

So Samuel gives them a king (9:1–10:16). God tells Samuel that Saul is the chosen king and Samuel anoints Saul. With the anointing comes the power and presence of God. Saul starts to prophesy (10:6, 9–13) and he is transformed. People who know Saul are somewhat surprised by this. "Is Saul a prophet?" they ask. Perhaps their surprise is a forewarning of the way in which, fundamentally, Saul's spirit is at odds with that of a true prophet.

Then Samuel calls the tribes together, and Saul is chosen—probably by the casting of lots (10:20–21). Saul is in some ways a curiously reluctant leader. He does not tell his relatives what has happened, and when the time comes to present him to Israel, nerves get the better of him and he has to be dragged out from hiding behind the baggage wagons! Saul's first actions, however, are successful and he defeats the Ammonites at Jabesh. The Israelites celebrate and Saul is confirmed as king.

❺ Samuel's farewell 12:1–25

Like Moses and Joshua, Samuel's farewell speech reminds the listeners of all that the Lord has done for Israel. His message is simple: "Don't worship idols, they can't help you; the Lord will take care of you. But if you do evil, you will be punished."

The reign of Saul
13:1–31:13

❻ Saul's first failure 13:1–15:34

Saul's success leads to a Philistine backlash. He appears to have made an arrangement to meet Samuel at Gilgal, but fearful of defeat, he takes it on himself to make a sacrifice. Saul's failure is more than a failure of nerve. He thought he could act independently of Samuel, that he could disregard the instructions of God, given through his prophet. It may not have been much in and of itself, but it is indicative of Israel's perennial failure from now on —a people and monarchy who simply would not obey the Lord and listen to his prophets. Samuel tells Saul that he will never found a dynasty. It will not be his son who succeeds to the throne of Israel. His reign is over almost as soon as it has begun.

Saul's unsuitability is further demonstrated when he makes a foolish vow, leaving his soldiers so weak that they are forced to eat unclean meat (14:31–35). Jonathan, Saul's son, unwittingly breaks the vow, so Saul believes that he must be killed, but the army rises up to save him (14:36–46). We're suddenly back in the time of the Judges, with men making foolish vows that lead to disaster. And God is silent.

This incident gives a clue to Saul's character. He was always trying to do the right thing, but managing to do it in the wrong way. It was not wrong to sacrifice, nor to fast, but it was wrong for Saul to take it on himself—

Questions, Questions
Is God a republican?

So, God is against the monarchy, then?
Sorry?
Well, it says in the Bible that he never wanted Israel to be a monarchy. He warns them against having a king.
That's right, but you have to see it in more of a spiritual context.
Um . . . meaning, what?
It wasn't just that they were asking for a king, it was that they were rejecting the fundamental kingship of God. God says, "I am really the one they have rejected as their king."
Where does he say that, then?
It's all in 1 Samuel chapter 8.
OK, but look what he says about kings—he says that a king will take their sons for the army, enslave their children, take their best lands, impose harsh taxes and force them to fill in lots of paperwork.
Sorry?
All right, maybe not the paperwork. But all the rest. God obviously isn't a big fan of kings. He's a republican.
No, he's not. The point is, Israel already had a king; God was their king. But that wasn't good enough for them. They wanted to be like other nations. All the nations around them had kings, so Israel wanted one as well. God gave them what they wanted. In fact, the country's second ruler—King David —was one of their most heroic figures. So, even though it wasn't God's plan, he still worked through the monarchy.

Puzzling Points

Why does God want the children killed?

God tells Saul to destroy the Amalekites completely —not only their soldiers, not only their possessions, but the women and the babies as well. It seems cruel and harsh. So why? Isn't this the God of love and forgiveness? This is a complicated question and no answer is entirely satisfactory.

We have to remember that the times were extremely brutal and cruel. It was a dog-eat-dog world. The Amalekites had killed children themselves, so they were not exactly innocent victims (1 Sa 15:33).

Throughout the Old Testament, God is concerned for Israel's purity. He wants it to be free from contamination by other people and cultures. These were cultures that were completely opposed to God, harsh, brutal regimes worshiping harsh, demeaning gods.

But two wrongs do not make a right. And the children! Why the children? In the end we just don't know. All we know is that God is a God of justice and those who are righteous will find an eternal rest with him. We cannot ignore these issues, but equally, they do not fit into our cozy schemes and neat theologies.

▷**81**

I can feel a headache coming on . . .

and to ask his men to fast when they were in active combat was foolish. When told by God to destroy everything that the Amalekites have, he kept back the cattle, intending to sacrifice them later. Samuel's reply sums up the problem with Saul: "Does the LORD really want sacrifices and offerings? No! He doesn't want your sacrifices. He wants you to obey him" (15:22).

❼ A new king   16:1–13

Samuel's final act as the Lord's prophet is to anoint a new king (16:1–13). Following the promptings of the Lord, he goes to Jesse, a resident of Bethlehem. Samuel rejects one tall, good-looking young candidate after another. Eventually he settles on Jesse's youngest son, David, a shepherd who has to be called in from the fields. Job done, Samuel returns to Ramah, where he was eventually to die (25:1).

David, a gifted musician, is invited to court to play for Saul. Saul has gone from bad to worse. Now he is suffering from an evil spirit—and becoming increasingly subject to mood swings and paranoia.

❽ David and Goliath
17:1–58

The story of David and Goliath is one of the most famous stories in the Bible. Much has been made of David's speed, being unencumbered by armor, and also of the fact that he didn't have to get into one-to-one contact with the giant. He was a sniper, not a wrestler. He picked the giant off with a well-aimed pebble, he didn't engage in a martial arts match. But the real point about David's defeat of Goliath is that he relied totally upon God. David's faith is in stark contrast to the fear of the rest of the army. The army was scared of a giant, but David trusted God.

It is this, above all, that Saul recognizes. He is envious of David, and jealous of his successes, but what really gets him going is that he knows David has a close relationship with the Lord. "Saul was afraid of David, because the LORD was helping David and was no longer helping him" (18:12). Whatever Saul tries against David doesn't work. He lures him into apparently suicidal battles with the promise of his daughter in marriage. He throws a spear at David when the boy is playing the harp, which by any measure is taking music criticism a bit too far. But nothing works. Everything David touches turns to gold. And Saul descends further into bitterness and increasingly erratic behavior.

Indeed, such is God's presence with the boy that, when David flees to Samuel's side, those who are sent to kill him start prophesying (19:18–24). Even Saul is struck down by the power.

⑨ The cave 24:1–22

Saul's attempts to capture and kill David are repeatedly frustrated—worse, he finds himself at David's mercy. Saul goes into a cave to relieve himself, unaware that David is hiding in there. David cuts off a piece of Saul's cloak to show that he could have killed the king, but didn't. Later he addresses the king from a distance, trying to make his case. Saul is struck with remorse and, weeping, promises to spare David, merely asking him to spare his family.

⑩ The Witch of Endor 28:3–25

Saul, ever more desperate, now consults a witch, in direct contravention of God's commands. This is a difficult passage—it may be that the ghost was truly Samuel's recently departed spirit, allowed by God to appear to the woman; it may be a deception, an evil spirit in the form of Samuel. Or it may be some early form of séance, where the witch simply pictured Samuel's words and presence in her mind. Samuel sounds more touchy than anything else. "Why are you bothering me by bringing me up like this?" he asks (28:15). It almost sounds as if he had to get out of the bath. And anyway, he doesn't have anything new to say to Saul. Saul has plumbed new depths in his desperation, but nothing has changed.

⑪ Death of Saul 31:1–13

The end has come for Saul. Facing the Philistines in a battle on Mount Gilboa, his sons—including Jonathan—are killed. Seriously wounded, in the end, Saul takes his own life. Then he is beheaded by the Philistines and his body nailed to the wall of one of their cities. His body is eventually retrieved by a rescue party from Jabesh and buried in relative obscurity, under a small tree. So died the first king of Israel. Saul—so gifted in many ways, so courageous, but so proud, unstable and tragically flawed.

Puzzling Points

Does God send an evil spirit on Saul? (16:14)

It doesn't necessarily indicate that God is causing this, but it indicates that it is only through God's permission that evil spirits can operate at all. We should also not forget Saul's role in this. His rebellious nature and disobedience are the direct cause of God's spirit leaving him. He is not some kind of innocent party at the mercy of forces beyond his control. His moods and violence and his future behavior are conditioned as much by his own character and his refusal to bow to God's will as they are by supernatural forces. The evil spirit is merely working on what is there already.

▷278

If David was already at court, why doesn't Saul know who he is? (17:55–8)

David wasn't a permanent resident at court, so there is no reason for Saul to know his family details. Equally, Saul may simply be wondering whether he came from a family of warriors. And he may well suspect that he is watching his successor.

2 Samuel
The reign of King David

This is the story of David's triumph—and his downfall. It is the story of how Israel's greatest king was to lose control of his family and almost his kingdom. Yet it is also the story of how he was to discover new depths of God's love and forgiveness.

Who and **When:** See Introduction to 1 Samuel.

What: 2 Samuel continues the story of Israel's first monarchs, from the accession of King David. The first seven years of David's reign are spent in civil war, with David battling against Saul's son, Ishbosheth. When this conflict is concluded, David becomes the king of Israel.

David goes on to conquer the enemies of Israel and develop the nation into a kind of small empire. Under his leadership, the country reaches its largest geographical area. He transforms Jerusalem into the capital of the country, installing the ark of the covenant in place and planning a magnificent temple. It was a golden age for the country.

And yet, the book of Samuel is nothing if not brutally honest. If it celebrates the political and military triumphs of the king, it also depicts his personal flaws and failures. David himself commits adultery and murder; his family is torn apart by incestuous rape, assassination and rebellion.

In the end, perhaps the second part of Samuel is less about national glory and more about personal forgiveness. David certainly defeated Israel's enemies, but he also discovered more about Israel's God—a God who was to show his forgiveness to the king by promising that his family would reign in the land forevermore.

Quick Guide

Author
Various sources

Type
History

Purpose
The history of the reign of King David—his God-given successes, and his human failings.

Key verses
7:11–13 "Now I promise that you and your descendants will be kings. I'll choose one of your sons to be king when you reach the end of your life and are buried in the tomb of your ancestors. I'll make him a strong ruler and no one will be able to take his kingdom away from him."

If you remember one thing about this book . . .
Sin has consequences, but God will always forgive if we ask.

Your 15 minutes start now
Read chapters 5–7, 11–12, 13, 15, 18

The Route Through 2 Samuel

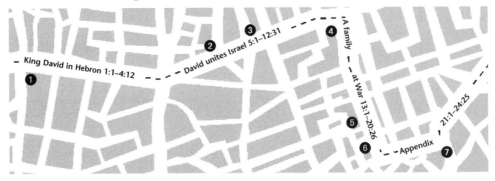

King David in Hebron 1:1–4:12

David unites Israel 5:1–12:31

A family at War 13:1–20:26

Appendix 21:1–24:25

King David in Hebron   1:1–4:12

Saul's death—Part 2

The second part of Samuel opens with David mourning Saul's death (1:1–16). This account seems to conflict with the account in 1 Sa 31:1–13, where Saul takes his own life. Perhaps the messenger was hoping to gain favor, thinking that, as Saul was David's enemy, he would be rewarded for killing the king. Instead he is punished and David sings a lament over the death of Saul and Jonathan (1:17–27).

With Saul dead, David is free to claim the kingship. However, there is still opposition. Saul's son Ishbosheth is installed as king over Israel by the commanders of Saul's armies. David rules Judah, the southern half of Israel, and is king in Hebron for seven and a half years (2 Sa 2:1–5:3). This is a time of civil war, of family feuds and bitter rivalries. As David's power increases, the feuds within the opposing army get worse.

❶ Assassinations and feuds

Ishbosheth fast loses credibility with his troops. His army commander defects to David—and is later assassinated by Joab, David's general and all-round enforcer (3:22–27).

David unites Israel   5:1–12:31

Finally Ishbosheth himself is assassinated and David becomes king of all Israel. He conquers Jerusalem by sending his troops up through underground water tunnels (5:6–12; 1 Ch 11:1–9; 14:1–2).

Once more, there is war against the Philistines, and David illustrates the difference between his approach and Saul's. David asks God what to do at every juncture. The Lord says that he will deliver the Philistines into David's hands, and David defeats them at Rephaim (5:17–25; 1 Ch 14:8–7).

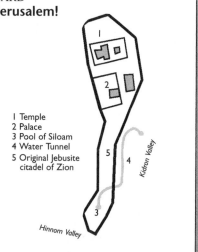

POSTCARD
Welcome to Jerusalem!

Set high in the hills of what is now called Judah, this ancient city has until very recently been home to the Jebusites—a Canaanite tribe who called the city "Jebus" and the fortress "Zion."

However, following the capture by King David, a new palace has been built, and Jerusalem, as it is now called, is the capital of the new United Kingdom of Israel.

However, the city is not just the home of royalty, it is also a religious center. King David has brought the ark of the covenant to Jerusalem and has also sought planning permission (from God) for a magnificent new temple.

As it is high in the hills, the water supply can be a bit problematic, but supplies are brought in through an ingenious underground tunnel. Visitors are advised to boil the water, though, especially if there are invading soldiers wading through it.

1 Temple
2 Palace
3 Pool of Siloam
4 Water Tunnel
5 Original Jebusite citadel of Zion

Kidron Valley

Hinnom Valley

PARALLEL LINES

Much of 2 Samuel is repeated in Chronicles.

	2 Samuel	1 Chronicles
List of David's sons	3:2–5	3:1–4
DAVID UNITES ISRAEL	5:1–5	11:1–3
David captures Jerusalem	5:6–12	11:4–9; 14:1–2
David's sons in Jerusalem	5:13–16	14:3–7
Fights the Philistines	5:17–25	14:8–17
ARK COMES TO JERUSALEM	6:1–19	13:1–4; 15:1–16:3
GOD'S PROMISE	7:1–29	17:1–27
David's wars	8:1–18	18:1–17
Israel fights Ammon	10:1–19	19:1–19
The Rephaim	21:15–22	20:4–8
David's warriors	23:8–39	11:10–47
THE EVIL CENSUS	24:1–25	21:1–22:1

A Little Local Difficulty
Uzzah's death   6:3–8

Once again the power of the ark is evident. A man called Uzzah, anxious that the ark was going to fall from the cart, put out a hand to steady it. "The LORD God was very angry . . . and he killed Uzzah right there beside the chest" (6:7).

Why did God do this? We know that anyone who touched the ark was in danger, that, in some ways it was a "dangerous substance," but this is not someone mistreating the ark or even treating it trivially. This is someone trying to help. So why is God angry?

Although Uzzah's intent might have been good, he violated the laws laid down for handling the ark (Ex 25:15; Nu 4:5–6, 15). The fact, is there are no easy answers to this. God appears inflexible and legalistic here.

Perhaps the only comfort we can take from this is that David was angry at God. He was as mystified as the rest of us.

▷**63, 67**

❷ The return of the ark   6:1–19 ▷133

David was keenly aware—more so than any other of Israel's kings—of his obligations toward God. He arranges for the ark of the covenant to be brought to Jerusalem, which is to be the capital of the united Kingdom of Israel.

Leading the procession, David literally dances for joy in front of the ark as it is carried into the city. He is half naked, and his dance disgusts his wife Michal. She welcomes him with sarcasm and insults, but David doesn't care. He knows that before the Lord we cannot and should not try to stand on our dignity. Michal, who could not appreciate the childlike joy in David, would never have children of her own.

❸ The temple and the future 7:1–29

With the ark back in the city, David determines to build a temple to the Lord. The prophet Nathan initially welcomes the idea, but God gives Nathan a message. It will not be for David to build the temple. Indeed, the Lord doesn't need a temple. Instead he gives David a great promise. David and his descendants—the house of David—will be kings long into the future.

This is another of God's covenants with humanity—this time specific to the descendants of David. From this covenant, the Jews understood that the Messiah, the chosen one, would come from David's line. Its true and eventual fulfillment was found in Jesus, who was a direct descendant of David.

❹ David and Bathsheba   11:1–12:23

David begins a period of expansion. He defeats longstanding enemies (8:1–13; 10:1–19; 1 Ch 18:1–13; 1 Ch 19:1–19) and rules Israel "with fairness and justice" (8:15), as is shown in his dealings with Mephibosheth, Jonathan's crippled son (9:1–13).

Then it all goes wrong. David, taking a walk on the palace roof (the roofs were flat, he wasn't mountaineering), sees a woman bathing. She is Bathsheba, the wife of one of his army commanders; she and the king have an affair and Bathsheba gets pregnant (11:1–5).

David panics. First he recalls Uriah from the front, and tries to get him to sleep with Bathsheba. Uriah refuses; his men are doing without all creature comforts, so why should he be different? David tries to get him drunk, but that doesn't work either. In the end, the desperate king sends orders that Uriah is to be left fighting alone in the most dangerous part of the siege. The cheated husband is killed. Someone else fired the arrow, but David committed the murder (11:6–26).

It is a defining moment in David's life—as defining as the moment when he strode out to face Goliath. He must have known that, even if no one else did, the Lord knew what had happened—and, indeed, the Lord *does* know. When Nathan the prophet reveals David's guilt through a story, David does not argue. He does not plead or excuse himself. He admits his sin, asks for, and receives, forgiveness. Despite David's prayers and fasting and painful entreaties, the child dies. Sin can always be forgiven, but it always has consequences (12:1–23).

> ### Details, Details . . .
> ### Paternity test (11:4)
>
> The Bible records that Bathsheba was "purifying herself" at the time when David saw her, and that when she came to him she had "purified herself from her uncleanness" (11:4 NIV). It indicates that Bathsheba had just finished her monthly period and was washing according to the ancient Levitical laws (Le 15:19–30). The implication is that she cannot have been pregnant when David slept with her. It is the closest the Old Testament gets to a DNA test.

In time, Bathsheba conceives another child—a son who turns out to be Solomon, the king to succeed David, a child whom the Lord loved so much that he called him by a special name (12:24–25).

A family at war   13:1–20:26

David's children   13:1–14:33

One of the lessons of the Bible is that virtuous parents do not guarantee virtuous children. Eli and Samuel both had children to be ashamed of, and David's family must rank among the most dysfunctional families ever. Here's a quick guide to the significant characters:

Solomon	Amnon	Absalom	Adonijah
Mother: Bathsheba	Mother: Ahinoam	Mother: Maacah	Mother: Haggith
David's chosen successor, and, despite the plotting of his brother and his brother's supporters, eventually a magnificent king.	A drunkard who raped Tamar, his half-sister. David refused to discipline his favorite son. Amnon was eventually assassinated by Absalom.	Killed his brother in revenge, and rebelled against his father, David. His big head was the death of him in more ways than one.	A rather pathetic figure Adonijah was eventually executed by his brother Solomon when he made an attempt to grab the throne.

Brief Lives: King David

Background: Youngest son of Jesse. Great-grandson of Ruth and Boaz.

Occupation: Shepherd, singer-songwriter, giant-killer, warrior, king.

Achievements: David is celebrated as Israel's greatest king. The shepherd boy who slew the giant, he became the ruler of Israel at the age of thirty, following the death of Saul. After reigning for seven years at Hebron, he captured the city of Jerusalem and made it his capital, bringing the ark of the covenant into the city and planning a glorious temple to the Lord. So close was his relationship to the city that it became known as the City of David.

So far, so triumphant. David was undoubtedly a great ruler —by the standard of kings. He triumphed in battle, brought prosperity to his country and had a large number of wives. Under his rule, Israel's borders spread to their furthest-ever extent. He brought success to the country and defeated its enemies.

Ultimately, however, what makes David special is not his success but his humanity. For despite his desire to serve God he committed some grievous sins. He was guilty of adultery. He was directly responsible for the deaths of Uriah, Joab and Shimei. His favoritism towards his eldest son caused murder and rebellion within the family.

The real David can be seen in the many psalms that bear his name. There, we see a man in all his moods. Scared, joyful, remorseful, triumphant, hesitant, desperate—above all honest. It is those that make David so special, for they record the prayers of a man who, despite the actions of himself and others, truly loved God. Indeed, he never could hide his feelings. When the ark returned to Jerusalem he threw off his gear and danced for joy, despite the disapproving looks of his wife (well, one of them).

Perhaps this is why God promised that his descendants would always reign and why it was from his line—the house of David—that the Messiah was to come. It was not because David was a mighty warrior and a powerful king. It was because he truly loved God and trusted in his promises.

Pros: Honest, courageous, passionate, faithful.

Cons: Human.

❺ Death of Absalom   18:1–18

Absalom, a handsome man with beautiful, abundant hair, starts to plot against his father. He begins a sort of PR campaign, telling people that he is on their side and treating them all like close friends (15:1–5). Eventually he has enough support to form a rebellion and David is forced to flee, accompanied only by close family and a few of his most faithful soldiers (15:13–22). Even in the midst of this, David is moved more to sorrow than anger. He decides to leave the ark in Jerusalem (15:23–29) and he even forgives an old madman who is insulting him and pelting the royal party with stones (16:5–13).

Not content with taking over the palace, Absalom humiliates his father by sleeping with some of his wives. This is basically an attempt to claim the throne. The succeeding king often staked his claim by "taking over" the harem of the preceding monarch. It is rather like a young lion taking over the pride. Eventually it comes to a battle and Absalom's troops are routed. Absalom tries to escape on a mule, but, riding under a low branch, his head is caught in the branches and he is left hanging there. Joab, David's commander, finds the rebel and stabs him with a spear. Absalom's big head is, truly, his downfall.

David hears the news about his son with terror and grief (18:33–19:8). Although he pulls himself together when confronted by Joab, he is to bear this wound for the rest of his life. There is, throughout this story, a sense of an old man who simply cannot bear it. He fights because he must, but he takes no pleasure in any of the killing. There is no real sense of victory here—just a sense of resignation and grief.

❻ Rise of Joab   19:1–8

David's inclination is to forgive and forget, but Joab is a hard, cruel figure. And Joab, over the next period, takes effective control of the army. He treacherously and brutally kills Amasa, who had served under Absalom (17:25; 20:7–13), and he puts down a revolt by a man called Sheba with characteristic efficiency. At the end of David's reign it is this iron commander who is in the ascendant.

Appendix   21:1–24:25

The book ends with some miscellaneous accounts.

It lists the death of seven of Saul's sons at the hands of the Gibeonites (21:1–10), tells how David had Saul's bones reburied in their family tomb (21:11–14), and includes two poems by David (22:1–51). It also records the last words of David, although this is probably a kind of final poem, rather than his actual deathbed speech (23:1–7).

❼ The evil census   24:1–25 ▷134

Finally we have another curious tale. David decides to take a census of his people. Joab tries to talk him out of it, but David is adamant and so the count goes ahead. God is angry and punishes Israel with a terrible disease. David goes to Araunah, buys a threshing floor, builds an altar and makes a sacrifice. Only then does the plague end.

Why is God angry against Israel? Why does he punish David for merely counting the number of people in the land?

Puzzling Points

Who killed Goliath? (21:19)

In a section dealing with various warriors in David's army we read of Elhanan who killed Goliath of Gath (21:19). Some have used this snippet to argue that this was the true victor over Goliath and that the story about David is nothing more than royalist propaganda.

It is a curious argument, given that we have a detailed account of David's fight and only one line here. But then, if you are predisposed to want to discredit the official line, you will pounce on any morsel. In fact, 1 Chronicles 20:4–8 contains the same information as 2 Samuel 21:15–22, only it records that the giant killed by Elhanan was not Goliath but Lahmi, his brother. The detail has presumably gone missing here.

It may be that this story should be placed after chapter 20 and the cause of the Lord's anger is therefore the people's support for the rebels Absalom and Sheba. But that doesn't answer the question of why David's census makes God so angry.

Some have argued that, since Israel was under no threat, David didn't need to know the numbers in his land—he was merely glorying in his achievements. Or it may be that he was trusting in numbers and doubting God's ability to protect Israel. Certainly he is aware of his own sin, and acknowledges it. He asks for the punishment to be on his family rather than on his people (24:17).

There is also the question of the angel—which David sees striking down the people of Israel (24:17). It is akin, perhaps, to the angel of death that struck at Egypt. It is a strange episode and one that is shrouded in mystery. But at the end of it there is a curious fact. The threshing floor that David buys from Araunah the Jebusite was to the north of the old city. Later it would become the site of the temple. David does build his temple, in a way. He buys the land and sets up the altar where, in future centuries, the temple would be located.

1 Kings
Prophets and kings

This is the history of the kings of Israel and Judah from the reign of Solomon to the final collapse of their kingdoms. Like Samuel, 1 and 2 Kings are actually one book, which has always been split into two parts because you couldn't fit it all on one scroll. The entire book contains forty-seven chapters covering the period from the accession of Solomon (975 BC) to the beginning of the exile (561 BC).

When: Kings was probably written when the Jews were in exile in Babylon. Kings seeks to explain what went wrong, to help the Jews in exile understand why everything had fallen to pieces. Thus, throughout the book, the author makes judgments on the kings. They are good, or bad, depending not on military success or foreign policy or expanding trade, but on whether they stayed faithful to God. Every king in the book is measured according to one simple standard: did he obey the commands of the Lord?

Who: Not known, but whoever he was, he worked from a wide variety of sources and was familiar with Old Testament books such as Deuteronomy.

What: The book of Kings is not just about the monarchs. It is also the story of some of those tempestuous, difficult, God-filled people, the prophets. This was the golden age of prophecy. Prophets had been before and would come again after, but this period saw prophets like Elijah and Elisha, Isaiah, Ezekiel, Jeremiah and a host of others. Some of these are mentioned in Kings, some have left prophecies that refer to those times. What comes across in Kings is their bravery and devotion. These were holy, inspired and hugely courageous men who confronted wickedness and encouraged obedience. They supported the poor and oppressed and condemned the cruel and powerful. They spoke out for God in a world that did not wish to hear what its maker had to say.

The Route Through 1 Kings

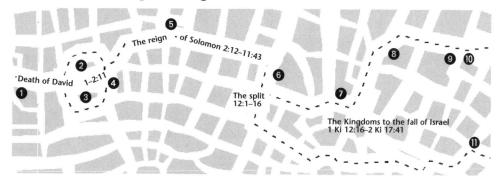

Puzzling Points

Why don't the numbers add up?

One of the problems with the book is that the numbers given for each king do not add up. It looks so simple—after all, the number of years for each king's reign is given and we can also date certain events from other records outside the Bible, such as Assyrian and Babylonian records. Thus we know that Ahab died in 853 BC, Jehu began to reign in 841 BC, and so on. Accordingly we can date other events from these points.

Except that it doesn't work. The years given for the kings of Judah and the kings of Israel don't tally. For example, Kings says that, in Judah, it was 95 years from Rehoboam's accession to Ahaziah's death. But add up the figures for the same period in Israel and you get 98 years. Take it on from there to the fall of Samaria and, if you add up the total for the kings of Judah you get 165 years, whereas the total for the kings of Israel only amounts to 144 years.

Some of the problems can be solved by the theory that some of the reigns may have overlapped, or that some kings may have reigned in tandem with their father or son, or that the timings began in a different part of the year. But in the end we have to face the fact that this is not history written to our expectations and conventions.

The important fact here is that this history has a moral truth to it. Whatever the numbers, the history has a spiritual and moral truth behind it. And that is what really matters.

Death of David   1:1–2:12

❶ Body warmer   1:1–4

During his final days David was given a young girl, Abishag the Shunammite, as a kind of human electric blanket, to keep him warm. We are told that he did not have sex with her (1:4), which, given he was about seventy and dying, is not really surprising.

❷ Battle for succession   1:5–53

As the great king prepares to die, the maneuvering to replace him begins. Adonijah makes the first move, securing the support of Joab. He invites his supporters to the wonderfully named Crawling Rock, where he performs a sacrifice—partly a ceremony to name him king. Nathan the prophet sends Bathsheba to David to let him know what has happened. David—although it is not recorded—had apparently sworn that Solomon would succeed him as king of United Israel. In the presence of Nathan the prophet, the old man renews this vow (1:28–36) and Solomon is declared king.

Adonijah reacts with abject fear. He grabs one of the corners of the altar for protection—on some ancient altars the corners were shaped like animal horns and it may be this that Adonijah held. The altar was supposed to be sacred, and anyone touching it was assumed to be safe from harm. Technically, however, this only covered those who had accidentally caused someone's death (Ex 21:14). Solomon guarantees Adonijah's safety, providing he behaves (1:42–53).

❸ Death of David   2:1–12

David's final words are a mixture of spiritual instruction and political revenge. He advises Solomon to (a) follow the teachings of God as laid down in the Law of Moses, (b) obey the Lord and keep the faith, and (c) have a few people killed.

The first of these is Joab. Solomon is advised, "Don't let him die peacefully in his old age." In the harsh realities of the time, Joab would have designs on the throne, but that was not the reason: Joab had killed two men when there was no war on. He had acted not like a warrior but like an assassin. The other target is Shimei, the mad old man who insulted the king at Mahanaim. David had always sworn not to kill him, but no such vow was to restrain his son. Mosaic law, admittedly, forbade the insulting of a ruler (Ex 22:28) but, even so, the event seems like a petty vendetta. In a way this final speech sums up the troubled final years of David's reign; the early hope and glory has been tarnished by rebellion and civil war, God's glorious promise accompanied by all-too-human ambition. So David died and was buried in Jerusalem, the city that ever after was to be referred to as the City of David.

The reign of Solomon
2:12–11:43

❹ The battle of the body warmer

Although Adonijah has been reprieved, he has not given up, and his scheme this time revolves around the beautiful young body warmer, Abishag. He asks for her hand in marriage, but the request is not as innocent as it seems. Possession of a royal wife or wives was seen as signifying the right to ascend the throne (which is why Absalom slept with some of his father's wives). Adonijah was trying to strengthen his case.

Solomon realizes that he can never be secure with Adonijah around—and he has him killed. Now the other conspirators are in danger. Abiathar the priest is sent into retirement (2:26–27), but Joab is hunted down. As he clings to the altar, he is dispatched by Benaiah, Solomon's new "enforcer."

Finally we learn the fate of Shimei. Initially Solomon grants him clemency, providing he does not leave the country. Evidently he viewed Shimei as a potential threat and did not want him conspiring with any of the surviving relatives of Saul. Shimei obeys the command, but then crosses the border to retrieve some slaves. It is the final straw. Once more Benaiah acts and the last of David's enemies is removed (2:36–46).

❺ Solomon builds the temple
5:1–6:38; 2 Ch 2:1–16 ▷136–37

It is left to Solomon to fulfill his father's wish to build a temple in Jerusalem. It takes thousands of workers, huge amounts of stone and precious metal and fine timber and takes seven years to achieve. After the temple, he builds himself a new palace that takes thirteen years to build (7:1–12). Hiram of Tyre, the finest craftsman of his time, is brought to furnish the building (7:13–51; 2 Ch 3:15–17; 4:1–5:1).

Finally, the ark is installed and, just as in the days of Moses, a cloud fills the temple (8:1–12). The light inside the cloud is so bright that the priests have to leave the room. In a long speech, Solomon asks God to watch over his temple, to protect his people, to act with justice and to listen to their prayers. The temple is not merely for Israel but for God-fearing people from throughout the world (8:41–44). Above all, he asks the Lord to forgive their sins and hear their cries for help (8:14–61). The ceremony is attended by people from all parts of the country (8:62–66). The inauguration of the temple takes place during the Feast of Tabernacles, the commemoration of Israel's wanderings in the wilderness and the protection of God. They are finally home (2 Ch 5:2–7:10).

Things you don't find in the Bible: The wisdom of Solomon

Well, you do find it, actually. But along with it you also find quite a high level of what you might call basic stupidity. Solomon was that most dangerous of things: a very clever idiot.

He is described as the wisest person in the world (4:29–34) and people came from all over the world to hear him teach. He left us proverbs and psalms, wise sayings and brilliant insights. His wisdom appears to have been what we might term astuteness. It helped him to solve problems such as the famous dispute between the two mothers (3:16–28), and it certainly enabled him to solve the political problems with which he was faced. Under his leadership, the United Kingdom of Israel reached its most prosperous state (4:20–27).

Yet, strangely, all this wisdom didn't stop him from doing stupid things. In the latter part of his reign he worshiped foreign gods. He treated one half of his kingdom with a harshness that led, after his death, to a rebellion and split. Their complaints were about the way in which he used their tribes as forced labor to build the temple. The building that was the crowning glory of Solomon's kingdom actually contributed to its downfall (12:4). Solomon's policy, as much as anything, brought down the kingdom.

Perhaps the lesson of Solomon's life is that there are times when obedience to God and faithfulness to his commands are the wisest course. Solomon was given everything, yet he threw it all away.

111

Landmark: Israel and Judah

After the death of Solomon, the kingdom split into two: Israel and Judah. However, Solomon's reign was only one of several factors that led to the division. In many ways the "crack" between north and south Israel had been present since the time of the conquest. There were a number of factors that led to the split:

• The tribe of Judah always had a looser connection to the other tribes in the northern part of the country. Only one of the judges came from Judah—and that was the pretty anonymous Othniel—and it did not get involved in many of the squabbles of that time.

• Across the middle of Israel there was a chain of Canaanite cities that had never been completely conquered, cutting Judah off from the central tribes. Though there was no barrier to communications, it meant that the Promised Land was, to some extent, divided from the start.

• Northern Israel had produced many of the judges and it was hard for them to accept David and Solomon—leaders from the tribe of Judah. Solomon only widened the gap, with unjust taxes, forced labor and a reign characterized by extravagance.

• There were cultural differences between the two areas, and different ways of living, based on the different type of terrain they inhabited.

This "distance" between the two halves of Israel was only ever overcome with difficulty and, indeed, some experts argue that even under David and Solomon the two sides might still have seen themselves as separate political identities—much like Scotland or Wales do as part of the UK. After all, under David's rule, the northern tribes rebelled twice. So, in many ways, the split was inevitable—although Solomon's behavior certainly didn't help.

The land of Judah was based around the territory originally assigned to the tribes of Judah and Benjamin, the land of Israel consisting of the territories of the other ten tribes. Israel was always the more unstable and, from the first, it was characterized by palace revolts, blood feuds, assassinations and a catalog of (mostly bad) kings, with a number of different families seizing the throne. Judah, on the other hand, preserved the royal lineage of David, though it has to be said that it, too, had more than its fair share of awful monarchs.

Judah's capital was the city of Jerusalem—David's city—with its temple and its palace. Israel's capital was first Bethel, and then Samaria. Of the two kingdoms, Judah was the better placed, because the chief enemy of the time—Assyria—would have to come through Israel in order to attack Judah. Judah could therefore use Israel as a kind of buffer zone.

Israel, meanwhile, was the wealthier of the two nations—especially after the wealth that Solomon had piled up in Jerusalem was carried away by Shishak of Egypt only four years into the split. The truth is that both kingdoms were weak, and although there were periods of relative prosperity and stability for both nations, there was only ever going to be one outcome. United, they might have stood: divided, they were doomed to fall.

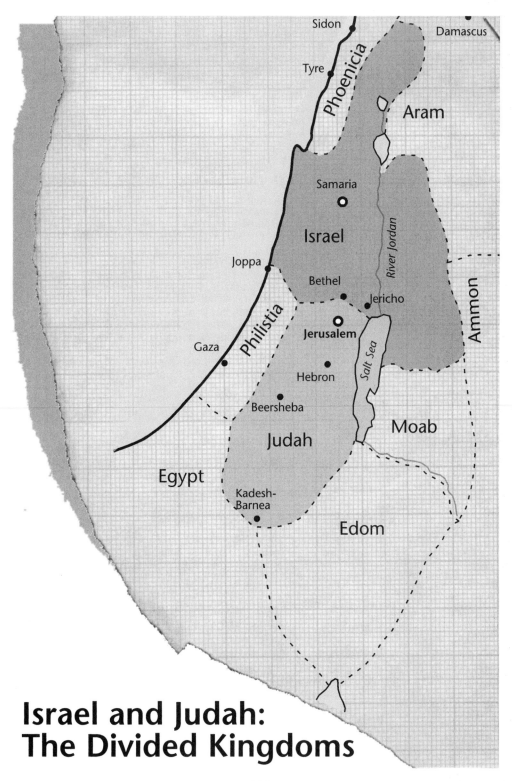

Israel and Judah:
The Divided Kingdoms

Questions, Questions

The Queen of Sheba
Who was the Queen of Sheba, then?
She was the queen. Of Sheba.
You know what I mean.
Well, no one is exactly sure. Sheba was probably a kingdom in Southwest Arabia. Perhaps where Yemen is today. It was a rich mercantile nation.
Eh?
Did a lot of trading with ships.
So this was a kind of trade agreement.
Maybe, but the queen didn't just come to see the sights and to make treaties. She came because she had heard of Solomon's wisdom. She even came with a list of questions for him to answer.
I hate people who ask too many questions.
Me too.

The Lord appears to Solomon again in a dream. He reminds Solomon to obey him and keep his teachings. His promise to David—that their house would always rule Israel—is conditional. There is also warning that reaches far into the future—one that points us to later events in the book. God came to the temple and he can abandon it. Its presence is no guarantee of God's presence with his people. If we place our faith in buildings, however sacred they are, we will be mistaken. Only faithfulness results in the presence of God (9:1–9; 2 Ch 7:11–22).

❻ Decline and fall   11:1–43

In the end it all falls to pieces. You'd have thought that after the presence of God in the temple, after all that God had promised and all that he had delivered, Solomon would remain faithful. But he didn't.

According to the figures, Solomon married an astonishing 1,000 women. Most of these relationships were merely diplomatic, done to seal treaties with kingdoms large and small. But even so, the number is excessive. Not only that, but Deuteronomy 17:17 explicitly warns against kings taking too many wives. This was an era of polygamy, but this is surely taking things too far.

As Solomon got older, his policy of "if it moves, marry it" caused disaster. Solomon, for all his wisdom, is led astray and starts to worship foreign gods. He worships Astarte and Milcom, described as "the disgusting god of Ammon" (11:5). His enemies gather against him and his officials start to rebel (11:14–40). One of these—Jeroboam—is given a message from the Lord: he will be a ruler of ten tribes of Israel.

And so, all the promise of Solomon is frittered away, and the promises of God are lost. God tells him that the United Kingdom of Israel will be taken from his son. The reign of the house of David over a united kingdom was to last for only two generations.

The split   12:1–16; 2 Ch 10:1–19

Wisdom is obviously not genetic. The son and successor of Solomon did not inherit any of his father's astuteness. When asked by the tribes if he was going to treat them better than his father, he replied that he would be harder. Perhaps he thought he was being tough. His foolishness meant the end of United Israel. Ten of the tribes rebelled against him and the country split into two: Israel in the north and Judah in the south. For a moment, he considered attacking the rebels, but Shemaiah the prophet forbade him to engage in civil war (12:21–24; 2 Ch 11:1–4).

Rehoboam assumed that the people would follow him because of his father, but he didn't earn their support. Like his father, he had a large harem and a luxurious lifestyle. Unlike his father, he had little political wisdom and no personal authority.

The Kings of Israel and Judah

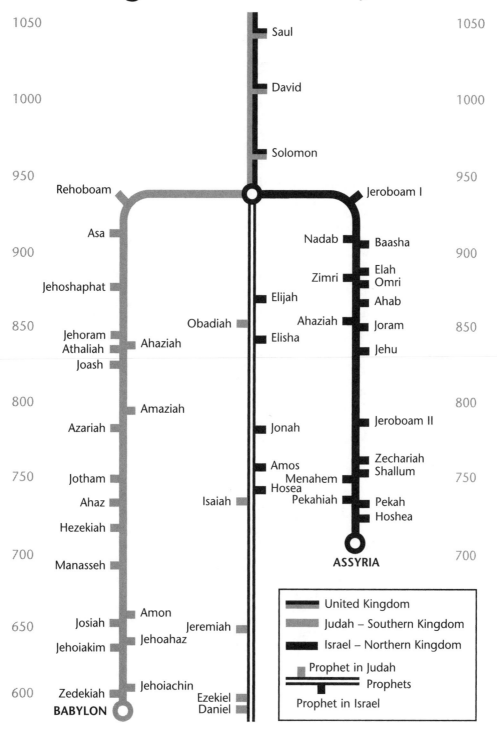

United Kingdom

Judah – Southern Kingdom

Israel – Northern Kingdom

Prophet in Judah

Prophets

Prophet in Israel

Two Kingdoms to the fall of Israel
12:16–2 Ki 17:41

Rehoboam, King of Judah 12:1–24; 14:21–31; 2 Ch 10–12

Rehoboam ruled for seventeen years. Rehoboam's reign was strengthened by a large number of priests and Levites who came to the southern kingdom to escape the idolatry of Jeroboam (2 Ch 11:13–17). However, they must have been disappointed, for Rehoboam also set up Asherah poles and allowed temple prostitutes. He strengthened some of the cities in his territory (2 Ch 11:5–12), probably to protect himself from attack from Egypt. It didn't work and King Shishak of Egypt invaded, getting as far as Jerusalem and ransacking the temple. All the valuable bronze and gold that Solomon had installed was taken.

Jeroboam, King of Israel 12:25–14:20

Although Jeroboam was appointed by divine command, he did not obey God. Instead he erected altars and built idols. The idea was to set up centers of worship to rival Jerusalem. The problem was that, unlike the temple, in Bethel and Dan the people had golden calves to worship (12:25–33). Anyone who liked could be a priest (13:33).

His actions led to outcries from prophets, which the king ignored. However, when his son was sick, he asked his wife to disguise herself and consult Ahijah, the prophet who had anointed him. Unfortunately you can't fool a prophet—at least, not a *real* prophet—and Ahijah had a terrible message for the woman: her husband's entire family would be wiped out (14:1–18).

> ### Details, Details . . .
> ### Asherah poles (14:15)
> Jeroboam set up sacred poles to his gods. These were fertility symbols, carved statues sacred to the goddess Asherah. Asherah was the consort of Baal—the old Canaanite religion was returning with a vengeance.

Abijam/Abijah, King of Judah 15:1–8; 2 Ch 13:1–22

Kings calls him Abijam; in Chronicles he is Abijah. In Kings he is represented as a sinner like his father, Chronicles presents a slightly more positive view—in particular he prays to the Lord for deliverance from the tribes of Israel. Probably the truth is that, like Rehoboam, he did a mixture of good and bad things.

Asa, King of Judah 15:9–24; 2 Ch 14:1–16:14 ▷138

In the first ten years, aided by the prophet Azariah, Asa brought peace, prosperity and widespread religious reform. He cleared out the evil ways that had seeped in, including the idols of his fathers and the male temple prostitutes (15:12–13). He even punished the queen mother, Maacah. Asa repelled an invasion attempt from Ethiopia (2 Ch 14:9–15). He restored the temple and sacrificed 700 oxen and 7,000 sheep in celebration. The only stain on his career is an alliance he made with Syria to defend himself against Baasha, king of Israel. This treaty was condemned by Hanani the prophet because he was not relying on the Lord (2 Ch 16:1–10). Asa was incensed and threw the prophet into prison. He also had bad feet (15:23).

Nadab, King of Israel 15:25–32

Only reigned for two years, but in that time managed to kill all the rest of his family. Kings says he killed them because of his father's sin, but still condemns him as a bad king. He was assassinated and succeeded by . . .

Baasha, King of Israel 15:33–16:7

Baasha, rather appropriately given his name, was a soldier. After killing Nadab, he carried on a long conflict with Judah and its king Asa. The prophet Jehu condemns him and his house and, although he reigned for twenty-four years, his family were murdered by Zimri.

Elah, King of Israel 16:8–14

A bad king, although to be fair he didn't get much of a crack at it. Son of Baasha. Only reigned for two years before he was killed by Zimri, his chariot commander, while Elah was drunk at the home of his prime minister. Politics was obviously a lot more fun in those days.

Zimri, King of Israel 16:15–20

At least he only lasted a week. Zimri assassinated Elah and then, a week later, killed himself by setting fire to the palace (16:18). Zimri had captured the throne through an opportunist killing. When the army heard that Zimri had proclaimed himself king, they crowned Omri instead. Omri marched to Tirzah and surrounded the palace. Zimri saw that he was surrounded, and the rest is history. Or arson, to be precise. His name became a byword for treason (2 Ki 9:31).

POSTCARD

The capital of the northern kingdom, Samaria occupies a commanding position 300 feet up on a hill overlooking the major trade routes.

The citadel—which took six years to build—was begun by King Omri, who originally purchased the land for development for the price of two talents of silver.

There is much to fascinate the visitor, including packed street bazaars with merchants from Damascus, the Ivory Palace of King Ahab and the temple that may or may not be dedicated to the worship of the Lord, depending on which king is currently in power.

Its prominent position atop the hill makes Samaria an easy place to defend—just as well, since one of the most popular pastimes in Samaria is to stand on the battlements, gaze out over the panoramic views and spot whichever invading army is heading our way next.

Welcome to Samaria!

Omri, King of Israel 16:21–28

Although he only merits a small passage in the Bible, he was one of the most important of Israel's kings and a number of archaeological discoveries testify to his activities in the field of foreign affairs. After seeing off Zimri, Omri fought a civil war against Tibni, a rival for the throne. He established the city of Samaria as his capital.

Brief Lives: Elijah

Background: Not known. Came from Tishbe, but as we don't know where this was, it's not much help.

Occupation: Prophet.

Achievements: Elijah's name means "the Lord is my God" and it sums up the message that he took to Ahab and Jezebel and the people of Israel. His whole life was a contest, a fight between the forces of evil and the God of justice and love. Elijah's acts are continual demonstrations of the power and presence of God—and therefore implicit condemnation of the empty and barren Baal worship. The contrast between his simple prayer and the frantic, desperate self-mutilation of the Baal prophets is striking (18:16–40). No wonder the king couldn't bear to meet him—the man was a living reminder of all his kingdom's sin and failure.

He had various posts:

Reminder: With his rough garments and wild appearance, Elijah was a reminder to Israel of the authentic faith that they had abandoned. Elijah was the spiritual successor to Moses. Several of the events of his life are in direct comparison. He spends time in the wilderness—forty days in fact, just like Moses on Sinai. He "sees" God on the mountain. He alone preserved the true faith.

Ambassador: Elijah's presence in the country is an indication of God's presence. When he goes to live in the ravine at Kerith it is a sign that God himself has left Israel. Many of his miracles take place outside Israel—a sign that God's favor is resting on other nations.

Warrior: In the showdown at Mount Carmel, Elijah humiliates the prophets of Baal. When they cannot raise fire he suggests it is because their god has gone for a walk, or is sitting on the toilet (18:27). He is an aggressive fighter for the Lord.

Miracle worker: Elijah demonstrates God's power through a series of miracles. The most spectacular one was probably the raising of the widow's son at Zarephath, the first recorded instance of the raising of the dead in Scripture (17:7–24).

Despite this, Elijah was prone to depression and fear. Surrounded by enemies and often running for his life, he sometimes felt that his best wasn't good enough. In the end, Elijah didn't just die, God came to collect him. Few people have had a closer relationship with their God than this strange, hairy man from Tishbe.

Character: Angry. Passionate. Courageous. Sometimes depressed and scared.

Pros: Served God in the teeth of fierce opposition. Handy to have at a barbecue.

Cons: Prone to self-condemnation and fear.

Ahab, King of Israel 16:29–22:40

A mixture of cunning strength and abject weakness, Ahab's reign is very important because it forms the backdrop to the activities of the great prophet Elijah. In foreign policy he was quite astute. He made peace with Jehoshaphat, King of Judah. Ahab formed an alliance with Phoenicia, the foremost commercial nation of the time, which was cemented by his marriage to the daughter of Ethbaal, King of Tyre. Her name was Jezebel.

Foreign policy, then, A+. Religious policy, however, F-. Ahab's idolatry outstripped any of his predecessors, largely due to his Phoenician wife. With Ahab it was a whole new Baal game. While paying token respect to God's laws, he set up a temple to Baal in Samaria and, in fact, tried to merge the two religions. In this he was encouraged by his queen, who combined an evangelical zeal for Baal worship with a vindictive streak and the temper of a bull hippo with a toothache. Jezebel organized the destruction of the altars to God, persecuted the true followers and killed prophets. Ahab probably did not agree with her zeal, but seemed too weak to stop her.

Let's hear it for Obadiah 18:3–16

One of the unsung heroes of Scripture, Obadiah is a kind of ancient Oscar Schindler, hiding prophets in a cave to save their lives (18:4). He was a God-fearing court official whom Elijah used to take messages to Ahab. Despite his fears about the king's response, Obadiah does his duty and the result is the great defeat of Baal at Mount Carmel (18:16–40).

❼ Elijah in the desert 19:1–18

The death of her prophets at Carmel enrages Jezebel and she threatens Elijah with death. Fearing for his life, he runs into the desert. Scared and isolated, he begs God just to let him die. Once again God provides miraculously for him—this time through an angel. The food strengthens him to spend forty days walking through the desert to Mount Sinai.

The allusion is obvious. This is Elijah's personal exodus. The forty days look back to the Jews' forty years in the desert and to Moses' forty days spent on Mount Sinai (Ex 34:28), and forward to Jesus' forty days' fast in "the wilderness" (Mt 4:2). The Lord asks Elijah, "Why are you here?" A question that implies the journey is as much to do with Elijah's emotional turmoil as the Lord's guidance. Elijah answers briefly: he has done his best, but he feels it wasn't good enough; all the prophets have been killed and the people have turned away. It should have been the time of his greatest triumph, but he is lost, alone and afraid for his life. As he did with Moses, God meets with his prophet. In a remarkable passage Elijah sees a mighty wind, a powerful earthquake and a blazing fire. But none of these is God. Instead God comes in a gentle whisper. And the whisper gives Elijah new instructions about a new king and a new assistant in his work.

There seems to be a shift here, from power to gentleness. The wind and the earthquake and the fire are all redolent of the previous manifestations of God. They speak of power and justice, of God's might. But the whisper? That is personal. That is a God working in a gentle way (19:1–18).

❽ The call of Elisha 19:19–21

From Mount Sinai, Elijah goes and finds his new apprentice—a young boy called Elisha. Elisha means "God saves"—similar to Joshua. He was handling the twelfth pair of oxen—the smallest pair, indicating that he was probably quite young when this call came. Elijah throws his cloak around the boy—a sign that Elisha is being "adopted." Elisha sacrifices the oxen and goes with Elijah.

A Little Local Difficulty

The man who would not hit the prophet.

20:35–36

Here we have a man who is asked by a prophet to strike him and refuses. The result? He is eaten by a lion. It seems something of an overreaction. The same punishment is meted out to a prophet who disobeyed a command from God to refrain from eating—even though he was tricked into eating. Complete obedience to the prophets was, evidently, a matter of life and death. Even so, it is a baffling occurrence and one that seems fundamentally unfair.

Meanwhile, Ahab is under attack from Syria. Miraculously—and somewhat confusingly considering his inherent sinfulness—Ahab is assisted by a prophet of the Lord to destroy the Syrian army (20:1–34). Ahab's mercy to the Syrian commander Benhadad is also an example of his astute foreign policy. Better a live friend than a dead enemy. He forgot, however, that God had told him not to let Benhadad live.... The Lord's protection of Israel is not the same as approval of Ahab's reign.

❾ Naboth's vineyard 21:1–29

Corrupt religions lead to corrupt behavior. Close to the royal palace in Jezreel was a vineyard (1 Ki 21:1) owned by Naboth. Ahab wanted it for a vegetable garden—but Naboth refused his offer. Jezebel solves this little difficulty by having Naboth accused of blasphemy and stoned to death. Elijah confronts Ahab in the vineyard. It is their final meeting, their gunfight at the OK Corral. Elijah pronounces judgment on Ahab. Even though the king repents, he cannot do more than delay the sentence. This judicial murder was the final straw in his discredited reign.

❿ The death of Ahab 22:1–40; 2 Ch 18:1–34

Ahab's prophets are a ragtag group of sycophants who will happily tell the king anything he wants to hear. Not so Micaiah son of Imlah. "I hate Micaiah," grumbles Ahab. "He always has bad news for me" (22:8). Micaiah is advised not to rock the boat and just to confirm what the other prophets have said. He does so (22:15–16), but he is mocking them. Ahab tells him not to lie and then Micaiah delivers the truth: his prophets are lying and if Ahab goes to Ramoth he will be killed.

Micaiah's reward for telling the truth is a slap in the face from Zedekiah, the leading official prophet, and being thrown into prison. But he is right. Ahab tries to disguise himself to avoid his fate, but he is still killed. He is hit by an arrow fired at random and he bleeds to death. His chariot is washed with a whore's bath water, and the dogs lick away his blood.

⓫ Jehoshaphat, King of Judah
22:41–50; 2 Ch 17:1–21.1 ▷138

He was a God-fearing, hard-working monarch who was widely respected by his people. He seems to have been a very "hands-on" monarch who would tour the country talking with the people and convincing them to "turn back to the Lord God and worship him, just as their ancestors had done" (2 Ch 19:4). He established a legal system that was fair and took account of what the prophets had to say.

Jehoshaphat's only real fault was that he tended to be too friendly in his relations with other, less God-fearing leaders. He was friendly with Ahab, even marrying his son Jehoram to the daughter of Jezebel, Athaliah. He made an alliance with Ahaziah that was criticized by the prophets (2 Ch 20:35–37). Indeed, his alliance with Ahab was the direct cause of Moab invading his country. Even then, however, Jehoshaphat's reliance on prayer, fasting and seeking the will of God brought success, with the Amorite, Moabite and Edomite troops fighting against themselves.

2 Kings
Decline and fall

Who, When: See 1 Kings

What: The second book of Kings continues the story of the long downward spiral. There is a sense of doom hanging over the book—a sense that the clouds are gathering and the storm is about to break. The clouds, in particular, are two great empires: Assyria and Babylon. Between them, these two mighty powers would spell the end, first for the northern kingdom of Israel, and then for Judah, its southern neighbor.

In 722 BC Israel was destroyed by Assyria, its capital city Samaria was demolished and the people were taken into captivity. The end for Judah came some 150 years later, in 586 BC when it was conquered by the Babylonian emperor Nebuchadnezzar. Jerusalem was completely destroyed and the majority of the population were taken away to Babylon. At the end of the book, King Jehoiachin of Judah is in captivity. Although he has personal freedom and eats at the emperor's table, he is still, like his people, a captive.

The root of all their problems lay in the godlessness of the kings and their people. Just as in the first part of the book of Kings, God sends prophets to warn the people of the fate that is awaiting them. In 1 Kings the chief character was Elijah; in 2 Kings the focus switches to Elisha, whose activities dominate the first 13 chapters of the book.

After his death, if we want to find out about the actions of the prophets, we must turn to their own writings. Isaiah, Jeremiah, Ezekiel, Amos, Hosea and many other great prophets were at work during the downfall of the two kingdoms. Although they are rarely mentioned in the text of Kings, the writings they left behind form a unique commentary on the action.

Quick Guide

Author
Unknown

Type
History

Purpose
See 1 Kings

Key verse
13:23 "But the LORD was kind to the Israelites and showed them mercy because of his solemn agreement with their ancestors Abraham, Isaac, and Jacob. In fact, he has never turned his back on them or let them be completely destroyed."

If you remember one thing about this book . . .
God's will *will* be done.

Your 15 minutes start now
Read chapters 2, 4–5, 9, 12, 17, 22–25

The Route Through 2 Kings

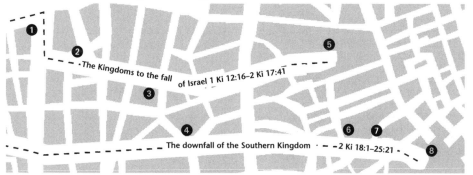

The Kingdoms to the fall of Israel 1 Ki 12:16–2 Ki 17:41

The downfall of the Southern Kingdom · 2 Ki 18:1–25:21

Ahaziah, King of Israel   1 Ki 22:51–3; 2 Ki 1:1–18

The first book of Kings ends with a brief résumé of the life of Jehoshaphat and an introduction to Ahaziah, the son of Ahab and, alas, a chip off the old block.

Elijah—who is here described in all his hairiness (1:8)—condemns Ahaziah for consulting a foreign god when the king is injured in a fall. Ahaziah sends troops to arrest him, and they are burnt up by fire from heaven. (Apart from the third commander, who, like all good military commanders, assesses the fate of his predecessors and beats a wise retreat.)

❶ Elijah's death   2:1–8

The tale of Elijah's death—or, since he didn't actually die, his transport to God—is not just about the miraculous manner of the prophet's passing. It is also about the faithfulness and dogged endurance of Elisha. Several times Elijah suggests to Elisha that he stay behind, but Elisha insists on accompanying the old man. In another echo of Moses, Elijah dries up the River Jordan to allow them both to cross. Offered a farewell gift, Elisha asks for double his master's power. It is, in some ways, an audacious request—typical of a young, zealously devoted man. Elijah realizes that such a gift is not in his power to grant, but God evidently approves the request. Elijah is taken up to heaven; Elisha returns across the Jordan, and demonstrates that he has, indeed, inherited his master's power (2:1–18).

Two miracles   2:19–25

At Jericho, Elisha purifies the water (2:19–22). As he heads toward Bethel some boys come out and jeer at his appearance. Hair was a significant symbol in Old Testament times—a symbol of masculinity and strength (for example Absalom, Samson). Elisha was bald. The youths mock him, mistaking the outward appearance for the inward power and showing a complete disdain for the Lord's prophet. Elisha curses them in the name of the Lord and straight away two bears attack them (2:23–25). Personally, this is one of my favorite stories in the Bible. Never, never, *never* mock bald men.

Joram, King of Israel   3;1–27

Ahab's son, although not as bad as his parents, was not much of an improvement. On a campaign with Jehoshaphat they consult—at Jehoshaphat's suggestion—Elisha. Elisha cuttingly informs Joram that he wouldn't even look at the king, were it not for his respect for Jehoshaphat. The war goes well, culminating in a desperate, horrific act by Mesha of Moab, who sacrifices his own son. Horrified, the Israelites return home.

❷ Two incidents with lepers   5:1–7:20

Leprosy was one of the most feared diseases of ancient times. An incurable disease, the skin was progressively covered with white marks, killing off the flesh. In the Levitical laws it rendered its victims unclean, which is why the Bible often talks of people being "cleansed" of leprosy rather than healed.

Details, Details . . .
Body warming

Elisha lies out on the body of the boy, just as his master Elijah did (4:34 and 1 Ki 17:21). Apparently the intention was to transfer bodily warmth from the living to the dead. However, it is clear in both cases that it is not this physical act that makes the difference, but the prayer that accompanies it.

Details, Details . . .
Anyone for donkey à l'orange? (6:24)

The donkey was considered unclean food under the Levitical laws, but here the situation is so bad that not only are the inhabitants of Samaria eating it, they are reduced to eating the most unappetizing part—its head. (Well, all right, perhaps the *second* most unappetizing part.) The pigeon droppings (6:25) were used as fuel for fires and not food. At least I *hope* they were used as fuel . . .

In the first incident, Elisha heals Naaman, the Syrian commander from the disease. Gehazi, Elishah's servant sees a chance for a bit of money and his greed is punished with the same disease that afflicted Naaman. It is one of the unwritten rules of the Bible: never try to profit from a prophet.

This was not the end for Gehazi, however, and there are signs that he learned from his sin. He is summoned before the king to tell him what Elisha has been doing and to help the Shunamite widow recover her home. His willingness to speak well of his master and the truth of his words give some hope that he had changed.

The second incident occurs during the terrible siege of Samaria, when food runs so low that the people are reduced to cannibalism and eating unclean food. King Joram considers Elisha responsible for this—although why is not made clear. Perhaps he felt that the disaster came from God, so God's representative on earth should bear the responsibility. When he is challenged, Elisha promises that the Lord will raise the siege. This time the Lord affects the hearing of the Syrians; they believe they are being attacked and they flee in panic. When four lepers come to beg for food they find a strangely deserted camp.... In the rush to go to the camp and grab whatever supplies are available, a guard at the gate is trampled underfoot—the same guard who disbelieved the prophet's words (6:24–7:20).

Questions, Questions
The limits of power
I don't get it. If Elisha could save himself from the Syrian army, why couldn't he prevent them from besieging Samaria?
Because he couldn't.
Thanks. Are you going to explain that at all?
Look, we don't know the rules by which prophecy works. It is clear that true prophets can only operate by the power of God. They don't own that power, it flows through them. So if other events happen, that is because God allows them to happen—for his own purposes.
This isn't really helpful.
I know. But the more you read the Bible the more you understand and the more you *don't* understand. There are always questions. The Psalms are full of questions. And here we have one of the greatest and most powerful prophets of Israel weeping because he knows what is going to happen—and HE CAN'T PREVENT IT.
There's no need to use bold capitals.
Sorry. Just got carried away there.

Joram was right in one sense: the Lord was with Syria rather than Israel. In Damascus Elisha encounters Hazael. Elisha stares at Hazael—apparently one of Benhadad's officials—and simply starts to weep. He can see what this man will do to Israel. He tells Hazael that the Lord says he will be the next king of Syria. Hazael promptly returns to his master and callously murders him. Elishah's prophecy does not excuse Hazael's actions—nor his later oppression of Israel. His acts arise out of his own sinful nature. God knows what is going to happen, but that doesn't mean that he approves of it.

Jehoram, King of Judah 8:16–24; 2 Ch 21:2–20 ▷138
His eight-year rule is notable only for Jehoram's inability to control Edom. He was king at the same time as his father Jehoshaphat, possibly because his father was ill or infirm.

Ahaziah, King of Judah   8:25–29; 2 Ch 22:1–6 ▷139
Related to Ahab through his mother, Ahab's daughter. Had, apparently, the same family values, i.e., bad.

❸ Jehu, King of Israel   9:1–10:35
Jehu killed off the family of Ahab and wiped out the prophets of Baal, but he didn't entirely stop the pagan worship. Jehu is an army officer—a charioteer—who responds to the news that he is to be king in a laconic, somewhat relaxed way. "What did that mad old prophet want?" ask his fellow officers. "Oh, you know," replies Jehu. "Just wanted to make me king" (9:11–13). However, his relaxed speech hides a man of considerable action. He drives his chariot way too fast (9:20) and kills not only Joram, King of Israel, but also Ahaziah, King of Judah.

Brief Lives: Elisha

Background: Not known.

Occupation: Farmer's son. Apprentice prophet. Prophet.

Achievements: Elisha's work extended through the reign of six kings and over fifty years. Elisha's acts are, in some ways, echoes of Elijah's. He provides a hard-pressed widow with a miraculous supply of oil (4:1–7). A Shunamite woman who provided hospitality for Elisha has her son brought back from the dead (4:8–37). In anticipation of one of Jesus' most famous miracles, he provides for one hundred people using twenty loaves and some grain (Mk 6:35–43). He miraculously makes a stew taste good, which may not sound impressive, but the implication is that the cook has accidentally thrown some poison in (4:38–41).

Indeed, there is an ordinariness about some of the prophet's miracles that makes them seem almost unimpressive. I mean, compared to the parting of the Jordan or raising someone from the dead, making an ax-head float seems a little, well, domestic. But the point is that Elisha's life was lived in the light of God. Therefore he made no distinction between "ordinary" life and "religious" life. Things were not "important enough for a miracle" or not. It was simply a question of asking in faith.

All of which does not mean that Elisha was not concerned with the big picture. Elisha was always on the move. He went from country to country, from court to court. He was involved in affairs of state. The king of Syria was thwarted so often by Elisha's insight that he believed there must be a spy in the army. When he learned the true nature of the Israelite's secret weapon, he sent an army to go and capture the prophet, but Elisha was surrounded by "the Lord's army" and the Syrians were taken into captivity. The Syrians were blind in more ways than one—even when they had their sight, they could not see the reality that Elisha saw.

Character: Impulsive. Compassionate. Perhaps slightly sensitive about his appearance.

Pros: A powerful man of God—more powerful, in fact, than his master.

Cons: Don't mention the hair.

Then he beats the traffic cops and goes after Jezebel. There is something almost admirable in the way that she puts her makeup on and brushes her hair. She evidently wants to look her best when she is thrown out of the window (9:30–32).

Jehu then completes the job. To establish himself as king he has to take Samaria, the fortress city. He writes to the people in Samaria and invites them to select one of Ahab's sons to be king. He will then attack them. The people are cowed into submission —they want to be on Jehu's side. They kill Ahab's sons and Jehu removes the rest of his family. All those associated with Ahab are eliminated. So much for Israel.

Then Jehu turns his attention to Judah. He appoints Jehonadab, son of Rechab, to take over the rule of Judah. Jehonadab was the leader of an anti-Baal movement—so much so that many decades after him those who followed similar principles were known as Rechabites (Je 35:6–10).

Jehu's final reforming act is to wipe out the prophets of Baal. He does this by simply inviting them to a sacrifice and pretending he is going to be a major-league Baal worshiper. They file into the temple and when they are in, the guards kill them. Simple, but effective.

Questions, Questions

Why kill the children?
In punishing the children for the sins of the father, isn't God breaking his own laws?
What do you mean?
Deuteronomy 24:16 says, "Parents must not be put to death for the crimes committed by their children, and children must not be put to death for crimes committed by their parents." But, surely, time and time again, we see God doing this?
Yes. Good point. Glad to see you're thinking about this.
Stop playing for time and answer the question.
Well, the actions of God in the Old Testament pose some interesting exegetical and ethically challenging issues we have to take in context . . .
You don't know, do you?
Er . . . no. The only thing we can do is have faith in God's justice. No one is punished who does not deserve it.
That's not much of an answer.
No. But I'm afraid it's the best we can do.

Queen Athaliah of Judah
11:1–21; 2 Ch 22:10–23:21 ▷139

Athaliah, mother of Ahaziah, is so upset by his death that she murders the rest of the family (or, at least, those who are left after Jehu had finished murdering most of them)—and secures the throne for herself (10:12–14). Probably her aim was to kill any direct descendants, i.e. her grandchildren. Going to visit Granny was evidently a more risky occupation in those days. However, her plans are thwarted by Jehosheba, who is married to the high priest. Joash, the baby son of Ahaziah, is hidden in the temple while Granny takes over the country.

After six years, Jehoiada the high priest arranges for a coup d'état. He secures the support of the army and then anoints the young Joash and gives him a book of instructions on how to rule the country (11:12). This may have been a copy of the Laws of Moses, or a more specific book on "how to be a king." Athaliah hears the people proclaiming and comes to have a look at what is going on. Bad move.

Joash, King of Judah   12:1–21; 2 Ch 24:1–16 ▷139

It was evidently a good guide, that book on being a king. Joash was a good king, but he relied heavily on the advice and support of Jehoiada the high priest. When that old man died (2 Ch 24:17–19) Joash was persuaded to start worshiping idols and the goddess Astarte. His country was attacked again and he was forced into paying a tribute to Hazael. In the end Joash suffered the same fate as his father—he was assassinated on the road, probably by hired killers.

Jehoahaz, King of Israel 13:1–9

The son of Jehu was a bad man and an even worse military commander. By the time Hazael had finished with him, his army was decimated.

Jehoash, King of Israel 13:10–19

Weak and ineffective. He did defeat the Syrians and recapture the territory they had taken, although that was a deathbed gift from Elisha.

Amaziah, King of Judah 14:1–22; 2 Ch 25:1–24 ▷139

Amaziah took revenge on his father's assassins, but had mercy on their children. He fought a successful campaign against Edom, but then grew arrogant and foolishly attacked Israel. He was defeated and captured by Jehoash. In his later years he turned against God and was then assassinated, just like his old dad.

Jeroboam II, King of Israel 14:23–29

Although it was a time of prosperity and military success, it was also a time of hypocrisy and wealthy cynicism. The prophets Amos and Hosea offer a true perspective on this reign.

❹ Azariah/Uzziah, King of Judah 15:7; 2 Ch 26:1–23

Azariah—who is also the Uzziah mentioned in Chronicles and Isaiah— came to the throne as the result of his father's assassination. Just as his father was the victim of a popular uprising, Azariah appears to have been a popular choice and, initially at least, he did not let the people down.

Generally a good king, although prone to skin diseases, he defeated many of Judah's enemies and developed the agricultural strength of Israel. Chronicles records that he loved farming (2 Ch 26:10). He reorganized the army and even developed new weapons. A man of many parts, then, but this was his downfall. He took it on himself to burn incense, usurping the role of the priests, and, as punishment, he was infected with leprosy.

His public life was now at an end and he lived in seclusion for the rest of his life, handing over the practical reign to his son Jotham. When he died he was not buried with his ancestors, but in a field. Chronicles records that this was because of his leprosy, but I don't think Uzziah would have minded. He always loved fields and farming.

Zechariah, King of Israel 15:8–12

Israel's kings now follow in bewildering succession. Zechariah only ruled for six months before he was assassinated by . . .

Shallum, King of Israel 15:13–16

No time to tell if he was good or bad, since he only made it to one month before he was killed by . . .

Menahem, King of Israel 15:17–22

A violent, bloody murderer who even attacked pregnant women. Threatened by Tiglath-Pileser of Assyria, he paid the Assyrian emperor by increasing taxation.

Pekahiah, King of Israel 5:23–26

As seems traditional by now for Israel's kings, Pekahiah was a bad king who was assassinated. His killer was one of his officials, a man called . . .

Pekah, King of Israel 15:27–31

He ruled for twenty years. He attacked Judah, prompting Ahaz to call on the Assyrians. They took over huge portions of Israel and took many of the inhabitants into captivity. In the end he was assassinated by Hoshea. What goes around comes around, as they say.

Jotham, King of Judah 15:32–38; 2 Ch 27:1–9

Meanwhile, back in Judah, Jotham finally succeeded old Uzziah the Farmer. He fought successfully against the Amorites and grew powerful.

Ahaz, King of Judah 16:1–20; 2 Ch 28:1–27

His son, however, was not like his father. The book of Kings records, with almost a sense of astonishment, that Ahaz was *even worse* than the kings of Israel. Which, given their history, is saying something. Ahaz bought into pagan practices big time, worshiping at every pagan shrine (or even large tree) he could find, and even sacrificing his own son (16:2–4). Under Uzziah and Jotham the Judaean army was well organized and powerful; Ahaz seems to have managed to undo all their good work and when he was attacked by Israel and Syria, he had to call in someone to help. He called in the Assyrians, which is a bit like protecting yourself from a dog by calling in a tiger. Sure, the dog will get eaten, but sooner or later, so will you. Ahaz, however, became such a fan of the Assyrians that he even copied their altars and changed the temple to mimic the Assyrian pattern.

❺ Hoshea, King of Israel 17:1–41

The man who assassinated Pekah took over a country on the very brink of annihilation. The Assyrian Emperor Shalmaneser was effectively in charge of the country and imposed punitive taxes on Israel. When Hoshea rebelled and refused to pay, Shalmaneser simply put him in prison and closed down the country. The kingdom of Israel was simply wiped out, and all the inhabitants were carted away into captivity in Assyria.

The author of Kings draws the story of the northern kingdom to a close by pointing out the truth: the country was annihilated because it insisted on worshiping "worthless idols," because it chose kings who were evil, because it turned its back on God. Shalmaneser repopulated Israel with exiles from other lands and, although he provided an Israelite priest to teach them, they worshiped a wide range of pagan gods. The Northern Kingdom was at an end.

Landmark: The Fate of Israel

In 722–721 BC, Shalmaneser V finally conquered Israel. According to Assyrian records, 27,290 people were deported from Israel to Assyria and foreign settlers were sent to Israel to take their homes and towns. The result was that the land lost virtually all traces of Israelite culture. In Samaria—which lay between Israel and Judah—the new inhabitants took on the Israelite religion and absorbed those Israelites who had not been taken into captivity.

Later the Samaritans were to develop their own version of Judaism, and build their own temple on Mount Gerazim. By the time of Jesus, Samaria became absorbed as a district within the Roman province of Palestine. However, for the rest of their history, the Samaritans were not viewed as "proper Jews" by those in Judah. They viewed the Samaritans as half-breeds, both in racial and religious terms. It was the beginning of a hatred that was to last for centuries.

The downfall of the Southern Kingdom   2 Ki 18:1–25:21

❻ Hezekiah, King of Judah
18:1–20:21; Is 37:1–39:8; 2 Ch 32:24–33 ▷140

The force that Ahaz had unleashed on the northern kingdom was about to be turned on Judah. But there was hope, for Hezekiah, the son of Ahaz, was completely unlike his father. "Hezekiah trusted the LORD God of Israel," says the Bible. "No other king of Judah was like Hezekiah, either before or after him" (18:5). The result was that Judah survived the Assyrian threat. Sennacherib, the Assyrian king, invaded Judah and captured everywhere except Jerusalem. As the Assyrian army massed outside Jerusalem, Hezekiah went to the temple and prayed to God. The Lord assured him that Sennacherib would not take the city. During the night the angel of the Lord visited the Assyrian army and they were decimated. The threat was lifted and the Assyrians were never as powerful again.

Manasseh, King of Judah   21:1–18; 2 Ch 33:1–20 ▷140

Hezekiah's son Manasseh was only twelve when he came to the throne, and reinstituted the profane practices that his father had swept away. He worshiped Astarte and "the stars in heaven" (21:3), put idols and pagan altars in the temple and even practiced witchcraft and sorcery. Those who opposed him were butchered in the streets (21:16). It was fortunate for him that his father's faithfulness had led to the collapse of the Assyrian army.

Amon, King of Judah   21:19–26; 2 Ch 33:21–25

Manasseh's son continued in his father's wicked ways. He only reigned for two years before being assassinated by his officials.

❼ Josiah, King of Judah   22:1–30; 2 Ch 34:29–36:1
▷141

Josiah reversed the trend and followed in his great-grandfather's footsteps. The most significant event of Josiah's reign was the discovery of the Book of God's Law during renovation work on the temple.

Judging by the reforms that followed, it appears to have been the book of Deuteronomy, although it could have been the entire Pentateuch. As to how it came to be lost, no one knows. Some believe it was buried in the foundations of the temple when it was built—a kind of symbol that the Law was the foundation of their worship. Others believe that the book was actually put together a lot later, in the time of Hezekiah, and that it had been conveniently "lost" during the reigns of his two evil successors. Whatever the case, its reappearance leads to widespread reforms. Josiah immediately calls together the elders of the country, reads the book to them and makes a solemn promise to obey its commands (23:2). He destroys the pagan shrines and, for the first time since the days of Solomon, the Jews celebrate Passover. Josiah even takes his reforms to the now defunct Israel, traveling to Bethel to destroy the pagan temple there, thus fulfilling a prophecy that had been given to Jeroboam (1 Ki 13:1–2).

It seems impressive, but it was too late. Jeremiah records that it was largely an outward reform on behalf of the people (Je 11:1–14); and God was still angry with them. Nor did the reign end happily for Josiah. For all his piety and reforming zeal, he was no military strategist and he perished at Megiddo in a battle against Pharaoh Neco of Egypt.

Jehoahaz, King of Judah   23:31–34; 2 Ch 36:2–4

Josiah's son, therefore, inherited a society with no real military power and he was captured and imprisoned by Pharaoh Neco.

Jehoiakim, King of Judah   23:35–24:7; 2 Ch 36:5–8

Such was the control of Pharaoh Neco, that he now chose Judah's kings and even renamed them. Jehoahaz's brother Eliakim was crowned King and had his name changed to Jehoiakim. Since both names mean roughly the same, it seems an odd move. Probably Neco was simply demonstrating his complete control.

However, Egyptian dominance was soon ended. The Babylonians defeated Egypt at Carchemish, establishing themselves as the unrivaled rulers of the region. Jehoiakim served the Babylonians for three years, but then he rebelled. Babylonian troops invaded and Jehoiakim conveniently died, leaving his son to face the music.

Jehoiachin, King of Judah
24:8–17; 25:27–30; 2 Ch 36:9–10; Je 52:31–34

Jehoiachin served only three months as king before surrendering to the Babylonians. He was taken to Babylon along with most of his people. The Babylonians took all the educated classes, all the soldiers and craftsmen. Only the very poorest people were left behind. Jehoiachin was eventually released from prison in Babylon, but he never returned to Jerusalem.

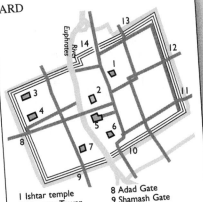

POSTCARD

Welcome to Babylon!

What a sight greets the visitor—or, more frequently, the captive—as they enter Babylon! First, the walls—so huge that you can drive chariots round them. Not so much a wall, more of a ring road. Each wall is decorated with enameled bricks and surrounded by a moat channeled from the mighty River Euphrates. No wonder the rivers of Babylon make people sit down and weep!

Inside the city, the splendor continues, with temples and towers around every corner. In the center is the mighty ziggurat, or temple tower, a kind of stepped pyramid leading to the heavens. The intrepid visitor should not miss the famous hanging gardens of Babylon. If they are too much, try the much smaller hanging basket of Babylon. Not as impressive, perhaps, but a lot easier to water.

1 Ishtar temple
2 Ziggurat Tower
3 Belitnina temple
4 Adad temple
5 Marduk temple
6 Gula temple
7 Shamash temple
8 Adad Gate
9 Shamash Gate
10 Urash Gate
11 Zababa Gate
12 Marduk Gate
13 Sin Gate
14 Hanging Gardens

❽ Zedekiah, King of Judah
24:18–25:21; 2 Ch 36:17–21; Je 52:3–30

The last king of Judah was Zedekiah, Jehoiachin's uncle, placed on the throne by Nebuchadnezzar. Zedekiah, in a last futile gesture, rebels against Babylon. Jerusalem is besieged and, after eighteen months of appalling suffering, the city is taken and Zedekiah is captured. After a show trial, the king has to watch his sons being killed. It is the last thing he sees, because Nebuchadnezzar has him blinded.

It is the end for Jerusalem. The temple is burned, the palaces destroyed, the walls broken. The temple fittings are dragged off to Babylon and the last shreds of the Judaean army rooted out and executed (25:8–21).

And the first one of you to sing "hi-ho, hi-ho" will get a slap.

Gedaliah 25:22–26; Je 40:7–9; 41:1–3

The epilogue to this sad history tells us that Gedaliah was appointed to be governor over what was left of the country. He was assassinated by the last fragments of the royal family, who viewed him as a collaborator, and who then fled into exile in Egypt.

Like the northern kingdom of Israel, the southern kingdom of Judah had been utterly destroyed. It lasted some 140 years longer, and it was not the Assyrians but the Babylonians who completed the destruction, but the effect was the same. The temple was a ruin, Jerusalem was in ashes, the dream of the Promised Land was, it would seem, at an end.

1 Chronicles
How it should have been

Kings was written to explain their history to the Jews in exile; Chronicles was addressed to those who had returned. Faced with the ruins of their land and their temple, the book asks the question, "Does God care about Israel anymore?"

Who: According to tradition, Ezra wrote Chronicles (not to mention Ezra and Nehemiah), but this is uncertain. The author was probably a priest, given the book's emphasis on the temple and priesthood.

When: Around the fifth century BC, after the Jews had returned to Jerusalem.

What: Chronicles is dominated by two great themes: the house of David and the house of God. The book aims to express the continuity of God's relationship with his people, arguing that the Israel that was re-established after the exile was the same nation that it had been before. That is why it begins with so many genealogies. Only by going right back to the beginning can Israel look to the future.

Quick Guide

Author
Possibly Ezra, but unknown

Type
History

Purpose
A reminder to Israel of their purpose and glory days.

Key verse
17:14 "I will make sure that your son and his descendants will rule my people and my kingdom forever."

If you remember one thing about this book . . .
God looks at the long-term, and he is in control of history.

Your 10 minutes start now
Read chapters 11, 14–17, 28–9

This continuity is also expressed through the worship practices of Israel. The writer of Chronicles places a great emphasis on the importance of the temple and the priesthood. Just as the "modern" kings were the successors of David, the rebuilt temple was the successor of Solomon's temple and Moses' tabernacle. The priests were the successors of Aaron.

There was a problem, though. The people who returned were from the kingdom of Judah. Those taken into exile in Assyria—the ten tribes of Israel—never did return. So how can it still be the same people? Chronicles makes it clear that many Jews came south throughout the history of the two kingdoms, often for religious reasons, either during times of persecution, or after the conquest by Assyria. The new nation, therefore, still has representatives of all twelve tribes. The line continues.

The Route Through 1 Chronicles

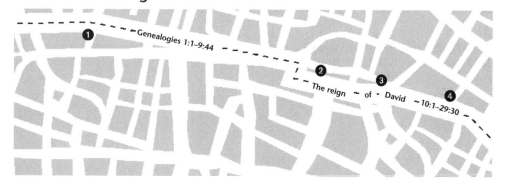

1 — Genealogies 1:1–9:44

2 — 3 — The reign ~ of · David ~ 10:1–29:30 — 4

Puzzling Points

You call this history?

If the book of Kings raises some problems with chronology and some difficulties between our understanding of history and the Bible's view, Chronicles blows the entire concept of history out of the water.

The problem is that Chronicles provides a blatantly sanitized view of the past. The bulk of the book, for example, is dedicated to David and Solomon—which would be fine, except that it leaves out anything that would tarnish their reputations. There are no civil wars, no rebellions and, most significantly, David's affair with Bathsheba is omitted entirely. Similarly, Solomon ascends the throne to unanimous approval. He takes no revenge on those who wronged David and no mention is made of his later idolatry or his incredibly numerous wives. There is no mention of Solomon's harsh treatment of the ten tribes, either. Blame for the split between Israel and Judah is, in this account, entirely placed on the shoulders of Jeroboam.

Chronicles offers a completely different account of the crowning of Solomon, where an apparently fit and healthy David hands over the crown to his son at a great ceremony. Kings records the handover as being organized over the old king's deathbed, secured by deathbed vows and by the necessary "removal" of Solomon's opponents.

Whatever else it is, Chronicles cannot be regarded as history in the same sense as Kings, let alone in the same way that we would understand the idea.

So what is it, then? What could justify this piece of Davidic propaganda?

The answer is that it is inspiration. It's more like an inspiring speech or sermon. The author selects from a wide range of material to provide a view of history that will inspire and encourage the readers. The author was writing for a group of people who were trying to put their nation back together. They needed to be inspired by the successes of their heroes, not depressed by their failures.

The chronicler wasn't really telling history as we would understand it. He wasn't claiming to. He was painting an ideal portrait of what kings should be like. He was inspiring the restored kingdom with a selection of "Israel's greatest hits."

It emphasized to the Jews who had returned to Jerusalem that they stood in a long line of faithful men of God, that the temple was vital as a sign of the God they worshiped and the heart of their nation and that, just as God had established the kingdom of Israel in the past, he would do so again. It reaffirmed their links with the past. Those who had been in exile in Babylon must have wondered whether God had forgotten them, whether they had been fooling themselves all those years. No, replies the chronicler. God's promises still stand. The people of David, of Moses, Abraham and Isaac, are alive and well and worshiping in Jerusalem.

PARALLEL LINES
Where have I seen that before?

	1 Chronicles	2 Samuel	▷ Page
Death of Saul	10:1–14	31:1–13	101
David becomes king	11:1–9	5:1–10	103
David's warriors	11:10–12:40	23:8–39	...
God's promise to David	17:1–26	7:1–29	104
David's victories	18:1–17	8:1–18	...
War with Ammon	19:1–20:3	10:1–19	...
The Philistine giants	20:4–8	21:15–22	106
The census	21:1–30	24:1–25	106

Genealogies   1:1–9:44

❶ Family matters

The idea here is to show that the restored Israel was a continuation of the past. The genealogies are a kind of shorthand reminder of all that God has done for the nation. So, although the early history of Israel is not recounted in detail, the roll call of names would have been enough to remind the Jews of the great saving acts of their God. So we have Adam and Noah (1:1), Abraham and Isaac (1:28). However, some notables are missing. There is no Moses, no Joshua. Why? Because after the list reaches the twelve sons of Jacob (Israel) (2:1) the focus narrows down onto the house of Judah. This book, remember, is going to be largely about David and Solomon—of the tribe of Judah.

After the extensive genealogies, the chronicler goes on to list the people who returned to Israel after the exile and their roles and responsibilities (9:1–34). Again, the emphasis is on the temple, with a detailed description of the guarding of, and provision for the house of God.

The reign of David   10:1–29:30

❷ David brings back the ark
13:1–14; 15:1–16:43; 2 Sa 6:1–22 ▷104

The details of David's preparations in chapter 15 are expanded from the material in 2 Samuel. It reflects the emphasis of the chronicler on the Levites and the music and the names of the people involved. The song that David sings in chapter 16 is actually made up of excerpts from three different psalms. Whether, therefore, David actually sang this psalm, or whether the chronicler has constructed a representative psalm, is open to debate.

PARALLEL LINES
Where have I seen that before?

	1 Chronicles	Psalm
First section	16:8–22	105:1–15
Second section	16:23–33	96:1–13
Third section	16:34–36	106:1, 47–48

❸ The plans for the temple 22:1–29:9

Again, the chronicler's theme of the temple leads to more information about the purchase of the threshing floor. In the Chronicles account, David cannot build the temple because he has too much blood on his hands—his involvement in wars means that he is in some way not pure enough (22:8–9). However, that doesn't stop him thinking about it.

In Chronicles, David makes specific plans for the place, bringing in stonemasons and laying down instructions for Solomon to follow. Even though David knows he is not to be the one to build the temple, he wants to pass on his ideas to his son. It is as if he builds it in his imagination. His preparation was not limited just to the stone and the architectural features, but also to the administration. Chronicles lists the duties of the priests (23:1–24:31), the musicians (25:1–31) and the guards (26:1–28), as well as officials such as army commanders, tribal leaders and those responsible for the royal treasury.

❹ Solomon is crowned king 28:1–29:9 ▷111

David hands over to Solomon the architectural plans for the temple and "officially" hands over the throne. This idealized account is very different from the tales of ambition, malice and greed for power that we find in the beginning of Kings. There is no mention of the aged David warming himself against a young woman, nor of the rebellion of Adonijah and the challenge to Solomon's succession.

David is paralleled with Moses in this book. Just as Moses did not make it into the Promised Land, so David does not get to build the temple. But equally, just as Moses received the instructions for the tabernacle from God, David receives the instructions for the temple (1 Ch 22–29 echoes Ex 25–30).

2 Chronicles
The time of the temple

When it comes to the temple, the chronicler is a complete anorak. He is obsessed with the detail of the rites and rituals, of who did what and when. Why should this be? The secret lies in the time that he was writing. He was writing for an audience who had just returned from Babylon and who were struggling to rebuild the temple. In that context it was vital that they understood as much as they could about what the temple was used for, what should be in it and what activities it should involve. The temple was the single biggest symbol of God's presence in the land of Israel. The chronicler therefore gives a huge amount of time and attention to its history and activities. This was what the new building should be aiming at.

A similar reason lies behind the inclusion of all the lists of names and tribes. These are not mere historical details—although to us they might seem irrelevant. To the people who had returned from exile, they were important because they could see the role that their ancestors, their tribe, had played. Thus the history was personalized for them. They were urged to continue the work that had been given to their ancestors.

The kings in the Chronicles

Many monarchs in Kings are "not quite" good, or "not all" bad. Even the good kings frequently fail to remove all the pagan altars from the land (e.g., 2 Ki 15:4 in the reign of Uzziah). Chronicles takes a much more "black and white" approach to history. There are no gray areas, no gradual descents into idolatry. He characteristically divides reigns into two parts, with kings starting out good and then turning bad. Thus, while Joash followed the example and advice of Jehoiada he was successful. The moment Jehoiada dies, everything changes and the result is catastrophic. This allows the chronicler to draw people's attention to one of his main themes: the consequences of good and evil.

The Route Through 2 Chronicles

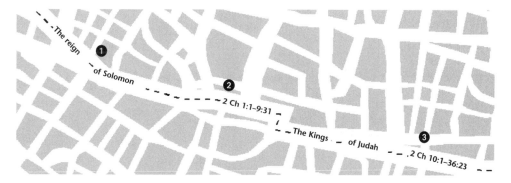

The reign ❶ of Solomon
2 Ch 1:1–9:31 ❷
The Kings of Judah
2 Ch 10:1–36:23 ❸

The reign of Solomon 1:1–9:31

As with David, this is an idealized picture of a monarch. The first book of Chronicles built a picture of David as comparable with Moses. Similar comparisons are drawn here, with Solomon and the builder Huram Abi likened to Bezalel and Oholiab in Exodus (Ex 35:30–36:7). The point here is to establish and reinforce the continuity of the history of Israel. Just as God gave instructions for the building of the tabernacle, he has also given instructions for the building of the temple.

❶ Building the temple   2:1–7:22 ▷111

The details of Solomon building the temple echo the account in 1 Kings. Again, some of the more contentious details are omitted—the forced labor that is used in the building is stated in Chronicles to have come from for-eigners (2:17–18), but the later complaints of the ten tribes indicate that some Jews were involved. The details of the building are slightly abridged —1 Kings 6:4–20 is omitted completely—but there is more detail about the furnishings in Chronicles.

❷ Other events in Solomon's reign   8:1–9:31

Solomon's riches, splendor and wisdom are all emphasized—and none of the later blemishes on his career are mentioned. There is no apostasy, no mention of foreign gods. This is a vision of a perfect time for Israel, with cups and dishes of pure gold, because silver was "almost worthless in those days" (9:20).

Solomon's temple

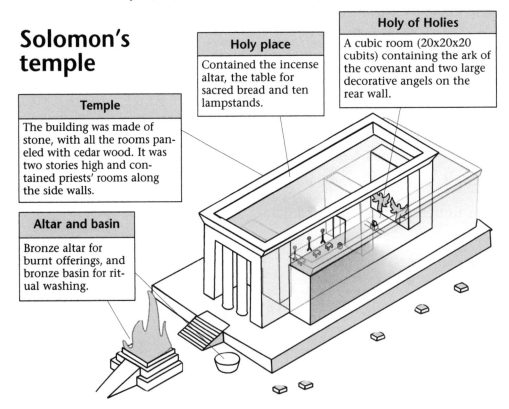

Holy place

Contained the incense altar, the table for sacred bread and ten lampstands.

Holy of Holies

A cubic room (20x20x20 cubits) containing the ark of the covenant and two large decorative angels on the rear wall.

Temple

The building was made of stone, with all the rooms pan-eled with cedar wood. It was two stories high and con-tained priests' rooms along the side walls.

Altar and basin

Bronze altar for burnt offerings, and bronze basin for rit-ual washing.

PARALLEL LINES

	2 Chronicles	1 Kings	▷ Page
Wisdom of Solomon	1:1–13	3:1–15	111
Solomon's wealth	1:14–17	10:26–29	...
Solomon starts the temple	2:1–17	5:1–12	111
The temple is consecrated	3:1–7:22	6:1–8:66	114

Landmark: Temples and Shrines

In ancient cultures, temples were the homes of gods. They were where the god lived and where his followers would bring offerings. The temple would often contain a statue of the god, as well as an altar for the offerings and even a throne for the god to sit on. Most early temples followed the same pattern, consisting of a main building and an inner sanctum, where the high priest would be able to consult with the god.

Israel's God was different. He did not need a house in which to dwell. And yet the Bible talks of a number of temples or shrines that were built in his honor, and where he spoke to his people.

Tabernacle

The first of these is the tabernacle, built by Moses. The tabernacle was a kind of mobile temple. It had all the paraphernalia of a temple—the altar, the priests, the inner sanctum where God could be consulted. As Israel was wandering in the desert, however, it could be packed up and transported from place to place.

Shrines

After the Israelites entered the Promised Land, the tabernacle was replaced by a number of permanent shrines, notably at Shiloh (1 Sa 3:3) and Bethel (Ju 20:26–27). Both sites housed the ark of the covenant at various times. After the kingdoms divided, Jeroboam of Israel made Bethel the religious center of his kingdom, installing a statue of a golden calf and making sacrifices to false gods (1 Ki 12:20–29).

Temple

Once David unified the kingdom and centralized the government in Jerusalem, it was natural that the ark would find its resting place in the city. David wanted to build a temple, but the work was completed by his son, Solomon. There were to be three temples on this site. Solomon's was destroyed by the Babylonians in 587 BC, but was rebuilt seventy years later. This second temple lasted for some 500 years, until it was massively redeveloped by Herod the Great. Indeed, the reconstruction work continued for many decades—the third temple was still under construction during the life of Jesus. The third temple was finally completed in AD 64, but it only stood for six years. It was completely destroyed by the Romans in AD 70, following a Jewish uprising. There was never a temple in Israel again.

▷60, 63, 147, 286

The kings of Judah   10:1–36:23

The section covering the kings after Solomon focuses almost exclusively on the kings of Judah. It is considerably shorter than the section in Kings and much of it is drawn from a different source. The chronicler is interested primarily in Judah and the kings of Israel are only mentioned where their activities impinge on Judah.

The main aim of the Chronicles account is to trace the lineage of the house of David, and therefore to demonstrate God's promise to secure for David an unbroken line of descent. The other aim is to reinforce for the returning exiles that they are the true remnant of all Israel. Hence there are accounts of people from the northern tribes crossing the border and moving south throughout the history of the divided kingdom. Often this would be in response to apostasy and unfaithfulness in the north.

Rehoboam   10:1–12:16; 1 Ki 12:1–20 ▷116

Abijah   13:1–22; 1 Ki 15:1–8 ▷116

The chronicler's account of Abijah is around three times as long as that in Kings. Some of this is due to a lengthy speech the king gives (13:4–12), but there is also a difference of interpretation of the reign. Kings takes a broadly negative view of Abijah, whereas the chronicler has a more positive view. Largely this is because the chronicler places the blame for the split between the two kingdoms on the shoulders of Jeroboam. In Chronicles, therefore, Abijah is seen as an instrument of vengeance.

Asa   14:1–15:19 ▷116

The chronicler introduces chronological sections in his account of Asa to indicate the way the king changed. For ten years he did the right things, and an invasion by the Cushites was therefore repulsed (14:1–7). He continued to be a "good king" until the thirty-fifth year of his reign, when he was confronted with an invasion by Baasha, king of Israel. There is a problem here, since according to the chronology in Kings, Baasha was dead by the thirty-sixth year of Asa's reign. Various solutions have been suggested, but it is likely to be a copyist's error—the invasion is undated in Kings.

However, the point is that Asa changed: he relied on Benhadad of Aram, paying him with silver and gold from the temple and even imprisoning Hanani the prophet. The chronicler emphasizes that faithfulness brings protection from the Lord, but that disobedience brings punishment.

Jehoshaphat   17:1–21:3 ▷120

This theme is picked up in the account of Jehoshaphat's reign, which again is much fuller in Chronicles than in Kings. Kings is concerned with the relationship between Ahab and Elijah, whereas the prophet is only mentioned once in 2 Chronicles, and then only because he sends a letter. Jehoshaphat is criticized for his unwise alliance with Ahab, but praised for his faithfulness to God and his emphasis on justice and fair judgment (19:1–11). His efforts against Moab and Ammon held a special relevance for the chronicler because these same people were harassing the Jews of the restored Israel.

Jehoram   21:4–20; 2 Ki 8:16–24 ▷123

Jehoram's assassination of his brothers is not mentioned in Kings—although plenty of the kings of Israel did exactly the same. Jehoram is criticized as "walking in the ways of the kings of Israel," which is about as big an insult as the chronicler could manage. Jehoram married into Ahab's family, and followed in his father-in-law's footsteps. Elijah's letter (21:12–15) predicts the consequences of Jehoram's unfaithfulness: his sons and wives will die, and he will die through disease.

Ahaziah   22:1–9; 2 Ki 8:25–29 ▷123

This account is shorter than in Kings. The Kings account concentrates on the rebellion of Jehu and the death of Omri, but the chronicler is not interested in the northern kingdom. The account of Ahaziah's death differs slightly from that in Kings. Here, Ahaziah is found hiding in Samaria, captured and killed. In Kings he is shot while trying to escape.

Athaliah   22:10–12; 2 Ki 11:1–3 ▷125

The only queen of Judah to reign in her own name, her approach to securing the succession (i.e., killing everyone remotely related to her) was obviously something she had learned from her husband Jehoram. If she had succeeded in this, she would have broken the chain of descent through the house of David. However, the real king, as it were, was in hiding.

Joash   23:1–24:27; 2 Ki 11:4–21 ▷125

The chronicler's account emphasizes the widespread popularity of the coup, and also renews the sanctity of the temple—only the authorized people were allowed in the temple (23:6–7). It is in Chronicles that the link between the presence of Jehoiada the high priest and the faithfulness of Joash is made plain. "As long as Jehoiada lived" sacrifices were made in the temple (24:14), but after his death, Joash was seduced by foreign gods.

Retribution was immediate—indeed, one of the themes of Chronicles is the swiftness of the consequences. Apostasy against the Lord had immediate and serious consequences for the kingdom. Joash's wickedness—and his killing of Jehoiada's son—resulted in an invasion from Syria and the assassination of the king. But it was not just the king—the chronicler records that the Lord sent prophets to the people who "refused to listen" (24:19).

Amaziah   25:1–28; 2 Ki 14:1–22 ▷126

Amaziah, like Joash, had a reign of two halves. The good years (25:1–13) are followed by years of wickedness (25:14–28). Ironically, it is at the moment of his greatest success that Amaziah falls from grace. He defeats the Edomites and brings back some of their gods. His arrogance leads him into a foolish challenge to the king of Israel, resulting in the conquest of Jerusalem and the capture of the king. "As soon as Amaziah started disobeying the LORD some people in Jerusalem plotted against Amaziah ... and killed him" (25:27).

PARALLEL LINES
Alternative accounts in the book of Kings

	2 Chronicles	1 Kings	2 Kings	▷ Page
Rehoboam	10:1–12:16	12:1–20	...	116
Abijah	13:1–22	15:1–8	...	116
Asa	14:1–15:19	15:9–24	...	116
Jehoshaphat	17:1–21:1	22:41–50	...	120
Ahab of Israel	18:1–34	22:1–35	...	120
Jehoram	21:4–20	...	8:16–24	123
Ahaziah	22:1–9	...	8:25–29	123
Athaliah	22:10–12	...	11:1–3	125
Joash	23:1–24:27	...	11:4–21	125
Amaziah	25:1–28	...	14:1–22	126

```
┌─────────────────────────────────────────────────────────┐
│                    PARALLEL LINES                        │
│          Alternative accounts in the Book of Kings       │
│                                                          │
│              2 Chronicles   1 Kings    2 Kings    ▷ Page │
│   Uzziah      26:1–23       ...        15:1–7      126   │
│   Jotham      27:1–9        ...        15:32–38    127   │
│   Ahaz        28:1–27       ...        16:1–20     127   │
│   Hezekiah    29:1–32:33    ...        18:1–20:21  128   │
│   Manasseh    33:1–20       ...        21:1–18     128   │
│   Amon        33:21–25      ...        21:19–26    128   │
│   Josiah      34:1–35       ...        22:1–30     128   │
│   Jehoahaz    36:1–4        ...        23:31–34    129   │
│   Jehoiakim   36:5–8        ...        23:35–24:7  129   │
│   Jehoiachin  36:9–10       ...  24:8–17; 25:27–30 129   │
│   Zedekiah    36:11–14      ...        24:18–25:21 130   │
└─────────────────────────────────────────────────────────┘
```

Uzziah   26:1–23 ▷126

Once again, Uzziah's reign is a dichotomy—good followed by bad. Wisdom and faithfulness leads to success, before arrogance leads to disaster. Blessings and success lead to power (26:1–15). Then Uzziah becomes arrogant and, as with some of his predecessors, illness strikes.

Jotham   27:1–9 ▷127

Jotham remained faithful to God and was rewarded (27:6).

Ahaz   28:1–27 ▷127

Ahaz's reign has, in this account, not one single redeeming feature. He does not start good and turn bad, he starts bad and gets worse. He invites Tiglath-Pileser from Assyria to come to his aid, which simply makes things worse (28:20), but instead of seeking the Lord, he sins even more than before (28:22). He closes the temple and takes away all the furnishings.

❸ Hezekiah   29:1–32:33 ▷128

The chronicler dedicates more space to Hezekiah than to any other post-Solomon king. His faithfulness is linked to that of "his ancestor David" (29:2) and the chronicler focuses particularly on the religious reform and reconsecration of the temple. He devotes—as we have now come to expect—a lot of time to the administration and the religious duties. In Kings, Hezekiah's reign is mainly noted for the conflict with Sennacherib. There are numerous parallels with the chronicler's description of Solomon, especially in the celebration in the temple (30:25–26), his wealth (32:27–29) and the extent of his kingdom (30:25). Hezekiah is, then, a second Solomon. However, the chronicler omits certain details that are in Kings. According to Kings, when Sennacherib comes to attack Jerusalem, Hezekiah sends out a bribe taken from the temple treasuries (2 Ki 18:14–16). Hezekiah, like Solomon and David, is presented in his best light. He does, admittedly, talk about Hezekiah's pride (32:24–26), but the event is dealt with quickly.

Manasseh   33:1–20 ▷128

Manasseh was the longest reigning of any of the kings of Judah and the account here differs greatly from that in Kings. Although both books record his evil deeds, only Chronicles records his journey to Babylon and his repentance. The writer of Kings sees Manasseh as almost completely rotten and, indeed, as the primary cause of the exile in Babylon (2 Ki 21:10–15). Chronicles does not dismiss this picture but adds later events.

Amon   33:21–25 ▷128

Josiah   34:1–35:26 ▷128

Both accounts of Josiah concentrate on his religious reforms and the discovery of the Book of the Law. Typically, the chronicler gives more emphasis to Josiah's celebration of the Passover, with attention to the detailed arrangements.

Josiah was a good king, whose ending came about because of pride. The prophet Jeremiah held him in high esteem and even composed a lament on his death (35:25). It is this that leads some to believe that Lamentations was written by Jeremiah.

Jehoahaz   36:1–4 ▷129

Jehoiakim   36:5–8 ▷129

Jehoiachin   36:9–10 ▷129

Zedekiah   36:11–14 ▷130

View Points

Manasseh in Kings and Chronicles

On one hand:	On the other hand:
Some experts argue that the chronicler's emphasis on divine reward and retribution led him to alter history. In order to explain the length of Manasseh's reign, he had to have repented. Otherwise surely the Lord would not have been treating evil with the swift retribution that it deserved.	Others say that the chronicler was drawing from an authentic source—he simply had access to material that the writer of Kings didn't have. After all, there are plenty of other long, evil reigns recorded in Chronicles.

Moving on: The point is that Manasseh is like the returning Israelites. He was punished, but he returned to do good things. They should follow his example.

The final four kings of Judah follow in quick succession. The game is up. Their continued unfaithfulness brings down the Babylonian forces on them and the country is captured. Pharaoh Neco takes Jehoahaz captive and replaces him with Eliakim, whom he renames. Then Nebuchadnezzar removes Jehoiakim and Jehoiachin and places their uncle on the throne—whom he renames Zedekiah. The renaming is a symbolic sign of ownership. These kings were owned by their conquerors to such an extent that even their names were changed.

The conclusion   36:15–23

The conclusion of Chronicles is different to that of Kings. The writer of Kings wanted to show how the exile had come about—and his history did not extend beyond the exile. The only way he could show that the Davidic descent was still in action was to point to the later favor bestowed on the kings while in Babylon.

The chronicler, on the other hand, writes from a postexilic viewpoint. For him, the exile was a time of purification. Just as the temple was repeatedly purified after being closed or abused, this was a chance for the people and the land to be made new. To this end he points to the Levitical "Sabbath rest" (36:21). According to Leviticus, the people had to allow the land to rest every seven years (Le 25:1–7). This was a Sabbath for the entire country—a period when the land could recover from all those kings, good and bad.

The book ends with the proclamation of Cyrus. There was to be a new temple again. The people were to return. The Sabbath was over and it was time to go back to work.

Ezra

The journey home

Ezra is the story of the return of the Jews from Babylon. Early manuscripts put both Ezra and Nehemiah together into one book. However, the beginning of Nehemiah indicates that they are two separate documents, although both cover similar ground.

Who: Ezra and others. Some argue that the same person who wrote Chronicles also wrote Ezra. Certainly the beginning of Ezra is virtually identical to the end of Chronicles, indicating that the same hand wrote both. There are also lots of lists from official sources and the usual genealogies. It seems likely, therefore, that the book of Ezra is "3 Chronicles"—a continuation of the Chronicle taking Israel past the exile and into the return. Whether the author of all three books was Ezra, we don't know, although the use of Ezra's memoirs and the first-person "I" offer some support.

When: Around 440 BC. Traditionally, Ezra arrived in Jerusalem in 458 BC and Nehemiah in 445 BC. However, some argue that Nehemiah arrived earlier.

What: The aim of the book is to show how God's promises were fulfilled. He promised through the prophets that the land would be restored to his people.

To achieve this, God uses foreign kings (Cyrus, Darius and Artaxerxes), Jewish leaders (Joshua, Zerubbabel, Ezra and Nehemiah) and prophets (Haggai and Zechariah). Through their endeavor the city is restored, the temple rebuilt and the people returned.

Quick Guide

Author
Ezra and whoever wrote Chronicles

Type
History

Purpose
The history of the return from exile and the rebuilding of Jerusalem.

Key verses

3:11–12 "Everyone started shouting and praising the LORD because work on the foundation of the temple had begun. Many of the older priests and Levites and the heads of families cried aloud because they remembered seeing the first temple years before. But others were so happy that they celebrated with joyful shouts."

If you remember one thing about this book . . .

God fulfills his promises—even when things seem bleak.

Your 10 minutes start now

Read chapters 1, 3–4, 7, 9–10

The Route Through Ezra

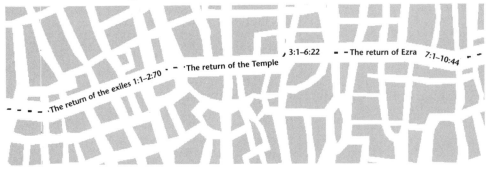

The return of the exiles 1:1–2:70

The return of the Temple 3:1–6:22

The return of Ezra 7:1–10:44

The return of the exiles
1:1–2:70

Cyrus has defeated Babylon and the first exiles are allowed to return. The governor of Judah was Sheshbazzar, who may well have been a Jewish official, given a Babylonian name as was the practice. Indeed, some claim that Sheshbazzar is the Babylonian name for King Zerubbabel, on the grounds that both were governors (5:14; Hag 1:1, 2:2) and both laid the foundation of the temple (3:2–8; Hag 1:14–15; Zec 4:6–10). The likelihood, however, is that they were two different people, with Sheshbazzar the "official" leader, and Zerubbabel the popular leader. The fact that both laid the foundations is probably due to the fact that so little was achieved under Sheshbazzar that the whole process was started again.

The long list of people who returned is almost exactly paralleled by Nehemiah 7:6–73. While in exile, the people obviously remembered their hometowns and villages.

Return of the temple
3:1–6:22

Joshua the priest and Zerubbabel the leader begin the huge task of rebuilding the city and the temple. The first thing they do is to rebuild the altar so that sacrifices can take place (3:1–6). Then, to huge joy and tearful delight, the foundations of the temple are laid (3:7–13).

The rebuilding is not without opposition and here we have to unravel the chronology, which gets very confused. Chapter 4 contains a brief history of opposition, spanning the reigns of several different monarchs. First we have opposition during the reign of Cyrus (559–530 BC) when the enemies offer their "help," perhaps intending to slow down progress and sabotage proceedings (4:1–3). When this is refused, they begin a propaganda war, aiming to discourage the workers and spread disinformation (4:4). Thus work stopped until the reign of Darius (522–486 BC). After this, chronologically speaking, we should hop to chapter 5, where Darius orders the rebuilding to continue.

Instead, the author inserts accounts of the opposition under Xerxes (486–465 BC) (4:6) and Artaxerxes (465–424 BC). This, rather confusingly, refers to a later time, *after* the temple had been finished. The work that is being hindered here is the defenses of the city. The enemies send messages to Artaxerxes I, the Persian emperor, accusing the Jews of rebuilding

Puzzling Points
Why don't the numbers add up?

Ezra 2:64–65 contains the total number of people who returned. But when you add up the individual figures given in 2:3–60 it adds up to just under 30,000: it's short by 10,000–12,000. Similar figures given in Nehemiah add up to around 31,000 people.

It may be that this missing 12,000 is made up of women and children and some extra priests who were not accounted for (2:62–63). The likeliest explanation, however, is that it is a simple copying error—which would also account for the differences between the lists in Ezra and Nehemiah.

Details, Details . . .

Want to read Ezra in the right order? Here's how:

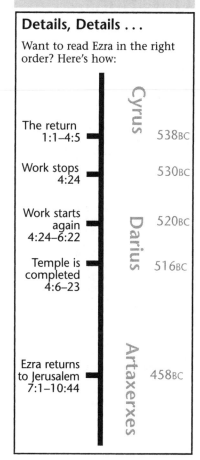

The return 1:1–4:5	Cyrus — 538BC
Work stops 4:24	530BC
Work starts again 4:24–6:22	Darius — 520BC
Temple is completed 4:6–23	516BC
Ezra returns to Jerusalem 7:1–10:44	Artaxerxes — 458BC

the defences purely so that they can rebel against Persia (4:6–16). The king investigates the history and decides to stop the work, on the grounds that the Jews have a long history of "troublemaking" (4:17–21).

After this interlude, we return in chapter 5 to the temple and to the year 520 BC. In a series of speeches, the prophets Haggai and Zechariah exhort the people to recommence the work (5:1–2; Hag 1:1; Zech 1:1).

The officials, concerned at what is happening, write to the king. A search of the royal archives reveals the edict of Cyrus, allowing the Jews to work on their temple and city (5:1–6:12). Darius authorizes—and even pays for —the rebuilding of the temple, which is completed on March 12, 516 BC (6:15), almost seventy years after its destruction. About a month later, Passover is celebrated in the temple again.

The new temple followed, broadly, the same ground plan as Solomon's, but the Holy of Holies was left empty because the ark of the covenant was now irretrievably lost. Haggai reports that those old enough to remember the original were disappointed at this new temple, but it was to enjoy a much longer life than Solomon's original.

Questions, Questions
Divorcing the foreign women

I thought divorce was bad? Why is it OK here?
Generally divorce is discouraged in the Bible, but what was at stake here was the future of the country. This is not a case of marital differences, it's about the way in which the foreign influence was pulling God's people away from their tasks and responsibilities.
So, if I can prove my wife is forcing me to worship foreign gods I can divorce her?
Ezra was faced with an immediate problem and had to come up with a solution. That doesn't mean that the solution can be applied to all instances. Marriage in the Old Testament times was hugely different from what it is today. So we can't just take instances of what occurred here and turn them into universals.
So you're saying I can't divorce her for disbelief, then?
No, the reason you can't divorce your wife is more fundamental.
What is it?
You're not married, you idiot.
▷331

The return of Ezra
7:1–10:44

There now follows a gap in proceedings, during which time the letters to Artaxerxes were written (see chapter 4). Work on the city comes to a standstill for some sixty years until 458 BC when Ezra decides to approach the king and ask for permission to return to Jerusalem. There were still Jews living in Babylon and, from these, Ezra took more back to Judah to restart the work on the city and bring order to the region.

Ezra gathers the people together in the town of Ahava and sets off on the long journey back to Jerusalem. When he gets there, he finds that the original returnees have married with people from the tribes around and are now "living just like the people around them." Far from keeping God's city holy, they are even accused of returning to the idol worship and false faith of the Canaanites (9:1–4).

It is clear that drastic surgery is needed. Ezra prays long and hard, and his prayer brings those who have fallen away from the Lord back to their senses. They agree to do whatever Ezra recommends, and what Ezra recommends is divorce. Despite a few objections, the foreign wives who have led the priests astray are divorced and their influence is removed (10:1–17). The book ends with a long list of those who agreed to divorce their foreign wives.

Nehemiah
Praying and planning

Nehemiah is a companion piece to Ezra. Indeed, in some early manuscripts, the two are formed into one book.

It begins twelve years after the end of Ezra, when Nehemiah, a Jew still living in Babylon, receives news of Jerusalem. The city is still in a state of disrepair, the gates have never been replaced and Jerusalem is still under threat.

Who: The author is unknown. It is possible that it was the same person who compiled Chronicles and Ezra.

When: Probably around the same time as Ezra, i.e., c. 330 BC.

Nehemiah goes to Jerusalem   1:1–2:10

Nehemiah is the king's wine bearer (2:1), a highly trusted official in ancient courts since he has to taste the wine and check it isn't poisoned. He hears the news of Jerusalem and, like his forerunner Ezra, responds with prayer and fasting. However, one of the key characteristics of Nehemiah is his patience. He heard about Jerusalem in November/December 446 BC and did not present his petition to the king until March/April 445 BC (1:1; 2:1). The reason for his delay may have been that the king was away in his winter palace, or simply that the time wasn't right and the king wasn't in the right mood.

Eventually, however, he goes before the king and his demeanor is noticed. It was usually the duty of courtiers and counselors to remain thoroughly cheerful in the king's presence, but Nehemiah could not pretend. His sadness is noticed, his trouble is explained and his prayers are answered (2:1–9). Nehemiah appears to have asked more for a leave of absence from the court—the king evidently expects him to return after some time (2:6).

Quick Guide

Author
Unknown, but probably the guy who wrote Chronicles

Type
History

Purpose
The account of Nehemiah's return to Jerusalem and the rebuilding of the walls.

Key verse
4:9 "But we kept on praying to our God, and we also stationed guards day and night."

If you remember one thing about this book . . .
Prayer and planning go hand in hand. (And hard work as well, but then you'd need three hands . . .)

Your 10 minutes start now
Read chapters 1–2, 4–6, 8–9, 13

The Route Through Nehemiah

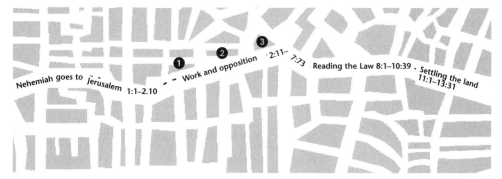

Nehemiah goes to Jerusalem 1:1–2.10   **1** Work and opposition 2:11–7:73   **2** **3** Reading the Law 8:1–10:39   Settling the land 11:1–13:31

Work and opposition 2:11–7:73

Nehemiah's journey provokes opposition, notably from Sanballat the Horonite and Tobiah the Ammonite. These were two local governors. Sanballat was the governor of Samaria. Probably Tobiah was the governor of Ammon. Their opposition was not religious but political—a strong Judah would reduce their power and influence. Nehemiah's task, therefore, is carried out with caution and carefulness. He inspects the walls discreetly (2:11–16), encourages the local leaders (2:17–18) and establishes his right to take action in the face of opposition (2:19–20).

❶ Nehemiah's organization 2:11–4:23

Chapter 3 describes Nehemiah's organization. Forty key individuals are named and allocated to about forty-five different sections. The account implies that most of the work concentrated on rebuilding the gates to the city. These were vital, since they were the obvious points where enemies might enter. The workers cover all sections of society, starting with the high priest himself, Eliashib (3:1), and including goldsmiths, perfume makers, merchants and temple servants.

Despite the ridicule of Sanballat and Tobiah, the walls are gradually increased in height (4:1–7). When their plots increase, Nehemiah responds in typical fashion: they "kept on praying" and also "stationed guards." This combination of faith and practical action is typical of Nehemiah's approach. He allies a deep faith in God with careful planning. His workers work with a trowel in one hand and a sword in the other—indicating their awareness of the task to be done and the threat facing them (4:9–23).

❷ Fighting oppression 5:1–19

Nehemiah was also concerned with the poor and oppressed and when evidence comes of Jews oppressing their brothers, he acts swiftly (5:1–13). Again, despite being angry, he thinks it over (5:7). He challenges the people publicly to set right their wrongs and they respond to his speech. Perhaps they were responding to his example (5:14–19), for he made sure that he provided for the poor and made no profit from his situation. Although he could have bought property very cheaply, he did not abuse his position and his workers followed his example (5:16).

❸ Threats and blackmail 6:1–7:3

Sanballat and Tobiah attempt to lure Nehemiah to a meeting—presumably to divert him from his task (6:1–4). When that fails, they try to blackmail him by threatening to spread rumors to the Babylonian king (6:5–8). They even bribe some of his own workers to try to kill him (6:10–14). Shemaiah tries to persuade Nehemiah to enter the sanctuary—something that was forbidden—in order to save his life. Shemaiah's ignorance of the Law alerts Nehemiah to the threat. Nehemiah's response is simply to turn to prayer and finish his work.

Reading the Law 8:1–10:39

With the walls finished, all the people gather to hear the reading of "God's Law." There are different views of what this book was, but it was probably either

---

Details, Details . . .
The Feast of Shelters or Tabernacles (8:13–18)

The Jewish festival of *Succoth* was a commemoration of the time spent in the desert and a thanksgiving for God's protection. The people were instructed to live under tents or booths. The Law was read and, in later times, part of the temple was lit by giant candelabra. This may be the reason why Jesus' statement "I am the light of the world" took place during the feast.

▷**151**

Deuteronomy or the entire Pentateuch. The people apparently stood for five or six hours in rapt attention, but the important thing is that they didn't just listen to God's Law, they responded, first in worship (8:6) and then in repentance and prayer (8:13–9:37), and finally in action (10:28–39). Their response to the Bible is not simply to listen, but to act: an example to all of us.

Their commitments are listed in chapter 10. With a "complete understanding" of what they are doing (10:29), they commit themselves to obey the Law, not only with regards to tithing and temple worship, but also reinstituting the Jubilee (10:31).

Settling the land   11:1–13:31

Finally, Nehemiah oversees the settlement of the land. Jerusalem needed inhabitants, but the size of the city meant that not everyone could live there. Lots were cast to see who else should live in the city (11:1). After lists of those who were settled in the city, the dedication of the city walls is described (12:27–47). Two groups march around the top of the walls, praising God and singing. This is followed by a service at the temple.

The final part of Nehemiah describes the other regulations and changes that Nehemiah implemented in the light of the reading of the Law. He ensures that the work of the temple is fully supported and saves the priests and Levites from having to take on "second jobs" (13:4–14). He restores the proper use of the Sabbath and outlaws—as did Ezra—mixed marriages (13:15–29).

At times, this sounds uncomfortably like ethnic cleansing, with "anyone who had any foreign ancestors" being sent away (13:3). The issue, however, was that, as we have seen repeatedly in Israel's history, foreigners led to Israel compromising their faith. The key to this action lies in Nehemiah's statement right at the end of the book: "Then I made sure that the people were free from every foreign influence" (13:30). It was drastic action, but the restored kingdom was too precious to risk.

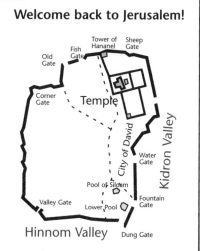

POSTCARD

In its postexilic state Jerusalem is even more picturesque than ever!

The intrepid tourist can explore the rubble of many famous buildings, including the temple, the gates and most of our defensive walls. But don't let the run-down appearance fool you— the city planners have big ideas for the city, including new walls and a brand new temple.

Indeed, the temple is one of the triumphs of the new city, although it cannot rival the temple of Solomon in its glory—especially since the Holy of Holies is empty and the ark of the covenant long since lost.

Nevertheless, this is still a city that centers around religion, and the visitor will be able to experience a number of religious festivals and ceremonies, and even spend five or six hours standing and listening to a guy read the Pentateuch. What more could you want?

Welcome back to Jerusalem!

Esther
God in the background...

The tale of a Hebrew girl who becomes a princess, Esther is a book with a certain fairy-tale quality about it. It is a story of court intrigue, danger and suspense. And God is never mentioned once . . .

Who: We don't know who wrote the book, but the evidence suggests a Jew living in a Persian city.

When: Around 460 BC-ish.

What: The book tells the tale of Esther, a Jewish girl who becomes queen of Persia and who rescues her people. What is really unusual about Esther is that the book doesn't mention God at all. Not once. Some experts believe that the letters YHWH—the Jewish letters for God (Yahweh)—are hidden in the book in the form of an acrostic. This, they argue, reflects one of the key themes of the book, the way that God's purposes are hidden from us, woven into the strands of history. With its message of liberation and justice for the oppressed, Esther remains as relevant today as it was when it was written.

The festival of Purim

Esther has remained a popular book with Jews because of its association with the festival of Purim. Purim is a celebration of the deliverance won by Esther. During the festival, the story is read in the synagogues and there are often plays and pageants based on the book. The name Purim may come from the Hebrew word for "lot," referring, perhaps, to Haman's casting of lots to decide the day of the Jews' destruction.

Quick Guide

Author
Unknown
Type
History
Purpose

To show how God rescues his people—even when we are unaware of his presence. To explain the history of the Jewish festival of Purim.

Key verse

4:14 "If you don't speak up now, we will somehow get help, but you and your family will be killed. It could be that you were made queen for a time like this!"

If you remember one thing about this book . . .

God is always at work in the world, even when we hardly notice he's there.

Your 10 minutes start now

Read chapters 2–7, 9. Or, if you want a *really* quick version, just read 9:24–32.

However, this link with Purim also casts some doubts on the book's authenticity as a historical account, since there is no mention of the festival anywhere else in the Bible, and no explicit reference to it being celebrated until the second century AD. Nonetheless, the book shows an intimate knowledge of Persian life and customs and the depiction of Xerxes is consistent with what we know of him from elsewhere.

The Route Through Esther

1 Esther becomes queen 1:1–2:23 · Haman's plot 3:1–15 · Esther foils the plot 4:1–9:19 · The Festival of Purim 9:20–10:3

Esther becomes queen 1:1–2:23

An everyday story of royal folk . . .

King Xerxes, the most powerful ruler of the world, has a disagreement with his wife, Queen Vashti, resulting in her dismissal. He succeeded Darius and ruled from 486–465 BC. Queen Vashti was, apparently, deposed in 484/483 BC. She reappears later as queen mother during the reign of her son Artaxerxes, but she obviously fell out of favor with her husband.

❶ The beauty treatment 2:1–18

Esther is recruited for the king's harem and given what appears to be extensive beauty treatment (2:12). Out of all the women, she is the king's favorite and she becomes queen. He is unaware that she is Jewish.

❷ The rescue 2:19–23

Her connections save the king, in fact. For Mordecai, her cousin, discovers a plot against the king. He tells Esther, who warns the king and the plot is foiled. Crucially, this fact—and Mordecai's role—is written down.

Haman's plot 3:1–15

Following the conquest of Babylon by Cyrus of Persia in 539 BC, many Jews returned to Jerusalem, but some moved eastwards, to the cities of Medea and Persia. There are, for example, texts from the time of Artaxerxes that list the names of around a hundred Jewish citizens in the city of Nippur.

Details, Details . . .
And my *real* name is . . .

Xerxes is the Hebrew version of the Greek name Ahasuerus. And Ahasuerus is the Greek version of the Persian name Khshayar-shan. (And, let's face it, if your name sounded like someone sneezing, you'd probably prefer the Hebrew version as well.)

Details, Details . . .
The laws of the Medes and Persians

Xerxes' advisers tell him to write a law that cannot be changed. This law is also mentioned in 8:8 and Daniel 6:8. The "laws of the Medes and Persians" have since become a synonym for anything that cannot be changed.

POSTCARD

The Persian Empire, we are proud to say, is the biggest empire yet seen on earth!

Following the defeat of the once-powerful Babylon empire by Cyrus the Great, we have continued to expand our empire, but, unlike our predecessors in the empire business, we are not interested in the wholesale movement of nations. On the contrary, we have pursued a policy of returning people and religious artifacts to the country from whence they came.

Our capital, Susa, is noted for its luxury and elegance and the work of our jewelers and goldsmiths is renowned. Our hairdressers aren't bad, either. Our main religion is Zoroastrianism, with its key principle "do good, hate evil." Some wonder how we can believe that while simultaneously invading small defenseless countries, but we like to think we're doing it for their own good.

Welcome to Persia!

1 Susa
2 Persepolis
3 Babylon I
4 Asshu
5 Nineveh
6 Damascus
7 Jerusalem
8 Memphis

However, being a follower of God in another land was never easy. Here, Haman, the top official in Xerxes' government, begins to get delusions of grandeur and orders everyone to bow to him. Mordecai—a Jew and Esther's cousin—refuses, with the result that Haman decides to kill the Jews. Orders are delivered with a chilling efficiency. All Jews—young, old, male, female—are to be killed. The date is settled by the casting of lots: the thirteenth day of Adar. It is clear that Xerxes does not know what is being planned. Haman does not tell Xerxes it is the Jews, he just refers to "some people" (3:8–9).

Esther foils the plot   4:1–9:19

When Mordecai discovers the plot, he puts on mourning clothes and goes to the palace gate. He gets a message to Esther about what is to happen to her people. She invites the king and Haman to a banquet.

❸ Reading the roll   6:1–14

Before this, we have an interlude where the king reads the book of records and remembers what Mordecai has done and decides to honor him. In an almost comic episode, Haman believes that the king is about to honor him, only to find out that the honor is due to go to Mordecai. And, much to his disgust, Haman has to organize the parade.

Haman now knows he is in serious trouble. When the king finds out what is going to happen to the Jews, Haman will be ruined (6:12–14). Indeed, the truth comes out almost immediately. At the banquet Esther reveals what Haman has been plotting. Haman is executed, in the very way that he had planned for Mordecai.

However, the danger has not yet gone away, for the orders have gone out to all parts of the kingdom. Esther pleads with the king to change the law. He gives her permission to write another law—overruling Haman's command—and the Jews take revenge on those who threatened them.

The festival of Purim   9:20–10:3

Mordecai orders that all Jews should commemorate their deliverance by celebrating the festival of Purim. The writer gives a short version of the story (9:24–32) and ends with a celebration of the greatness of Xerxes and his faithful servant Mordecai.

Landmark: Jewish Calendar and Festivals

There were three main festivals in the Jewish calendar. Passover commemorated the exodus from Egypt; Pentecost, or the Feast of Weeks, celebrated the wheat harvest; and Tabernacles (*Succoth,* or the Feast of Shelters), which was both a harvest festival and a commemoration of Israel's wanderings in the desert.

Other significant days included the Feast of Trumpets, which called people to fast in preparation for the Jewish new year (*Rosh Hashanah*), and the Day of Atonement (*Yom Kippur*) which was a day of national fasting and repentance. Lesser festivals included Purim, which recalled the Jews' deliverance in the time of Esther.

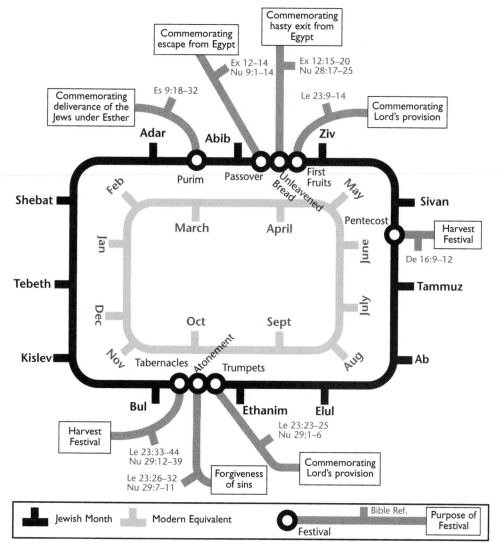

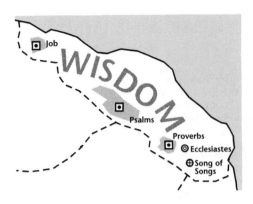

Wisdom

The five books that make up this section are extremely varied. All human life is here. Pain, pleasure, love, hate, sex, anger, cynical boredom, wild jubilation—all the emotions and attitudes that fill our days can be found in these five books.

In many ways they are the most "human" books of the Bible. They ask difficult questions and reflect bleak and often depressing moods, but just as they talk about the bad things, they also celebrate the good. There is often an almost awestruck appreciation of the physical world and what it means to be human. The Hebrew word for "wisdom" has a meaning similar to "life skills": the Jews have always regarded wisdom as something intensely practical, something to help you live your life. However, these are not just pragmatic skills to get us through the day. They are focused on God, on his relationship with humanity and how all wisdom and knowledge are based on a proper respect for him and his works.

Job

Job is a long meditation on the problem of suffering. Most of the book consists of a lengthy series of arguments between two opposing viewpoints at the end of which God appears and, it seems, doesn't answer the question.

Psalms

Psalms is a collection of 150 poems or songs. Some are joyful, some are sad, some are desperate, some are thankful. They are an intensely personal reflection of what it means to have a relationship with God.

Proverbs

Proverbs is a collection of wise and helpful sayings on all aspects of human life, from work to women to wine. The aim of Proverbs is to help us live right: it is a kind of mini-manual on human behavior.

Ecclesiastes

Ecclesiastes is one of the strangest books of the Bible, a dark, cynical meditation on the futility of existence. There are moments of recognition of God's greatness, but the prevailing mood of the book is that mood you have on a really bleak winter morning as you wait for the bus in the rain.

Song of Songs

Song of Songs is a love poem, joyously extolling the virtues of sex. Despite some efforts by well-meaning theologians and experts to make out that it is some kind of allegory, it is really about men and women. Not to mention gazelles.

Job
Faith and suffering

Job is one of the most powerful and mysterious books of the Bible. It is a poetic masterpiece, an exploration of suffering and faith and, above all, the power of God.

Who: It is not likely that the author was Job himself; more likely it was a later author, bringing the story together from a number of sources.

When: It is difficult to date the writing of the book—it could have been written any time from the reign of Solomon to the exile. However, the action takes place much earlier. The hero, Job, is a figure akin to Abraham, a patriarch, rich in livestock, blessed with a large family, who lived to a great age. So the setting of the story is around 2000–1500 BC.

What: Job is described as "a righteous man." He is firmly established as undeserving of all that befalls him. He is described as upright, blameless, a man of integrity. Just as importantly, he is a resident of "the land of Uz" which lies "somewhere in the east." In other words, he is not an Israelite. And rightly so, for Job's experiences and his questions are universal to mankind.

Job may be concerned with the problem of suffering, but in the end it provides no real answers. Job does not tell us why suffering happens. Instead it shows us the shallowness of most theories. Job's friends, his comforters, are certain that he must have sinned. They want a nice, straightforward theory to explain why suffering occurs. Job does not answer the question; but it does question all the answers.

In the end, all these questions are swept away by the presence of God himself. In the face of his power, Job's questions seem trifling and insignificant—and his friends' theories seem trite and superficial.

Quick Guide

Author
Unknown

Type
Wisdom literature

Purpose
The book is concerned with one fundamental question: why do innocent people suffer?

Key verses
7:1 "Why is life so hard? Why do we suffer?"

19:25–26: "I know that my Savior lives, and at the end he will stand on this earth. My flesh may be destroyed, yet from this body I will see God."

If you remember one thing about this book . . .
We do not know why people suffer—but God is still worthy of our faith and worship.

Your 15 minutes start now
Read chapters 1–3, 28, 38, 41–42

The Route Through Job

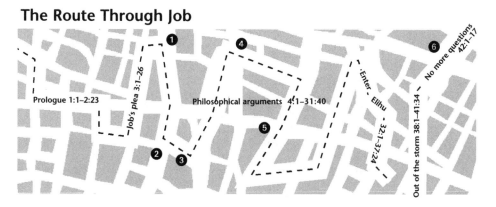

Prologue 1:1–2:23

Job's plea 3:1–26

Philosophical arguments 4:1–31:40

Enter . . . Elihu 32:1–37:24

Out of the storm 38:1–41:34

No more questions 42:1–17

Things you don't find in the Bible: The patience of Job

People who are resigned to their suffering, who demonstrate a saintly endurance in the face of trial or disaster, are often described as having "the patience of Job."

But the whole point of the book is that Job isn't patient. He shouts. He argues. He rants and raves. He is not prepared to wait until the ordeal is over; he wants an explanation. And he wants it *now*.

Prologue 1–2:13

Job begins with a kind of "once upon a time" scenario. We are introduced to Job, a resident of the mysterious land of Uz (as opposed to the land of Oz, which is an entirely different place). In the very first verse, Job is described as "truly good," and throughout the book his upright nature and inherent goodness are restated. Having introduced the main protagonist, the scene switches to the courts of heaven, where Satan challenges God. "Sure," he says, "Job worships you because you give him all this stuff. The sheep, the property, the 6-litre supercharged camels. But you take those away, and he will soon curse you."

God disagrees, and allows Satan to remove all of Job's wealth. In the subsequent verses Job's cattle, property and even his family are taken away from him. Everything he once had is gone. Satan is even given permission to make Job ill.

And so, as the prologue ends, Job sits on a rubbish heap, scraping his sores. His wife calls on him to "curse God and die." But Job wants something more than mere release from his suffering. He wants answers ...

Job's plea 3:1–26

Job's first speech is a summary of the key issues of the book. It is a heartfelt, despairing cry, not a philosophical inquiry. Job curses the day he was born, and wishes he had died at birth. Yet he does not curse God. His cry is familiar to all who have suffered deeply: "Why do I have to go on?"

Philosophical arguments
4:1–31:40

The bulk of the book is taken up by the arguments between Job and three of his friends: Eliphaz, Bildad and Zophar. There are, basically, three cycles of arguments where each side successively puts its point of view. The two viewpoints—that of Job and that of his three friends—may be summarized as follows:

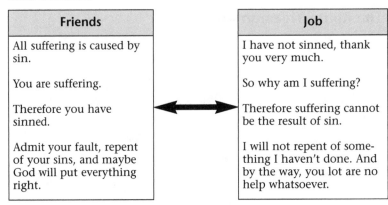

Friends	Job
All suffering is caused by sin.	I have not sinned, thank you very much.
You are suffering.	So why am I suffering?
Therefore you have sinned.	Therefore suffering cannot be the result of sin.
Admit your fault, repent of your sins, and maybe God will put everything right.	I will not repent of something I haven't done. And by the way, you lot are no help whatsoever.

Job's friends are merely voicing the traditional, orthodox view of the time: that all suffering was deserved. Even today there are many religions and viewpoints that argue the same way, that your fate in this life is directly affected by your actions in previous lives. Even some Christians would sympathize with this viewpoint, arguing that success and "prosperity" are a sign of God's blessing, while failure and suffering are a sign of his displeasure. This viewpoint is denied by the book of Job which, with regard to the causes and origin of suffering, makes only one simple observation: "suffering happens."

❶ Round one 3:1–14:22

It is not that Job's opponents are entirely wrong. They argue that God destroys the guilty, not the innocent (4:7), that nobody is entirely blameless (4:17), that trouble comes to everyone (5:7). The problem is that, even though these statements are correct in themselves, they do not solve the problem. Job *knows* that the reality is very different from their easy words.

The first round of arguments gradually increase in anger and bitterness. Eliphaz starts quite quietly, Bildad takes a stronger line (8:1–22) and Zophar's words are the harshest of all the "friends." Job replies with vicious sarcasm—there is nothing his friends can tell him that he doesn't already know. He even accuses them of "telling lies for God" (13:7). They are acting like God's spin doctors, spewing out words that make no sense. Finally, Job appeals to God (13:20–14:22), begging him for mercy.

Puzzling Points

Why does God make a bet with Satan?

This is not necessarily Satan, as we understand him later in the Bible. In Job, the person who raises questions about Job's integrity is referred to as *the* Satan. It could be Satan himself, or it could be a servant of God with a specific role as an investigator—a kind of celestial quality control inspector. The Satan questions whether there is such a thing as disinterested faith, or whether people merely worship God for the money (not to mention the camels, donkeys, sheep, etc.). It is this challenge that God sets out to answer.

There are two possible reasons, therefore, why God allows Job to suffer.

Because it resulted in good

Out of Job's suffering comes, not only his own deep personal encounter with God, but a piece of literature that for thousands of years has helped and sustained those who suffer.

It's the only way to prove the truth

The second reason is simpler. Ultimately God "accepts the bet" because it is, in fact, the only way to prove the truth. The only way to disprove the Satan's accusation is to let Job suffer. Anyone can follow God during the good times. Job's example shows that God is there for us in the bad times as well. His faith survived the acid test—but to do so, it had to go through the acid.

Does this mean that all suffering is a deliberate test from God? Well, all suffering is certainly a test, for the bad times we all go through will be a "test of faith." Like Job we will be tempted to turn our backs on God. But as to whether it is *deliberate* on God's part, that is a more complex question and one with which philosophers and theologians have wrestled for centuries. Still it remains, at heart, a mystery.

The message of Job is that suffering will happen. We don't know why it happens—Job is never aware of the cause of his suffering—but whatever the reason, we must have faith.

▷**276**

❷ Round two   15:1–21:34

The second round of this contest is shorter and more violent. The same arguments are rehashed. By now, Job's friends have become his tormentors. They will not listen (17:4) and all they can do is to offer "empty hopes" (17:12).

Don't panic, I'm only metaphorical.

Details, Details . . . Who is Leviathan?

The creature of Leviathan is mentioned frequently in Job. The name refers to a mythical sea monster who represented the forces of chaos. When Job refers to this monster, therefore, he is talking about chaos and meaninglessness, the sense that life has no explanation, no purpose, no sense.

Some commentators have interpreted the description in Job 42 as a crocodile, but the symbolic interpretation is more important here. It is God who has tamed this creature—this powerful, primeval force of chaos. Life may seem meaningless, Leviathan may seem to be triumphant, but God is greater, and God is in control.

❸ I will see him   19:23–27

Suddenly, in the middle of all this gloom and bitterness, there is a ray of hope, like sunshine breaking through the storm clouds. Verses 23–27 show a different Job, one who longs to see God. "I know that my Savior lives," he says, "and that at the end he will stand on this earth. My flesh may be destroyed, yet from this body I will see God. Yes, I will see him for myself, and I long for that moment." The chapter is, in a way, typical of Job's dilemma. He rails at God, shouts at him, accuses him of injustice and callous uncaring. Yet he also knows that God is a magnificent God, a merciful God, a God who loves his people. It is these two contradictory aspects that Job seeks to reconcile.

❹ Round three   22:1–31:40

The contest drags on. This time only Eliphaz and Bildad get their arguments in. For the last time they repeat the same, stubborn line. They have nothing new to add, no new comfort to bring. Eliphaz tries listing Job's sins (22:5–9), Bildad points out, yet again, that nobody is perfect (25:4). Job, in words that positively drip with sarcasm, thanks them for their help (26:1–4) before launching into a final speech.

❺ Depths of the earth   28:1–28

This is another magnificent poem, a hymn to Wisdom. Though men dig to the depths of the earth, though they discover hidden places in their search for jewels and gold, what is really precious is wisdom. Where is it to be found? Only with God and in our relationship with him. "Wisdom means that you respect me, the Lord, and turn from sin."

Enter Elihu   32:1–37:24

Finally, Job's friends stop arguing with him, because "he refused to admit that he was guilty." But a new voice enters the fray—a young man called Elihu, who has been listening to the debate with increasing anger and frustration. Elihu is a mysterious individual, the original angry young man. He believes that suffering is God's way of turning us away from sin. He questions whether Job is truly innocent and points out, rightly, how often those who call on God to help them out of trouble forget him the moment things get better . . .

Elihu's argument is that suffering may be some kind of advance warning, causing us to turn to God. Suffering, in Elihu's terms, is a kind of red alert: "Hard times and trouble are God's way of getting our attention!" (36:15). This too has been a popular theological argument over the years, and while there is some merit in it, it is hard to see how anyone can reasonably argue that the death of Job's children and the loss of everything he owned are merely God's way of attracting his attention. Elihu's argument, though full of passion, does not really lead us any further toward a solution. Perhaps towards the end of Elihu's argument the weather turns and the rain starts to fall, for he ends his speech by describing God's power expressed in thunder and lightning. Ironically, it is out of the very storms described by Elihu that God speaks.

Out of the storm   38:1–41:34

"From out of a storm, the LORD said to Job . . ." Finally God speaks. Now, the reader might be forgiven for saying, now we are going to get the answers to all those questions. Now we are going to find out the truth.

And God does answer Job's questions. With another load of questions.

"Why do you talk so much when you know so little?" he asks. And then he goes on to show how little Job really knows of the world. "How did I lay the foundation for the earth?" "Did you ever tell the sun to rise?" "Have you ever walked on the ocean floor?" "From where does lightning leap or the east wind blow?"

Using these questions, God establishes his awe-inspiring power. He follows them up with a veritable roll call of animals. We start with lions, mountain goats, wild donkeys and wild oxen. Then ostriches get their own section, followed by horses, hawks and eagles. Then we have "Behemoth"—which some translations translate as "hippopotamus"—followed by Leviathan, the great sea monster of the deep.

No more questions . . .   42:1–17

In the face of all this, Job's arguments seem to dissolve. "Who am I to answer you?" he says. "I did speak once or twice, but never again." Why does Job give in so meekly? This is a man who has spent thirty chapters rehearsing his arguments, preparing what he would say to God if he had the chance. What better time than now?

The truth is that, in the face of who God is, all Job's questions melt away. "I have talked about things that are far beyond my understanding," he adds. "I heard about you from others; now I have seen you with my own eyes." Job realizes that, for all his questions, he has to trust God based on who God is.

Then God says a very strange thing to Eliphaz: "What my servant Job has said about me is true, but I am angry with you and your two friends for not telling the truth." What can God mean? After all, Job spent most of the book accusing God of all manner of injustice and crime, while the three friends were trying to uphold the orthodox, official viewpoint. Perhaps God prefers honest doubt to dishonest certainty. He welcomes questions, he wants real attempts to understand him, even if, as in the case of Job, the ultimate answers are too mysterious for our comprehension.

❻ A happy ending?   42:7–17

In the end Job is blessed by God. His goods are recovered (double the amount he had before), he has children and great-grandchildren. But is this really enough? The questions raised by Job cannot simply be forgotten now that "everything has turned out all right in the end." I do not think that this is the message of Job. God's blessing on Job was not really the 22,000 assorted livestock, nor even the children and grandchildren. God's blessing on Job was to speak with Job and share the truth with him.

Good people suffer. We don't know why God lets this happen, but it does not mean that God is unjust, uncaring or powerless. Job is not ultimately about why suffering happens, but about how we should react to it. Even when our lives are full of darkness and despairing questions, we must remember that God still loves us, listens to us, and will lead us home.

Psalms
The poetry of the believer

Who: Various authors (see opposite). There is a lot of debate over the authorship. Most psalms contain information telling who wrote it, what collection it was in, what type it is, what it is commemorating and when it is to be used.

Notations such as "a psalm of David," however, are ambiguous. They might mean "written by," or they might equally mean "concerning," or even "for the use of." David might even mean "of the house of David," i.e., applied to the royal family. What we do know is that David was a lyricist and songwriter, whose prowess on the harp was well attested, so it is not unreasonable to assume that his works had been preserved from the very earliest times. And there is certainly no strong reason to doubt the antiquity of most of the poetry.

When: The collection as we have it was brought together over many centuries. Opinion varies over how long, but it was at least 400 years. It was probably completed in the third century BC, where it probably served as a prayer book for use in the temple and synagogues.

What: Psalms is a book of poetry. More than that, it's a book of poetry collections, a book of books, an anthology made up of other anthologies. "Psalms" is a Greek word that comes from the psalterion—a kind of ancient stringed instrument. (Nowadays it would be like calling the book "Guitaros.") The Hebrew title is "Praises."

An even better title, however, might be "The Book of Mood Swings." Each "chapter" of Psalms is a separate poem, composed at a different time for a different purpose, and often by a different person. Reading them end to end, therefore, is an emotional roller coaster: one minute you hit the heights, the next you're in deepest despair. The book of Psalms is more like a spiritual journal, a record of feelings and circumstances. The psalms reflect how life is. One day you feel like drinking champagne, the next you feel like drinking strychnine. This is poetry, not logic. Enjoy the ride.

The Route Through Psalms

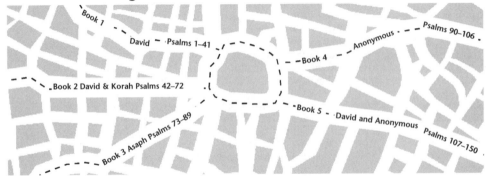

Book 1
David — Psalms 1–41

Book 2 David & Korah Psalms 42–72

Book 3 Asaph Psalms 73–89

Book 4

Book 5 — David and Anonymous

Anonymous — Psalms 90–106

Psalms 107–150

Who wrote the psalms?

According to the traditional view, they break down like this:

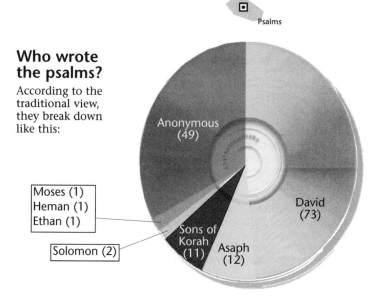

- Anonymous (49)
- David (73)
- Asaph (12)
- Sons of Korah (11)
- Solomon (2)
- Moses (1)
- Heman (1)
- Ethan (1)

You call this a rhyme?

You might think that Hebrew poetry doesn't rhyme. In fact, it does, but it "rhymes" ideas, rather than words. Here are three basic types:

Synonymous Parallelism

This is where an idea is stated and then "rhymed" with a similar statement.

First Statement	Parallel Statement
The LORD is a shelter for the oppressed,	a refuge in times of trouble. (Ps 9:9 NIV)

Contrasting Parallelism

This is where the second half of the "rhyme" contrasts with the first.

First Statement	Completed Statement
The LORD protects everyone who follows him,	but the wicked follow a road that leads to ruin. (Ps 1:6)

Progressive Parallelism

This is where the second half of the "rhyme" echoes the first, but adds something extra to it.

First Statement	Additional Statement
The LORD is my light and my salvation—	whom shall I fear? (Ps 27:1 NIV)

There are other variations on this theme, but those are the basic patterns.

Types of psalms

Any attempt to squeeze the psalms into neat little boxes is bound to end in failure. Although the categories below may help to identify some of the psalms, you will find on reading that many of them blur the boundaries. Some start as laments and end up as praises. Pilgrimage psalms can contain thanksgiving. Nevertheless, we can identify some different types.

Cries for help

Ps 3–7, 10, 12–13, 17, 22, 25–28, 35, 38–40, 42–43, 51, 54–57, 59, 61–64, 69–71, 77, 82, 86, 88, 102, 109, 130, 140–43

These psalms are laments—individuals crying out to God for help. They are direct, passionate, emotional prayers, full of bones that break, bodies that crumble, waters that threaten to drown, savage beasts about to attack. There are frequent protestations of innocence (7, 12, 26), and even reproaches for God's apparent forgetfulness (9, 10, 22, 44). Equally frequently they end with a reassurance, a confidence that the prayers have been heard, and a thanksgiving in faith (6, 22, 69, 140).

Sometimes the lament comes on behalf of a nation, such as before an army goes into battle (44), or in times of natural disaster (60). Two psalms (not to mention the very psalm-like book of Lamentations) reflect the emotions of a nation in exile after the destruction of Jerusalem (74, 137). Other national laments include 79, 80, 83, 85 and 90.

Thanks to God

Ps 18, 30, 32, 34, 41, 65–68, 75, 106–7, 116, 138

These psalms offer thanks for God's works, for his rescue or for answers to prayers. They may be giving thanks for a danger averted, for a successful harvest, for victory in battle, or for God's goodness to the writer.

Praises

Ps 8, 9, 16, 19, 23, 29, 33, 36, 81, 91, 95, 100, 103–5, 111, 113–14, 117, 135, 136, 139, 145–48, 150

Although all psalms offer praise of one sort or another, these psalms—which are sometimes called "hymns"—praise God generally for his greatness and power. Some are loud blasts on the trumpet, others quiet expressions of trust. All praise God.

A special subgroup of these are what are called "kingship" psalms, which celebrate God's reign over all (47, 93, 95–99). Another subset are the "royal" psalms, which are a little like the kingship psalms, but are based around a comparison of heavenly and earthly kings (2, 20–21, 45, 72, 89, 101, 110, 115, 118, 144).

Pilgrimage songs

Songs of Zion: 43, 46, 48, 76, 84, 87, 122, 126, 129, 137. Pilgrimage Psalms: 120–34

They are often termed "songs of ascent"—pilgrimage psalms sung by those climbing up the hill into Jerusalem. They may have been sung by pilgrims going to the city for one of the three annual festivals of Passover, Purim and Succoth. A subset of these are the songs of Zion—psalms specifically in praise of Jerusalem, the city of God.

Wise thoughts

Ps 1, 15, 37, 53, 112, 119, 127

These psalms are more instructive in character and closer to proverbs. They are wisdom poems, that aim to impart moral or ethical teaching to the reader or listener.

Cries for vengeance

Ps 7, 35, 40, 55, 58, 59, 69, 79, 109, 137, 139, 144

There are also a number of psalms that curse either individuals or enemies of Israel. They are dark and unsettling screams of vengeance, when the cries for help have tipped over into darkness. The psalmist wishes to wash his feet in his enemy's blood (58:10), or asks the Lord's blessing on any-one who smashes a Babylonian child's head against a rock (137:9). To the modern eye they seem outrageously bloodthirsty. However, the psalmist saw the success of his evil enemies as a direct affront to divine justice, as a rebellious outrage against the rule of God.

The other factor that drives this is an important one to remember: the psalmist, as far as we can tell, had little idea of judgment after death. (Whether he had any idea of life after death is open to debate.) The pleas are more urgent, therefore, because he wishes to see the triumph of God in *this* life.

Words, words, words

Like all great poetry, the psalms are rich in imagery and metaphor. They abound in word play and alliteration, and in repetition. Again, this is one of the reasons why the psalms continue to speak to so many people. Poet-ry, like story, speaks across the generations. Great metaphors are universal: we still find mountains as majestic and awe-inspiring as the ancient Hebrews did.

Like all great poets, the psalmists worked with an overall design in mind. These were not spontaneous and unplanned prophetic outbursts, but crafted songs. That is not to say that they do not contain nuggets of prophecy, but the form of the prophecy has been carefully shaped and crafted. There are several acrostics—psalms where each line or stanza begins with the successive letter of the Hebrew alphabet. The most famous of these is Psalm 119, which consists of 22 stanzas, each beginning with a letter of the Hebrew alphabet. Some have suggested that this was an aid to memory, but in fact the Hebrews were far better at memorizing than we are, and didn't need such aids. More likely it is illustrative of a sense of completeness: everything is covered, from A to Z, as it were.

Research has also indicated that some other forms were used. There are psalms that echo the opening and closing stanzas (33, 86), there are psalms that use the same number of lines in each stanza (12, 41), and there is even one shaped like a stepped Babylonian pyramid—a ziggurat. (Can't see it myself, but maybe you have to look at it from a certain angle.) The point is, someone has worked at these. We get most out of the psalms, therefore, if we work hard at understanding them.

Emotion unplugged

The psalms are not manuals of theology. They are not moral lessons or lists of laws or nuggets of history—although they contain all those things. The psalms are personal human expressions. They are often raw in their emotional tone. They can appear pleading, even petty at times. More than perhaps any other part of the Bible, they record real feelings and raw emo-tion. Perhaps this is why Jesus, dying on the cross, screamed out a line from a psalm.

Psalms: the greatest hits

All the psalms deserve reading, but here are some of the most famous ones.

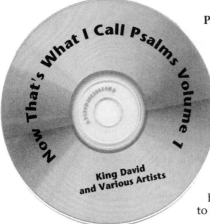

Psalm 8: A praise psalm directed at the Creator. The creator of the earth, the maker of the heavens and the stars, is also the God who cares about individual humans.

Psalm 9: Another praise psalm that some scholars believe should be put together with Psalm 10 since, when combined, they show some indications of forming an acrostic. It is a powerful mix of thanksgiving and praise, singing of God as a refuge for all those who are oppressed.

Psalm 13: A simple, plaintive cry to the Lord, perhaps during a time of illness. The psalmist is close to death, but still he trusts in God.

Psalm 15: More of a wisdom psalm than anything else. The psalmist argues that what qualifies someone to enter the temple, to have access to God, is not sacrifice and ritual, but moral righteousness and a pure heart.

Psalm 18: This psalm occurs with minor differences in 2 Samuel 22, where it celebrates David's escape from Saul. Just as David was to hide in rocks and caves, the Lord is his safe hiding place. There are two sections recounting how God has rescued him (18:1–19, 30–45), and in between comes a statement of his faithfulness toward God (20–29).

Psalm 19: A wonderful hymn of praise to God, extolling the glory of God, and saying how the heavens testify to the might of their creator. There is no nation or language where God's voice cannot speak through his creation. Nature is not divine in itself, but it points to the true divinity. From nature, the psalmist moves to the Law, which he describes as "sweet as honey." These are hardly the words that I might choose to describe Leviticus, but the psalmist is aware that it is the Law that gives life to Israel.

Psalm 22: An anguished lament of loss and abandonment. No other psalm fits so exactly the feelings that Jesus must have felt on the cross: the sense of darkness and distance. Equally, no other psalm fits so perfectly the end result of the cross experience, where all people, from the rich to the beggars, will kneel before the Lord, and where the ends of the earth will remember what the Lord has done for them.

Psalm 23: Probably the most famous psalm of them all. An expression of complete trust in God, where the Lord is likened to a shepherd leading his sheep. He guides, protects, refreshes and anoints his people, and leads them home to dwell with him forever.

Psalm 27: A confident statement of trust in the Lord. Whatever happens, the Lord will protect his child. It ends with the psalmist's belief that God will show his goodness among the "land of the living." This is not a distant God, but one who dwells with, and acts among, his people.

Psalm 42: A plea for deliverance, notable for the strength of its imagery. The psalmist is like a hunted deer whose soul thirsts for God. Indeed, the whole psalm is drenched with water imagery—in the streams, the tears, the thundering waterfalls and the roaring seas. From the depths of his need, he calls on the depths of the Lord's love.

Psalm 46: A song of Zion. More waters, more dangerous seas, but this time contrasted with the stream of God's blessing that flows out from Jerusalem. Jerusalem doesn't have a river, but the river here is the out-pouring of God's love and blessing to the rest of the world.

Psalm 51: A great psalm of forgiveness and mercy. Set in the time after David had committed adultery with Bathsheba, the king pleads with God to be made clean, to be washed white again. He does not argue that it was a momentary aberration, but recognizes the innate sinfulness of humankind (51:3–5). Equally he knows that only the Lord can cleanse him, only the Lord can make him as new again. There is a recognition, as well, that sacrifice and ritual are not enough: the only offering God really wants is true repentance and a contrite heart.

Psalm 66: A psalm of thanksgiving. God has saved his people and delivered them from their enemies. Verses 11–12 describe the fortunes of war —people in prison, prisoners enslaved, chariots driven over the troops. Some suggest that this was written after Judah's deliverance from the threat of the Assyrians (2 Ki 19).

Psalm 89: Ethan the Ezrahite's only hit, but what a great psalm it is. It is a repeated assertion of God's promise to David—probably written during the time after David, when the activities of the kings of Judah made this promise seem unlikely to be fulfilled. It may have been after the fall of Jerusalem and the exile of King Jehoiachin in 597 BC. Despite this bitter background, there is a jubilation about this psalm, a defiant joy that knows the truth of God's promises. Chaos is all about—here typified by the sea and by Rahab, another name for Leviathan, but God is all-powerful. Even though the psalm ends with a plaintive cry, the Lord is still to be praised.

Psalm 95: A call to joyful worship, probably sung by a Levite or priest to the assembled people. God is the great king above all other gods, and the song leader reminds the people not to rebel against him as the Israelites did during the time in the wilderness.

Psalm 96: Another call, this time beyond Israel to all nations, urging them to acknowledge the reign of God. It is not just the psalmist or the nations who "sing to the Lord a new song"; the whole of creation joins in with praise to God. (See also Psalm 98 for similar imagery.)

Psalm 100: A short, simple thanksgiving psalm. The psalm is in two parts: a call to praise followed by the reasons why the Lord should be praised.

Psalm 102: No author is named here, but many can identify with his circumstances—a suffering man who asks the Lord for help. The power of the imagery adds to the intensity of the emotion. This seems to be a picture of physical affliction (although the references to the restoration of Zion might imply that the suffering is caused by being in exile). The writer wants his words recorded for posterity. His suffering may be intense, but he keeps faith in the Lord's promise.

Psalm 104: A wonderful creation hymn that draws on Genesis for its imagery. The Lord is wrapped in light, he spreads the heavens out like a tent (104:2). The earth is a fertile place, abounding in wildlife; the sea teems with fish and in the center is man, with his appointed work. There is both order and creativity, a sense of purpose and a sense of joy. Even our old friend Leviathan goes in for a bit of splashing about.

Psalm 107: A thanksgiving psalm that was probably composed for a special festival. It tells of the return to Jerusalem of the exiled and the lost: those who never thought they would see their city again have been led home, those who suffered in chains have been released. Some have been freed from disease (17–22), others rescued from the chaotic turmoil of the sea (23–32). But the Lord is not just rescuer, he is judge as well. He turns the waters into deserts (some interpret this as referring to the sieges of the Babylonians and Assyrians) to bring judgment on his people, because of their wickedness. Finally, however, he lifts the needy again and brings them back to fruitful life.

Psalm 110: A mystical vision of a great king. David refers to this king as "my Lord," and it is David's "Lord" who is given ultimate authority and power. Although David may have been writing it for his son Solomon, Christians generally interpret this psalm as pointing to Jesus—indeed, Jesus used it in that very way (Mt 22:43–45) and Peter and the author of Hebrews also used its imagery (Heb 5:6–10; 7:11–28; Ac 2:34–36).

Psalm 119: The biggie. The biggest psalm in the collection, the longest chapter in the Bible, this psalm is a kind of microcosm of the whole book. It consists of 22 eight-line stanzas, each beginning with a different letter of the Hebrew alphabet. Its fundamental theme is the Word of God, which it describes using different Hebrew words. Thus we have "law," "statutes," "precepts," "commands," "decrees," "word," "promise," etc. The psalm is really a collection of mini-psalms, each with their own mood and theme. Songs of praise mix with cries for deliverance; meditations on the Word of God mingle with proverb-like instruction. There are two fundamental themes: devotion to the Word of God and a belief in his promises.

Psalm 121: A "song of ascents"—a pilgrimage song probably sung on the journey to Jerusalem for one of the great festivals—and revolving around the theme of watching. The pilgrim looks up to the Lord, but all the time the Lord is watching over him—both now and forever.

Psalm 131: One of the simplest and most beautiful of the psalms. This is another pilgrimage song, but filled with a humble, childlike trust in the Lord. When Jesus speaks of becoming like a child, one thinks of the attitudes reflected here: simple, trusting, still and quiet, like a child being cuddled by its mother.

Psalm 137: A song of the exile, notable not only for its moving evocation of lost souls in a faraway land, but also for the bloodthirsty ending. The Babylonians have ordered them to sing, but how can they, when their hearts are still in Jerusalem?

Psalm 139: A psalm of devotion. This is reminiscent of Job in its understanding of the awesome greatness of God, a greatness that knows us intimately. Our thoughts and words are not hidden from God. He was there when we were made in our mother's womb, he has ordained the days of our life and fills them with his thoughts. The psalmist asks for God to examine him, to test him, not out of a sense of pride, but from a heartfelt desire to live in the best way possible.

Psalm 150: The final great hymn of praise to the Lord—a psalm of where, why and how. Where should God be praised? Everywhere—from the temple to the heavens above. Why should God be praised? For his power and greatness. How should God be praised? Through singing, dancing, music, just breathing—a mighty song of love in which everyone can join.

And now, here's one from my last album.

Landmark: Life after Death

For the most part, the Old Testament is concerned with life before death, rather than life after death. The psalmist cries to God to rescue him now, in this life. The dead were thought to live in sheol, the underworld, a shadow world, very different to later images of heaven.

It is one of the remarkable facts of the Bible, that throughout virtually all the writings of the Old Testament there is no real mention of life after death. There are odd verses that might be interpreted in this way, Psalm 49:15 for example, but in general they did not believe that righteousness would be rewarded in this way. They obeyed God because he was God, not in the hopes of reward. It was only later that a belief in life after death began to develop, a belief that Jesus was to vindicate when he died and rose again.

▷ 390

Proverbs
Getting you to think

Proverbs is an anthology of sayings on life, character and conduct. In some ways, however, the term "proverb" doesn't quite give the true flavor of these writings. The Hebrew word can also be translated "taunt" (Isaiah 14:4), "oracle" and "parable." Perhaps the best way to understand these words is that they are there to stimulate, to provoke, to get us to think.

Who: Various. Some are attributed to Solomon, some to Agur the son of Jakeh, some to King Lemuel, and some to a being known only as "the Oracle." Also the "men of Hezekiah" are credited with compiling some of the book. There are also sections simply attributed to "the wise."

When: Assuming Solomon had a hand in some of the book, it dates from the tenth century BC. The mention of Hezekiah's men implies that it was edited between 715 and 686 BC, tying it in with King Hezekiah's interest in the writings of David and Asaph (2 Ch 29:30).

What: The book does not develop an argument, or narrate a history. It is a collection—or rather, a series of collections. Just as Psalms is a collection of poetry collections, Proverbs is a collection of proverb collections.

Most proverbs are intensely practical, but then the Bible is a deeply practical book. God cares about the way we behave, the way we live our lives, our actions here on earth. In the eyes of the writers of Proverbs, to act justly, to keep our mouths from lying, to work hard, to avoid sinful relationships—these are what it means to "fear the Lord."

Quick Guide
Author
Various, including Solomon and King Lemuel's mom
Type
Wisdom literature
Purpose
A collection of sayings offering advice on all aspects of life.
Key verse
1:7 "Respect and obey the LORD! This is the beginning of knowledge. Only a fool rejects wisdom and good advice."
If you remember one thing about this book . . .
Wisdom is a fundamental attribute of God. Look for wisdom, learn from it, and treasure it when you find it.
Your 10 minutes start now
Read chapters 1, 3, 8, 15, 27, 31

The Route Through Proverbs

The way of wisdom 1:8–9:18

Introduction 1:1–7

Solomon's proverbs 10:1–22:16

Sayings of the wise 22:17–24:34

Hezekiah's proverbs 25:1–29:27

Proverbs of Agur 30:1–33

Proverbs of Lemuel 31:1–9

Epilogue 31:10–31

Themes in Proverbs

"A recurring theme is like something that recurs a lot. And is a theme."
Nick's not-very-useful proverbs 1:1

The proverbs in this book cover a huge range of topics, but several themes recur. Certain characters also crop up regularly, such as the nagging woman, the idle man, the gossip and the dishonest tradesman.

Seek wisdom

The overarching theme is the need for us to actively seek wisdom. Again and again, Proverbs urges the reader to think about things; to pursue wisdom and to treasure it when we find it. See, for example, 2:1–5.

Avoid bad companions

Chapter 1:10–19 is a classic example, a picture of a kind of ancient Jewish gang culture—the young man is warned away from these paths. Wise friends, on the other hand, are to be welcomed (13:20).

Help the poor

Proverbs, like so much of the Bible, stresses the need for social responsibility. There are numerous "one-shot" proverbs on this topic, but see, for example, 3:27–35.

Watch your language

Gossip, lies and foolish talk are all condemned in Proverbs. One of the emphases is on how we live together as a society, and nothing causes more division in society than gossip, innuendo and lying. Chapter 26:20–28 warns against gossip, against lying, flattery and "smooth talk" that hides evil intent. It's not just lies, either: there is also an emphasis on saying the right thing at the right time. You don't, for example, go into a house of sorrow and sing a jolly song (18:20). But the right "word of correction" from a friend is to be welcomed.

Get out of bed

Many proverbs have to do with the virtue of hard work and the rejection of idleness. Chapter 6:6–11 paints a picture of the sluggard, the idle person who sleeps and dozes and does nothing. This is not someone who has no work, it is someone who simply can't be bothered.

Don't get into bed

Few things illustrate the contemporary relevance of Proverbs better than its observation of the destructive effect of adultery and faithlessness. Chapter 5:1–23 is all about staying faithful to your wife and avoiding the lures of another woman, and there are many other parts of the book which warn of the dangers. Sometimes this is a warning against prostitutes, often it is simply about women who don't see anything wrong with their actions (30:20). Chapter 7 tells a story of a man who is lured to destruction because he can't say no.

Details, Details . . .
Add a little sage

Sages were important figures. They were founts of knowledge, counselors, people who had natural leadership skills and a high reputation. They were to some extent the schoolmasters and educators of the Israelites, hence the frequent references to "the young."

Solomon is, perhaps, their finest example: a man who showed exceptional judgment as well as creative problem-solving skills. Although it has to be admitted he was less and less wise as his life went on.

Introduction 1:1–7

Introduces the concept of wisdom and what the book is to be used for: as a guide to life, as a rule of conduct, as a moral and ethical help. The basic approach is summed up in verse 7: the fear of the Lord is the beginning of knowledge, but fools despise wisdom and discipline. This is the bedrock of all wisdom, the source from which true understanding and insight flow (Job 28:28; Ps 111:10).

The way of wisdom 1:8–9:18

This section introduces the idea of wisdom. Much of it is addressed from a father to a son, or sons.

Wisdom here is given a human form—a woman's form. She cries in the street, rebuking and challenging those who ignore her (1:20–30); she fights against the "folly" (9:1–6, 13–18), depicted in alluring, seductive terms. Throughout the book there is a strong link between adultery and prostitution and foolishness, a reminder that this book is particularly addressed to sons. Nothing, it appears, leads a man into folly as quickly as a wicked woman.

This is contrasted with the figure of wisdom, who is pure and, well, wise rather unsurprisingly. She walks with kings and rulers, she brings prosperity and righteousness. She describes how she has been with God from the beginning (8:22–31). The fact that the Jews imagined wisdom in terms almost akin to a deity shows how important they felt it to be: it is a fundamental attribute of God.

Solomon's proverbs 10:1–22:16

This large collection of proverbs seems to have been the core of the collection. The proverbs follow a similar couplet format, contrasting one line against the other. So, a wise son brings joy to his dad, a foolish one grief to his mom (10:1); lazy hands bring poverty, busy hands bring wealth (10:4), and so on. The only exception is 19:7—and that's probably because there's a line missing. This was the classic form of proverb.

From chapter 16 onwards the form changes slightly, with one half of the couplet reinforcing or developing the first line, rather than contrasting with it. Thus we have: "share your plans with the Lord, and you will succeed" (16:3).

The proverbs in this collection cover the whole range of subjects: righteousness, laziness, wealth, fidelity, friendship, careful speech, worship, honesty . . . the whole of life, in fact.

Details, Details . . .
All at sixes and sevens

A strange literary device, which always gives the impression that the Lord has forgotten something the first time round. There are six things he hates, seven he detests. It's a device, like saying "once upon a time" or "you know what I think."

Sayings of the wise 22:17–24:34

This short section contains two parts. The first part contains thirty proverbs, which appear to have been written for someone in an official position, someone who will have to give "sound answers to him who sent you" (22:21 NIV). These are mostly four-part proverbs, although one, dealing with wine-drinking, runs to 17 lines!

The second part consists of an even smaller section that seems to deal with social justice and community advice. It includes a favorite topic, the sluggard or lazy person (24:30–34). This is similar to a section in Solomon's collection (6:6–11) and may even have been a part or a continuation of the original poem.

Hezekiah's collection   25:1–29:27

More proverbs of Solomon, this time collected by Hezekiah's men. This may mean that some of them are Solomon's originals, or it may mean that these are proverbs "in the style of Solomon."

They are predominantly in the classic couplet form. Here, for the first time, there is a tendency to group proverbs by subject—for example, the group on the king (25:2–7). They are more poetic than the first section, with more use of simile and metaphor, perhaps because these were products of a later, more literary age.

Proverbs of Agur   30:1–33

We know nothing of Agur, beyond this little collection of proverbs. His message is summed up in 30:8. "Make me absolutely honest and don't let me be too poor or too rich. Give me just what I need."

It's not much, maybe, in the history of great sayings, but I can't help thinking that if we could all grasp this perhaps the world would be a better place. There is also a series of proverbs that use the "three, no, four" approach. His proverbs have an almost surreal visual appeal, such as the delightful prospect of people who do not respect their parents being pecked to death by birds (30:17). Hang on, I'm just going to check that the budgie's cage is closed ...

Proverbs of Lemuel
31:1–9

These Proverbs were, apparently, taught to King Lemuel by his mother. We don't actually know who Lemuel was, but he had a clever old mom. Probably, Lemuel and Agur were not Jews: the tradition of wisdom was spread widely across the ancient Middle East. (For example, neither Job nor any of his friends were Jewish.) Lemuel's mom focused her advice mainly on the virtues of chastity, temperance and justice.

> **Details, Details ...**
> **Oracle (30:1; 31:1)**
> The proverbs in this section and in Lemuel's collection use the word "oracle"—a slightly mysterious word, but one that implies the importance that the Israelites attached to these sayings, grouping them on a level with prophecy.

Epilogue   31:10–31

Experts are divided as to whether the final part of chapter 31 belongs with Lemuel's sayings or not. It is an acrostic poem in praise of a good wife. Although the poem, naturally given its time, concentrates on her domestic skills, its key message is true of all generations: her husband depends on her, and she never lets him down (31:11).

Ecclesiastes
Why bother?

Who: "Quoheleth" or "teacher." The teacher is identified as "son of David, king of Jerusalem," which is usually taken to mean Solomon, although it could mean any other king of that lineage. Equally it might represent an ideal king, a sort of archetype. Whoever he was, I think we can rule Mr. Happy out of the equation.

When: Probably around 400 BC, but if the author was Solomon, then much earlier.

What: Ecclesiastes is one of the most surprising books of the Bible—a cynical, weary dismissal of life from one who has seen it all, and rejected it. As it says again and again, "everything is meaningless."

Ecclesiastes has moments of humor and lightness, and passages of startling and moving beauty. It also recognizes that God is supreme—that if nothing on earth matters, then the same cannot be said of him. But the overriding feeling is one of tiredness and cynicism. The psalms might raise their hands in praise of God; Ecclesiastes just gives a weary shrug of the shoulders.

Quick Guide

Author
"Quoheleth" or "teacher"—often attributed to Solomon

Type
Wisdom literature

Purpose
A dark reflection on the apparent futility of existence. (Still, you've got to laugh, don't you?)

Key verse
1:2 "Nothing makes sense! Everything is nonsense. I have seen it all—nothing makes sense!"

If you remember one thing about this book . . .
Life is not always a load of chuckles.

Your 10 minutes start now
Read chapters 1, 3, 7, 11–12

For these reasons, many Christians would prefer that it wasn't there at all. They feel uncomfortable with its corrosive cynicism, its penetrating rejection of superficial optimism and cheerful platitudes. But perhaps that is what gives Ecclesiastes its unique strength. Ecclesiastes is *real*. It represents the thoughts of many, many people. People who are close to despair, who see no purpose in life. Exactly the kind of people we pass every day in our modern towns and cities. (And, to be honest, in my home, before I've had the first coffee of the day.)

Whether this book is the genuine record of one man's anguish, or a deliberate attempt to portray a way of thinking, is difficult to judge. Whatever it is, it serves as a wake-up call to us. This is the flip side of the Bible, and we should do all in our power to help those who are trapped in the kinds of attitudes that are depicted in Ecclesiastes.

The Route Through Ecclesiastes

Everything is meaningless ~ 1:1–2.26
Everything has its moment ~ 3:1–22
Life is unfair 4:1–6:12
No one knows the future 7:1–11:6
Respect God ·11:7–12:14

Everything is meaningless
1:1–2:26

We begin with a bang. "Nothing makes sense!" cries the teacher. "Everything is nonsense." Life is pointless, and even boring (1:8). There is nothing new anywhere and trying to make sense of it all is like trying to catch the wind (1:14). It's not exactly a cheery introduction. Not what you might call "uplifting." But it does have a universal appeal, for, if we are honest, who has not thought this way at some time?

The speaker goes on to describe more about his life. He has lived in luxury and fame (2:4–8). He is the wisest man of his time (1:16; 2:9). But he cannot make sense of any of it.

For a moment he decides that it is better to be wise than foolish (2:12–14), but even this gets him nowhere. He will lose it all in the end. Why did he bother? What has he really gained from his hard work?

Perhaps the best thing to do is simply to live in the moment—to eat, drink and be merry. If we please God we will be rewarded—but then he sees that this doesn't work either (2:26).

Everything has its moment 3:1–22

Bringing God into the equation does bring a more positive outlook—if only momentarily. Chapter 3 begins with one of the most beautiful passages of the Bible, a poem that argues that everything has its moment.

Despite his cynicism, the writer cannot "reject" the idea of God, and he knows that God "makes everything happen at the right time" (3:11). And some things will last forever—things created by God. We don't know what will happen—and this writer at least isn't even sure what will happen when he dies (3:21). All we can do, apparently, is to trust in God to judge fairly, and enjoy our work.

Life is unfair   4:1–6:12

For a moment there things looked mildly positive—or at least less suicidal—but then he veers back toward darkness again. Injustice is all around him; he would be better off dead, or, better yet, never born at all (4:2–3). Now even work is pointless to him. His cynicism, like acid, is destroying everything.

Friends, now, friends might be good. If nothing else, they can protect you from being beaten up (4:9–12). And wisdom does have some advantages (4:13–16).

He now turns his cynical eye to worship. Again there is a sense of pointlessness in his thinking, a sense in which God comes across as a grumpy old man, ready to take offense at our slightest remark. It is better to say nothing than to say the wrong thing.

The way of the world

Chapter 5:8–12 raises one of the core issues of the book. We shouldn't be surprised at injustice, he argues, because that's just the way of the world.

Maybe this gives us a clue to this uncomfortable book. Who is supposed to be speaking here? The king. The head honcho. So if life is so unfair, why doesn't he do something about it? He is supposed to be the king. His thinking, however, is morally bankrupt. He knows what is wrong, but he won't even lift a finger to change things. Perhaps that is part of what Ecclesiastes is all about—it is showing exactly what happens to society when you think this way. It is less a statement of facts than an imaginative attempt to portray a way of thinking, a philosophy that is utterly bankrupt. Perhaps the real point of the book is not to say that life is like this, but to push us to the realization that life *isn't* like this.

No one knows the future 7:1–11:6

As the book goes on, indeed, there is a gradual change. The positive experiences start to shine through a little more brightly. We never exactly get to grinning, but just now and then a slight smile breaks through. Wisdom does offer some protection (7:12). Perhaps we should be cheerful in the good times and reflective in the bad times (7:14).

At times it is almost as if he is persuading himself, through a series of random proverbs. Nobody is perfect (7:20). Don't eavesdrop (7:21). Obey the king (8:2–5). Generosity will be rewarded (11:1–3). It is better to be wise than foolish (9:13–18). Wisdom can even make you smile (8:1).

In between these more positive thoughts there are still plenty of black moments. Most men are bad, but all women are evil (7:26–28). We have twisted minds (7:29). Thieves do prosper (8:10–13). Foolishness infects and contaminates everything (10:1–3). The arguments seesaw back and forth. Positives are followed by negatives. But what can he know, compared to God who gives us all breath (11:5)?

Respect God 11:7–12:14

Suddenly the gloom is broken by a beautiful sunrise. But that only accentuates the darkness that will follow, just as the gloom of old age replaces the joys of youth (11:7–12:8). All this thought and writing is also pointless. "There is no end to books," the teacher warns us, "and too much study will wear you out" (12:12).

Ecclesiastes doesn't so much end as fade away. At the end there is only a kind of reluctant resignation. "Respect and obey God! This is what life is all about" (12:13). It's not exactly a leap of faith: more like a very small hop.

And yet I think it is a kind of triumph, in its own way. Having explored the alternatives, having faced the apparent meaninglessness of his life, the writer wearily turns back to the only thing he can believe in: that God will somehow sort it all out in the end.

No, it's not a leap of faith. But it is a step in the right direction.

Song of Songs
Wonderful love!

The full title of the book is "The Song of Songs which is Solomon's" or "The Most Beautiful of Songs." It's a collection of love songs, a celebration of spontaneous and natural love.

Who: Traditionally ascribed to King Solomon (although which of his many wives he is addressing is not made clear), but the language of the book is more typical of a later period than Solomon's.

When: Probably in the third century BC although it may be earlier.

What: It's a love poem, one of the most startling things in the Bible—eight chapters celebrating erotic, physical love.

Many commentators have found this somewhat difficult to come to terms with. Jewish rabbis taught that the song is an allegory of the love between God and his people. Christian teachers saw it as an allegory of the love between Christ and his Church, or even between Christ and the believer's soul. Indeed, for a thousand years this was the official line.

The problem with these theories is that there is not a hint of them in the book itself, nor in the rest of the Bible. If this had been a common image of God's relationship with Israel, we might expect to find it elsewhere. And, although Israel is sometimes described as a bride, the image is left there; there is certainly no description of the wedding night.

The problem is not with the song, but with us. The Bible has a lot to say about the bad side of love, about degradation, lust, perversion, rape. Here it celebrates what is good about physical love, affirming its spontaneity, power and mystery. The Song of Songs is about love—both physical and emotional. If you're uncomfortable with that, then you'll be uncomfortable with this book.

Quick Guide

Author
Unknown. Traditionally attributed to Solomon, but probably not by him.

Type
Wisdom literature

Purpose
A celebration of love and sex.

Key verse
8:6 "Always keep me in your heart and wear this bracelet to remember me by. The passion of love bursting into flame is more powerful than death, stronger than the grave."

If you remember one thing about this book ...
Love between husband and wife is mysterious, passionate and awe-inspiring.

Your 5 minutes start now
Read chapters 1–2, 5, 8

The Route Through Song of Songs

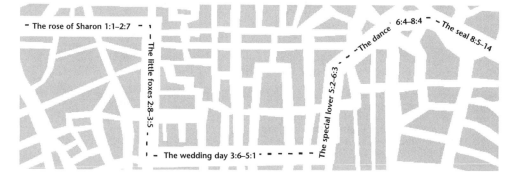

- The rose of Sharon 1:1–2:7
- The little foxes 2:8–3:5
- The wedding day 3:6–5:1
- The special lover 5:2–6:3
- The dance 6:4–8:4
- The seal 8:5–14

> **Details, Details . . .**
> **The rose of Sharon (2:1)**
>
> Sharon is a fertile plain to the south of Mount Carmel. Although usually translated as "rose," the nature of this flower is not known. It may have been some kind of crocus.

> **Details, Details . . .**
> **Foxes in the vineyards (2:15)**
>
> "Vineyards" is used as a metaphor for the lovers themselves, for their appearance (e.g., 1:6). This probably means "keep us safe from whatever might mar us." Or, more colloquially, "keep us this way forever."

The rose of Sharon
1:1–2:7

We are introduced to the lovers. She describes herself as "dark skinned." In ancient times, unlike our own, being tanned was not considered desirable. But love does not obey conventional fashion. The man is a shepherd of sorts, although he is also described as a king.

The little foxes   2:8–3:5

This poem is not merely about love, but also about companionship. The lovers' joy is not merely in physical love, but in simply being in the presence of one another.

Having said that, the physical side is celebrated throughout—this is not some kind of platonic love. Chapter 2:16–17, although difficult to translate, is obviously a metaphor for sex.

The wedding day   3:6–5:1

This section describes the wedding day between the two. The groom is likened to the great Solomon, the bride is described in glowing, if somewhat zoological, terms. The passage is full of tastes and smells—pomegranates, grapes, honey, henna, nard, saffron, cinnamon, frankincense, myrrh—their love invades all their senses.

The special lover   5:2–6:3

The lover appears at the door, late at night. By the time she opens it he is gone. It echoes the search in 3:1–5, perhaps indicating the difficulty of finding true love, a search that even results in violence—perhaps to show her desire and dedication.

Questions, Questions
Oh, baby, I love your armadillos . . .

Er . . . a word please.
I know what you're going to ask. It's the gazelles, isn't it?
Not just the gazelles. The "hair like a flock of goats" and the "teeth like a flock of sheep."
Not to mention the "nose like the tower of Lebanon."
Right.
Well, it's not the imagery that we would use, but you have to remember that this poem is at least 2,300 years old. So their ideas of what was beautiful are different from ours.
So you wouldn't recommend using these in casual conversation?
Not if you want the relationship to go anywhere, no.
Thank you for your advice. And can I just say before I go that you have ears like a pair of giraffes?
No. And stop looking at me like that.

I've never been so insulted in all my life.

The dance 6:4–8:4

The lovers engage in a dance together. "Shulam" in 6:13 may be a variant of Shunam, or Shunem, a village near Jezreel. The most famous Shunamite was Abishag, the concubine of King David (1 Ki 1:3). Mandrakes (7:13) are pungent herbs associated with fertility.

Undoubtedly 8:1–4 are difficult verses. They seem to imply that the lovers must keep their liaison a secret. Or it may be that the woman wants to display her affection all the time, but is prevented from doing so by social taboos.

The seal 8:5–14

Seals were important items in the ancient world—an individual's seal was a representation of his or her own name (Ge 38:18). It was an extension of his or her being. But the lovers are so close that they have become one person. Their love will conquer all, for it is stronger than death.

Details, Details . . .
Tirzah and Jerusalem (6:4)

Tirzah was an ancient Canaanite city (Jos 12:24). It was Jeroboam's choice for the capital of the northern kingdom and its name meant "pleasure" or "beauty." Jerusalem was, of course, the capital of the southern kingdom. The lover is picturing his beloved as the two finest cities. Comparing a woman to a city was not so rare in ancient times, when cities were generally thought of as female.

Landmark: Marriage

Marriages in ancient times—and this includes New Testament as well as Old Testament times—were very different from marriages today.

Marriages were arranged, with the parents choosing a suitable partner for their son or daughter. Although Samson, for example, chose his mate, he asked his parents to arrange it (Jg 14:1–3).

Engagements were much more like legal contracts. Usually the bride was "purchased" by the payment of the "bride price," which was supposed to compensate the bride's father for the loss of a useful and valued member of the household. (As a father of three girls, may I say here and now that I am always open to offers.) However, brides could also be captured in wars (De 21:10–14), taken away in raids (Jg 21:1–12) or gained by seduction, when the seducer was obliged to marry his conquest (Ex 22:16).

In the early times, polygamy (i.e., having more than one wife) was allowed, but by the time of the monarchy only members of the royalty indulged in this practice.

Prophecy

The section of the Bible called "The Prophets" contains seventeen books. The first five are known as the major prophets; the remaining twelve are called the minor prophets. Each section is arranged broadly in chronological order, with the earliest prophets first, and so on.

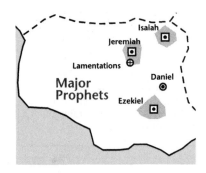

Major prophets

Isaiah

Isaiah prophesied in Judah during the reigns of four kings. His primary message was to warn them of the threat of Assyria and Babylonia, but he also gave a message of hope for the future.

Jeremiah

Jeremiah prophesied in Jerusalem. He warned of the impending punishment of Judah and looked toward the time when the Lord would make a new agreement with his people.

Lamentations

An acrostic poem—possibly by Jeremiah—that depicts the fall of Jerusalem at the hands of the Babylonian army.

Ezekiel

A priest and a prophet, Ezekiel was an exile in Babylon who had a series of visionary messages both for fellow exiles and for those left in Jerusalem.

Daniel

The book of Daniel tells the story of an exiled Jew in Babylon and is a mix of narrative account and a series of visions of future empires.

Minor prophets

This section consists of twelve books: Hosea, Joel, Amos, Obadiah, Jonah, Micah, Nahum, Habakkuk, Zephaniah, Haggai, Zechariah and Malachi.

The phrase "minor prophets" refers not to the contents of these books, but to their length. Some of these books are only one chapter long.

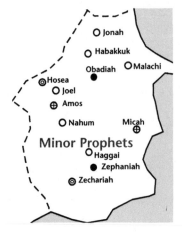

Most of these men prophesied during the decline of the kingdoms of Israel and Judah, although two of them—Haggai and Zechariah—are associated with the return to Jerusalem after the exile, and the last book—Malachi—is dated a century or so after the return. Some are very different from what we would normally expect of a book of prophecy. Jonah, for instance, is more of a story *about* a prophet than a book of prophecy itself, and Habakkuk is similar to Job in the way it asks difficult questions of God.

The themes they deal with are similar to those of the major prophets—themes such as the unfaithfulness of the people, social injustice and oppression, the future redemption of God's people, and the coming of a Messiah, a person chosen by God who would rescue his people from their foes.

Landmark: Prophecy

Prophecy is often confused with *prediction*, with the ability to see into the future. In the Bible, prophecy is much broader than that. Prophets were people of truth—they spoke the truth that God gave them. Often that did, indeed, involve predictions of the future, warnings of impending punishment or promises of future blessing. But just as frequently it involved challenging people about their conduct. Prophets encouraged, criticized and exhorted the kings, the priests and the people. This emphasis on truth meant that being a prophet was a risky business. If a prophet's words were not proved to be true—if he or she was a "false prophet"—they could be taken and stoned. Job assessment was tough in those days.

Prophets played a significant part in the life of Israel. Although many of them were abused and ignored, many were accorded respect and allowed to exercise their gifts—even if that made for uncomfortable listening. Descriptions of the experience of prophecy in the Bible are often physical: prophets shake, and the message burns inside their bones. They cannot help but speak out, and several of them receive the gift of prophecy with a certain amount of reluctance.

The prophets in the Bible bring many different messages from God, but it is possible to spot some themes, especially in the messages of the later prophets.

Calling the people back to God

The leaders and people of Israel and Judah repeatedly turned away from God and toward false religions—an act that was a direct factor in their fate as nations. Time and again, the prophets called the Israelites back to true faith. Time and again, they were ignored.

Calling for justice

The books of the prophets are full of condemnation of the rich, the powerful, the self-righteous and the way they were oppressing the poor. Rarely has God's heart for the poor and oppressed been more clearly demonstrated than through prophets such as Amos and Micah.

Calling judgment on Israel and Judah

Continually the prophets warned Israel and Judah what would happen to them. Continually they warned them that they would be destroyed, taken away, if they persisted in their evil ways. And, just as continually, the inhabitants of those countries ignored them. Right up until the Assyrians and Babylonians came to their doors . . .

Calling judgment on other nations

It was not just Israel and Judah who came under the scrutiny of God. The prophets also had warnings of destruction for Israel's neighbors and oppressors. The Babylonians, the Assyrians, the Cushites, the Medians, the Egyptians: they would all be judged by the Lord.

Calling out rude names

One of the most astonishing things about the prophets is the language they used. These were not gentle diplomats. They spat out the passion of God, they shocked people into listening, they were outrageous and outspoken. God is passionate about his people, and his prophets reflect his anger and his passion.

Calling to God

There is another thing that runs through the words of the prophets: the saving mercy of God. If the prophets saw the near future in all its awfulness, they also saw the far future in its glory. They saw the destruction that would come on Israel and Judah, but also the salvation that was to come for all humanity. They contrasted the world around them with the world that was to come. Most of all, they pointed to Jesus, the Messiah, who would usher in God's reign of peace, justice, mercy, compassion, safety, shelter and love.

Isaiah
The Lord saves!

Who: Isaiah's name means "the Lord saves." Married with two sons, he lived mainly in Jerusalem, reportedly wrote a biography of King Uzziah (2 Ch 26:22) and, according to Jewish tradition, died a particularly gruesome death: he was sawn in half (Hebrews 11:37 makes reference to this). However, some experts believe the book to be the work of different "Isaiahs."

When: He began his ministry in 740 BC (6:1). He lived at least until 681 BC, when the Assyrians were defeated.

What: The core themes of Isaiah are judgment and redemption. God will punish his people, but he will also rescue them. Isaiah constantly emphasizes God's power and might—he is a "fire" that will scorch the earth. But if God is a fire in judgment, he is also a stream in the desert, and a road back from exile. Isaiah points to the exile that will come, but he also points beyond, to a wonderful new age, an age of peace and wholeness when the Messiah will reign.

Reading Isaiah can be difficult. It is not really chronologically arranged and readers are thrown from one standpoint in time to another. Political observations and historical accounts jostle with visions of the far future and calls to repentance. Signs of the near future mingle with Messianic announcements. Condemnations of Israel's enemies are interrupted by visions of glory and even put-downs of palace officials.

His most sustained passages are visions of redemption and glory, when the exiles are brought back to Mount Zion. They are passionate visions of a glorious future —visions that must, during the hard times, have given Isaiah and his disciples a rock to cling to.

Quick Guide

Author
Isaiah. Or "Isaiahs," depending on your point of view.

Type
Prophecy

Purpose
To show how God would punish his people—and rescue them.

Key verses
65:17–19 "I am creating new heavens and a new earth; everything of the past will be forgotten. Celebrate and be glad forever! I am creating a Jerusalem, full of happy people. I will celebrate with Jerusalem and all its people; there will be no more crying or sorrow in that city."

If you remember one thing about this book . . .
God is a God of judgment and forgiveness.

Your 15 minutes start now
Read chapters 1, 5–6, 9, 26, 44, 53, 65

The Route Through Isaiah

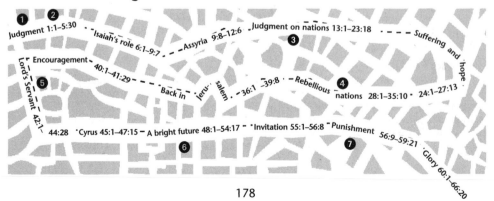

Judgment 1:1–5:30 · Isaiah's role 6:1–9:7 · Assyria 9:8–12:6 · Judgment on nations 13:1–23:18 · Suffering and hope

Encouragement 40:1–41:29 · Back in Jerusalem · 36:1–39:8 · Rebellious nations 28:1–35:10 · 24:1–27:13

Lord's Servant 42:1– · 44:28 · Cyrus 45:1–47:15 · A bright future 48:1–54:17 · Invitation 55:1–56:8 · Punishment 56:9–59:21 · Glory 60:1–66:20

Judgment
1:1–5:30

The introductory chapters outline the problems: wickedness and corruption abound (1:2–6, 21–23); the enemies are gathering (1:7–9); they perform the rituals but they carry on sinning (1:10–17). Yet even now, forgiveness is possible (1:18–20).

❶ Three pictures of Jerusalem

Chapters 2–4 contain three pictures of Jerusalem:
- her future glory (2:2–5; 4:2–6)
- her present decay (2:6–3:15)
- her coming judgment (3:16–4:1)
- her eventual purification (4:2–6)

❷ The vineyard

Isaiah 5 begins with a parabl about a vineyard that produced only bitter grapes. Israel is constantly likened to a vine or vineyard in the Old Testament, an image later used by Jesus. This leads into a condemnation of Israel's moral decay (5:8–12) and a warning of what the future holds (5:13–30). The picture is strikingly modern: a society that knows how to party, but not how to worship; how to break rules, but not how to obey them.

Isaiah's role
6:1–9.7

The year is 742 BC and Isaiah has a vision. His mouth is touched by a "burning coal" to purify him and he is sent to speak to the people. Verse 6:9 shows what a fruitless task it will be, but the chapter ends with a promise that a few chosen ones will be left.

Chapters 7–12 deal with political events in Israel, mixed with predictions about someone called Immanuel, or "God with us." Ahaz is proposing an alliance with Assyria, a foolish policy that will only delay Israel's destruction. The core of Isaiah's message is in 7:9: if they do not stand firm in their faith, they will be lost.

View Points

How many Isaiahs?

On one hand:
The book is the work of different "Isaiahs," based on stylistic differences between different sections and on the fact that different parts of Isaiah reflect political situations at different times. For example, the historical context of chapters 1–39 is that of the second half of the eighth century BC; whereas chapters 40–66 have references to the exile that would fit with the fifth and sixth centuries BC. They also point to different themes—with "first Isaiah" talking about God's punishment and the threat of Assyria, and "second Isaiah" talking of the collapse of Babylon and the rise of Cyrus.

On the other hand:
If there are enormous differences between the two sections, there are big similarities as well. Phrases crop up *throughout* the book that are not found elsewhere in Scripture. So if they were different people, they used the same phrase book.

As to the specific mention of Cyrus, either you believe in prophecy or you don't. If God gives predictions of the future, why shouldn't he go into detail? It's not as if he doesn't know what's going to happen.

Moving on: The general agreement is that the book was the work of different hands (indeed, some experts argue that there is another one—Trito-Isaiah). Does it matter? Not necessarily. Prophecies given by God to different people at different times are still prophecies and still have much to say to us. However many "Isaiahs" there were, the core message of judgment and redemption remains true.

How do you want your coal—medium or well done?

Puzzling Points
The virgin and the child (7:14)

The Hebrew word used in 7:14—*almah*—is usually translated "virgin," but it actually means "young woman." Certainly the term could include virgins, but it didn't mean "virgin" as such. In fact, Isaiah was probably talking about his own family. The young woman may refer to his wife-to-be (8:3). First, he is talking about a "sign from God" that would usually be fulfilled in a few years. Second, the next verse, about eating "yogurt and honey" (7:15), implies that the child will not have enough to eat, i.e., he will be living in an area of devastation and famine.

Far from being a prophecy of a distant time, therefore, Isaiah seems to be saying that, in a short time, despite the hardships they will have to endure, many women will name their children Immanuel—"God with us." Their faith in God will be in marked contrast to Ahaz's lack of faith.

So how come this verse pops up every Christmas? Simply because in the Greek version of the Bible, used by Matthew, the Hebrew word *almah* was translated as *parthenos*, which could mean "virgin," so Matthew saw it as a prophecy of Mary. Some use this confusion to argue that the Virgin Birth was a made up story, based on a mistranslated verse, but it could equally work the other way. Both Matthew and Luke believed the Virgin Birth to be a fact. This passage may not have been a direct prophecy of Christ, but it was certainly a pattern, a distant echo of what Christ would do.

Isaiah knew that tough times were ahead, but he knew ultimately that God would be with his people. Which is exactly what Christmas is all about.

▷**250**

A close shave 7:1–9:7

Chapter 7:18–25 describes the desolation of Israel if they side with the Assyrians. They will even have their beards shaved off—considered a great dishonor in ancient times. The king dismisses Isaiah's message, so he writes it down on a scroll for his followers (8:1). His son is born—his wife was also a prophetess, making it something of a family business. The name Maher-Shalal-Hash-Baz is a difficult one, but roughly means "suddenly attacked, quickly taken."

Isaiah calls the people to have faith, to trust in the Lord rather than in mediums and false prophets (8:17–22). There is a wonderful passage that looks far into the future, to the coming of Jesus, the true king who would bring light in the darkness and establish an everlasting kingdom (9:1–7).

Assyria 9:8–12:6

This section continues the theme of impending ruin, with the king of Assyria poised to walk on the people of Israel "like mud in the streets" (9:5). In 10:5–34, Assyria is described as an instrument of the Lord, a tool being used by him to show his anger. Chapters 11–12 contain another great hymn of praise and prophecy of the Messiah, with a vision of a reign of perfect peace. It is a return to Eden, with man and nature in harmony (11:6–10) and all nations brought together (11:10–16). It ends with a song of praise to God (12:1–6).

Other nations 13:1–23:18
Captive clothing 20:1–6

In Isaiah 20, the prophet dresses like a captive to illustrate the fate of Egypt and Ethiopia at the hands of Assyria. After Assyria had captured the northern kingdom in 722–21 BC, Hezekiah was under pressure to make alliances with Egypt. Isaiah is warning him of the folly of such a course. Sargon is probably Sargon II who ruled Assyria from 721–705 BC.

❸ The valley of vision 22:1–14

Isaiah 22:1–14 is an oracle against the "Valley of Vision," i.e., Jerusalem. The leaders have fled, the people have died "not by the sword"—probably meaning that they have succumbed to famine or disease. They put their faith in man-made defences, but not in God. Instead of repenting, they celebrate and drink (22:13). Then Isaiah suddenly gets personal, with an attack on one Shebna, a high-ranking government official. He appears to have been a foreigner who was getting above himself, coveting a grave worthy of a king. He occurs later, in a different post, perhaps having been demoted (36:3; 37:2).

Judgment on other nations
13:1–23:18

Isaiah 13–23 is a long section, mainly containing prophecies of judgment on other nations. Similar patterns can be found in Amos 1–2, Ezekiel 25–32 and Jeremiah 46–51.

Philistia (14:28–32)

Some starved, some killed, an invasion from the north.

Damascus and north Israel (17:1–11)

Starvation and war.

Tyre (23:1–18)

Devastation, commercial collapse (23:9), loss of power. Tyre will one day worship the Lord (23:18).

Assyria (14:24–27)

A brief prophecy that they will all be wiped out.

Egypt (9:1–22)

Civil war, drought, plague. But 19:23–25 is a remarkable prediction of unity, when Egypt, Assyria and Israel will join together in repentance and worship.

Ethiopia or Cush (18:1–7)

Destroyed by Egypt. Ethiopia is described as a land of "whirring wings," which may refer to locusts or simply imply that the country is in a complete panic.

Moab (15:1–16:14)

A sad, mournful poem predicting famine, exile and even attack by lions. Unlike his attitude to the other nations, Isaiah seems genuinely moved by Moab's distress and by the cries of her refugees.

Arabia (21:13–17)

War and conflict.

Seir or Edom (21:11, 12)

A brief prediction of oncoming "darkness." Not specified, but it doesn't look good.

Babylon (13:1–14:23 & 21:1–10)

The utter destruction of the city (13:2–22), the death of the king (14:4–23). Military defeat is followed by betrayal, violence and destruction.

Suffering and hope 24:1–27:13

Now the Lord looks beyond Israel's neighbors to the world. This section is closely related to chapters 13–23. They are a picture of the final judgment, when the Lord will punish not only the wrongdoers on earth, but also the "powers above" (24:21). This passage is not only a commentary on the events around Israel, but also a message of future salvation.

In chapter 24 Isaiah depicts the judgment of the earth. God will also punish the heavenly powers—i.e., Satan and the fallen angels.

In the midst of this, Isaiah seems to hear songs of joy, but they are premature. In chapter 25 the focus shifts and we are at the period after Assyria has been destroyed. All nations are invited to a banquet on Mount Zion, featuring—and I am fond of this part—fine and aged wines (25:6). Death itself is destroyed (25:7–8). Moab in 25:10–12 is symbolic of all those who would oppose God. They are shown swimming in a cesspit. A song of victory is sung (26:1–19) to the eternal rock (26:4). Leviathan is overthrown and now Israel is the true vineyard (27:2–5).

**Details, Details . . .
Ariel (29:1 NIV)**

"Ariel" is a pun on "altar hearth." Isaiah means Jerusalem, the center of their worship. They worship without understanding or thought, and will have to be shocked out of their apathy (29:13–14).

Rebellious nations 28:1–35:10

A mix of passages on rebellious nations, and also on rebellious people. Samaria (28:1–13) and Jerusalem (28:13–29:8) are warned. In particular, Isaiah condemns the false priests and prophets, and the ignorant, corrupt leaders, wallowing around in a haze of drink and hypocritical religion (29:1–14).

❹ The useless monster 30:1–31:9

Chapters 30 and 31 contain more warnings against placing faith in Egypt, but once again Israel will not listen. The pro-Egypt party have, apparently, won over the king, and now, like some modern spin doctors, they want to hear only good news and pleasant falsehoods (30:10). Isaiah likens Egypt to a useless monster (30:7). He warns against placing faith in their men and horses (31:1). He reminds Israel that the Lord will deliver them, that Assyria will be destroyed.

Chapter 32 begins with a wonderful picture of a new world order, a new society, where clear thought and helpfulness are the norm. The carefree, careless women will be taken away and the land will become fertile again. Chapter 33 is a picture of the doomed Jerusalem and a warning to the Assyrian attackers. It is contrasted with the ideal Jerusalem of the future, ruled over by the Messiah-King (33:17–24). Chapters 34 and 35 are cries for justice against "all the nations," but against Edom in particular. The scattered Israel will return and "sorrows and worries will be gone far away" (35:10).

Back in Jerusalem . . . 36:1–39:8

These are link chapters, bringing us back to the real historical situation of the time and serving as an introduction to the second half of Isaiah. They are paralleled in 2 Kings 18:13–27 and 2 Chronicles 32:1–19.

Sennacherib makes two attempts to conquer Jerusalem (36–37). The Assyrian leader who confronts Hezekiah is confused, believing him to have torn down all the altars to the Lord. In fact, Hezekiah had torn down all the altars to false gods. The mocking officer offers to give them some horses to fight with, and warns them that they will be forced to eat their own dung and drink their own urine (36:12). Hezekiah's response is to seek the Lord through Isaiah. Isaiah reports that the attack will come to nothing: the Lord is in control and Sennacherib is just his puppet (37:21–29). The Assyrians are visited by an angel and struck down (the Greek historian Herodotus attributed this to the plague) and, back in Nineveh, Sennacherib is assassinated.

Chapter 38 deals with Hezekiah's illness and recovery. The Lord gives him a remarkable sign of his recovery—the shadow which goes back ten steps (38:8), God's sign that the king has some years left "in the sun." The king then makes a tactical error, showing envoys from Babylon around the city, revealing everything to them (39:1–8). Perhaps he was seeking help, perhaps he was simply showing off, but one day that knowledge gained would come back to haunt Israel.

Encouragement 40:1–41:29

Chapter 40 is about the glory of the Lord, and much of it is similar in its questions to the way the Lord answers Job. The beginning has three voices at work, each showing how the "comfort" of verse 1 will be brought about. Verses 3–5 are often seen as a prophecy of the role of John the Baptist. Isaiah then shouts about the frailty of man, particularly with reference to the human forces that have been oppressing God's people. Verses 9–11 are an announcement of the coming of the Lord, the Good Shepherd. God has not forgotten his people, but they must have faith and wait for salvation (40:27–31).

Chapter 41 shows that God is in control of the future, and only he can know what is going to happen. The idols, on the other hand, are dumb (in every sense of the word). Verse 25 brings the first hint of Cyrus, the hero who would defeat Babylon and release the Israelite captives.

The Lord's servant 42:1–44:28

These chapters return to the theme of the chosen one, the Lord's servant. Just as Cyrus will be the physical agent of Israel's freedom, the Lord's servant will be a spiritual agent of redemption.

He is not depicted as the great warrior who many would have been hoping for, but as someone who will bring healing and justice. This is contrasted with Israel the servant (42:19) appearing as blind and deaf to what the Lord wants.

❺ Fruit and wood

Chapters 43 and 44 contain wonderful passages about forgiveness and deliverance. God will be with his people and protect them. He loves his people (43:4), who come from all nations (43:9). Nothing they can do can earn his forgiveness; it is for his own sake that he offers salvation (43:25). This is one of the high points of the Old Testament. The contrast between the dumb idols and this life-giving, loving, forgiving God could hardly be more marked. The Lord gives life, bringing dry deserts to fruitfulness, while the idols are worthless, pointless concoctions of men. The irony is that they are fashioning gods out of wood and minerals, while ignoring the God who made the trees and the rocks in the first place (44:6–23).

Cyrus 45:1–47:15

At last Isaiah names the one whom the Lord will use to redeem Israel: Cyrus (44:24–45:25). Through him the exiles will return, the temple will be rebuilt. It is a difficult passage, because he speaks of Cyrus in messianic terms, as the shepherd, the anointed, the chosen ally.

Part of this is because, once again history and prophecy are combining. Cyrus is seen as a "type" of Christ, a kind of forerunner, or image. But Cyrus is still in the future—indeed, some argue that this language is proof of this being a prophecy of Cyrus, rather than a description, for the real Cyrus would hardly have deserved such plaudits.

Similarly, Isaiah sees his effects as far more wide-reaching than they actually were, particularly in passages where the victory of Cyrus is supposed to bring together all the nations in worshiping God. Even the most optimistic of Cyrus's contemporaries would have had trouble arguing that one.

Chapters 46 and 47 describe the collapse of Babylon—not just the city, but the entire civilization. The walls have fallen, but, more importantly, so have the gods.

A bright future 48:1–54:17

Isaiah 48 sums up the main arguments in the previous seven chapters.
• God alone can predict the future (48:1–8).
• God alone is the true God, the first and last (48:9–13).
• God alone has brought Cyrus to power (48:14–16).
• God punished Israel for Israel's own good (48:17–19).
• God alone will rescue Israel from exile and punish those who are evil (48:20–22).

❻ The suffering servant 49:1–53:12
Chapter 49 returns to the theme of the Lord's servant, but by the Lord's servant Isaiah means two things: Israel and the Messiah.

Israel is described as the Lord's servant because it is a light for other nations, God's representatives taking his saving power to earth (49:1–6). However, Israel proved to be a bad servant, one that rarely obeyed its master's commands. God came to its rescue simply because he could not stop loving his people. Like a mother and her child, God loves his children (49:15–18). So Jerusalem has a bright future, as the center of worship for many nations, many servants of God.

In their place is another servant, a strange figure, one who has come to teach, yet who is beaten and tortured, one whom Isaiah describes in a series of "servant songs" (50:4–11). Is he describing a person here? Or are we talking about Israel as a nation again? The same figure appears in 52:13–53:12, a suffering, ill-treated servant, beaten until he looks scarcely human. People look on him and "think about things they have never seen or thought about before" (52:15).

It culminates in Isaiah 53, where this person—for it is clearly a person now—is described. He is not a handsome Prince Charming, but a figure of hatred and rejection. Isaiah makes clear, however, that his suffering is for us, for God's people. For *our* sins he has been wounded and crushed; to bring us back to God he took our punishment. Isaiah 53 is the high point of messianic prediction. It throws away the old images of a mighty warrior who would drive the enemies out by force. This is a figure working at a far deeper, more mysterious level, and fighting a far more deadly enemy. The final verse of chapter 53 contains a powerful, stunning promise: "The LORD will reward him with honor and power for sacrificing his life. Others thought he was a sinner, but he suffered for our sins and asked God to forgive us." This historical figure would undergo the punishment on behalf of everyone. And his name was to be Jesus.

Invitation   54:1–56:8

After this it is party time. Israel has been washed clean and it is time to celebrate, to put sin and guilt and shame behind them. Now, the Lord promises love and mercy forever (54:8). A new Jerusalem is promised and invitations are issued to everyone. This is a new order, with the thirsty and the poor on the guest list (55:1–5). Foreigners too will be part of his nation (56:3–7). This is a society for all who worship the Lord and obey his commands.

Through all this the grace of the Lord is evident. He has never given up on his people. His servant is prepared to dare anything on our behalf. We are reminded of God's power. His ways are not our ways, his thoughts are not our thoughts (58:6–11). No. And we should be eternally grateful.

Punishment for the unfaithful
56:9–59:21

The suffering servant forms a stark contrast to the real leaders of Israel. They are blind watchdogs, stupid and greedy. They are drunken, unrepentant shepherds who lead their flock astray (56:9–12).

Meanwhile, God's people suffer, or worse, follow their leaders' stupidity. They are obsessed with a terrible mixture of the occult and the sexual. In terms that occur throughout the prophets, Israel is accused of a kind of spiritual adultery, of sleeping with foreign gods. Of course, this was also a part of their idolatrous worship (57:1–13). Only those who are contrite will be saved; only those who humbly call on the Lord will receive his help (57:15–21).

❼ Integrity and justice   58:1–59:21

Isaiah 58 contains a great injunction on those who follow the Lord to act responsibly and fairly. They are to think of their workers (58:3), free the prisoners (58:6), feed the hungry, house the homeless and clothe the naked (58:7). They must respect the Sabbath and take their worship seriously (58:13). Then they will be known for their honesty, for their true religion and their light will shine like the dawning sun.

Details, Details . . .
Job description

When Jesus preached at the synagogue in his hometown, his text came from Isaiah 61:1–3. This was his job description. This was his declaration that he was the servant predicted in Isaiah.

> **Details, Details . . .**
> **Burial caves and pigs (65:4)**
>
> It was forbidden for Jews to eat pork or to come into contact with the dead. This may imply that they have been engaging in heathen rituals, or even occult practices with the dead.

Chapter 59 returns to familiar ground, with Israel urged to leave their old ways. It ends with the Lord promising to rescue his people. They will form the nucleus of a new nation, with whom the Lord will enter into a new covenant. He will give them his Spirit to live with them forever (59:20–21).

Glory   60:1–66:20

The final chapters of Isaiah tread familiar ground, starting with the future glory of Jerusalem and the saving justice of the Lord (60–61).

Chapter 62 sees Jerusalem dressed like a bride or a queen, and given a new name to describe her character better: Hepzibah, or "my delight is in her," and Beulah, or "married." Later, both John and Paul use the same imagery for the Church, talking of it as "the bride of Christ." Chapter 63:1–6 is a short poem portraying God as a victorious soldier, who has trampled Israel's enemies like grapes beneath his feet. In 63:15–64:12 comes a desperate cry for help from the Lord, a prayer to their Father. They believe that God has abandoned them, their temple is burnt and their land laid to waste (64:11).

The answer comes in a final restatement of the main themes. The guilty will be punished and the hypocrites silenced (65:1–7). Those who worship false gods will be slaughtered (65:11–12), but the faithful servants will be rewarded (65:13–16). There will be a new heaven and a new earth, free of death and illness and sadness and pain. Nature will live in harmony with humankind and God will be among his people (65:17–25).

There is another call to true worship (66:1–4) and further condemnation of apostasy (66:5–17). The book ends with a promise that God will never forget his people and a dire warning of the fate of those who choose another path. It ends virtually as it has begun, but if the gloom is still there, the messianic promises are brighter, more distinct, than before.

Was there one Isaiah or two? Did he write in the eighth century alone or in the sixth as well? Such questions are, in the end, impossible to answer for sure. What we do know, however, is that this whole book is drenched with the Spirit of God. There might have been one person writing these messages down, or three people, or thirty-three people—but there was only one author.

Jeremiah
Judgment on Judah

Who: Jeremiah, son of Hilkiah the priest. Jeremiah lived in Anathoth, about three miles north of Jerusalem. A contemporary of Zephaniah, Habakkuk and Ezekiel, Jeremiah lived and prophesied in Judah.

When: Between 622 and 580 BC. He began his career in the reign of Josiah (a good king) and after that lived through a succession of increasingly ineffective and appalling monarchs: Jehoahaz, Jehoiakim, Jehoiachin and Zedekiah.

His prophecies break into three broad periods:
• 627–605 BC Judah is threatened by Assyria and Egypt.
• 605–586 BC God's judgment against Babylon.
• 586–580 BC In Jerusalem while the city is captured.

What: Jeremiah was a political and social revolutionary. Few people in the Bible have led lives of such conflict: he was forever being thrown into jail, or tried for his life, or forced to flee. He was publicly humiliated by false prophets and even thrown into a sewer. Time and time again, Jeremiah calls the people to repent; time and time again, he is ignored, reviled or abused. The reward for his prophecies is beating, exclusion and imprisonment.

Quick Guide

Author

Jeremiah

Purpose

A record of his prophecies during the last years of Judah.

Key verse

31:33 "Here is the new agreement that I, the LORD, will make with the people of Israel: 'I will write my laws on their hearts and minds. I will be their God, and they will be my people.'"

If you remember one thing about this book . . .

The Lord punished his people for their unfaithfulness—but he also promised them forgiveness.

Your 15 minutes start now

Read chapters 1–2, 7–8, 12, 16, 25, 31, 39, 52.

The reason for this harsh treatment is simple: the powers that be simply did not want to hear his message. Jeremiah's prophecies encompass the downfall of the kingdom of Judah. Jeremiah prophesied in the dark, final days of Judah's destruction. The country had turned away from God, while all around the forces of destruction were gathering.

Jeremiah is a surprisingly honest book. The prophet was originally a timid figure and, despite promises that he would receive strength from God, he often struggled with his calling (not surprising, when you see what happened to him). He often calls for vengeance on his enemies and he often breaks down in tears. Yet he does remain strong. He keeps the memory of his first calling close to his heart and he keeps going. While all around him collapses, Jeremiah's foundations remain firm.

The Route Through Jeremiah

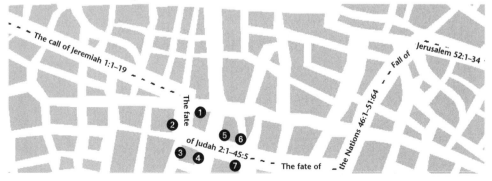

The call of Jeremiah 1:1–19

Although Jeremiah is only young, his age is no barrier to God, who has been preparing the prophet since before he was born (1:5). Jeremiah's authority comes from God and it is God's message that he will speak.

Details, Details . . .
Bunch of almonds (1:11–12)

God makes a pun. The Hebrew for "almonds that ripen early" sounds like "always rise early." All right, it's not the *best* joke in the world, but the point is that God is ready.

The fate of Judah 2:1–45:5

Judah has turned to other gods. The nation is described as an unfaithful wife, someone who has made the whole land filthy (2:1–8). Instead of the living water God offers, they have tried to collect their water in their own faulty, cracked wells. The country is like a prostitute who chases one god after another (3:1–5).

Warnings of destruction 3:6–6:30

Judah didn't learn from the example of Israel. They watched their sister go into captivity and now they are heading the same way (3:8–10). They make pretenses of repentance, but they don't mean it. "At least," says God, "Israel didn't pretend."

Disaster is coming. Throughout Jeremiah we can hear the distant hoof-beats coming ever closer, as the invading armies close in on the rebellious people. What is going to happen to Judah fills Jeremiah with horror. He sees the darkness and devastation as Jerusalem dies. She is like a cheap whore who has been beaten to death by one of her lovers (4:27–31).

The instrument of destruction is going to be a "foreign nation" (5:15–17), an ancient power that will strip the land of everything. They will attack without warning. Armies normally did not fight in the heat of noon, but this army will attack when and where it pleases (6:4–5).

Outside the temple 7:1–8:3

Jeremiah stands outside the temple and warns the people. Theirs is a superstitious faith, a belief that if they attend the temple regularly it will all be OK. God likens their temple to a thieves' hideout—an image that was later used by Jesus (Mt 21:13). Their lives are immoral and they are worshiping false gods, including Astarte, the so-called queen of heaven (7:18). So, no more sacrifices. "Take the meat home and cook it yourselves," says God.

The people of Judah have even sacrificed children (7:31) to false gods. The place where they have done this is called Hinnom Valley. Later it was to be renamed Ge-Hinnom or Gehenna, and Jesus used it as a synonym for hell. It is a place where the bones of idolaters and murderers are scattered and where a deathly silence shrouds the land (7:30–8:3).

❶ The tears of a prophet 8:3–11:17

Jeremiah has sometimes been called the weeping prophet, and this section certainly shows that. The reason is that he knows what is going to happen. These are not vague feelings that he has, they aren't hunches or guesses. He knows what will happen. He can see the bodies on the streets, the land in ruins. Unlike the people who trust in idols or try to spot the future in the sky (10:1–5), Jeremiah knows exactly what the future holds.

Judah has broken their agreement with God, an agreement that dates back to the time when God brought his people out of Egypt. Now they will be uprooted and discarded (11:1–17).

The plot against Jeremiah   11:18–12:17

Such is the strength of opposition to Jeremiah that the people of his hometown plot against him. This raises serious issues for Jeremiah. How is it that the evil men are having such an easy life, while he, the Lord's prophet, is suffering? God replies that judgment will happen, and that it will be terrible. But he also points to a restoration in the distant future.

❷ Visible signs   13:1–19:15

The next few chapters contain several "visible signs" as Jeremiah either acts out the message from the Lord or points to images that give a message.

The Linen Cloth 12:1–11	Wineskins 13:12–13	Drought 14:1–15:21
Judah is like a piece of clothing worn by God. But it will be discarded. It will rot away in the darkness.	The people will be senseless and disorientated, as if they were drunk. They will be discarded like smashed bottles.	In the midst of a terrible drought, Jeremiah prays for rain, but nothing comes. The drought is a picture of what will happen—the death of a country.

Loneliness 16:1–21	The Jar 19:1–13	The Potter 18:1–23
Just as God called Ezekiel not to mourn his dead wife and Hosea to marry a prostitute, he calls Jeremiah to remain unmarried. The cost of being a prophet was immense, not only in physical terms, but in emotional turmoil. Jeremiah's isolation was to show to the people around him that they were approaching a time when it would be better to be childless, better to be unmarried and alone.	Jeremiah buys a clay jar, stands in front of Jerusalem's leaders, and smashes it. God is going to shatter their country and their city. Simple, but effective.	Jeremiah goes to a potter's shop, where he watches the potter mold his clay. The message is clear: God changes his mind. He can create and uncreate. He can make and he can destroy.

During these chapters, Jeremiah's complaints reach new heights (or depths, depending on your point of view). He is injured and in pain. He feels as much in the grip of a drought as the country (15:18).

The people's reaction to Jeremiah's messages is to plot against the prophet. Jeremiah reacts with raw emotion, in a prayer remarkable for its vitriol (18:18–23). He wants to hear his enemies scream. He wants God to condemn them forever. Significantly, God does not respond to this impossible prayer.

Jeremiah's arrest   20:1–18

Jeremiah's message brings punishment and he is arrested by Pashhur, the head of the temple security force. He is put in the stocks at the temple gate, and in his humiliation he cries out to the Lord again.

Prophecies against kings   21:1–22:30

The chronology in these chapters is mixed up. The prophecies in chapter 21 are earlier than the prophecy in chapter 20. Zedekiah came after the other kings.

Perfect kings and false prophets   23:1–40

Jeremiah preaches against the false prophets, those who do not speak the words of God, but lure the people into false worship. They encourage those who do evil (23:14). They claim to speak for God, but they never even listen to him (23:21). Their visions and dreams are lies (23:25). Not so Jeremiah's visions, and he has a vision of a true King, one who will rule with justice (23:1–8).

The basket of figs   24:1–10

This vision comes after the initial collapse of Jerusalem, sometime after 597 BC. The figs in exile will be protected and will grow; those left behind will rot away.

Seventy years of exile   25:1–38

A prophecy from 605 BC. For 23 years Jeremiah has been at work, and no one has been listening to him. Now he predicts the captivity that will come. Seventy years is a round figure for the exile, probably meaning simply "a long time." In fact, the Jews were in exile in Babylon from around 605 to 538 BC.

❸ The trials of Jeremiah   26:1–29:32

Throughout his life, Jeremiah was under threat and trial. These incidents span his life and career.

In 609 BC comes a message that links with 7:1–15. Jeremiah's message almost costs him his life, but some brave people speak up for him (26:1–24).

Forward to 597 BC. Jeremiah stands, humiliated and isolated, wearing a yoke on his shoulders. The yoke—which was usually used to harness cattle—is a sign of how Judah should approach the Babylonians. This is a deeply political message, for Zedekiah is trying to stand against Babylon, but Jeremiah is saying that servitude is the only way out. The false prophets flatly deny this, and they tell the king what he wants to hear. Hananiah breaks the yoke—a fatal move, and he dies two months later.

In the same year, Jeremiah sends a letter to those who have already been taken into exile (29:1–32). The false prophets were predicting that the exiles would swiftly return; Jeremiah advises them to settle down for a long wait.

❹ Let's hear it for Uriah   26:20–24

Uriah, son of Shemaiah, pays the ultimate price for his faithfulness to God's commands. Jehoiakim is so intent on punishing Uriah that he even sends kidnappers to bring Uriah back to Egypt. Uriah's body is dumped in the pit, but his obedience to God has never been forgotten.

❺ The new covenant 30:1–40

In the midst of all this turmoil and despair, Jeremiah is granted a vision that will change everything. God secures a future for his people; they will return to the land and they will rejoice.

More than the restoration of the land, however, God promises a new covenant, a new agreement with his people (31:31–37). This will be an agreement of their hearts and minds. God will be their God and they will follow him willingly. This promise looks far, far ahead. Jeremiah may have thought that he was talking about the return from Babylon, and in some ways he was, but equally he was speaking words from God that referred to events that would only be fulfilled in the time of Jesus (He 8).

The field and the slaves 32:1–33:26

588/87 BC. In this remarkable act of faith, Jeremiah buys a field. The point is that his hometown, where the field is situated, is already under foreign occupation. On the face of it, it seems a foolish thing to do, but Jeremiah obeys the Lord and pays the money for a field he will probably never see. God is saying to Judah that, one day, they will own the land again. One day, they will return and tend their fields and own their property. In the midst of all the destruction, Jeremiah was sending a signal. The land would not always be occupied by foreign powers. One day it would return to the rightful owner.

This theme of future restoration is picked up in chapter 33, where the Lord gives another promise of the future king (33:14–26).

With the enemies at the gates of Jerusalem, Zedekiah tries to curry favor with God by celebrating the Jubilee (De 15). However, the selfishness of the Jews wins out and the slaves are all taken back into captivity, the king breaks his word, and they are worse off than before.

> **Details, Details . . .**
> **Rechabites (35:1–18)**
>
> A nomadic group who lived near the Israelites. Their obedience to the Lord is a direct criticism of the Israelites' disobedience. This is a flashback to the reign of Jehoiakim (609–598 BC).

Jehoiakim burns the scroll 36:1–32

This exciting chapter offers a unique insight into the writing methods of an Old Testament prophet. It is 605 BC. Jeremiah is banned from the temple, so he writes down his prophecies, dictating them to Baruch, his scribe.

The message, which impresses and moves the royal officials, does not go down so well with the king. In a wonderfully graphic description we see the king listening to the words, and then, after every few paragraphs, cutting up the scroll and throwing it into the fire. It is a stupid and futile gesture. Jeremiah simply repeats his dictation and this time adds a lot more (36:32).

❻ Jeremiah in prison 37:1–39:14

In 588 BC, Jeremiah is arrested on suspicion of joining the Babylonians. The king summons him secretly to the palace to ask him questions. Typically, Zedekiah does not release Jeremiah; he just puts him in a nicer cell. This, perhaps, was Zedekiah's fatal flaw. He knew what was right, but could never quite bring himself to do it wholeheartedly.

Zedekiah is a weak man and a weak king. He condemns Jeremiah and the prophet is thrown into a well. The well has mud at the bottom, the terrible idea being that, once Jeremiah runs out of strength, he will drown in the mud. Then Zedekiah is persuaded to do a U-turn and rescues the prophet. He can't even make up his mind whether to surrender (38:19).

In the end (Je 39) he is captured by the Babylonians while trying to sneak out of the city at night. The sad, pathetic figure of Zedekiah is blinded, and the last thing he sees is his sons being killed.

Ironically, it is Nebuchadnezzar who shows most respect to Jeremiah. He makes sure that, although only a handful of the very poorest people are left in Jerusalem, Jeremiah is looked after. He stays at Mizpah "with the few who were left in the land."

❼ The final days of Jerusalem   39:15–42:22

The last few left in Judah manage to make a disastrous situation even worse by fighting among themselves. The passage is frighteningly reminiscent of the days of the judges—the same kind of social breakdown, the same reliance on violence, the same struggle for power.

Ishmael, son of Nethaniah, is a guerrilla leader who views the surrender to the Babylonians as treachery. He assassinates the governor, Gedaliah, then the Judaean officials and Babylonian soldiers (40:7–41:15).

Although the remnant are promised the protection of the Lord provided they do not flee to Egypt, they do not believe Jeremiah and flee the country, taking Jeremiah and Baruch with them (41:16–43:13). In Egypt they carry on exactly as before, turning to foreign gods, so the Lord tells them that punishment is coming (44:1–30). Babylon will capture Egypt as they captured Jerusalem.

Let's hear it for Baruch (45:1–5)

Baruch, it seems, shared his master's cheery outlook. However, God understood his anxieties and reassured him of his protection. Baruch was a faithful servant and wrote an awful lot of words. I know how he feels.

The fate of the nations
46:1–51:64
See map opposite

These chapters present a series of prophecies against the nations surrounding Judah. They might have thought they were the powerful ones. This is a reminder that they are merely tools of the Lord. Egypt, Philistia, Moab and Ammon will all fall to the rule of God.

Jeremiah's prophecies against the nations were written on a scroll and sent to Babylon. There, Seraiah read it aloud and sank the scroll in the Euphrates. It was a symbol of the eventual fate of Babylon.

The fall of Jerusalem   52:1–34;
2 Ki 24:18–25:30; 2 Ch 36:11–21

This passage, which is a later addition to Jeremiah, says that only 4,600 people were taken from Jerusalem. This number clashes with the huge number given in 2 Kings 24—but it may not include women and children.

The book ends with a new ruler in Babylon, Evil-Merodach (not a good name from the PR point of view). He is kind to the captured king, but nothing can disguise the fact that Jehoiachin is still a captive and the entire country is still enslaved.

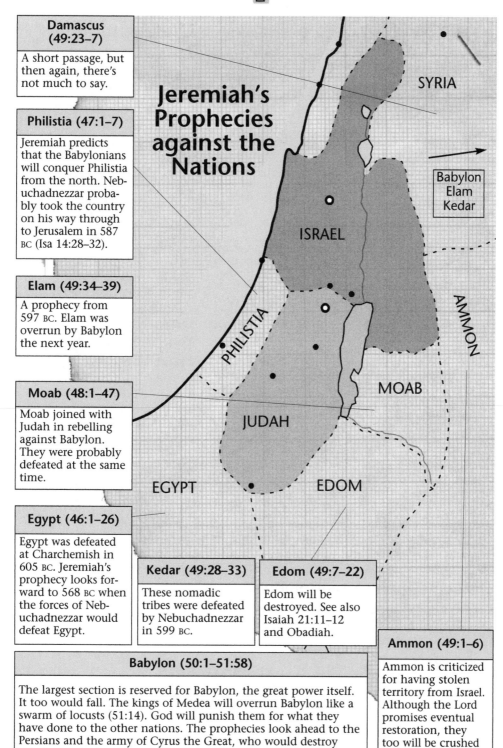

Jeremiah's Prophecies against the Nations

Damascus (49:23–7)

A short passage, but then again, there's not much to say.

Philistia (47:1–7)

Jeremiah predicts that the Babylonians will conquer Philistia from the north. Nebuchadnezzar probably took the country on his way through to Jerusalem in 587 BC (Isa 14:28–32).

Elam (49:34–39)

A prophecy from 597 BC. Elam was overrun by Babylon the next year.

Moab (48:1–47)

Moab joined with Judah in rebelling against Babylon. They were probably defeated at the same time.

Egypt (46:1–26)

Egypt was defeated at Charchemish in 605 BC. Jeremiah's prophecy looks forward to 568 BC when the forces of Nebuchadnezzar would defeat Egypt.

Kedar (49:28–33)

These nomadic tribes were defeated by Nebuchadnezzar in 599 BC.

Edom (49:7–22)

Edom will be destroyed. See also Isaiah 21:11–12 and Obadiah.

Ammon (49:1–6)

Ammon is criticized for having stolen territory from Israel. Although the Lord promises eventual restoration, they too will be crushed by Babylon.

Babylon (50:1–51:58)

The largest section is reserved for Babylon, the great power itself. It too would fall. The kings of Medea will overrun Babylon like a swarm of locusts (51:14). God will punish them for what they have done to the other nations. The prophecies look ahead to the Persians and the army of Cyrus the Great, who would destroy Babylon and release the captive Israelites.

SYRIA · **ISRAEL** · **AMMON** · **PHILISTIA** · **MOAB** · **JUDAH** · **EGYPT** · **EDOM**

Babylon
Elam
Kedar

Lamentations
The funeral of Jerusalem

Who: Traditionally Jeremiah, although no authorship is mentioned in the book.

When: After the fall of Jerusalem, around 588–587 BC.

What: Perhaps the least read book of the entire Bible. It consists of five incredibly depressing poems, written by Jeremiah as the city of Jerusalem was descending into chaos and defeat. Surprisingly, there is one passage where Jeremiah breaks out into a hymn of praise (3:21–40). In the midst of all this, he "dares to hope."

The structure of the poem is unusual, for it is an acrostic—or at least the first four chapters are—with each verse of each chapter beginning with the appropriate letter of the Hebrew alphabet. (Chapter 3 has three verses for each letter). Chapter 5 is different, although it has twenty-two verses. Acrostics are used to indicate completeness. Perhaps the prophet is indicating that the suffering of the people has gone from A to Z—across the complete range of experience.

While the prophet understands that Jerusalem's suffering is deserved, he questions whether they really deserved this much.

Perhaps the worst feeling of all is that sense that God has deserted them, that he is on the side of their enemies, that he and his people are no longer even on speaking terms. It is not merely that Jerusalem is crushed, not merely that their own sins have brought them to this—it is the feeling that the Lord has turned his back on them.

Yet the prophet knows that this will not last. The Lord will build up his city and his people again. There is hope among the rubble.

Acrostic
A poem or song that
Begins with successive letters of
   the alphabet. You
Can find examples in
Different parts of the Bible.
Every reader misses out on these,
For nowadays we don't
Get taught the
Hebrew alphabet.
I can't keep this up any longer . . .

The Route Through Lamentations

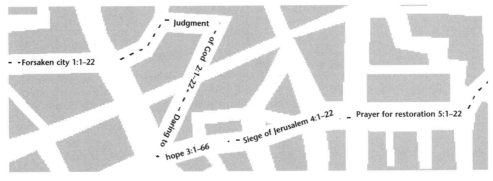

- Forsaken city 1:1–22

Judgment of God 2:1–22

Daring to hope 3:1–66

Siege of Jerusalem 4:1–22

Prayer for restoration 5:1–22

194

Forsaken city   1:1–22

Jerusalem is lonely and deserted. The poet paints a picture of a city that is abused on every level. The roads are empty and one interpretation says "Young women are raped . . ." (1:4). It is a chilling picture. In the poem, Jerusalem—the city itself—speaks out: "I never stop groaning—I've lost all hope!" (1:22).

Judgment of God   2:1–22

The prophet describes what has happened to the city. In graphic terms he relates the anger of the Lord. It was not the Babylonians, but the Lord who attacked the city with bows and arrows (2:4). The temple was swept aside as if it were a garden shed (the walls of a garden) (2:6). Children die in the streets (2:12) and there are even accounts of cannibalism in 2:20 and 4:10. There is a terrible, lonely silence (2:10). The chapter ends with Jerusalem speaking again, lamenting the scale of the Lord's attack. "Have you ever been this cruel to anyone before?"

Daring to hope   3:1–66

And yet, there is hope. The prophet laments that he is in darkness, his bones have been crushed, he has been torn to shreds and—a little strangely —he has been reduced to eating gravel (3:16—although, frankly, it's preferable to eating your own children). Then he remembers. "The LORD's kindness never fails!" he says (3:22). "The LORD can always be trusted to show mercy each morning" (3:23). "We're still alive!" he says. "We shouldn't complain when we are being punished for our sins" (3:39). It is a momentary respite, however, and once again the prophet becomes aware of the dangers around him (3:48–66). He asks for protection, even though God has not protected the city.

Siege   4:1–22

It was better for Sodom—at least that city was destroyed quickly. "Being killed with a sword is better than slowly starving to death" (4:9). The people of Jerusalem are hunted down like wild animals—they even behave like beasts.

A prayer 5:1–22

This is a final plea for the Lord to remember his people. The poet knows that the only one to set them free will be the Lord; there is no one else to call on. There is no justice (5:14) and no mercy (5:11–12). The poem ends with a chilling uncertainty—maybe the Lord really doesn't want his people anymore.

View Points

Did Jeremiah write Lamentations?

On one hand:
2 Ch 35:26 records that the prophet Jeremiah composed funeral songs for Josiah, so he was obviously familiar with the form. There are also passages that relate to Jeremiah's life, such as 3:55–63 which ties in with the prophet's little trip down the sewer.

On the other hand:
In 4:17, the writer looks to Egypt for salvation and in 4:20 he calls Zedekiah "the Lord's chosen leader." Since Jeremiah considered Zedekiah to be about as much use as a basket of rotten figs (Je 24:8–10), this doesn't fit. Experts also see differences in the way the poems are ordered that point to different authors.

Moving on: What is obvious, however, is that the author was in Jerusalem, he saw what was happening and, more importantly, he grasped *why* it was happening and what the future held.

Ezekiel

When: The events described in Ezekiel take place from around 580 BC. The book was probably edited together fairly soon after the prophet's death—sometime around 570 BC.

Who: The third of the "big three" prophets (alongside Isaiah and Jeremiah), Ezekiel was a priest (1:3). He was, apparently, among the first group deported to Babylon in 597 BC (but see ViewPoints on the opposite page). A later tradition asserts that he was murdered in Babylon and was buried there.

What: Ezekiel is one of the most eccentric, bizarre and outrageous prophets of the Old Testament. I mean, let's face it, the man ate a scroll. He lay for 390 days on his left side—followed by a rather restrained 40 days on his right side. He also knocked a hole in the wall of his house and climbed through.

There is, it seems, a thin line between "prophet" and "nutcase." However, it is important to remember that all these actions had a purpose. Ezekiel was a shock-tactic prophet. He was like a performance artist, only he was giving messages from God. At times his message is couched in almost obscene language (for example, chapter 16). Ezekiel was inflamed by the seriousness of the situation—if his listeners were offended, then so be it. They needed to be shocked out of their apathy.

Ezekiel's fundamental themes are to remind his fellow exiles of the faults that led to their predicament, and to point to their future restoration. Even though they were living in a foreign land, they could and should clean up their act.

Quick Guide

Author

Ezekiel

Type

Prophecy

Purpose

To warn those in Jerusalem of what will happen to them, but also to tell them that the Lord will forgive his people and bring them home.

Key verses

37:12–14 "So tell them, 'I, the LORD God, promise to open your graves and set you free. I will bring you back to Israel, and when that happens, you will realize that I am the LORD. My Spirit will give you breath, and you will live again.'"

If you remember one thing about this book . . .

The Lord is a God of judgment, but also a God of forgiveness and new life.

Your 15 minutes start now

Read chapters 1–4, 12, 16, 24, 37, 47

Like his fellow prophets of the time, he knew what was coming, but he also knew that there would be a future restoration. He understood that there would be peace and security, that there would be a return (43:4–7). God takes no pleasure in all that has happened, and, even in exile, wants to bring his people back to him (33:11–20).

The Route Through Ezekiel

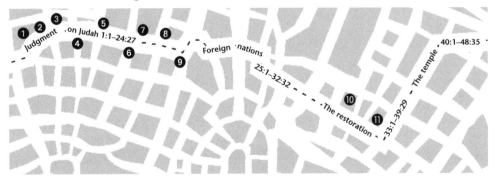

Judgment on Judah 1:1–24

❶ The four creatures

Ezekiel begins with a bang. We are introduced to the writer and then plunged straight into his first vision.

Each creature has four faces (eagle, lion, human, bull) and two wings. Their wings make a roaring sound when they fly (1:24) and fold against the bodies when they stop (1:23). They move in straight lines, because with four faces a part of them is always looking ahead (1:12). They glow like coals (1:13) and fire seems to move between them. Next to them are wheels made of chrysolite, a precious stone with an olive-green color. The wheels have eyes all the way round them and accompany the creatures when they fly through the air. The creatures fly about within a dome, which sparkles like ice (1:22). Above the dome there sits a figure on a sapphire-blue throne, a figure of fire, blazing with flames below the waist, glowing like hot metal above and surrounded by light.

Is this God? Ezekiel describes the figure as "the Lord's glory" (1:28) Perhaps it is one *appearance* of God—and Ezekiel is left to describe God in the only language he has. So we get mystical creatures, roaring noises, bright lights, rainbow colors—an assault on the senses.

❷ Eat the scroll 2:1–3:27

Ezekiel is chosen to be God's prophet. He is to speak to the people of Israel (2:3). He is to give his message to the "people who were brought here to Babylonia with you" (3:11). To symbolize this, he is given a scroll to eat. The message is taken into his very core, absorbed into his body. Prophecy was not a "job," but a calling that took over the complete being.

View Points

Did Ezekiel go to Babylon with the first group of exiles?

On one hand:	On the other hand:
Of course he did. The Bible says he did, and anyway, to argue that he had to be on the spot is to misunderstand the nature of prophecy—which by its nature is visionary and not tied to a specific place or time.	No he didn't. This is a later insertion. His sermons make more sense if they were delivered to the audience in Jerusalem. After all, there doesn't seem much point warning an audience in Babylon to change their ways. It's too late for them.

Moving on: A compromise might be that Ezekiel went to Babylon and came back, before the final exile, or that he stayed in Jerusalem until 586 BC.

Details, Details ...
Tel Abib or the Abib Hill (3:15)

This is the only mention of the place where the exiles lived in Babylon. It means "Hill of the flood"—a pile of rubble caused by destruction. I think we can assume they weren't given the *best* quarters.

Puzzling Points

Why isn't Ezekiel pleased?

Ezekiel describes how, when the Lord's power took hold of him, he was "annoyed and angry" (3:14). Other translations talk of him being bitter and angry. This could mean that he was identifying with the Lord's anger. Or it could mean that he was only too aware of what lay in store.

Some people yearn to be "specially chosen" by God, to be a prophet. Old Testament prophets knew—or if they didn't know they soon discovered—that the calling was incredibly hard and difficult. Here, Ezekiel is warned that he will feel as if he is in the middle of "thorn bushes or scorpions" (2:6).

When God calls someone to prophecy it is a serious task, not to be undertaken lightly. It was not something that those called went into lightly. Indeed, Jeremiah asked to be relieved of the responsibility. A prophet is not something you *do*, however, it is someone you *are*.

▷177

A Little Local Difficulty
The years don't add up

The numbers in chapter 4 have caused scholars a lot of argument and hard thinking. Each day is supposed to represent a year of punishment, but that is difficult to reconcile with the chronology as we know it.

Some argue that the 390 years start with the reign of King Solomon, but even then it doesn't quite add up. A more satisfactory interpretation is that the days of Ezekiel's ordeal correspond to the actual days of the siege, which began on January 15, 588 BC and ended on July 29, 587 BC. Although that adds up to 560 days, the siege was raised in the middle because of the Egyptian army approaching, which might lead to a total of 430 days. Or it might not. Your guess is as good as anyone's.

After eating the scroll and being given his final calling from God, Ezekiel is returned to Babylon. Seven days later he sees the Lord again. There may be a link here to the period of ordination of a Levitical priest (Le 8:1–33). Ezekiel is preparing for his work. He is struck dumb by the Lord. He is "tied" and from now until the fall of Jerusalem he can only utter what the Lord tells him.

❸ The brick 4:1–17

Ezekiel acts out the tragedy of Jerusalem. The city is represented by a picture on a brick. Ezekiel lies on his left side for 390 days to represent the suffering of Israel, then for 40 more days on his right side to represent the number of years of Judah's suffering. He eats a truly horrible meal cooked over dried cow dung (it was going to be human dung, but God allowed him to substitute the less offensive substance). He is acting out the starvation, the awful conditions, the terrible truth. "Everyone will be shocked at what is happening, and, because of their sins, they will die a slow death" (4:17).

❹ The hair 5:1–7:27

OK, the dung part was bad enough, but now it gets really weird. Ezekiel shaves off his hair and weighs it. Of all his hair, only a few strands will survive, just as only a few people will survive. He follows this demonstration with a series of graphic messages (5:7–7:27) from the Lord telling how the people's sins will lead to disaster.

❺ Jerusalem 8:1–11:25

Once again, Ezekiel is carried to Jerusalem—whether bodily or in spirit is not made clear. He sees the Jews worshiping idols in a temple where the walls have been decorated with unclean animals. He sees them bowing down to the rising sun (8:16). Tammuz (8:14) was the Babylon fertility god. In an episode reminiscent of the angel of death passing over Pharaoh's city, seven "men"—the guardian angels of the city—hunt through the streets (see also Re 8:2, 6). One marks the heads of those who show any sign of repentance or upset at what is happening. The others kill all those who are unmarked.

The four creatures from chapter 1 make a return appearance—although here the bull's face is replaced by a cherub or "winged creature." Now they also have extra wheels (10:10), either intersecting or revolving within the original wheels. Their bodies are also covered with eyes. They give one of the angels coals to scatter on the city. The Lord's glory leaves the temple and moves above the winged creatures. Ezekiel is told to speak against the leaders in Jerusalem, then the Lord's glory leaves the city. Ezekiel is returned to Babylon.

❻ The hole 12:1–16

Having spent a year or so lying on his side and cooking over cow dung, Ezekiel now digs a hole in the side of his house and crawls through it. He packs a bag and, hiding his face, leaves in the darkness. Unfortunately, although lots of people are watching, nobody questions his actions (12:7–9). Presumably by now they are used to him. So he has to go back and explain. The leader in Jerusalem will have to sneak away at night—exactly what did happen to Zechariah. The king's capture and blinding are predicted (12:13).

❼ The whore   16:1–63

One of the most shocking chapters of the Bible. In harsh, uncompromising language, Ezekiel talks about Jerusalem as a young girl. He paints a picture of her life, from her troubled birth to a life of degradation and immorality. Jerusalem was just another unwanted baby until the Lord took her under his care. She grows to adolescence and she is clothed in the finest clothes. She is under God's care and protection, "as beautiful as a queen." "I, the LORD God, had helped you become a lovely young woman" (16:13–14).

And how does she respond? By offering herself to anyone who passes by. Jerusalem in this chapter becomes a nymphomaniac, sleeping with whoever she can—and even paying them for it (16:34). Ezekiel is pointing out the way in which Jerusalem offered herself to false gods, or allied herself with other nations—when she should have been following what God wanted for her. She must now face the prescribed punishment for adultery: she will be stripped of her finery and stoned to death (16:40). The chapter ends with a promise. The Lord really does love Jerusalem. She will be restored— but only when she faces the truth about her sins and herself: a truth she is too ashamed even to talk about (16:63).

❽ The cedar tree   17:1–24

One of the few parables in the Old Testament, this story is recounted in verses 1–10 and then explained in 11–21. It's a political parable. The first eagle is Nebuchadnezzar; the cedar tree represents David's dynasty, the tip of which is King Jehoiachin. Nebuchadnezzar plants a new king—Zedekiah—who grows into a low vine. The second eagle is an Egyptian pharaoh—either Psammetichus II or Hophra—to whom Judah turned for help. The point of the parable is that the second eagle will not help them; the east wind is coming—in the shape of Babylonian forces—and that will blow the vine away once and for all. God, however, will replant the cedar tree. A shoot of David's family will become the greatest tree ever. It is a beautiful image of the true king, which would only be fulfilled in Christ.

Details, Details . . .
The oversized Egyptians

Verse 16:26 is generally mistranslated, because it is so, well, *rude* actually. In the NIV it appears as "the Egyptians, your lustful neighbors," but the original Hebrew word translated as "lustful" actually means "having oversized organs." In the CEV the phrase is virtually ignored altogether. The Authorized Version is better, with the verse running, "Thou hast also committed fornication with the Egyptians thy neighbors, great of flesh."

Why is this important? Because it shows that God is not always polite. Most Bible versions actually tone down Ezekiel 16—but God's language is rougher and more shocking than we imagine. He wanted to shock people, he wanted people to realize just how low their sins had brought them. The people of Judah were behaving like characters out of some cheap, disgusting porn film—that's how God viewed their behavior. We might find such language offensive—but it is not half as offensive as the way that the people in Jerusalem betrayed God.

The blindness of the people   18:1–23:49

Ezekiel issues a series of prophecies against Jerusalem, warning of the coming destruction. He delivers a history of Israel to a group of Israel's leaders, showing that this cycle of disobedience has been going on since they left Egypt. There is a wonderful verse at the end of chapter 20 when Ezekiel complains that "people already say I confuse them with my messages." (v. 49). Another version reads, "People will say I speak in riddles." Ezekiel was communicating in the way God told him, but people's eyes were so blinded that they chose to believe he was speaking nonsense.

In 21:22 he describes how the Babylonian leader will decide which way to go —by divination with arrows and consulting a sheep's liver. Of course, the truth is, as this passage shows, God is using him and his army. He might think that his gods are directing him, but the one true God is really in charge. Admittedly, that's small comfort to the sheep . . .

Chapter 23 is another parable. Oholah is Samaria, Oholibah is Jerusalem. Once again, their infidelity is described in shockingly graphic terms. This time, however, Ezekiel seems to be talking about political alliances, rather than idolatry.

⑨ Do not mourn   24:15–27

Few episodes illustrate the sheer cost of being a prophet more than the death of Ezekiel's wife. Usually, mourners would go barefoot and bareheaded, covering their faces and eating "mourning food." Ezekiel will do none of this. His wife was the person he loved most in the world (24:16), but it is to be another sign to the people: they too will lose what they loved most. This is a poignant and personal moment, the only time apart from the very beginning of the book where Ezekiel is referred to by name. God promises an end to the prophet's lack of speech. When the final news is brought to him, he will be able to speak freely (24:26–27).

Foreign nations   25:1–32:32

Although these prophecies were uttered at various times, they have been collected together in the book. They serve as an interlude, between Ezekiel's prophecies before and after the fall of Jerusalem. Ammon (25:1–7), Moab (25:8–11), Edom (25:12–14) and Philistia (25:15–17) are all rebuked for their glee over the fate of Israel. There is then a long prophecy against Tyre (chapters 26–28). Tyre was a Phoenician seaport. Although initially acknowledging Babylon's rule, it later joined with other states in a rebellion. Ezekiel predicts its eventual destruction at the hands of Nebuchadnezzar. Tyre was a magnificent city, but, despite its beauty, it would fall. Sidon (28:20–26) was another harbor port to the north of Tyre that had joined in the rebellion. It too would fall.

Finally, there are seven oracles against Egypt, all dated (29:1–32:32). These oracles were probably given at the time when Egypt had created a temporary lull in the siege. Egypt is pictured as a great monster, or crocodile, lying in the Nile (29:3). The word is actually "Leviathan," as in Job. Despite its boasting, the country will fall. It is criticized for being unreliable, for proving no stronger in its help to Israel than a reed (29:7). Never again would Egypt be as powerful as in the past.

The restoration   33:1–48:35

⑩ Watchman   33:1–34:31

This chapter ushers in a new work and role for Ezekiel. He is described, as before, as "a watchman," but his message has changed. Before he was warning of judgment, but now that judgment has begun. Now he has to explain to the people how they should respond. Where they used to ignore him, now they listen to his words (33:10). He promises them that, unlike their leaders, the Lord is a good shepherd (34:11–17). This is an image that Jesus picked for himself many years later—an image that clearly identified him with his father. Indeed, chapter 34 is full of images that Jesus used—God talks of separating the good sheep from the bad sheep, in a way similar to Jesus in Matthew 25:32. Ezekiel was looking forward, though he did not know it, to the arrival of the one true king.

⑪ The valley of the bones   37:1–28

The restoration promised by God is seen in chapter 37 when the prophet is taken to a valley of dry bones. Before his eyes, the bones come together—a sign that God will bring life to his "dead" people. Then Ezekiel is told to get two sticks and join them together, to indicate that, for the first time since the death of Solomon, Israel will be one country again.

The temple 40:1–48:35

The last few chapters of Ezekiel strike the reader as rather dull—like the work of some kind of prophetic building inspector. But Ezekiel is trying to give a picture. He is describing the ideal temple—a temple that will never be built, but which symbolizes what the real temple should be about. It is a building from the center of which flows a river that brings life to all the land around it—the spiritual heart of the nation.

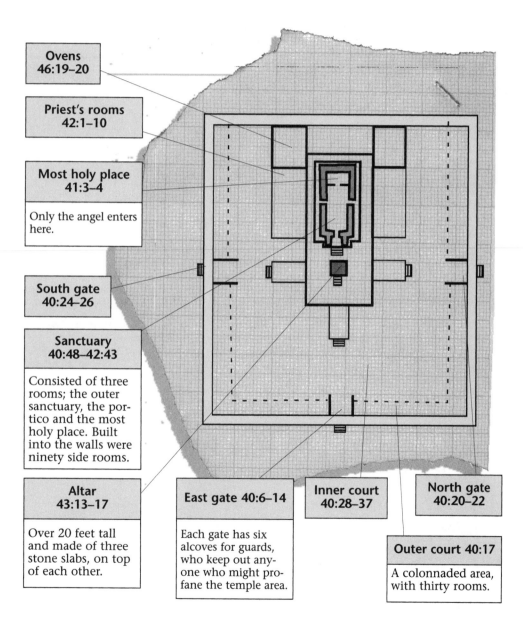

Ovens
46:19–20

Priest's rooms
42:1–10

Most holy place
41:3–4

Only the angel enters here.

South gate
40:24–26

Sanctuary
40:48–42:43

Consisted of three rooms; the outer sanctuary, the portico and the most holy place. Built into the walls were ninety side rooms.

Altar
43:13–17

Over 20 feet tall and made of three stone slabs, on top of each other.

East gate 40:6–14

Each gate has six alcoves for guards, who keep out anyone who might profane the temple area.

Inner court
40:28–37

North gate
40:20–22

Outer court 40:17

A colonnaded area, with thirty rooms.

Ezekiel's vision is remarkable in its precision—he knows the dimensions of every part of the temple. The key fact, however, is not really the dimensions of the temple, but what it produces. In Ezekiel 47, the prophet sees a river flowing out from the temple, getting ever deeper and stronger, and bringing new life. (This image is picked up in Revelation 22.)

The river comes from the temple—from the pure presence of God (47:1–2). It is powerful and ever deepening. As Ezekiel wades in, he finds it growing ever deeper and stronger. This river brings new life. Even the Dead Sea is brought back to life by its presence (47:8–11). The fruit grown along its bank brings nourishment and healing (47:12). It is everlasting. The water never dies out, the stream never runs dry (47:12).

Details, Details . . .
Son of man

Ezekiel's title is used ninety-three times in the book. It emphasizes his humanity, but also that he is representative of humanity. Jesus frequently used the title for himself. In Daniel 7:13ff the phrase seems to indicate the people of Israel, as opposed to the beasts who represent the other nations. Why Jesus used the title is the subject of much debate.

The water is not a literal description, but an image of the powerful, life-changing presence of God. Like the wind that blew new life into the dry bones, dry and dead lives will be brought back to life by this life-giving stream.

Daniel
God among the captives

Who: Daniel. Or someone a lot later, depending on your point of view (see ViewPoints later on).

When: Either sixth century BC, or second century BC, depending on your view of the authenticity of the book (see ViewPoints, if you haven't already).

What: Daniel is an odd mix of narrative and prophecy. It tells the tale of a group of Jews in exile in Babylon, but also recounts prophecies that point to future times. The stories are set in the reigns of three Babylon emperors: Nebuchadnezzar, Belshazzar and Darius. They feature Daniel and his friends—and particularly their struggle to keep their integrity under pressure. Daniel is a kind of modern-day Joseph, rising to power and influence in a foreign court through his God-given wisdom and insight.

Along with this, the book is full of weird dreams and prophecies of empires in the future. The final four chapters detail Daniel's own prophecies of the future.

One central theme of the book is especially relevant to us today: the pressure to conform and to change our customs and practices. Babylon was a "multicultural" empire that had absorbed knowledge and customs from those it had conquered. Daniel, however, is all about integrity—retaining a purity of worship in the face of enormous pressure to conform and to change. In today's world, where there is always pressure on us to worship other gods or to water down our faith, Daniel has an important message about the need to stay faithful and the way that God will support us in that struggle.

Daniel lived in a time and a place where every day brought a challenge to his faith, but he did not waver—and his courage changed the society around him.

Quick Guide

Author
Attributed to Daniel

Type
Prophecy

Purpose
To show how God remained with his people, even when they were captive in Babylon.

Key verse
7:13 "I saw what looked like a son of man coming with the clouds of heaven, and he was presented to the Eternal God."

If you remember one thing about this book ...
Do not conform to the culture around you: do what God wants and he will give you strength.

Your 15 minutes start now
Read chapters 1–3, 5, 6, 7, 11

The Route Through Daniel

- - - Daniel in Babylon 1:1–4:37 - - - Belshazzar's feast 5:1–31 - - - The lion's den 6:1–28 . Daniel's visions 7:1–12:13

Landmark: Angels

The word "angel" comes from the Greek word for "messenger," and refers to one of the primary functions of these beings: to bring messages to people from God. They also perform actions on behalf of God; they were active in the destruction of Sodom (Ge 19), they brought food to Elijah (1 Ki 19:5–7), and even gave military assistance (2 Ki 19:35).

As to their exact nature, it seems clear that they are created beings, capable of moral judgment and rebellion. Their appearance depends on the circumstances, but frequently they are creatures of dazzling brightness, who strike fear into the hearts of those who encounter them. Angels are portrayed as holy, uncorrupted figures, able to see God face-to-face. In the early parts of the Old Testament angels are not given names, but from the time of Daniel, angels have names and specific tasks.

Angel of the Lord

This specific angel is so closely identified with God himself, that, at times, it is hard to spot the join. It is as if he were some direct extension of God's personality. He speaks in the first person, as God himself (e.g., Ge 16:7; Ex 3:2). At other times he is distinguished from God (2 Sa 26:16). In the New Testament he is specifically identified as Gabriel. Generally speaking, when the angel of the Lord appears to men, he is addressed as God—he is God's representative, his "spokes-angel."

Fallen Angels

A group of angels who, led by Satan, rebelled against God and were cast out of heaven (Mt 25:41; Re 12:9; Lk 10:18). They fight against the forces of good, but will one day be totally defeated.

Daniel in Babylon 1:1–4:37

Daniel is a member of the royal family, in exile in Babylon. He and his three friends, Hananiah, Mishael and Azariah, are among a group selected to be educated in the royal palace. They are given Babylonian names and a Babylonian education. The idea is clearly to induct them into the superior ways of the Babylonian culture.

From the start, therefore, Daniel's task is clear—to remain uncontaminated by the culture that surrounds him. He begins by only eating "clean" food (1:8), a decision that is vindicated when he ends up looking healthier than those around him.

❶ The first dream 2:1–49

Nebuchadnezzar is a complicated figure. Like many dictators and tyrants, he is cruel on a whim, changeable, irrational and a borderline nutcase. He places a great importance on occult and magic. Here, he is tormented by nightmares that his wise men cannot interpret. That's hardly surprising, for he won't actually tell them what those nightmares are. If you claim to be psychic, however, you ought to be able to prove it. Ultimately, the wise men failed.

Daniel is motivated, not by the desire to demonstrate wonderful prophetic insight, but because he wants to save lives. He sees the king's wise men being rounded up for execution and intervenes to rescue them.

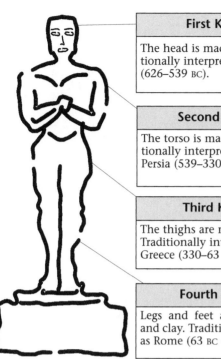

First Kingdom

The head is made of gold. Traditionally interpreted as Babylon (626–539 BC).

Second Kingdom

The torso is made of silver. Traditionally interpreted as Medeo-Persia (539–330 BC).

Third Kingdom

The thighs are made of bronze. Traditionally interpreted as Greece (330–63 BC).

Fourth Kingdom

Legs and feet are made of iron and clay. Traditionally interpreted as Rome (63 BC onwards).

Having intervened, of course, he has to deliver—and he does so, through the power of prayer. Through prayer, Daniel receives from God the content and meaning of the dream (2:31–45). Throughout his explanation, he is careful to give the glory to God and not himself (2:28–29).

There are many interpretations concerning which kingdoms are indicated by the statue. However, the traditional view identifies the statue with the four great empires of Babylon, Medeo-Persia, Greece and Rome. The kingdoms fall because of a stone cast by the hand of God, setting up "an eternal kingdom that will never fail" (2:44–45). This was the reign of Jesus.

❷ The fiery furnace   3:1–30
The king's recognition of the power of God (2:47) is, apparently, short-lived. Now he sets up his own statue and commands everyone to worship it. Shadrach, Meshach and Abednego refuse and are cast into the furnace. Instead of burning, they are perfectly fine. Amazingly, the king sees not three men, but four walking around in the flames—a fourth figure who "looks like a god" (3:25).

Christians interpret this fourth figure as being Jesus, and the whole incident as an image of the way in which Jesus walks alongside us in our troubles. When we are in the furnace, he will be there with us.

❸ The second dream of Nebuchadnezzar   4:1–37
In his second dream, Nebuchadnezzar imagines a mighty tree that is cut down. Daniel again interprets the dream: God will "cut Babylon down to size," for the dream prefigures Nebuchadnezzar's fall. Twelve months after the dream the emperor does, indeed, have some kind of breakdown—God speaks to him and he becomes like an animal, living off grass and running wild. Finally, desperately, he prays to God and is healed.

Belshazzar's feast 5:1–31

Belshazzar was not, in fact, the son of Nebuchadnezzar, but the son of Nabonidus. The writer may have got the name wrong, or it may be that the word is used in a more general sense, as in ancient times it was possible to refer to a previous king as "father."

Belshazzar's downfall, like Nebuchadnezzar's, is due to pride. He uses the sacred objects from the temple as drinking goblets (5:2). A hand writes a mysterious message on the wall—one that only Daniel can interpret. The message is one of judgment. Daniel receives rapid promotion, but it is too late. That night the king is killed. (Still, at least he was saved from a hangover.) Darius the Mede takes over the kingdom.

Daniel in the lion's den 6:1–28

Once again, Daniel rises to a position of prominence, this time through his organizational abilities rather than his interpretive skills. When Darius is maneuvered into declaring all prayer illegal (other than prayer to himself), Daniel carries on as normal and the king is forced to throw him to the lions. Once again, God intervenes and Daniel is saved. The unfortunate officials—and their even more unfortunate wives and children—are thrown into the pit and eaten alive.

Daniel's visions 7:1–12:13

The second part of Daniel is straight out of the drawer marked "Ezekiel." It is full of strange and disconcerting images, weird beasts, talking horns and helpful angels. It recounts various visions that Daniel has had during the reigns of Belshazzar and Darius.

❹ The four beasts

Like the four parts of the statues, Daniel's beasts represent four superpowers: Babylon, Medea, Persia and Greece. The fourth beast is the most frightening, a monstrous creature, and the empire he represents will "speak evil of God Most High" (7:25). The horns of this beast probably represent Roman emperors, or authorities that are opposed to God. God gives authority to a figure called "the son of man," which refers back to Ezekiel and forward to the title that Jesus chose for himself.

❺ The ram and the goat 8:1–27

Two years later, Daniel has another vision—this time of a goat and a ram. The interpretation is supplied by the angel Gabriel. It is largely a restatement of the first vision with the "goat" of Greece superseded by the "ram" of the Romans. There is a more detailed statement about the length of time of the exile—2,300 days (8:14).

The "little horn" is a reference to Antiochus IV, the ruler of Syria from 175 to 164 BC. He was a persecutor of the Jews who closed down the temple and put a Greek altar in the Holy of Holies. The closeness of this description to the actual events leads some to believe that Daniel was written after the event. It all depends on your view of prophecy.

❻ Daniel's prayer 9:1–27

Daniel prays for his people. The seventy years' captivity predicted by Jeremiah is almost finished, and Daniel and his people are desperate to return to Jerusalem. Daniel is again visited by the angel Gabriel, who predicts a "chosen" or "anointed" leader who will be replaced by another empire. The numbers are even more confusing here than in the other parts of Daniel. It may be that the days stand for years, in which case the chosen one would arrive 483 days after the rebuilding of Jerusalem.

❼ Final visions 10:1–12:13

The final chapters contain Daniel's visions of the far future, including an awesome vision of a shining figure. This is similar to John's vision in Revelation. The last chapters are full of obscure references to guardian angels and spiritual warfare, as well as the now rather obligatory reference to the future empires.

This time there is more detail about the empires, with a prediction of four more kings of Persia (11:2), Alexander the Great (11:3–4) and his successors, and the rise of new powers.

The prophecy is a detailed description of what happened to the area after the death of Alexander the Great (the great king of 11:3). Alexander's kingdom was split between his four generals and the region was a field of conflict for the next two hundred years.

Again we have a reference to the desecration of the temple by Antiochus IV (11:29–32) and finally some obscure verses that may be a reference to events in Antiochus's life, or may refer to events still in the future.

Daniel ends with a vision of resurrection (12:1–4). This is the first book of the Old Testament to make such an overt reference to the resurrection.

A Little Local Difficulty
"A time, two times and half a time" 7:25

This might mean three and a half years. Or it might not. Difficult to tell with Daniel.

WARNING: DIFFICULT TERRAIN

The difficulties with Daniel make it a difficult book to interpret—and also, frankly, a rich ground for cults and extremists. Many extreme Christian and non-Christian beliefs have been built on the rather shaky ground of verses from Daniel taken out of context. For example, chapter 10 talks about "guardian angels" —angels responsible for certain places. It introduces the idea of angels at war with other "spiritual" beings. Paul, indeed, talks of "forces and powers" both "seen and unseen" (Col 1:16), so it is clear that there is a lot going on around us of which we are largely unaware. But it is equally clear that God is in charge, and that he is our protection and strength.

We should be very careful of trying to build a theology around what is essentially a vision. These are not literal descriptions, but pictures and images. Even discounting the debate over the authenticity of Daniel, the book is too obscure to be used as a definite description. Instead it is a language all of its own, a language of pictures and impressions. Some of it is open to clear interpretation—much of it is more mysterious and hidden.

Hosea
God's everlasting love

Hosea is a dramatic tale of one man's love for an unfaithful wife—and through that, of God's love for his unfaithful people. Hosea personifies the merciful, forgiving love of God.

Who: Hosea lived in the northern kingdom of Israel and prophesied soon after Amos. His father was called Beeri, which—despite what it sounds like—means "well-man." He prophesied, according to his writings, for the best part of forty years, but nothing is known of him outside this book.

When: 750–715 BC. The troubled, final years of Israel before it succumbed to the Assyrians.

This is a violent and unsettled society with kings being ousted by coups, moral corruption and the idolatry of the priests and the people. Like Amos, Hosea condemns social injustice and the false gods and fake worship that bring it forth.

The most startling thing about Hosea is the extent to which he lived his message. Both Ezekiel and Isaiah "acted out" their prophecies, performing dramatic acts to get their message across to the people. Hosea's whole life was a prophetic act: marrying an unfaithful prostitute, naming his children "Not pitied" and "Not my people," this was a man who was a living metaphor.

The overriding message of the book is clear: despite their faithlessness, God still loves his people. He doesn't want to punish them, but their continued "adultery" with other gods gives him little choice. God repeatedly urges Israel to stop "sleeping around," but Israel is too interested in material gain to notice.

Quick Guide

Author
Hosea

Type
Prophecy

Purpose
To show how God loves his people—despite their unfaithfulness.

Key verse
6:6 "I'd rather you were faithful and knew me than offered sacrifices."

If you remember one thing about this book . . .
God loves us, despite our sin—and he wants us back.

Your 10 minutes start now
Read chapters 1–3, 11, 13–14

The Route Through Hosea

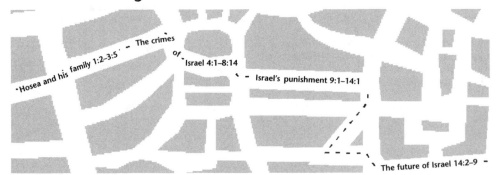

Hosea and his family 1:2–3:5

The crimes of Israel 4:1–8:14

Israel's punishment 9:1–14:1

The future of Israel 14:2–9

Hosea and his family   1:2–3:5

Hosea's marriage is an act that mirrors the relationship between God and his people. Israel, in language reminiscent of Ezekiel 16, is a whore who chases after anyone with a bit of cash. Hosea's children are prophetic messages from God—"God Scatters" (1:4), "No mercy" (1:6) and "Not my people" (1:8).

However, Israel, like the children themselves, does have a future. One day, says God, there will be a time when Israel shall be called "children of the Living God" and when his people shall be shown pity (2:1).

In chapter 2, God is depicted as a jilted husband who wants to win his wife back. He is angry with her and warns her of the punishments and restrictions he will set up (2:6–10). Nevertheless, he does not want to punish her, to treat her harshly; instead he wants to marry her (2:19) and win her back to a life of righteousness and mercy and love. Hosea is a book full of these sudden oscillations on the part of God, these emotional swings between the urge to punish and the desire to hold. Like any jilted husband, he want to punish his wife, but more than that, he wants her back.

The crimes of Israel   4:1–8:14

Chapter 4 shows the extent of the unfaithfulness. "Cursing, dishonesty, murder, robbery, unfaithfulness—these happen all the time. Violence is everywhere" (4:2). They worship "objects of wood" (4:12). The "living metaphor" of Hosea is no mere picture—the Israelites were actually indulging in prostitution, for their false worship involved the use of cult prostitutes (4:14).

True worship

The heart of Hosea's message is found in 6:6: "I'd rather you were faithful and knew me than offered sacrifices." The Israelites believed that it didn't matter what they did as long as they turned up at the temple and took part in the necessary rituals. But God says that true worship is not found in merely saying the right words or obeying the right rituals, but in trying to live according to the will of God.

They have trusted in their own judgment, setting up their own kings and princes without listening to God (8:4). They believe their salvation lies in their allies (8:10), or even in their fine buildings and defences (8:14), but they have forgotten their maker.

Israel's punishment   9:1–14:1

Israel must be punished. Hosea speaks out at the festival to mark the grape harvest, using the image of the vine. There will be no more sacrifices, no more festivals. The days of punishment are coming. They may call him a fool or a madman, but he knows what the future holds for them. They are like a vine that is dried up and discarded, uprooted and left to die. They planted evil, and harvested injustice (10:13). Now there is nothing but disaster awaiting them, and Hosea paints a vivid, horrific picture of the cruelties that the Assyrians will inflict on the people (10:14–15).

Throughout the book of Hosea, there is a sense that God is struggling to hold back the tears. This is an emotional God, a heartbroken God. He is like a mother who taught her children to walk, only to see them run away. Yet he cannot forget the strength of that relationship. He knows that Israel must be punished, but he will not destroy his children. One day they will return to him, like fluttering birds (11:11).

Doom will come to Judah and Israel. As in the time of Moses, they will have to enter the wilderness again before they can find their way back to the Promised Land (12:9). They will suffer for their unfaithfulness, wiped out, like a stream in the desert sands (13:15).

The future of Israel 14:2–9

It is a vision of future hope that ends the book. After the rejection there will be forgiveness, and in a beautiful, lyrical passage, God describes himself as the dew showering the olive tree in a world where he loves "without limit." All it requires is repentance and obedience, and God and his people can walk together.

Joel
The day of the locust

Who: Joel, son of Pethuel. We don't really know any more about him, although he probably lived near Jerusalem.

When: Again, uncertain, but probably ninth century BC. Some put it later, but it makes no real difference. Locusts were, unfortunately, a regular feature of life in the Middle East at that time.

What: Joel is a book that seeks to interpret a huge, natural disaster. Judah has been laid waste by a plague of locusts, with Jerusalem stripped clear of all vegetation. Joel looks beyond the disaster to ask questions about why it happened. He interprets it as a warning from God, a forerunner of the day of judgment, when God's army will invade.

The invasion of the locusts   1:1–2:11

Joel's picture of the locusts is vivid: they are like a powerful nation, without number (1:6). They grow and multiply rapidly (1:4) and they eat everything—there is no food for the cattle (1:18), no food even for the wild beasts (1:20). They appear in the sky like a black cloud, turning a garden of Eden into a barren desert (2:3).

The description of the locusts is horrifyingly real. The cities are invaded, the noise is like an earthquake, the walls are black with their crawling bodies (2:9).

Joel calls for a day of mourning and prayer—the only thing that will alleviate this catastrophe (1:13–14).

Quick Guide

Author
Joel
Type
Prophecy
Purpose
Helping Judah to understand why they have suffered a natural disaster.
Key verse
2:13 "Don't rip your clothes to show your sorrow. Instead, turn back to me with broken hearts. I am merciful, kind, and caring. I don't easily lose my temper, and I don't like to punish."
If you remember one thing about this book ...
We should repent—before it's too late.
Your 5 minutes start now
Read chapters 1–3

I'm going to sue for defamation of character.

The Route Through Joel

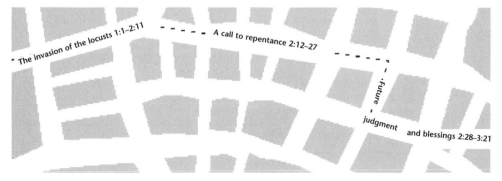

The invasion of the locusts 1:1–2:11

A call to repentance 2:12–27

Future judgment and blessings 2:28–3:21

A call to repentance   2:12–27

It was usual in ancient societies to show stylized expressions of grief. People tore their clothes, put ashes on their heads, even ate certain foods. But Joel calls for a repentance that is not superficial. It is Judah's heart that needs tearing, not clothes. He calls for a response that goes beyond ritual displays and barren emotion and actually involves a change of heart.

If Judah changes its ways, then the "soil will celebrate" (2:21). The fruit will return, the grass will grow, the ravages of the locusts will be undone. It is a vision of material abundance, of a time when the Lord will rid the land of the locusts and bring back the abundant crops.

Future judgment and blessings   2:28–3:21

The abundance will not just be in terms of fruit and crops. There will be an abundance of God's Spirit. Old and young will be aware of the presence of God. Ordinary people—servants, both men and women—all who faithfully worship God will be saved. It is a wonderful prediction of the way that Christ was to reach out to all sectors of society, slave and free, male and female, highborn and low. No wonder Peter used this passage in his first sermon (Ac 2:16).

At the same time, God will punish the nations that oppose him (3:1–16) and they will be harvested like grapes. There will be a time when a greater judgment than the locusts will arrive and nothing will protect the evil people from his judgment.

Landmark: The Day of the Lord

Joel talks of the day of the Lord, a day of judgment and punishment. The phrase was to become a way of referring to the end of time, the point when God's purpose would finally be fulfilled. The day of the locusts might have been bad, but it is nothing compared to the day of the Lord.

The Israelites originally saw the day of the Lord as the moment when God would intervene—finally and dramatically—in human history. They believed it would be the point when God turns up, destroys their enemies and sets everything right. But, increasingly, the prophets began to warn them that the day of the Lord was not necessarily going to be the great celebration that Israel was expecting. As the country turned to foreign gods and wallowed in wealth and luxury, Amos warned his countrymen that the day of the Lord might be turned against them, that it would be a day of judgment against Israel (Am 5:18–27). The destruction of Jerusalem was seen as fulfilling this prophecy.

In the New Testament, however, the day of the Lord was reinterpreted as referring to the second coming of Jesus (2 Co 1:14; Ro 2:15–16). This would be both a day of judgment *and* a day of victory. It would be the time when God—through his Son—would end human history, judge humankind and establish his rule forever.

Amos
Plain speech for the poor

Who: Amos, a shepherd from Tekoa. His name meant "burden." Amos was a "cross-border" prophet: although his home was in Judah, he went to preach in Bethel, at that time the capital of Israel.

When: In the reign of Uzziah, sometime around 760–750 BC. We don't know how long his preaching lasted—but he was ordered to leave the country.

What: Amos was not a part of the court like Isaiah or Zechariah. He was not a priest like Jeremiah. He was a small businessman. Although he is described as a shepherd, he was really a sheep owner as well as having a fig business (7:14). But when the word of the Lord came on him he had to speak out.

Like many small businessmen, he was in favor of plain speaking. His message is a straightforward condemnation of Israel's smug, self-satisfied veneer of religion, a savage swipe at their idolatry, their luxuriousness and their corrupt and unjust society.

Amos is an impressive character. Although not a "professional," he has a true prophet's passionate commitment to the truth, a deep respect for God and an understanding of the significance of all that God has done for his people. He has seen God at work and heard him speak. Now he must pass that message on, an ordinary person who has been suddenly promoted to the prophets' ranks. As he says, "Everyone is terrified when a lion roars—and ordinary people become prophets when the Lord God speaks" (3:8).

Quick Guide

Author

Amos

Type

Prophecy

Purpose

Urging Israel's leaders to pay attention to the needs of the poor and to act with justice.

Key verses

5:23–24 "No more of your noisy songs! I won't listen when you play your harps. But let justice and fairness flow like a river that never runs dry."

If you remember one thing about this book . . .

God's love has to be expressed in love and concern for the poor and oppressed.

Your 5 minutes start now

Read chapters 1, 4–5, 9

The Route Through Amos

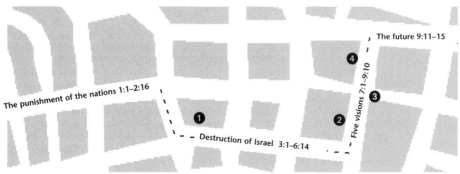

The punishment of the nations 1:1–2:16

Destruction of Israel 3:1–6:14

Five visions 7:1–9:10

The future 9:11–15

The punishment of the nations
1:1–2:16

After establishing his origins, Amos runs through a roll call of Israel's neighbors and the punishments awaiting them. Their crimes are a catalogue of horrific violence, from ripping open pregnant women (1:13) to rolling spiked logs over people's heads (1:3). It is interesting to note the order in which he takes each neighboring nation.

He begins with the farthest—Syria (1:3–5), Philistia (1:6–8) and Phoenicia (1:9–10). One can imagine his listeners nodding with approval at the fate awaiting their enemies. Then he moves nearer to home with Edom (1:11–12), Ammon (1:13–15) and Moab (2:1–3). By now his audience might be wondering where all this is going to end—for it is circling ever nearer their own land. And so it proves, for he touches briefly on Judah and their disobedience and apostasy, before ripping into Israel.

His listeners must soon have realized that the judgments on other nations were just a prelude to the real message—a full-on indictment of Israel and all its crimes. People are bought and sold (2:6), father and son sleep with the same girl (2:7), they dishonor the temple with their drunkenness and greed. Punishment is coming, and there is no escape.

Destruction of Israel   3:1–6:14

This judgment is spelled out in the next section, where Amos concentrates on the injustice and depravity of Israel and Samaria. It is full of his characteristic language. Talking about how little will be left after the enemies descend on Israel, he describes how a shepherd has to retrieve part of a maimed sheep to prove that it has been eaten by a lion (3:12). He describes the women of Samaria as "cows" (4:1). He talks of how he had to become a prophet when the Lord called him (3:8).

Above all, he lists Israel's many sins and offenses. This is a society where some live in luxurious summer and winter houses decorated with ivory (3:15) while others are oppressed and abused (4:1). The situation is summed up in his passionate plea to his listeners to "choose good instead of evil" (5:15). It is up to them. They can carry on as they have been doing, cheating, lying, swindling, or they can turn back to the Lord.

❶ God hates religion   5:21–6:14

It is the hypocrisy that God hates most. In the midst of this terrible society, they were still "going to church." They still went to the temple, and made sacrifices. "I, the LORD, hate and despise your religious celebrations and your times of worship," God says. "No more of your noisy songs! I won't listen when you play your harps." Instead he urges them to let justice flow like a river. It is one of the first of many such cries that were to come from the lips of the prophets over the centuries: never mind the volume of the singing, it's the quality of life that matters. Never mind the frequency of attendance, it's what's inside the heart that God cares about.

The section ends with dire predictions of Israel's punishment. They feel smug and safe (6:1), they live lives of idle luxury (6:4–6), but that will all end. They have chosen a path as stupid as trying to gallop on rocks, or plow the sea. The rich people will be dragged off first into captivity. The days of ivory-clad houses and fine wine will be over.

Five visions   7:1–9:10

Amos backs up his prophecy with five visions of disaster.

❷ The first three prophecies   7:1–9

Locusts attack the crops (7:1–3). They attack at the worst possible time, when the first few grains have been harvested but before the bulk of the crops have been gathered in. Amos pleads for the people and the Lord relents. Then the Lord threatens to send a fireball (7:4–6). Again Amos pleads, again the Lord relents. Then Amos sees the Lord standing beside a wall, measuring it with a plumb line. The people no longer measure up to God's standards. The wall will be torn down.

❸ Amos go home!   7:10–17

Amos's prophecies have been noticed by the authorities and he is hauled before Amaziah, the priest at Bethel. Amaziah, however, completely misunderstands the nature of Amos's ministry and tries to force Amos to move on. His reward for dismissing Amos is to hear what will become of his family: his children killed, his wife sold into prostitution, his land taken, Amaziah himself dying far from home in a foreign land.

❹ Two final visions   8:1–9:10

Amos does not depart immediately. There are two more visions. The first is of a basket of ripe fruit (8:1–3). The inference seems to be that Israel is ready to be plucked from the tree and consumed. Chapter 8:4–14 repeats some of the accusations of earlier chapters, but here the Lord promises a more serious shortage than famine or drought, a shortage of God himself, a silence, an absence. They will search throughout the country, but he will have left them (8:11–12). They thought they could live without him, they thought they could turn to other gods. Now they will truly be alone.

The final vision is of the Lord in the temple at Bethel. From the very place where people expect to receive blessing and forgiveness, God is about to launch their destruction. Wherever they go, destruction will follow. Climb as high as you can, dive as deep as you dare, you can never outrun your own sin. The people of Israel believed that they were too "special," but God points out that he has made all nations. In a startling passage, he declares that other nations are just as important to him (9:7). His purposes will be fulfilled, whether Israel cooperates or not.

The future   9:11–15

After all this, it is something of a surprise to find that the book ends on an upbeat note. Some scholars have argued that it must have been a later addition—but the same kind of future promise can be found at the end of many prophetic books. Just because Amos had a predominantly gloomy message doesn't mean all his messages were like that.

Instead he is granted a final vision of glory, a vision of the time when God will restore his land, when all seasons and harvests will run into each other (9:13). Israel will be firmly planted in God, and nothing will ever uproot it again.

Obadiah
Doom for Edom

Who: Obadiah. His name means "worshiper of the Lord," but beyond that we know nothing.

When: Not known. There are two main theories, both relating to verses 11–14.

1. If it is referring to the invasion by the Philistines, that would mean Obadiah was a contemporary of Elisha, writing sometime in the ninth century BC.

2. If it refers to the Babylonian invasion, then the date would be two hundred years later.

What: Obadiah is the shortest book in the Old Testament: only one chapter. Its theme is the destruction of Edom—a nation south of the Dead Sea—and the victory for Israel. Edom was also a symbolic name, referring right back to Esau and the choice of Jacob by God. In that sense, Edom stood for all those whom God did not choose, the people whose wickedness made them outcasts (Mal 1:3). Although, therefore, this is about a mountainous nation that had stood by and watched Judah suffer, it is also about all those who stand passively by while evil is committed, all those who are rejected by God for their sin and their callous disinterest.

Quick Guide

Author
Obadiah

Type
Prophecy

Purpose
A prediction of the destruction of Edom.

Key verse
15 "The day is coming when I, the LORD, will judge the nations. And, Edom, you will pay in full for what you have done."

If you remember one thing about this book . . .
You cannot escape the judgment of God.

Your 2 minutes start now
Read chapter 1

Details, Details . . .
Obadiah vs. Jeremiah

Obadiah 1–9 is very similar to Jeremiah 49:7–22. There is much argument over whether Obadiah quoted from Jeremiah, or Jeremiah from Obadiah, or both of them from another, earlier book. This would affect the date of the book, but not much else.

The Route Through Obadiah

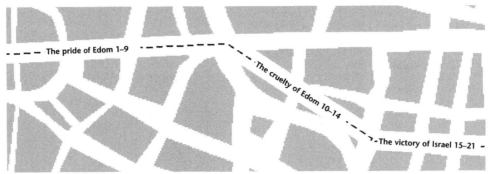

- - - The pride of Edom 1–9
The cruelty of Edom 10–14
The victory of Israel 15–21

The pride of Edom 1–9

Edom is a mountainous kingdom, proud and smug in its ability to withstand attack. Since the Lord made the mountains, however, they will afford the Edomites no refuge. They will lose everything (5–6).

The cruelty of Edom 10–14

The Edomites were related to the Israelites—a fact that makes their cruelty all the worse. Their ancestor was Esau, the brother of Jacob. Although God chose Jacob, that does not absolve them of responsibility. Yet they stood and watched while evil was committed. They should have helped their kin, but they stood by, safe in their mountain strongholds, while Jerusalem fell. More than that, they picked over the bones of Israel, looting whatever was left. To stand and watch, when we have the power to stop evil happening, is to be part of the crime.

The victory of Israel 15–21

The day of the Lord is coming, when the Edomites will get their just deserts. Previously it has been implied that other nations will conquer Edom (7), but now it is clear that Israel will defeat them. The captives will return to take possession of the land (20). The Edomites stand accused of profaning God's holy mountain by drinking on it (16). Now that mountain will be reclaimed and it will be greater than all the hills of Edom put together (21).

Jonah
God's love for all

This little book contains one of the most famous stories of the Bible, and its four chapters have given rise to almost as much debate as the first four chapters of Genesis.

Who: We don't know who wrote it, but the story is about Jonah, whose name means "dove." Traditionally the book is believed to have been written by Jonah himself, but it may have come from the same source as the tales of Elisha and Elijah.

When: The action takes place around 800–750 BC. Jonah was a contemporary of Amos. Some date the book later, after the exile, or at least after the fall of Nineveh in 612 BC. However, it may well have been written earlier—it would certainly make more sense if the prophet went to the superpower when it was still a superpower, rather than after it had collapsed.

What: For a book in the "Prophets" section, Jonah is remarkably light on prophecy. Indeed, we only have one line of prophecy from Jonah in the whole book: "Forty days from now, Nineveh will be destroyed!" Hardly a complex message.

However, the real point of the book lies not so much in Jonah's message as in his destination. Jonah was being sent with a message of God's forgiveness to the most brutal place on earth. "See?" God is saying. "Even your worst, most brutal enemies can repent." Israel believed that the truth was theirs alone and they wrapped it in ritual and rite and sanctimonious piety. But God implies that the Assyrians—the hated, feared Assyrians—were children of God as well. And when they repented and listened to his message, he forgave them.

Jonah, therefore, is much more than an entertaining story about a dude and a big fish. It's a story about how even your worst enemies can receive God's forgiveness.

Quick Guide

Author
Unknown

Type
Prophecy

Purpose
To show how God's message could even reach Israel's worst enemies.

Key verse
4:2 "Our LORD, I knew from the very beginning that you wouldn't destroy Nineveh. That's why I left my own country and headed for Spain. You are a kind and merciful God, and you are very patient. You always show love, and you don't like to punish anyone, not even foreigners."

If you remember one thing about this book . . .
There is no one who is beyond the reach of God's forgiveness and love.

Your 10 minutes start now
Read chapters 1–4

The Route Through Jonah

Jonah runs away 1:1–17

Jonah in the fish 2:1–10

Jonah in Nineveh 3:1–4:11

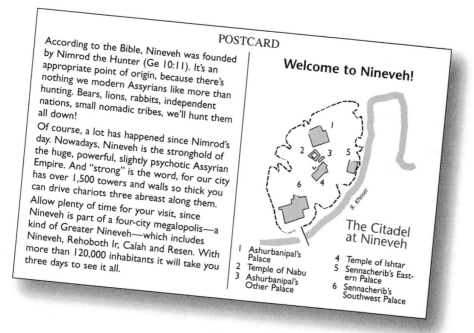

POSTCARD

According to the Bible, Nineveh was founded by Nimrod the Hunter (Ge 10:11). It's an appropriate point of origin, because there's nothing we modern Assyrians like more than hunting. Bears, lions, rabbits, independent nations, small nomadic tribes, we'll hunt them all down!

Of course, a lot has happened since Nimrod's day. Nowadays, Nineveh is the stronghold of the huge, powerful, slightly psychotic Assyrian Empire. And "strong" is the word, for our city has over 1,500 towers and walls so thick you can drive chariots three abreast along them. Allow plenty of time for your visit, since Nineveh is part of a four-city megalopolis—a kind of Greater Nineveh—which includes Nineveh, Rehoboth Ir, Calah and Resen. With more than 120,000 inhabitants it will take you three days to see it all.

Welcome to Nineveh!

The Citadel at Nineveh

1 Ashurbanipal's Palace
2 Temple of Nabu
3 Ashurbanipal's Other Palace
4 Temple of Ishtar
5 Sennacherib's Eastern Palace
6 Sennacherib's Southwest Palace

Jonah runs away 1:1–17

The story of Jonah is often told as if Jonah was some kind of naughty schoolboy, disobeying the Lord because he didn't want to travel. But the truth is that he was being asked to go to the most dangerous place on earth. Imagine being asked to go and stand on the steps of the Reichstag in Hitler's Berlin and to tell the assembled Nazis that they need to repent. That's what Jonah was asked to do.

Previously he had been a prophet in Israel, a prophet who told Israel good news. Jonah features elsewhere in the Bible, in 2 Kings 14:25, where he predicts good things for Jeroboam II. His prophecies, and their successful fulfillment, must have made Jonah "prophet of the month" in Israel.

However, one of the key factors in Israel's military success was the emergence of a new and frightening power. Damascus—the country with which Israel had been at war—was only quieted because it had been attacked by the Assyrians, a powerful, brutal and savage empire. Israel, therefore, had no reason to feel smug, yet that is exactly what happened and prophets like Amos and Hosea were sent to shock Israel out of its complacency.

Jonah, however, was sent in a different direction. He was asked to go to Nineveh itself. He was being asked to go to a huge city, the center of the most powerful nation on earth, to tell them that they should be ashamed of themselves. He was told to go and tell a nation of psychotic, rampaging, violent people that the Lord didn't like what they were doing. No wonder he ran in the opposite direction.

So Jonah runs away from God. This is not a great plan, since it involves running away from someone who, by definition, is everywhere. You cannot run away from God, you can only ever run toward him.

It is important to note that the pagan captain is a god-fearing and humane man. It is Jonah who says that he must be thrown overboard, but the captain makes every effort to reach shore (1:13). When the situation becomes impossible, he jettisons Jonah with great reluctance and in full acknowledgment of God's power. It is another reminder to Jonah that people of other nations are much more ready to obey the word of the Lord than the prophet is himself.

Jonah in the fish   2:1–10

Inside the fish, Jonah prays, not unnaturally, for salvation. He knows he deserves death, but the Lord saves him. It is a prayer that all Christians echo: only through God's grace are we brought up from the depths.

Questions, Questions
The fish

Er, excuse me . . .
Look, I know what you're going to ask. It's the "fish" part, isn't it?
Well, it does seem a bit . . . er . . . unbelievable.
Absolutely.
Sorry?
Yes, it is. If you look at it only from our scientific perspective, it is unbelievable. Impossible.
Oh. Then it's not real.
I never said that. I said that from our scientific perspective it's unbelievable. But miracles don't happen from our perspective. They happen from God's side. So he can do what he wants. He did make the fish, after all.
Mammal.
Sorry?
Whales are mammals, not fish.
Look, this is Ancient Israel we're talking about here, not your biology class. They didn't care. As far as they were concerned it was a big wet thing that came up out of the sea.
So you're saying it could have happened?
The Bible describes loads of "unbelievable" things—many around the time of Jonah. Elijah and Elisha were always making ax-heads float, or delivering jars of oil that never ran out, or bringing people back to life. It is perfectly possible to regard the story of Jonah as a kind of allegory, but if you're going to reject it on the grounds of the fish business, then you have to reject much of Genesis, Exodus, Kings . . .
I get the point. By the way, did you know that blue whales have blood vessels so big that a man could swim along them?
No. Tell me more . . .

Jonah in Nineveh
3:1–4:11

Back on dry land, Jonah is reminded of his task and this time he obeys. He goes to Nineveh—a huge city on the banks of the Tigris—and preaches a simple message of repentance: if they don't change, the city will be destroyed in forty days.

Throughout the Bible we get used to prophets being ignored, derided, beaten up, lowered into sewers, etc. It comes as a welcome surprise to find that the Assyrians immediately obey Jonah. The king declares a fast and a day of repentance and prayer. "Perhaps," he says, "God will change his mind" (3:9).

Which he does. Much to the irritation of Jonah. Jonah appears to be annoyed that his journey is wasted and that God will not punish foreigners. "I knew from the very beginning that you wouldn't destroy Nineveh," he says. "You always show love, and you don't like to punish anyone, not even foreigners." (One of my favorite, favorite Bible lines.)

The Lord's answer is to show that he is in control. He creates a vine to shield the sulking Jonah from the sun, then makes it wither and die, leaving Jonah at the mercy of the wind and the heat. The message is clear. It is God's world and it is filled with God's creations. If Jonah can care about something as trivial as a vine, should God not care about the inhabitants of Nineveh?

It is one of the great missionary statements of the Bible. The city is full of people who cannot tell right from wrong, who have no moral or spiritual leadership, but God cares for them. Even if they are foreigners.

View Points

Jonah—Fact or Fiction?

On one hand:
Jonah is a fable or parable about Israel's lack of faith and responsiveness to God compared with that of the so-called ungodly nations. It is certainly a good story, told in a highly exciting style, but the events are told in the manner of a legend, and the repentance of the Assyrians is too good to be true.

On the other hand:
In terms of style, Jonah fits quite well alongside the accounts of Elisha, Moses, Elijah and the things that happened to them. Why couldn't God preserve a man in a whale? He made whales, after all. He's God. And just because the book is arranged neatly doesn't mean it didn't happen. The Old Testament writers were always carefully arranging their material. All historians do that.

Moving on: The key is the meaning. Jonah can be viewed as a story or as fact, but it remains true: God loves all the world and wants everyone to repent.

POSTCARD

For some 500 years Assyria has been the empire of choice in the Middle East. Our policy of expansion has been ably pursued by powerful emperors such as Tiglath-Pileser (I, II and III), Sargon, Sennacherib and Esarhaddon. Crazy names, psychotic guys.

Indeed, under Esarhaddon, and his son, Ashurbanipal, our empire has reached its greatest extent. Our influence now extends from the Persian Gulf all the way into Egypt.

Some would like to portray us as a cruel and brutal regime and, it has to be admitted, many of our sculptures do show a succession of kings glorifying in violent destruction and happily looking on while their captives are gruesomely punished. But you can't build an empire without brutally crushing the opposition, stealing their treasure, destroying their cities and taking their entire nation into captivity.

As the saying goes, you can't make an omelette without breaking legs. Sorry, eggs.

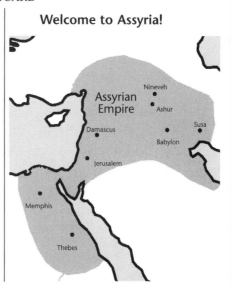

Welcome to Assyria!

Assyrian Empire

Nineveh
Ashur
Susa
Damascus
Babylon
Jerusalem
Memphis
Thebes

Micah
Judgment and hope

Who: Micah, a resident of Moresheth, a small town in southern Judah.

When: Between 750 and 686 BC. Micah prophesied during the reigns of three kings: Jotham, Ahaz and Hezekiah. He was a contemporary of Isaiah and Amos.

What: Another prophet crying out against injustice and trying to get the people to change their ways. The seven chapters of Micah oscillate between condemnation of Israel's conduct and great prophecies of a future hope.

Micah uses language in a strong and powerful way. He creates vivid pictures: people shave their heads "as bald as a vulture" (1:16); mountains melt like wax; there are images of people sitting at peace under their own vine, and majestic images of a future king who will shepherd his people into a time of great peace.

A bit of background: both kingdoms were under threat of attack and invasion. In 734 BC the wonderfully named Tiglath-Pileser III of Assyria conquered most of Israel; in 722–721 the capital Samaria fell and the northern kingdom was conquered. In 701 Judah revolted against the Assyrians and was defeated by Sennacherib. Say what you like about the Assyrians (and you *can* say what you like as they're all dead), they had great names.

The Route Through Micah

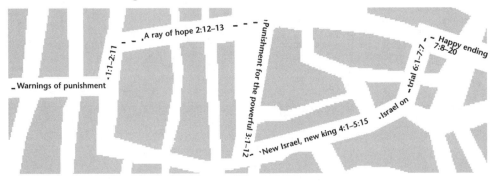

Warnings of punishment · 1:1–2:11 — A ray of hope 2:12–13 — Punishment for the powerful 3:1–12 · New Israel, new king 4:1–5:15 · Israel on trial 6:1–7:7 — Happy ending 7:8–20

222

Warnings of punishment 1:1–2:11

The first part of Micah pronounces judgment: judgment on Samaria, the capital city of Israel, and Jerusalem, the capital city of Judah. These are supposed to be great cities, centers of holiness and faithfulness, but they have become abhorrent, given over to false gods and evil practices.

First Micah tells Samaria that it will be crushed underfoot; then he tells Jerusalem that it is doomed. It will be like a "going-away gift" (1:14), a dowry given by the bride's father to the husband when she leaves home. This is a prophecy of the fate of Judah, when entire towns were literally "taken away" into captivity.

Why should this happen? Because the people are evil and immoral. They cheat families of land, they steal the clothes from people's backs, they throw women out of their homes and disinherit their children. Their false gods have changed the way they act. Their false religion has false morals, and the outcome is oppression, injustice and dishonesty.

> ## Details, Details . . .
> ## Temple prostitutes (1:7)
>
> At many pagan temples, men were encouraged to pay "temple prostitutes" for sex. The official line on this was that it was a way of worshiping whichever god the temple happened to support; the real truth was that it was a way for the priests and temple officials to fill their coffers. Few things show more obviously the man-made origin of these false religions than their emphasis on sex. Whereas God sees sex as something pure and sacred between husband and wife, the pagan religions turn it into something shameful and sordid.

A ray of hope 2:12–13

After this depressing catalog of crimes, there is a sudden, brief ray of hope. Micah turns the lights on in the gloom and points to a time when the Lord will bring together the people of Israel again. The shepherd will bring his sheep to safety.

Punishment for the powerful 3:1–12

Just as the capital cities should be places of holiness and righteousness, so their ruling elite should be holy and righteous. But they abuse their power. Their prophets lie, telling people anything they like, as long as there's a meal in it for them (3:5). Their leaders are cruel and murderous and corrupt (3:9–11). Their priests care more about money than truth. It is their behavior, more than anyone else's, that has led to Israel's and Judah's plight—for they take the people with them.

New Israel, new king 4:1–5:15

Micah now looks forward to an ideal society, a new city where God's Law will be obeyed. This fantastic passage shows what the world could be like, if only God was worshiped and obeyed.

It is universal—with people from all nations coming to worship (4:2). It is inclusive—the outcasts, the lame, the grieving will all find a welcome there (4:7). It is peaceful in the truest sense of the word. The Hebrew word for peace meant much more than the absence of war. It meant wholeness and rest—the image here is of people resting beneath their fig trees. Weapons of war will become instruments of growth as spears and swords become plows and pruning forks (4:3).

Most of all, it is ruled by a mighty king. Micah foretells how the Messiah, the chosen King, will come from Bethlehem, a small, disregarded town.

This King will shepherd his people and "the whole earth will know his true greatness." The whole of this part of Micah is looking forward to an ideal world, to the world as it should be and one day will be, when it is ruled by Jesus, mixed with more immediate prophecies of the eventual fate of Assyria and the other enemies of Israel.

Israel on trial   6:1–7:7

After this picture of the truly just and righteous society, Israel is called to account. First God appears as a witness for the prosecution, reminding them of their history (6:3–5). The "jury" are the hills and mountains—jurors who have been there forever and have seen everything that has happened.

Then they are called to account for their actions. God demands more than just lip service. His demands are, in essence, very simple: "See that justice is done, let mercy be your first concern, and humbly obey your God" (6:8).

Chapter 7 paints a picture of a society in collapse. No one trusts anyone else, there is no loyalty, no honesty, and the only time people cooperate with one another is when they are committing a crime (7:3). Families hate one another, and even your best friend and loved ones cannot be trusted.

Details, Details . . .

Weights and measures (6:11)

This emphasis on weights and measures and boundary stones recurs frequently in the Bible. The reason is simple: fairness and honesty. There was no Better Business Bureau in ancient times, no Consumer Affairs programs to complain to. Keeping your weights and measures accurate—and therefore giving people what they paid for—was a very basic and fundamental demonstration of honesty. What is more, it is one that had a huge impact on ordinary people. God's emphasis on it is a reminder of what he said elsewhere: faithfulness in the little things is what really matters.

A happy ending   7:8–20

In the midst of this chaos and carnage, Micah waits in hope. "I know that I will see him making things right for me and leading me to the light," he says (7:9). The walls will be rebuilt, the people will be led to the good pasture again. Micah prays to God to lead them home, and God replies that he will work miracles once again. The people will be brought home and their sins will be thrown far away, into the depths of the sea.

God is angry, God is sad, but above all God is faithful. The message of Micah is that God keeps his promises—and that the vision granted to the prophet would come true, when the true King came out of a little town called Bethlehem.

Nahum
The end of Nineveh

Who: Nahum is described as an Elkoshite, a resident of Elkosh. Which doesn't in fact help much, since we don't know where Elkosh was. His name means "comforter," although, since he prophesied the complete destruction of Nineveh, he wasn't much of a comfort to the Assyrians.

When: Around 620 BC-ish. He talks in the past tense about the fall of Thebes, which happened in 663 BC, and he seems to imply that the fall of Nineveh is imminent, which was to happen in 612 BC. This makes him a contemporary of Zephaniah and a young Jeremiah.

What: The theme of the book is the destruction of Nineveh —and by Nineveh, Nahum means the entire Assyrian empire. This cruel, oppressive empire was to be destroyed and, indeed, the book ends with the destruction of Nineveh.

God is depicted in Nahum as slow but sure. He is "slow to anger," but he will not leave the guilty unpunished. Evil will not triumph.

The fall of Assyria

Under Esarhaddon (681–669 BC), and his son, Ashurbanipal (669–631 BC), the Assyrian empire reached its greatest extent. But the clouds were gathering: the neighboring empires of the Babylonians and the Medes grew in strength and eventually the fall of Assyria—so long predicted by the prophets of the Bible—came about. Nineveh was first besieged in 633 BC, finally capitulating in 612 BC. Rather than be captured, the besieged emperor Sinshariskun set fire to his palace, a gesture made slightly less noble by the fact that he took all his wives with him. Thus the words of Nahum and Zephaniah came to pass. Assyria melted into the mists of history. It made one final attempt at rebellion against the Medes, failed completely and disappeared.

The Route Through Nahum

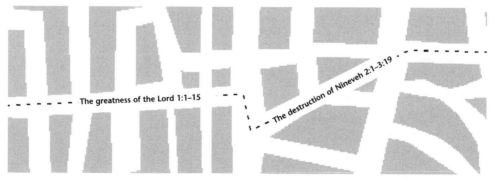

The greatness of the Lord 1:1–15

The destruction of Nineveh 2:1–3:19

Puzzling Points

How can God be vengeful?

Nahum describes a God who "takes revenge on his enemies" (1:2). It is difficult for us—in the light of Jesus' injunction to "love our enemies"—to understand what is going on here. Surely God loves everyone?

God does love everyone—in fact, God is love. But love is not, despite what the poets say, blind. People don't have the right to abuse God's love. He is forgiving, but people have to ask for forgiveness, and they have to change their ways. To those who turn to him he is a caring refuge. But those who fight him, those who are cruel and heartless and brutal—these people he will punish. And let's not forget, these are harsh, brutal people we are talking about here, not someone who stole your pencil case or ran into your car. Nahum 2:12 shows that the Assyrians were once like lions, and now they are being savaged themselves.

Even so, they could repent. Jonah went to Nineveh to preach, so no one is beyond God's reach. But for those who will not repent, there will be consequences.

God does not delight in meting out punishment—in fact several times in the Bible it talks of him weeping, and shows him reluctant to act. But he will act against the guilty—the universe demands it.

Wickedness and tyranny must be defeated. Love that just lets everyone do what they want is not love but a kind of uncaring.

There is love, but there has to be justice as well. God embodies both.

The greatness of the Lord   1:1–15

The first chapter of Nahum is a meditation on what God is like. For those who trust in him he provides a refuge, but for those who plot against him, he is an overwhelming flood.

Assyria has made "evil plans against the LORD" (1:11) and will be utterly destroyed and forgotten. The good news for the people of Judah is that they will be freed to keep their "promises to God" (1:15).

The destruction of Nineveh   2:1–3:19   ▷219, 221

In a series of pictures, Nahum shows the destruction that is on its way for Nineveh. We see the soldiers struggling to defend the city (2:3–4), the gates on the Euphrates being burst open (2:6), short, staccato, almost poetic images that conjure up the panic of war (3:1–3). Nineveh is described as a disgraced and dishonored queen, dragged off, publicly humiliated. In a shocking image, her skirts are lifted in a humiliating display of her nakedness (3:5).

This is an image that recurs in the works of the prophets—it was the classic punishment for prostitutes. Nineveh is a harlot who will be publicly pelted with filth and humiliated.

Nineveh's fortresses look fine (3:12), but they fall easily. The merchants and soldiers who were once its strength will strip the land and then disappear when the trouble comes.

"You're fatally wounded . . ." (3:19). God was true to his word. Within a few centuries of the collapse, Nineveh was nothing more than a pile of ruins covered in sand. The merchants, the princes, the proud, cruel people were all gone, to be replaced by sand and, eventually, archaeologists. A fate worse than death, as anyone who has ever stood next to an archaeologist at a party will tell you.

Habakkuk

Why is this happening?

Who: Habakkuk. Lived at the same time as Jeremiah.

When: Sometime around 605 BC. Habakkuk predicts the Babylonian invasion of Judah and the attack on Jerusalem, which took place in 597 BC.

What: These were troubled times. The land of Judah was riven by violence and conflict, justice was scarce, people were suffering, and invasion was just over the horizon.

Habbakuk's question was simple: why was God allowing this to happen? What was God—the God of justice—doing? He raises the same questions as Job, but from a slightly different perspective. Whereas Job asks, "How could you let this happen to me?" Habakkuk asks, "How could you let this happen to us?"

The book is a conversation—it is set out as a dialogue between man and God. Habakkuk argues with God, trying to understand God's actions, which seem to him meaningless and mysterious. God replies to Habakkuk and the prophet responds with a moving, passionate declaration of faith.

Quick Guide

Author

Habakkuk

Type

Prophecy

Purpose

Why does God allow bad things to happen to his people?

Key verse

3:19 "The LORD gives me strength. He makes my feet as sure as those of a deer, and he helps me stand on the mountains."

If you remember one thing about this book ...

No matter what those in power might think, they cannot escape judgment.

Your 5 minutes start now

Read chapters 1–3

First question   1:1–11

Habakkuk looks at the world around him and asks God one simple question: why do you allow this?

God's answer to Habakkuk's question is equally simple: the Babylonians are coming and they will punish Judah. This, it has to be admitted, is not exactly comforting. God is going to replace the murderous, unjust, decadent Judaean rulers with ... er ... the murderous, unjust, decadent Babylonian rulers. Worse, Babylon is a nation that does not acknowledge God's rule.

The Route Through Habakkuk

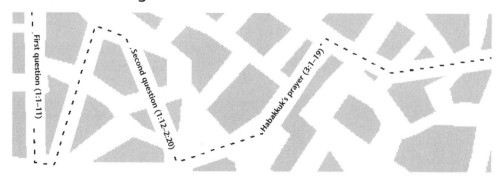

First question (1:1–11)

Second question (1:12–2:20)

Habakkuk's prayer (3:1–19)

Second question   1:12–2:20

Habakkuk's second question to God is, roughly, "You call that justice?" The Babylonians are worse than the Judaeans, so how can God let them succeed? How can he let them go on capturing one nation after another?

God responds with a message about the fate of the Babylonians. They too will fall. They will get what is coming to them. God is using them, but he does not approve of them.

He lists Babylon's crimes. They are arrogant and greedy and want to take over the world (2:5); they steal, cheat and murder (2:6–8); they lure their neighbors into traps so that they can strip them of everything they own (2:15); they destroy the trees and the animals (2:17) and worship false gods (2:18–20). The Babylonians sound, in this passage, astonishingly like the multinational, greedy, rapacious corporations of today.

The message is clear: the Babylonians will get their just deserts. God is not blind, and they too will be punished.

Details, Details . . .
Teman and Paran (3:3)
Teman means "south" and Paran probably refers to the land near Sinai, so this is a reference to the exodus, picturing God marching out from the wilderness in judgment. The exodus theme is picked up in the mentions of plagues (3:5), chariots being crushed by water (3:8) and the deliverance of the people (3:13).

Habakkuk's prayer 3:1–19

Habakkuk responds with a prayer of praise to God—a prayer that was evidently turned into a song by succeeding generations. Like Job, he can only answer his questions by concentrating on what God is. God is mighty and powerful—therefore the forces of darkness cannot succeed. God is just, therefore justice will be done in the end.

Even though hard times are ahead, Habakkuk will trust in the Lord, who will give him strength.

Zephaniah
The day of the Lord

Who: Zephaniah was a member of royalty. A distant member, admittedly, but his great-great-grandfather was King Hezekiah. And he would have been of considerable social standing—which makes his message all the more shocking.

When: During the reign of King Josiah (640–609 BC). Given that Josiah was a good king and a reformer, this prophecy probably belongs to the early part of his reign (2 Ki 22:1–23:30; 2 Ch 34–35).

What: Judah was to be judged. Those who were following false gods would face the judgment of the one true God.

Zephaniah concentrates on the theme of "the day of the Lord," which the Judaeans smugly believed would be the time when they had the power and control. Instead, Zephaniah tells them that it is a day when they too will be judged.

Josiah was, in fact, a reforming king, raising the possibility that Zephaniah's message actually hit home. We may be dealing with that unique phenomenon here—a prophet who was actually listened to.

Quick Guide

Author
Zephaniah

Type
Prophecy

Purpose
To warn Judah of the coming judgment of the Lord.

Key verse
2:3 "If you humbly obey the LORD, then come and worship him. If you do right and are humble, perhaps you will be safe on that day when the LORD turns loose his anger."

If you remember one thing about this book . . .
Judgment is coming, but God has a glorious future in mind for his people.

Your 5 minutes start now
Read chapters 1–3

The Route Through Zephaniah

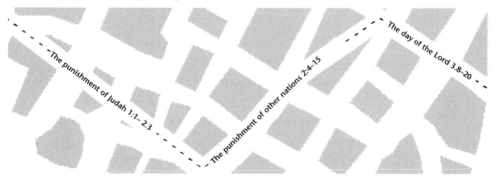

The punishment of Judah 1:1– 2.3

The punishment of other nations 2:4-15

The day of the Lord 3.8–20

Punishment of Judah 1:1–2:3

The judgment on Judah is proclaimed in apocalyptic terms—reminiscent of the flood in Genesis. Those who bow to the stars (1:5) and worship Baal (1:4) while proclaiming their allegiance to God will be wiped away.

Zephaniah describes people in Jerusalem, from the Fish Gate to the Lower Hollow, crying out (1:10–11). Their money is gone, their possessions are taken, their food is destroyed. In graphically bloody lines, the sins of the people result in physical destruction—their guts and blood rush out (1:17).

Yet there is always hope. In words that are echoed throughout the works of the prophets, the Lord declares that all the people have to do is turn to him and they will be safe (2:1–3).

Details, Details . . .
Cush (2:12)

Sometimes translated as Ethiopia, the Hebrew text has "Cush"—an area that included parts of present-day Ethiopia and Sudan. Not that it matters, for it too will be chopped down.

The punishment of other nations 2:4–3:7

It is not just Judah—other nations will also be judged by the Lord. Philistia will be destroyed and given over to those who remain faithful (2:7). Moab and Ammon will suffer for their sneering and contempt for the Lord. Assyria, the mighty, will also fall. Nineveh will turn to rubble and animals will graze there, while ravens will fly in its once beautiful palaces.

Finally the prophet returns to Jerusalem and its continual rebellion against God. Here we see the traditional complaints—priests who disgrace their places of worship, false prophets, corrupt and oppressive officials. There is a note of real sadness among all God's declarations of punishment. "God felt certain that Jerusalem would learn to respect and obey him" (3:7). Alas, they were eager to start sinning again.

The day of the Lord 3:8–20 ▷212

The day of the Lord will come. The world will be cleansed—even the languages purified (3:9). Those who are truly humble will find safety. Those who "live right and refuse to tell lies" will eat and sleep in safety (3:13).

This will be a time of celebration. Zephaniah paints a wonderful picture of God and his people delighting in one another, shouting and singing at the tops of their voices. But God will also celebrate. "He celebrates and sings because of you, and he will refresh your life with his love" (3:17).

We think that our relationship with God is only a one-way thing; we forget that God delights in us. Jesus talks about the angels throwing a party every time one sinner repents (Lk 15:10). The Bible makes it clear that when people follow God he is thrilled, just as he is saddened when they turn away.

Finally, in language very similar to Micah, Zephaniah says that the lame and the outcasts will be welcomed into the new kingdom. Sorrow is no more: the day of the Lord has brought judgment, it is true, but it has also brought wholeness, peace and glorious celebration.

Haggai
Rebuilding the temple

Who: Haggai. We don't know anything more about him, other than that he was an exile in Babylon and that he returned to Jerusalem in the second wave of returnees. Oh, and by the way, "Haggai" is not the plural of "haggis."

When: 520 BC: September 21, October 17 and December 18, to be precise.

What: Morale was low in Jerusalem. It had been twenty years since their liberation from Babylon, with the defeat of the Babylonian empire by Cyrus the Great. Enthusiastic and committed, they returned to Jerusalem vowing to rebuild the place and reinhabit the land. It was a second exodus. God would be with them again and would bless them.

And then reality set in.

When simply staying alive was a major challenge, other tasks such as rebuilding the temple were pushed a long way down the list of priorities. Weariness and hardship, combined with local opposition, had led to the abandonment of the temple rebuilding project.

Haggai and Zechariah are two prophets who preach broadly the same message. Israel must reconsider its priorities. The temple is more than a building project; it is a sign that the land will be dedicated to God.

Quick Guide
Author
Haggai
Type
Prophecy
Purpose
To inspire the people who have returned from exile to continue with the rebuilding of the temple in Jerusalem.
Key verse
2:4 "But cheer up! Because I, the LORD All-Powerful, will be here to help you with the work, just as I promised your ancestors when I brought them out of Egypt. Don't worry. My Spirit is here with you."
If you remember one thing about this book . . .
What you spend your time and energy on reflects your real priorities.
Your 5 minutes start now
Read chapters 1–2

Let's hear it for Cyrus
Archaeological evidence about Cyrus shows him to have been a tolerant leader—although he may just have been hedging his bets. The Cyrus Cylinder records his words: "May all the gods whom I have placed within their sanctuaries address a daily prayer in my favor . . ." Although he personally worshiped the Babylonian god Marduk, he was clearly not above asking a few other religions for the odd favor.

The Route Through Haggai

Putting God first 1:1–15

Promises of glory 2:1–9

Promises of blessing 2:10–23

Putting God first   1:1–15

Haggai calls on the Jews to reexamine their priorities. Times are hard. Food is in short supply, the weather is cold. They don't have time to spend on the temple. But Haggai responds that it is because they have not completed the temple that these things are happening. The temple is a sign of their allegiance.

Every city, every culture proclaims its gods through its buildings. In our own culture the tallest, grandest buildings used to be churches and cathedrals. Nowadays, they are banks and shopping centers. We worship money. In Haggai's time the buildings that were the best—although "best" is a relative term here—were the individual homes and houses. The temple lay abandoned. "Who do you worship?" asks Haggai. "The person who rescued you or your own comfort?"

The message hits home and the rebuilding begins.

Promises of glory   2:1–9

Haggai's second message comes a month later. No doubt the first flush of enthusiasm following Haggai's message has worn off. The people are discouraged—especially when they look at the building itself. How can this pile of stone and timber be called a temple? How can this shabby structure compare with the temple in Solomon's time? But Haggai's message this time is one of encouragement. He urges them to dream dreams about this place and to imagine what it could be. He promises them that God will intervene and help them.

Promises of blessing   2:10–23

Two months later Haggai gives two prophecies on one day. The first message is to the priests and people, urging them to keep holy and free from contamination by sin. The foundation for the temple has been completed, but something is getting in the way. We don't know what the "unclean" elements were to which Haggai is referring, but he urges the people to keep free from contamination and corruption and to stay holy. "From now on," he says, "things will get better."

The second message that day is for King Zerubbabel, telling him of his special status and how the Lord will bless him. The Hebrew for 2:23 says that Zerubbabel is to be the Lord's "signet ring." A signet ring was engraved with the king's seal and was used to stamp official documents. It was a symbol of authority. In Genesis 41:42 Pharaoh takes his signet ring from his finger and puts it on Joseph's finger to illustrate that Joseph has his authority.

God told Zerubbabel's grandfather Jehoiachin that he was like a signet ring that had been pulled from the Lord's finger and thrown away. Now his grandson is back. The ring has been put back on the Lord's finger.

Zechariah
The future king

Who: Zechariah, the son of Berechiah, and the grandson of Iddo. This was probably the Iddo who is mentioned in Nehemiah 12:4 and Ezra 2:2 as returning from exile in 536 BC. Iddo was a priest, which means that Zechariah probably followed in his footsteps. He was a contemporary of Haggai (see Ez 5:1; 6:14).

When: Zechariah's first vision occurred in about mid-October, 520 BC. His work continued for at least two years until 518 BC (Zec 7:1), but in all probability he preached and prophesied beyond this date.

What: Few books of the Bible are as difficult to interpret as Zechariah. Many experts, both Christian and Jewish, have spent long hours studying the text, only to be forced to concede that they have no idea what the prophet is going on about.

However, there is plenty we *can* understand. No book of prophecy has more to say about the Messiah, or points more clearly to Jesus. In the future, Zechariah saw a wounded King, a shepherd, the one for whom all creation was waiting. He glimpsed what was coming and his excitement is found in virtually every line.

Quick Guide

Author
Zechariah

Type
Prophecy

Purpose
A vision of the far future of Israel.

Key verses
7:8–9 "So once again, I, the LORD All-Powerful, tell you, 'See that justice is done and be kind and merciful to one another!'"

If you remember one thing about this book . . .
The future is in God's hands—and he knows what is going to happen.

Your 10 minutes start now
Read chapters 1–2, 7–8, 13

Such excitement must have been in stark contrast to the world around him. Like Haggai, his contemporary, Zechariah faced a demoralized people in a damaged city. The foundations of the temple had been laid, but nothing more. There were no priests worthy to make sacrifices, and any glory seemed long gone. Like Haggai, Zechariah sought to inspire people to get back to work and see the temple through to completion.

His first series of prophecies consists of messages given on three distinct occasions. These include eight strange visions. The second section consists of a series of messages to Israel and its leaders as well as a final, awe-inspiring vision of the far future. One day, he is saying, the glory will return. One day, the king will be back in Jerusalem.

The Route Through Zechariah

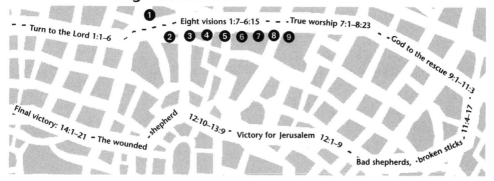

Turn to the Lord 1:1–6 · Eight visions 1:7–6:15 · True worship 7:1–8:23 · God to the rescue 9:1–11:3 · Bad shepherds, broken sticks 11:4–17 · Victory for Jerusalem 12:1–9 · The wounded shepherd 12:10–13:9 · Final victory: 14:1–21

First message: Turn to the Lord
1:1–6

This is an introduction to Zechariah, preached in the eighth month of the second year of the reign of King Darius—October/November 520 BC. Zechariah sets the tone and theme for his ministry, calling the people to repentance and warning them not to follow the examples of their ancestors.

Second message: Eight visions
1:7–6:15

Zechariah's second message was received three months later, on February 15, 519 BC—exactly two months after the cornerstone of the temple was laid. It consists of eight strange nighttime visions. These were not dreams—later on the angel wakes him from sleep precisely so that he can receive more visions (4:1).

❶ Strange riders   1:7–17
The prophet sees strange riders, the leader of whom is on a red horse. They are the Lord's news reporters, riding through the world to find out what is going on. While other nations relax in security, the Lord will restore Jerusalem.

❷ Four animal horns, four craftsmen   1:18–21
The horns represent the powerful nations that, for centuries, oppressed Israel. If four is meant literally, then Zechariah probably meant Assyria, Babylonia, Egypt and the Medeo-Persians. They are destroyed by four craftsmen or blacksmiths. Why they are craftsmen is uncertain, but the point is that there is no longer any opposition to rebuilding the temple.

❸ The measuring line   2:1–13
A man with a measuring line is sent to measure Jerusalem, but the city is simply too big. God will expand the city so that it will be without boundaries. The Lord will be its protection—a wall of fire, which recalls his presence in the wilderness—and its glory (2:5). He calls his people back from their exile (2:6) and points to a future when all nations will recognize his presence and come to him.

❹ Joshua versus Satan   3:1–10
Joshua, the high priest, stands before the Lord and the Satan, or accuser. He is dressed in filthy clothes, which are removed and replaced with rich clothes and a priestly turban.

This obviously refers to the high priest in Jerusalem at the time, Joshua, son of Jehozadak (6:11). He would officiate at the sacrifices in the new temple. But it also looks forward, for Joshua or Jeshua means "the Lord saves" and the Greek version of the name is, of course, Jesus. It is a symbol of what will happen. There will be a "branch"—a Hebrew term for the Messiah or Chosen One—who will remove the sins of the land.

❺ Lamps and olive trees   4:1–14
Wakened by the angel, Zechariah sees a lampstand, with seven lamps and a bowl of oil acting as a kind of reservoir to feed them. Two olive trees are on either side.

The oil represents the Holy Spirit. It is by God's Spirit that Israel achieves what it does; not in its own power or force. The two olive trees are Joshua and Zerubbabel, the high priest and the king, two functions that ultimately would be combined in the figure of Jesus.

❻ Flying scroll   5:1–4
Zechariah sees a huge scroll, unrolled and flying through the air. The scroll is the written law of God, which condemns those who break it.

❼ Evil in a basket   5:5–11
A woman in a basket is taken away by flying women to Babylon. The basket is literally an *ephah*—a measuring basket. The implication is that the completion of the temple will remove evil from the land.

❽ The chariots   6:1–8
Zechariah sees four chariots roughly corresponding to the horsemen he saw in his first vision. They emerge from between mountains of bronze to go throughout the world.

God's power will go out and conquer the world. The mountains may represent Mount Zion and the Mount of Olives, but then they might represent Mount Everest and Mount Rushmore for all I know. (And don't ask me about the "bronze" part.) What is obvious is that nothing can stop these charioteers: they conquer everywhere, even the evil, Babylonian land of the north (6:8).

❾ The chosen one   6:9–15
These visions are followed by an instruction to Zechariah to go and crown Joshua the high priest. As in the fourth vision, this is not just about the actual high priest of the time, it was also looking forward. For God points to one who will "reach out from here like a branch." The coming king would also be a priest—a combination not allowed in Israel. For this reason some believed that the Messiah would actually be two people: one priest and one king. Those listening may have believed that Zechariah was referring to Zerubbabel—perhaps even Zechariah believed that he was referring to Zerubbabel. In fact, he was pointing far, far ahead.

Third message: True worship
7:1–8:23

A deputation comes to Zechariah to ask about fasting. Zechariah challenges them about the depth of their sincerity. In words that echo Micah and Amos and Jeremiah and, well, most of the prophets actually, he reminds them of what true religion really is. It is not mere observance of ritual, but justice, mercy, compassion, generosity, goodwill (7:9–10). His message is reiterated in 8:16–17. As in the very first lines of the book, Zechariah exhorts his listeners not to make the same mistake their forebears made. Only if they love truth and peace (8:19) will their fasts be joyful and meaningful.

Zechariah paints a picture of true peace in the city of truth. It will be a place where people can grow old in safety and security (8:4), where children play in the streets (8:5), where there will be water and good fruit (8:12). It will be a place where people of all nations gather, because they have heard that God is at work (8:23).

God to the rescue   9:1–11:3

The second part of Zechariah is different in style and tone, but contains the same kind of visionary imagery, the same message of encouragement and exhortation to the people to keep going and obey the Lord.

It begins with a section on the doom that will fall on Israel's enemies. Hadrach and Damascus will fall, as will Tyre and Sidon. The Philistines will "no longer eat meat with blood in it"—that is, they will become a part of Israel, and follow their laws.

Verses 9:9–10 celebrate the future king, the Messiah. He is not a warrior king on a warhorse, but humble, riding on a donkey—an image that was to find fulfillment in Jesus' entry into Jerusalem (Mt 21:5). Before the horse became common, the kings of Israel rode on mules or donkeys (2 Sa 18:9; 1 Ki 1:33). His appearance is followed by a series of images of rescue —from captivity (9:11), from defeat (9:16), from drought (10:1), from exile (10:8–10), from drowning (10:11). The Lord will provide the security and safety the people need. In particular he will provide them with good shepherds to lead them. They have relied on fortune-tellers (10:2) and bad leaders (10:3), much to the Lord's anger, but now he will raise up new leaders to lead them.

Bad shepherds, broken sticks
11:4–17

The image of shepherds continues, first with the shepherds of Lebanon wailing because their pastures have been destroyed. The meaning of this passage is uncertain. The pines, oaks and cedars may represent certain countries, hewn down by God and following on from the condemnation of Egypt, Assyria and Lebanon in 10:10–12. An alternative interpretation sees it as a description of Lebanon, Bashan and Jordan following their rejection of the Messiah. This would link it in with the next section, which talks of Israel's rejection of the Good Shepherd.

Suddenly the tone changes dramatically. Zechariah acts as a shepherd. This seems to be a case of "action prophecy," such as performed by Hosea and Ezekiel. The sheep represent Israel. As the good shepherd, he gets rid of bad leaders (11:8), and he rules his flock with two sticks, "favor" and "unity." But the flock hates him, the agreement is canceled and he is paid a paltry sum, which he gives to the potters at the temple—the people who make special bowls considered acceptable for temple sacrifices. The people have rejected the good shepherd, they are broken up and ruled by shepherds who do not care for them. This is a difficult passage, but it appears that, despite the pleas in Zechariah for the people not to repeat what their ancestors have done, their actions will be the same: they will reject God's leadership, and they will face division and destruction.

Victory for Jerusalem   12:1–9

And yet, Jerusalem will survive. It will face a final siege that the Lord will enable the people to repulse. When this will happen, and whether the vision is an actual event or a figurative one, is not made clear. Probably it ties in with earlier predictions of the destruction of Jerusalem's enemies.

The wounded shepherd
12:10–13:9

Suddenly the tone shifts again, and from here the prophecies become darker and even more difficult to fathom. It is not hard to see the figure of Jesus in the wounded shepherd, mourned by representatives from throughout Israel (12:10–14), and his death certainly opened up a fountain of forgiveness, washing away guilt and sin (13:1). Then, however, there is a difficult passage talking about what appears to be the death of prophecy. Yet Zechariah is talking about false prophets, for the land has been swept clean. It is these prophets who, should they dare to prophesy, will be killed —even by their own parents. Indeed, false prophecy continued well after Jesus's time, but those depicted by Zechariah are so desperate to disguise themselves that they will deny their own power and pretend to be farmers.

The striking down of the Good Shepherd will bring about a dispersal of the sheep, or rather a refining. The chosen people will become refined, tested, but purer. Jesus himself quoted this verse before his arrest to indicate the dispersal of the apostles. They would regather, however, and become pure gold. Thus the apparent disaster of striking down their leader actually brings the people into a closer walk with God (13:9).

The final victory   14:1–21

Another victory in the midst of defeat, for Jerusalem is pictured as being in a state of siege, its treasures plundered, its women raped (14:2), its inhabitants fleeing (13:5). Then the attackers will literally fall apart (13:12) and start to attack each other (13:13). This horrible apocalyptic scene is the day of the Lord, the day of judgment, and mixed in with the horrific scenes of disaster are visions of new life, streams flowing from Jerusalem (14:8), and finally people from all nations coming to worship God. Those who refuse to go will suffer drought and disaster.

Finally everything in Jerusalem will be sacred, from the bells worn by the horses to the simplest pot. There will be no need to buy special pots in which to make sacrifices, for the whole city will be sacred and the whole of life an act of worship.

And so this strange book ends in a strange way, with God worshiped throughout the world and everything made holy. The Lord has promised his people a king, a chosen one who will save them. In Zechariah, he rides on a donkey. In the New Testament, he was to do exactly the same.

Malachi
You cannot cheat God

Who: His name literally means "messenger." Nothing more is known about him. Malachi could be a name, but could equally be simply a title.

When: Malachi was probably the last prophet of Old Testament times. This prophecy probably comes from Jerusalem, after the exiles had returned. The situation he describes fits exactly with what Nehemiah found on returning for his second visit. So it is likely that Malachi's message dates from just before that, in 433 BC. He was a contemporary of Ezra and Nehemiah.

What: The temple was rebuilt, sacrifices were being offered again, but times were difficult. The old sins of Israel were creeping back. God's Laws were being disobeyed, his instructions ignored, the people were once again suffering under a regime of injustice and greed. The glory prophesied by Zechariah and Haggai had not come about; the temple, far from being a spiritual powerhouse, was a place where they simply went through the ritual.

Malachi has a particular style—almost like a teacher. He uses questions and answers. He makes a statement, then poses an objection raised by those listening, and then dismisses their objection. It's called the didactic-dialectic method. Apparently.

Malachi was an intense, sometimes severe patriot. Faced with a disheartened and disobedient people, he reminded them that religious ritual is no good on its own. It only has value if it is a true expression of sincere belief. The Law is important. The priests should guard it carefully, but more than that, they should obey it. God has a purpose for these people—a particular role for them to play. By weakening their culture they are hindering that purpose.

The Route Through Malachi

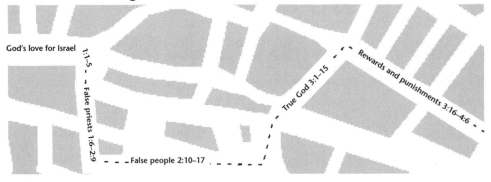

God's love for Israel 1:1–5

False priests 1:6–2:9

False people 2:10–17

True God 3:1–15

Rewards and punishments 3:16–4:6

God's love for Israel
1:1–5

The book starts with a reminder: God still loves Israel. He has chosen them to be special, right from the point when Jacob was blessed instead of Esau. And he will still make his chosen people great.

False priests
1:6–2:9

It is not merely that the priests show no respect for the Lord, they don't even understand what they are doing. They offer cheap religion—sacrificing worthless animals, complaining of the hard work, and even turning their noses up at the smell (1:13).

God would rather shut the temple completely than accept this mealy-mouthed, halfhearted religion. Throughout the Bible God shows his rejection of half-hearted religion. There is nothing about going to the temple (or even going to church) that automatically results in holiness. Only wholehearted faith makes worship acceptable to God. Indeed, halfheartedness makes God so angry that he will take the offal from their rotten sacrifices and smear their faces with it (2:3). One possible translation is that God will smear their faces with manure from their sacrificial animals and then throw them on the dung heap. I told you he took it seriously.

False people
2:10–17

The unfaithful people are likened to a husband who has left his wife and is sleeping with another woman. Indeed, this might be the literal situation—there may well have been those who married foreign women. The danger in this is not in marrying a woman from a different nation, but in following her god. The Israelites were to keep themselves pure—and that meant keeping the faith. They have rejected their wives and chosen foreigners, just as they have rejected their first, true faith and dallied with foreign gods. Now they weary God, wondering why there is no justice, why God does not punish evildoers. They should put their own house in order before asking such questions.

True God
3:1–15

God does, in fact, answer their question, although perhaps not in a way that would give them much comfort. There will be a day of justice, but it will descend on their heads.

God is on his way, and it is clear who he will punish: those who dabble in witchcraft, those who cheat their spouses, who lie, who cheat, who steal, who oppress those less powerful than they are, who "steal the property of foreigners"—in other words, those who cannot stand up for themselves—who, above all, show no respect for God (3:5).

Puzzling Points
Why does God hate Edom?

In 1:3 some versions have God saying "but Esau I hated," or "I rejected Esau." Paul was later to explain this in terms of election (Ro 9:10–13)—in other words, God chose one and rejected the other. We might also remember that Leah was "hated" in Genesis 31, yet God did bless her. God has clearly chosen one group of people through whom to work his purposes, but that does not mean that everyone else is excluded. The prophets repeatedly talk of all nations coming to worship God, and the message of Christianity went out to all nations. Indeed, in 1:11, God talks of his name being worshiped by all nations and praises them in comparison with the Israelites.

Edom here is, perhaps, more symbolic of those people who chose a different way. Those who live in the land of wickedness will always be rejected by God. Indeed, the message of Malachi is that this will be Israel's fate, unless they change their hearts.

**Details, Details . . .
The messenger (3:1)**

The messenger is usually taken to be a prophecy of John the Baptist. John prepared the way for Christ himself, the person who would confirm and fulfill the agreement between God and man. John brought a message of the promise, the new agreement between man and God, which was to be found in Jesus.

**Details, Details . . .
A scroll of remembrance (3:16)**

It was the custom in ancient times to write down the names of those who had done good deeds so that they would be remembered, much as today we would give an award or a medal. (See Es 6:1–3; Is 4:3, Da 7:10.)

This is not difficult to understand. This is not brain surgery. It shows what true religion isn't and therefore what God really wants. He wants us to look after those less powerful, to stand up for their rights, to be honest in our lives, to keep our promises and be faithful to our husbands and wives, to reject the occult, to respect God and all he stands for.

You cannot cheat God. The priests thought they could get away with not paying their tithes (3:8–11). They looked around them and wondered why they were worshiping God when it was not helping them; they never thought that the problem might be with their own cheating, halfhearted worship.

Rewards and punishments
3:16–4:6

God knows the truth. The end of Malachi shows that his message hit home—at least with some. God promises to be with them, but he also reminds them once more of the day of judgment. To those who reject God, it will be a day of burning, of complete destruction. To those who follow him, he promises not burning flames, but warming sun (4:2). Before that, however, he will send Elijah. Again, Christians believe that this is a reference to John the Baptist, who challenged people "in the name and spirit of Elijah" (see Lk 1:17 and Mt 11:13–14).

Between the Testaments

Between the last book of the Old Testament and the first book of the New Testament is a period of around 400 years. When we leave the Israelites they are reestablishing the kingdom after the exile. At the opening of the Gospels, 400 years have passed.

After the exile, Israel became a minor territory in a succession of empires. After the Persians, there came the Greeks under Alexander the Great. Alexander was committed to a policy known as Hellenization—imposing a uniform Greek culture on all the lands he conquered.

On his death his kingdom was divided between his generals, with two of them, Ptolomy and Seleucis, founding dynasties that would greatly affect the future of Israel. The Ptolomies settled in Egypt and ruled Israel for over a century. Then the Seleucids took over and Antiochus IV imposed an even more radical Hellenization policy. His aim was nothing more than the eradication of the Jewish faith. He made a concerted effort to destroy every copy of the Pentateuch and he insisted that the people make offerings to Zeus. Most awful of all, he marched into the temple, set up a statue of Zeus and sacrificed a pig—an unclean animal.

These outrages led to an uprising headed by Judas Maccabeus and the inauguration of the Maccabean revolt, which successfully ousted the Seleucids, and led to 100 years of Jewish independence.

And then the Romans came along.

In 63 BC the Roman general Pompey took Jerusalem after a three-month siege of the Temple Mount. He massacred priests and marched into the Holy of Holies. (He was disappointed and a little baffled to find that there was nothing in it.) Thus, at the beginning of the New Testament, we have an Israel that is once again under foreign control, and occupied by a vicious, brutal, sacrilegious and much hated army.

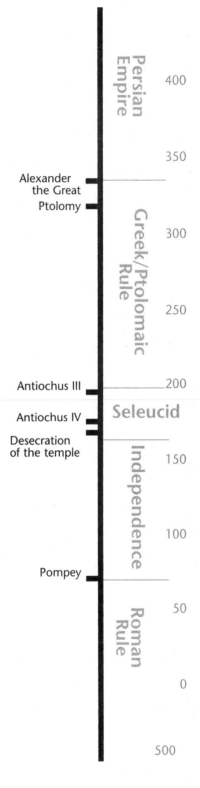

Persian Empire — 400

350

Alexander the Great

Ptolomy

Greek/Ptolomaic Rule — 300

250

Antiochus III — 200

Antiochus IV — Seleucid

Desecration of the temple

Independence — 150

100

Pompey — Roman Rule

50

0

500

241

Judaism in change

During the exile, there was no temple at which to worship, no central point to which to travel to make sacrifices. The Jewish faith became much more centered on personal faith and on the reading and discussion of the Scriptures. Personal prayer became an acceptable alternative to sacrificial ritual. This attitude persevered on their return to Jerusalem. Judaism became a faith that could be practiced anywhere there was a scroll and someone to read it.

This led to the growth of small local synagogues—local meeting places, where Jews met for worship, prayer and the study of the Scriptures. Many synagogues also served as schools where the local boys were educated. The people sat on benches around the walls and much of the teaching took the form of discussion—a leader or rabbi would be invited to read a passage and then talk about it, after which he would answer questions.

By the time of Jesus, therefore, the Jewish faith had become, to an extent, decentralized. There was less reliance on the temple—although most good Jews made their way to Jerusalem on pilgrimage at least once a year.

This decentralization led to something of a split in Judaism itself. Orthodox Jews were split into two camps. The Pharisees were the "synagogue" party. They strove to enforce the Law, and, although few in number, were enormously influential. They were, if you like, the local priesthood, concentrating on the synagogues and at odds with the powers that ran the temple. They spent a great deal of time updating laws involving things like Sabbath-day observance, tithing and ritual cleanliness. Although Jesus criticized the Pharisees for hypocritical displays of religion, he also had friends who were Pharisees and later, Pharisees were to become Christians (Ac 15:5).

The Sadducees ran the temple and controlled the high priesthood. They were the aristocratic party. They were traditionalists. They rejected all religious writings except the Pentateuch and therefore threw out any theories —such as the resurrection of the dead—that were not found in those five books. The two parties were generally at war with each other, except on special occasions when they could both agree to hate someone else—such as at the trial of Jesus.

There was also a third group—the scribes. These were students of the Law, whose job was to interpret the Scriptures and pass on their knowledge. They built up a large body of oral law—unwritten decisions and pronouncements that sought to apply the Mosaic Law to daily life. They were mainly associated with the temple and the high priests. They are sometimes referred to in the New Testament as "lawyers" or "teachers of law."

This, then, was the religious background to the work of Jesus. He taught in synagogues, he was opposed by the Pharisees and Sadducees and questioned by the scribes. But he was not like any of these groups. Unlike them, he didn't just obey the Law, or interpret the Law, or enforce the Law. Instead, he *made* the Law—which is why people were always so struck by his authority.

Part Three
The New Testament

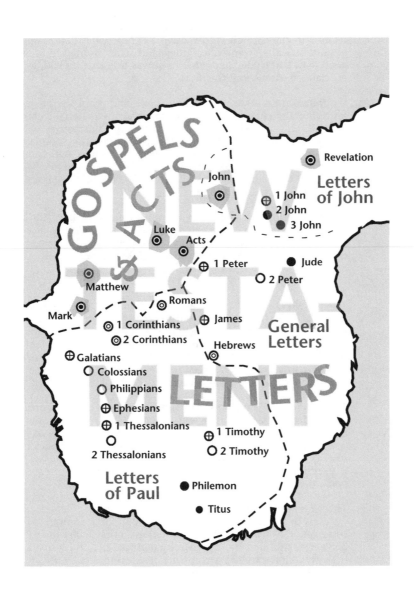

The New Testament

At first there were only the stories

After Jesus died, stories of his life and works were remembered and recounted. Jesus himself left no writings, but such was the power of his preaching and teaching that many of his most famous utterances were remembered by his followers. Initially these were simply passed from person to person, but gradually they were collected and written down.

As Christianity spread, there became a need for a more permanent record. Those who had witnessed Jesus firsthand were dying and there were new recruits in the Church who wanted to know what had happened. More importantly, they wanted to understand. They wanted to know why this good man had to die, and whether it was true that he had, as his followers claimed, risen from the dead.

So, four writers—Matthew, Mark, Luke and John—wrote accounts of Jesus' life, drawing on all the evidence and the material they could find. Before that, however, the leaders of the early Church were writing letters to their congregations. These were answering questions, explaining teaching, reminding the first followers of Jesus of what he had said. Gradually, these letters began to be passed round from one group of followers to another. Eventually the most authoritative of these were collected into what is now known as the New Testament.

The New Testament is probably the most influential book in the world. It has been translated into more languages—and read by more people—than any other book. Its teachings have dominated the social and political landscape of the Western world for 2,000 years.

Here are some things to bear in mind when reading the New Testament:

There is no church. Church, as we understand it, did not exist for the followers of Jesus. It is tempting to think that the moment Jesus rose, the first followers set up an entirely new organization, built some buildings with large pointy towers and started to wear dog collars. The first Christians were Jews and they did not see themselves as a separate organization. Even after Jewish opposition had led to the inevitable split, there were still no church buildings as we know them; the first followers met in houses.

They were not intending to found a new religion. There has always been a debate over whether Jesus intended to found Christianity or not, but certainly the early followers did not see Christianity as a departure from Judaism, but as a fulfillment. The New Testament sees itself, therefore, as a fulfillment of the Old Testament. That is why the New Testament is so full of references to the Old Testament: they weren't starting a new book, they were finishing the old one.

The New Testament is about Jesus. Whereas the Old Testament introduces us to a succession of figures, the figure of Jesus dominates the New Testament. His teaching, actions, opinions, miracles are the subject of this book and, although there are strong personalities and individuals among his early followers, their writings are all concerned with the life and teaching of this one man. He was the one toward whom the Old Testament had pointed: the Messiah, the chosen one, the fulfillment of prophecy.

Palestine in the time of Jesus

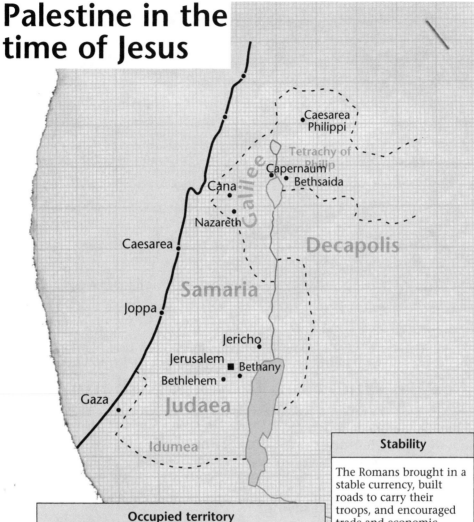

Caesarea Philippi

Tetrachy of Philip

Galilee

Capernaum
Bethsaida

Cana

Nazareth

Decapolis

Caesarea

Samaria

Joppa

Jericho

Jerusalem ■ Bethany
Bethlehem

Gaza

Judaea

Idumea

Occupied territory

By the time of Jesus' birth, Israel was an occupied territory, under the control of the Roman Empire. The nation of Israel had become "Palaestina" or "Palestine"—a Roman province ruled by a Roman governor. Palestine was further divided into a series of administrative regions such as Galilee, Judaea and Samaria. These regions were parceled out by the Romans to local rulers. Herod the Great controlled Judaea, and several more areas, for thirty-three years and on his death the territory was controlled by his three sons. Archelaus ruled Judaea, Samaria and Idumaea; Antipas ruled Galilee; Philip ruled several small regions northeast of Galilee. These rulers were the tetrachs—the Roman word for a ruler of any part of a province. There was also the Decapolis, a group of ten cities founded by Alexander the Great.

Stability

The Romans brought in a stable currency, built roads to carry their troops, and encouraged trade and economic expansion. There were common languages—not only Latin, but *koine*, or common Greek.

This stable background helped the spread of Christianity. Travel was easy, communication was straightforward and, while the Romans worshiped their own gods, they were generally tolerant of other religions and only ever interfered if their political interests were threatened.

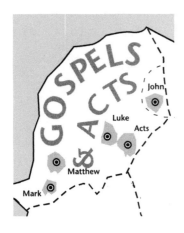

Gospels and Acts

The four gospels and the book of Acts record the origins and early history of Christianity. Gospel means "good news" and that is what Christians saw the content of these books to be—good news about Jesus.

Synoptic Gospels—Matthew, Mark, Luke

Out of the four gospels, Matthew, Mark and Luke are noticeably similar, covering many of the same events, using broadly similar language, and narrating the history in roughly the same order. This has led to them being dubbed the Synoptic Gospels (syn = "together" and optic = "seeing"). They see things, as it were, with the same eyes. Most experts agree that Mark was the earliest of the Gospels to be written. Both Luke and Matthew used Mark as one of the main ingredients of their own works.

The gospel of John

The fourth gospel, John, is very different. Written a lot later, it focuses on relatively few events in the life of Jesus, preferring instead to treat each incident in greater depth. We also get far more reported speeches of Jesus.

Acts

Or, to give it its full title, the Acts of the Apostles. This is a continuation of Luke's gospel, from the resurrection of Jesus through the foundation of the early Church. It focuses on three main characters: Peter, Paul and Jesus, present both after his resurrection and then through the Holy Spirit.

Where did they get it all from?

We have already seen how Luke and Matthew used Mark for much of their source material. But there were also other key sources for these books.

Memories and recollections

The Gospels draw heavily on firsthand memories and impressions. Acts, also, was written by someone who was actually there, and many times in the book Luke says "then *we* did this or that . . ."

Treasured sayings

Christians remembered the words and actions of Jesus. This was not a literate culture and people were used to memorizing facts, stories, important sayings. Some of these sayings were collected together and circulated among the early Church. Paul may have had one of these sayings in mind when he quotes Jesus in Acts 20:35: "It is more blessed to give than to receive" is a statement of Christ not found in any of the Gospels.

Early "gospels"

Although Mark is the first we have, that doesn't mean it was the first. There may well have been earlier biographies and accounts.

Inspiration

Certainly in the case of John's gospel, there is another element: divine inspiration. John knew Jesus and worked alongside him and spent many years thinking about and praying over what he had heard. His gospel, therefore, includes reflections and comments from the writer himself, ideas that came to him direct from God, rather than from other sources.

The main events of Jesus' life

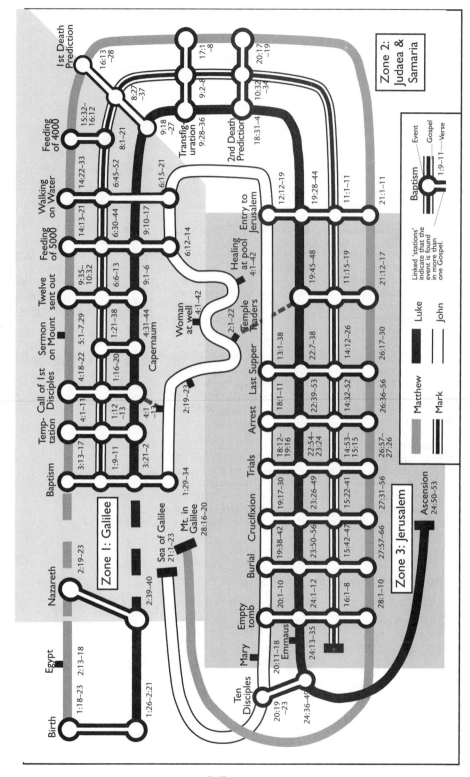

247

Matthew
Good news about the Messiah

Who: The traditional view is that this was written by Matthew the disciple. He was a tax collector, also known as Levi, who left his job to follow Jesus. Some experts question this on the basis that, if Matthew wrote it, why did he use so much out of Mark? After all, he was an eyewitness. The easiest answer to this objection is that he used Mark because he agreed with it. What we can say is that the author is Jewish, probably living in Palestine and addressing a Jewish audience.

When: Depends. Some say as early as the late 50s AD, others the 70s AD or even later.

What: Matthew is the most Jewish gospel. Although the gospel was written in Greek, it is obviously aimed at a Jewish readership. It is, for example, hugely concerned with the fulfillment of Old Testament prophecy and it uses typically Jewish terminology, such as calling Jesus the "Son of David."

Matthew has a specific aim: he wants to prove to his Jewish readers that Jesus is the Messiah, the Promised One. He begins his gospel by emphasizing Jesus' family link with David and he uses more quotes from the Old Testament than any other gospel writer to drive his point home.

Quick Guide

Author
Matthew, the Disciple

Type
Gospel

Purpose
To explain the life and work of Jesus to a mainly Jewish audience.

Key verses
28:19–20 "Go to the people of all nations and make them my disciples. Baptize them in the name of the Father, the Son, and the Holy Spirit, and teach them to do everything I have told you. I will be with you always, even until the end of the world."

If you remember one thing about this book . . .
Jesus was the Messiah—God's chosen one.

Your 15 minutes start now
Read chapters 1–2, 5–7, 17, 21, 25–28

Matthew's aim was to show that the Jewish faith found its ultimate expression in Christ, in Joshua ben Joseph, the Jewish rabbi from the small town of Nazareth. More, the implication was that if Jesus was the true Messiah, then Christians were the true Israel. That is why, in Matthew, Christ is depicted in his most kingly fashion, from the Magi coming to worship at the birth of the new king, to the triumphant entry into Jerusalem, to the sign attached to the cross. This man, argues Matthew, was the true King of the Jews.

The Route Through Matthew

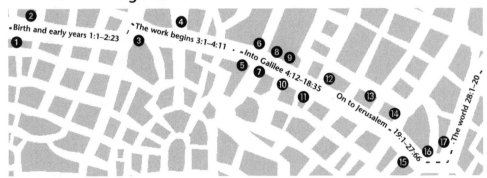

- Birth and early years 1:1–2:23
- The work begins 3:1–4:11
- Into Galilee 4:12–18:35
- On to Jerusalem 19:1–27:66
- The world 28:1–20

If he was a king, however, it was not how the Jews had been accustomed to expect him. This is one of the reasons why Matthew spends so much time pointing to prophecies that were fulfilled in the life of Christ. They had been looking for a particular kind of king—a warrior prince like King David—mighty in battle and, hopefully, quite handy with a harp. Matthew aims to show that all the prophecies point to Jesus and that, if they did not recognize him, it was because they were looking for the wrong things.

The emphasis on the kingship of Christ in Matthew is echoed by the amount of talk about his kingdom. Matthew repeatedly uses the phrase "the kingdom of heaven." This was the new Israel, a kingdom, not of earthly location, but carried everywhere in the hearts of the believers. Wherever two or three gathered for prayer, Christ would be with them and the kingdom would burst into life.

For all this Jewishness, Matthew is not a narrow gospel. This kingdom is open to all, from whatever nation. At the end of Matthew's gospel we get what is known as the Great Commission, where the disciples are told to go and spread the good news throughout the world (28:18–20).

Finally, there is also an emphasis on the rules of this kingdom. Matthew talks about righteousness—about what the people must do to be a part of the kingdom. If he is the king, then we are the subjects. Like God with the old kingdom of Israel, he will lead us, but we must follow.

POSTCARD
Welcome to Bethlehem!

Five miles south of Jerusalem, Bethlehem is a small, but important town.

Our humble community (formerly known as Ephrath) is associated with some of the greatest names in Israel's history. The great King David was born and raised here and, as Naomi's hometown, Bethlehem was the setting for much of the book of Ruth. It is also the traditional site of the tomb of Rachel, wife of Isaac.

Our importance is not just in the past, but in the future, for the prophet Micah has foretold that the Messiah himself will be born in this place.

If that is so, we can offer him a wide range of top-class accommodation. (Warning, guests are advised to book well in advance.)

L. Galilee

Nazareth

ISRAEL

R. Jordan

Jericho

JERUSALEM

Bethlehem

Dead Sea

Birth and early years   1:1–2:23

Only Matthew and Luke give details of Jesus' early life—and both offer different accounts.

❶ Family tree   1:1–17; Lk 3:23–38

Matthew begins, typically for this most Jewish of writers, with a long genealogy. It differs from that of Luke, choosing to begin with Abraham, the father of the Jewish people, while Luke goes back to Adam, the father of everyone. Both family trees follow the same line up to David, but differ after that. Various explanations have been put forward, but the most likely is that Matthew is following Joseph's line, while Luke is following Mary's. Matthew follows Jesus' legal parenthood, while Luke follows the bloodline. This, however, does not entirely remove the difficulties, since both genealogies end up with Joseph.

What is interesting about the lists is the people they include—not just the great and the good like David, Solomon, Isaac and Jacob, but also Tamar, the woman who posed as a whore; Rahab, the prostitute who hid the spies; Ruth, the faithful foreigner; and Bathsheba, the adulteress. The women and the foreigners also play their part. Although Matthew states that the genealogy is in blocks of fourteen generations, he "telescopes" it, omitting some of the lesser known or less important names. The number 14 seems to have been a significant number for him, possibly because it was a multiple of the perfect number 7, possibly because it was a numerical version of the name David.

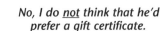

No, I do __not__ think that he'd prefer a gift certificate.

Things you don't find in the Bible: Three kings

These were not kings, nor were there three of them (I mean, there *might* have been three, but the Bible doesn't say). They were "Magi"—astrologers from the East, probably from Persia or Arabia. Herod's instruction that the men should kill all children under two implies that it may have taken the Magi up to two years to reach their destination.

❷ The Virgin Birth

1:18–24; Lk 1:26–38
▷180, 272

One of the most disputed passages of the Bible. Matthew's concern is to show that Jesus had a divine origin; that he was, literally, the Son of God. The story is developed much more fully in Luke, but only Matthew mentions Joseph's reaction. Joseph is described as a "righteous" man and his sensitivity shows this. This is not someone who will have the young girl punished, but someone who will do what he thinks is best for her.

There are significant differences between the two accounts of the birth. There is no mention in Matthew's account of the shepherds or the census, or the baby in the manger. And in Luke's account there is no reference to the Magi or Herod. Matthew begins in Bethlehem, a town significant both for its links with David and for the prediction in Micah that the chosen one would be born there. He leaves out the account of the census that Luke records. In Matthew's version, Jesus and his family flee to Egypt because of the king's wrath, but in Luke he appears to return home to Nazareth straight after visiting the temple.

Matthew's statement about Jesus being called a "Nazarene" (2:23) is mystifying, because the statement does not actually occur anywhere in the Old Testament. Probably, Matthew is referring to a tradition in the prophets that the Messiah would be despised, for at the time of his birth the phrase "Nazarene" was virtually synonymous with calling someone a "nobody."

PARALLEL LINES
Now where have I seen that before?

	Matthew	Luke	▷ Page
ANNOUNCED TO MARY	1:18	1:26–38	272
Announcement to Joseph	1:19–21	...	...
Mary's song	...	1:46–55	273
TRAVEL TO BETHLEHEM	2:1	2:1–7	273
Birth	...	2:6–7	273
Shepherds and angels	...	2:8–20	274
Presentation in the temple	...	2:21–38	274
Visit of the Magi	2:1–12	...	250
Flight to Egypt	2:13–15	...	274
Herod's revenge	2:16–18	...	251
RETURN TO NAZARETH	2:19–23	2:39–40	274

Let's *not* hear it for Herod

In Matthew's account, Jesus' birth is followed by drastic opposition from Herod the Great, who ruled from 37 BC to 4 AD. Herod was not a Jew, and was placed on the throne by the occupying Roman forces. This event is not recorded elsewhere in history, but it is not out of character for a man who murdered his wife, three sons, mother-in-law, brother-in-law, uncle and many others (although the cat probably escaped). He had his good side, though, in that he was responsible for rebuilding the temple in Jerusalem, begun in 20 BC. Not *much* of a good side, admittedly, but about the best you can expect from a psychopath.

The work begins   3:1–4:11

❸ Baptism of Jesus   Mk 1:9–11; Lk 3:21–22

This is the start of Jesus' ministry. He comes to John, not because he needs to repent—indeed, John recognizes his own unworthiness to perform the baptism—but because it is a demonstration to others of what they ought to do and an announcement of the arrival of the Messiah. Jesus' baptism brings together an appearance of the Trinity—the Father speaking from heaven, the Spirit descending on the Son.

❹ Temptation in the desert Mk 1:12–13; Lk 4:1–13

Jesus spends forty days and forty nights in the desert—in a conscious echo of some of the heroes of Israel's past. While there he is "tested." Jesus' temptations are not merely attempts by Satan to divert his ministry; they show us very clearly the type of Messiah he *wasn't*. He would not use his power for his own ends (4:3). He would not gain followers by pointless displays of miraculous power (4:5–6). He would not switch allegiance in order to gain earthly power and influence (4:8–9). Following his confrontation and defeat of this temptation, he is ready to go out and begin his ministry.

Brief Lives: John the Baptist

Background: John was Jesus' cousin, born around 7 BC, the son of the priest Zechariah and his wife Elizabeth.

Occupation: Prophet. Baptizer.

Achievements: John was the forerunner of Jesus, a wilder, rougher figure, who preached in the desert. He lived on a diet of grasshoppers and honey, which is a lot more appetizing than it sounds. (At least, I *hope* it's a lot more appetizing than it sounds.) John's message was simple: repent, for the kingdom of heaven is coming. Repentance called for the people to change their hearts and make a new start. He would baptize anyone who truly repented—but he sent away the Sadducees and Pharisees because they did not show any signs of genuine repentance (3:7–10). As a symbol of their repentance, John baptized people in the Jordan —drenching them with water to symbolize their new cleanliness.

Never noted for his tact, John incurred the wrath of Herod Antipas by criticizing his marriage to his brother-in-law's ex-wife. Herod, who had a sneaking admiration for John, was tricked into beheading the prophet (Mt 14:1–12; Lk 9:7–9; Mk 6:14–29).

Character: John presented something of a wild figure—much like the description of Elijah. He lived on a diet of insects and honey and wore rough clothes.

Pros: Radical. Honest. Unafraid.

Cons: Difficult to cater for.

The work in Galilee   4:12–18:35

❺ Calling of the disciples   4:18–22
Mk 1:16–20; Lk 5:1–11 ▷283

Disciples were special followers of a particular teacher. We know that John had disciples (Mk 2:18), as did some of the Old Testament prophets such as Isaiah (Is 8:16). Jesus appears to have two levels of disciples: a larger group of seventy (Lk 10:1, 23) and a smaller, inner circle of twelve (Mt 10:1). These are not just here to learn, but to be trained to carry on the task after the leader has gone.

Jesus heals and teaches

4:12–25;
Lk 6:17–19 ▷281

Jesus' ministry was holistic—calling to all parts of humanity. He came to teach about God, but he was more than a teacher. He came to cast out demons, but he was more than an exorcist. He came to heal people, but he was more than a medicine man. He came to free prisoners, but he was more than a revolutionary. He came to feed the hungry and clothe the naked, but he was more than a charity worker. He was God, and that meant that he attended to all levels of human life.

❻ The Sermon on the Mount

5:1–7:29

Unique to Matthew, this large section is probably a composite collection of linked teaching, rather than a record of one single discourse. Luke has much of the same material, but a lot of it is spread throughout his book, rather than brought together in one place. Matthew is probably consciously placing Jesus alongside Moses. Moses came down from Mount Sinai with the Law, Jesus' sermon on a mount is a new law, a new foundation for life.

Ideals

Jesus speaks in ideals. Indeed, many have found the standards set in the sermon utterly unrealistic, but there is no indication here that Jesus is speaking hypothetically. Jesus frequently spoke in ideals, just as God did through the Law in the Old Testament. God, after all, told Israel to "be holy, just as I am holy" (Le 11:44), and there is no indication that he was joking. The Sermon on the Mount, therefore, sets out a target, an ideal standard of human behavior for us all to aim at.

Reversal

The kingdom of heaven that Jesus talks about is an upside-down world. In the Sermon on the Mount, it is the poor who are blessed and the humble who receive the reward. This kingdom does not fight its enemies, but forgives them. It is a kingdom intended, not for the powerful and the rich, but for the poor and the outcast and those who have no other supporter than God.

The spirit of the Law

The relationship of Jesus' teaching to the Law is a matter of much debate and disagreement. What Jesus says in the sermon is that his disciples must go beyond the Law. By his time the Law had become a thing of ritual and regime, a rigid set of rules people had to follow. Jesus dismisses this. Indeed, on several occasions he deliberately breaks the rules. What Jesus preaches is the spirit of the Law. He sums up the Law in one sentence, almost completely ignoring the rules and heading straight for the heart (7:12). It is as bad to think about sinning as to sin itself. God demands obedience in all areas of our life—including the part between the ears.

The Beatitudes

5:1–12

The first part of the sermon is made up of the beatitudes—a series of nine blessings showing a complete reversal of accepted values. It is not the powerful but the meek who will really inherit the earth. When difficult times happen they are times of rejoicing—not because of what is happening on earth, but because of what is happening in heaven (5:12).

How we should live

5:13–6:18

After the Beatitudes there are a series of instructions on how we should act. Those who follow Christ are to be the "salt of the earth." Salt is used for flavoring—for making food taste better. It is also used for preserving.

Details, Details . . .
The Lord's Prayer
(6:9–15; Lk 11:2–4)

Wrongly titled, really, since it's actually the disciples' prayer—or, at least, the prayer that Jesus taught them.

This is one of the central points of the Sermon on the Mount and picks up many of the themes of the discourse. It talks of the kingdom of God being made real on earth (6:9–10), of reliance on God to provide the food we need (6:11), and of conditional forgiveness—we are forgiven, but we should also forgive (6:12). Jesus was later to illustrate this in a parable (Mt 18:21–35).

It is, in fact, a prayer that we should be able to put into practice the kind of love that Jesus talks about in the sermon that surrounds it.

In the same way, our behavior should make life better for people and save them.

This behavior is outlined in a series of examples dealing with hatred and revenge (5:21–26, 38–42), adultery (5:27–30), divorce (5:31–32), speaking the truth (5:33–37), and love (5:43–48). Chapter 6 moves into religious areas, with Jesus' teaching on giving (6:1–4), prayer (6:5–15) and fasting (6:16–18) with the emphasis on the spirit behind the action, rather than the legalistic observance of the Law itself. The hypocrites' observance of the Law misses the point entirely: the value is not in the action itself, but in the spirit in which it is done.

Trust in God   6:19–7:28
Finally, there is a section dealing with our trust in God and reliance on his provision. We are enjoined not to store up money and riches on earth (6:19–24), not to worry about the future (6:25–34), to refrain from self-righteous judgment (7:1–5), and to go to God for all our needs (7:7–11).

The section on judging others is about hypocrisy rather than judgment itself. Where people are acting in an evil manner, it is right that we should condemn their behavior. Jesus does not call on us to accept any behavior, or to refrain from judgment altogether. What he warns us about is self-righteous judgment: we should always look at our own actions and motives with as critical an eye as we are keen to turn on others.

The Golden Rule   7:12; Lk 11:9–13
The spirit of the discourse is summed up in what has been called the Golden Rule: "Treat others as you want them to treat you. This is what the Law and the prophets are all about."

❼ The Gadarene swine
8:28–34; Mk 2:1–12; Lk 5:17–26 ▷278

From the start of his ministry, Jesus went about healing those who were possessed by demons. In our age, demon possession is the subject of some controversy. Some deny it altogether, arguing that what is meant here is a mental health problem, or epilepsy. Others argue that demon possession is real and that exorcism it is still part of the Church's ministry today. Whatever your view, there is no doubt that the events detailed in the Gospels have a supernatural aspect and that the healing and release experienced by those whom Jesus helped are immense. God's kingdom extends over all the areas of our lives: physical, mental and spiritual. God is the God not only of the seen, but of the unseen.

This supernatural power had an unsettling effect on those who watched it. Those critical of Jesus accused him of operating in the name of Beelzebub, arguing that only a ruler of demons could have power over demons (12:22–29; Mk 3:20–30; Lk 11:14–23). Jesus, however, made it clear that he was operating in God's power; his power was a testimony to the might and immediacy of God's kingdom (12:28).

Faith and miracles
8:1–9:38

Chapters 8 and 9 contain instances of healing, including returning sight and speech (9:27–34), healing leprosy (8:1–4), raising the dead (9:18–26) and even controlling the weather (8:23–27). The faith of the army commander (8:10) contrasts with the panic of the disciples during the storm. These are signs of who Jesus really is. His power over life and death, and over the natural world, his ability to "know" people's thoughts, and, most importantly, his claim to be able to forgive sins, all point one way. In the Jewish mind, only God could forgive sins. Jesus claims that he too has that power (9:1–8).

The wrong sort of people
9:9–13; Mk 2:13–17;
Lk 5:27–32

One thing that really annoyed the Pharisees was that Jesus spent so much time with the wrong sort of people. He enjoyed going to parties—so much so that he was even accused of being a drunkard (11:19). And he associated quite freely with sinners, including tax collectors and prostitutes. Jesus' answer is simple: they are exactly the kind of people who need God's mercy and forgiveness.

❽ The sick woman and the dying girl
9:18–26; Mk 5:21–43; Lk 8:40–56

A woman who has been "bleeding" for twelve years touches Jesus. This was a severe menstrual discharge that under the old Law made her ritually and permanently unclean. Her faith in Jesus not only heals her physically, but purifies her in terms of the Law. Then Jesus raises a dead girl to life, clearing out the mourners and the funeral musicians, and waking her from her "sleep."

Jesus' healing, therefore, is a physical sign of his spiritual power. He not only heals people, he forgives sins. He heals the blind and opens their eyes to faith. He stops the bleeding and makes someone "pure."

❾ The work of the apostles   10:1–42

A disciple means a "learner." An apostle means "one who is sent out." In this chapter, "disciples" become "apostles," sent out by Jesus to carry the message into the towns of Galilee. Luke records that Jesus prayed all night before selecting the twelve.

Landmark: The Kingdom of Heaven

Jesus talks repeatedly about the kingdom of heaven (or the kingdom of God in Luke's gospel). "Go and tell people that the kingdom of God is near," he tells his disciples.

Jesus was not talking about a worldly kingdom, but a kingdom that crossed borders and was beyond nationality. He was fundamentally talking of the way in which our lives are ruled by God. For Jesus, people entered the kingdom when they gave their allegiance to God, when they acknowledged him as their ruler.

What Jesus was concerned about when talking of the kingdom was the way in which life was lived. Being part of the kingdom meant living in a certain way, following the unique laws of the kingdom. There are no social distinctions—the poor and the outcasts are specifically invited to be a part of it. It is a kingdom of forgiveness and love. One day, the kingdom will be a physical reality as well, when Jesus returns. In the meantime, it is up to all of his followers to act as true representatives of God's country.

Details, Details . . .
Tax collectors (9:9)

Tax collectors were reviled people in the time of Christ. They basically paid the Romans for the tax-collecting franchise. They would buy the right to collect taxes on behalf of the Romans, and then recoup their initial outlay by adding a percentage on top of whatever taxes they collected. It was a mix of collaboration with the enemy and plain, old-fashioned extortion.

Details, Details . . .
Wineskins (9:17)
Mk 2:18–22; Lk 5:33–39

New wine is still fermenting, which causes expansion. Therefore, if you put it in old, brittle leather wineskins, they would crack and break. Jesus is saying that the old ways are too brittle to contain his message. The Pharisees with their hard, inflexible legalism couldn't cope with the joyful salvation brought through Christ.

The list of apostles in Matthew differs slightly from that in Luke, but the "Judas, son of James" in Luke is the same as the Thaddeus in Matthew and Mark. They are a mixed group, including not only the fishermen Simon Peter, John, James and Andrew, but also Matthew the tax collector, and Simon the Zealot (Zealots were a radical political group of which Simon may have been a member before joining Jesus).

Jesus was aware that the task he was giving them had dangers and difficulties. Some places would not welcome them. And Jesus' message was one that brought conflict, even though it was a message of peace and love (10:34–39). Jesus even came up against his own family, who thought he was mad (Mk 3:21). Many of those who have followed Jesus down the years have encountered fierce opposition and even martyrdom. The conflict that Jesus predicted for his followers is still around today.

PARALLEL LINES
Now where have I seen that before?

	Matthew	Mark	Luke	John	▷ Page
Jesus and the law	12:1–8	2:23–28	6:1–5	...	265
Jesus and parables	13:10–17	4:10–12	8:9–10	...	265
Death of John the Baptist	14:1–12	6:14–29	9:7–9	...	266
Feeding the thousands	14:13–21	22:34–40	9:10–17	6:1–13	267

Puzzling Points
The sin against the Holy Spirit (12:30–32; Mk 3:28–29; Lk 12:10)

There is, apparently, an unforgivable sin. The puzzling point is working out what it actually is. Jesus describes it as "speaking against the Holy Spirit." The context of this statement—where Jesus has been accused of casting out demons by satanic power—implies that he is talking about a complete inversion of values. Someone who deliberately calls evil "good" and good "evil" cannot be forgiven because they no longer know that they are sinning. The Bible is clear that anyone who asks for forgiveness will receive mercy—ask and it will be given to you. But those who call God evil can never ask for forgiveness, because there is no one to ask.

Jesus and his hometown
13:53–58; Mk 6.1–6; Lk 4.16–30; Jn 6.41–42

The response of the people in Jesus' hometown is more willful obstinacy than anything else. These people knew Jesus when he was growing up, a fact that colors their entire perception of him. He is described as "the son of the carpenter" in Matthew and as "the carpenter" in Mark, indicating that for many years he was a simple workman like his father. The word used is *tekton*, which can also mean "craftsman." A *tekton* was not just a carpenter but a sort of odd-job man, one who would come round and fix your windows or mend the door or make a table. They could not believe that the odd-job man was a teacher and healer of power.

❿ Walking on water
14:22–32; Mk 6:45–52; Jn 6:15–21

After all the pressure of so many people around him, Jesus sends his disciples away by boat. He escapes to pray and to avoid the crowd, who, as John records, were determined to make him king. Jesus has his own timetable. The key thing here is not just a display of supernatural power for its own sake, but as a response to the fact that the disciples were in difficulty. Mark places the time between 3 a.m. and 6 a.m.—that dead time of night when all seems dark and hopeless. And the remarkable thing is not that Peter sinks, but that he manages a few steps before his faith falters. Jesus' rescue of Peter opens the disciples' eyes to the truth: "You really are the Son of God!"

The sign of Jonah
16:1–4; Mk 8:11–13; Lk 12:54–56 ▷279

⑪ Who are you?
16:13–20; Mk 8:27–30; Lk 9:18–21

This encounter takes place near Caesarea Philippi. The town was originally called Paneas, but it was rebuilt and renamed in honor of Philip the Tetrarch, and Caesar, the Roman emperor.

It is in the shadow of this tribute to earthly rulers, therefore, that Jesus asks his disciples the one crucial question: "Who do you say I am?" (16:15). They had already answered this at a number of other times and places (Jn 1:41, 45; Mk 1:16–20; 2:14), but as the time grew nearer for Jesus to go to Jerusalem it was even more important for them to be sure that he was the Messiah. The times ahead would test their faith to its very limit.

Peter's answer that Jesus is "the Messiah, the Son of the living God" is commended and Jesus changes his name—just as God changed the names of Jacob and Abraham. The exact nature of the name change is the matter of some debate. Jesus actually used the term *Kepha* or *Cephas*, the Aramaic term for "rock." (We get Peter from the Greek word for rock, *Petros*.)

The cost of discipleship
16:21–28; Mk 8:31–9:1; Lk 9:22–27

Jesus counsels the disciples not to tell anyone of their conclusion. Peter is shocked at Jesus' prophecy of the future for him, but Jesus rebukes him. The disciples, like most people, believed that the Messiah would bring military glory and material riches. There will be glory, but it will be a heavenly glory, and it will only be achieved through suffering and death.

⑫ The transfiguration
17:1–13; Mk 9:2–13; Lk 9:28–36

Jesus, accompanied by a handful of his closest disciples, goes to a mountain. It is not clear where this was; possibly it was Jebel Jermaq in the north of Palestine. Matthew says it took them six days to get there, Luke says eight days, but whoever was correct, it was obviously a long journey.

As they are praying, Jesus is "transfigured"—his clothing and face shine with an incredibly bright light. The

Puzzling Points
Dog food
(Mt 15:21–28; Mk 7:24–30)

A woman possessed by a demon follows Jesus. At first glance, Jesus appears to give a very negative answer, claiming that he was only sent for the Jews and talking of Gentiles as "dogs." In fact he is deliberately mocking this viewpoint. Just as the heart makes a person clean or unclean, the heart can make someone a true Israelite. Although Jesus sent his apostles initially to the Jews he did not restrict his ministry in this way. Jesus' questions may be seen as an ironic challenge to the traditional view of the Messiah. He was not just here for the Jews, but for the whole world.

Puzzling Points
On this rock (Mt 16:18)

There has been enormous debate about what Jesus means by the phrase "on this rock I will build my church." Some believe that it refers to Peter himself, who is given absolute authority and the leadership of the Church. While Peter did go on to be the effective leader of the early Church, there is no strong evidence that he was viewed as some kind of ordained leader.

More likely is that "the rock" Jesus was talking about was Peter's confession. The Church will be built on "the rock of faith"—faith in Jesus as the Messiah. Therefore the keys of the kingdom will be given to all those who believe— a promise that is echoed in Matthew 18:18.

disciples who are there see two other figures with him: Moses the great law-giver, and Elijah the great prophet. Peter suggests making three tents or booths for the great figures, but God rebukes him. Jesus is not on a par with Moses and Elijah: he is greater than them.

Jesus again warns the disciples not to reveal this until later. The appearance of Elijah prompts the disciples to ask why he had not appeared earlier—it was a traditional view that the appearance of the Messiah would be preceded by the return of Elijah (based on Mal 4:5). Jesus answers that John the Baptist was the embodiment of Elijah.

Jesus predicts his death
17:22–23; Mk 9:30–32; Lk 9:43–45

From now on, Jesus speaks increasingly about what must happen in Jerusalem and the shadow of the cross falls across these chapters. In Mark's account the disciples are afraid to ask any more questions: they don't like what they are hearing, they prefer not to believe it.

Sin and forgiveness
17:6–35; Mk 9:42–48; Lk 15:3–7

> ### Details, Details . . .
> ### The temple tax (17:24–27)
>
> The temple tax was originally a voluntary tax of a third of a shekel (Ne 10:32), but in Jesus' time it had become a compulsory half-shekel tax payable by every male twenty and over. Jesus uses it as a kind of parable, claiming exemption because he is, in fact, the king. The whole affair has a kind of lighthearted, almost jokey feel about it, down to the miraculous provision of the money in the mouth of a fish.

Jesus is outspoken on both the causes and the response to sin. First, those who cause others to sin are warned. Jesus' "little followers" are all those who have become like children and entered the kingdom. Not children, therefore, but the *childlike*. There are heavy penalties for those who lead others into sin. This is not to negate personal responsibility and, to emphasize this, Jesus repeats the message from the Sermon on the Mount: if your eye offends you, get rid of it. Do all you can to avoid sinning, and don't cause others to sin either.

But what if you do sin? The second part of this discourse deals with forgiveness and redemption. It tells of the Good Shepherd who will go to the limit to find one sheep. God *never* gives up on anyone, so when people sin we, too, should do all we can to put the situation right, first one-to-one, then with some others as witnesses, then before the church (18:15–16).

Anyone who refuses to listen must be treated like "an unbeliever or a tax collector" (18:17). And how did Jesus treat these? He spent time with them, associated with them, died for them. Peter asks how many times we should forgive and is told "seventy times seven" (18:21–22). Peter probably selected the perfect number seven as his upper limit for forgiveness, but Jesus multiplied it to imply a number beyond measure. God *never* gives up on anyone. As I might have mentioned before.

On to Jerusalem   19:1–27:66

Jesus and divorce   19:1–12; Mk 10:1–12
Jesus emphasizes the importance of the marriage vows and the need for lifelong commitment. In New Testament times only the husband could divorce his wife; she could not, unless there were exceptional circumstances, divorce her husband. Jesus argues for a much greater commitment. He does not rule out divorce completely, but he only permits it in the case of "serious sexual sin" or, in some versions "marital unfaithfulness." There

is considerable debate about what this means—some argue that it means repeated and prolonged acts of adultery rather than a one-time affair. The principle was that everything possible should be done to achieve forgiveness and reconciliation.

Jesus and riches 19:16–30; Mk 10:17–31; Lk 18:18–30

Wealth gets in the way of worship. In the Sermon on the Mount, Jesus pointed out that a man cannot serve two masters, that money becomes a god to rival the one true God. Here he issues a direct challenge to the rich young man before him. How much do you want this? How much, really, are you prepared to follow me?

Most commentators have argued that this particular incident does not mean that we all have to give up our possessions; they argue that it was a specific response to a specific inquiry. Jesus identified the one thing that was stopping this young man and challenged him on it. But Jesus widens the discussion from one rich man to rich people in general. The popular interpretation that the "eye of the needle" was a gate in Jerusalem that camels could get through providing they weren't carrying too much is without any evidence whatsoever. Jesus means what he says: for rich people to get into the kingdom of heaven is as difficult as threading a large, bad-tempered beast of burden through the smallest gap imaginable. In the end, all we can do is test ourselves and our attitudes—and rely on the grace of God.

PARALLEL LINES
Now where have I seen that before?

	Matthew	Mark	Luke	John	▷ Page
James and John	20:20–28	10:35–45	...	...	267
The temple	21:12–17	11:15–19	19:45–48	2:13–22	281

⓭ The entry into Jerusalem 21:1–11; Mk 11:1–11; Lk 19:28–38; Jn 12:12–19 ▷286

Jesus approaches Jerusalem from the east. His entry is, at last, a public expression of his Messiahship—he enters the city riding a colt that had not previously been ridden, in fulfillment of a prophecy in Zechariah 9:9. John and Matthew include the detail that it was a humble donkey he was riding and not the horse of a warrior or an earthly prince. Nevertheless, the fact that the people think the time has come is evident. They throw their cloaks down before him, they wave palm branches and shout "Hosanna," a word that means "save us now."

The true workers 21:23–22:22

The religious leaders start to question Jesus' authority, with both sides seeking to undermine that authority (21:23–27; 22:15–33, 41–46), but he turns the tables on them. More, he tells stories that completely undermine not only their authority, but their self-righteousness. In a series of parables, he shows that the kingdom of heaven will not be filled with those you might expect.

The parable of the two sons in the vineyard contrasts the elder son who disobeyed his father with the younger son who obeyed. The moral is clear:

Landmark: Messiah

The Hebrew word means "anointed," a rescuer sent from God to save his chosen people. The Greek word for "anointed" is *christos*, from which we get Christ.

Of course, people only need saving when they are in peril, but the history of Israel from the time of the prophets onwards is of a nation constantly under attack and oppression. Between the two Testaments, Israel was occupied first by the Greeks and then by the Romans, and the cry for the Messiah to come was ever more desperate. The Jews interpreted the Messiah as being primarily a military hero, someone who would drive out the forces of occupation from their country. Before Jesus there were those who claimed to be the Messiah. Judas of Galilee led an insurrection in 6 AD and there were others, including Simon of Jericho and Athronges, a shepherd who claimed to be a king. All of these revolutions were brutally suppressed.

Jesus was recognized by many as the Messiah, but tried to play down these expectations. He didn't like to be called Messiah and appears to have been reluctant to apply the term to himself. The point was that he was not the figure they wanted him to be, and he had no intention of being connected with violence and insurrection. He was preaching a revolutionary message and he was setting up a new kingdom, but it was not in the way that the Jews were expecting.

In the light of Christ's crucifixion and resurrection, his followers understood that he really was the Messiah and they began to see how the many prophecies of the Messiah were fulfilled in Jesus. Gradually the word *christos* turned into Christ and became more of a name. But it means, really, what it always meant: Jesus Christ, the anointed one, the Messiah.

the priests and the Pharisees might have been first, but their place will be taken by the "less worthy" tax collectors and the prostitutes. Unlike the religious leaders, they actually believe. The message—that God's kingdom has been taken from the so-called holy people and given to those who deserve it—is backed up in two other parables: the tenants in the vineyard and the parable of the banquet. The tenants do not treasure the property that has been given to them and treat the messengers from the owner with disdain. In the end they are evicted. It parallels Israel's response, over the centuries, to the prophets and those calling for repentance. The banquet guests refuse to come and in the end their places of honor are given to those on the street corners, good and bad alike. God chose Israel to join him at the feast, but they found better things to do.

The greatest commandment
22:34–40; Mk 12:28–34; Lk 10:25–28

The relentless testing of Jesus by the experts in the Law leads to one of the greatest insights in the Bible. Asked to choose which is the most important commandment, Jesus sums up the entire Law and the prophets in two simple statements: love God and love your neighbor.

The teachers of the Law
23:1–36; Mk 12:38–40; Lk 11:37–52

A coruscating attack on the teachers of the Law, who preach without practicing (23:3) and burden people with guilt (23:4). Interested merely in display (23:5–6), not only are they not going to heaven, they also lock others out (23:14). They fuss over the minutiae, but fail to see the bigger picture (23:23–24). Like painted tombs, they are attractive on the outside but dead within (23:27–28).

The end times
24:1–25:46; Mk 13; Lk 21 ▷285

⑭ The anointing at Bethany
26:6–13; Mk 14:3–9; Lk 12:1–8; Jn 12:1–8

While at Bethany a few miles outside Jerusalem, Jesus has his head anointed by a woman. Judas objects, pointing out that the money for the highly expensive perfume could have been spent on the poor. And so it could. But there is a time for worship and a time for preparation. In this context, Jesus recognizes that the act is one of worship and of preparation for his burial to come. John's account names the woman as Mary and describes the perfume as being poured on his feet. Although some believe it to be a different occasion, it does seem to be in the same place at the same time.

The plot and the trial
26:1–5; Mk 14; Lk 22; Jn 11–13 ▷289

After his attacks on the religious establishment, they plot to kill Jesus. They recruit Judas Iscariot into their plan. Why Judas did it has been the subject of enormous debate. Some argue that he was trying to force Jesus into revealing himself. Others that he was greedy for the money. Some believe he was disenchanted with the kind of Messiah Jesus was turning out to be. Whatever the case—and we will never know—Judas agrees to deliver Jesus into the hands of his enemies.

⑮ The Passover meal
26:17–45; Mk 14; Lk 22; Jn 13 ▷288

It is Passover—the time when the Jews celebrate their rescue from Egypt, when they recall how the blood of the lamb was painted on the doorways to spare them all from death. Jesus uses the occasion to prepare his disciples for what must inevitably follow and institutes a meal to be eaten in remembrance of him.

Puzzling Points
Why doesn't Jesus want people to know who he is?

It's called the "Messianic secret." Several times in the Gospels Jesus counsels people not to tell what he has done for them, or not to tell people that he is the Messiah. Why should he do this?

The most likely explanation is tied in with the expectations of the people. It was not that Jesus was denying that he was the Messiah, rather that he was not the type of Messiah they wanted. He was refusing to be pigeonholed, he was refusing to be the kind of Jewish superman of the popular imagination. There were times when the people wanted to crown him king (Jn 6:15), but his was not an earthly kingdom, it was a heavenly one.

It is a sign of how deep this popular perception of the Messiah had gone that Peter, after acknowledging Jesus as the chosen one, simply cannot believe that God will allow him to suffer and die. Even his disciples thought like everyone else.

Jesus knew he still had a lot to do. He had teaching to impart and a message to get across; he did not want to be forced prematurely into a confrontation with the Romans or the religious authorities. He knew that this would happen, but it was to happen at the right time.

After the meal, Jesus goes to the Mount of Olives to pray. He is so sad that he feels as though he is dying (26:38), but even so his disciples are unable to stay awake with him and pray. He is increasingly alone. It was the custom in Israel for men to greet each other with a kiss on the cheek. Judas uses this to identify Jesus to the guards—although it is hard to imagine that they needed much help, given Jesus' notoriety since entering the city. After a brief fight he is arrested and taken away for trial.

Peter and Judas   18:15–18, 25–27

Peter—in a blind panic—denies that he ever knew Jesus. This is Cephas, the strong one, the one always willing to jump in feet first, the one who tried to walk on water. And yet, at the point of trial, he turns away.

⑯ Crucifixion and death   27:31–56;
Mk 15:22–41; Lk 23:27–49; Jn 19:17–30 ▷290

Jesus is savagely beaten, dressed up in a mockery of royal robes and taken out to be killed. On the cross he is taunted and abused. On either side of him are two thieves. Matthew reports that they said cruel things to him, Luke that one of them was deeply affected by this man. There is no real contradiction here: a man can start off mocking and be changed by the person's response. Clearly the second criminal realized that this was no ordinary man; his reward was that he was to be with Jesus that night in paradise.

Burial 27:57–61 ▷304

His death is attended by some of his followers and family—watching from a distance. The body is taken down and put in the tomb of a supporter. Tombs in the Middle East were not subterranean like in our culture. They were caves cut into the rock and sealed with boulders. Pilate puts guards on the tomb to ensure that Jesus' body is not taken by his followers.

⑰ Resurrection 28:1–10; Mk 16:1–8
Lk 24:1–12; Jn 20:1–10 ▷291

The women were the first to see the truth. They find that the tomb is empty, the guards are on the ground. An earthquake has struck and an angel has rolled away the huge stone as if it were the wheel of a cart. The guards positioned there by Pilate have fainted with fear. The women hear from the angel that the Lord has risen and rush to tell the disciples. On the way they encounter Jesus himself. They pass on the message from Jesus for the disciples to go to Galilee. Matthew also uses this occasion to counter a specific story that had been circulated since the time of the event. Sensitive to the accusation that Jesus' disciples stole the body, Matthew specifically denies it. He claims that this was a story put about by the soldiers who were bribed to spread the rumor around.

The world 28:1–20

Matthew ends his account with what is called the Great Commission. Although Matthew says that the disciples were there, the implication is that more than just the inner circle were present. In verse 10, Jesus instructs his "followers" to go to Galilee, so it may well be that more than the eleven were present.

If so, it would reinforce the fact that this instruction is for all Jesus' followers and not just for the original eleven. It is an instruction to the Church as a whole. The disciples—all disciples—are to go from Jerusalem to the ends of the earth, spreading the good news. The news about Jesus is for all people in all nations, and Jesus will be with his followers every step of the way.

Puzzling Points
It is finished

Jesus' cry on the cross—*Eli, Eli, lama sabachtani*—My God, My God why have you deserted me?—is probably a quote from Psalm 22, but as it is Aramaic and the psalm is in Hebrew this is open to debate. The New Testament offers no explanation of this cry and it may, in fact, be beyond our comprehension. Certainly it expresses the humiliation and extreme sense of loneliness Jesus must have been feeling.

Jesus' final shout is also ambiguous at first reading. Matthew refers to one final shout (27:50). "It is finished!" can mean many things in the context. Ultimately your interpretation of these cries depends on your view of Jesus. Those who do not believe in Jesus' resurrection tend to view it as an admission of failure: "The game is over. I've lost." Those who view him as savior see it as the cry of someone who has reached the end of the race: "The task is done. I have endured."

Landmark: The Names of Jesus

Throughout the Bible there are many names and terms given to Jesus.

Proper names

Jesus

The Greek version of the Hebrew name Joshua. The name means "God saves."

Christ

A version of the Greek word *christos*, meaning "Messiah."

Terms Jesus used for himself

Alpha and Omega

The beginning and the end. Alpha and Omega are the first and last letters of the Greek alphabet (Re 1:8).

Bread of life

The fundamental thing we need to nourish and sustain us. Also used the term "bread of heaven" referring to the manna sent by God to keep the Israelites alive in the desert (Jn 6:35, 41).

Cornerstone

The foundation stone used for any building. The one stone on which all the rest of the building depends (Ep 2:20).

Good shepherd

Protecting and rescuing his sheep (Jn 10:11).

Light of the world

Bringing hope, revealing truth, banishing darkness (Jn 9:5).

Messiah

Jesus only publicly used this term during his trial. It means "God's anointed king" (Mt 26:63–64).

Son of man

A difficult term that refers to Jesus' Messiahship and seems to indicate that he is the "supreme" or "ideal" man (Mk 8:38; Lk 17:24).

Terms others used to describe Jesus

High priest

Someone who can permanently mediate between man and God (He 6:20).

Immanuel

A name that means "God is with us" (Mt 1:23).

Savior

The one who destroys death and rescues those who trust him (2 Ti 1:10).

Word

With God at creation, the reason behind the universe (Jn 1:1).

Mark
The simple truth

Who: There is no named author in the gospel, but tradition ascribes the book to John Mark.

John Mark lived in Jerusalem with his mother Mary during the early Church times (Ac 12:12). His home was a meeting place for the first Christians and it has even been speculated that it was the location of the Last Supper. Later he accompanied Paul and Barnabas (who was also Mark's cousin) on their first missionary journey (Ac 13:4–13). Eventually he lived in Rome, where he was probably with Peter (1 Pe 5:13). It seems likely then, that if we accept Mark as the author, this gospel was written in Rome while Mark was working alongside Peter. This theory is backed up by references from early Church historians (Papias of Hierapolis writing in AD 130 records that an old man told him that Mark wrote down Peter's recollections of Jesus' life), as well as by the amount of Latin terms that creep into the gospel.

When: Sometime between AD 58 and 65. A Thursday.

What: Mark's is the most action-packed gospel, mainly because it is the shortest. There is nothing about Jesus' birth and upbringing, and no details about his age or the length of his ministry. The gospel begins with John the Baptist and Jesus' baptism. It also ends the most abruptly—with no resurrection appearance, just two women, an empty tomb and an angel with a message from God. Although some versions of Mark include alternative, longer endings, these are probably editorial additions to the original gospel.

Mark's theme is simple: Jesus Christ is the Son of God. This is recognized not only by his Jewish followers, but also by people like the Roman centurion as Christ is on the cross. This factor is important, because Mark was probably writing for a predominantly Gentile, Roman audience. So Mark is careful to explain Jewish customs and translate Aramaic words and phrases.

Quick Guide
Author
John Mark
Type
Gospel
Purpose
Telling the story of Jesus to a predominantly Roman audience.
Key verse
16:6 "Don't be alarmed! You are looking for Jesus from Nazareth, who was nailed to a cross. God has raised him to life, and he isn't here."
If you remember one thing about this book . . .
Jesus had an action-packed life, but it was also one of suffering and service.
Your 15 minutes start now
Read chapters 1, 6, 10, 14–16

The Route Through Mark

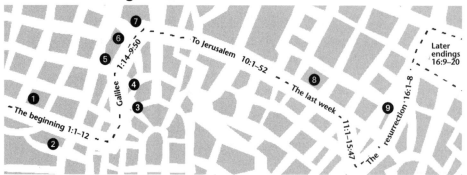

264

The beginning 1:1–12

❶ John the Baptist 1:1–8

Mark's gospel begins with a bang—or a yell, at least. There is nothing of the birth of Jesus, just the sudden arrival of John the Baptist shouting in the wilderness and preparing the world for the ministry of Christ.

❷ Baptism and temptation 1:9–12

Mark spends much less time on the temptation of Christ than the other gospels. He records no individual temptations, just that Satan tested him. He also records that angels took care of him and that wild animals surrounded him. He is not mentioning this to depict Jesus as some kind of nature boy; on the contrary, the description is probably intended to show how dangerous the experience was.

Galilee 1:14–9:50

❸ The first disciples 1:14–20 ▷252

Jesus and the Law 2:23–28; Mt 12:1–8; Lk 6:1–5

The relationship between Jesus' teaching and life and the Law in the Old Testament is a difficult one to work out. Jesus himself declared that he had come not to break the Law but to fulfill it (5:17–20). Yet he and his disciples often incurred the wrath of the Pharisees because of their attitude to the Law, especially their attitude to the Sabbath. All four gospels record that he healed people on the Sabbath—which the legalism of the Pharisees viewed as work. Jesus' point is that they were not interested in the Law, but in legalism. The Law for them had become a trap to catch sinners, whereas God always intended it as a means of bringing people toward him. They were like blind people leading the blind (Mt 15:14).

Jesus' attitude to dietary and cleanliness laws is also revolutionary (Mk 7:14–23; Mt 15:10–20). It is not what we eat that makes us unclean, but what comes out of us. Jesus often spoke of the fruit of a man's life being proof of what kind of tree he was. Good trees would provide good fruit, bad trees, bad. Likewise a person's cleanliness or uncleanliness can be gauged, not by their diet but by their words. Our words reveal our heart. We might be holy on the surface, but it is inside that matters.

Jesus truly understood the Law—so much so that he managed to sum it up in two commands (22:34–40; Mk 12:28–34; Lk 10:25–28). But he came to supersede the Law, to go beyond it. He came to rescue God's Law from being an external set of petty rules and regulations and to turn it into an inward attitude of heart.

Jesus and parables 4:10–12; Mt 13:10–17; Lk 8:9–10

A parable is a story with a message. Much labor has been expended over the interpretation of Jesus' parables with every detail scrutinized for its significance, but they were not intended as allegories where every detail has a meaning. It is usually quite simple to distinguish between the main point of the tale and the details that establish the setting and turn it into a good story.

Jesus used stories because they were memorable, because they engaged with people's lives and helped them to visualize his teaching in more understandable terms (13:34–35). He also used stories because, well,

Landmark: The Family of Jesus

The Bible tells us relatively little about the family of Jesus. His father, Joseph, is not mentioned outside of the infancy narratives. The fact that Jesus is referred to as "Mary's son" (Mk 6:3; Mt 13:55–56) has been taken to indicate that Joseph was dead by the time Jesus' ministry began. Indeed, one theory is that he waited until he was around thirty to start his preaching and teaching ministry because, before that, he was responsible for supporting the family.

Jesus had, as far as we know, four brothers: James, Joses, Judas (or Jude), and Simon (Mt 13:55; Mk 6:3). Apocryphal writings suggest that he had two sisters, Salome and Mary, but there is no biblical evidence for this.

His family struggled at first to make sense of Jesus' mission and life (Mk 3:21), but we know that later they were well known in the early Church. Along with Mary, the mother of Jesus, the most prominent of them was James, who became the leader of the church in Jerusalem. Two of the disciples—James and John—may also have been related to Jesus. If the Salome mentioned by Matthew (Mt 27:56) is the same as Mary's "sister" mentioned by John (19:25) then that would make James and John Jesus' cousins.

Things you don't find in the Bible: Salome and the seven veils

Mark doesn't identify which daughter danced before Herod Antipas. Salome is merely the only daughter of Herodias that we know about. For all we know, the real Salome might have been a shy, retiring type who liked to sit and do the crossword. (Admittedly, she later married her uncle, Philip the Tetrach, but that doesn't necessarily mean she was a glamorous showgirl.) Nor does the Bible tell us anything about the type of dance. The idea that she performed some kind of striptease—the dance of the seven veils—is a complete myth, invented in the nineteenth century by playwrights and film-makers to sell tickets. We don't know the daughter's name, and we don't know the dance; all that matters is that Antipas was so drunk and lecherous he made a stupid promise. And, as we see elsewhere in the Bible (e.g., Ju 11:34–40), stupid vows have a way of coming back and haunting you . . .

humans have *always* used and loved stories. As Chesterton wrote, "Literature is a luxury, stories are a necessity."

In Jesus' time it was usual for rabbis and teachers to use stories to illustrate or explain their teaching. Usually the rabbinic parable was very simple and obvious—indeed, many of Jesus' parables fall into this category and caused no difficulty to those who heard them. But some of his parables caused a lot of perplexity. Here, Jesus argues that this is part of the point. Referring, probably, to the parables that were to be brought together in Matthew 13, Jesus quotes from Isaiah 6. People will listen to these stories and not understand. Jesus is not talking here about people who genuinely don't understand, he is talking about those who simply refuse to grasp the point of the stories. The implication is that the act of telling the stories is judgmental, that people's response to these parables will indicate whether they are close to the kingdom of heaven or not. These parables are a kind of spiritual litmus test; the listener's response is all important. Stories have power and none more so than the parables of Jesus.

Death of John the Baptist
6:14–29; Mt 14:1–12; Lk 9:7–9

John the Baptist was always an audacious, outspoken preacher and eventually he comes into conflict with the authorities. Herod Antipas has married illegally, according to Jewish law, in taking the divorced wife of his half-brother Herod Philip (not to be confused with Philip the Tetrach, who was yet *another* brother). Anyway, leaving all these family confusions aside, the point is that Antipas and Herodias are in contravention of the Jewish law—presumably based on Leviticus 18:16 and 20:21. It is Herodias who plots the death of John. Antipas was actually interested in what he had to say and was often "glad to listen to him" (6:20). Later, Antipas was to show a similar interest in Jesus. The Jewish historian, Josephus, states that John was imprisoned in the fortress of Machaerus, near the Dead Sea.

❹ Feeding the thousands   6:30–44; 8:1–10;
Mt 14:13–21; 15:32–39; Lk 9:10–17; Jn 6:1–14

Jesus' life is a little like that of a modern pop star. Wherever he goes the crowds follow him. There are two distinct occasions recalled where he performs broadly the same miracle. On the first occasion he uses five loaves and two fish to feed 5,000 on the second he uses "seven loaves and a few small fish" to feed 4,000. Some have seen these as the same event, but there is a distinction. One event takes place in Jewish territory, the other in Gentile territory. Jesus answers the spiritual needs of people through his preaching and their physical needs. There is also a parallel here to the exodus—once again, God is providing miraculously for his people in the desert.

❺ The deaf and dumb man   7:31–37

This incident, which is only recorded in Mark, is interesting for a couple of reasons. It records Jesus' use of spittle in the healing process. Generally Jesus could heal with simply a word, but here there is obviously some importance in the man himself feeling what is going on, perhaps to help him to faith. Jesus groans before issuing the command; maybe he was feeling the pressure and the weight of expectation, or maybe he was simply responding to the illness. Illness and death were never meant to be a part of God's order at the beginning of the world. Jesus uses saliva again with a blind man at Bethsaida (8:22–26). The spittle is applied to the man's eyes and his sight gradually returns.

❻ Who is the greatest?
9:33–37; Mt 18:1–5; Lk 9:46–48

People's inability to escape from the standard view of the Messiah is shown in the next episode, where the disciples argue about which of them is the greatest. Jesus overturns their idea of greatness—just as his Messiah was the exact opposite of the one they imagined. In his kingdom, it is those who serve who have true greatness—an idea that he was to demonstrate in action on the eve of his crucifixion. Unless we have the same attitude as children—humble, trusting, not ambitious or arrogant—we will never enter Christ's kingdom.

❼ For and against   9:38–41; Lk 9:49–50

It was not only the disciples and Jesus himself who were performing miracles. Here we have an account of an independent exorcist, but one who is working in Christ's name. The disciples try to stop him, because he is not one of the "official" followers. Jesus is not interested in forming some kind of exclusive club. Anyone who has faith in his name is on his side.

Puzzling Points
Some people will not die . . . (Mk 9:1)

Jesus states that some people will not die before they see the kingdom of God come in power. Various interpretations have been put forward for what Jesus means. Some argue that it means his transfiguration, or that it refers to his resurrection, or even the descent of the Holy Spirit as depicted in Acts. However, the fact that Jesus implies that some people will be dead when it comes may point to an event further in the future—perhaps the spread and effectiveness of the early Church.

To Jerusalem   10:1–52

James and John   10:35–45; Mt 20:20–28

In Matthew it is not James and John but their mother who requests the best jobs for her boys. She—and they—have a limited understanding of what it means to be a disciple. They request to sit in the places of honor, on either side of Jesus. Jesus describes a new vision of leadership, one where all leaders are true servants, and where the Son of man has to become a slave, in order that all the slaves may go free.

Questions, Questions

The fig tree (11:12–14, 20–24; Mt 21:18–22)

It seems a bit unfair. After all, it's not the fig tree's fault that it hasn't got any fruit. And if he was hungry, why didn't he have a proper breakfast?
It's prophetic symbolism.
Sorry?
Think "actions speak louder than words." Think taksh.
Did you just sneeze?
No, I said "Taksh."
Ah, you mean, of course, the small edible growths on the Mediterranean fig tree that appear around March and later drop off before the actual figs ripen.
Exactly.
So you are implying that this tree had no "taksh."
None whatsoever. Which meant that it wasn't going to have any fruit and should therefore be condemned.
So what is it symbolizing?
Well, it could stand for the nation of Israel. The Jews had made a fine show of religion . . .
. . . i.e., the leaves . . .
But without producing any fruit. As a tree they were useless and therefore would have to be replaced.
Perhaps it's the origin of the phrase "I don't care a fig."
Perhaps it isn't.

The last week
11:1–15:47

❽ The widow's offering
13:41–44; Lk 21:1–4

Jesus was always focused on looking at the heart rather than the surface. The rich people at the temple who are assuring themselves of their faith because of the amount they give are contrasted with the widow who gives all that she has. It is not the amount that matters in terms of our giving, but the cost; not the appearance but the reality.

❾ Resurrection   16:1–8;
Mt 28:1–10; Lk 24:1–12;
Jn 20:1–10

Mary Magdalene, Mary the mother of James, and Salome go to anoint the body—even though it had already been anointed at the interment by Nicodemus (Jn 19:39–40). They wanted to do something, to be involved. At the tomb they find the

---

PARALLEL LINES
Now where have I seen that before?

	Mark	Matthew	Luke	John	▷ Page
Jesus and divorce	10:1–12	19:1–9	...	...	258
Jesus and riches	10:17–31	19:16–30	18:18–30	..	259
ENTERS JERUSALEM	11:1–11	21:1–11	19:28–40	12:12–19	259
THE TEMPLE	11:15–19	21:12–17	19:45–48	2:13–22	281
The fig tree	11:12–24	21:18–22	...	...	268
Greatest commandment	12:28–34	22:34–40	10:25–28	...	260
TEACHERS OF THE LAW	12:38–40	23:1–36	20:45–47	...	260
The end times	13:1–27	24:1–25:46	...	...	285
The widow's offering	13:41–44	...	21:1–4	...	267
ANOINTING AT BETHANY	14:3–9	26:6–13	12:1–8	12:1–8	261
THE PLOT AND THE TRIAL	14	26:1–5	22	11–13	289
THE LAST SUPPER	14	26:17–45	22	13	288
CRUCIFIXION AND DEATH	15:22–41	27:31–56	23:27–49	19:17–30	289–90

stone rolled away and a young man sitting in the tomb. The young man tells them to go and tell the disciples that Jesus has been raised. In particular he mentions Peter—perhaps because of Peter's denial of Christ. They emerge from the tomb, shaking with fear and afraid to speak up.

And there it ends. In the earliest manuscripts we have, Mark's gospel ends here. It is far too abrupt an ending, even for a writer like Mark. Maybe Mark was unable to finish his manuscript, either through death or illness, or perhaps the final scroll was lost before it could be copied.

Later endings 16:9–20

The verses that, in most Bibles, are numbered 16:9–20 are a later account dating probably from the early second century. They include details that are in other gospels, such as the appearance to Mary Magdalene (Jn 20:10–18) and the encounter on the road to Emmaus (Lk 24:13–35). However, there is no mention in the New Testament of disciples drinking poison or handling snakes with impunity, and great caution should be used in treating these words as "gospel."

Some Bibles have another ending—called the shorter ending—which talks of the disciples going to the east and the west with the news. This too is a later addition.

Details, Details . . .
Rufus (15:16–21)

Mark includes a detail that may give a further clue about the origin of this gospel. Men who were to be crucified were normally made to carry the horizontal beam of the cross, which weighed between 30 and 40 pounds. Jesus starts out carrying his cross (Jn 19:17), but, having been so badly beaten, is unable to carry on. So the Romans commandeer a man who just happened to be passing, a man called Simon. Simon was from Cyrene, which was a major city in Libya, north Africa. He was probably a Jew in Jerusalem for the Passover.

Although both Luke and Matthew record that Simon of Cyrene carried Jesus' cross, only Mark gives details of Simon's sons Rufus and Alexander. His readers must have known one or other of these people. They must have been prominent Christians in the community that Mark was addressing.

The only other mention of Rufus in the Bible is in a letter from Paul to the church at Rome. It is certainly possible that the Roman church contained someone whose father had carried the cross of Christ.

Luke
The case for Jesus

Who: The author's name—as in all of the Gospels—does not appear in the book, but traditionally, this book has been ascribed to Luke, Paul's companion. He was a doctor (Col 4:14), probably a Gentile and not a Jew. He also wrote Acts.

When: Probably written around AD 65–70, although many experts argue for a later date, around AD 80–85. If Theophilus (see opposite) was a high-ranking Roman official, the book was probably written in Rome, although Antioch, Achaia and Ephesus have all been suggested.

What: Luke's aim is to write a proper history of what actually happened. He declares at the beginning that he carefully studied the sources and he aims to present a careful survey of the life and teaching of Jesus. Luke's intention is to argue the case for Christianity; to counter ignorant and ill-founded reports.

There is a joyful, optimistic feel to the gospel. Most importantly, it is a gospel for the poor and marginalized. Luke's gospel is full of tax collectors, prostitutes, lepers and thieves. The news of Jesus' birth comes not to the foreign dignitaries as in Matthew, but to humble, despised shepherds. Significantly, Luke's gospel shows a respect for women that is highly unusual for the time. The Bible has often been criticized for its view of women, but in comparison to the time, women in the Bible are remarkably liberated and respected. Luke's gospel begins with two mothers celebrating and features throughout significant encounters of women with Jesus.

Luke writes not for Jews like Matthew, nor for Romans like Mark, but for Gentiles of all nationalities. "Heroes" in the gospel include a Gentile centurion and a Samaritan rescuer, and the genealogy of Christ goes back to Adam, the father of all. He also inserts into his gospel songs or poems that must have been traditionally associated with the leading characters. These include the Magnificat of Mary (1:46–55), the Benedictus of Zechariah (1:68–79) and the Nunc Dimittis of Simeon (2:29–32).

Quick Guide
Author
Luke
Type
Gospel
Purpose
An attempt to put together a detailed, well-researched account of Jesus' life.
Key verses
1:3–4 "So I made a careful study of everything and then I decided to write and tell you exactly what took place . . . I have done this to let you know the truth about what you have heard."
If you remember one thing about this book . . .
The good news is especially good for the poor and oppressed.
Your 15 minutes start now
Read chapters 1–2, 4, 12, 14–15, 19, 22–24

The Route Through Luke

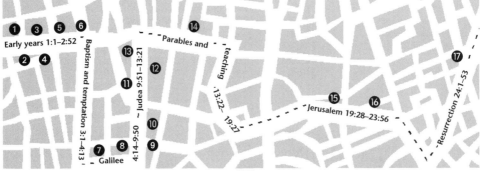

270

Early Years   1:1–4:13

Theophilus   1:1–4

The book is directed at one person: Theophilus, a name that means "lover of God." He is addressed as "Honorable," indicating that he was probably a high Roman official. Luke indicates that Theophilus had already heard something of the story and wanted to find out more, but equally, the official may also have served as Luke's patron, responsible for paying for the copying and distribution of the book—a kind of first-century publisher.

❶ Birth of John the Baptist 1:5–25

Matthew says nothing of the birth of John the Baptist, but Luke emphasizes John's relationship with Jesus and the miraculous aspects of his birth. Zechariah and Elizabeth are both of priestly descent, descended from Aaron. Elizabeth, like many other notable wives, is advanced in years and unable to have children, e.g. Sarah (Ge 17), Rebekah (Ge 30) and Hannah (1 Sa 1). In Luke's account, John's birth is foretold by God. Zechariah is literally dumbstruck by the angel's visit, his lack of faith resulting in his losing his voice. The son prophesied by the angel will have the spirit and power of Elijah (1:17). He will also be subject to a Nazirite vow of abstinence (Nu 6:1–4), linking him with other Old Testament characters such as Samuel and Samson.

> **Details, Details . . .**
> **Zechariah's service in the temple (1:23)**
>
> Each priest had to spend a week in the temple at Jerusalem once every six months. Zechariah was given the duty of keeping the incense burning on the altar in front of the Holy of Holies. Some priests never had to do this. Priests were chosen by lots. It was the priestly equivalent of jury duty.
>
> ▷366

❷ The Virgin Birth   1:26–45 ▷250

Luke also gives an account of the Virgin Birth—an account that contains more detail than Matthew's. Luke does not quote the verse like Matthew does and perhaps the fact that he omits the reference reinforces the idea that the early Church viewed the Virgin Birth as a historical fact. Mary goes to visit her relative Elizabeth, who, inspired by the Holy Spirit, recognizes the importance of both Mary and the child she is carrying.

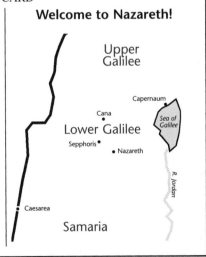

POSTCARD

Nazareth is a thriving, bustling town. No, really.

Admittedly our town is not mentioned in the Old Testament. Or the Talmud. Or the histories. But that doesn't mean we're completely obscure.

We may be a little out of the way, but we're certainly not out of touch! Sepphoris (the capital of Galilee) is only an hour's walk away, and since the city is currently the focus of a major rebuilding program, there is plenty of work for local carpenters and builders.

We are near to several major trade routes, while our relatively high altitude (1,200 ft above sea level) allows us fine views of the world around us and the sightseer can stand and watch Roman legions marching by to the north, and trade caravans passing by to the south. In other words, we're a pretty normal place to grow up. And proud of it.

Welcome to Nazareth!

Upper Galilee

Capernaum

Cana

Sea of Galilee

Lower Galilee

Sepphoris • Nazareth

R. Jordan

Caesarea

Samaria

The Magnificat   1:46–55

Mary's song of praise is known as the Magnificat, because in Latin the first word is *magnificat,* which means "glorifies." The song is very similar to a psalm and its theme is the way in which God has glorified the poor. It is not the proud, the highborn or powerful who have been chosen to carry the Son of God, but this humble teenage girl. This song is a spontaneous outpouring of emotion, the New Testament equivalent of the song that Hannah sang on the birth of Samuel (1 Sa 2:1–10).

Brief Lives: Mary

Background: Her real name is Miriam. Mary is the Greek version. She is known as "the Virgin Mary" because Jesus was born by the Holy Spirit, but after Jesus' birth she had several more children with her husband, Joseph.

Occupation: Mother.

Achievements: Mary was probably a young girl at the time of her marriage to Joseph. Brides at that time could be as young as twelve, but given the maturity of her response she was probably a few years older.

Most of what we know about Mary comes from the accounts of Jesus' birth. She came from a poor and ordinary family, but her response to God's choice of her shows remarkable spiritual insight. Although she "treasured" all the events of Jesus' upbringing, she appears to have had her doubts about his mission later in life (Mk 3:21). However, at the end of his life, Mary was there, standing by the cross while her son died a horrific death. She was also among the first to know of his resurrection after she visited the tomb.

Character: Mary was undoubtedly a brave and thoughtful woman, prepared to endure ridicule and even punishment in obedience to God. She had the courage and faith to obey God, in the face of the scorn of the world, and that is surely reason enough for us to honor her.

Pros: Honest, courageous, obedient, young.

Cons: Later in life had worries about her son's career. But what mother doesn't?

❸ Birth of John the Baptist   1:57–80

A similar outburst of praise is heard on the birth of John, but this time from his father, the elderly priest Zechariah. He has received the power of speech again, and he and his wife have announced—to their neighbors' surprise—that their child will be called John. Zechariah's song is known as the Benedictus, after the first word *benedictus*, which means "praise be." It recalls God's promises to Israel and how God has given his people a "horn of salvation" (1:69), animal horns being a symbol of great strength. He looks forward to the role that his son will play (1:76–77) and to the light that will break in on all those who live in the "dark shadow of death" (1:78–79).

John grows up in the desert (Lk 1:80), leading some to conjecture that he was part of the Dead Sea community at Qumran. But there is no evidence for this. He could have made his dwelling anywhere, as long as there was a bit of honey and a few insects for lunch.

❹ The Birth of Jesus   2:1–7 ▷250

Matthew simply records that Jesus was born in Bethlehem. Luke gives us the reason why he was there. However, Luke's reason raises some historical difficulties. Luke assigns the census to the time when Quirinus was governor of Syria, but this would place it in AD 6 or 7, which is probably too late. Luke could mean "before" Quirinus, or he could simply have got his censuses confused. It is also highly unusual that the census required Joseph to go back to Bethlehem. Roman censuses were usually about where you lived—just as modern censuses are. Finally, there are no historical references to this census at all. That doesn't mean that the event didn't happen: there is evidence of a similar census in Egypt some years later, and Luke is a reliable historian.

Whatever the case, Luke's story emphasizes the poverty of the event and those who attended it. Luke is the most socially aware gospel. Mary's song celebrated the fact that God's grace was being showered on someone who was poor. Jesus came from poor parents —Joseph had to offer the poor man's offering when he visited the temple (2:24).

Shepherds   2:8–20

Matthew brought us the Magi, Luke brings us the humble shepherds. Just as Jesus' birth was given to a poor family, the news is given first to some of the poorest people in Palestine—the shepherds, sitting out on the dark hills.

Luke's picture is of a birth in makeshift accommodation, of a baby lying in the filth of an

Landmark: Baptism

Baptism is a ritual whereby those who wish to repent are symbolically "washed" in water. Jesus was baptized by John and he also baptized others (Jn 3:22). He told his disciples to go into the world and "baptize them in the name of the Father, the Son, and the Holy Spirit" (Mt 28:19).

Baptism isn't found anywhere in the Old Testament, although certain Old Testament events are held to be symbolized by the act, such as the crossing of the reed sea and the way that Noah passed through the waters.

Baptism, as portrayed in the New Testament is a symbolic and powerful act. Baptism was primarily a sign of repentance and cleansing—an indication that the person's sins had been washed away. As it was a public event—taking place in the rivers and lakes—it was also a public sign of commitment. It also had a symbolic function: the act of going under the water and coming up again was seen as echoing Jesus' death and resurrection (Ro 6:3–5). Baptism was a sign that the believer's old life was dead and buried—now there was new life in Christ.

For all these reasons, baptism remains a vital part of the church's rituals today. Today it is still a sign of repentance, of commitment and of new life in Christ.

Things you don't find in the Bible: The stable

The traditional picture of the baby Jesus lying in a snug stable, surrounded by neatly dressed cattle and freshly scrubbed shepherds and lit by the 60-watt glow of his halo, is about as far from the truth as you can be. There is no mention of the stable in the Bible—we infer it from the fact that Jesus is lying in an animal's feeding trough. But all this directly implies is that they were unprepared for the birth: they didn't have a cot.

Details, Details ... Jesus' birthday

We cannot date this with any real certainty. It must have happened before 4 BC because that was the date of Herod's death. As to December 25, all that is a later invention. There are no clues in the narrative as to the date; if anything it was in the summer, since sheep were generally kept out on the hills from March to November. So if you want to eat your Christmas lunch on June 25, you would probably be more accurate. (Oh, and the millennium should have been celebrated in 1996 at the latest.)

animal's feeding trough, of the news being presented to the poor and excluded. It was good news for all people —but especially the poor.

❺ The presentation in the temple
2:21–38

The law prescribed that after eight days the baby should be circumcised. This probably happened in Bethlehem, after which they took the boy to Jerusalem to be presented to the Lord. The law prescribed that this presentation should happen thirty-three days after the birth (Le 12:4–8). A rich man would have offered a lamb as a sacrifice. Joseph offers the poor man's sacrifice of two doves or pigeons.

Their visit to the temple brings them into contact with two more characters: Simeon and Anna. Simeon is described as a righteous man who has received a prophecy that he will not die before he has seen the Messiah. He takes the baby in his arms and utters what is known as the Nunc Dimittis (from the first words meaning "Now dismiss ..."). It is the song of a slave who is finally released, of a servant who has done his duty and is now requesting leave to go. However, Simeon's message has a harder side—he tells Mary that her son will bring not only a light for the nations, but suffering for his mother. The truth about Jesus is also recognized by an old woman called Anna (2:36–38). She is an eighty-four-year-old widow (or the Greek could mean that she had been a widow for eighty-four years), whose devotion to prayer and fasting is as notable as her age. Although her words are not recorded, she is a female counterpart to Simeon.

❻ Jesus in the temple 2:41–52

This single incident is the only account we have of Jesus' childhood. Although the Old Testament recommended that Jews travel to Jerusalem for the three major annual feasts (Passover, Pentecost, Tabernacles) by Jesus' time it was generally only a once-a-year visit

A Little Local Difficulty
The return to Nazareth 2:39–40 ▷271

Luke's account makes no mention of Herod's persecution and of the exile in Egypt, but implies that Jesus, Mary and Joseph went straight from Jerusalem to Nazareth.

The only way to solve this problem is to assume that they went home to Nazareth and then back to Bethlehem again, where the wise men visited them. After all, Herod's command to kill all children under two indicates that the wise men may have visited when Jesus was a toddler, rather than a baby. As they stand, the two accounts cannot be harmonized. However, it has to be said that the clear implication in Luke is that they stayed in Nazareth—which was seen as Jesus' hometown.

for most Jews. Jesus here is twelve years old—legally still a child. His parents, traveling as part of a large party, lose sight of him and don't discover him until three days later, when he is found still in the temple, debating with the teachers. At festival times, with all the visitors around, rabbis would gather at the temple and find audiences for their teaching, just as Jesus did later in his life (19:47). Jesus' reply to their anxious inquiries implies that he was already aware of his destiny and role.

This is the only event recorded of Jesus' upbringing, right up to the age of about 30. All we know of the silent years—as they are called—is that Jesus increased in wisdom and many people began to recognize something about his character.

John the Baptist   3:1–20 ▷252

Luke gives us the historical setting by dating the next events in the fifteenth year of the reign of Tiberius. This probably means around AD 25 or 26. However, the names he includes indicate a general period, rather than a specific date. Annas and Caiaphas were successive high priests rather than simultaneous, although Annas was deposed by Rome and many Jews continued to recognize his authority.

Luke gives us a few more details about John's ministry than the other gospels. John insists that repentance is more than skin deep. People are required to share their possessions. Tax collectors and soldiers are not required to leave their jobs, but they are required to change their ways (3:12–14).

Baptism and temptation   3:1–4:13
Mt 3:13–17; Mk 1:9–11 ▷251

Galilee   4:14–9:50

❼ In the synagogue   4:16–30
▷242

Luke 4 records two incidents at two different synagogues: one in Jesus' hometown of Nazareth and the other in Capernaum.

The service in the synagogue followed a fairly set pattern. After an introductory series of prayers there were readings from the Old Testament. Jesus had obviously gained a reputation as a preacher, as he was given a scroll to read from and invited to preach. His scroll is the *Haphttarah*, the Prophets. As he talks, his listeners are at first amazed at his wisdom and then enraged by his implications. He tells them that the reason they cannot accept him as a prophet is that they are too blinded by their own preconceptions. He tells them, basically, that lepers and Gentiles are actually their superiors, because they are more open to God. The mob is prepared to kill him, but he escapes.

Landmark: Temptation

To be tempted is not the same as to be sinful. Jesus was sinless, but he was not immune to temptation. Hebrews says that he was tempted just as we are (4:15)—indeed, there would be little identification between Jesus and humanity if he wasn't tempted. Temptation turns to sin, or not, depending on our response.

Satan gave Jesus the opportunity to turn away from God—and that's all temptation really is. It is a choice that is presented to us —an appealing choice on one level, a choice that would make life easier, or more gratifying or more pleasurable. But temptation is always a choice. It is not an irresistible force.

Jesus answers all the temptations with quotes from Scripture—actually all from Deuteronomy (8:3, 6:13 and 6:16). This is an indication of how we too can combat temptation when it comes.

Brief Lives: Satan, aka Lucifer, the Devil, Beelzebub, etc.

Background: Angel.

Occupation: Angel. Then Fallen Angel.

Achievements: As the adversary of God, Satan has pursued a relentless, if ultimately pointless career. In the Old Testament he makes few appearances, although he is traditionally identified with the "serpent" in Genesis. Most of our information about him comes from the New Testament, where he is in charge of demonic forces. Jesus refers to the story of Satan being an angel who fell from heaven because of rebellion against God (Re 12:9; Lk 10:18). He tries to tempt Jesus away from his true path (Mt 4:1ff). His demons can possess individuals, but they cannot possess Christians, who have a superior protection. His area of authority is limited, however, and he is only allowed to do what he does at the express permission of God. Eventually he will be defeated by God and thrown into oblivion.

Character: Just evil.

Pros: Um ... I'll get back to you on that one.

Cons: Too many to mention.

❽ A day in the life   4:31–44; Mk 1:21–34

This passage gives us an intriguing glimpse of a day in the life of Jesus. He teaches in the synagogue in the morning. The reaction of those in Nazareth is the direct opposite of the people in Capernaum. There the people receive his teaching with amazement. More, they watch while the demons recognize the power of Jesus and are expelled.

After that he leaves the synagogue and goes to Simon Peter's house, where he heals Peter's mother-in-law. After sunset the Sabbath ends, and people come to him to be healed. Early the next morning he gets up and prays alone in a deserted place. Before long the others come looking for him—there are still a lot of people who want to see him. However, despite the pleas from the people of Capernaum for Jesus to stay, he prepares to leave. There are other synagogues to preach in and other people who need to encounter Jesus.

❾ Sermon on the plain   6:17–49; Mt 5:1–7:29

Luke's version is very different from that in Matthew. For a start it's on a plain and not up a hill. But more than that, Luke's version is much, much shorter. Luke has only four beatitudes and matches them with four "woes." They obviously share a common tradition, and it is not impossible that Jesus preached two different sermons at two different times, containing much of the same material, but the likeliest explanation is that Matthew chose to gather a large amount of teaching in one place, while Luke spread it more evenly throughout his gospel.

One of the key differences, however, is that Luke has "blessed are the poor," where Matthew has "blessed are the poor in spirit." Similarly, Luke talks about those who hunger, where Matthew has those who "hunger for righteousness." An enormous amount of discussion has gone on about the difference between the two. In Matthew's account, Jesus is looking beyond the merely physical to the spiritual dimension as well, but Luke retains his emphasis on the poor and the outcast.

Jesus raises the dead   7:11–17

There are three accounts of the dead being raised in the Gospels (excluding the resurrection of Jesus himself). The widow's son (Luke 7:11–17); Jairus's daughter (8:40–56; Mk 5:21–43) and Lazarus (Jn 11:1–44). Jesus' activity is welcomed as a sign that he is a great prophet: both Elijah (1 Ki 17) and Elisha (2 Ki 4) brought back sons to life.

❿ The perfumed feet   7:36–50

During a meal at a Pharisee's house, a prostitute enters and pours a bottle of expensive perfumed ointment over Jesus' feet. Weeping, she wipes the perfume away with the only thing she has available—her own hair. The Pharisee is not only shocked by this display of unashamed emotion, he cannot believe that a holy man would let this person near him. Any holy man worth his salt would surely know that she was a sinner. Of course Jesus knew she was a sinner—that was the point. Her gestures do not earn the forgiveness of sins —they are merely an expression of her love and faith. It is the faith that is rewarded, not the perfume.

> ### Details, Details . . .
> ### Dinnertime
>
> On special occasions, people in the New Testament ate lying down on their left side and eating with their right hand. Their feet would extend away from the table. Jesus follows this custom here and, more noticeably, in the Last Supper, when the disciples are described as "reclining."

Judaea   9:51–13:21

The cost of discipleship   9:51–62

Jesus' journey to Jerusalem is indicative of the cost of discipleship. First a Samaritan village refuses him because he is going to Jerusalem. The Samaritans believed their shrine in Gerizim to be the equal of Jerusalem, therefore they took offense. The disciples want to punish them, but Jesus demonstrates that the disciple's life means not returning evil for evil.

The three people who wish to follow Jesus demonstrate the costs of discipleship. Disciples will have no true home on earth, because their allegiance is to a different kingdom (9:57–58). Following Jesus is a matter of urgency. There is no indication that the man's father is actually dead—he is wanting to postpone the time when he joins Jesus' followers. But the urgency overcomes all other considerations (9:59–60). Finally, disciples must say goodbye to the past. You cannot march into the future with confidence if you are always looking over your shoulder. Becoming a disciple of Jesus means making a clean break and never looking back (9:61–62).

Landmark: Evil Powers

We do not have to look far in our world to find evil. It is there on our TV screens. It fills the newspapers. Wars, famine, hatred, bigotry, abuse, violence—this is an evil world. But where does it come from? Who is responsible for all this?

According to the story of Genesis, evil began with an act of rebellion against God. This is fundamentally what it remains. Every act of evil is an act of rebellion against the will of God. By the time of the New Testament, however, evil was seen more as being concentrated in particular beings with a leader called Satan. These beings were pure evil, who could invade and "possess" individuals.

There appears, then, to be two levels of evil. There is the evil that man does as a conscious act. And there are evil powers who are at work in this world. The relationship between these two has long been the cause of debate. What is true is that man remains responsible for his own actions. Leaving aside the thorny issue of demon possession, there is no indication that the Devil can make anyone do anything. He can tempt them, he can bring suffering on them, he can attack them, but they retain the responsibility for their own conduct and lives. They can choose to ask for God's protection, or they can give in to their own selfish desires.

The other thing to remember about evil is that God is more powerful. Demons cannot possess Christians, because a Christian is someone with the Spirit of God in them, and God cannot be defeated by the Devil. Satan is not the opposite of God. Satan is a fallen angel—if he has an opposite, it is Michael. God has no opposite. And one day he will act and all evil will be banished forever. In the meantime we do well to remember that we are in a war.

⓫ The sending of the seventy-two 10:1–24

Jesus followed the sending out of the twelve by sending out the seventy-two. Some manuscripts have "seventy" followers; the Jews believed that there were seventy nations in the world, and we have already seen the importance of seventy in their thinking. This action, therefore, can be seen as symbolic of the mission that Jesus was to give the disciples at the end of Matthew: go into all the world and tell people about me.

The instructions for the seventy are similar to those for the twelve, but there is an added sense of urgency —so much so that they cannot stop to greet people on the road (10:4). The success of their mission fills Jesus with joy, but he also has to temper their pride.

The Good Samaritan 10:25–37

Luke fills his account of Jesus' journey to Jerusalem with a series of parables told along the way. In answer to a question by "an expert in the Law of Moses," Jesus tells one of the most famous stories in history. Because of the level of detail in this story, many have wondered whether it was a real event. It could well have a basis in fact, because the road from Jericho to Jerusalem was notorious for its robbers, but all good storytellers choose an appropriate location for their story – and that doesn't mean it actually happened.

The two people who ignore the injured man are both religious: a priest and a Levite, a high official in the temple and one slightly lower in status. Their reluctance to get involved might be from religious scruples (it was against the Law for a priest to come into contact with a dead body), or from fear that the body might be a lure so that, while they were attending to it, other robbers would attack them. Or it might be simple callousness and selfishness. But the point of the story is that the despised Samaritan, a member of the nation that all Israel hated, turns out to be the hero. Given that just a little while earlier Jesus himself had been rejected by the Samaritans, the choice of hero is even more surprising.

⑫ Martha and Mary 10:38–42

Martha and Mary appear regularly in the gospel of John: this is their only appearance in the Synoptic Gospels. This is a lesson in priorities. Martha wanted to make everything perfect for Jesus, but his needs were simple. The many things she was worried about might be an abundance of dishes, but all Jesus needed was a simple meal. Activity is not the same as productivity. Sometimes the best thing is to sit and listen.

⑬ The Lord's Prayer 11:1–4

Like the Sermon on the Mount, the Lord's Prayer in Luke is different from that in Matthew. It is shorter and written in a simpler, less figurative language. "Debts" in Matthew becomes "sins" in Luke. "Our Father in heaven," becomes "Father." The prayer itself is followed by a story illustrating the need for persistent, earnest prayer (11:5–13).

The teachers of the Law 11:37–52; Mt 23:1–36; Mk 12:38–40 ▷260

The sign of Jonah 12:54–56; Mt 16:1–4; Mk 8:11–13

It seems odd, given all that had happened already, that the Pharisees and Sadducees were still asking for a sign. Probably they were asking for a huge apocalyptic vision, perhaps the very kind of thing with which Satan tempted Jesus (4:5–6). Jesus promises them only the sign of Jonah—the prophet who was in the belly of the fish for three days and nights. He is referring to his death and resurrection.

Warnings and punishments 13:1–9

Jesus uses two topical events to talk about the need for repentance. The people believe that bad things happen to those who deserve them. Jesus does not subscribe to this view for the simple reason that no one is less or more deserving than anyone else. Since we are all sinners, the only moral to be drawn from these disasters is our need for repentance. The parable of the fig tree that follows indicates that we will get a chance to repent.

Parables and teaching 13:22–19:27

Humility 14:7–14

The seating plan at the banquet is always a sign of importance. If you are the best guests you get seated nearer the front. The rest of us get pushed to the back. Jesus argues that the desire to be important and to achieve honor is to be avoided. Instead, approach with humility; that way anything that happens is a bonus! Similarly, when inviting guests, don't head for the

---

Details, details . . .
I saw Satan fall (10:18)

Traditionally, this has been interpreted as a reference to the fall of Lucifer in the remote past. But it may be that Jesus is using the fall of Satan as a symbolic response to the disciples' action—saying that their actions have overthrown the powers of darkness.

Landmark: Jesus and Women

There has always been debate and disquiet about the prominence of women in the New Testament. Why doesn't Jesus have any women disciples?

The point is not that women aren't prominent enough, but that they feature at all. In the culture of the time a woman was virtually invisible. She had no legal status and hardly any rights. She was there to cook the meals, raise the children, or simply to be the object of desire and pleasure for men.

Jesus didn't treat women this way. Luke 8:1–3 lists women who accompanied him on his journeys around the towns and villages. His followers not only included wives and mothers, but prostitutes and foreigners—people with whom no "respectable" Jewish male would associate.

They saw in Jesus someone who would view them with compassion, with respect and understanding. They responded to him with a deep and profound faith. Often they perceived the truth about Jesus, a truth that many of the male "experts" failed to see.

Questions, Questions

God the Father

So, if God is a father, does this mean that he is male?

No.

But he must be. I mean, my dad is male. At least, we're pretty sure he's male.

No, it hasn't anything to do with gender, but characteristics. Jesus called God "Abba," which is a more intimate word for father, similar to our word "Dad." He's trying to change our view of who God is. The point is that any human term when applied to God comes short of the reality. When people in the Bible encountered God face-to-face they were hardly able to speak about the experience, so any words we use will fall short of the reality.

But didn't he appear as a man to people in the Old Testament?

Sometimes. But then he also appeared as a cloud, a pillar of fire and a bush. God is above gender and when we use the term "father," we are talking about particular characteristics that he possesses. Jesus described God as a father, it is true, but he also described him as pure spirit (Jn 4:24).

So we could describe him as a mother, then?

Father, mother, parent—as long as the term accurately captures the reality of what God is like. In Isaiah 66:13 God likens himself to a mother comforting her children; in Psalm 131, the psalmist talks about his relationship with God as similar to that of a young child sitting on his mother's lap. God is the perfect parent—caring, loving, merciful and always willing to give us his wisdom.

influential and the important. Invite the outcasts, the unimportant, the uninfluential. It's the opposite of social climbing. Social potholing, perhaps.

⓮ The prodigal son 15:11–31

The second of the great stories that are unique to Luke and probably the best story ever told. It continues the theme of the parables of the lost sheep and lost coin, but this time places the action in a human setting. It is a story of forgiveness, of reconciliation, of total, unwavering love; the story of an old man who does not mind looking foolish but who rushes toward his son and hugs and kisses him. God does not stand on his dignity when it comes to returning sinners.

The attitude of the elder son is the attitude of the Pharisees. These—the elder son, the "true" Israelites—did not welcome returning sinners, because of who these people were. It was the same attitude that condemned Jesus for spending time with prostitutes and tax collectors. Far from rejoicing that these sinners repented, they did not want those kind of people in the kingdom.

The dishonest servant 16:1–13

At first glance this parable appears to reward dishonesty, but that is to miss the point. The parable is about the shrewd use of money to gain friends. Jesus' view is that wealth is wicked anyway (16:9), so you might as well make the best use of it.

Rich man and beggar 16:19–31

Repeat after me: this is a story, not an accurate description of hell. Jesus is telling a story about the need for repentance and right behavior now. After death, reality sets in and God's justice can be seen to be at work. This is a companion piece to parables such as that of the Rich Fool. It is a story telling of people who stored up treasure in heaven. Or not. And, as the life of Jesus was to show, some people don't ever listen, not even when the truth is staring them in the face. Not to mention walking among them, performing miracles and telling great stories.

The Pharisee and the tax collector

18:9–14 ▷255

The contrast is between the self-righteous, "religious" person and the truly contrite "sinner." The Pharisee doesn't really pray at all—he just indulges in self-congratulation and arrogance. The tax collector, on the other hand, really prays, although his words don't have eloquence and basically all he does is thump himself. But God listens to our hearts, not our words. This is seen in real-life action in the story of Zacchaeus (19:1–10) the tax collector who truly repents and who becomes a "true son of Abraham."

Jerusalem
19:28–23:56

The temple 19:45–48; Mt 21:12–17; Mk 11:15–19; Jn 2:13–22 ▷287

Those who wanted to make a sacrifice at the temple had to buy their sacrifices from the "official outlets." Animals, wine, oil or salt—these were only available from the authorized retailers in the temple yard. Similarly, if you wanted to pay the temple tax, you could only do so in the form of shekels, so anyone coming from outside Palestine had to change their Roman and Greek currency.

All of this would have been fine, were it not for the fact that the stallholders were ripping off their customers. Shoddy animals were being sold for high prices, and the money changers were charging an exorbitant exchange rate. Jesus, uniquely, is roused to physical anger by these abuses, which basically made a profit out of people's desire for forgiveness. He wrecks the stalls and throws out the stallholders. The ordinary people, the blind, the lame, are now even more sure that he is the Messiah and start to call him "Son of David." The religious authorities, however, are not amused. They are on a collision course.

Puzzling Points
Why does Jesus tell his disciples to buy swords? (Lk 22:35–38)

Jesus tells his disciples that hard times are coming. He is preparing them for conflict and persecution. His statement that they should all go out and buy swords is obviously ironic—a point underlined when the disciples produce two swords and Jesus tells them to put them away.

Landmark: Teaching of Jesus

Jesus taught people. One of the tasks he engaged in most was to explain the Scriptures and to debate the issues they raised. Indeed, he did this from an early age—when he was lost as a boy, his parents found him in the temple debating with the teachers (2:41–50). Later, he was called "Rabbi" and "Teacher." *Rabbi* was to come to mean an authorized, official teacher, mainly at the synagogues, but Jesus was, in a way, a very *unauthorized* teacher. There is no indication that he had any formal training and he did not teach in the recognized centers. Although some of his teaching took place in synagogues, a lot of it took place in fields, in a boat, on the side of a hill, in houses—wherever the opportunity afforded itself.

Typically, teaching of the time drew attention to previous teachers and "authorities," piling up references and quotations. Jesus made no such references, teaching with his own authority.

His teaching is characterized by a number of approaches:

He told stories
Jesus told lots of stories. Loads and loads of stories. In fact, he never taught without using parables.

He encouraged questions
Teaching was as much a matter of debate and discussion as it was one man making pronouncements.

He demanded a response
Jesus was not interested in making debating points or floating nice theories, he was interested in recruiting followers and in changing lives.

He made people think
Lots of times Jesus made provocative statements or told difficult stories and did not explain them. He wanted people to think about his words and make their own discoveries. He still does.

He challenged pointless discussion
If people tried to open a debate that was merely theoretical, or even pointless, Jesus changed direction. He wasn't in the entertainment business.

He walked the talk
He was not just words. He lived what he taught.

PARALLEL LINES
Now where have I seen that before?

	Luke	Matthew	Mark	John	▷ Page
ENTERS JERUSALEM	19:28–40	21:1–11	11:1–11	12:12–19	259
THE TEMPLE	19:45–48	21:12–17	11:15–19	2:13–22	281
Teachers of the Law	20:45–47	23:1–36	12:38–40	...	260
The widow's offering	21:1–4	...	13:41–44	...	267
THE PLOT AND THE TRIAL	22	26:1–5	14	11–13	289
THE LAST SUPPER	22	26:17–45	14	13	288

⓯ Jesus before Herod   23:6–12

Luke inserts a third trial. As well as the trial before the religious leaders and the trial before Pilate, he has Jesus taken before Herod. Herod views Jesus with curiosity more than anything else. He questions him, but Jesus does not answer. Herod is a distraction in the great events that are unfolding. Jesus is not going to waste his time on intellectual trivialities. He has a greater purpose to fulfill.

PARALLEL LINES
Now where have I seen that before?

	Luke	Matthew	Mark	John	▷ Page
CRUCIFIXION AND DEATH	23:27–49	27:31–56	15:22–41	19:17–30	289–90
RESURRECTION	24:1–12	28:1–10	16:1–8	20:1–10	291

⓰ The Emmaus road   24:13–35

Cleopas and his friend are trudging, dejectedly, back to Emmaus from Jerusalem. They are followers of Jesus and now the mission that promised so much has, apparently, ended in ignominious failure. Suddenly, they are joined by an unknown stranger, who begins by asking questions and ends by providing answers.

The importance of this event is huge, for it shows how Jesus himself "taught" the events of his life in the context of the Scriptures. One of the key ideas that Jesus explains here is the idea that the Messiah would suffer. The Jews were keen on the princely Messiah, the man of power; they could even get their heads around the idea of the Good Shepherd leading the flock of Israel. But the idea that the Messiah would suffer and die for his people, the idea that he would be treated with contempt by the enemies of their nation, the idea that the Messiah would be seen by some as a failure, this was too much for them to believe.

And yet, Jesus shows them, through Scripture, how that must happen. Thus, the two men have their eyes opened. They thought it was a failure, but it was the greatest success; they thought it was a disaster, but it was the greatest triumph. After the questioner becomes the answerer, there are more role reversals: the guest becomes the host when he joins them for a meal and breaks bread. And in that moment they recognize him. The stranger turns out to be the closest friend.

Jesus appears to the disciples
24:36–49; Mt 28:16–20; Jn 20:19–23; Ac 1:6–8

The two men rush back to Jerusalem to tell the others of these experiences, and in the middle of their discussion, Jesus appears again. He is no ghost— they can touch him and he eats their food. He repeats some of the lessons from the road to Emmaus and ends with the promise that he will send someone else to be with them—the Holy Spirit, as we will learn in Acts.

⓱ Ascension   24:50–53

There is a gap of six weeks between verse 49 and 50—a gap we get from Luke's account in Acts (Ac 1:3). The actual account of Jesus being "taken up to heaven" is not in the earliest manuscripts of Luke. Instead Jesus simply lifts his hands in blessing and departs. However, this time it is a different departure. The first time he raised his hands and departed, he was on the cross and his disciples fled. This time they return in joy and triumph, to spend their time at the temple praising God.

Landmark: The Disciples

The Gospels are agreed that Jesus chose twelve men to be his special disciples, but there are minor differences about the actual names. The accounts agree on eleven of them: Simon Peter, Andrew, James, John, Philip, Bartholomew, Thomas, Matthew, James son of Alphaeus, Simon the Zealot and Judas Iscariot. However, Matthew and Mark have Thaddeus, while Luke lists Judas, son of James. The likelihood is that these were the same person, that Thaddeus was his nickname (Mt 10:2–4; Mk 3:16–19; Lk 6:13–16). John doesn't provide a list, but he does mention a "Nathaniel," who was probably the same as Bartholomew.

They were a diverse group. Matthew was a tax collector, a collaborator with the hated Roman occupying forces. Simon is described as a zealot —a member of a political group that was actively opposed to Roman occupation. Many were married, and their wives were later to accompany them on their missionary journeys (1 Co 9:5). Peter, Andrew, James and John were fishermen. Philip may also have been a fisherman, since he came from Bethsaida, a well-known fishing village. Indeed, John and James may have been more "in the fish business" than fishermen—their father was sufficiently well-off to have hired servants (Mk 1:20) and their mother provided financial support for Jesus' work (Lk 8:3).

Perhaps what is more important about the disciples is their attitude. They were often afraid, frequently baffled and, when the going got tough, they ran away. Yet they were also genuinely committed to Jesus and, after his resurrection, they took the message of the good news to all who would listen. Ultimately, this group of ordinary individuals was to change the world.

Jesus—The Last Week

Known as "Holy Week," or "Passion Week," the last week of Jesus' physical life on earth is treated at length in all the Gospels, the events and sayings associated with it taking up about a third of their combined writings.

The reason for this is simple—it was the most crucial moment in his career. This was the defining moment, the tipping point that would decide the success, or failure, of his work. This section brings together several landmarks, looking at the timing, the location and some of the central issues concerning Jesus' death and resurrection. In the meantime, it is worth bearing in mind some points about Jesus' entry to Jerusalem.

It was planned

Some argue that Jesus did not expect the events of this week, that he only went to Jerusalem because he had not taught there much and that things after that got out of hand. Others believe that the whole event was a gamble that went wrong; they believe that Jesus was trying to turn public support into a rebellion, or even to force God into proving that he was indeed the Messiah. In this view, the event ended "wrongly," with Jesus neither a successful revolutionary nor the proven Messiah.

The evidence of the Gospels, however, indicates that Jesus did know what was going to happen. His entry into Jerusalem did not happen by accident; he didn't just "find himself in the area." All the Gospels suggest that he was aware of his unique relationship with God, he knew what his role was to be, and he knew, therefore, that the time was right for these events to take place.

It is easy to think that "something went wrong" because, by human standards, Jesus did it all the wrong way round. He refused to capitalize on the triumphant entry to the city by overthrowing the authorities; he demonstrated his leadership, not by seizing political power, but by washing the feet of his disciples; and he secured his greatest victory by dying like a common criminal. God's thinking is not our thinking, God's ways are not our ways. God's plans are greater, and more potent, than our plans.

It challenged the political powers

For most of the time, the Romans took little or no interest in Jesus. They were always suspicious of anyone who attracted large crowds of followers, but the fact that Jesus mainly operated away from the "centers of power" meant that they were content to let him be. Such Romans as took an interest in him had personal reasons—and expressed a personal faith. Jesus' triumphant entry into Jerusalem changed all that. Now there was a man with a following. And he was right on their doorstep.

It challenged the religious powers

Jesus always challenged the religious authorities of his day, condemning the teaching of the Pharisees and Sadducees and showing how their teachings had perverted true faith in God. His entry to Jerusalem, however, was in a different league. The triumph of his entry must have really unnerved them. After all, if this man really was the Messiah, then their power would be gone in a flash. And throwing out the money lenders and traders from the temple was a direct, and violent, attack on their authority. This troublemaking false messiah would have to be dealt with.

The time: Sunday to Wednesday

Jesus arrived in the region six days before Passover. Most of the time Jesus spent in the temple area in Jerusalem, teaching his disciples and the crowds. The evenings were mainly spent in the nearby village of Bethany, at the home of Lazarus, Mary and Martha, or on the Mount of Olives overlooking the city.

End times

During the last week, Jesus gives a series of "apocalyptic" discourses—statements that deal with the end of the world, describing events that will precede his return. Interpreting these passages is very difficult. Jesus mixes events near to his time with events that were—and still may be—a long way off. This is not a literal description, nor is it a timetable. However, certain key events are mentioned:

• The destruction of the temple

Most experts believe this to be a reference to the events of AD 70 when the Romans destroyed the temple. However, it is bound up with less identifiable elements: wars, rumors of wars, earthquakes, darkness.

• False messiahs and false prophets

Jesus warns of others who will claim to be the returned Messiah. They will have powers and be able to perform miracles, but they are not the real thing.

• A visible return

Christ is pictured returning in a cloud of glory. All earth will see him—from east to west.

• It will take everyone by surprise

No one knows the day or time, even though the signs might be there. Even Jesus doesn't know the exact timing (Mt 24:36).

• A final judgment

Christ will return to judge and the judgment will be final. People will not be judged on their observance of religious ritual, or even on the soundness of their philosophy, but on how their religion and their philosophy affected their lives. Did they really believe it and live it out? Or did they merely go through the motions?

Sunday

Triumphant entry

Mt 21:1–11;
Mk 11:1–11;
Lk 19:28–44;
Jn 12:12–19

Monday

Traders at temple

Mt 21:10–13;
Mk 11:15–18;
Lk 19:45–48

Returns to Bethany

Mt 21:14–17

Leaders begin to plan

Mk 11:18–19

Tuesday

Leaders challenge Jesus

Mt 21:23–27;
Mk 11:27–33;
Lk 20:1–8

Jesus teaches on the Mount of Olives

Mt 23:1–26:5;
Mk 12:1–13:37;
Lk 20:9–21:38

Mary anoints Jesus

Mt 26:6–13;
Mk 14:3–9;
Jn 12:2–8

Judas plots

Mt 26:14–16;
Mk 14:10–11;
Lk 22:3–6

Wednesday

The place: Jerusalem

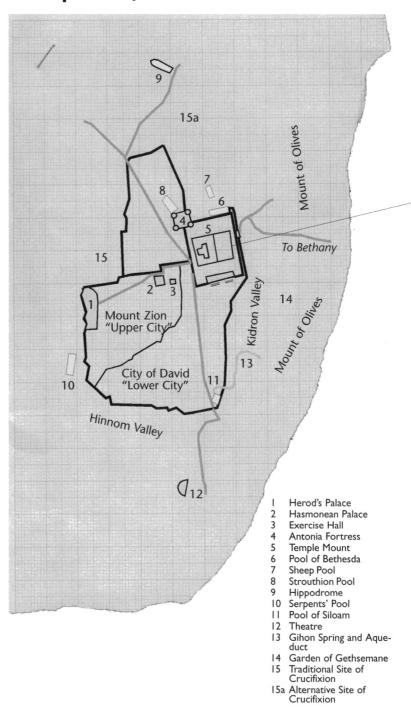

1 Herod's Palace
2 Hasmonean Palace
3 Exercise Hall
4 Antonia Fortress
5 Temple Mount
6 Pool of Bethesda
7 Sheep Pool
8 Strouthion Pool
9 Hippodrome
10 Serpents' Pool
11 Pool of Siloam
12 Theatre
13 Gihon Spring and Aqueduct
14 Garden of Gethsemane
15 Traditional Site of Crucifixion
15a Alternative Site of Crucifixion

The place: the temple

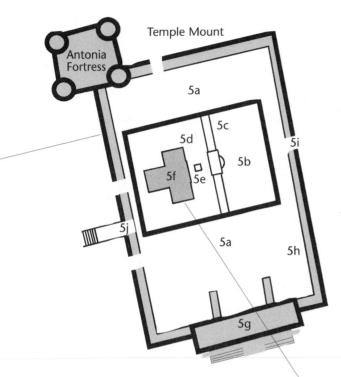

Temple Mount

Antonia Fortress

5a

5c

5d

5b

5i

5f

5e

5j

5a

5h

5g

5a **Court of Gentiles**
This was the only area open to non-Jews. This was also where the traders and money changers did their business.

5b **Court of Women**
The farthest point where women were allowed in the temple.

5c **Court of Israelites**
Only for male Jews.

5d **Court of Priests**

5e **High Altar**
A huge altar where animals were sacrificed.

5f **Temple Building**
Consisting of the entrance, the holy place and the Holy of Holies (see below).

5g **Royal Portico**
A large covered porch where the Sanhedrin met.

5h **Solomon's Portico**
A covered porch that surrounded the temple area. It provided a place for meeting and teaching, and Jesus taught here.

5i **Shushan Gate**
Leading to the Mount of Olives.

5j **Bridge and Gate to the Lower City**

The area for the temple was on a hilltop over-looking the city. In order to make room for his ambitious design, Herod had to level around thirty-five acres of ground.

Herod's temple was a magnificent building. Some fifteen stories high, it was twice as high as Solomon's building, made of cream-colored stone and decorated with gold. The floor plan followed that of earlier temples, with the holy place, and the Holy of Holies—which was empty, of course, the ark being long since lost.

And the Jews were never allowed to forget who was really in charge. In the northwest corner of the mount stood the Antonia Fortress, where Roman troops were garrisoned. The high priests' robes were stored there as a sign of the Jews' subjection to the Romans.

In the end this was proved only too graphic-ally. In AD 70 the temple was completely destroyed by the Romans. The huge golden candlesticks, the sacred table and all the other sacred objects were carried off to Rome in tri-umph. The temple was never rebuilt again.

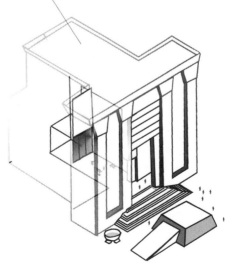

Landmark: Last Supper

What is called "The Last Supper" appears in all four gospels, although there are differences between the accounts. Interestingly, the earliest written account of it comes in 1 Corinthians, which was probably written before the first gospels.

There are two central questions about this.

Was it the Passover meal?

Matthew, Mark and Luke are all clear: this was the Passover meal. But against that, John is equally clear that it wasn't the Passover, but happened the night before. It certainly shares some features with Passover —the disciples were reclining, they dipped their bread in sauces and they sang a hymn before leaving. All of these customs fit in with Passover. On the other hand, there is no mention of the lamb or the unleavened bread and many experts believe that the authorities would never have interrupted such an important event as Passover in order to arrest Jesus.

In the end there is no consensus on the solution. The synoptic writers believed that the Passover festival was on a Friday, and John believed it was on a Thursday. There is obviously a confusion about the calendars, but at present no one has come up with a real solution.

What did Jesus intend by it?

This, perhaps, is the more important question. What was Jesus actually doing? Was he meaning for us just to drink the wine and eat the bread, or are we to partake of a meal? Did he mean it to be a special occasion or are we supposed to remember him every time we eat bread and drink wine?

The answer lies in the actions of the early Church. They, after all, were close to the action and included people who had been at the original meal. To fulfill Jesus' command to "eat this as a way of remembering me" (Lk 22:19), they instituted a celebration called "Eucharist," which means "thanksgiving," otherwise known as the "Lord's Supper."

It was part of a shared meal, to which all kinds of people were invited. This surrounding meal was known as the *agape* meal, or "love feast." This was open to everyone in the community, rich or poor, highborn or low, young or old. The "Lord's Supper," then, was not just a religious ritual for a holy huddle, but was placed in the context of practical love for the community. It is mentioned first in Acts 3:42 and also by Paul in 1 Corinthians 11. Paul's account clearly indicates that there was to be a communal meal during which wine and bread were to be taken. The whole point of the meal, says Paul, is to bring us together in shared remembrance (1 Co 10:17). Jesus clearly intended his followers to remember the new covenant—the new agreement that God was making with his people (Lk 22:20). He used bread and wine—staple, ordinary ingredients—to inaugurate a regular celebration in which all those who follow him could take part. The early followers of Jesus joined together in unity and equality to remember what Jesus had done for them, and to celebrate the new promise of forgiveness and salvation that God gave to them through Jesus' death.

And followers of Jesus still do that today.

The time: Thursday and Friday

Earthquakes and torn curtains

The moment of Jesus' death is attended by shattering noises and startling events.

Earth shakes and rocks split (Mt 27:51) and darkness fills the sky (Lk 23:44). It is as if creation itself is reacting against the event. In the temple, the curtain guarding the Holy of Holies is torn in two from top to bottom—not a natural occurrence, for the curtain was too high for any human to reach the top (Mt 27:51; Mk 15:38; Lk 23:45). The place where only the high priest could go was now open for all.

The earth opens and dead men walk around (Mt 27:52–53). A curious event, only found in Matthew. It is, perhaps, symbolic of what Jesus' death was to achieve—the defeat of death. And those watching the event are struck with fear and wonder—they know that something unique has happened (Mt 27:54; Mk 15:39; Lk 23:47).

The trials of Jesus

The religious council

The religious leaders are concerned about Jesus' blasphemy. This is a highly charged, emotional affair, with the high priest screaming and shouting and Jesus being spat on and beaten. John also adds in a brief interrogation with Annas the deposed high priest (Jn 18:12–14), but this is not a trial as such—just a prelude to the main council meeting.

The Roman trial

The Roman trial of Jesus is conducted by Pilate, the governor. He asks Jesus, "What is truth?" but he is less interested in truth than convenience. Pilate insists on knowing the charges—which are incitement to riot, urging nonpayment of taxes and claiming to be the king (Lk 23:1–2). He tries to offer Jesus in exchange for a political prisoner called Barabbas, but this ploy fails. Although Pilate finds Jesus innocent of all three charges, still he passes sentence. He is fearful of a Jewish riot, fearful of bad reports going back to his superiors.

Herod's trial

Herod is merely curious. He asks lots of questions, none of which Jesus answers, so Herod has him beaten and sent back to Pilate.

So, the different trials have different agendas, but all three feature brutality and humiliation and, in the end, there is a consensus between the three parties that Jesus should be removed.

Thursday

Preparing for Passover
Mt 26:17–19
Mk 14:12–16
Lk 22:7–13

Passover meal
Mt 26:20–35
Mk 14:17–31
Lk 22:14–38
Jn 13:1–17:26

To Gethsemane
Mt 26:36–46
Mk 14:32–42
Lk 22:39–46
Jn 18:1

Friday

Arrest
Mt 26:47–56
Mk 14:43–52
Lk 22:47–53
Jn 18:2–11

Annas
Jn 18:12–24

Council
Mt 27:1
Mk 15:1
Lk 23:66–71
Jn 18:24

Peter's Denial
Mt 26:67–75
Mk 14:66–72
Lk 23:54–62
Jn 18:12–18, 25–27

6:00 a.m.

Herod
Lk 23:8–12

Pilate
Mt 27:2, 11–26
Mk 15:1–15
Lk 23:1–5, 13–24
Jn 18:28–19:16

Death of Judas
Mt 27:1–10
Ac 1:18–19

Crucifixion
Mt 27:26–44;
Mk 15:15–32;
Lk 23:24–43;
Jn 19:16–24

9:00 a.m.

Darkness covers land
Mt 27:45
Lk 23:44

12:00 p.m.

Death
Mt 26:45–55
Mk 15:33–41
Lk 23:44–49
Jn 19:28–30

3:00 p.m.

Burial
Mt 27:57–66
Mk 15:42–47
Lk 23:50–55
Jn 19:31–42

6:00 p.m.

Landmark: Cross

The cross was an instrument of torture or execution used by the Romans. It was considered the most demeaning of all methods of execution and reserved for the lowest of the low. It was the degrading, lowly aspect that made Jesus' death so shocking: the Son of God treated like the scum of the earth.

Generally, the physical form of the cross was more like a "T" shape, with a central stake stuck into the ground and a crossbeam on top. The description of Jesus' cross implies, it was the *crux immissa,* with an upright beam above his head, onto which a sign was pinned. Sometimes the victim's offense was written on a board and hung around his neck. The condemned criminal had to carry his own crossbeam to the place of execution, which was always outside the city, and usually a piece of wasteland. At this place, the criminal was tied or nailed to the crossbeam, and then hung on the stake. The victim's feet were just clear of the ground—Jesus was not high in the air as has often been depicted. He bore his weight by straddling a peg that stuck out from the upright post and, in the end, died from blood loss and exhaustion. Often the victim's legs were broken, meaning that they could no longer support themselves and their heart would no longer stand the strain.

The cross leaves us with one very simple, deeply profound question: Why? Why was it necessary for Jesus to die in this way? Why was it necessary for him to die at all? There are different explanations.

Example
Some see in it an example that we should follow. Jesus suffered unjustly and was treated brutally, but he did not fight back and he did not complain. Although, therefore, he seems to have lost, morally and ethically he was superior to his persecutors.

Revolution
To the Romans, Jesus was a political agitator. To the Jewish authorities he was a false messiah who was challenging the fundamental Law and insulting their authority. Many people see in Jesus a revolutionary who fought, and defeated, the oppression around him.

Sacrifice
A dominant theme of the New Testament is the way that Jesus died in our place. My sin means that I should be punished for my death, but Jesus has taken my punishment. He has served my sentence for me, paid my fine. Although I might physically die, I will not suffer the punishment I ought to suffer, because someone has already done that for me.

Identification
Jesus' life and death means that there is nothing I can go through that he does not understand. People may question God about the issue of suffering, but the one thing they cannot accuse him of is not knowing about it. Jesus lived and died and was a full part of humanity. He therefore knows what it means to be tempted, to be tired, to be lonely, to laugh, to drink, to sweat, to die.

In the end, the cross is a mystery. Jesus had to take all the sin and shame on himself, he had to die in our place. In some way too deep for us to fully comprehend, this was the way it had to be done.

The time: Sunday

The different gospels contain different details about the resurrection, with Jesus appearing to different groups and with varying numbers of angels present at the tomb. Although many attempts have been made to make the accounts harmonize, in the words of one commentary "an exact harmony eludes us." Which is a posh way of saying you can't fit it all together.

Some argue that this means the accounts are inherently unreliable, but eyewitness accounts can often differ—and when something as remarkable as the resurrection is concerned, there must have been a considerable amount of confusion and surprise. Nevertheless, there is a complete agreement on the core details: the tomb was empty and Jesus appeared to his followers after his death.

Landmark: Resurrection

The resurrection is crucial to the story of Jesus. The earliest evidence we have lies in the sermons given by Peter immediately after the events took place (Ac 2:14–36). Experts believe that the language used in these speeches is different from that of the rest of Acts, indicating that they are, indeed, very early records.

So, from the earliest times, the disciples were quite clear that Jesus had risen again. Matthew, Mark and John were all clear that Jesus rose in bodily, physical form. Paul—who was writing less than twenty-five years after the event—reminds his readers of what they have always known, that Jesus rose from the dead. He also points to resurrection appearances that were known to his readers but that the gospel writers did not put into their accounts.

The accounts themselves are told very simply. There is no attempt to introduce symbolism or even make allusions to the Old Testament. Instead they concentrate on two simple facts: the grave was empty and Jesus was seen by many people on several different occasions. These are important facts. His body was not still in the grave while his spirit moved around like a ghost. He had changed—Mary Magdalene and some other disciples did not immediately recognize him—but he had actually, physically, risen.

The final piece of evidence lies in the behavior of the disciples. Something turned this dispirited, scared, disillusioned bunch into a group of powerful, motivated witnesses. They, at least, were convinced of the truth: Jesus had risen. And their conviction and faith spread like wildfire through the city of Jerusalem and beyond.

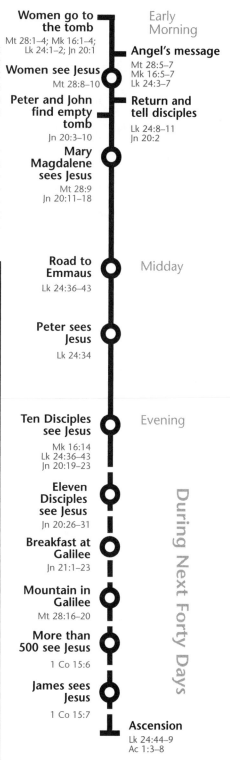

Women go to the tomb
Mt 28:1–4; Mk 16:1–4; Lk 24:1–2; Jn 20:1

Early Morning

Angel's message
Mt 28:5–7
Mk 16:5–7
Lk 24:3–7

Women see Jesus
Mt 28:8–10

Peter and John find empty tomb
Jn 20:3–10

Return and tell disciples
Lk 24:8–11
Jn 20:2

Mary Magdalene sees Jesus
Mt 28:9
Jn 20:11–18

Road to Emmaus
Lk 24:36–43

Midday

Peter sees Jesus
Lk 24:34

Ten Disciples see Jesus
Mk 16:14
Lk 24:36–43
Jn 20:19–23

Evening

Eleven Disciples see Jesus
Jn 20:26–31

Breakfast at Galilee
Jn 21:1–23

Mountain in Galilee
Mt 28:16–20

More than 500 see Jesus
1 Co 15:6

James sees Jesus
1 Co 15:7

Ascension
Lk 24:44–9
Ac 1:3–8

During Next Forty Days

291

John
The Word of God

Who: Tradition has it that this book is the work of the apostle John. One argument supporting this is the fact that he is not named in this gospel, but referred to as "the disciple that Jesus loved" (13:23; 19:26; 20:2; 21:7). This would be natural if he was the author. The book shows a definite Jewish background and has many tiny details that could only have come from an eyewitness.

Some have argued that the book is the work of several hands, with a core block of material supplied by the "witness," explanatory material supplied by someone they call the "evangelist," and the whole lot brought together by an editor. The main difficulty with this view is that no one can say who did which part.

Another view is that the work was originally issued in two versions—a Jewish version which aimed to show that Jesus was the Messiah, and a Greek version, which was the same as the Jewish version, but with a new prologue and explanations of some of the Jewish terms.

When: Again, tradition places this as the last of the Gospels, dating from around the end of the first century AD. However, some experts believe it was written earlier—around AD 70.

Clement of Alexandria claimed that John wrote his gospel as a supplement to the other three, which would obviously make it the last. It is also the most complex theologically, which might indicate that it was written at a time when the theology had developed.

However, it is no more complex than Romans, which was written around AD 57. People started trying to figure out what it all meant the day after Jesus died. So the complexity does not necessarily indicate a late date. Indeed, there is a lot of agreement between John's theology and Paul's. Both demonstrate that Jesus is the image of God, that he created all things, and that by placing our faith in him we will have everlasting life.

Quick Guide
Author
John, the apostle and friend of Jesus
Type
Gospel
Purpose
To explore not only what Jesus said and did, but who he really was and what it all means.
Key verses
3:16–17 "God loved the people of this world so much that he gave his only Son, so that everyone who has faith in him will have eternal life and never really die. God did not send his Son into the world to condemn its people. He sent him to save them!"
If you remember one thing about this book . . .
Jesus is God. Faith in him will save all who believe.
Your 15 minutes start now
Read chapters 1, 3–4, 8, 11, 13, 15–16, 19–20

The Route Through John

292

What: John is unique. The language, the imagery, the style of the book are like none of the other gospels. There are places where he may have used material from the Synoptic Gospels, but the differences are striking. John's Jesus does not speak in parables, but in a series of speeches or discourses that use far more complex language and imagery.

There is more interpretation in this book, and times when the writer himself adds comments and explanations. It is more reflective than the other gospels. Some see the synoptics more as history, and John as theology; that what *happens* in the synoptics is *explained* in John. This is too simple a view, and it ignores the vast amount of historical detail that John contains. The book includes names and places that are missing from the other gospels and many of these details have been confirmed by archaeology. Nevertheless, it is true that John expands on areas that are less developed in the other gospels. The synoptics tell us of Jesus' authority to forgive sins, but John tells us where this authority came from. In the synoptics Jesus' claim to be God in human form is evident through his actions, but never overtly stated. In John it is right there on page one, line one.

For these reasons—the style, the complexity, the sheer amount of reported speech—many people find it hard to view the gospel of John as having the same level of authenticity as the other three. How is it that Jesus sounds so different here? Why doesn't he teach in the same way? Where did all these long conversations come from?

John is different. But then people's lives have different aspects. People who only know me through my work, will record a very different figure from the one my family might record. When John recounts episodes that we find in the synoptics, he doesn't use the same language. He is seeing the same event, but from a different perspective.

There are, undoubtedly, times when the writer records things that are interpretive and explanatory. The book begins with one such passage that sums up the entire life of Jesus in what you can only call cosmic terms. But that doesn't make it any less authoritative or inspired. Throughout the Bible God gives his followers pictures and visions to explain history. The entire output of the prophets is based on the idea of direct inspiration. John is the work of one who was with Jesus and knew him intimately. It is also the work of one who, prayerfully and over many years, asked God what it all meant.

And what it meant was life. Life in all its fullness, life in all its power, life everlasting.

Landmark: Word of God

This title for Jesus is found almost exclusively in the gospel of John. As a concept it is an important one, not only for what it tells us about Jesus, but because it is truly multicultural. John is using an image that speaks to both a Greek and Jewish audience.

The Jewish meaning

"The Word" meant "the Word of the Lord." God said something and it happened. So, to a Jew, the Word of God represented God's purpose and intention, the very mind of God.

The Greek meaning

Greek Stoic philosophy argued that the universe was not random or senseless, but that there were fundamental, rational principles that governed all things. These principles were the *Logos* or "word," the principles behind existence itself. The "word" also became a kind of shorthand for rational thought.

John brings together these two principles into one being: Jesus. Jesus is the *Word* of God, the living, breathing purpose of the Creator, the fundamental truth of the universe.

The beginning   1:1–18

The beginning of Matthew takes us back to Abraham. The beginning of Luke takes us back to Adam. The beginning of John takes us back to the time before the world even started.

The book begins with a kind of poem, a statement that makes it clear that Jesus was with God from the very start. Indeed, he was more than with God, he *was* God. Jesus is described as "the Word." It was through this being, through this Word, that all things were created. Christ is then referred to as the light, echoing the very first words that God spoke: let there be light. Christ is the "light of the world," the one who comes to defeat the darkness. This is reinforced by John the Baptist, who spoke of the light, but who was not the light itself.

This "poetical" preface is a summary of the gospel. Jesus was with God from the beginning, for he was, in fact, God. John the Baptist prepared people for Jesus' coming, but when he arrived, few people recognized him. Those who did recognize him, however, became children of God, not because of their own efforts, but because of God's love. No one has ever truly seen God, but Jesus shows us what God is like.

John the Baptist 1:19–34

When John the Baptist is challenged about his nature and mission, he makes it clear. He is not the reincarnation of Elijah, he is not the Messiah, he is merely one who is paving the way. John doesn't recount the baptism of Jesus, but he refers to it, for the very next day John the Baptist talks of having seen the Spirit come down on Jesus.

The first disciples   1:35–51

Two of John the Baptist's followers join Jesus. One of them is Andrew, the brother of Peter. The other is not named, but the theory is that it was John, the author of this gospel. Andrew, from the first, recognizes Jesus as the Messiah. In John's account Jesus renames Peter straightaway. In the other accounts it takes place after Peter's profession of faith. Nathaniel, who is commended by Jesus for being a true Israelite, recognizes Jesus as well. Like Jacob —another true Israelite—Nathaniel will see angels ascending and descending from heaven (Ge 32: 22–32).

Landmark: Incarnation

Incarnation means to appear in person. The incarnation of God means that God took human form and lived among humans. This was first done in the form of Jesus. The incarnation teaches us several things.

If you want to change the world, you have to be in the world.

God did not stay in heaven and keep his distance. He took human form and lived with us. For Christians the lesson is still valid. We have to get alongside people if we are to save them.

If you want to understand, you have to experience.

God understands what it is to be human because he has been a human. Hebrews, for example, says that God understands temptation, because in the form of Jesus he was tempted (He 2:18).

If you want to teach, demonstrate.

Jesus' life on earth shows us how we should live. It provides a model that we should follow.

Following Jesus' resurrection, the Church has taken on the job of making God known in the world. Empowered by the Holy Spirit, we are encouraged to make God visible to the world around us through our faith and actions. God is still incarnate in the world. He appears in person, through those who follow him.

The Ministry of Jesus 2:1–12:11

John structures his account of Jesus' life around seven special signs and seven "I am" statements.

The signs are special miracles that point to the true nature of Jesus. These miraculous signs lead frequently into discourses or to confrontation with the authorities.

The seven statements are known as the seven "I am's" because each time, Jesus likens himself to something—bread, water, a door—to illustrate his true nature. There is also a special "I am," the eighth and greatest, where Jesus, deliberately and overtly, identifies himself with *Yahweh*, the unspoken name of God.

Brief Lives: Peter, aka Cephas, Simon, Rocky, etc.

Background: Brother of Andrew. Married and lived in Capernaum.

Occupation: Fisherman. Disciple. Apostle.

Achievements: Jesus renamed Simon the "rock." In the Gospels, however he was more like lava than granite. He was hot-headed and impulsive, always getting into scrapes and rarely able to open his mouth without putting his size twelve sandals in it. He could say great things one minute and foolish things the next; one minute he would be walking on water, the next drowning under the waves.

Jesus named him "the rock," not for what he was, but for what he would become, for in the early Church Peter was to be the strong man, the one on whom all the others relied. The catalyst for this was his denial of Christ and his subsequent forgiveness. He knew what it was to fail his Lord completely; and, after Jesus reinstated him and restored him, he did not fear failure again.

He proved to be a clear-headed and courageous leader of the early Church, sensible enough to recognize his own limitations, and spirit-filled enough to do more for the Lord than he ever imagined he could.

Character: Impulsive, hot-headed, full-on enthusiasm.

Pros: Never does anything by halves.

Cons: Never thinks before he never does anything by halves.

❶ Sign 1: The wedding at Cana   2:1–12

Jesus' first miracle, where he turns dishwater into wine. It is a picture of what Jesus does for all people who believe in him: he transforms the ordinary into the extraordinary, the sinner into the son of God, the dishwater into the best wine of all. This is specifically referred to as Jesus' first miracle (2:11). The Greek word used means "sign."

❷ Jesus in the temple   2:12–25

The synoptics paint a picture of Jesus' life which is broadly in two parts: a main ministry in Galilee and Judaea, and a final week in Jerusalem. In their accounts, Jesus gradually moves toward Jerusalem, the climax of his work. In John's account Jesus moves between Jerusalem and the other areas. He makes several visits to the city before the climactic last week.

John places the temple scene much earlier in his gospel. Opinion is divided as to whether this means that Jesus cleansed the temple twice, or whether John has simply put one event in a different chronological order. It's not impossible that Jesus should have done this twice—once at the beginning of his ministry and once at the end. What makes John's account significant is that Jesus drives the animals out of the temple as well. It is a sign that the need for sacrificing animals was at an end.

Jesus and Nicodemus   3:1–21

We do the Pharisees a disservice if we portray them solely as a bunch of unthinking zealots. Their teaching could be oppressive, their emphasis on the externals could lead to hypocrisy, but nevertheless, many were good, faithful men. Here Nicodemus, one of their number, recognizes Jesus' importance (3:1–2). Even so, he visits Jesus at night—perhaps an admission of the sensitivities surrounding this controversial preacher.

The conversation is a prime example of why the Pharisees saw Jesus as such a threat, for he argues that, to enter the kingdom of God, it is not enough to be born a Jew. Instead, you must be born again. Few verses in the Bible have inspired more books, sermons, speeches and general discussion than the phrase "you must be born again." In fact, it can easily be translated "you must be born from above." What Jesus is saying is that to enter the kingdom of God, you have to make a completely new start.

Over the years, the phrase has been turned into a kind of test, and many Christians have spent long hours wondering whether they are really "born again" or not. Politicians and preachers declare that they are "born again" as if they have just joined the yachting club or something. It is not that kind of process that Jesus is talking about here. He describes it quite succinctly in the famous verse 3:16: "God loved the people of this world so much that he gave his only Son, so that everyone who has faith in him will have eternal life and never really die." Jesus goes on to make the point that we also have to live by the truth (3:21). It is all very well for people to claim to be "born again," but they have to live in the light as well.

John the Baptist again   3:22–30 ▷252

This incident is difficult to fit in with the chronology of the synoptics, because Mark records that Jesus did not begin his work in Galilee till after the arrest of John (Mk 1:14). Probably this records an earlier incident, where John the Baptist recognizes that his ministry is only preparing the way. Now that the bridegroom has arrived, it is time for the best man to leave the party. Verses 31–36 were probably not uttered by John the Baptist, but are a kind of summing up of all that we have learned so far in this gospel about Jesus.

❸ The woman at the well   4:1–42

In Samaria, Jesus encounters a woman drawing water from the well and asks her for a drink. This was a radical and revolutionary act. Jews and Samaritans hated each other and would not even use the same cups, but Jesus came to save not just the Jews but the whole world. What starts as a simple request turns into a personal, challenging, life-changing experience. Several times she tries to divert the conversation into areas of theological controversy, proof positive that theology can sometimes be a convenient way of escaping the real issues. Finally she tries to evade the issue by saying that they will just have to wait for the Messiah to explain everything. Unfortunately her escape plan is scuttled: "I am the Messiah," says Jesus. Startled, the woman rushes off to get her townsfolk. They come; they listen. Many become believers.

❹ Sign 2: Healing of the official's son
4:43–54; Mt 8:5–13; Lk 7:1–10

This miracle of healing is similar to that of the centurion's slave in Matthew and Luke and may even be the same incident. The event shows that Jesus did not need to be physically present for the healing to occur. What makes the difference is faith.

> ### Details, Details . . .
> ### The Samaritans
>
> The antagonism between Jews and Samaritans goes back to the sixth century BC. When the Jews returned from exile in Babylon they regarded themselves as the pure race; the mixed race that still lived in the area was regarded as unclean. The Samaritans responded to this attitude—and to the restoration of the temple in Jerusalem—by building their own temple at Mount Gerazim. By Jesus' time the antagonism was so strong that Jews were forbidden even to drink from the same vessels as Samaritans. The Samaritans lived in the land between Judaea and Galilee. When people want to insult Jesus they call him a Samaritan (8:48).   ▷**127**

❺ Sign 3: The Pool of Bethesda   5:1–18

Again this has similarities with other miracles in the synoptic accounts (e.g. Mk 2:1–12 and Lk 5:18–26). The emphasis is not only on Jesus' power to heal, but on his ability to forgive sins. This was blasphemy to the Jews —only God has the power to forgive sins. Where the synoptics leave it to the reader to work it out, John underlines the point unequivocally: Jesus was claiming to be equal with God (5:18). Jesus goes on, in a lengthy speech, to back up this statement, claiming to have the authority to judge individuals and to give eternal life (5:19–30). The Jews may search the Scriptures to back up their own preconceptions, but they cannot recognize the truth when it is sitting in front of them (5:31–47).

❻ Sign 4: Feeding the five thousand   6:1–15
Mt 14:13–21; Mk 6:30–44; Lk 9:10–17 ▷267

❼ Sign 5: Walking on water   6:16–21
Mt 14:22–27; Mk 6:45–52 ▷256

"I am" 1: The bread of life   6:22–59 ▷67

The crowd are puzzled to know how Jesus got to the other side of the lake without a boat. Their question leads into the first great "I am" statement: "I am the bread of life."

Jesus likens himself to bread—not just a basic foodstuff of life, but the manna that came down from heaven. He is the bread that sustains us and gives us life. He goes on to talk about the symbolism of the bread and wine. In the synoptics he institutes what came to be known as the Lord's Supper. Here he does not refer to the feast directly, but points to its true meaning. To drink his blood and eat his flesh is to reflect on the meaning of his death and to remember who he is and what he has done for us.

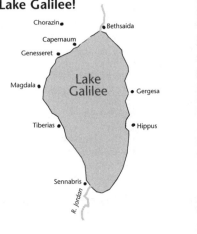

POSTCARD

Welcome to Lake Galilee!

Also known as Lake Tiberias, Lake Gennesaret, the Sea of Galilee or the Sea of Tiberius, this popular fishing resort is home to a thriving community of villages and industry. The lake is justly famous for the quality and abundance of its fish, many of which are pickled and sent to Jerusalem and beyond.

Situated in northern Palestine, it is a freshwater lake that separates two parts of the River Jordan. In the middle it spreads to a width of about 8 miles, and it is about 13 miles long.

As it is surrounded by hills, it is subject to squalls and sudden changes of temperature. Fishermen are warned that severe weather conditions can sometimes arise. It's always advised to wear a life jacket, or travel with someone who can control the weather.

The family of Jesus   7:1–9 ▷266

Jesus' brothers have not yet become his followers. They urge him to go to a more public arena and show what he can do. He refuses their suggestion, which was similar to the temptation in the desert. The fact that they were not all believers at the time of Jesus' ministry might be a clue as to why Jesus entrusted the care of his mother to one of his disciples, John. However, the odd thing is that after telling them he isn't going, he goes. Why he does this is not explained. It may be that John is trying to marry together two different narratives, or it may be simply another example of Jesus waiting for the right moment.

Whatever the case, Jesus uses the occasion to assert his divine origin again. We often think of Jesus as "gentle Jesus meek and mild," this slight, hippie-like figure who wanders around Galilee with a lamb on his shoulders. However, anyone who actually reads the Gospels, as opposed to looking at Victorian stained glass, will find a figure full of passion and energy. He angrily throws out the traders in the temple. In debating with the Pharisees he shouts at them (7:28). He gets so excited that people think he's mad (7:20). He is deliberately confrontational and unsettling—a side of him that comes out very clearly in the gospel of John.

As this passage in John shows, Jesus doesn't just gently talk about God, he SHOUTS it at people (7:37). His approach causes as many people to turn against him as toward him. John tells us that they take sides in their argument about his claims (7:40–44).

❽ The woman caught in adultery   7:53–8:11

This passage is almost certainly a later addition to the gospel, inserted here in the middle of Jesus' passionate arguments with the Pharisees. However, even though it is an insert, many believe that it is an authentic story.

It fits in perfectly with the way that Jesus answered all the tests that the hard-line religious leaders brought before him, illustrating a perfect balancing act: Jesus condemns the woman's sin, but not the woman herself. It also includes a wealth of detail, such as Jesus doodling in the sand and the fact that it was the oldest men who began to drift away first. (Older people often have more self-knowledge than the zealous young.) Most of all, it is a perfect example of how Jesus treated individuals. He made demands of them, but all the demands took place in the context of forgiveness and grace.

"I am" 2: The light of the world   8:12–20

Darkness and light are powerful metaphors in the gospel of John. Indeed, the whole book begins with God "shining a light" on the world. The Pharisees and religious zealots are unable to see the truth about Jesus because they have been blinded by their own self-righteousness and preconceived ideas. We miss out on the threatening nature of darkness in our culture of twenty-four-hour facilities and electric light. In the ancient world the dark was dangerous. Bad things happened at night. Light brought safety and understanding. Light was linked to life, for only with light could people live without fear. Light brings freedom, a theme that Jesus goes on to elaborate in 8:31–38.

❾ The great "I am"   8:48–59 ▷51–2

This is not usually listed with the other "I am's" in the gospel—mainly because it kind of sums all of them up. This is the clearest indication of Jesus' identification with God. When the people accuse him of being demon possessed because he claims to be greater than Abraham, Jesus replies with the startlingly ungrammatical statement: "Before Abraham was, I am." Although there is much debate about this statement, the Jews recognized that Jesus was referring to the divine name. They are prepared there and then to stone him to death, but he hides.

The Jesus that John portrays is a confrontational figure. He enrages people so much that he has to hide. Taken out of context, Jesus' speeches in John seem lyrical and almost poetic. Placed in context, they become incendiary statements, igniting the passions of those who saw him as a threat to the entire religious establishment. In the other gospels, "official" opposition comes in later. In John it is there from the very earliest chapters.

❿ Sign 6: The blind man sees   9:1–41

This has similarities to some healings in Mark (e.g., Mk 8:22–26). The disciples assume that something the man has done has caused his blindness, the same glib explanation of suffering that we find in Job. Jesus dismisses the idea that sin is connected with physical disability and points to attitude: what matters is not the disability, but the opportunity to show God at work in people's lives.

Once again, the healing leads to confrontation, since it happened on a Sabbath. The Jewish religious leaders instigate a thorough investigation, even bringing in the man's parents to give a proper identification. The man himself, however, pours scorn on their arguments, even mockingly suggesting that they are only asking because they want to join the disciples! The Pharisees end by taking refuge in the very philosophy raised by the disciples at the beginning of the chapter: this man is a sinner. Anyone, in fact, who does not see things their way, is a sinner.

> **Details, Details . . . The temple festival (10:22)**
>
> This was the feast of dedication or Hanukkah. It celebrates the rededication of the temple in the time of the Maccabees. It was celebrated by the lighting of lamps in the temple and surrounding houses.

"I am" 3 and 4: The gate and the good shepherd
10:1–42

God is frequently depicted as a shepherd in the Old Testament (the most famous example being Psalm 23). Jesus once again identifies himself with God, and explains that his care for the sheep extends as far as laying down his life to save them. But he is also the gate—the way in which people can enter into eternal life.

Puzzling Points
Why does Jesus weep?

Jesus is described as being terribly moved by this scene (11:33, 38). As he nears the tomb he starts to cry (11:36). Why? He cannot be mourning for Lazarus because he knows that Lazarus will rise again. And he cannot be joining in with Martha and Mary because he knows that in a few minutes their tears will turn to joy. One theory is that it was the simple fact of death itself that was causing him to cry. He was weeping because death was never meant to be. God never intended death to be a part of life on earth; its very presence was a terribly sad fact (Ge 1:9, 22). Jesus was not weeping because Lazarus was dead. He was weeping because of death itself.

Another theory is that Jesus weeps because he knows that he will have to face death himself. Indeed, it is this very act of raising Lazarus that intensifies the plotting that will, ultimately, lead to his death.

Puzzling Points
When was the perfume incident? (12:1)

There is a difficulty in the chronology between John and the synoptics. John places this meal six days before the Passover. Matthew places it two days before Passover. Various schemes have been suggested to account for the difference, but ultimately their accounts just seem to differ.

⑪ Sign 7: Raising of Lazarus
"I am" 5: The resurrection and the life
11:1–44

Jesus has already claimed that he had the power to give life (5:21). Now he proves it. The episode with Lazarus is unique because it involves one of Jesus' personal friends. Lazarus, along with his sisters Mary and Martha lived in Bethany, a village close to Jerusalem. (Mary is described as pouring perfume on the feet of Jesus and wiping it with her hair. This refers to the incident in 12:1–8. There is no need to identify her with the woman mentioned in Luke 7:36–50.)

Jesus is caught between two sets of expectations. Mary and Martha want him to rush to Bethany straightaway. The disciples know that if he ventures too close to Jerusalem he will be stoned. In the end, Jesus waits two days before setting off. "Oh great," says Thomas, "let's all go and die with him." (Perhaps the other twin was the cheerful one.) By the time Jesus gets to Bethany, Lazarus has been dead for four days. Martha greets him with all the faith she can muster—even now, with her brother lying in the tomb, she still has faith that he can act. Jesus confirms her faith with another of his great "I am" statements: I am the resurrection and the life. I am the one who brings people back from death (11:25). And he proceeds to demonstrate this with Lazarus.

The plot to kill Jesus
11:45–57

John points to the raising of Lazarus as the crucial event that turns the tide against Jesus. The synoptics imply that it was the cleansing of the temple. It is noticeable here that the Pharisees and the Sadducee high priests are not just concerned about the religious issues: they believe that if many more people follow Jesus, the Romans will step in. They are protecting not only their religion, but their political power and influence. Caiaphas, the high priest, issues a statement that has been echoed by many cold, callous leaders: better for one man to die than for the nation to perish. Jesus is, in their eyes, expendable. And they start to put out requests for information.

Curiously enough, they also decide to kill Lazarus, which seems a bit unfair (12:9–11). I mean, the man has only just been resurrected. They were obviously getting desperate and were intent on covering up all the evidence of Jesus' activities. Even if that meant getting rid of people he had brought back from the dead.

The last week 12:12–19:42

⑫ The entry to Jerusalem 19:28–40;
Mt 21:1–11; Mk 1:1–11 ▷259

⑬ The voice from heaven 12:23–36

After the triumphant entry, Jesus talks, not of triumph but of loss. He talks of dying, of falling like a grain of wheat into the ground. There is a hint of uncertainty— he doesn't know what to say (12:27). And then some hear a voice from heaven while others hear mere thunder. In John, this is the end of Jesus' public ministry. From now on, he teaches his disciples in a series of small, private locations. John tells us that he went into hiding and then gives a brief summary of the main contents of the previous chapters. Many had faith in Jesus, including some of the leadership. But ranged against them were the forces of the Pharisees, and many of the leaders fell away, because they liked the praises of men more than praise from God.

⑭ The upper room

John does not give the details about the Last Supper that appear in the other gospels. There is nothing about the arrangements for the room and his date for the supper is slightly different. While in Matthew, Mark and Luke it seems to be a Passover meal, John records it as happening the evening before Passover (13:1). The only way that scholars have resolved this issue is to suggest that the Pharisees held their Passover a day before the Sadducees, but there is little proof for this.

Washing the feet 13:1–20

The act of washing his disciples' feet is a reversal of all the worldly rules of kingdom. Their leader should have his feet washed, not the other way round. But the key thing is that Jesus acts like a slave. He takes off his outer clothing, he washes the dust and the dirt from the feet of his disciples. It is an act that brings to mind some of the prophetic actions of Ezekiel. Jesus is showing them a new vision of what it means to be a leader.

The betrayer 13:21–30; Mt 26:20–25; Mk 14:17–21; Lk 22:21–23

In eastern meals it was often the custom for the host to offer a special morsel to one of the diners. It was a sign of special friendship. Jesus seems to indicate that, despite what Judas was to do, he would still love him.

New commandment 14:31–35

He picks up this theme in the command he gives to his disciples. They must love one another. The quality of their love for each other will be what identifies them as his followers—the love that led Jesus to act like a slave to his followers.

Details, Details . . .
The Greeks in Jerusalem (12:20–22)

At Passover Jerusalem attracts Jews from all over the world. Even Greek Jews have heard about Jesus and want to meet him. They approach Philip, who discusses the proposal with Andrew. The outcome is not recorded.

Puzzling Points
What about other faiths?

John 14:6 has often been interpreted as meaning that only those who believe in Jesus will enter heaven. What Jesus is saying here is that those who see him see the Father. In that sense it becomes a question of who you think Jesus is. The key concept, then, is not the paraphernalia of Christianity. It's not whether you sing hymns in tune or whether you can quote the Bible for hours at a time. It's who you think Jesus is. That is what will ultimately decide your future.

This encounter with Jesus is crucial. Elsewhere Jesus says that, because he has come and spoken to them, they have no excuse for their sin. In other words, those who encounter Jesus but do not respond must take the responsibility for their decision. But those who don't encounter Jesus, or those who see a distorted picture of him through the bigotry of false followers—what of them?

We cannot say. God is a God of love and a God of justice and, at the end of time, it will be up to Jesus to judge who has followed him and who hasn't. Our job is simple: to help people encounter Jesus by offering them love.

"I am" 6: The way, the truth and the life   14:1–31

Jesus has already described himself as the gate. He does not show us the way to salvation—he is the way to salvation. He points us heavenwards because those who have met him have met the Father. After he has promised the Holy Spirit, the meal is ended.

"I am" 7: The true vine   15:1–17

Some believe this passage to be inserted out of place here, arguing that Jesus could hardly have taught all this while walking from the upper room to the Garden of Gethsemane. The issue is what is meant by 14:31: "It is time for us to go now." Some experts argue that this actually means something like "it is time for action," or "time to get serious." In which case, Jesus might have been speaking metaphorically, indicating his spiritual determination to challenge the forces of darkness.

Either way, the image is fundamental to what Jesus claims for himself. The image of the vine is a standard image in the Old Testament for the nation of Israel, but Israel had failed to live up to the standard God set, so Jesus came. Jesus is the true vine, producing life-giving fruit for his Father. Anyone who would follow him can be grafted onto the stem, can "join" the vine and bear fruit like Jesus.

Details, Details . . .
I chose you (15:16)
Jesus is talking about the disciples. He chose them for his friends. When they were sent out, they produced the same fruit that he did. Jesus is indicating that they will continue to do so, providing they remain rooted in him.

Opposition of the world   15:18–16:33

To be rooted in Jesus is not to opt for an easy existence. The world hates the leader and it will hate the followers. They will be abused and thrown out of synagogues.

⑮ The great prayer   17:1–26

This is Jesus' longest recorded prayer. The prayer falls into three sections.

First, Jesus prays for what he is about to do, asking that his Father will return him to his previous position of glory, and that he will exchange humiliation for glory (17:1–5). Second, he prays for his disciples. He doesn't ask that they be removed from the world, but that they be protected from the world and from the evil one (17:6–19). Finally, he prays for all his future followers (17:20–26). He prays for unity both with each other and with God. The prayer makes clear that it is through his followers that people in the future will find out what God is like. People will see it through God's love and Christ's presence in their lives (17:26).

Betrayal and arrest   18:1–11
Mt 26:47–56; Mk 14:43–50; Lk 22:47–53 ▷261

⑯ Trial before the high priest   18:12–14, 19–24
Mt 26:57–58; Mk 14:53–54; Lk 22:54 ▷289

This encounter is not recorded in the other gospels, which merely recount that Jesus was taken to the house of the high priest. It is not a trial as such, but an interrogation by Annas, a relative of the high priest. Annas had been deposed from the high priesthood in AD 15, but many Jews may still have regarded him as the "real" high priest. Jewish law decreed that a man could not be sentenced on the same day as his trial. It may be that this interrogation and that of Caiaphas were hurried through in order to meet with this stipulation.

Peter's denial

18:15–18, 25–27
Mt 26:69–75; Mk 14:66–72; Lk 22:55–62 ▷261

John inserts a scene with Jesus and Annas in between Peter's denials. It is like watching a scene from a film, with the camera cutting between locations. In the exterior shots we see Peter denying his Lord. Cut to the interior, and we see the high priest ill-treating Jesus.

Brief Lives: Judas Iscariot

Background: Unknown. Iscariot might mean that he came from Kerioth, or it might simply mean "thief."

Occupation: Disciple. Spy.

Achievements: The figure of Judas is a difficult one to make out. Part of the problem is that Jesus seems to have known from the start that Judas would betray him. Indeed, he seems to have picked him almost for that purpose. In the Synoptic Gospels Judas does not appear to turn against Christ until they arrive in Jerusalem and Jesus doesn't mention the fact until during the Last Supper. In John's gospel, however, Judas is always shown in a bad light. John, for example, records the incident with the perfume that is also found in Matthew 26:6–13 and Mark 14:3–9. But he adds that Judas was in the habit of helping himself to their joint funds (12:6). He also records that Jesus called Judas a devil (6:71) and knew from early on that he would betray him. That Judas did a terrible thing is certain. That he bitterly regretted it is also certain. But the statement that he was a thief is confusing. If he was that shifty, why did they give him control of the money? It may have been only later that these facts about Judas came out. Or it may be that they reflect a later tradition.

Character: Difficult to fathom.

Pros: Committed enough to follow Jesus in the first place.

Cons: In the end he could not be trusted.

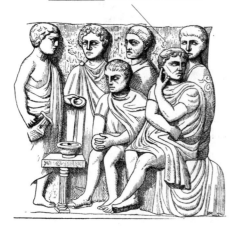

It's no use arguing—I am absolutely <u>determined</u> to sit on the fence.

⑰ Jesus and Pilate 18:28–19:16; Mt 27:15–31; Mk 15:1–20; Lk 23:1–5, 13–25 ▷289

The encounter between Jesus and Pilate in John is fundamentally the same as that described in the other gospels, but John paints a far more detailed picture. In John's account, Pilate comes across as an uncertain, slightly desperate figure. His constant references to Jesus as "the king of the Jews" are, perhaps, intended to curry favor with the crowd, but have the opposite effect. Pilate wants to release Jesus, but he is outmaneuvered by the mob. In the end they pass his sentence for him, and this rather pathetic leader is forced to have Jesus executed.

"What is truth?" he asks in this gospel. Pilate's tragedy was that he let other people decide for him. He asked the right questions, but he never had the courage to answer them.

Crucifixion and death 19:17–42; Mt 27:31–56; Mk 15:22–41; Lk 23:27–49 ▷290

The spear 19:31–37

Only John records this incident. The spear thrust might have been to kill Jesus, or it might simply have been a random act of brutality. At any rate, what appears to have happened is that the spear pierced Jesus' heart, releasing the fluid in the pericardium. John affirms that this is an eyewitness account. This is important because there were some who, in later years, denied that Jesus had died on the cross. John refutes their theories. Jesus was dead; the spear thrust proved it.

Burial of Jesus 19:38–42; Mt 2:57–61; Mk 15:42–47; Lk 23:50–56 ▷262

Let's hear it for Joseph of Arimathea

All the Gospels record that it was Joseph who provided the tomb for Jesus. Joseph was a member of the Sanhedrin who had not voted for Jesus' death. His position meant that he had to act in secret, but it also allowed him influence with Pilate. As a rich man, he provided the body with wrappings of fine linen. The idea that Joseph came to England later, carrying the Holy Grail, is a legend, not recorded anywhere in the Gospels.

Resurrection 20:1–21:25

⑱ Appearance to the women 20:1–10; Mt 28:1–10; Mk 16:1–8; Lk 24:1–12 ▷291

John records that it was Mary Magdalene who went to the tomb, whereas the other gospels record that there were several women. However, Mary's use of the phrase "We don't know where they have put him!" seems to indicate that she was not the only one present.

**Details, Details . . .
The unclean Romans
(18:28)**

According to Jewish law, anyone who came into contact with "unclean" foreigners would not be allowed to eat the Passover meal.

Peter and John investigate, but they do not see the risen Christ. Mary, however, accompanies them to the tomb, but does not return with them to the city. She is standing weeping outside the cave when she sees two angels. Then she turns round and sees the gardener.

It is a curious fact that in several of his resurrection appearances, his close friends do not recognize Jesus. Something has changed, and the transfigured body is not the same as before. All he has to do is speak her name, however, and she knows who it is. She calls him "Rabboni," which means "my teacher." Jesus tells her not to hold him, perhaps because he knows that she will see him again, or perhaps because he is implying that she can only "hold" him through the Holy Spirit now.

Appearance to the disciples 20:19–29; Mt 28:16–20; Mk 16:14–18; Lk 24:36–49 ▷283, 290

John records that Thomas was the disciple who was missing when Jesus appeared. Although at first he insists that he will need physical contact with Jesus to prove that he has risen, when Jesus actually appears before him, Thomas doesn't need to touch him. Straightaway Thomas acknowledges his Lord. It is not necessarily a bad thing to doubt, as long as it leads to renewed faith.

The first ending 20:30–31

It is probable that the last two verses of chapter 20 were the original ending of the gospel of John. The author ends with a summary of why he wrote it all down and what he hopes for his readers.

⓲ The second ending 21:1–25

The final chapter was possibly added to record a genuine appearance and to tell the story of what happened to Peter. Verse 21:24 implies that it was written by another hand, from original testimony by John.

It is a period of uncertainty over the future and, during this time, some of the disciples have returned to their former occupation and gone out fishing. But they appear to be rusty after so long away from their profession and their catch is negligible. After recognizing Jesus, Peter impetuously throws off his clothes and swims to him. After a barbecue Jesus challenges Peter. Three times he asks him to affirm his love, a balance for the three times that Peter denied him.

Peter then asks Jesus about John. But Jesus isn't going to get into any more discussions: they must simply have faith and follow him.

Details, Details . . .
You will hold out your hands . . . (21:18)

There are different views about this. The traditional view is that it refers to Peter's death, which was said to be crucifixion upside down. However, Jesus may simply be stating that Peter will be at the mercy of others as he travels and spreads the gospel.

Details, Details . . .
All those books (21:25)

Slightly over the top, maybe, but no doubt true. The writers of the Gospels—or the compilers of the original sources from which the Gospels were formed—must have selected from a large number of incidents, speeches and events. This may be a comment added by a later editor or compiler.

Acts
The birth of the Church

Who: The traditional view is that this is the second book written by Luke the doctor. The author was a companion of Paul on his journeys (the historian starts to use the word "we" from around chapter 16).

When: Probably written about AD 64 or 65. It ends a little after Paul's imprisonment in Rome but does not give any result of his trial, which it surely would have done had the result been known.

What: Luke's gospel was about the origins of Christianity; this book is about the origins of the Church. It tells the story from the resurrection of Jesus in Jerusalem to the imprisonment of Paul in Rome.

This is a period of conflict. There is conflict with the Jewish and Roman authorities, and conflict within Christianity itself as to what the Church should be like. In the book of Acts we see them grappling with some difficult questions. What laws should the Church obey? Should they talk to Jews or Gentiles? How should the followers of Jesus be organized?

Luke includes several long speeches that argue that Jesus is the Messiah and that Christianity offers hope and forgiveness. He also shows how Christianity is life-changing—the most potent example of which is the conversion of Saul, the Christian-hunter, into Paul, the great evangelist.

The biography of the Holy Spirit

Acts also explores the role of the Holy Spirit in the Church. Acts is a kind of biography of the Holy Spirit —at least in his interaction with the first Christians. The Holy Spirit is a constant figure in the background of Acts; inspiring, protecting, punishing, informing, pushing the first Christians to ever greater lengths as they spread the good news of Jesus Christ.

Quick Guide

Author
Luke. Or, at least, the same person who wrote the book of Luke.

Type
History, really.

Purpose
A history of the spread of Christianity and the coming of the Holy Spirit.

Key verses
2:33 "Jesus was taken up to sit at the right side of God, and he was given the Holy Spirit, just as the Father had promised. Jesus is also the one who has given the Spirit to us, and that is what you are now seeing and hearing."

2:44–45 "All the Lord's followers often met together, and they shared everything they had. They would sell their property and possessions and give the money to whoever needed it."

If you remember one thing about this book . . .
God's Spirit is at work in the world.

Your 15 minutes start now
Read chapters 1–2, 7, 9–10, 15, 19, 28

The Route Through Acts

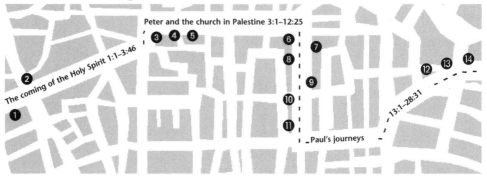

The coming of the Holy Spirit
1:1–3:46

Resurrection appearances 1:1–11

Acts begins with the figure of Jesus still very much present. Jesus appears after his death for forty days speaking to the apostles and even eating with them (1:4). His followers are to wait for the coming of the Holy Spirit. It is that event that will empower them to take the message to the whole world (1:8). Finally, Jesus returns to heaven in a cloud—linking us back to the Old Testament appearances of God as a cloud in the tabernacle and the temple (Ex 40:34; 1 Ki 8:10–12).

❶ The new apostle 1:12–26

The followers continue to meet together in a group that includes members of Jesus' family. The details given about Judas' death differ from the account in Matthew. Although various attempts have been made to harmonize the two accounts, the most likely explanation is that Luke was probably inserting details from a different tradition.

Judas' replacement is chosen by drawing lots, which we might find odd today, in societies that are used to voting. However, the principle had a long tradition in the Old Testament where the Israelites used the mysterious Urim and Thummim (Ex 28:30). This was not seen as "magical" or "lucky," it was assumed that the Lord was in control of the outcome. The exact method used isn't certain, but some experts think that the "lots" were stones that were cast out of a jug. The result depended on which colored stone came out first.

❷ The Holy Spirit 2:1–47

The Day of Pentecost (2:1) was an annual Jewish festival that drew Jews from all over the known world. It was fifty days after Passover and ten days after the last appearance of Jesus and, as the followers wait in a room, the Holy Spirit descends on them with a sound like a roaring wind and what looks like fire. They start to speak in other languages—languages that can be understood by the other Jews present. Inspired, Peter preaches the first ever sermon of the Christian Church. Some argue that this should be the model for all sermons, but it is difficult to draw any overriding principles about preaching from this speech apart from the facts that it concentrated on Christ and was thoroughly grounded in Scripture. And it was short. Hang on, maybe we should take it as a model after all . . .

Puzzling Points
Was Matthias really necessary?

Some have argued that the apostles made a mistake, that they should have waited for the Lord to reveal who should have been the twelfth apostle. The theory is that they should have waited for Paul to come along. They back up the argument with the observation that Matthias is never mentioned again in the Bible.

However, lots of the apostles are not mentioned again and Matthias, like the other eleven, would have been someone who observed firsthand the ministry of Jesus (1:21–22). There is no evidence that Peter did anything wrong. Paul was not so much the "real" twelfth apostle, as a sort of added bonus.

Peter and the Church in Palestine
3:1–12:25

❸ The first church 3:41–47

The response to Peter's simple sermon is amazing: over 3,000 people repent and believe. The followers start meeting together and these verses describe the activities of the first church. They are like a family and their openness, distinctiveness and love lead others to join them (3:47).

They did not just listen to the apostles, but met with them in the temple (3:46) and discussed issues, as had happened in Jesus' day. They prayed together (3:42), shared what they had, and lived in community (2:44–47).

They also "broke bread" together (2:42, 46) which is usually interpreted as meaning that they celebrated the Lord's Supper. However, it took place in the context of a collective meal and was also held in their own homes.

The impression is of a radical, active, joyful group of people, living in a true commonwealth, caring for each other and welcoming new followers with warmth and love.

❹ Healing and opposition   3:1–4:22

This incident sums up much of Acts, with a miraculous sign of the Spirit followed by religious opposition.

From a worldly point of view, the followers of Jesus had little going for them. They had no political or religious recognition, no temples and little in the way of administrative structure. What wealth they had was shared among believers. But what they did have, which set them apart from the rest, was power. Jesus had promised his followers that they would perform miracles (Jn 14:12–26) and in this incident, Peter and John act in the name of Christ to perform a miraculous healing, and Peter explains what has happened to the crowd. His speech (3:12–26) brings him into conflict with the Sadducees, because their theology denied the idea of a resurrection. However, the Holy Spirit has transformed these two ex-fishermen and, indeed, the other followers into people who will bravely speak the message (4:31). They can no longer be dismissed as an ignorant, ill-ordered rabble of fanatics and now have to be treated with caution (5:34–40).

Details, Details . . .
The time of prayer (3:1)

At this stage Peter and the other followers were still attending the temple. The apostles did not imagine, in the early years, that they were establishing a new religion; they did not get together in a small room and "decide" to found Christianity. Instead they saw themselves as a fundamental part of, and indeed culmination of, Judaism.

They were still attending the temple, and the miracles that they performed were done in the name of the Messiah—as is made clear when Peter speaks (3:18). Peter's early messages are rooted in the Jewish Scriptures and show how Jesus came to fulfill all the prophecies. They were still meeting in Solomon's Porch and the increasing hostility made bystanders keep apart, even though they felt attracted (5:12).

A Little Local Difficulty
Annanias and Sapphira   4:32–5:11

The early Church placed a great emphasis on sharing possessions. Here, a couple keep back money for themselves and are struck dead because they lie about it. The problem was not that they kept back the money—they had a right to do that—it was that they *pretended* not to have kept anything back. This is a very difficult passage, not least because over the years many Christians have done the same thing and survived. So why were they picked out? It may be that this was a one-time act of discipline, to impress on the early Church the need for total commitment and honesty before God. In that way it serves as a New Testament parallel to the deaths of Nadab and Abihu (Le 10:2) which took place as the Israelites were beginning to worship in the tabernacle. It may also be that, just as in the time of the ark of the covenant, the presence of God through the Holy Spirit was much more powerful (and therefore dangerous) in the early Church. Ultimately, though, it is another case of apparently inexplicable divine punishment. Perhaps the lesson is that all who lie and deceive will face punishment—it's just that some face it sooner than others.

Landmark: Holy Spirit

Before Jesus there was no clear indication of the existence of the being known as the Holy Spirit. When the Old Testament talked about the Spirit of the Lord, they used the word "breath," indicating that the Spirit is a kind of basic, powerful energy that comes from God. This Spirit would empower, lead, create and inspire the prophets and the leaders of Israel. However, the key thing is that in Old Testament times the Spirit came only temporarily. He did not dwell permanently on earth.

In Jesus' life the Spirit is much more evident, descending on Jesus at his baptism. After Jesus finished his work, he promised that the Holy Spirit would come to his followers to dwell with them forever (Jn 14:16). He is also depicted as a person— a being who can be grieved, lied to, and who takes direct action.

He has several roles:

Redirector: The Spirit points people to Jesus. His aim is to direct followers to what Jesus was like and to help them to be more like him (Jn 16:13).

Motivator: The Spirit guides the Church in mission, sending them out and even telling them where to go (Ac 13:2).

Empowerer: It is the Spirit who gives the Church its power. Only through the Spirit can the Church find the power to love each other, to forgive, to be joyful, to be, in fact, what we ought to be (Ga 5:22–23).

Giver: The Spirit brings gifts to the followers, such as powers of healing, teaching, administration, helping others (1 Co 12:28).

Trainer: The Spirit also brings wisdom and insight, allowing us to learn more about God and each other (1 Co 2:13).

Security: The Spirit's power in us protects us from sinful thoughts. The more of the Spirit we have, the less likely we are to stray (Ro 8:5).

Communicator: The Spirit gives the followers messages from God, through visions, through direct messages (Re 2:7).

Without the Spirit, Christianity is just a set of political and philosophical ideas. With the Spirit, Christianity is a relationship with a powerful, comforting, caring God.

Questions, Questions

The Trinity
OK, then, if you're so clever, tell me where the Trinity is mentioned in the Bible.
It isn't.
Sorry?
It isn't mentioned anywhere in the Bible. In fact, it wasn't formally agreed to be the case until the fourth century AD.
So it's not a biblical concept?
I didn't say that. It's not overtly stated, it's true, but it came about because in the end it was the best explanation for all the facts.
Meaning?
Well, they knew about God. Everyone knew God was God. But then along came Jesus. And he claimed to be God as well.
Where did he do that, then?
He claimed to forgive sins, he claimed that he was the Son of God, he used the phrase "I am" to refer to himself, which everyone knew was a name of God.
See page 52.
Sorry?
Just helping the readers.
Oh. And most of all, he was raised from the dead. So the early Church concluded that Jesus wasn't just someone sent from God, he was God. When Thomas saw the risen Christ he exclaimed "My Lord and my God!"
See page 305.
Thank you. Anyway, when Jesus departed, along came the Holy Spirit. Jesus told them that the Holy Spirit would be with them "forever." He transformed the followers of Jesus through his power. He comforted them, guided them and empowered them. So they came to the conclusion that the Spirit was an equal partner with Jesus and God.
I see. But ... well, doesn't anyone mention the Trinity anywhere?
Of course. In John 15:26, Jesus talks about the Spirit coming from the Father. And there are a large number of references to the three of them together, especially in places like 2 Corinthians 13:14 where Paul links them as one.
See page 337.
Will you stop doing that?
Sorry.

Details, Details . . . Peter's shadow (5:14)

Peter's shadow held no intrinsic power, it was more what it represented. The same is true with Paul's clothing in Ephesus (19:11). In the Gospels, too, there is the woman who reaches out to touch Jesus' clothing. Jesus makes the point that it is not the touch but the faith that heals her (Mk 5:24–34). He put mud on the eyes of a blind man (Jn 9:6–7), but it was his power as God, not the mud, that made the difference. The mud merely helped the blind man to faith. The book of Acts doesn't condemn relics as such, but they are not necessary for healing. They are not ends in themselves. They are the signpost, not the destination.

The medieval church placed a great faith in relics, but that was the problem: the faith lay in the object, not in Jesus. This led to the medieval Church collecting huge numbers of fragments of the true cross, thorns out of the crown of thorns and bones of various apostles. You don't have to be an archaeologist to work out that these things are extremely unlikely to be authentic. (For a start, there were at least three heads of John the Baptist knocking around.) This is not faith, but superstition.

❺ Stephen   6:1–8:3

The growth in the numbers of converts leads to an administrative problem, so a new group of people are appointed to oversee the material needs of the Church, allowing the apostles to concentrate on preaching and spreading the message. The complaint seems to center on a communication problem between the Aramaic-speaking leadership and a section of the followers who spoke Greek. It is probably to bridge this communication gap that several of the seven were appointed, because they have Greek names.

The men chosen were "respected," "wise" and "full of God's Spirit." Although they were chosen to fill what was an administrative and organizational post, we know that two of them, Stephen and Philip, become famous for other ministries. Their number also includes a Gentile—Nicolaus—who had converted to Judaism.

Stephen, in particular, starts to perform miracles and signs among the people. The fact that the opposition suddenly clusters around him may be accounted for by the type of people who oppose him, the Greek-speaking Jews attacking one of their own kind. These are the freedmen, Jews who had been freed from slavery in places such as Cyrenia, Alexandria and Cilicia. Their charge implies that Stephen recognized that the temple and the Laws would be changed in the light of Jesus (7:14).

Stephen's defense is a long history lesson, but it should be remembered that he is up against a religious court. His message cannot have been welcome to his judges. Stephen doesn't actually mention Jesus by name, he calls him "the Righteous One," or "the One Who Obeys God," but the conclusion is clear: the Jews have repeatedly rejected God's prophets and now they have rejected God himself. Finally, Stephen sees a vision of Jesus standing at the right hand of God—a vision that tips the council leaders into violence (7:54–57). Stephen becomes the first martyr of the Christian Church. He is stoned to death while a young man called Saul looks after the coats (7:58).

The persecution in Jerusalem   8:1–4

The death of Stephen was a trigger for a widespread persecution in Jerusalem, forcing many of the followers to flee. Saul was a prime mover in this—a kind of Christian-hunter. The attack may have centered on the Greek-speaking Jews, since the disciples seem to have remained in Jerusalem. Ironically, it was this persecution that led to an even greater spread of Christianity, for the followers took the message with them wherever they went. Christianity in Jerusalem might have been suppressed, but it was about to break out elsewhere.

❻ Philip   8:4–40

Philip's success as a preacher and evangelist leads to a visit from Peter and John, to check him out. We are seeing the beginnings of one of the problems that the Church would have to address in future years; the need to check that teachers and evangelists were passing on the true message.

No such problems in Philip's case, however, and the gospel is soon spread even farther afield with the conversion of a high-ranking Ethiopian (actually from Nubia). In their culture the king was considered a god and could not be seen, so the actual government devolved on Candace, the queen mom. The Ethiopian was the equivalent of the secretary of the treasury. He believes Philip and is baptized. Ethiopian tradition believes that he was the country's first evangelist—and he undoubtedly would have spread the message to his countrymen. Presumably in a high voice.

> **Details, Details . . .**
> **Eunuch (8:27)**
>
> He had probably started out his career as an attendant in the king's harem and had been castrated to stop him taking his work home with him, as it were. However, the key thing is that his emasculation and his race would have barred him from being accepted as a Jew under the old Levitical law (De 23:1). Christianity has no such barriers.

❼ The conversion of Saul   9:1–18

Saul's conversion marks a turning point for the Church, and is such an important event that it is told three times in Acts—once by Luke and twice by Paul himself.

Some skeptics have argued that this "vision" was really because Saul was epileptic. They base this on (1) the fact that he mentions a "thorn in his side" that he cannot get rid of (2 Co 12:7), and (2) the fact that he falls off his horse. It's not exactly a compelling argument and certainly Saul's later determination on behalf of Christianity cannot easily be explained by the fact that he once had an epileptic fit while riding along a road.

This is, rather, an extreme spiritual experience. It may well be inflamed by his own guilty conscience—sometimes we fight most strongly against that to which we are most strongly attracted. He was trying so hard to wipe out all the Christians, but in the end he saw the Lord himself. The experience was overwhelming, so overwhelming that he lost his sight. His three days in blindness are perhaps symbolic of Jesus' three days in the tomb.

When he was a Pharisee, Saul was an argumentative, disruptive figure. When he was a Christian he was still an argumentative, disruptive figure. He was just a *saved*, argumentative, disruptive figure. From his very early days as a Christian he was "trouble." In his first few months as a Christian he had to escape from Damascus because of death threats (9:22–25). Then he had to escape from Jerusalem because of death threats (9:28–30). I'm beginning to spot a thread here . . .

Let's hear it for Ananias   9:10–18

If there was one person you would not want to meet face to face, it was Saul. Ananias is the very kind of person that Saul has been persecuting. He knows what Saul has been doing, and why he has come to Damascus. Nevertheless, he goes and prays with Saul.

Let's hear it for Barnabas   9:6–27

Barnabas's real name was Joseph (4:36–37), but it was changed to reflect his encouraging nature. Barnabas was a real believer, not just in Christianity but in people. It is Barnabas who lays his reputation on the line and speaks up for Saul before the apostles.

POSTCARD

Welcome to Damascus!

The ancient capital of Aram (that's Syria to you and me), Damascus is the oldest continuously inhabited city in the world. Admittedly, under the Romans, our influence has waned slightly, but we are still a major commercial center.

Although surrounded by desert, the city is irrigated by the rivers Abana and Pharpur, meaning that it is full of orchards, gardens and lush vegetation. Visitors will want to visit the many bustling stalls along the city's main thoroughfare—Straight Street.

People from many nations come here, as the city is at the center of several major trade routes. In particular, the city has a large Jewish community—hardly surprising given our proximity to Palestine—but visitors are asked to be careful what they say in the synagogues, otherwise they'll be taking you out in a basket!

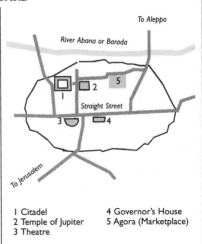

1 Citadel	4 Governor's House
2 Temple of Jupiter	5 Agora (Marketplace)
3 Theatre	

Details, Details . . .
The Italian regiment

This regiment (10:1) is known to have served in Palestine during AD 69. Cornelius was a centurion, in charge of one hundred troops. However, he was probably a wealthy individual, since he kept a large household.

❽ Joppa and Caesarea 9:36–11:18

There was now a time of peace for the Church (9:31), possibly because Saul was out of the way. Peter starts traveling around, going first to Lydda and then to Joppa, and, as he moves around, he begins to realize that the old boundaries within the Law no longer work in the light of Christ. This is vividly illustrated by the fact that in Joppa he stays with Simon, a man whose job as a leather worker made him unclean in Jewish Law because it meant contact with the skin of dead animals. (The actual address was Simon the Tanner, Sea Road, Joppa—10:32). Peter has a vision where clean and unclean animals are mixed together and where all can be eaten. Perhaps Peter was staring out to sea, for the animals were contained in something that looked like a sheet or a sail.

When Peter goes to Caesarea, he has had time to digest the vision and understand its meaning. There is no longer "clean" and "unclean." When someone worships God and does right, then nationality no longer matters. Peter concludes, "Now I am certain that God treats all people alike" (10:34–36). Previously it was not that Gentiles could not be saved, it was that they had to become Jews first. But now the Holy Spirit comes on them without any of the trappings of Judaism, without circumcision or dietary laws. The death and resurrection of Jesus opened the way for *all* of humankind to be saved: Jew and Gentile, equal in their need for repentance and their hope of salvation.

Peter's activities cause consternation back in Jerusalem, and when he returns the apostle is forced to explain himself. Although his explanation is accepted, there was still a conservative party of Jewish Christians who held a hard line. These "circumcisionists" believed that the message could be preached to the Gentiles, but still held that, on acceptance, the Gentile should be circumcised. The argument was not finished yet.

Brief Lives: Paul, aka Saul

Background: Born in Tarsus, Asia.

Occupation: Pharisee. Christian-hunter. Evangelist.

Achievements: Paul is, perhaps, the most important figure in the early Church. We don't know what he looked like, although a not-too reliable work of the second century describes him as bald, bow-legged, short, with eyebrows that met in the middle and a hooked nose. From which I think we can assume that it was his mind that attracted people.

Paul was born into an orthodox Jewish family and raised as a Pharisee. He studied under Gamaliel (Ac 22:3) and eventually became a kind of religious secret agent, traveling around Palestine seeking out Christians to punish. This Jewish background is vital in understanding Paul's importance to the Church, for, after his miraculous conversion, he brought his immense knowledge of the Scriptures and his keen intellect to bear on the key issues of the early Church.

Indeed, he seems to have embodied those issues. One of the most contentious problems was the difficult relationship between Jewish and Gentile Christians. Paul was both in one body. He was a Jew who was a Roman citizen; a Pharisee who had become a Christian. He saw both sides of the story.

He was probably not a tremendously powerful speaker; his strength lay in his writing, and it is his letters that formed the basis for the doctrine of the early Church. It was Paul, as much as anyone, who sat down and worked out what it all meant, who sought to explain exactly what had happened when Jesus was nailed to the cross.

The cross and its implications form the core of Paul's teaching. Paul believed that the death and resurrection of Jesus meant salvation for all who believed. Jew or Gentile, rich or poor, slave or free, all that mattered was faith in Jesus.

He traveled widely with this message, making at least three missionary journeys throughout Asia Minor. On the way he established churches, spoke in synagogues, challenged false teachers and generally riled a lot of feathers. His name change came about not because he became a Christian, but probably because he was working among Greeks, and therefore chose a Greek name.

After being arrested and sent to Rome in AD 51, he was probably released and then imprisoned again a few years later. Tradition says that he was executed in Rome in either AD 62 or 64.

Character: Strong. Outspoken. Courageous. Humble. Demanding. Irritable.

Pros: Spoke the truth fearlessly.

Cons: Spoke the truth a little *too* fearlessly for some people's liking.

Puzzling Points
The baptism of the Holy Spirit

The Bible here seems to make a distinction between the acceptance of the message of Christ and the descent of the Holy Spirit. Some Christians argue that there is a distinction between being baptized in the faith and being baptized in the Holy Spirit. Others argue that later events show that repentance and the Spirit's arrival occur simultaneously (10:44–48) and that this separate instigation was symbolic, showing that the followers in Samaria were not distinct and separate from those in the hated city of Jerusalem. In Ephesus, Paul encounters a group of people who have put their faith in Jesus, but have not received the Holy Spirit—simply because they haven't heard of it. He baptizes them "in the name of the Lord Jesus" and they experience the Holy Spirit in a powerful way.

Details, Details . . .
What happened to Saul?

When he leaves Antioch, he is called Saul; when he comes back, he is called Paul (13:9). The change of name marks the change of outlook. Saul is his Jewish name, but in the Roman world he will be known as Paul. As his mission is now one to the Gentiles, he uses his Roman name from now on. This duality is characteristic of Paul: the Jew who was also a Roman, the Pharisee who became a Christian.

❾ Antioch and beyond 11:19–30

With the mission to the Gentiles now formally recognized, Jewish Christians began to take the news to the Gentiles. It particularly thrived in Antioch, where the first Gentile church was established and where the followers are first called Christians (11:26). Barnabas is sent to oversee the situation and he in turn calls in Saul, who comes to help in overseeing the Church. It was, as they say, the start of a beautiful friendship.

❿ Renewed persecution 12:1–25

Back in Jerusalem, however, a renewed bout of persecution had broken out. Herod Agrippa I, the grandson of Herod the Great, was trying to gain the support of the Jewish religious leaders. He beheads the apostle James and imprisons Peter.

Paul's journeys
13:1–28:31

Peter is almost entirely absent from the second half of Acts. Instead, the attention switches to Paul, the ex-Pharisee, the great thinker and strategist of the early Church. It is Paul who sees the need to establish Christian centers in the major cities and centers of communication. It is Paul who, from now on, is tirelessly preaching and traveling and writing.

⓫ The council 15:1–35

Peter's vision had convinced the followers of the rightness of reaching out to the Gentiles. But there were still some who held that a Gentile, once converted, had to be circumcised.

The argument gets more and more serious until Paul and Barnabas are called to Jerusalem to face the apostles and the leaders of the Church. After much discussion, Peter speaks out against the need for circumcision. Given his position in the Church, his speech is remarkable for its simplicity and humility. James, the brother of Jesus, endorses this approach.

In the end the decision appears to be something of a compromise. Gentile converts are not required to undergo circumcision, but they will have to obey some dietary laws. Why should this be? The answer might lie in the need to build communities that would work and live together. It would be difficult to build a community if one half of the community was engaging in activities the other half thought repugnant. This meant not eating food that had been sacrificed to idols (1 Co 8:7–13) or food with blood in it. It also meant abstaining from sexual sin, which may indicate that the Gentile population thought more lightly of certain sexual activities than the Jews.

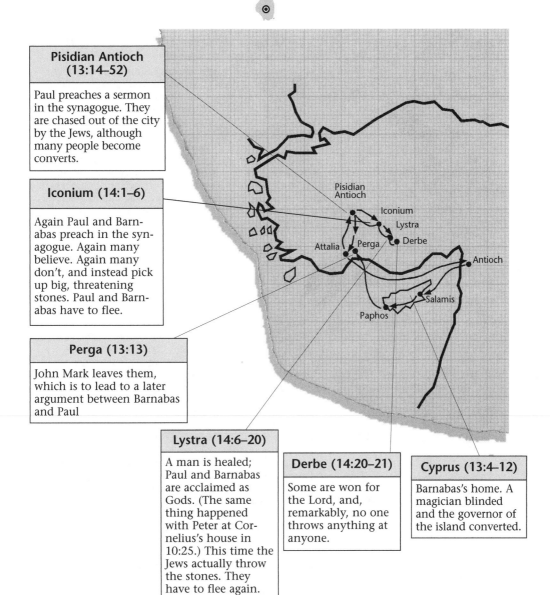

**Pisidian Antioch
(13:14–52)**

Paul preaches a sermon in the synagogue. They are chased out of the city by the Jews, although many people become converts.

Iconium (14:1–6)

Again Paul and Barnabas preach in the synagogue. Again many believe. Again many don't, and instead pick up big, threatening stones. Paul and Barnabas have to flee.

Perga (13:13)

John Mark leaves them, which is to lead to a later argument between Barnabas and Paul

Lystra (14:6–20)

A man is healed; Paul and Barnabas are acclaimed as Gods. (The same thing happened with Peter at Cornelius's house in 10:25.) This time the Jews actually throw the stones. They have to flee again.

Derbe (14:20–21)

Some are won for the Lord, and, remarkably, no one throws anything at anyone.

Cyprus (13:4–12)

Barnabas's home. A magician blinded and the governor of the island converted.

Map labels: Pisidian Antioch, Iconium, Lystra, Derbe, Attalia, Perga, Antioch, Salamis, Paphos

Paul's first journey   13:1–14:28

The journey is a remarkable account of trial and triumph—of converts made and many hardships suffered by the evangelists.

In virtually every town and city they are threatened, beaten or simply expelled. And yet, they have the courage to revisit the same places on the way home, setting up the churches and appointing leaders. Paul tells them that "We have to suffer a lot before we can get into God's kingdom" (14:22), which, given what happened to him on the outward journey, is one of the understatements of the Bible.

Paul's second journey
15:36–18:21

Let's hear it for John Mark   15:36–41

Many commentators assume that Mark was in the wrong when he left Paul. They talk of Mark "repenting" and Mark "coming good." The truth is, we don't know why Mark left Paul on their first journey. He could have had perfectly good reasons. If anything, the signs are that Paul was in the wrong, since later he was to change his mind about Mark and even ask for Mark to join him in Rome (2 Ti 4:11). Paul was not a perfect man and, like all leaders, he made mistakes. This may well be one of them.

Puzzling Points
Timothy's circumcision (16:3)

After the debate of previous chapters, this comes as a shock. If Christians didn't need to be circumcised why does Paul force the act on Timothy? Elsewhere we have accounts of Paul refusing to allow another of his followers to be circumcised (Ga 2:3–5). So why the inconsistency?

The answer appears to lie in their background and their task. Timothy was a Jew with a ministry among both Jews and Gentiles. It was a cultural act that would enable Timothy's ministry. He refused to allow the Gentile Titus to be circumcised because it would have indicated that Titus had not been made perfect by his faith.

Let's hear it for Gallio

Gallio was a figure of considerable importance in the area. The brother of Seneca, the Stoic philosopher and tutor of Emperor Nero (not one of his best pupils), his decision that the disagreement between Christians and Jews was an internal religious squabble was probably a major factor in allowing Christianity to spread without interference from Rome.

Philippi (16:11–40)

The conversion of a prominent businesswoman and the freeing of a demon-possessed slave girl. Paul and Silas are thrown into jail and during an earthquake they convert the jailer and his family. When the charges are dropped, they insist that the Roman officials come and let them out in person. Paul was not above using a little free publicity for the cause.

Paul wrote to the Philippians, expressing his joy and thanking them for their unceasing prayer.
▷ 344

Thessalonica (17:1–9)

Preaching in the synagogue. The Jewish leaders try to catch Paul, but have to content themselves with arresting some of the local Christians. He wrote twice to the Thessalonians.
▷ 350

Berea (17:10–15)

A personal favorite. The Bereans didn't just blindly accept the gospel, nor did they unthinkingly reject it. They thought about it long and hard. Even though the Thessalonian envoys cause trouble for Paul, the other followers can stay on. The Bereans are genuinely open-minded people.

Corinth (18:1–17)

Paul spends some two years here, preaching and working as a tentmaker which, apparently, was his profession. It was at Corinth that he wrote to the Thessalonians. An attempt to have him arrested ends with the Jewish ringleader being beaten up (18:12–17). Paul appears to have made a kind of Nazarite vow while he was in Corinth. It may have had something to do with his vow not to preach to the Jews (18:6).

He wrote twice to the Corinthians. Priscilla and Aquila are also mentioned in his letter to the Romans (Ro 16:3–4).
▷ 328–29

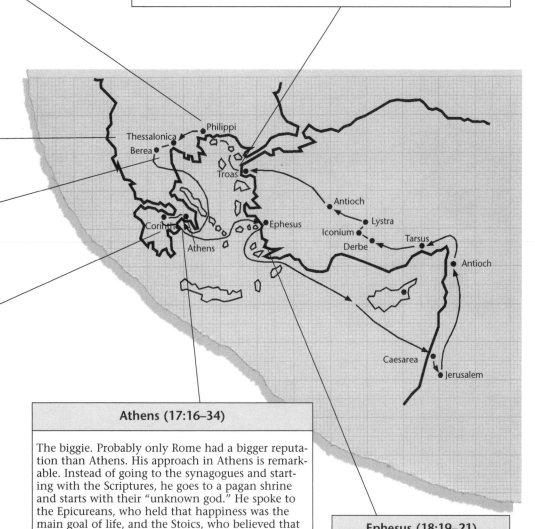

Troas (15:6–9)

Paul's journeys are directed not only by his strategic aims, but by the Holy Spirit. Indeed, there are times when Paul's steps are altered. Here he planned to go into Asia, but is stopped. We don't know how this happened—presumably one of their number had a vision or a message. Perhaps it was Paul himself, because he has a vision of someone from Macedonia appealing for help. At this point the historical account starts to talk about "we," indicating that Luke joins them at Troas, probably staying on in Philippi when the others left. He rejoins Paul when he travels from Philippi to Troas in 20:6.

Map labels: Philippi, Thessalonica, Berea, Troas, Antioch, Lystra, Iconium, Tarsus, Ephesus, Derbe, Antioch, Corinth, Athens, Caesarea, Jerusalem

Athens (17:16–34)

The biggie. Probably only Rome had a bigger reputation than Athens. His approach in Athens is remarkable. Instead of going to the synagogues and starting with the Scriptures, he goes to a pagan shrine and starts with their "unknown god." He spoke to the Epicureans, who held that happiness was the main goal of life, and the Stoics, who believed that what mattered was human reason and self-discipline. Here, in the home of philosophy, he takes on the philosophers on their own turf. With, it has to be admitted, mixed results.

Ephesus (18:19–21)

A brief stop. He was to return on his third journey.

Paul's third journey

19:22–21:16

Troas (20:7–12)

A comforting story for all preachers. It is late at night, the room is hot with the heat from the lamps. A young man literally dies from boredom. Paul revives him and then the believers share communion. And Paul continues preaching . . .

Let's hear it for Apollos
19:24–28; 1 Co 18:23

Apollos was an Alexandrian Jew who seems to have heard only the partial gospel. We don't know exactly how his message differed—it may be that it was a message of repentance, rather than faith in Jesus, or it may be that he did not teach about the Holy Spirit (19:1–7). Nevertheless, Apollos was to be a major teacher and leader of the Corinthian church.

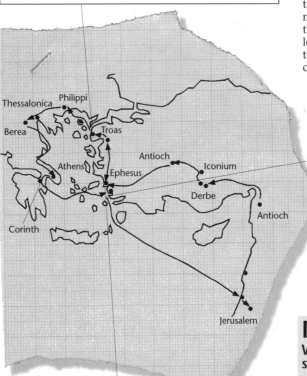

Miletus (20:17–38)

Paul's journey ends in a somber mood. He is returning to Jerusalem in the knowledge that it will mean imprisonment and suffering (20:22–23). At Miletus he leaves his friends in Ephesus with a tearful farewell: they will not meet again.

Puzzling Points
Why does the Holy Spirit say two different things?

Paul has been told by the Spirit to go to Jerusalem (20:22). But on Cyprus, the followers receive a message from the Holy Spirit telling Paul *not* to go to Jerusalem (21:4). Probably the Cypriot believers knew of the trials that were awaiting Paul and took this as a warning not to go. The same thing happens with the prophet Agabus at Caesarea (21:10–12), when even Luke and the rest of his followers urge Paul not to go. Paul knew that he had to go, regardless.

Ephesus (19:1–41)

Paul's work at Ephesus is, initially, one of bringing completeness. He encounters a group of the followers who seem to follow the teachings of John the Baptist rather than Jesus (19:1–7). There is also a group of Jewish mystics who use Jesus' name without understanding the faith (19:11–20). They use the names of Jesus and Paul as a kind of magic word. Paul's message also undermines the idols made by the Ephesian silversmiths. Paul's stand against evil is not just against spiritual forces, but against material exploitation of the gullible and the foolish.

▷**340–41**

Landmark: Church

By the end of Acts, the Church had spread throughout Asia Minor, into Greece and as far as Rome. However, the "churches" in question were not like those we are familiar with today.

The word church comes from the Greek word *ecclesia*, which was the word used for a gathering of people at the call of a herald. And that is what churches were—groups of people who had come together in answer to the call of Christ. Thus, in the New Testament "church" never means either a building or a denomination, for the simple reason that neither existed.

Church services

As far as we can tell (which is not very far), early churches held open services of worship that included prophecies, teaching, singing and reading from Scriptures. They seem to have met every day of the week, with the Lord's Supper celebrated on the first day of the week (1 Co 16:2). Sometimes a collection was taken up for those in need.

Locations

The early Church had no official buildings of their own. The earliest identifiable separate church buildings date from around AD 200. Before then, the groups met in houses and, in the early years, in synagogues. Paul mentions several "house churches," including those run by Priscilla and Aquila (Ro 16:5), Nympha (Col 4:15) and Philemon (Phm 2). This means that the groups were probably not more than 20–30 strong—few houses had rooms big enough for any more to meet.

Church organization

There was no priesthood in the biblical accounts of the early Church—not in the sense that it has now come to be understood. The idea of some functions only being allowed to be done by one man is more of an Old Testament concept. In the New Testament all believers are described as being part of the priesthood (1 Pe 2:5, 9).

However, any group has to develop leadership structure and there are three types of church leader identified in the New Testament.

Apostles

These were the twelve chosen by Jesus. Judas was replaced by Matthias and later Paul was added as an "honorary" apostle. These were held to have the ultimate authority through their close association with Jesus.

Elders

The word used is *episkopos*, which is sometimes translated as bishop, but actually means overseer. These appear to be the strategic and spiritual leaders of the local Church. It was probably these leaders that Paul met with at Miletus and at Jerusalem, where there was a council of elders, including James, that debated difficult issues.

Deacons

The Greek word *diakonos* means servant. Male and female, the role of these people may have been more practical. Certainly the first deacons were set up to "serve tables," to take responsibility for the charitable action of the church. The elders may have been the teachers, but it is difficult to define the exact roles of the two groups.

Paul's journey to Rome
21:17–28:31

Jerusalem 1: Arguments   21:17–26

At Jerusalem the same old argument resurfaces. Paul's labors are being undermined by the circumcisionists. Paul takes part in a series of traditional Jewish rituals to convince them that he is not being divisive. It seems ridiculous that a man who achieved so much should have to go to such lengths to prove himself, but Paul never stood on his reputation.

Jerusalem 2: Riots   21:27–22:23

The riot is started not by local Jews, but by Jews from Asia (22:27), the same kind of Jews who always tried to make trouble for Paul on his journeys. They accuse him of taking a Gentile—Trophimus—into the temple, in direct contravention of Jewish law. Gentiles were allowed in the outer court, but not beyond. The riot gives Paul the opportunity to tell his story (22:1–21), but he is arrested by the Romans.

⑫ Jerusalem 3: Trial   23:1–22

There is almost a sense of mischief here. First, Paul claims not to recognize the high priest. There have been various explanations for this, ranging from a genuine mistake to the fact that Paul had bad eyesight. But it all sounds more ironic than that. Paul is, perhaps, pointing out that the official is not exactly behaving with high-priestly dignity.

Then, as soon as the trial begins, Paul lobs an incendiary statement into the arena. He claims to be a Pharisee who believes in the resurrection of the dead. Both statements are true, but Paul was no longer a Pharisee in the same sense as those before him. And the resurrection he believed in was the resurrection of Jesus Christ. Nevertheless, the statement works superbly. The two sides immediately start fighting among themselves. Paul is dragged away, and eventually sent to Caesarea.

Details, Details . . .
A Roman Citizen (22:24–29)

A Roman citizen had many privileges not afforded to others. For a start he had a right to a fair trial and he was not allowed to be flogged. The Roman whip was a cruel and brutal instrument—so cruel that the Romans reserved it for use on the races they oppressed. It normally maimed its victims for life, and frequently killed them. Only a small number of people in the Roman provinces had the right to claim Roman citizenship. Paul knew very well the rights of a Roman citizen and was about to use those rights to ensure that the gospel was heard by the widest possible audience.

⑬ Caesarea: Investigation
23:23–26:32

Gradually Paul's strategy becomes clearer. Jerusalem was only ever a staging post. Paul's aim is to use the trial to take the message of the gospel into the heart of the Roman empire. At Caesarea he is investigated by Felix, Pilate's successor as governor of Palestine. Paul spends two years in Caesarea. He is called to give testimony three times, first to Felix (24:10–23), then to his successor Porcus Festus (25:6–12), finally to Festus and King Agrippa (26:1–32). The latter is a good-humored exchange. Festus accuses Paul of being slightly mad, Agrippa jokes that Paul is trying to convert him and Paul says, "I wish everyone could be like me . . . apart from the chains."

Malta: Shipwreck   27:13–28:15

Paul's demand to appeal to the emperor meant that he would be sent to Rome. He makes his journey in three stages: from Caesarea to Myra, Myra to Malta, and finally Malta to the Bay of Naples. Luke tells the story in some detail, including the incident of the shipwreck at Malta. Throughout the journey Paul appears calm, confident and good-humored, winning the friendship and approval of the people through his faith.

⓮ Rome: Arrival
28:16–30 ▷324

At Rome, Paul is placed under house arrest. Although he might well have been imprisoned with a light chain, he would have had plenty of time to preach and to write and to think. He never stops talking to people about the Way. The first people he talks to are local Jews, "to try to win them over to Jesus" (28:23).

Puzzling Points
The ending

Luke ends his account abruptly. Given the wealth of detail in the preceding chapters and the drama of the court appearances before Festus and Agrippa, it seems odd that the final court appeal is not recounted. In all probability the case was simply dropped, although the legal requirements would have taken two years. Most scholars agree that, from the evidence in the letters, Paul was a free man from AD 62 to 65. He probably went to Crete and traveled round the Aegean Sea and may even have achieved his stated aim of going to Spain. Tradition tells us, however, that when Nero ascended the throne Paul was arrested again. He wrote his final letter, 2 Timothy, from Rome and from a far more serious imprisonment than the fairly benevolent house arrest he had in Acts. This imprisonment was to end less happily as well: he was probably executed in AD 67.

Paul's journey to Rome

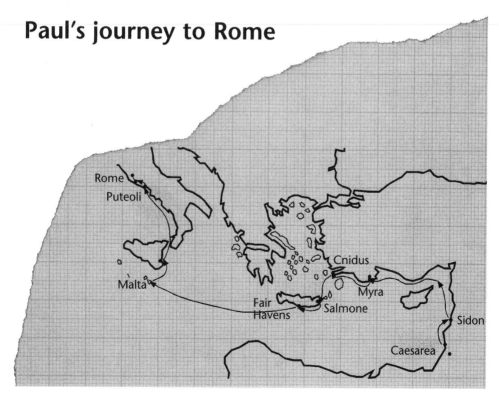

Letters

The remaining twenty-one books of the Bible consist of letters from the apostles. These were written to churches and individuals in the early years of the Church. They address a group of people, rather than an institution; they talk to those who had decided to follow Jesus, rather than the members of "the Church."

The majority of these letters were written by Paul. Paul was the great evangelist and teacher of the early Church, and most of his teaching is found in his letters to various churches in Asia Minor. However, there are other letters written by—or attributed to—other apostles, and by one unnamed writer.

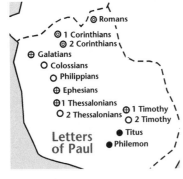

Letters by Paul

Romans, 1 and 2 Corinthians, Galatians, Ephesians, Philippians, Colossians, 1 and 2 Thessalonians, 1 and 2 Timothy, Titus, Philemon.

The bulk of Paul's letters are written for churches—although there are a few written to individuals. For the most part, these were churches where Paul had had some involvement—either in establishing the Church or in being involved in the training and teaching. Indeed, the letters are primarily public letters—intended to be read aloud or circulated and continuing Paul's role as a teacher.

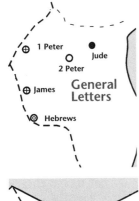

General letters

Hebrews, James, 1 and 2 Peter, Jude.

These letters were addressed, not to a specific community, but to the Church in general. Accordingly, they don't really deal with specific problems or issues as many of Paul's letters do. They take broader themes. Hebrews, for example, deals with the relationship of Christianity to the Old Testament Law, while James is a practical guide on how to live as a Christian.

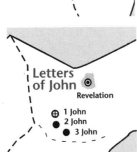

Letters of John

1, 2 and 3 John, Revelation.
Finally we have letters by John. John's letters are much shorter than Paul's and deal primarily with the issue of false teaching.

And then there's Revelation.

Revelation is only really in with the letters because nobody knows where else to put it. It's a massive, sprawling, obscure vision of the future, filled with mystical imagery and symbolic numbers.

Romans
The gospel truth

Who: Paul.

When: Probably around AD 57. Paul still hadn't been to Rome, so he was writing to tell them about himself and his beliefs and a little of his plans. It was probably written in Corinth, since there are references in the letter to people living there.

What: Paul was probably writing to introduce himself and his thought to those at Rome in preparation for a visit there. He doesn't say anything very much about the Roman church, for the simple reason that he didn't know much about it. However, he does touch on the thorny issue of the relationship between Jewish and Gentile Christians, indicating that he might have heard of difficulties between the two groups.

The subject of the letter is faith: faith in Jesus Christ. Salvation comes to us not through what we do, but from whom we put our faith in. It is God's forgiveness and love that rescues us, not our own efforts.

This is a key theme for Paul, and one that recurs throughout his letters. It was a controversial view at the time—and in many ways has remained a controversial view throughout history. Paul argued that salvation is not a matter of obeying the Jewish Law—nor even a case of obeying natural laws or morality. It is a gift of God.

That is not to say that it does not matter what we do. As followers of Jesus we are obliged to live lives of love, hope and sacrifice. But, Paul argues, we do this as a response to salvation, not in order to obtain it.

Quick Guide

Author
Paul

Type
Letter

Purpose
To explain the gospel.

Key verse
1:17 "The good news tells how God accepts everyone who has faith, but only those who have faith. It is just as the Scriptures say, 'The people God accepts because of their faith will live.'"

If you remember one thing about this book . . .
Only faith makes us right with God.

Your 10 minutes start now
Read chapters 1, 4–5, 8, 10, 12

The Route Through Romans

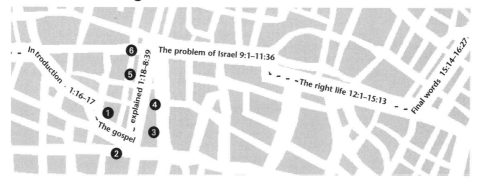

Introduction 1:16–17

The gospel explained 1:18–8:39

The problem of Israel 9:1–11:36

The right life 12:1–15:13

Final words 15:14–16:27

POSTCARD

Welcome to Rome!

Rome is the most famous city in the world. Center of the Roman Empire and home to the emperor, this wealthy, cosmopolitan city contains people from all nations and faiths. It is famous for its many buildings, including amphitheaters, temples and palaces. The city has been home to a succession of glorious, powerful, and often completely insane emperors.

Those of other cultures will find our city a real "Rome away from Rome." As our glorious empire has expanded, so the numbers of foreign slaves have grown and our population includes such groups as 40,000–50,000 Jews. The city is ideally situated on the River Tiber, with the port of Ostia only seventeen miles away. The heart of our social life is the Forum, where the visitor will be able to meet with people from all classes.

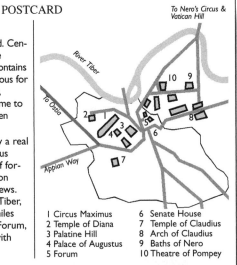

1 Circus Maximus	6 Senate House
2 Temple of Diana	7 Temple of Claudius
3 Palatine Hill	8 Arch of Claudius
4 Palace of Augustus	9 Baths of Nero
5 Forum	10 Theatre of Pompey

Puzzling Points
Righteousness

Paul uses this word a lot in Romans. In the Old Testament the word is used more in a legal state—it means that a man is in the clear, "in the right." Thus Israel is often compared to other nations and found more "righteous." But the term came to have a wider meaning, and to imply a moral code, a type of righteous behavior. A man could be called "righteous" because he did what was right (e.g. Joseph in Mt 1:19).

In Romans, Paul uses the term to describe the relationship between man and God. The fundamental question is, how can we be "right" with God? Does it depend on us keeping the Law in all its aspects? If that is so, we're all doomed, because no one can keep the Law. Instead, Paul argues that what makes us "right" is faith. It is through faith in Jesus that we become "right with God."

Greetings   1:1–15

Paul begins with a rather formal introduction and a brief history of his role and message (1:1–7). This is followed by a prayer of thanks and notice of Paul's desire to visit Rome. He wants to help them grow stronger as Christians and to share with them the blessings of the Holy Spirit (1:10). But he also wants to "win followers" (1:13). Paul's vision of a church is always one that is reaching out to others.

Introduction   1:16–17

In two verses, Paul sums up the message of this letter. It is only through faith that we can receive salvation. Jew or Gentile, faith is the only way to life.

The gospel explained
1:18–8:39

❶ We are all guilty   1:18–2:16

An old advertising dictum says, "Start with the problem, then show the solution." This is what Paul does. He starts with the indissoluble problem: everyone is guilty. He catalogs a long list of practices that get between us and God, not just big sins like murder, but "everyday" sins, like gossip, cheating, causing strife between one another (1:29).

Admittedly, Paul says that some have tried to do what is right—either through their own consciences or through following the Jewish Law (2:6–16), but everyone has fallen short of what is right. None of us can claim to be guilt-free.

❷ Being Jewish   2:17–3:20

Paul was constantly speaking and arguing in synagogues, and the core of his argument is distilled here. First he deals with circumcision. Without obedience to the Law, circumcision is useless. Circumcision is an outward symbol of an inward reality. Without what Paul calls a "circumcision of the heart," it is useless. So is it any good being a Jew? The only advantage that Paul can list is that the Jews received the message first. Ultimately, he concludes that both Jews and Gentiles are "ruled by sin" (3:9). All the Law has done is to draw our attention to our own failings. We're all, frankly, in the same boat.

❸ Problem solved   3:21–4:25

From stating the problem, Paul goes on to explain how people can be "made right" with God. In fact, he states that the answer is already there in the Old Testament (3:21). The answer lies in a free gift. God sent Jesus Christ to be our sacrifice, to take the punishment that we should bear for sinning. Once again, Jew and Gentile are brought together, this time not in sin, but in faith in Jesus (3:29–31). It is only through faith in him that we are saved. Paul uses the story of Abraham to illustrate this. God accepted Abraham, not because of his good deeds, but because of his faith (4:3). Abraham, the father of the Jewish race, was not made faithful by circumcision. His circumcision was a sign of his faith. So Abraham is the father, not just of the Jews, but of all those who have faith (4:16).

> ### Details, Details . . .
> ### Miscellaneous quotes (3:10–18)
>
> This is not one quote but a series of quotes from various places. Paul is drawing together lots of sayings—mostly from Psalms.

❹ Adam and Jesus   5:1–21

Faith in Christ, then, is what makes us right with God. But here Paul has another fundamental question to answer. How does Jesus' death affect us? What difference does one man's death make? His answer lies right back at the beginning, with Adam. Paul argues that through Adam's decision we are all infected with sin. It is part of our human nature, in the world from the beginning (5:12–14). And just as one man brought sin into the world for everyone, so one man brings forgiveness into the world for us all (5:19).

❺ A new start   6:1–8:17

This new freedom does not mean that we can carry on as before. Once we put our faith in Jesus, our old selves are dead. We should be like Christ, and live our lives for God (6:8–11). Paul is not arguing that we can do what we like, or that, because we cannot work our way to heaven, we shouldn't even try to do what is right. Instead we are enjoined to be "slaves" of God, obeying the commands of our master (6:15–23); we are now "married" to God and should be faithful to what he wants (7:1–6). We know what is right to do, but our sinful natures rebel. That is why God gives us a further gift—the Holy Spirit. The more we are ruled by the Holy Spirit, the more we will be able to do what is right (8:5–11).

As Paul writes, you can sense the excitement pouring out of him, so much so that he alters one of his previous images. Did he say that we were God's slaves? No, the truth is that God's Spirit doesn't make us slaves but children—we "call him our Father" (8:15). One is reminded of Jesus' parable of the prodigal son. The boy would have been content to return home and be a slave, but his father views him not as a slave, but as a son.

Puzzling Points
Predestination (8:28–30)

Paul implies, in these verses, that God has selected —has predestined—those he chooses to save. The problem with these verses is that, taken alone, they seem to imply an inscrutable, almost malignant God, who selects some to be saved and others to be condemned. There is nothing we can do about it, we're either in the club or out.

Some, indeed, have argued that this is the case. The verse means what it says: that only those whom God chooses are to be saved. And there is no doubt that, throughout the Bible, God chooses people to bless. He selected Abraham (9:6–13). He chose Jacob over Esau (9:10–13). God "can either have pity on people, or he can make them stubborn." God has the right to choose who he wants. Paul implies that God has deliberately hardened the hearts of the Israelites until the "complete number" of elect Gentiles has come in (11:25–26).

This is a somewhat joyless argument—and the predominant feeling that comes through Paul's writing here is joy—joy that we have been chosen. I'm not sure how much joy one could have if one was aware that one was chosen, while millions of others—through no fault of their own—have been deliberately discarded.

Another major issue is that this narrow view of predestination doesn't fit with some of Paul's other statements in Romans, let alone the rest of Scripture. After all, John states that Christ came so that "all men" might believe, not "some men" (Jn 1:7). Paul himself writes that "no one who has faith will be disappointed" and talks of how all people have disobeyed God, but he still wants to show them all mercy (11:32).

Indeed, Paul's own examples point to individual responsibility. For example, God chose the Jews to be his people, but rejected them when they disobeyed his commands. Paul doesn't dismiss them as the "non-elect," but yearns for them to believe. So humans too have the right to choose.

In the end there isn't a clear answer. God is sovereign, but people have free will. Perhaps the only answer is in the words of Charles Haddon Spurgeon, the great Victorian preacher. Spurgeon believed in election, but he wanted everyone to know Christ. In the end he declared, "Oh Lord, save the elect . . . and then elect some more!"

❻ A wonderful future
8:18–39

Another question presents itself: if Christ has achieved all this, why isn't everything perfect for those who follow him? Paul's answer is that creation is still imperfect and that our hope lies in the future. The Holy Spirit is like a foretaste of what is to come, offering a taste of what we will experience in the future. He helps us in our weakness (8:26–27) and strengthens our faith (8:23).

The problem of Israel   9:1–11:36

Paul is torn over the issue of Israel. God chose them, but they have rejected him. How can this be? The other nations have welcomed God's offer of friendship, but the Jews are sticking stubbornly to the Law (9:30–33). God has not turned his back on his people, and Paul hopes that the faith of the Gentiles will provide the inspiration the Israelites need (11:14–15). Gentiles should not pride themselves that they have been "chosen." Instead they should remember their roots (11:18). The tensions between Jewish and Gentile Christians might have had something to do with this—but also, no doubt, the resentment felt by Christians at the persecution and opposition they suffered at the hands of the Jews.

The right life   12:1–15:13

The fact that we are saved by faith doesn't give us the right to sit back and relax. We express that faith through what we do and Paul goes on to talk about how the Church should act. Once we let God change the way we think, then we will know what to do to please him (12:2). Paul presents a challenging, but inspiring, list of things that all Christians should try to do. Simple things, all of which express our love for God and reflect the great love that he has shown us (12:9–21).

Living Together   14:1–23

This has been a letter dominated by thoughts about Gentiles and Jews. Now Paul turns his attention to Gentile and Jewish Christians and how they should live together. Paul's principle is to do what we can to avoid disagreement. Paul accepts that different Christians will have different beliefs and practices (14:1–3). We shouldn't judge others, but each of us should make up our own mind (14:5). We should live in peace with each other, and help each other to have a strong faith. (Much of the history of the Church shows, unfortunately, that they never read this part. See below for Paul's example.)

Final words   15:14–16:27

Toward Jerusalem   15:14–33 ▷320

Paul has been an apostle for the Lord for over twenty years. In all that time he has tried to boldly go where no preacher has gone before (15:20–21). He has two worries about his trip to Jerusalem; will the Jewish authorities attack him? And will the Jerusalem church accept his gifts and the validity of his ministry? In fact, although James accepted it, Paul was forced to "prove" his orthodoxy to his fellow Christians—a living example of all he had written about in chapter 14.

Goodbyes   16:1–27

As was customary in his letters, Paul ends with a list of personal greetings and messages. In particular we might note Phoebe, who appears to have been a female church leader at Cenchreae, and Ampliatus, which was a common slave's name. Paul also mentions Rufus, who may well have been the son of Simon of Cyrene, mentioned in Mark's gospel (Mk 15:21).

Details, Details . . .
Different roles (12:4–8)

This is not an exhaustive list, nor are the roles listed in order of merit. Paul, indeed, does not distinguish between the different parts of the body, so he doesn't distinguish between the relative importance of the gifts. The body is one of Paul's favorite images, developed more fully in 1 Corinthians 12.

Puzzling Points
Obedience to authorities (13:1–7)

Paul's view of worldly authorities is that they have been given their power by God. "People who oppose the authorities," he writes, "are opposing what God has done, and they will be punished."

This raises problems. Does it mean we are to submit silently to those in charge, whatever they do or say? What about the Old Testament prophets who routinely opposed their rulers? What about Paul himself, who was imprisoned by "the authorities"?

The key is surely in 13:3, where Paul writes that rulers are a threat to evil people not good people. In the context of the time, Paul is writing to Christians who found themselves ruled by pagan authorities and some of whom took the view that they therefore did not have to obey them. "Not so," says Paul. Unless the commands the authorities gave were contrary to the will of God, Christians should do all they could to live as model citizens.

Details, Details . . .
Tertius (16:22)

Paul's secretary. Paul dictated the letter and Tertius wrote it down.

1 Corinthians
The greatest is love

Who: Paul

When: Around AD 54, toward the end of Paul's time in Ephesus (Ac 20:31).

What: There were problems in the church at Corinth. The followers were being affected by the sexual immorality of the city, there were arguments and factions within the church, and several people were giving false teaching.

Corinth was one of the most cosmopolitan cities in the ancient world. A hugely wealthy trade center, it was also a byword for debauchery and corruption—a kind of mixture of London, Las Vegas and Amsterdam. Such was the emphasis on sex within the city that the Greeks used the word "corinthianize" as a verb: if someone was doing a bit of "corinthing," they were sleeping around. This atmosphere seeped into the church, turning it into a group of followers infected by wealth and sex. The Corinthian church had many of the signs of a true church, but they were behaving like spoiled brats rather than children of God.

It's the culture, stupid

Few books in the Bible illustrate more clearly the need to understand the culture and society to which the letter was addressed. Paul was writing to a particular church, with particular problems, at a particular time.

Quick Guide
Author
Paul
Type
Letter
Purpose
To challenge the behavior of the Corinthian church.
Key verse
13:13 "For now there are faith, hope, and love. But of these three, the greatest is love."
If you remember one thing about this book . . .
Our actions should be guided by love.
Your 10 minutes start now
Read chapters 1, 3, 12–13, 15

This, of course, doesn't mean we can't draw principles from his writing, but it does mean we have to be very careful to understand what he meant *at the time of writing*. Culture and social customs change. In Paul's world women were supposed to cover their hair, and long hair on men was seen as sinful. Few Christians today would argue that women should still do the same. Marriages of the time were very different from those of today. Similarly, Paul's views on celibacy were given in the context of a city notorious for its sexual profligacy, in the knowledge that the time was dangerous for Christians, and in the belief that the Lord's return would be imminent. So in all his writings, we must be careful to take account of the *people* to whom Paul was writing, and the *reason* he was writing.

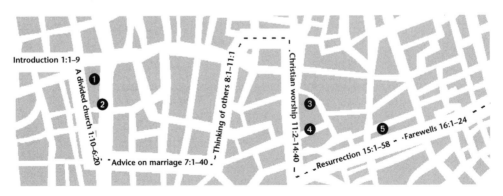

Introduction 1:1–9

A divided church 1:10–6:20

Advice on marriage 7:1–40

Thinking of others 8:1–11:1

Christian worship 11:2–14:40

Resurrection 15:1–58

Farewells 16:1–24

Paul and Corinth

Although it is called 1 Corinthians, this is actually the second letter that Paul wrote (and for all we know he might have slipped them the odd post-card as well). Still, this is the first letter we have, hence the name. Paul's relationship with the followers in Corinth was not always an easy one. For several years he had trouble in the city and trouble with the church.

First, Paul came on his own. He was joined later by Timothy and Silas (Ac 18:1–18). He worked as a tentmaker, but it was a difficult, nervous time (1 Co 2:1–5). Paul was attacked and harassed by Jewish religious leaders. After helping establish the church, he went on to Syria.

His first letter was written mainly to warn the believers against sexual immorality and against associating with "immoral people." Nothing more is known of the letter.

His second letter is the letter we call 1 Corinthians. Paul's meaning in the first letter had not been clear and the situation had deteriorated, with arguments in the church and accusations of sexual immorality. He wrote from Ephesus and dispatched Timothy to try to deal with the situation.

His second visit is referred to in 2 Corinthians 2:1 as a "painful visit." It was an attempt to sort out the dissension within the church, but it did not go well. This is not recorded in Acts, but probably was a brief visit some-time during his three years at Ephesus.

Following this visit, Paul wrote again—a hard and "severe" letter that is referred to in 2 Corinthians (2 Co 2:4; 7:8). It was so outspoken that Paul seems to have had second thoughts about sending it. Nevertheless, it seems to have worked and some of the church at Corinth seem to have repented of their behavior.

Relieved at his success, Paul sends a fourth letter, declaring his intention of making another visit.

First Visit — AD 52

First Letter

Second Letter — AD 54–55

Second Visit

Third Letter — AD 55–56

Fourth Letter

POSTCARD

Welcome to Corinth!

Corinth is the commercial hub of Greece! Our unique position makes us a crossroads for travelers and goods going to and from Rome and Athens. After the unfortunate destruction by the Romans in 146 BC, our newly rebuilt city boasts a wide range of cutting-edge facili-ties, including an amphitheater, several shop-ping malls and over twelve temples.

Corinth is one of the biggest cities in Greece with a population of some 250,000 people. And to make sure that your visit is comfort-able we are also home to 400,000 slaves.

Our modernity also extends to our habits—and we are proud to say that our city is known for its sexual freedom. Not for nothing is our favorite goddess Aphrodite—goddess of love. Indeed, much of our sexual activity is mixed up with our religion.

To Lechaeum

To Philius

To Cenchrea

Acrocorinth

1 Theater
2 Temple
3 Meat market and Temple of Apollo
4 Synagogue
5 Amphitheater
6 Temple of Aphrodite
7 Upper Fountain House

Introduction   1:1–9

Paul introduces himself and commends the church. They are a gifted church—they don't lack any spiritual gift. The issue here is how those gifts are put to use.

A divided church   1:10–6:20

❶ Gang warfare   1:10–4:21

The church was divided amongst itself, with factions lining up behind Paul, Apollos (a prominent leader and preacher in Asia) and Cephas (i.e., Peter). There was also another group rather superiorly calling themselves "Christians" (1:11). The mention of Peter doesn't necessarily mean that he visited the church; more likely it indicates a group of Jewish Christians.

Their factions came with a sense of intellectual authority; they believed that their group was philosophically and theologically correct. So Paul addresses the whole issue by stating that we are all, basically, fools. Human cleverness is foolishness in God's eyes, but those whom the world calls fools—the humble believers in the cross of Christ—are the truly wise ones (1:18–2:5). Their behavior, therefore, is not "spiritual," but "worldly." These "mature and wise Christians" are squabbling like infants (3:1–4).

There is no place for pride among Christians—and especially among Christian leaders. There is no place for empire building. On the contrary, the role of an apostle is one of hardship and struggle, not glamour. Sarcastically he compares the foolishness and poverty of a "simple" apostle with the wisdom and comfort of the "mature" followers (4:6–13).

❷ Incest and immorality   5:1–6:20

The Corinthians are so "intellectually superior" that they are condoning incest. "Even the pagans don't stoop that low," says Paul. He argues that the man who is doing this should be handed over to Satan (5:4–5)—which doesn't mean some kind of magical rite, but that he should be expelled from the church in the hope that he comes to his senses.

Paul reserves his sternest words for those who call themselves Christians but behave otherwise. He argues that the severest measures should be taken, that Christians should not even associate with these people (5:11). This seems extreme; how are they to be turned round if they are ostracized? But the phrase usually translated "do not associate" means "do not get mixed up with." Paul is arguing, not for ostracism but for avoiding anything that implies approval of their behavior.

Details, Details . . .
Is he coming or not?
(4:18)

Some of Paul's opponents in the church argue that Paul is unstable: that he says one thing and does another. "He says he is going to visit, but then he changes his mind." "He is scared to come in person, so he sends someone else." Such arrogant assertions were to resurface again and again (2 Co 1:17; 10:10).

Paul uses the image of the law court to show the way that the church should deal with its own discipline. Orthodox Jews would never take their case before a Gentile court, for to do so would imply that the Jewish people were unable to operate their own laws. Similarly, Paul argues that the church should deal with its own problems (6:1–11).

The key thing is, however, to stop the kind of behavior that leads to these disputes, to control the passions and desires of the body. Although 6:12–20 deals with sexual immorality—a particular problem for the Corinthian church—Paul's list also includes theft, greed, drunkenness, slander and cheating. Just because we are free to do something doesn't mean it is right to do it. In Paul's argument, you cannot separate the soul and the body; you cannot sin with the body and leave the soul intact. Each affects the other.

True and false marriage   7:1–40

After his very first letter, the Corinthian Christians asked Paul some specific questions regarding relationships. It must be taken into account, when reading this passage, that Paul was addressing these specific questions. He talks to the unmarried, the married and the intending-to-be married.

Thinking of others   8:1–11:1

Food sacrificed to idols was one of the burning issues of the Greek and Asian churches. Meat left over from pagan sacrifices might be eaten in feasts and banquets, and might even be sold in the market. Was a Christian somehow participating in idol worship by buying a chunk and taking it home?

Paul's answer is that the Corinthians should always assess their own actions in the light of the faith of others. Some might feel free to eat such meat, but if it damaged the faith of others, they should think again (8:1–13). He illustrates this by showing how he has sacrificed his own freedoms. He has become a slave to others and sacrificed his own "rights" so that others might be brought to faith (9:1–18). He points out the danger of anything to do with idols—lessons from the history of Israel that show how overconfidence can lead to a fall (10:12–13). Paul concludes, therefore, that it is better to refrain from partaking. "I always try to please others instead of myself," he writes, "in the hope that many of them will be saved" (10:33).

Christian worship   11:2–14:40

Paul's instructions for worship are the result of specific questions and issues raised by the Corinthian church. This raises problems when we try to discern the principles underlying his instructions. In Paul's world, for example, covering your head was a sign of submission to authority. Women rarely appeared in public with their heads uncovered and men, in Paul's view, dishonored themselves if they prayed with their heads covered. In our culture, covering your head is much more about keeping the rain out.

This section, therefore, has engendered a lot of debate as to what is "eternal principle" and what is "cultural practice." Perhaps the most important principle underlying the whole debate is the seriousness of intention.

Puzzling Points
So is all divorce wrong? (7:10–11)

Paul takes his lead from Jesus (Mk 10:9; Lk 16:18). However, he doesn't mention the words reported in Matthew (Mt 5:32; 19:9). Paul's clear belief is that divorce between Christians is not permissible. However, the issue is not quite as clear-cut. For one thing, Paul was addressing a specific culture and time. The idea of marriage was completely different in the society Paul is addressing, as was the position of women. Second, he does not reflect the teaching of Jesus in Matthew, where divorce is permitted under certain circumstances (Mt 5:32; 19:9). Third, he is talking about a marriage between two Christians—the principles he lays down for marriages where one or the other partner is not a believer are different—and a great many difficulties are caused in marriages where one partner's behavior is obviously un-Christian. Whatever Paul's strictures, they must be viewed in the light of particular circumstances. Should a woman remain with a husband who beats her up? Clearly not. Compassion and love will always play a part. All divorce is a failure, but all failures can be restored by the love of God.

331

Puzzling Points
Are men in charge of women? (11:3–16)

There are three views about these verses.

• A permanent mandate. Some see these verses as a divine, permanent instruction indicating not only that men are in authority over women, but also that women should keep their heads covered in public.

• A bit of a mandate. Some argue that the principle of headship is a divine mandate, but that covering the head is a cultural expression. The wife should show respect for her husband by godly living, as much as by a particular form of clothing.

• Not a mandate at all. Some see these verses as reflecting the culture of the time. Paul was dealing with marriage relationships at Corinth, and was giving a reason why women should cover their heads. Verses 11–12, in this view, emphasize marriage as a relationship of equality and mutual dependence.

▷ 279, 334

Details, Details . . .
The cloudy mirror (13:12)

Mirrors in Paul's day were made of polished metal, rather than mirrored glass. So, if the metal was dull, the image was blurred and poor.

Whatever conclusions we come to concerning the role of women in worship, or the administration of communion, Paul is arguing that these things must be approached seriously. It is no trivial matter to pray, to prophesy or to take part in communion.

❸ Spiritual gifts   12:1–14:40

The church at Corinth was marked by a wide diversity of spiritual gifts. With the differences and divisions at Corinth, these too had become a matter of division, with some arguing that one was more important than the other. In particular, the gift of speaking in ecstatic tongues was seen as a spectacular sign of holiness and Christian maturity. Paul uses the image of the body to state that each gift has its role. He does not dismiss the gift—on the contrary, he displays it himself (14:18)—but he does not rate it as being of the highest importance. Paul rates higher those gifts that build up the church. And he does not argue that everyone has to display it. We are all different, but the same God works in all of us (12:4–11).

❹ The greatest is love   13:1–13

In the middle of this argument, Paul breaks off to speak about love. Chapter 13 is one of the most famous passages from the Bible and, indeed, one of the greatest pieces of writing ever. Paul explores what has really been the theme of his whole letter: the need for love. It is a kind of summary of the book. We don't know everything, but one day we will see all these difficult issues more clearly. In the meantime the best thing to do is work on what we know really matters: faith, hope and best of all, love.

Resurrection   15:1–58

Some have argued that Paul "invented" Christianity, that he created the theology and principles of the early Church. This chapter, in fact, shows how much Paul was indebted to the historical tradition. It is Paul's classic account of what the resurrection means, but it is based on real appearances. Paul here states that the resurrection of Christ is of the utmost importance. If Christ didn't actually come back to life, then everything that Paul preaches is a lie (15:5) and the Christian faith is useless (15:17). That is why Paul points to well-known accounts, real people and real events. As to the type of bodies that we will have, Paul's only conclusion is that they will be different. They will be eternal bodies, free from decay and disease, outshining the old body as much as a flower outshines the seed.

A Little Local Difficulty
Baptized for the dead   15:29

No one really knows what Paul means here. Three different theories have been suggested:

• Living Christians were being baptized on behalf of dead Christians, who could not be baptized before they died.

• Christians were being baptized in anticipation of being reunited with friends or relatives who had died.

• New converts were baptized to "replace" baptized believers who had died.

In the end we don't really know. Since Paul mentions it only in passing, and only this once, it's not a major feature of first-century faith.

❺ The early Church in Corinth

Paul's letter gives us an intriguing picture of what went on in the church at Corinth.

We can see that they had regular worship that included a "prophecy" or message, which was distinct from the teaching or speaking (14:29). They would take up a weekly collection for the poor (16:1–2). They included a celebration of the Lord's Supper. They included the exercise of spiritual gifts, including speaking in tongues. They included someone singing and teaching. Much as happens today, in fact. Except that the women kept their hats on, of course.

Farewells   16:1–24

After directions for collecting money, Paul gives his farewells and some details of what he plans to do. He ends with what may be the most potent message of this letter: "I love everyone who belongs to Christ Jesus" (16:24).

Puzzling Points
Should women remain silent? (14:26–40)

I'm getting a strange sense of déjà vu here . . .

The problem here, as with the "head covering/authority" part, is working out what problem Paul was addressing. Some have taken these verses to mean that women should never preach. Others argue that what was happening was that women were either shouting out questions or talking among themselves.

There are three views here:

• A permanent mandate. Women should always be silent in church and this is an expression of their subordination as reflected in Paul's view on "headship."

• A principle. There may be appropriate roles for them to play in worship, but they should be subordinate to the roles played by men.

• A cultural expression. Churches had been formed out of the synagogue model, where women and men were separate. The position of women in first-century society was entirely different. All Paul is reflecting here, in this view is that he was a cultural product of his own times.

▷279, 334

Landmark: Men and Women

We live in a society where men and women are considered equal. Even though sexism is still rife in some areas, in the eyes of the Law men and women have the same rights and the same responsibilities.

The Bible was not written at a time like that. The time during which the Bible was written was a time when women were second-class citizens. Or even third-class, ranking slightly behind the livestock. The Old Testament comes from an age where women had no powers, and no legal standing. Divorce was only available to husbands; women were not allowed to own property and were declared impure at times when their bodies were only performing naturally.

This creates some difficulties and tensions for us when we read the Bible. The sexism seems shocking. But we have to look beyond the cultural values of the time if we are really to understand what the Bible says about men and women.

The Bible has often been accused of being male dominated—and there is no doubt that most of the stories are about men. But that is hardly surprising, given the kinds of cultures with which we are dealing. What is more notable, in fact, is not that women don't feature so prominently, but that they feature to the extent that they do. There are many, many heroines in the Bible. There are people like Rahab and Tamar, Deborah and Miriam. There are teachers like the mother of King Lemuel; there are prophetesses and princesses.

In the New Testament times the position of women was not much better. Their testimony was still not accepted in a court of law. They could not teach the Torah. Jewish men still gave thanks to God that they were not born female. Into this culture, God chose a young, unmarried teenager to bear his son. Women were among the first to recognize Jesus' power and the Bible describes how Mary and Martha—as well as their brother Lazarus —were "loved" by Jesus (Jn 11:5). It was not the strong men but the faithful women who met the risen Jesus first.

Jesus had a radical attitude to women. Here was a man who did not look down on women, but who engaged them in conversation, who challenged them to change their lives, who refused to go along with the sexist attitudes of his day.

Paul is often cited as an example of misogyny, but a closer look at his life indicates that the issue may not be as simple as it is often made out to be. Paul's statements on the role of women in church are just as likely to be pronouncements on local problems, rather than global, divine directives. True, Paul saw the man as the "head" of the relationship, but in the rest of his views about marriage he was radically different from the general views of his age. In Paul's view, marriage was a partnership of two servants, each willing to serve the other. Paul had women on his team and worked alongside them.

In the light of these observations, it is important to remember that God created men and women equal. "God created humans to be like himself; he made men and women" (Ge 1:27). We were created to help each other, to be part of a team. God sees no distinction between men and women, despite the traditions of the ages and the attitudes of history.

▷ **279**

2 Corinthians
Jars of clay

Who: Paul

When: AD 55–56. This second letter was probably written from northern Macedonia. Paul had only been able to visit Corinth for a short, and difficult, visit, not the promised "long stay" (1 Co 16:6). Although he had promised to return, he decided that another painful visit would serve no purpose, so he returned to Asia. His opponents used this decision to accuse Paul of unreliability. They were also saying that Paul was not a real apostle, even accusing him of pocketing the money he had collected for the Christians in Jerusalem.

Paul was stung into sending them a strong letter. He waited, worried, to hear their reaction, even traveling to Troas in order to find out the news. When Titus told him that the letter had worked, his relief was immense (7:6–16).

This is one of the most personal of Paul's letters. In it we feel the weight of his anxiety for the Corinthian church, and the depth of his concern for them. We also see a vulnerable side of Paul—a side that feels the need to assert his own integrity and honesty.

The problem of chapter 10 . . .

Two Corinthians refers to the "severe letter" that Paul had sent to the Corinthian church. However, some scholars have argued that part of this letter is preserved within 2 Corinthians. Their theory is that chapters 10–13 are, in fact, from the "severe" letter. They point to the sudden change in tone, the fact that the flow of the letter has been completely interrupted: one moment Paul is encouraging the Corinthians to give generously, the next moment he is criticizing them and threatening them with punishment. It is a compelling argument and it would certainly explain some of the references within those chapters. However, the earlier chapters indicate that the criticism of Paul has not entirely disappeared, so Paul may simply be reinforcing the message from the "severe" letter.

Quick Guide

Author
Paul

Type
Letter

Purpose
To put right the rumors about Paul's conduct and to encourage the church to deal with troublemakers.

Key verse
4:16 "We never give up. Our bodies are gradually dying, but we ourselves are being made stronger each day. These little troubles are getting us ready for an eternal glory that will make all our troubles seem like nothing at all."

If you remember one thing about this book . . .
Though times are tough, we do not lose heart, because God is at work with us.

Your 10 minutes start now
Read chapters 3–6, 10, 12

The Route Through 2 Corinthians

First defense 1:1–7:16 · Collection for Jerusalem 8:1–9:15 · Second defense 10:1–12:21 · Final comments 13:1–13

First defense 1:1–7:16

❶ Why didn't he come? 1:1–2:17

Paul begins with a justification of his work and a defense of his conduct. He talks, first, of the hardships he has endured in Asia (1:8–11). He has not been on vacation; he has been enduring huge physical and emotional strain. He explains that he did not want to visit Corinth again because he did not want another painful experience. But that doesn't mean he has had an easy time. He has been in fear of death, he has been suffering terribly (2:1–4).

❷ Jars of clay 3:1–6:14

Throughout the letter Paul treads a tightrope. He does not want to appear to be boasting, but he has to defend his actions and integrity. He feels fragile and threatened, like a jar of clay (4:7–12), but the point is that the power comes from elsewhere. Paul is establishing here that, whatever glory he has achieved, whatever troubles he has had to go through, the power at work in him comes from God. On his own, he can do nothing; and, therefore, when he talks about his achievements, he is talking about the work of God through a fallible, fragile human being. What keeps him going is the hope of exchanging his tired, battered old "tent" for a wonderful new home in heaven (5:1–6). In chapter 6, he deals specifically with the sufferings he has endured and with the integrity with which he has responded. He is poor, but rich; dying, yet still alive. He has nothing, yet he has everything (6:8–10).

❸ Light and darkness 6:14–7:16

Paul urges his readers to stay away from the darkness. Part of the problem with the church in Corinth was the way that they made accommodation with the pagan world all around them. Their behavior was not all that it should have been. That is why he wrote to them in such a tone. He did not enjoy hurting their feelings, but the result was worthwhile, because he received the news that they had turned around (7:8–16).

Collection for Jerusalem 8:1–9:15

Now that the relationship between Paul and the Corinthian church is restored, he feels confident enough to test their love by asking them to contribute to the collection for Jerusalem. Christians should give of their riches, because Jesus gave everything he had (8:8–9). Giving, therefore, should not be a reluctant act. Paul is not forcing anyone to give; he is encouraging his readers to develop a joyful spirit of generosity (9:7).

Second defense 10:1–12:21

The change in tone from the end of chapter 9 to the beginning of chapter 10 is noticeable. Suddenly Paul is moved to defend himself again. There is still a group of people at Corinth who are hostile to Paul and who are spreading rumors about him. He is worried that they have not given up their old ways. It is this difference that makes many scholars believe that this is part of a different letter, which has been inserted here.

First, he answers the charge that his bark is worse than his bite (10:1–11). When he comes, he assures them that he will "walk the talk." Those who underestimate him do so at their peril.

Second, he defends his role (11:1–15). He may not be a "super-apostle," he may not be eloquent, but he is convinced of the God-given nature of that role. Being an apostle does not necessarily mean that he has powers of persuasion and eloquent oratory; it means that he has a mission given to him by God. He was given a vision—taken into the third heaven (12:1–5)—and it is this that underwrites his mission and gives him the power to continue. Paul is no superman; he talks openly of the suffering he has endured and the punishments he has faced. Indeed, he talks about an ongoing suffering, a thorn in his flesh that remains with him despite prayer (12:7). Not a superhero, then, but a jar of clay filled with the Spirit of God.

Final comments
13:1–14

Paul promises to visit the Corinthians for a third time. Before he comes he gives them a chance to make sure that their house is in order. Only they can put things right; only they can test themselves; only they can follow the truth. The final verse is, perhaps, testimony to an early Christian belief in the Trinity, bringing together Father, Son and Holy Spirit in one prayer.

Details, Details . . .
The trouble in Jerusalem

The church in Jerusalem was in financial trouble from the very beginning. The probable explanation is that the vigorous opposition from Jewish families and employers meant that Christian converts lost their homes and employment. Early in his Christian life, Paul raised money for famine relief in Jerusalem (Ac 11:27–30). Paul might also have seen a benefit from this collection in bringing the Gentile and Jewish Christians together. He believed also that the Gentile Christians had an obligation to the Jerusalem church —for without their witness there would be no church in Asia Minor.

Details, Details . . .
The third heaven (12:2)

This seems to mean the highest heaven. Paul also uses the word "paradise" (which was originally a Persian word for park or garden) to describe the state he was in. This vision appears to have come to Paul around AD 41 or 42, some six years after his conversion, but before he set out on his first journey. The experience was so overwhelming that even now, fourteen years later, Paul is unsure whether it was a bodily experience or not.

Galatians
Faith and obedience

Galatia is a region and not a city. Normally the term refers to the northern part of the region, but there is no evidence that Paul ever visited that part. It is likely that the letter was sent to the churches Paul had established on his first missionary journey—churches in Derbe, Lystra, Antioch and Iconium (Ac 13).

When: Probably written around AD 48/49, making it the earliest of the New Testament writings.

What: Acts 15 tells of Jewish Christians visiting churches in Syrian Antioch and insisting that all believers must be circumcised. Paul and Barnabas argue with them, then take their argument to the council in Jerusalem. It seems that these teachers reached the Galatian churches as well and Paul is writing to counter their theories.

The "circumcisionists" argued that Paul was not a "proper" apostle, and that he was diluting the requirements of the Jewish Law in order to make the gospel acceptable to Gentiles. In response, Paul asserted his right to be called an apostle and argued that the gospel is a gospel of love and grace. It is no longer about laws and regulations, but about faith in God. His anxiety that people were being taken in by the pro-circumcision lobby is reflected in the fact that this letter is the most strongly worded of all Paul's writings.

Throughout the years, the circumcisionists sought to undermine Paul's work. The circumcisionists seem to have been most strongly at work in the Jerusalem church, their influence even extending to the leadership of the church, who were pressured into conforming to Jewish law (2:11–21). The circumcisionists were suspicious of Peter as much as anyone, because Peter had been the one whose vision showed that the old laws were not in place anymore (Ac 10–11). They claimed the support of James, the leader of the Jerusalem church (although there is no evidence that James supported them). In the end, Paul was so impassioned on this subject that he even confronted Peter himself.

Quick Guide

Author
Paul

Type
Letter

Purpose
To combat the ideas of those who thought Christians still had to be circumcised.

Key verse
5:6 "If you are a follower of Christ Jesus, it makes no difference whether you are circumcised or not. All that matters is your faith that makes you love others."

If you remember one thing about this book ...
What matters is not outward show, but inner commitment.

Your 5 minutes start now
Read chapters 1–3, 5:1–15

The Route Through Galatians

The true apostle 1:1–2:21

The true faith 3:1–4:31

True freedom 5:1–6:18

The true apostle   1:1–2:21

This is a vigorous, urgent book. Paul has no time to waste here, he leaps straight in with the core of his message: he is a true apostle, chosen and appointed by God (1:1–2).

Already on the offensive, he carries straight on to attack those who are teaching false messages. To Paul this would undo all he had tried to achieve and all the work that the Holy Spirit had done through him. The issue is clear: if the circumcisionists get their way, Christianity will be reduced to an obscure Jewish sect. He therefore goes straight for the theological jugular: it doesn't matter if these people are angels, if they are preaching a false gospel they will be punished. Paul has been more Jewish than the rest of them put together (1:13–14). He knows all about the Law. And as to their claim that Paul is not a "proper" apostle, he dismisses it. His mission was given by God and approved by Peter and James and John (2:9–10).

Paul had seen firsthand what slavish obedience to the Law had done to people. He had seen its failure to save anyone. There was no way he was going to let the Christian faith be taken back down that road.

The true faith   3:1–4:31

Calling someone "stupid" (3:1) is not the polite way of starting theological debate, but then Paul was not interested in being polite. This is grievous bodily theology—Paul is pulling no punches.

The Law was a temporary measure until the promises given to Abraham could be fulfilled by Christ (3:19–20). It was supposed to teach us, but now we have a better teacher (3:24). Paul is simply baffled that the Galatians, who had so eagerly accepted his message, should now choose to return to a kind of slavery. They were freed from slavery to man-made gods; why would they want to go back to slavery again (4:8–11)? Paul urges them to look beyond the false friendship of the Judaizers and to try to understand what being under the Law actually means. It means the difference between being a slave and being free (4:21–31).

True freedom   5:1–6:18

Paul's language is as strong as any of the Old Testament prophets in this chapter. He is so angry at those who advocate circumcision that he wishes they would cut the whole thing off (5:12). We have been set free by Christ, it makes no difference whether we are circumcised or not, what matters is faith that leads to love for others (5:6). Freedom, however, should not be abused. It should be seen as an opportunity to exercise love. If you want to follow a law, love your neighbor as yourself (5:14).

Paul is not against works. On the contrary, he argues continually in his letters for the importance of doing the right things and avoiding immorality. But the works spring from faith. It is faith that makes us love others (5:6) and obedience to Christ that makes us offer others a helping hand (6:2).

Details, Details . . .
Large letters (6:11)

Some have seen in this reference an implication that Paul had bad eyesight. But he may just have been wanting to emphasize his final, simple message: the cross of Christ is what matters. Paul nearly always ends his letters with a very simple summary of his message. "It doesn't matter if you are circumcised or not. All that matters is that you are a new person" (6:15).

Ephesians
The wonder of God

Who: There has been debate over whether Paul actually wrote this letter. It doesn't have the usual personal greetings and parts of it seem to be based on Colossians. Some believe, therefore, that this letter was written by a follower of Paul, rather than the apostle himself.

However, it may well be that this is a circular letter, a sort of inspirational newsletter sent to other churches as well as the one in Ephesus. The similarity to Colossians is certainly nothing to wonder about. It might well have been written around the same time, and no writer likes to waste good material!

When: Paul was probably writing from prison in Rome in the early AD 60s.

What: Ephesians is a general letter, in that it does not address a specific concern or problem. Instead it is a statement of the way in which God's love will bring all people together in Christ. God has a plan and a purpose and this encompasses the whole universe.

Ephesians brings together many of the major themes of Paul's teaching, as a kind of summary of his thought. For that reason—and the debate about authorship—it has sometimes been speculated that this is a kind of *Introduction to Paul*, written not by the apostle but by a follower who was bringing together a collection of his work. The one tiny flaw with this theory is that there isn't a shred of evidence to support it, but actually it catches an important facet of this book. It *is* a superb introduction to Paul's theories.

Quick Guide
Author
Paul
Type
Letter
Purpose
To show how God's love should bring unity among those who follow him.
Key verses
4:4–6 "All of you are part of the same body. There is only one Spirit of God, just as you were given one hope when you were chosen to be God's people. We have only one Lord, one faith, and one baptism. There is one God who is the Father of all people. Not only is God above all others, but he works by using all of us, and he lives in all of us."
If you remember one thing about this book . . .
All Christians are part of the same "body"; we should all remain united in love.
Your 5 minutes start now
Read chapters 2, 4–5

One of the key themes of the book is unity—the need for followers of Jesus to recognize that we are all joined together and that we should all work for and support one another. Christ has brought together Jew and Gentile, we all have our role to play, and no one is more important than another.

The Route Through Ephesians

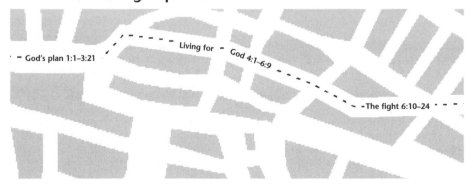

God's plan 1:1–3:21

Living for God 4:1–6:9

The fight 6:10–24

POSTCARD
Welcome to Ephesus!

Ephesus is the shopping center of the ancient world.

Located at the meeting point of both the major land and sea routes to the east, Ephesus is a major commercial center and port. The state-of-the-art port facilities are built round a man-made harbor, connected to the nearby Aegean Sea by a narrow channel. Constant maintenance ensures that this harbor does not silt up.

The city is packed with impressive monuments, including the temple to Artemis or Diana—one of the seven wonders of the world. The visitor should make a point of visiting the silversmiths and taking home a statue of the goddess, or spending time in the stadium where, along with various entertainments, many exciting and fascinating riots take place.

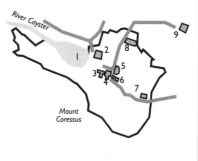

1 Harbor
2 Gymnasium
3 Temple of Serapis
4 Marketplace (Agora)
5 Theater
6 Bath Houses
7 Council Hall
8 Stadium
9 Temple of Artemis or Diana

God's plan   1:1–3:21

Paul begins with an almost breathless tone of wonder at the magnitude of God's kindness, wisdom and love. The overriding theme in this letter is the way in which God has planned all this from the start. Christ has died to give us freedom (1:7–8), and the same Christ now sits with God and rules over all things (1:19–22). Christ has given us life and he has given us a future (2:4–6). This is God's gift to us. There is nothing we can do to earn it. Our response has to be to "do good things and to live as he has always wanted us to live" (2:8–10).

This free gift, this love of God, means that all barriers are broken. The Law of Moses has been "destroyed" (2:15) and the barrier between Jew and Gentile has been torn down. We are now united in one body (2:16). Nationality, color, social status—all these distinctions don't matter. "Because of Christ, all of us can come to the Father by the same spirit" (2:18). We are all being built together into one magnificent temple.

In chapter 3, Paul reflects on his role in the great plan. It was his job to spread the good news to the Gentiles. He ends with a prayer that the Church will realize how great God's love is and how much his power can achieve through the Church.

Living for God   4:1–6:9

For Paul, Christian unity has to be more than a theory; it has to be lived out as a fact. This section repeats some of his arguments from 1 Corinthians 12–13 in his emphasis on unity and the different roles Christians play within the Church. Paul has a reputation for complex theology—and certainly his arguments can be complex and difficult—but he is always careful to frame the application in a simple way. Living in unity is a matter of simple principles, all springing from the forgiveness and love of Christ (4:25–5:5).

Puzzling Points
Wives, husbands and children (5:21–32)

Another contentious part. Here Paul talks about submission within relationships. But this is a *mutual* submission. Paul argues that wives should submit to their husbands, but he also argues that husbands should love their wives "as Christ loved the church." Christ's love was expressed in serving and dying for his followers. The emphasis here is on mutual support and value. Husbands should treat their wives as themselves. So authority doesn't really come into it.

The keynote of family relationships is in trust and respect. Children are enjoined to obey their parents, but fathers are told not to be hard on their children. Both have their own responsibilities and their own rights.

▷175, 359

Slaves　　　　　　　6:5–9 ▷363
The fight　　　　　　6:10–24

Paul ends with one of the most enduring images of his writing, that of the Christian putting on the armor of God. Much verbiage has been expended explaining precisely the appropriateness of each piece of armor, but it is really the whole suit that counts. Any weakness —any chink in the armor—will lead to fatal results. Accordingly, the Christian should be a person of truth, justice, peace and faith. They should pay attention to the Word of God and they should pray. All of these things form the Christian's "armory."

Paul never makes any bones about Christianity being an easy option. On the contrary, it often leads to conflict and oppression. But we can endure, if we are properly equipped for the fight.

Philippians
Running the race

Who: Paul.

When: Probably written from imprisonment in Rome, sometime around AD 61. Some have argued for an earlier date—and an earlier imprisonment—but it does seem to fit well with the account of Paul's imprisonment in Acts 28, when he was under house arrest in Rome. However, the conditions that he describes seem harsher than we would expect at this time, so we cannot be certain.

What: This is a thank-you letter. The Philippians, hearing of Paul's imprisonment, had sent him a gift. Paul is writing to thank them, but along the way he takes the opportunity to encourage them and to warn them about possible pitfalls. He encourages them to keep on running, because the race is not yet won.

Paul founded the Philippian church on his first missionary journey (Ac 16) around AD 50, probably the first church founded on European soil. When he and Silas first arrived, they met with some women who were praying by the riverbank (Ac 16:13–15). This indicates there probably wasn't a synagogue in the city. One of these women was Lydia, a businesswoman who dealt in expensive purple cloth, who became Paul's first European convert. Luke stayed in Philippi after Paul left, which may be because it was Luke's hometown.

Quick Guide
Author
Paul
Type
Letter
Purpose
Thanking the Philippian church for their gift and urging them to keep going.
Key verses
3:13–14 "My friends, I don't feel that I have already arrived. But I forget what is behind, and I struggle for what is ahead. I run toward the goal, so that I can win the prize of being called to heaven. This is the prize that God offers because of what Christ Jesus has done."
If you remember one thing about this book . . .
We are moving toward heaven —so we have to keep going!
Your 5 minutes start now
Read chapters 1:12–2:18; 3:12–21

Evidently the church at Philippi was very close to Paul's heart. From the first time they met they identified with Paul's message and took an active part in his work—a position that is reflected in their support for him while he is in prison. This, perhaps, is why his prayer for them is so full of joy (1:3–11). This is not a church that needs chastising or correcting. Instead he encourages them to continue in the faith, despite the persecution they face.

The Route Through Philippians

Greetings 1:1–11
Prison life 1:12–30
Humility 2:1–18
Paul's friends 2:19–30
Warnings 3:1–4:9
Thanks and farewell 4:10–23

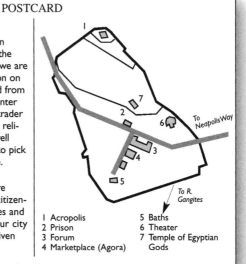

POSTCARD

Welcome to Philippi!

Philippi is one of the key cities of northern Greece. Our city is named after Philip II, the father of Alexander the Great. However, we are very much a modern city, and our situation on the Egnatian Way—the great Roman road from Rome to the East—makes us the ideal center of communications for the businessman, trader or those seeking to establish strange new religions in Asia Minor. The marketplace is well worth a visit and the tourist will be able to pick up some of our famous purple-dyed cloth.

Our town is primarily a Roman colony, refounded in 42 BC, and all those who are born here enjoy the benefits of Roman citizenship, along with our many other amenities and facilities. Many military folk have found our city the ideal place to retire and have been given land in the region.

1 Acropolis
2 Prison
3 Forum
4 Marketplace (Agora)
5 Baths
6 Theater
7 Temple of Egyptian Gods

Greetings   1:1–11

The letter is sent not only from Paul but also from Timothy. Timothy would be known to the Philippians, because he was with Paul when the church was founded. Paul addresses three groups in his opening sentences: "saints," "overseers" and "deacons."

- Saints refers to the whole church—all the Christians.
- Overseers probably means those in leadership of the church.
- Deacons were responsible for both spiritual and practical matters.

This, however, is not a hierarchy. Paul places the body of the church first. The leadership exists for the church, not the other way round.

Prison life   1:12–30

Paul's journey to Rome has not been easy and his future is uncertain. He doesn't know whether life or death will be better. He is quite happy to go to Jesus, but is also aware that there is much still to do (1:21–26).

Humility   2:1–18

What is important are unity and humility. There are some who are taking the opportunity of Paul's imprisonment to further their own ends (1:17). Paul knows that there are signs of division within the Philippian church as well, so he encourages them to remain united and to serve one another with humility.

Working out what it means to live as a Christian is a serious business. Paul describes it as a matter of "fear and trembling." This doesn't mean that we should be scared of it, but that we should take it seriously and do our utmost to shine with the light of Christ (2:14–15).

Paul's friends
2:19–30

Epaphroditus was the person who brought the gift from Philippi to Paul, a journey that almost cost the man his life. Now Paul is returning him to his home church, carrying this letter with him.

Warnings
3:1–4:9

Paul begins this section with the word "finally" (3:1) but is only half-way through his message—an example that has been taken up by preachers throughout history. Paul has obviously written before to the Philippians, but now he repeats his message: be on your guard.

Once again, the problem is with the circumcisionists within the church (3:2–11). They are arguing that people must be circumcised even though they are Gentile Christians. Paul uses exceptionally strong language in putting them down here—just as he does in Galatians. Once, as the truest of true Jews, he thought these kinds of regulations valuable. Now he describes them as "rubbish"—although the word he actually uses is *skybalon*, which means "dung." Paul is saying that, compared to what he now knows to be true, all he once believed is a load of . . . well, you get the point.

All he now wants is Christ and that is the goal toward which he is running. He will not achieve perfection this side of the finishing line, but he is pushing on. Others, however, are running in the opposite direction (3:17–19).

Details, Details . . .
An early hymn (2:5–11)

Paul is probably quoting here from an early Church hymn. He may have been the author, but some scholars believe that it comes from an Aramaic original. If that is so, this is one of the very earliest statements from the Church about Christ. It affirms his divine origin (2:6), his sacrifice on earth (2:7–8) and his present position, reigning with God (2:9–11).

Details, Details . . .
Euodia and Syntyche (4:2–9)

These women are quarreling and Paul exhorts them to make up (4:2). That Paul mentions them at all indicates that they must have been people with considerable influence in the church. They have certainly worked alongside Paul in the past, helping him to spread the good news. Who the "true partner" is to whom Paul refers (4:3) is a matter of debate. The most obvious person is Epaphroditus, although it has been suggested that the word used for "true partner"—*Syzygos*—is a personal name and one of the leaders of the church at Philippi.

Details, Details . . .
The race (3:12–16)

Paul uses this image several times in his letters (1 Co 9:24; Ga 2:2; Ga 5:7; 2 Ti 4:7). It was an image familiar to all Greeks and Romans who prized athletic prowess and chariot racing. Every major town had its stadium where athletes would compete against each other. The winner of the race would be given a prize—a laurel crown for their heads and sometimes a cash reward. Nowadays our runners receive much the same kind of thing—with a gold medal replacing the laurel. For Christians the finishing line means heaven, and the prize means eternal life with Jesus. But like all athletes we must keep training, keep learning, keep striving to make every performance our personal best (4:8–9).

Thanks and farewell   4:10–23

Paul ends with renewed thanks to the church that has helped him so much. Their gifts have not been easy donations, but sacrifices that have cost them dearly. Paul is certain that these people, whom he loves so much, will be blessed because of their sacrificial love.

Colossians
Don't be fooled . . .

Who: Paul.

When: Paul is probably writing from Rome, where he was in prison awaiting trial. Around AD 61.

What: Although Paul had never been to Colossae, he had learned of their faith from a man called Epaphras who had lived in the town and was now working with Paul. Indeed, many experts believe that Epaphras founded the church at Colossae. Epaphras's account indicated that the Colossians were being affected by some very strange ideas—so Paul is simply writing to set things right and to attack these "senseless arguments" (2:8).

We can't be sure exactly what the false beliefs were—they seem to have been a sort of mutant form of Judaism, with some dietary laws mixed with mystical pagan festivals. This is what is called "syncretism," which means mixing together Christianity with ideas from other philosophies and religions that are viewed as equally true. We live in a syncretistic society today, where ideas from all faiths are mixed together. For Paul it depends entirely on what the ideas are: here they include the dietary laws of Judaism along with ideas about angel worship and new moon festivals. Paul argues for the fundamental truth of Christ.

By the time Paul was writing, Colossae was in decline. Once, it had been an important city, but now it was more of a market town, overshadowed by nearby Laodicea and Hierapolis. The city, to some extent, dwelled in the past, and some of that attitude might account for their continued adherence to old faiths and rituals.

Quick Guide

Author
Paul

Type
Letter

Purpose
The church at Colossae was being influenced by false ideas and practices. Paul is writing to tell them about Christ.

Key verse
3:10 "Each of you is now a new person. You are becoming more and more like your Creator, and you will understand him better."

If you remember one thing about this book . . .
We should fix our eyes on Jesus: he is all that matters.

Your 5 minutes start now
Read chapters 1–3

The Route Through Colossians

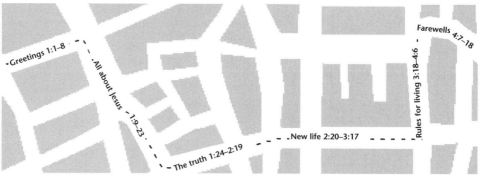

Greetings 1:1-8

All about Jesus 1:9-23

The truth 1:24–2:19

New life 2:20–3:17

Rules for living 3:18–4:6

Farewells 4:7-18

Landmark: Gnosticism

One of the problems facing the early Church was the growth of what is called Gnosticism. The word comes from the Greek word *gnosis* meaning "secret knowledge." Gnosticism developed in a variety of ways, but fundamentally it was about secret knowledge. Only certain "spiritual" people were allowed to know the hidden mysteries. Only certain people had received "enlightenment."

Another of their key beliefs was the idea that the material world was inherently evil. Creation, the body, the things around us, were bad. Thus they had two approaches. One was to try to "punish" the body through asceticism, through living without any luxury or indulgence whatsoever and only eating and drinking a very few things. This appears to be the approach in Colossae.

The other approach was to ignore matter, to pretend that it didn't exist. This led to them indulging in all sorts of sinful acts on the grounds that they somehow weren't real. This is the approach that is condemned in 1 John.

This view of matter also changed their view of Christ. The Gnostics believed that Christ couldn't have had such an evil, nasty thing as a human body. Some believed that he must have been a spirit in human form (this view is also called Docetism, from the Greek word *dokeo* which means "to seem"); others argued that the "spirit" Jesus joined the "man" Jesus at his baptism, but left before the crucifixion. The spirit sort of moved into the body for three years but left before the nasty part. (This is called Cerinthianism after Cerinthus, its most prominent spokesman.)

Today there is a considerable interest in Gnosticism and even some academic argument that it is the true Christianity. Which only goes to show that people will always be interested in philosophies that tell them secrets not revealed to the common people.

Gnosticism is alive and kicking. The bookshelves are packed today with people promising hidden knowledge and secrets only revealed to them.

Paul's approach was that self-discipline was important, but also that the material world was real. Reality had to be dealt with. He had no time for hidden mysteries. Paul wrote his letters to everyone in the church. God was for everyone, not for the mystically enlightened few. The only key to the mystery of God is Jesus: know him, and you will know all you need to know.

Greetings   1:1–8

Paul begins by assuring the Colossians that they are in his prayers. He is generous in his prayers for the church and encouraging in his statement that "the good news is spreading all over the world with great success" (1:6).

All about Jesus   1:9–23

Paul pointedly begins with an express wish that the Colossians will be given all the wisdom and insight they need (1:9). This will not come from Gnostic teachers, but from a knowledge of Christ. Jesus is the way to God, because he *is* God. He created all things and he is all-powerful (1:15–20). It is through Christ that we have become friends with God (1:21–22). All we need to stand in the presence of God is to remain rooted in the faith (1:23).

Let's hear it for Epaphras

Epaphrus was probably the founder of the Colossian church. He was a native of the town and was a courageous and faithful evangelist, having also taken the gospel to Laodicea and Hierapolis. Paul talks about working with Epaphras in Rome (1:7), but actually he was imprisoned with Paul (Ph 1:23).

The truth   1:24–2:19

The Gnostic philosophers would only give hints and suggestions about the "deeper mysteries." They used their philosophy as a way of establishing power and maintaining themselves as masters. Paul, on the other hand, becomes a servant in order to help people understand the "mystery." And the mystery is really very simple: "Christ lives in you, and he is your hope of sharing God's glory" (1:27).

Throughout this letter Paul talks about "understanding" and unlocking "the mysteries." His job is to reveal, not to conceal. It is easy to sound mystical and full of wisdom, but Paul warns his readers not to be fooled. They don't need complicated dietary laws or special pagan festivals (2:16). They don't need to worship angels or experience mystical visions (2:18). They need to remain part of the body of Christ.

New life   2:20–3:17; Ep 5–6

All these things are the old ways. As Christians we have new life in Christ, which means changing the way we think and no longer being controlled by "earthly" desires. Paul is explicit about the need for determination and self-discipline and he is also clear on what we might call the "equality" of sin. Being greedy is the same as worshiping idols (3:5). It's not just about putting away certain sins, but avoiding mundane things like insulting people, lying and cruelty.

Instead, we should concentrate on what will build up the body: kindness and love, wise teaching and praising God (3:12–15).

Everyone has the chance to be a new person. And the more we understand Jesus, the more we will be like him and the more we are thankful to God.

Details, Details . . .
Forces, powers, rulers and authorities (1:16)

These are not worldly powers, but angelic powers. One of the features of the Colossian muddle was a belief in different orders of angels and prayers to them. Paul is not here describing a hierarchy, or even giving a description of different groups as such, he is pointing out that everything is under Christ's authority. The New Testament is quite clear that there are unseen powers and forces at work in the world, but it is equally clear that Christ is more powerful than all of them.

▷ **278**

Rules for living   3:18–4:6

Most of this is treated more fully in Ephesians 5–6. Paul talks about our relationship with non-Christians. Conversation is to be interesting and full of kindness. Paul uses the phrase "seasoned with salt" (4:6 NIV) which has been interpreted in different ways. It might mean salt as a preservative, pointing to our role in saving others; or it might mean flavor, which means making our conversation interesting and "full of flavor" rather than dull and dreary. Or it might mean both.

Farewells   4:7–18

Several of Paul's key followers are listed here. Tychichus was a native of Asia—perhaps of Ephesus—who accompanied Paul on his third missionary journey (Ac 20:4). Aristarchus was a Jew from Greece who had been with Paul during the riots at Ephesus (Ac 19:29). Mark is back in favor with Paul, and Dr. Luke is also there. Demas was to let Paul down (2 Ti 4:10–11), and Onesimus was to be the subject of the letter to Philemon.

Details, Details . . .
Barbarians and Scythians (3:11)

"Barbarian" was a general term for anyone who didn't speak Greek. The stereotype of these people was that they were rough and uneducated. "Scythian" was a byword for cruelty. Paul's point is that whatever the background, we are all equal in Christ.

1 Thessalonians
The return of the Lord

Who: Paul.

When: Dating from around AD 51, this may well have been the first letter that Paul wrote to a church. Written only twenty years after the death and resurrection of Christ, this letter is probably earlier than the Gospels.

Paul arrived in Thessalonica in the winter of AD 49 after a difficult and traumatic experience at Philippi. He only stayed in Thessalonica for a short while, then he was forced to leave in the face of fierce opposition. Timothy joined Paul at Athens, and was almost immediately sent back to Thessalonica to find out how the fledgling church was doing. He then joined Paul in Corinth and gave Paul good news. Paul, full of joy at the news, sat down to write this letter.

What: Paul had been forced to leave Thessalonica hurriedly after a brief stay (Ac 17:5–10). The church, therefore, was left without much support and needed to hear from Paul on various issues.

The letter deals with some issues that had arisen and repeats some of his teaching. The signs of the youth of the church are evident—there is little evidence of any organization and structure and one of the key issues addressed is about when the Lord would return. Paul's emphasis is to explain these matters more clearly and give practical guidance as to how they should live in the meantime.

What comes through most clearly in the letter, however, is Paul's delight in the church. He is like a father watching his child take its first steps: full of joy and love for their efforts, while at the same time exhibiting a parental concern that they should walk safely. Paul praises the church for being an example to all the churches in Macedonia. Their welcome for Paul—and, more important, their acceptance of his message—has caused a real stir in the region (1:4–10).

The Route Through 1 Thessalonians

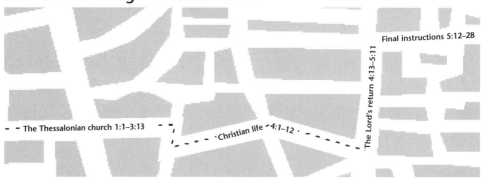

- - - The Thessalonian church 1:1–3:13

Christian life 4:1–12

The Lord's return 4:13–5:11

Final instructions 5:12–28

The Thessalonian church 1:1–3:13

Paul contrasts his behavior in Thessalonica with other, false leaders. He isn't in it for profit or personal power or ego. He is, apparently, replying to charges leveled at him by his enemies, and these same enemies have also been attacking the new Thessalonian church (2:14). Paul speaks harshly of those who attacked him, but that is partly because the wounds are still so fresh. In later years—after literally decades of opposition—he was able to be more philosophical about it. Nevertheless, their responsibility remains. They attacked the church in the same way that they attacked Christ—and, indeed, in the same way that they attacked the prophets (3:15–16).

Perhaps the strength of feeling Paul has about the Jews who are opposing the church is related to his strength of feeling about the Thessalonian Christians. They are his children; he would willingly give his life for them (2:7–8). Now, the news of their faith has brought Paul a breath of new life (3:8) and his love for them grows by leaps and bounds.

Christian life 4:1–12

Part of Paul's teaching was about the practical steps needed to live a Christian life. Here, he reiterates his teaching, reminding them of their responsibilities, particularly in the area of sex. Compared to the Jewish world, the pagans had a very different outlook on sex. Prostitution was not just a feature of their society, but also of their religion. The low standards in this area meant that churches in Roman and Greek cities were under constant threat. Paul reminds his children of the need for hard work, constant vigilance and love for one another.

The Lord's return 4:13–5:11

Paul's teaching at Thessalonica left some questions unanswered. The Christians were worried that those who had died would miss out on the event; that only those still living would benefit. They were also anxious to know the time of the Lord's return.

Paul answers both questions in turn. Those who have died will lose nothing; they will be the first to be raised, followed by all those followers who are still alive (4:13–18). As to the time of the Lord's return, all we know is what he told us—that he will come suddenly and unexpectedly. We should stay alert and prepared for his return.

Details, Details . . .
The thief in the night (5:2)

This image is also found in Matthew, but this letter was written before the gospel of Matthew was completed. So Paul is probably quoting from a collection of sayings of Jesus, which were later incorporated into the Gospels. The same is true for 4:15, where Paul records that Jesus said the dead would not precede the living into heaven. There is no such saying in the Gospels, so it must come from a different source.

Final Instructions 5:12–28

Paul ends with a machine-gun rattle of instructions and requests: pray continually, be joyful, keep thanking God, test everything . . . the requests just pour out of this proud father. It is as if he is rushed for time, or running out of space on the page—he crams so much in. Characteristically, he commands the reader to read the whole letter to the whole church—Paul doesn't want his teaching edited in any way.

2 Thessalonians
Keep the faith

Who: Paul. Probably. Let me explain. Few experts doubt that 1 Thessalonians is an authentic letter from Paul, but 2 Thessalonians, on the other hand, has attracted a lot of debate about its authenticity.

The main difficulties lie around the change in style. This second letter is more formal, with greater use of the Old Testament. It seems odd that the writer who was writing so passionately a few weeks ago is now so reserved. Critics also point to the teaching—which appears to be different. Chapter 2 talks of "signs" preceding the return of Jesus, whereas the first letter emphasizes the suddenness of the Lord's return. "If Jesus is a thief in the night," they argue, "he is a thief who rings the doorbell a lot before breaking in."

However, the letter had a lot of support from early Christian writers and the differences, such as they are, are not huge. Paul may simply be going into more detail about the second coming, perhaps in answer to questions from the Thessalonians. And "signs" are not the same as the event itself. Puffs of smoke from the top of a volcano do not tell us the time of the eruption. Indeed, some believe that this was the cause of these new instructions—that some of the Thessalonians mistook Paul's insistence on suddenness for immediacy, and they thought that the event was imminent. In these circumstances it would be entirely natural for Paul to write again, reaffirming the need for people to keep on with their normal, Christian lives.

When: AD 51/52.

What: The situation hasn't changed since the first letter. Paul is writing to the Thessalonians to encourage them, to reaffirm that the Lord will return, and to reassure them that he will bring justice. He corrects some false teaching, and warns against those who would use his name to back up their own ideas.

The Route Through 2 Thessalonians

Praise and judgment 1:1–12 - - Christ's return 2:1–12 - - Faithfulness and prayer 2:13–3:15 - - Conclusion 3:16–18 - -

Praise and judgment   1:1–12

Paul repeats his pride in the Thessalonians and his thankfulness for their faith. And now it appears that they need this encouragement, for they are encountering suffering. Paul reminds the church that God is also a God of judgment. Those who are causing the suffering will be judged and punished. This leads Paul into a renewed discussion of the subject of his first letter—"the day when the Lord returns" (1:10).

Christ's return   2:1–12

This is a complicated and difficult passage, possibly the most difficult in all of Paul's letters. Even Peter couldn't really understand it, so I'm not sure what hope we have (2 Pe 3:16). What is clear is that some teachers were going around claiming that the Lord had already returned. Worse, these people were claiming to have read it in Paul's letters, or to have heard it from the mouth of an apostle. These teachings were unsettling—in fact, Paul uses a nautical phrase that means that men have been driven from their moorings. They are literally "all at sea" (2:2).

To counter these teachings, Paul goes into more detail about the future, claiming that, before the Lord will return, there will be the advent of someone he calls "the wicked one" or "the man of lawlessness" (2:3–4). Paul refers to teaching already given to the Thessalonian church, but it is teaching that we no longer possess, so any theorizing on this is mostly speculation (2:6–7). The wicked one is normally identified with the Antichrist—a figure who will appear before Christ's return. He will head up a final, terrible rebellion against God (Re 13; 1 Jn 2:18–25). Someone, or something, is holding this being back—but what it is we don't know (2:6–8). What we do know is that when the Lord comes the wicked one will be totally, utterly destroyed.

Faithfulness and prayer   2:13–3:15

In the meantime, Paul turns to happier subjects—the faithfulness of the Thessalonians and the faithful love of God. In contrast to those foolish people who will refuse the love and follow the wicked one (2:9–12), the Thessalonians responded to Paul's message of hope, putting their faith in the truth (2:13).

He follows this, as in the first letter, with exhortations to the Thessalonians to continue with their good work and their prayer. The Thessalonian church seems to have had a tough time with idle people—perhaps people who stopped working because they thought "the end was nigh." But Paul points to his own example: never be tired of doing what's right (3:13).

Conclusion   3:16–18

Finally Paul ends with a blessing, adding his own signature—which some see as proof of the letter's authenticity.

1 Timothy
How to run a church

Who: Paul. But see ViewPoints on page 356.

When: AD 65/66.

What: The letter is addressed to Paul's loyal coworker, Timothy, a man whom the apostle had known from the days of his youth. Paul knew Timothy's mother and grandmother well and regarded the boy as a kind of son.

Timothy was now at Ephesus, helping to lead the church there. He was faced with many problems, most notably the false teaching that was being spread about by renegade Christians.

Church life   1:1–3:13

❶ False teaching   1:1–11

Paul begins by addressing one of the main themes of the letter: false teaching. These teachers are characterized by a delight in Jewish myths, obscure genealogies and an emphasis on the Law (1:4–7).

❷ Paul's life   1:12–20

Much of Paul's argument is similar to that given in Ephesians (Ep 3:1–13). He refers to prophecies given to Timothy that, although not recorded in Acts, probably were similar to the prayers prayed for Paul and Barnabas (Ac 13:1–3).

❸ Prayer and worship   2:1–15

Paul's advice is for the early Christian Church rather than individuals, probably what we are talking about here, therefore, is prayer during worship. We should pray for those with political power, we should pray in a spirit of peace and love, and we should pray in recognition of what God has done for us.

The Route Through 1 Timothy

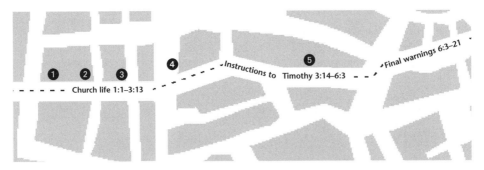

❹ Church leaders 3:1–13

This passage identifies two types of church leaders: elders (3:1–7) and deacons (3:8–13). This is fundamentally the same structure as can be seen in Acts 14:23, where Paul appoints elders. The elders are responsible for the overall leadership of the church; the deacons' role is to assist the elders and take on a variety of practical tasks. However, deacons could also teach, as in the case of Stephen and Philip (Ac 7–8). Eldership appears to be a male preserve, whereas deacons could be male or female (3:11).

Instructions to Timothy
3:14–6:3

Some, at least, of Timothy's instructions were probably intended to be made public. However, there are also instructions of a personal nature. Timothy is told to work hard, to concentrate on teaching the essentials, to earn, and expect, respect from others, and to read the Scriptures in worship (4:6–16). He is also to counter false teaching about marriage and clean and unclean foods (4:1–4) and to govern the church wisely (5:17–25).

❺ Widows and the elderly 5:1–16

This was an age without pensions and social security. The widows, the orphans and the poor were often left without any help. Paul places the responsibility for helping first on the families (5:3, 8) and, for widows without relatives, on the church. Young widows should remarry whenever possible. From the day of its birth, the Christian Church had been known for helping the poor, but there had to be guidelines. Not everyone was deserving and Paul gives guidelines for sorting out who should be helped and how.

Details, Details . . .
Hymenaeus and Alexander (1:20)

Hymenaeus was a false teacher who cropped up again in 2 Timothy (2 Ti 2:17–18). Alexander was a metalworker (2 Ti 4:14). Since Timothy was at Ephesus, he may have been one of the silversmiths mentioned in Acts (Ac 19). "Handed over to Satan" basically means excluded from the church. The church was seen as a sanctuary from evil; to be excluded from it was to be left to face the forces of evil alone.

Puzzling Points
Should women teach men? (2:12–15)

Paul's teaching on women here is much in line with his statements elsewhere: they should act and dress in a way that will not cause offense. But Paul also adds that they should not be allowed to "teach or to tell men what to do." There are, as you might expect, differences of opinion on this one.

• Some believe that Paul was talking specifically about the situation at Ephesus, where women might well have been involved in the false teaching, and which might explain the lines about Eve "fooling" Adam. Elsewhere Paul doesn't restrict women from speaking in church (1 Co 11:1–5), and he used them to teach men about the good news.

• Others believe that this represents the divine order of things, pointing to teaching from Paul on headship. The problem with this point of view is that it is difficult to define what is "teaching." If a woman can never teach a man, how can we learn, for example, from the Song of Deborah (Jg 4–5)? Or the proverbs of King Lemuel, which were passed on by his mother (Pr 31)?

▷**332, 334**

A Little Local Difficulty
Saved by Childbirth 2:15

A difficult and obscure verse that, if taken at face value, would imply that only those women who have children are saved. It cannot mean this, for that flies in the face of virtually everything else Paul writes. Some believe that it means that a godly woman will find fulfillment in the role of a mother. Others argue that the verse should run "women are saved by the birth of a child" and therefore Paul is referring to the birth of Christ. Another interpretation is simply that Paul is saying that the godly woman will be kept safe during childbirth. Ultimately, however, there is no real agreement and the verse remains a mystery.

Final warnings

6:3–21

Paul concludes with a final warning about false teaching, especially about wealth. Religion is not supposed to make anyone rich—not in monetary terms, anyway. Money is not wrong in itself, but the desire for money "causes all kinds of trouble" (6:5–10). Those who have money should not put their trust in it, but should use it to bless others (6:17–19).

View Points

Did Paul write 1 and 2 Timothy?

On one hand:
• The language is different from Paul's earlier letters. There are words here that are not found anywhere else in the New Testament and some of them have changed meanings.
• The issues that Paul raises include the type of Gnosticism that occurred in the second century.
• Paul seems to tell Timothy and Titus a lot of things that they would have known already, or which do not seem appropriate. Why, for example, give Timothy advice on how to behave "if you are a slave" (6:1)? He wasn't a slave, unless he was planning a sudden career move.
• The history refers to events and journeys that cannot be found in Acts.

On the other hand:
• The language varies in Paul's other letters as well. It depends on the purpose of the writer. Equally, Paul wrote using an amanuensis—a kind of secretary —who might have used some of his own words and done some editing. Paul was writing late in his career, and may have had to rely on help much more than in the past.
• Gnosticism in this form may not have arisen as late as people think. There is not much difference between the kind of thinking condemned here and the Judaistic/pagan mix found at Colossae.
• They contain instructions that must have been passed on to the wider church.
• Paul may well have been released from Rome and allowed to travel once more. The tradition of the early Church was that Paul was released and went on one more journey, before being finally captured and executed.
• The personal details reinforce the genuine nature of the letters.

Moving on: There is no authoritative external evidence that they are not the work of Paul. The letters are filled with numerous personal references that have a genuine feel. If they are the work of a later author, he had an excellent eye for personal detail. 2 Timothy in particular abounds in the kind of detail we expect to find in Paul's letters. There may well be parts of the letters that date from later times, but equally there is much in them that could genuinely have come from the hand of Paul.

2 Timothy
"I have finished the race"

Who: See introduction to 1 Timothy for debate over authorship.

When: Probably around AD 65/66. Paul was probably writing from Rome, where he had been imprisoned. This was a very different imprisonment from his first experience, when he was largely under house arrest. Now he was chained in a dungeon, far away from comfort and friendship. Paul had no illusions about the future: he realized that his race was almost run. In this light, he passes on final advice to Timothy.

What: This is Paul's final letter. In it, he writes an intensely personal letter to one of his closest friends. He addresses Timothy as "a dear child" a sign of the affection between them. Timothy was, in many ways, the son Paul never had.

In 1 Timothy Paul is writing to Timothy to help him with the problems he is encountering in the Ephesian church. In 2 Timothy the aim is broader. Here, Paul is facing the last days of his life, and his final letter is a deeply personal message of encouragement to his "dear child." One simple reason that Paul writes is through loneliness. His friends have deserted him and only Luke is there with him. At this time, more perhaps than any other, Paul is missing his "son."

Certainly Paul was a kind of spiritual father to Timothy. He reminds Timothy how he had laid hands on him and commissioned him for the special work he was to do. He prays constantly for Timothy.

Quick Guide

Author
Paul, but see the introduction to 1 Timothy.

Type
Letter

Purpose
To ask for Timothy's help and to encourage him to be strong in the faith.

Key verses
3:15–16 "Since childhood you have known the Holy Scriptures that are able to make you wise enough to have faith in Christ Jesus and be saved. Everything in the Scriptures is God's Word. All of it is useful for teaching and helping people and for correcting them and showing them how to live."

If you remember one thing about this book . . .
The Bible teaches us the truth—and how to live it.

Your 5 minutes start now
Read chapters 2–4

However, Paul was also concerned for the churches, especially given the wave of persecution that was to be unleashed by Nero. He is therefore writing to Timothy to encourage him to continue in his work. Through Timothy he hopes to pass on the same message to the church at Ephesus and beyond.

The Route Through 2 Timothy

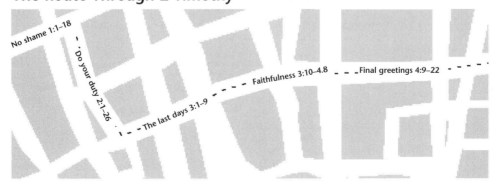

No shame 1:1–18

Do your duty 2:1–26

The last days 3:1–9

Faithfulness 3:10–4.8

Final greetings 4:9–22

No shame
1:1–1:18

Paul is in chains in a prison, yet he feels no disgrace. Suffering for the Lord is not, for Paul, a sign of failure or disgrace, but an opportunity to see the power of God at work. "God's Spirit doesn't make cowards out of us," he writes. "The Spirit gives us power, love, and self-control" (1:7). There is no cause to be ashamed of Paul or of the message.

However, even the great apostle can feel alone. It feels as though everyone has turned against him (1:15). But there were also friends like Onesiphorus—evidently a friend from Ephesus, who cheered Paul and who was not ashamed (1:16–18).

Details, Details . . .
Godless chatter (2:16)

Not, as it has often been interpreted, aimless or silly chatter, but teaching that is opposed to God. Paul links this phrase to Hymenaeus and Philetus and their false teaching. The precise nature of their teaching is not known, but it probably denied that the resurrection was a physical event and preached a purely spiritual resurrection.

Do your duty
2:1–26

With all that is happening to Paul and to the church in general, Timothy is urged to be strong. In a series of images, he is likened to a soldier on duty in the cold and rain; an athlete running the course with discipline and control; and a farmer, up early in the morning working in the fields (2:3–7). The emphasis is on strong, focused faith. In the Christian life it is easy to get wrapped up in words, to end up arguing about the secondary matters. Instead we are to work hard and teach the true message (2:14–15).

The last days
3:1–9

Paul believed—as did most of the Church at that time—that they were in the last days, the time before the return of Jesus. (Peter believed that the "last days" had begun immediately after Pentecost—see Ac 2:17.) He urges Timothy not to have anything to do with the evil, silly, self-obsessed, selfish people who will characterize the times. Now, 2,000 years after these words were written, Paul's description seems an uncannily accurate representation of the world around us.

Details, Details . . .
Jannes and Jambres (3:8)

In Jewish folklore, these were the names of the two Egyptian magicians who opposed Moses. There is no need to interpret Paul's reference to them as meaning that the story actually happened. He is using a well-known story to make a point.

Faithfulness
3:10–4:8

Instead Timothy is encouraged to remain firm to all he has learned. In particular, he is urged to remain faithful to the Scriptures. From his early years, his mother and grandmother Lois and Eunice taught him what was right (so much for not allowing women to teach men).

Paul points to Scriptures as the sure source of knowledge. In particular he draws attention to the practical usefulness of Scripture. This is not some handbook of esoteric philosophy. It is used for "helping people and for correcting them and showing them how to live." Scripture has to be put into practice, and the purpose of Scripture is twofold:

• To make us wise enough to have faith in Christ Jesus and be saved (3:15).
• To train God's servants to do all kinds of good deeds (3:17).

To be faithful in such a society is to go against the trend. People will look for teachers who please them, and hear what they want to hear. Even though it might not be popular, Timothy is encouraged to preach the message, and to correct people and confront them with their sins. But the Christian message isn't just about pointing out what's wrong, it's about helping people find what's right. Timothy is also to cheer people up and be patient in instructing them.

Finally, Paul describes the end of his life. He likens himself to a drink offering—a reference to the wine being poured on the altar of God in front of the temple. But he is also a soldier who has fought well and, in one of his favorite images, he is a runner who has finished the race and won the crown.

Details, Details . . .
The leather scroll (4:13)

Scrolls were made of papyrus—a kind of paper made out of reeds—or of animal skin, usually sheep's skin. Here Paul asks for the more important—and perhaps more durable—version. It is like asking for a hardback Bible rather than a paperback.

Final greetings   4:9–22

Some of Paul's colleagues have deserted him, some have had to go elsewhere, and only Luke remains. He asks Timothy to bring some personal items and gives news of mutual friends. He has been given a preliminary hearing, at which he escaped death. The reference to lions may be metaphorical, or it may be a literal reference to the lions in the Roman arena. Whatever the case, Paul knows that there are more trials in the future. Winter is coming, and Paul wants the warmth of friendship as much as he needs his coat.

Landmark: The Family

Families in the Bible—particularly in the Old Testament—meant much more than just Mom, Dad and the kids. The biblical concept of the family was a larger group, what we would call an "extended" family, and would encompass the father, his wife (or wives), their children, various other dependent relatives and even the servants.

Perhaps the stronger concept is the idea of "household," that is, those dwelling together under the same roof. Certainly in the New Testament the household included slaves and employees as well as the core "family" members. The household of Cornelius, for example, included Cornelius and his family, his servants and even some close friends (Ac 10:7, 24). Indeed, the spread of Christianity to some extent relied on these households, as they provided the setting for the early Church to meet.

The father was the undisputed head of the household and children remained under his control generally until marriage. Young children were looked after by their mother, but as soon as the boys were old enough, they started to work alongside their father. The blood ties between members of the same family were strong—and members of the family had the right to expect protection and provision from their kinsfolk.

▷175, 334

Titus
God never tells a lie!

Who: Paul.

When: Probably between AD 63 and 65.

What: The aim of the letter is to encourage Titus in his leadership and help him with some of the issues he is facing. Titus appears to have worked with Paul in Greece and Asia Minor, and Paul has appointed him to oversee the work in Crete. Many of the instructions are similar to Paul's letter to Timothy—but then they were facing broadly similar issues.

What we know of Titus comes from Paul's letters. When Paul went to Jerusalem to defend his ministry among the Gentiles, he took Titus with him (Ga 2:1–3), and Titus's conversion—the conversion of an uncircumcised Gentile—was vital to the vindication of Paul's case (Ga 2:3–5). He was later sent to Corinth to help with the church there, and his tact and sensitivity seem to have helped enormously (2 Co 2:12–13; 7:5–7).

After Paul's release from house arrest in Rome, he went to Crete and worked with Titus there. Paul had already visited the island—or, more correctly, he crashed into the island—during the journey to Rome (Ac 27:7–13). Perhaps the reception afforded him on that occasion made him keen to return there as soon as possible. He left Titus to complete the work he founded, but in the hopes that Titus would join him at Nicopolis as soon as a replacement could be found (3:12). Later, when Paul was imprisoned in Rome, Titus went on a mission to Dalmatia—modern Yugoslavia (2 Ti 4:10).

The Route Through Titus

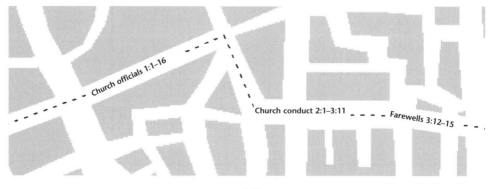

Church officials 1:1–16

Church conduct 2:1–3:11

Farewells 3:12–15

Church officials 1:1–16

Paul's teaching here is similar to that in Timothy. Elders should be mature, respected people. But Paul especially emphasizes their faithfulness in marriage and their ability to "stick to the true message." By Paul's time Crete had become a byword for cheating behavior. The Greeks even had a word for lying—"to cretanize."

Indeed, the church was at the mercy of some blatant "cretanization," with some of the Jewish followers raising the same myths and emphasis on rules and regulations that are found in Timothy's Ephesus. But to the pure, all is pure—that is, to those whom God has made pure, nothing is ritually unclean anymore.

Church conduct 2:1–3:11

Paul gives Titus advice for different groups within the church, for the old men and women, the younger women and men (2:1–6). He tells Titus to "keep it simple" when he preaches and advises slaves how to behave.

The way we act communicates as much as we say. Therefore, in the society that was Crete, the attitude and actions of the Christian community would have a huge impact. They are to live kind, decent and honest lives (2:11–12), quick to help others and never indulging in cruel words or stupid arguments (3:1–2).

To reinforce his arguments, Paul quotes an early Church hymn, or saying, that encapsulates the argument: Christ has saved us through mercy, we have been washed clean and given a new start and the hope of eternal life (3:4–7). Paul wants Titus to make sure that "all who have faith in God will be sure to do good deeds." Stupid arguments about foolish theories will only undermine their credibility with the Cretan people (3:8–11).

Farewells 3:12–15

Paul's letter has apparently been sent with Zenas the Lawyer and Apollos. Presumably this is the same Apollos who worked in Asia Minor (Ac 18; 1 Co 3). They should be given all the help that they need. But then, one of the core messages of the letter to Titus is that *everyone* should be given all the help that they need.

Details, Details . . .
A lying prophet (1:12)

This is one of those famous paradoxes. A Cretan prophet says, "Cretans always lie." Then Paul says that he is telling the truth. But if Cretans always lie, then he's lying and they always tell the truth. But if they always tell the truth, how can he be lying? . . . It just goes to show that you can take the Bible too literally.

The quotation is actually from the poet Epimenides who worked in Knossos around the 6th century BC.

Philemon
More than slaves

When: AD 60. Paul was in Rome, where he was under arrest. The letter was probably written at the same time as his letter to the Colossians.

What: Philemon is a unique letter—a private letter from Paul to Philemon with regard to a runaway slave. Onesimus was a slave who had, apparently, stolen money from Philemon and run away to Rome. Under Roman law this was an offense punishable by death, but Onesimus had met Paul and become a Christian. Now he was returning to his master to throw himself on Philemon's mercy.

Philemon was a rich Christian who had many slaves and in whose house a church met. We don't know exactly where he lived, but it was probably in Colossae, since Onesimus is mentioned in Colossians (Co 4:9, 17), and Paul sent Onesimus and Tychichus back together.

Paul is writing to Philemon, therefore, to ask for clemency for the slave. The letter is lighthearted in tone and full of wordplay. Paul employs great tact to argue his case. Some experts have pointed out that he uses a very formal structure, a format prescribed by Greek and Roman writers, in which he first builds rapport with his reader, then argues the case, then appeals to the emotions. The same basic structure has been a commonplace in every court of law ever since.

Quick Guide

Author
Paul

Type
Letter

Purpose
A plea on behalf of a runaway slave.

Key verse
16 "Onesimus is much more than a slave. To me he is a dear friend, but to you he is even more, both as a person and as a follower of the Lord."

If you remember one thing about this book . . .
There is no discrimination in Christianity; all are children of God.

Your 2 minutes start now
Read chapter 1. That's all there is.

The Route Through Philemon

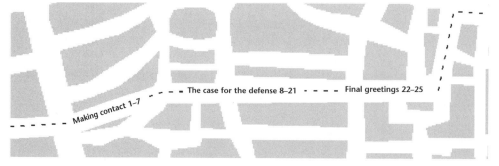

Making contact 1–7 - - - - The case for the defense 8–21 - - - - Final greetings 22–25

Making contact   1–7

Paul begins by assuring Philemon of his prayer and love. Tactfully the emphasis is on Philemon's faith and love and the way it is recognized by all around him.

The case for the defense   8–21

Paul now raises the crucial issue. Onesimus has become like a son to Paul; before he was a useless slave, now he is a valued friend. Paul offers to pay for whatever Onesimus has taken, emphasizing the message by writing it in his own hand.

Final greetings   22–25

Paul mentions others whom we know of from other letters. Epaphras was his friend from Colossae, Mark and Luke were probably the writers of the Gospels that bear their names, and Demas was a friend of Paul's who eventually deserted him in Rome.

Landmark: Slavery

The Roman Empire was built on slavery. Slaves probably made up a third of the population of the major cities of Greece and Asia Minor. Indeed, in major cities such as Rome or Athens, the percentage could have been as high as 80 percent.

The main point to remember about slavery in these times is that it was not thought of as degrading or particularly abhorrent. Slaves were the immigrant labor of their day. Admittedly, they did the basic jobs such as building, mining and cleaning, but they might equally work in administration and commerce. Many slaves were well educated, and were even responsible for the education of the children in the household. They were often freed from slavery, or allowed to earn enough money to buy their freedom. In the context of the time, masters were far more like employers.

Given all this, it is not surprising that Paul does not call Christians to free the slaves. Slavery was an economic reality. For Paul, what mattered was freedom through Christ. Paul's view is that Christianity takes no account of social status. It doesn't matter if you are a slave, because Christ's love is for all. God's Spirit has baptized all of us, whether Jew or Gentile, slave or free (1 Co 12:13; Ep 6:7–8). Paul addresses slaves as full members of the church; when it comes to following Jesus, he draws no distinction between slaves and their masters. He repeatedly points out that all men are equal (Col 3:11; Ga 3:28; Ep 6:8).

This is not to say that Paul necessarily approved of slavery. He advised slaves to obtain their freedom if possible (1 Co 7:21) and listed slave traders among the "ungodly," grouping them with adulterers, liars and murderers (1 Ti 1:20 NIV). He argued that masters should treat slaves with fairness and compassion. He believed, indeed, that all Christians were slaves, owned by God and called to work tirelessly in his service.

Hebrews
A people of faith

Who: We don't know who wrote Hebrews. For a long time it was assumed to be by Paul, but, although it agrees with his teaching, most experts now agree that he didn't write it. The style is totally different and the author has not had a direct encounter with Jesus (2:3). Since Paul set great store on his direct "meeting" with Christ, he wouldn't write such a thing. Barnabas has been suggested, as has Apollos, but we just don't know. For the sake of accuracy, I shall simply refer to the author as The Writer of Hebrews. Or TWOH for short. (Or possibly Bernard.)

When: Almost certainly before the destruction of Jerusalem in AD 70. Had the writer known of this, he would certainly have mentioned it. And when he does refer to the temple, he uses the present tense. Probably, therefore, sometime in the late 60s.

What: Hebrews was written to the … er … Hebrews, actually, to Jewish Christians. These knew the Scriptures, and may well have been established as Christians for some time, but they were insular and uncertain and wondering whether to turn back to Judaism. The Jews, after all, had a wealth of history and heritage, a magnificent temple, rich worship services and a magnificently robed high priest. What did Christianity have? No temples, no magnificently adorned high priests, just a load of slaves, Gentiles, widows, orphans and slightly manic ex-Pharisees.

Quick Guide
Author
Unknown
Type
General letter
Purpose
To show that Jesus is the true fulfillment of Old Testament history.
Key verses
7:26–27 "Jesus is the high priest we need. He is holy and innocent and faultless, and not at all like us sinners. Jesus is honored above all beings in heaven, and he is better than any other high priest. Jesus doesn't need to offer sacrifices each day for his own sins and then for the sins of the people. He offered a sacrifice once for all, when he gave himself."
If you remember one thing about this book …
There is no longer anything between us and God: faith in Jesus has brought us together.
Your 10 minutes start now
Read chapters 2, 5, 8, 11–12

In response, TWOH writes that Christianity is the fulfillment of Judaism. The Greek words for "better" and "superior" occur fifteen times in this letter. The message is clear: the old system has found fulfillment in the new. The rules and regulations have been superseded, the barriers torn down. The prophets, Aaron, Moses, Melchizedek, Abraham, angels, Joshua—they all must bow to their superior—the one true high priest, Jesus Christ.

The Route Through Hebrews

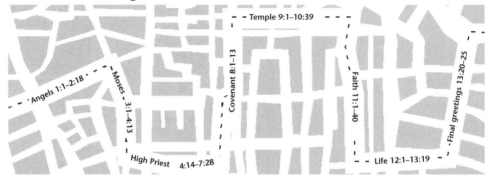

Angels 1:1–2:18

Moses 3:1–4:13

High Priest 4:14–7:28

Covenant 8:1–13

Temple 9:1–10:39

Faith 11:1–40

Life 12:1–13:19

Final greetings 13:20–25

Angels   1:1–2:18

TWOH kicks off with a simple, powerful affirmation of the uniqueness of Jesus. Many years ago, God's prophets spoke throughout history to the Jews. But now God has sent his Son to speak to everyone directly. This Son has washed away our sins and now has authority over all things.

This first section establishes that Jesus is greater than the angels. In a series of quotations, TWOH shows that the angels—whom some Jews were tempted to worship—worship Christ. Angels are, after all, merely spirits, not worthy of worship in themselves. They are only important because of the one who sent them (1:14).

The angels brought messages about the truth and this truth was proved when Jesus performed miracles and wonders (2:4). The most wonderful thing, however, was that this supreme being, whom even the angels worshiped, took the form of a man and came and died on earth (2:9).

God became a man and died to defeat evil and rescue humanity. And because he was made a man he understands us fully (2:14–18).

Moses   3:1–4:13 ▷53

Moses was the ultimate hero of the Jews. He was the one who, empowered by God, had led the people from Egypt and to the very edge of the Promised Land. He was the one who had met with God on the mountain, and brought back the Law. And Jesus is greater than Moses. Moses was a faithful servant, but Jesus is the master (3:1–6).

TWOH draws a parallel with the Israelites under Moses. They saw many miracles, and still turned away, with the result that they did not enter God's "rest." It is a warning to us all (3:16–19).

Even those who did enter the "rest" (i.e., the Promised Land) only entered a temporary solution. The real rest that God was speaking of was heaven, not the Promised Land. TWOH proves this by pointing out that psalm writers were still inviting people to enter God's rest, hundreds of years after Joshua had entered the Promised Land (4:7–10). It is through salvation that we enter the true rest of God (4:3). The true Sabbath is yet to come and it is greater than they imagine.

High priest   4:14–7:28

The Jewish high priest was the only one permitted to enter the Holy of Holies. Aaron was the original high priest, but Jesus is greater than Aaron.

Puzzling Points
Why does he misquote Scripture? (1:5–14)

One of the remarkable things about the book of Hebrews is that the writer gets the quotes wrong. Well, not exactly "wrong," but they differ from the original text in some ways. Part of the reason for this is because TWOH is using the Greek Septuagint, which is an ancient translation of the Old Testament into Greek. Most modern versions are taken from the original Hebrew, therefore there are differences.

However, even allowing for this, he treats his quotations rather freely. He merges comment and quotation into one whole. He takes individual verses and then gives them a meaning that is far beyond their original context. Sometimes he can't quite remember where the quotation came from or who said it, falling back on the phrase, "someone said somewhere ..." Let's face it, the man would fail most of his theology exams.

This is not an easy charge to answer. All we can say is that TWOH was inspired in his writing, but not perhaps in his memory. The truth of what he says is found not just in Hebrews but throughout the Bible. But as for his references ...

In the middle of this passage, TWOH breaks off to warn his readers that they must pay close attention to this difficult subject. He is giving them meat, not baby's milk. He is treating them with respect and not trying to feed them simple things, but is getting them to grasp difficult concepts. They know the basics of the Christian life (6:1–3). It's time to move on to some advanced studies.

Some apparently *have* moved—although not deeper into the Christian faith, but away from it. TWOH urges his friends not to fall into that sin, but instead to cling to their faith, to believe in God's promises and to run to God for safety (6:13–18). These promises are found in Jesus, who is greater than the greatest high priest. The curtain that formerly divided the people from the Holy of Holies has been torn in two. Jesus has gone ahead into that space and is waiting for us in heaven (6:19–20).

Landmark: The Priesthood

The priesthood was instituted by Moses in the wilderness, with the consecration of Aaron, first high priest of Israel (Ex 28–29). From that moment, all priests were supposed to come from within the tribe of Levi, from whom Aaron was descended. Later, descendants of Zadok, David's high priest, also claimed the right to be priests—indeed, by New Testament times, the Zadokites were the dominant family at the temple in Jerusalem.

I put down my Urim and Thummim earlier and now I can't remember what they look like.

The priest's main function was to offer sacrifices. In fact, they relied on sacrifices and offerings to make their living, because they were entitled to a proportion of all the offerings brought to the temple. At least until the exile, they also had some teaching duties, teaching the Law.

They wore a special uniform, which consisted of a two-piece apron called an ephod, and a chestpiece inset with twelve precious stones, representing the twelve tribes of Israel, and engraved with the names of the tribes.

The chestpiece had a pocket, directly over the priest's heart, which included the Urim and the Thummim (Ex 28:30). These were some kind of device-like stones, which were cast to determine the will of God.

Only the high priest could enter the Holy of Holies, the sacred inner room in the tabernacle and the temple, and then only for one day a year—on the Day of Atonement.

The priests were the intermediaries between the people and God—a role that disappeared with the advent of Jesus, after whom all Christians are described as a "royal priesthood." Jesus had no need to offer sacrifices—he was the sacrifice, once and for all (He 7:27–28).

Covenant 8:1–13

The old covenant made with Moses was temporary and inadequate. The laws could not be kept and the system of sacrifices, the temple and the tabernacle were only dim copies of the real thing. Christ brings a new agreement, a new covenant that requires faith and love, not endless sacrificial animals. TWOH quotes from Jeremiah to show that, even way back in his time, it was clear that the old ways weren't working. Jeremiah looks forward to a new covenant, written in the hearts and minds of the people. That covenant was to be fulfilled in Christ.

Temple 9:1–10:39

TWOH takes the reader back to the time of the exodus, when the first rules for worship were given, when the Law was established and the tabernacle was made. After describing the setup (9:1–5), he points out the inadequacy of the whole affair, which he argues was the Holy Spirit's way of showing that man and God were separated (9:8).

Man had no right of access to God, except through the high priest. Sacrifices could not totally remove sin, they could only remind people of their sin (10:2–4). But Christ is the perfect High Priest and he offers us free access for all time. More than that, he is the perfect sacrifice, which means that, to receive forgiveness, we no longer have to offer sacrifices. His one, perfect sacrifice means that we can be made clean for all time (9:25–26).The tabernacle, the Holy of Holies, all the fittings and the rules and the sacrifices and the ceremonies—all are just shadows of the truth. That truth has been shown in Jesus. And "when sins are forgiven, there is no more need to offer sacrifices" (10:18).

In the light of this awesome truth, TWOH again encourages his friends to persevere in their faith. They have already been through much hardship, but they did so in the light of a promise of better things to come (11:32–34). To turn away having come this far would be to invite God's judgment and punishment. To carry on will be to gain the reward of eternal salvation (11:35–39).

Details, Details . . .
Melchizedek (5:6, 10; 7:1–28)

Little is known of this Old Testament figure, except that he was a high priest to whom Abraham looked for blessing (Ge 14:18–20). TWOH uses Melchizedek as a symbol of Christ.

Melchizedek was a king and a priest. He was a priest because he was chosen by God, not because he came from a particular tribe (he wasn't even an Israelite, in fact). And TWOH uses the mysterious origins of Melchizedek—the fact that neither his ancestors nor his birth and death are recorded—to remind us of Christ's divine origins.

TWOH argues that the old order of high priests simply wasn't good enough. So God, just as he had with Melchizedek, chose Jesus. "And he is the perfect high priest forever" (7:26–28). ▷40

Faith 11:1–40

Faith is what is needed; and faith is nothing new. TWOH launches into a huge list of all those in the Old Testament who had faith in God, who lived and died in the confident belief that the Lord would keep his promises. It is a roll call of all the heroes of the Old Testament. Great heroes such as Abraham, Isaac and Moses are here, along with those who are not so famous—all those who suffered for their faith, who were beaten with chains and whips, who were "poor, ill-treated and tortured." These people were not great because they obeyed the Law. They pleased God because of their faith. None of them lived to see these promises fulfilled (11:13). God had something better in store for them. He was waiting for millions more heroes to join them through faith in Christ.

Life   12:1–13:19

It is as if all these heroes are watching us, surrounding us like a crowd in an athletics stadium. They are there in the stands, cheering us on, encouraging us, helping us to run the race with determination (12:1).

In the final section of the letter TWOH concentrates on our response to his message, on what we have to do about it. We must obey Jesus (12:25). We must remember the examples of those who, in the past, had given up the race. TWOH ends with a list of the simple things that Christians should do to keep running the race: hospitality, concern for the welfare of others, respect for individuals, and faithfulness to our partners.

Altars and camps   13:10–14

The meaning is obscure. Probably the passage is talking about the split between Christianity and Judaism. In the Old Testament, the priests ate the food that was sacrificed on the altar, but they were not allowed to eat the sacrifices on the Day of Atonement, when the bodies were taken outside the camp and burned. In other words, Christians can receive forgiveness through Christ's sacrifice in a way that the old atonement sacrifices could not achieve for the priests. We "share in his disgrace" by going to him, by following in his footsteps, and those footsteps take us outside the "camp" of the Law and into a new faith, a new relationship with God.

Final greetings   13:20–25

This, apparently, was a brief letter (13:22)! TWOH mentions that Timothy has been released from prison. Whether this is the same Timothy who accompanied Paul is unknown. Verse 24 could mean that the letter was sent to Italy, or from Italy.

James
Faith and works

Who: Authorship is generally agreed to belong to James, the brother of Jesus. He became a Christian when he saw a resurrection appearance of Jesus (1 Co 15:7). He is mentioned frequently in Acts, and seems to have been the leader of the church in Jerusalem. Paul visits him on his final, fateful return to the city and, along with Peter, James is involved earlier in the great debate about the mission to the Gentiles.

When: Some date the letter in the late AD 60s, but it may date from much earlier. For a start, the term "synagogue" is used to describe the place where Christians meet (2:2). The church structure, with just elders and teachers, is a very simple one, and there is no mention of the debate over such matters as circumcision. For these reasons, this may be one of the earliest of the New Testament writings. It represents an early attempt to put flesh on the bones, to map out a way for the first Christians to live their lives.

What: James was probably written for Jewish Christians. It uses Jewish terms and reflects what we might term a practical, Jewish outlook. The reference to the twelve tribes (1:1) has been taken by some to indicate the Jews scattered by the persecution that followed the death of Stephen (Ac 8:1).

Quick Guide

Author
James, brother of Jesus

Type
General letter

Purpose
To urge Christians to put their faith into action.

Key verse
2:14 "My friends, what good is it to say you have faith, when you don't do anything to show that you really do have faith? Can that kind of faith save you?"

If you remember one thing about this book . . .
Faith without deeds is no faith at all. What we believe is proved through what we do.

Your 5 minutes start now
Read chapters 1, 3, 5

James is one of those letters that you either love or hate. The reformer Martin Luther hated it, because in his eyes it didn't mention "faith" enough. Or "Jesus," come to that. However, the letter contains more quotes from Christ than the other New Testament letters put together. James doesn't talk overtly of Christ's death and resurrection, but he calls Jesus "glorious," he refers to the second coming (5:7) and he talks of Jesus as a judge (5:9).

Those who love James love it because it is the most intensely practical of all the New Testament letters. This is a book that tells us how to live, a book that challenges the reader to express their faith in practical and loving ways. More, it says that if the practical, loving deeds aren't forthcoming, there is something badly wrong with the faith.

The Route Through James

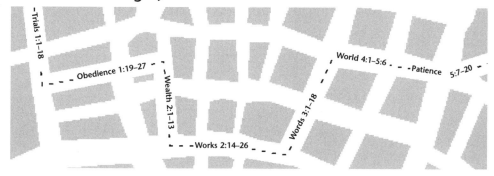

Puzzling Points
Paul versus James

Traditionally, James has always been held to be in opposition to Paul's letters. Whereas Paul emphasizes salvation through faith, it is argued, James seems to imply that works are what count.

In fact, there is not much real difference between them. If you read Paul's letters (you *have* read them all, haven't you?) you will find that he nearly always ends them with a list of things to do. Paul understood that faith always results in works, and that faith that does not result in good works is not real faith at all.

Consider this verse: "The only thing that matters is faith expressed through love."

That could come straight out of James's letter, but it was written by Paul (Ga 5:6 NIV). Anyone who reads Paul cannot be unaware of the emphasis he places on deeds, on doing good works. He says it time and time again. James never says that works can save anyone. What he does say is that faith without works is not faith at all. Which is precisely what Paul says.

Trials   1:1–18

The opening of the letter raises most of the issues that the rest of the letter will discuss. It begins with faith—a faith that is being tested by times of suffering and trial. James makes it clear that only those with faith will survive these trials. Those who doubt will be lost (1:6–8), those who trust in wealth and riches will be burned up (1:9–11), but those who hold fast will be rewarded with a glorious life.

James paints a picture of what Christians should be like during the hard times. They do not blame God for the suffering; they do not go under the waves; they trust in the one, unchanging God and in the message he has sent to his special people (1:16–18).

Obedience   1:19–27

It is one thing to listen and another to obey. Religion is more than just sitting in a pew, hearing the words and nodding in agreement. It is about not doing immoral and evil things. It is about controlling your words and your deeds.

Wealth   2:1–13

Jesus identified wealth as one of the prime opponents of people coming to God. James here talks of the love of wealth, prestige and power that so often corrupts the Church. The Church is not a social club, where only the best dressed can attend and where all the poor are carefully herded together at the back. Christianity is nothing if not a new community, a community where all are equal—a message that can be found throughout Paul's letters. James draws us back to the fundamental law—what he calls the "royal" law: love your neighbor as much as yourself.

Works   2:14–26

Faith without works is not faith at all. Words are no substitute for actions. James answers the "stupid people" by drawing on the example of Abraham. Whereas Paul took Abraham's belief in God's promise of children as the crowning example of his faith, James takes his willingness to sacrifice his son, if that is what God wants. It was the fact that he went and (almost) did it that showed Abraham really believed in God. Both Paul and James quote from the same verse (Ge 15:6).

Words   3:1–18

James sees the importance of words as paramount. Words show what is truly inside us. Words can cause more damage than forest fires.

He begins with public speaking, issuing a stern warning to teachers. He is not just talking about false teaching, but about integrity. It is very easy, as a speaker, to give the impression that you are wise and holy, that you have got it all sorted out. It is easy, as well, to put words in the mouths of your opponents, to misrepresent their views, to ridicule and demean. Teachers have power, and therefore they also have responsibility.

From public speaking, James moves to general speech, to those uncontrolled words that cause so much damage. It is so easy to speak ill of others; it is so much fun! But words born of jealousy and selfishness can have a catastrophic effect.

Words are revealing. A man who praises God one minute and curses his neighbor the next reveals the hypocritical attitudes that lie inside him. Instead we should seek integrity and wisdom, so that all our words are good fruit, revealing us to be a good tree.

World   4:1–5:6

You cannot love the world and love God. The two are opposed to each other. For thousands of years the history of the Church has been a history of people trying to do both things at once. Frequently, the Church has been much more concerned with power and wealth than with justice, service and love.

Instead we should focus on God and what he wants. That means acting justly. James warns against condemning people (4:11–12) and then he has another bash at the rich—not so much for their wealth this time as for the manner in which it was obtained. They are criticized for exploiting their workers, for not listening to the cries of the oppressed, for stuffing their faces while the innocent go to their graves. For anyone living in the rich Western Church today, these are challenging and chilling images. Greed will be punished, those who behave in this way are like turkeys being fattened up. Eat all you want, Christmas is coming . . .

Patience   5:7–20

There is a better way. James shows us the role of patient love. We should pray with others. We should seek forgiveness from one another. We should always try to lead people back from the abyss and to help them walk in the truth.

Landmark: Persecution

In the beginning, Christianity was seen by the Roman authorities as just another Jewish sect. Provided the Christians behaved themselves they were granted the same freedom as the Jews, a freedom that allowed Christianity to spread quickly throughout the empire.

Jewish opposition

In the early days of Christianity, therefore, the persecution came mainly from Jewish elements, who regarded Christians as blasphemers. It soon became clear that these people were not some subset of Judaism. They believed that the Law had been superseded, that Jesus was the Messiah, that there was no longer any such thing as clean and unclean food. The martyrdom of Stephen (Ac 6:14) launched a wave of Jewish persecution in Jerusalem and elsewhere and forced many of the Jerusalem Christians to escape the city. Indeed, most of the persecution mentioned in Acts is persecution of Christians by Jews. James, the leader of the Jerusalem church, was executed in AD 44 by Herod Agrippa. Christians were banned from the synagogues and took to meeting in their own homes.

Roman opposition

The freedom granted to Christianity by Rome did not last. Just as the Jews soon realized that Christianity was diametrically opposed to their beliefs, the Romans began to realize that Christians marched to a very different drum. In Rome the Christians were so unpopular that when the city was ravaged by fire in AD 64, Nero used them as a scapegoat. Both Peter and Paul are believed to have been martyred in Rome during this period. The Christians' refusal to participate in pagan ceremonies or to worship the Roman emperor, and the widespread suspicion that they were cannibals who ate the body and drank the blood of Christ, meant that the persecution increased. The persecution of Christians under the emperor Domitian (AD 81–96) forms the background to the book of Revelation, but it was not until the third and fourth centuries that persecution really became widespread. Diocletian was probably the most vicious of the Roman emperors, releasing a wave of torture, mass execution and the destruction of church buildings. Christians were often taken to the local stadiums, where they were attacked by wild animals as a form of public entertainment.

By that time, however, it was too late. Christianity had spread too far and become too well established. The Christians' bravery in the face of torture and death only served to promote their cause. Like it or not, the faith was here to stay.

1 Peter
Coping with suffering

Who: The traditional view is that the author is Peter, the fisherman, brother of Andrew and friend of Jesus. From the earliest records, it has been widely accepted that he was the author, but in recent times this has come under some doubt. (See ViewPoints, opposite.)

When: Probably sometime between AD 62 and 64. It shows familiarity with the late letters of Paul, so it cannot have been any earlier. The writer is in "Babylon" according to 5:13. This could mean that he was actually in Babylon—which by this time had become a small, ramshackle town on the Euphrates—or it could be code for "Rome." Both raise problems. There is no tradition of Peter going anywhere near Babylon, and the use of the code for Rome does not occur elsewhere any earlier than Revelation, which was written at the end of the century. The jury, as they say, is still out.

What: This is a not a letter to a person, or even to one church. It is a circular letter written to people who were facing, or about to face, suffering. His letter is intended to encourage them, to urge them not to lose faith, and to remind them that they were a special, holy people. The letter is not about the philosophical question of why suffering exists, but the far more practical question of how Christians should respond.

Quick Guide

Author
Probably Peter, the apostle

Type
General letter

Purpose
To encourage and strengthen Christians in the face of suffering.

Key verse
2:9 "But you are God's chosen and special people. You are a group of royal priests and a holy nation. God has brought you out of darkness into his marvelous light. Now you must tell all the wonderful things that he has done."

If you remember one thing about this book . . .
Bad times will happen, but God is always faithful.

Your 5 minutes start now
Read chapters 1–2, 4

The consequences of becoming a Christian in Peter's day were serious. It very often led to being ostracized, mocked, expelled from family or work. In many cases it led to death. Even today there are many societies where to be a Christian is to face danger and isolation. Peter is realistic. Suffering comes with the territory; it is part and parcel of being a Christian. The big issue is how we respond to it. "It's going to happen to you," says Peter. "The question is, how will you respond?"

Christ's suffering was the prelude to glory, and Peter argues that our suffering is a prelude to the glory that is awaiting us. In the meantime, we are to show love to one another and to use our God-given gifts wisely.

The Route Through 1 Peter

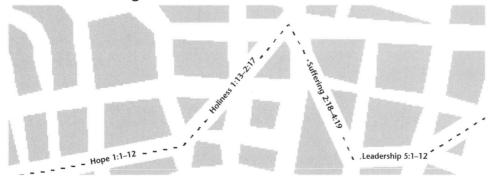

Holiness 1:13–2:17

Suffering 2:18–4:19

Hope 1:1–12

Leadership 5:1–12

ViewPoints

Did Peter write these letters?

On one hand:
• The Greek is too good to have come from an Aramaic-speaking fisherman.
• The situation described in the book did not exist until after Peter's death in the time of Emperor Domitian.

On the other hand:
• He could easily have used a secretary to help him write the letter—indeed, the reference to Silvanus (Silas) at the end might indicate that this was the case.
• The situation described in the book could just as easily reflect the persecution under Nero when Peter was still alive. So there.

Moving on: We can't tell. Best, perhaps, to concentrate on the message.

Details, Details . . .
Stone and priests (2:4–10)

Peter uses the imagery of the temple. Built around the idea of Christ as the foundation stone (Mk 12), we are being built into a kind of temple. We are not only the temple itself, but also the priests who serve within it. Ironically, this holy, life-changing edifice is built around a stone that other builders view as useless and ill-shaped. They can't ignore this stone, it keeps tripping them up and getting in their way. For many, Christ is a foundation to their lives. For others, he is a problem that simply will not go away.

Details, Details . . .
Good news for the dead (4:6)

This probably means that the good news has been preached to those who have now died. Despite their physical death, they will live. Paul addresses a similar theme in Thessalonians (1 Th 4).

Hope   1:1–12

Christians are people of hope. If we have to go through hard trials, we should remember that our ultimate destination is heaven. Just as gold is made purer by burning away the impurities, suffering can "refine" our faith (1:5–7). Old Testament prophets were given a message about Christ, but they did not understand all they spoke about. Their words, although spoken hundreds of years before, serve a later generation by affirming the truth of Christ (1:10–12).

Holiness   1:13–2:17

Pressure from the world is immense, but Christians should not allow this pressure to shape their thinking. We should think clearly and remember that we are God's "holy people," saved by Christ. We have been given a new nationality, citizens of heaven who are refugees on earth (1:13–17). In Peter's time malicious and cruel rumors were spread about Christians. They were accused of indulging in orgies, of cannibalism, of practicing magic. The truth was, they were often a misunderstood and hated minority.

Holiness, however, does not mean sitting back with a smug grin and a stick-on halo. It means conquering our selfish desires, obeying Jesus, not behaving with childish spite. Even though we are citizens of a different country, we should behave with respect and honor the authorities where we are living. This quite clearly draws on Paul's teaching (Ro 13:1–7).

Suffering   2:18–4:19

The emphasis in this letter is on suffering that is brought on people by the abuse of power. In Peter's view the answer is not rebellion, but trust in the example of Jesus. He does not condemn slavery, but instead argues that slaves should accept their position with their eyes fixed on Christ (2:18–25). Wives of non-Christian husbands should still accept their authority and should trust in their own example to win their husbands over. Husbands should not oppress their wives. It is a question of doing what is right, rather than insisting on "my rights" (3:1–7).

All Christians should be people who honor Jesus and put him in charge of their lives (3:15). If we are going to suffer, let us suffer for doing the right thing!

Leadership
5:1–12

Peter ends with advice and instructions for leaders. They should exercise their responsibilities out of love, rather than to make money or to enjoy power (5:2–4). Peter says that young people should obey their elders, but then adds that everyone ought to be humble towards everyone else. This is a community of servants serving one another. Peter learned about the humility of leadership when his feet were washed by Christ. His life was to show it in action.

Puzzling Points
Christ in prison (3:18–22)

This is the most obscure passage in the letter. It begins clearly enough, with the innocent Christ dying for the sins of many and rising again. But the next part is curious, apparently meaning that Christ went to a prison somewhere and preached to spirits who had been disobedient in the time of Noah.

Some argue that this means that Christ preached to fallen angels, specifically the "sons of God" who "married the daughters of men" during the early times (Ge 6:1–2). The problem with this theory is that Genesis doesn't necessarily say these people were angels or spirits. And anyway, even if they were, why go to them?

Another theory is that between his death and resurrection Christ went to the place of the dead and preached to Noah's contemporaries. In which case, the same problem arises: why just them? And what did he preach? And why use the term "spirit" if you mean men?

Peter seems to be using the whole story of Noah in a symbolic way, implying that, as in Noah's day, only a few were saved in the ark, so only a few will "sail to safety" through Christ.

2 Peter
How we should live

Who: The second letter of Peter, like the first, has excited a lot of argument about its authenticity. Most of the letters have a debate about their authorship, but with this letter there are real difficulties reconciling some of the features with the traditional author.

First there is the style, which is totally different from that of 1 Peter. Second there is the fact that much of the letter is a rehash of Jude. Third there are historical problems. The letter, for example, refers to Paul's letters as Scripture and the evidence suggests that these were not brought together as a collection before around AD 90, some twenty-five years after Peter's death. Finally there is the fact that the early Church itself didn't set much store by this letter. There is no reference to it until the third century AD.

It is certainly possible that Peter wrote it, especially if you take the view that he employed a secretary/editor to help him shape it. Similarly, there is no reason why Peter should not borrow from Jude's letter—if it said what he wanted to say. And Paul's letters could have been viewed as authoritative before they were collected together—we know that Peter set great store by Paul's opinion.

When: Not known. If Peter is accepted as the author, then sometime toward the end of his life, around AD 65–68. If not, then much later.

What: Whatever the decision about authorship, there is much that the letter can teach us. There are memorable descriptions of the day of the Lord's return, and practical instructions for how we should be living our lives. And in reference to Paul, the author of this letter finds Paul's letters hard to understand. Which always cheers me up when I get lost. After all, if *Peter* couldn't understand them . . .

Quick Guide

Author
Possibly Peter, but equally possibly someone else.

Type
General letter

Purpose
To urge Christians to live lives that please God.

Key verse
1:3 "We have everything we need to live a life that pleases God. It was all given to us by God's own power, when we learned that he had invited us to share in his wonderful goodness."

If you remember one thing about this book . . .
We *know* what we should do; the key thing is to get on and do it.

Your 5 minutes start now
Read chapters 1–3

The Route Through 2 Peter

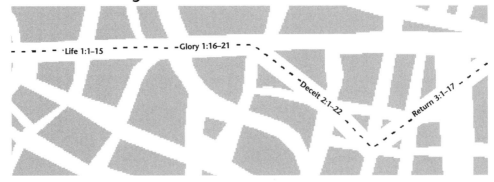

Life 1:1–15 — Glory 1:16–21 — Deceit 2:1–22 — Return 3:1–17

Life   1:1–15

Jesus claimed to have come to give us life in all its fullness (Jn 10:10) and that is where 2 Peter starts. "We have everything we need to live a life that pleases God" (1:3). God's power in us helps us to escape our evil desires. Instead we should focus on what is right. In a passage reminiscent of James, the author shows us how to "improve" our faith.

One of the theories about 2 Peter is that it was, like Jude, written to combat Gnosticism and "secret" mysticism. Hence the emphasis on having all we need. No secret knowledge is required. We know what to do, all we have to do is get on and do it.

Glory   1:16–21

Our faith is not based on made-up stories but on the testimony of eyewitnesses, people who were with Jesus on the mountain and who heard what God said about him (Mt 17:1–5). The testimony of these witnesses and the Spirit-inspired words of the prophets are like guiding lights to the truth about Jesus.

> **Details, Details . . .**
> **Morning star (1:19)**
> The morning star refers to any star that is the precursor to dawn. If we concentrate on what we know to be true, then the darkness will go away and faith will rise in our hearts.

Deceit   2:1–22

Most of this chapter is closely linked to the letter of Jude. It denounces false teachers (2:1–3), and makes references to incidents in Israel's history such as Noah, Sodom and Gomorrah, and Balaam. These false teachers promise a false freedom. They think they are free, but are slaves of their own desires. What makes their guilt worse is the fact that they knew what was right and they had the chance for true freedom. Yet they turned their back on the truth, and now they are in a worse state than when they started (2:20–22).

Return   3:1–17

The author concludes by looking to the return of the Lord. Already people are mocking the Christians because their leader has not returned as he said he would. The Lord's return was one of the major issues for the early Church. It was not just that Christians were expecting it, it was also that it was seen as a test of their beliefs. One can imagine the questions: "Why hasn't he come back yet?" "Can't he see that people are making fun of us?" Peter argues that these people have no perspective. This is God we're talking about here, the being who created everything in the first place. His time is not our time. What we mistake for lateness is mercy, because God wants everyone to have a chance to receive his forgiveness (3:8–9). But he will keep his promises. He will return, and that event will be final (3:10–13).

The author refers to Paul's letters—probably referring to Thessalonians—where these things are discussed. Even if they are hard to understand (3:15–16).

In the end, he urges us to make sure that we walk the right path. The ways of evil will take us in an unsafe direction. The kindness and wisdom of Jesus will keep us walking in the light.

1 John
Living in the Light

Who: John the apostle, son of Zebedee, brother of James.

Although the author is not mentioned in the book, it has been a tradition from very early in the history of the Church that John wrote this letter. As far as we can tell, no other name was ever put forward. There is plenty of internal evidence to back up this view, in particular phrases and expressions that are found in both this letter and the gospel of John, and the mention of eyewitness testimony.

When: Not really sure, but it was probably written between AD 85 and 95, probably after the gospel was written.

What: The letter was written to counter the threat of Gnosticism—an early form of Christianity that had changed the message of the Bible in several key ways.

John's purpose, therefore, was to expose false teachers and their utter lack of morality. He wanted to assure his readers that they had been saved. And because he had seen Christ, known Christ, he wanted to refute the idea that this human Savior was some kind of unreal spirit being.

Quick Guide

Author
John the apostle

Type
General letter

Purpose
To combat false teaching and call for pure lives.

Key verses
2:3–4 "When we obey God, we are sure that we know him. But if we claim to know him and don't obey him, we are lying and the truth isn't in our hearts."

If you remember one thing about this book . . .
If we claim to be children of God, we must live in the way that he wants us to live.

Your 5 minutes start now
Read chapters 1–3

The Route Through 1 John

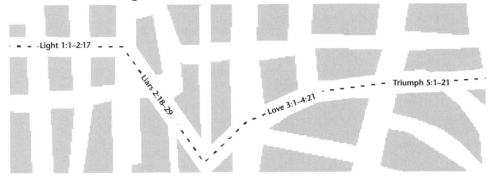

Light 1:1–2:17

Liars 2:18–29

Love 3:1–4:21

Triumph 5:1–21

Puzzling Points
Which John wrote these books?

There is a lot of debate about whether the person who wrote Revelation and the letters of John was John the apostle.

Those who deny his authorship center their argument around the style of the book; the Greek—certainly the Greek of Revelation—is very unlike the rest of John's writings. The author of the letters calls himself "the Elder." Papias, who was a church leader in the early second century seems to imply that there were two well-known "Johns" in the early Church: the apostle John and "John the Elder." Some experts believe, therefore, that the person who wrote Revelation and the letters was John the Elder, rather than the apostle. It's important to note that this view is not a recent one—the first person to disagree with the traditional view was Dionysius of Alexandria in the third century AD.

However, if there are differences, there are also similarities. Both John's gospel and Revelation refer to Jesus as the Word or *logos* of God, and also refer to him as the Lamb. The letters use imagery that is familiar throughout the gospel, images of light and darkness, of truth and error. Both the book of Revelation and the letters of John demonstrate links with Ephesus, and there is a tradition from the early Church that John the apostle lived in the city. There is also the testimony of early writers. Justin Martyr writing around AD 150 stated that the author was John the apostle and the account of Papias, mentioned above, is ambiguous to say the least.

There is also a third view. (There are probably a fourth and a fifth view as well, but I haven't got all day.) In this view there was a "school" of John working at Ephesus, a group of disciples who used his images and followed his teaching. John the apostle was the leader and mentor of this school. He was their inspiration and their source of information. In this argument, the books of John—the letters, the gospel and the book of Revelation—were all products of a group of writers.

In the end it is probably easiest to view the books as originating from the apostle himself. They might have been edited by others, they might have been collected and preserved by members of a "school," but they originate from John, the son of thunder, the apostle of Jesus Christ.

▷386

Light   1:1–2:17

John begins in a way that reminds us strongly of his gospel: with "the Word" giving life to the world. He affirms the physical presence of this "Word"—he has seen and touched him. Three times he says "we have seen." This is an eyewitness account of a real man.

"Anyone who has seen the light cannot go on living in the dark." This is not physical light—although that is a characteristic of God—but the light that drives away fear, light that reveals the truth, light that shows us where to walk. Everyone has sinned and everyone fails, but when that happens Jesus will speak on our behalf. We are to follow Christ's example and obey God's commands (1:5–2:6).

Details, Details …
My children … (2:12–14)

John is so excited he breaks into poetry. This brief, two-part poem addresses children, parents and young people. He is not addressing them as age groups but as different types of attitude. We should combine the innocence of children with the wisdom of parents and the energy of youth. We are forgiven; we know God; we have defeated the darkness.

Details, Details . . .
Antichrists (2:18)

The name "antichrist" is only used by John, although Paul embodies the same concept in his "lawless man" of 2 Thessalonians. These teachers are followers of the Antichrist. Antichristians, if you like. Their teaching is also identified at 4:1–3.

Details, Details . . .
Self-condemnation (3:19–20)

All Christians are sinners. That's where it starts. But sometimes it is difficult to feel that God has truly forgiven us; sometimes it is difficult to understand how much he truly loves us, and we feel uneasy. At these times it is good to remember the words of John: "God is greater than our feelings." Christianity is fundamentally based on the *truth* of God's love, not the *feelings* of God's love. Sometimes those feelings will surround and envelop us, sometimes they will seem very far away. But God is greater than our feelings and loves us still.

Puzzling Points
Water and blood (5:6–8)

Many Bibles have an additional verse about the Father, Son and Holy Spirit being one. This is a later addition. In fact the text is about Jesus' baptism and sacrifice. John is responding to the Cerinthians who taught that God "took over" the body of Jesus at his baptism, but left before his death. In their view, Jesus only came through water—that is, at his baptism—but not by blood—that is, by his death. But John affirms that it was the same Jesus who was baptized and who died. There was no trick substitution, no switch of identities. The one who was washed in the River Jordan was the same one who endured the muck and grime and nails of the cross: God, who died and rose again.

A Little Local Difficulty
The deadly sin   5:16–17

Some believe that, given the context of this letter John probably means the willful, deliberate denial of Christian truth, as practiced by the Gnostics. Others believe that he means any sin that actually leads to death—although it is not clear what sin is actually referred to. It may be that John is talking about events like Ananias and Sapphira (Ac 5) where a sin is met with immediate death. Or it may be that he isn't. No one is really sure.

And the command that we should aim to follow is the new command that is really as old as time. In John 13:34–35, Jesus tells us to "love each other, as I have loved you." When we do this, then the darkness is defeated. We cannot love darkness and light. We cannot love the world and God. We have to walk in the light.

Liars   2:18–29

Having set the scene, John now moves to the issue that has led to this letter: the doctrines that are being spread by false teachers. He sees the sudden emergence of these teachers as a sign that the Church is in the last days. These people deny the truth of Jesus. John emphasizes that the true followers know all they need, they know the facts. He calls on them to stay strong, to stay united and to keep close to Christ by following his example.

Love   3:1–4:21

The sign of a Christian is love. Love is how we tell God's children from the devil's children (3:10). Christian love is revolutionary—the world doesn't understand it at all (3:1, 13). People who have lived all their lives in darkness will find that the light hurts them. True love is expressed in actions rather than merely in words (3:16–18). Love brings us into the presence of God (3:19–21). Love is a test—it shows who knows God and who doesn't (4:8). Again and again the apostle repeats the word: love, love, love . . . But this is no mantra or meaningless phrase. It is expressed in real actions and real relationships.

Triumph   5:1–21

All who place their faith in Jesus are children of God. This love is expressed in obedience and, as John puts it, God's commandments are not hard to follow. Every day, when we choose God's way, we "defeat the world."

2 and 3 John

John's second and third letters are closely linked. So closely, that it is easier to deal with them together.

Who: It is generally accepted that these letters were written by John the apostle, although here John refers to himself as "the Elder" which, given that he was in his eighties, is something of an understatement. A comparison of the language again shows marked similarities with John's gospel.

When: Around the same time as 1 John, i.e., AD 85–95.

What: In 2 John, the apostle is warning of false teachers. From the start, the gospel had been spread by traveling evangelists, who would stay with supporters and friends. Now the original teaching was becoming tainted with falsehoods. It is time, then, for churches to tighten up on the hospitality being offered to these traveling teachers.

Third John continues this theme. In verse 9, John reveals that he has written "to the church" but that Diotrephes would not pay attention. We don't know who these people are, but here's one theory ...

Diotrephes is the leader of a church, who, influenced by the Gnostics, is teaching that Christ did not have a physical body. He is refusing to give hospitality to true Christians and those of his own flock who do welcome these true followers are excluded from the fellowship. So, John writes a "test" letter (the one we call 2 John). He writes to the church itself, in the hope that the letter will get read out, and trying to "turn the tables" on Diotrephes by warning the church not to give hospitality to the false teachers. However, Diotrephes refuses either to read out the letter or to obey its message. So, John writes to a member of the fellowship—Gaius—saying that he will visit in person to sort things out.

It's just a scenario, but it makes sense of the reference to a previous letter in verse 9. And it would account for another oddity: early writers talk of only two letters of John rather than three. It has been suggested, therefore, that 2 and 3 John were originally one letter, showing two successive episodes in the troubled history of an early church.

Quick Guide

Author

John the apostle

Type

Letter

Purpose

To challenge false teaching.

Key verses

2 Jn 6 "Love means that we do what God tells us. And from the beginning he told you to love him."

3 Jn 4 "Nothing brings me greater happiness than to hear that my children are obeying the truth."

If you remember one thing about this book ...

Hold firm to the truth—and love one another.

Your 5 minutes start now

Read the whole thing. Hang on, read *both* whole things.

The Route Through 2 and 3 John

Demetrius 12–15

Diotrephes 9–11

3 John

Gaius 1–8

2 John

Farewells 12–13

Truth 4–11

Greetings 1–3

381

Greetings   2 Jn 1–3

John writes to "a very special Lady and her children." We don't know who the lady was, but certainly the children means not her offspring, but members of the church. John uses the word in the same sense in his first letter. It may be that John is referring to the church itself as a "lady," as at the end he refers to her "sister." John, then, is probably writing from the church at Ephesus to one of their "sister" churches.

Truth   2 Jn 4–11

John's message boils down to one simple command: love one another. That is what God has told us to do; that is what we should get on with. In the meantime, there are dangers: the Gnostic belief that Christ was not truly human is being propagated. John writes to warn the church not to provide hospitality for the people who are teaching this nonsense.

The identification of the lady with a church group also makes more sense of the command not to offer them hospitality. At first glance it seems churlish and unloving not to offer these people hospitality. But if the lady is really a church and not an individual, then that objection disappears. John is not talking about "putting them up for the night and buying them a burger." He is talking about welcoming them into the fellowship and thereby giving tacit approval to their ideas. In that sense, John is not forbidding dialogue with those who have different ideas; he is saying that the church, as a group, has to keep firmly to the basic truths of Christianity.

Farewells   2 Jn 12–13

John evidently feels very warmly toward this church. Perhaps it was one that he himself founded. The sister he refers to here is probably the church at Ephesus.

Gaius   3 Jn 1–8

Gaius is a trusted friend of John's. Once again, the apostle places an emphasis on obedience. Love of God is expressed in obedience of his commands. Gaius has been faithful in offering hospitality to those who are working for the gospel and has a reputation for showing practical love.

Diotrephes   3 Jn 9–11

Gaius's character is contrasted with that of Diotrephes. Gaius supports those who follow the truth, whereas Diotrephes rejects them. Diotrephes wants to be the top dog and will suppress the truth if he can. He is abusing his power and organizing a whispering campaign against John.

Demetrius   3 Jn 2–15

Finally John commends Demetrius, indicating that perhaps Demetrius is the one who will take over from Diotrephes. John hopes to visit the church soon. They have only a short time to sort things out, before the eighty-year-old Son of Thunder will fall on them!

Jude
Encouraging the faithful ...

Who: Traditionally ascribed to Jude, brother of James and Jesus (Mt 13:55; Mk 6:3). The author refers to "the apostles" as a separate group, so we can probably rule out the apostle Jude as the author. Some experts believe that it was written by an anonymous author.

When: It could be as early as AD 65. Or as late as AD 80, depending on the relationship between Jude and 2 Peter.

What: The letter was written to encourage Christians to stay strong in the faith and to reject false teaching. It was written at a time when the Church was established, but still growing. New churches were being founded and new teachers coming forward. And some of those teachers had very different ideas about the Christian faith ...

Jude is similar to 2 Peter. Very similar. So similar, they may have been sitting in the same chair when they were writing. One theory is that 2 Peter was written by Jude as well. Jude refers to a letter he was going to write in the opening verses and, since 2 Peter contains most of Jude, perhaps 2 Peter was the full version and Jude only the "edited highlights." Whatever the case, the fact that both letters feature the same issue shows how widespread the problem of false teaching and failing leadership was.

It doesn't take a genius to guess at some of the unusual activities that the false teachers were introducing. Jude says that they abuse anything they do not understand. They are more like animals. There is an emphasis on the dirtiness, the almost physical manifestation of their sin that indicates that they were abusing their authority by luring others into sexual acts— a sad feature of cults and false teaching throughout the ages.

Quick Guide

Author
Probably Jude, brother of James

Type
General letter

Purpose
Defending the faith and challenging false teaching.

Key verses
20–21 "Dear friends, keep building on the foundation of your most holy faith, as the Holy Spirit helps you to pray. And keep in step with God's love, as you wait for our Lord Jesus Christ to show how kind he is by giving you eternal life."

If you remember one thing about this book ...
Do not live by your own selfish desires; try to live in the way God wants.

Your 2 minutes start now
Just read it.

The Route Through Jude

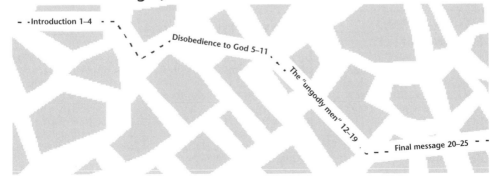

- - Introduction 1–4 - -

Disobedience to God 5–11

The "ungodly men" 12–19

Final message 20–25

Introduction   1–4

The letter starts with almost a hint of regret—Jude wanted to write an upbeat letter, a letter of positive encouragement about the salvation we all share, but he is forced to deal with problems. Instead of a joyful celebration, the letter is about grit and determination, and the need to reject false teaching.

He talks about "godless people," who are saying that because God is a God of grace "it is all right to be immoral" (4 CEV). Because they have been saved and forgiven, they assume they are free to do anything they want.

Disobedience   5–11

Jude is a letter that is steeped in the Old Testament and in Jewish myth and tradition. Its intended recipients were obviously from a Jewish background, and they would have understood the references that Jude is making in this section. His examples are not picked at random, but illustrate particular failings and sins, including rejection of God's authority (the fallen angels), murder (Cain), rebellion (Korah), idol worship (Balaam) and anything else that you can possibly think of (Sodom and Gomorrah).

The early Church was faced with a constant dilemma: Jesus had promised to return, but as the years went by, he hadn't yet turned up. Some began to doubt it would happen, others began to use his "absence" to attack the established teachings and replace them with their own ideas. Jude's response is to encourage his readers to trust in the Lord. The Lord rescued Israel from Egypt and took them into the Promised Land. Jesus will return, for God keeps his promises.

Ungodly people   12–19

Jude uses a series of powerful metaphors to show the devastating effect of these false prophets. They are bad shepherds, feeding on their own flock; like clouds without rain, or trees without fruit, they promise much but deliver nothing; like waves they are blown in every direction by their own desires.

Final message   20–25

Jude's final lines, however, show us what godliness is like. It is summed up in verse 22 where Christians are encouraged to show mercy to people who have doubts and to do all we can to rescue those who are about to be burned. After a letter that has, by necessity, had to concern itself with darkness and lies, Jude shows the light and truth of God. He can keep us from falling and carry us home. He has the authority and power and majesty—no one else.

Revelation
God wins

Who: Generally attributed to the apostle John, while he was a prisoner on the isle of Patmos. The tradition appears as early as 140 when Justin Martyr talked of the work of "a certain man, whose name was John, one of the apostles of Christ." Although the author simply refers to himself as John, it is clear from the book that he had a position of some importance among the Asian churches. However, some argue that it is a different John altogether, known as John the Elder (see 2 and 3 John).

When: Around AD 95. The early tradition states that John was in exile on a small, rocky island called Patmos, where he had been sent during the reign of the emperor Domitian (AD 81–96). Again, very early tradition records that John was 90 years old when he received the vision. Other theories as to its date revolve around different interpretations of the various symbols in this book, but there seems no strong reason to reject the traditional view of the book.

What: John wrote Revelation because he was told to. I mean, if you get a vision from God and you are told to write it down, you go ahead and do it. The book also gives a picture of the future—albeit one that is illustrated with obscure images. And it was written at a time when the churches were facing persecution of a type they had not experienced before.

In the early years, Rome, the great imperial power, didn't take much notice of what it saw as just another strange Jewish sect. By the time Revelation was written, however, the situation had changed. After about AD 60 the Roman authorities viewed Christianity as something to be suppressed. In AD 64, fire broke out in Rome and Emperor Nero avoided blame by accusing and then persecuting the Christians. Although Nero was on the "mad" side of "dysfunctional," subsequent, saner, emperors continued his work. They did it more officially and more efficiently, and for the next 250 years Christianity had no legal right to exist.

Quick Guide

Author
"John"—probably the apostle.

Type
Well, it's sort of a letter, but it's more of a vision-thing, really.

Purpose
To record a vision of the end times. And to encourage certain churches to pull their fingers out.

Key verses
21:3–4 "I heard a loud voice shout from the throne: God's home is now with his people. He will live with them, and they will be his own. Yes, God will make his home among his people. He will wipe all tears from their eyes, and there will be no more death, suffering, crying or pain. These things of the past are gone forever."

If you remember one thing about this book . . .
We have seen the future: God wins.

Your 15 minutes start now
Read chapters 1–3, 14, 18, 20–22

The Route Through Revelation

- The vision 1:1–20 — Seven churches 1:21–3:22 — The scroll and the Lamb 4:1–5:14 — Seven seals, seven trumpets, seven bowls 6:1–16:21
- Final comments 22:7–22:21 — New heaven, new earth 20:11–22:6 — Satan's downfall 19:6–20:10 — Babylon 17:1–19:5

It is against this background that Luke wrote his "official" account of Christianity to combat the more ludicrous rumors that were doing the rounds, while Peter urged his readers to live respectably and quietly and to face suffering with fortitude. Later, John is imprisoned on Patmos, a small island off the coast of Asia Minor, and he is granted a vision for these tough times. "The battle is tough now," he says, "but I've seen the ending. And we win."

That is the key message of Revelation: Christ wins. Whatever else the book brings up, whatever obscure theories and strange details we encounter along the way, the book is about God's victory over evil.

However, it would be wrong to see the book as entirely about the future. There is plenty in it that talks to us now. Jesus, through John, addresses the churches of the day, and the messages he gives them are as much about the need for Christians to stand against idolatry, sin and oppression as they are about the future of the planet.

Brief Lives: John

Background: Son of Zebedee, brother of James. Cousin of Jesus. A fisherman by trade and probably a disciple of John the Baptist, whom he left to follow Jesus.

Occupation: Fisherman. Disciple. Apostle. Writer. Exile. Visionary.

Achievements: John met Jesus when he was with the disciples of John the Baptist. He already knew Jesus, since his mother was Salome and Mary was his aunt (Mt 27:56; Mk 16:1; Jn 19:25). He spent three years with Jesus, later committing his memories to what we know as John's gospel. This gospel was not just his recollection of what Jesus said and did, but also his reflections on the nature of Jesus himself; who he was and where he came from. After the death and resurrection of Jesus he was with Peter in Rome for a while, and then he fades from the scene. Tradition has it that he went to Ephesus. Later, during the time of the Domitian persecutions, he was exiled to the Greek isle of Patmos, where he had the visions that were written down as Revelation. He also wrote letters to the Church.

Character: John and James are described as the "Sons of Thunder," indicating, perhaps, a fiery temper. Later in life he seems to have mellowed: his letters are notable for their emphasis on love.

Pros: Thoughtful. Caring. Insightful.

Cons: Fiery temper. Hyperactive imagination.

Dangerous ground

There is something very important to say about Revelation right here at the beginning: *no one really understands it.*

Oceans of ink and forests of paper have been spent trying to decipher this most obscure of all Bible books. But the truth is, there is much in there that we cannot understand. There are two main reasons for this:

• We don't live in the first century AD. The imagery John uses is imagery and iconography that would have been familiar to his readers. He was writing in the tradition of apocalyptic literature. A few experts now can make guesses about what most of it means. But even they are stumped at certain points.

• Even those in the first century probably couldn't understand it. Someone very wise once said that "life can only be lived forward and can only be understood backward." Revelation is a bit like this. It can really only be fully understood when we reach the end and look back.

This difficulty with the book should sound alarm bells when we meet anyone who claims to know exactly what it all means. They don't. And it means that we cannot take Revelation necessarily as a literal or chronological account. This is not a timetable, it's a vision. The events may lead on from one another and they may appear exactly as described. Or the pictures may point to a different, but no less true, reality.

The vision   1:1–20

John is on Patmos, where he has been exiled for preaching the gospel (1:9). On the Lord's Day—presumably while John was worshiping or praying—he hears a trumpet blast and turns to see the Lord. Jesus appears in a blaze of light, his appearance reminiscent of Ezekiel's visions of God (Ek 40:3), and the description of him as a "son of man" takes us back to Daniel (Da 7:13). It basically means one who looks like a human.

Jesus is the Alpha and Omega—the A to Z, the beginning and the end. He charges John to "write what you have seen and what is and what will happen after these things." Many have taken this statement to provide a sort of basic framework for the book. "What you have seen" refers to the vision itself, "what is" refers to the situation at the time of the vision, and "what will be" refers to the future prophecies.

Details, Details . . .
Nicolaitians (2:6, 15), Balaam (2:14) and Jezebel (2:24)

Nothing is known of the Nicolaitians, but they appear to be some kind of Gnostic sect. Gnosticism of one sort or another crops up three times in the messages to the churches. Twice it is identified with people—"Balaam" and "Jezebel." Of "Balaam" we don't really know anything. "Jezebel" was obviously a prophetess who was leading the followers astray, a situation similar to that which Paul encountered in Corinth. She was offering hidden knowledge—Satan's so-called "deep secrets," which may reflect a later Gnostic belief that in order to combat evil you had to experience it (i.e., an excuse for indulging in sin).

Details, Details . . .
White stone
(2:17)

Possibly a reference to God's habit of renaming people. He will claim ownership over them, by giving them a new, special name. It may refer to a *psephos*, an inscribed pebble that sometimes served as an admission ticket to special events.

Pergamum (2:12–17)

God's words to the church at Pergamum are as sharp as a two-edged sword: they have kept true and faithful despite tragedy, but they are following false teaching. They must turn back before it is too late.

Thyatira (2:18–29)

Thyatira was a garrison town and also the birthplace of Lydia, Paul's first convert in Philippi (Ac 16:14). The church is praised for its endurance and service, but warned against the teaching of a woman called "Jezebel"—a reference to the notorious queen—who is spreading false teaching. The church is urged to hold to the teaching they already have.

Smyrna (2:8–11)

A prosperous town and a faithful ally of Rome, Smyrna was famous for the magnificence of its public buildings. The church, however, had known suffering, poverty and persecution by local Jews. God reassures the church and promises that if they keep the faith, they will be rewarded.

Sardis (3:1–6)

Sardis was living on former glories. Once a great city, now it had lost much of its greatness. The church reflects the city: although it has a reputation of life, it is virtually dead. God urges the church to wake up, to recover its strength, to hold firmly to the truth.

Pergamum
Thyatira
Sardis
Smyrna
Philadelphia
Ephesus
Laodicea

Ephesus (2:1–7)

The church is praised for its integrity, work and endurance, but it is threatened by apathy and complacency. The followers are urged to turn back to first principles.

Philadelphia (3:7–13)

Though small and weak, the church has remained faithful in the face of persecution. God praises them for their faithfulness and assures them of victory.

Laodicea (3:14–22)

Laodicea was a rich and prosperous city that lay on the main trade route. The only problem with the city was that the water had to be piped from hot springs to the south, meaning that it arrived lukewarm. The church, like the city, is smug and complacent. And as lukewarm as its water.

Seven churches   1:21–3:22

The comments on the seven churches follow a set pattern. They start with the good things, move to the bad things and then end with a challenge—"let him who has ears hear!"

The scroll and the Lamb
4:1–5:14

From the churches on earth, the action moves to a kind of church in heaven. From the struggling churches in Asia, we see the reality in heaven, the power and the majesty, the purity.

Heaven is pictured with a series of thrones in concentric circles around one great throne in the middle. The figure on the throne shines like a gem. Or many gems, in fact. The elders might represent the faithful followers of Christ. There are also four beasts, reminiscent of, but slightly different from those in Ezekiel (Ek 1:6, 10). They may represent the whole of creation, in which case we have the whole Church and the whole of creation worshiping God (4:1–11).

The figure on the throne is holding a scroll that cannot be opened. The scroll represents the destiny of the human race and it is sealed with seven seals that can only be opened by the Lamb. John weeps because, unless someone can open the scroll, the divine purpose cannot be fulfilled. The figure who will open the scroll is not only a Lamb, but a dead Lamb. He takes the scroll and prepares to open the seals, surrounded by praise and worship. The inference is that God's purpose for the earth is in the hands of Christ. He has the right to set things in motion, not because of his power, but because of his sacrificial death.

Seven seals, seven trumpets and seven bowls
6:1–16:21

❶ Seven seals   6:1–8:1

Action in heaven results in action on earth. One by one the seals are broken. The first four seals release a series of riders on horses representing conquest (6:2–3), war (6:3–4), famine (6:5–6) and death (6:7–8). These are the classic punishments used by God throughout the Old Testament, and the horses refer back to Zechariah (Zec 6:2–3). The horsemen are given authority to wipe out a quarter of the earth (6:8).

The fifth seal reveals the souls of those who have already died for the cause, praying for judgment. The sixth seal brings darkness on the land, and the cataclysmic disintegration of the earth. It is the great day of God's wrath and it is about to descend.

Some scholars argue that the first six seals represent things that have already happened by the time of John's vision. They argue that the Lamb opening the first seal takes place at the time of Jesus' crucifixion and resurrection, and that the next six seals span the sixty or so years since.

Questions, Questions

Seven

What's all this seven business? I mean, seven lampstands, seven stars, seven seals, seven trumpets, seven dwarfs ...
Sorry?
Er, no. Not the dwarfs. That's something else. But you have to admit it's full of seven.
Yes, we're in seventh heaven. Not just here, either, but throughout the Bible. Seven crops up over 600 times and in Revelation there are tons of sevens sprinkled throughout the book.
So why?
From the very earliest times seven has represented completeness, wholeness. It was said to be the "perfect number." Ancient Babylonian texts used the phrase "seven gods" to mean "all the gods." The number was also used in this way as far afield as India and China.
And in the Bible?
Well, you have events like Naaman being asked to bathe seven times in the Jordan to cure his leprosy (2 Ki 5:10). He's being made perfect, you see. Circumcision took place after seven days (Le 12:3). An animal must be seven days old before it could be offered in sacrifice (Ex 22:30).
I get the point ...
And then there's the multiples. Because if 7 was good, 14 was super, 49 was great. And 70 was fantastic. So the seven churches in Revelation are kind of shorthand for *all* the churches. And in heaven, everything is perfect, so you have seven lamps (4:5), seven seals (Re 5:1), even the Lamb has seven horns and seven eyes (5:6).
And the seven dwarfs?
Oh, be quiet ...

Others argue that all this is in the future, and that the Lamb will open the seals when he is ready.

Either way there is a pause before the opening of the seventh seal, while an angel goes through identifying the servants of God. God is identifying all who belong to him. There has been a lot of debate over the number 144,000, but it is undoubtedly a symbolic number (let's face it—every number in Revelation is symbolic) signifying a complete total of God's people. This multitude stand before the throne and worship the Lamb. They have won through the times of trial and suffering and now they stand, clean, pure and holy in their final haven. After the seventh seal is opened, there is a silence. It is the lull before the storm.

❷ Seven trumpets   8:2–11:19

After seven seals, we have seven trumpets, each bringing disaster and destruction onto the earth. Trees burn up, the sea dies, the fresh water turns poisonous and a great darkness covers the sky. And above them all an eagle flies, warning that yet worse is still to come.

Landmark: Hell

Hell is an issue that most Christians don't like to think about. It raises too many difficult issues. Where is it? How can a God of love create a place of eternal punishment? Is it really full of flames?

Most of the images of hell are pictures; they are not intended as accurate descriptions. Jesus spoke of the "outer darkness" and talked of fire, weeping and lost, aimless people. However, he wasn't necessarily describing the physical details of the place. More likely he was using a metaphorical language to talk about alienation, loneliness and despair.

There are three names for hell in the Bible:

Sheol

Sheol is the name used in the Old Testament and seems to indicate a place of the dead. It was a place where the soul went after the death of the individual. It was not a place where the dead enjoyed the presence of God. There are several places where God promises to rescue those in Sheol and bring them into his presence (Ps 16:9–11).

Hades

In the New Testament, Sheol is called Hades, the Greek term for the realm of the dead.

Gehenna

Jesus spoke of Gehenna (Mt 10:28; Lk 7:5). Gehenna was a real place that had become an image of hell. Gehenna referred to *ge-hinnom*— the valley of Hinnom—which was a valley outside Jerusalem. It was the place where children were sacrificed to Molech (Je 7:31) and later it was noted for being the city's rubbish dump, where fires were kept burning day and night. Gehenna was outside the sacred city, beyond the walls. It symbolizes, therefore, a kind of spiritual wasteland, a rubbish dump, marked by the absence of God.

The Bible is clear that there are places where the dead go. However, it is also clear that which destination—heaven or hell—depends on the choices they make.

The fifth trumpet unleashes demonic forces, opening up the abyss from which weird, armored locusts emerge. The locusts are given strict limits. They can only harm those without the seal and then for a period of five months. Some have seen in the description of the locusts a prediction of bomber planes, but this is not easily proved. After all, not many planes have women's hair and the teeth of lions. The locust was another picture for a divine punishment.

The sixth trumpet releases four angels who unleash yet more destruction. Yet still the people do not repent. These judgments are intended to bring people to their knees, both literally and figuratively. God wants people to repent, but still they do not change their ways.

Before the seventh trumpet there is the interlude of the little scroll and the two witnesses. A glorious angel brings the watching John a message that is sweet as honey yet which turns his stomach. It is very similar to the experience of Ezekiel (Ek 2:8–3:3). Because the message is from God it is sweet, but its contents are a bitter message to communicate. Again, like Ezekiel, the temple is measured, but this time by the prophet himself rather than an angel. Chapter 11 is very difficult to understand—which, given the nature of this book, is really saying something. It uses symbols from Ezekiel and Zechariah, notably the olive trees and the temple. The temple probably represents God's people, the olive trees their twin functions as king and priest. They are defeated by a beast, but return to life after three and a half days. Some have identified the two witnesses with Peter and Paul, martyred in Rome, but the whole passage seems more a comment on the eternal witness of the Church, which condemns the ungodly but which can never be killed.

The seventh trumpet sounds and the door to heaven is opened. The ark of the covenant, previously hidden in the Holy of Holies and inaccessible to all but the high priest, is now open to all.

> ## Details, Details . . .
> ### Armageddon (16:16)
>
> The forces of evil gather for a final, symbolic, battle against God at the field of *Har Megiddo*, meaning Hill of Megiddo, a place where many battles were fought in the Old Testament (Jg 5:19; 2 Ki 23:29–30). Here it is called Armageddon. This has become one of the myths of Revelation, the idea of a massive earth battle resulting in the destruction of the planet. But this is a spiritual battle, for it is fought against God and the kings are gathered by evil spirits.

❸ The woman and the beasts   12:1–13:18

These chapters represent a step back in time, rather than the next stage in the process. They tell the gospel story and the history of the early Church in pictorial symbols.

The woman stands for the chosen people (she wears a crown on her head with twelve stars for the twelve tribes of Israel). She gives birth to a mighty ruler who is taken to reign with God.

The dragon represents the forces of evil, Satan himself, but based on the figure of our old friend Leviathan, the forces of chaos. The dragon is defeated by Michael, leader of the angels, and is thrown down to earth. This fall brings to mind Christ's words in Luke: "I saw Satan fall to earth like lightning!" The dragon eventually starts a war in the desert against the woman and her children—representing the persecution of the Church in Palestine and then in the rest of the world.

Landmark: The Millennium

Millennium means "thousand" and, in Christian terms, is applied to the thousand-year reign of Christ and the saints that is mentioned in Revelation 20:4–6. This is the only time that this event is mentioned in the Bible and, like a lot of Revelation, it has led to a number of different theories as to what the writer is on about.

Postmillennialists

These expect Christ to return *after* the thousand-year reign. There will be an age of peace and righteousness at the end of which Christ will return. Some postmillennialists believe this "millennium" has already begun, although if it has, no one is quite sure when it started.

Premillennialists

These believe that Christ will return *before* the millennium and then will reign on earth for 1,000 years with his saints. This tends to be a literal viewpoint, with Satan bound and thrown into a bottomless pit (20:2–3) and the dead raised to share in Christ's reign (20:4).

Amillennialists

In this view, this is not a literal timetable, but a symbolic description. Thus, we are not talking about a literal 1,000 years, but just a "long time," and God's promises to Israel and threats to Satan are symbolic, rather than literal.

Personally, I'm a pan-millennialist. I'm not sure what will happen, but it will probably all pan out in the end.

The dragon is followed by two beasts that bring to mind the beasts of Daniel. It seems clear that John understood the first beast to be the Roman empire and the second—the one that forces others to worship —as the emperor worship that caused so much persecution for the Church. However, some have interpreted the second beast as the Antichrist. The number of the beast is 666, which could represent Nero, or equally could represent total imperfection—repeatedly falling short of the "perfect" 7.

❹ Seven plagues 16:1–21

The situation on earth, then, is one of destruction and persecution. Contrast this with heaven, where the saved stand with Jesus. After the smoke and darkness of the previous chapters, what comes across is the joy. Those who refused to worship the beast are given special places of honor (15:2–4).

However, it is also a place for judgment on all those who worship the beast, and that judgment is announced (14:8–11) and carried out by angels (14:14–20).

All this is in preparation for the final group of seven. We have had the seven seals and the seven trumpets, now we have seven bowls, pouring out seven plagues (16:1–21). These plagues are reminiscent of the plagues on Egypt, but as with Pharaoh, no one turns, no one repents.

Babylon   17:1–19:5

The fall of Babylon has already been proclaimed (14:8). Now we see God's judgment. Babylon had, by the time of John, become a kind of code word for human sin and degradation. In John's time, Babylon referred to Rome, the hub of the evil empire, the place where saints were martyred and people lived in decadent immorality, and clearly that is the meaning it carries here. It is tied in with the first beast and there is a clear reference to Rome's famous seven hills (17:9). However, what these chapters show is that God will judge all evil, corrupt, oppressive regimes. The celebration resounds throughout heaven.

Satan's downfall   19:6–20:10

First Christ is depicted as a bridegroom, coming to a wedding feast. His bride is the true Church, with a dress woven out of the good deeds that they have done through the ages.

Then he is depicted as a warrior—the rider on the white horse—who fights a war against the beast and the false prophet and defeats them (19:11–21). Satan and his henchmen are rounded up and imprisoned and the souls of the dead are resurrected to reign with Christ for the "millennium"—a period of 1,000 years. At the end of this period, Satan is released again and there is a battle at which the forces of evil are utterly destroyed. Is this a literal 1,000 years? Or does John mean "a long time"? And if it is a literal 1,000 years, then when will it happen? Or is Satan already in prison and is it happening already? Or did it end in 1030? There has been an enormous amount of debate about this chapter, but the plain fact is we just don't know.

This is not a timetable. It doesn't tell you where and when events will happen. It just says, Christ will reign and Satan will be destroyed.

New heaven, new earth   20:11–22:6

Jesus sits at a final judgment of the dead. They come before Christ and are judged according to what they have done. Even those who died at sea return to face Jesus. Finally death and hell are destroyed, shut up, locked away forever (20:14–15).

The old earth has gone. Death and hell are no more. There is no longer any sea—that symbol for the Jews of all that is unknown and fearful. It is time to go back to the beginning, and for God and humanity to live together forever. The picture here is of a wonderful new life, a wedding party that simply goes on and on. In words that echo the wonderful prophecies of Isaiah, John paints a picture of a world without pain, without fear, without separation or guilt or death or sadness. Instead there is a new Jerusalem, a new "Holy City" where God can dwell with his people. One major difference though, there is no temple. Why do you need a temple when God is living all around you?

Final comments   22:7–21

John records a series of rather disjointed comments at the end. Typically, given his fight against any form of secret knowledge. The book is not to be sealed up or made secret in any way (22:10). Instead, each can respond. But we are warned against tampering with it. The book must stand as it is —obscure, baffling, incomprehensible at times, but moving, powerful and challenging at others. And overall the single message: "I've seen the ending. God wins."

Who's who

Where's where

ICONIUM city in Asia Minor 315, 338, *315, 318*

ISRAEL 1. the united kingdom 24–25, 29, 42, 45, 47–48, 59, 68–69, 74, 77, 79, 81, 82, 89–90, 95, 99, 100, 103, 111; 112, 137; *85* **2.** the northern kingdom 112–13, 121, 123, 126, 127, 128, 137, 176–77, 179–80, 183, 208, 213, 221–24; *113* **3.** the restored kingdom 132–33, 137, 142, 147, 182, 184, 200, 233, 241, 260

JERICHO ancient city N of Dead Sea 56, 83–84, 88, 122, 260, 278; *56, 84, 85, 113*

JERUSALEM the holy city and capital of Israel 24–25, 39–40, 42, 63, 79–80, 102–4, 110–12, 116, 128–30, 137, 142, 145, 147, 160, 163–64, 175–76, 179, 182–86, 194–95, 223, 230–31, 233–37, 241–42, 259, 271, 274, 277–78, 284–86, 301, 310–312, 320, 337–38, 364, 366, 372, *85, 86, 103, 113, 147, 149, 244, 286, 318*

JOPPA seaport in N Israel 312; *113, 244*

JORDAN Israel's main river 23, 56, 74–76, 80, 83–84, 86, 122, 124, 236, 252, 298, 380, 389

JUDAH 1. tribal region 112; *85* **2.** southern kingdom area originally given to tribe of Judah and later the southern kingdom 24, 48, 79, 103, 112–13, 121, 125, 127, 128, 130, 176–77, 187–88, 190–92, 197, 199, 211, 221, 227, 229–30; *113*

LAODICEA city in W Asia Minor 346, 348, 388; *388*

LYSTRA Roman colony near Iconium 315, 338; *315*

MEGIDDO Canaanite city and symbolic setting for Armageddon 128, 391; *85*

MESOPOTAMIA area between the Tigris and Euphrates rivers 32, 42

MIDIAN ancient desert country in NW Arabia 53, 73, 89

MILETUS port in Asia Minor 318–19

MOAB neighbor of Israel, east of Dead Sea 73, 75–76, 78, 88, 94–95, 120, 122, 139, 181–82, 192–93, 200, 214, 230; *181*

MORIAH ancient site of Jerusalem 41–42

NAZARETH town in Galilee, boyhood home of Jesus 248, 251, 264, 271, 274–76; *244, 271*

NILE major river of Egypt 51, 200

NINEVEH capital of Assyria 39, 183, 218–21, 225–26, 230; *39, 149, 219*

PALESTINE Roman province covering most of ancient Israel 127, 244, 248, 257, 273, 282, 298, 307, 312–13, 320, 391; *244*

PATMOS small island off coast of Turkey 385–87

PERGA city in Pamphylia 315; *315*

PERGAMUM capital of Roman province of Asia 388; *388*

PERSIA Mesopotamian country and empire 79, 144, 148–49, 206–7, 241, 250; *149*

PHILADELPHIA city in Asia Minor 388, *388*

PHILIPPI city in NE Greece 316–17, 343–45, 350; *317, 344*

PHILISTIA country to W of Israel on the coast 56, 91, 93, 98–101, 103–4, 133, 181, 192–93, 200, 214, 216, 230, 236; *91, 113, 181*

PHOENICIA coastal nation N of Israel 119, 200, 214, 220; *113*

PISIDIAN ANTIOCH see Antioch

RAMESES Egyptian city 50–51, *56*

RED SEA sea not crossed by Israelites 57

REED SEA sea crossed by Israelites 57

ROME Capital of Roman Empire 20, 22, 24, 44, 48, 127, 137,

205, 264, 270, 287, 306, 313, 316, 317, 319–21, 323, 324, 329, 340, 343–44, 346, 348, 355, 357, 360, 362, 372, 385, 391; *321, 324*

SALEM see Jerusalem

SAMARIA originally a city, then a region in N Palestine 48, 110, 112, 117, 119, 121–23, 125, 127, 139, 146, 182, 199, 214, 222–23, 244, 270, 277–78, 297, 311; *113, 117*

SARDIS capital city of Lydia 388, *388*

SEIR, see Edom

SHECHEM ancient city N of Jerusalem 39, 46–47, 90; *39, 86*

SHILOH ancient sanctuary town N of Bethel 63, 98, 137; *85*

SIDON Phoenician port 200, 236; *113, 321*

SINAI mountain in S of Sinai peninsular 51, 56–57, 70–71, 119, 253; *56*

SMYRNA city on W coast of Asia Minor 388; *388*

SODOM ex-city originally on S coast, and now on bottom of of Dead Sea 38, 40–41, 92, 195, 204, 377, 384; *39*

SUSA capital of Persia 149, *149*

SYRIA/ARAM nation NE of Israel 42, 116, 120, 123–24, 127, 139, 207, 214, 221, 273, 312, 329, 338, 138, 312; *113*

TARSUS city in SE Asia Minor 313

THESSALONICA city in N Greece 316, 350–53, 374, 377; *317*

THYATIRA city NE of Smyrna 388; *388*

TIGRIS major river in Mesopotamia 32, 220

TROAS port on NW coast of Asia Minor 317–18, 335; *317, 318*

TYRE 111, 181, 200, 236; *113, 181*

UR ancient city on River Euphrates 38–39; *39*

ZION hill in Jerusalem 178, 182, 235; *286*

ZOAR town near Sodom 41

What's what

We want to hear from you. Please send your comments about this book to us in care of zreview@zondervan.com. Thank you.

GRAND RAPIDS, MICHIGAN 49530 USA
WWW.ZONDERVAN.COM